RAIL VENTURES ®

PRESS

Ouray, Colorado

Editor: Jack Swanson
Contributing Editor: Jeff Karsh
Contributing Writers: Den Adler - Pere Marquette, Lake Cities and portions of
 Empire Builder, Lake Shore Ltd. and Algoma Central
 Ted Scull - Portions of Northeast Corridor
Copy Editor: Doris Swanson
Field Researchers: Dave Worden, Debbie Worden,
 Jeff Swanson and Karen Karsh
Cartography: Jim Swanson
Cover Design: Pat Wilson, Country Graphics
Cover Photo: City of New Orleans near Hammond,
 Louisiana.

Published by Wayfinder Press, P.O. Box 1877, Ouray, Colorado 81427
Manufactured in the United States of America

Fourth Edition, 1990 - Second Printing

Photo Credits: Robert R. Harmen - 213
 Scott Hartley - 27, 58, 68, 84, 126
 Jeff Karsh - 81
 Doris Swanson - 88, 112, 313
 VIA Rail Canada - 409
 Jack Swanson - All other photos

ISBN 0-943727-12-X

Additional copies may be ordered directly from Wayfinder Press, Box 1877,
Ouray, CO 81427. Add $2 to retail price for postage and handling.

Table of Contents

Passenger Train
Routes in the U.S.

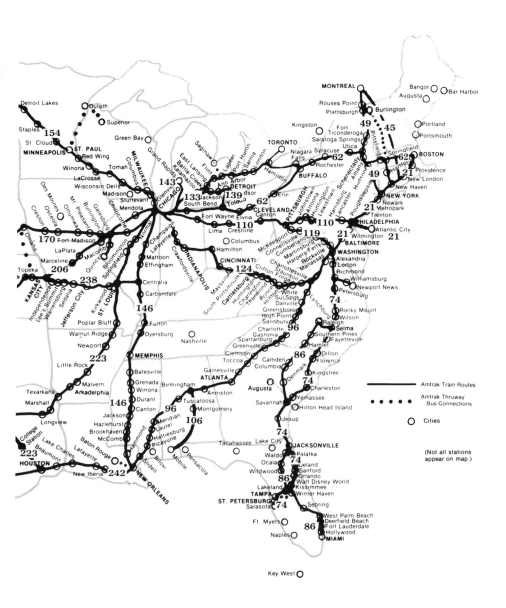

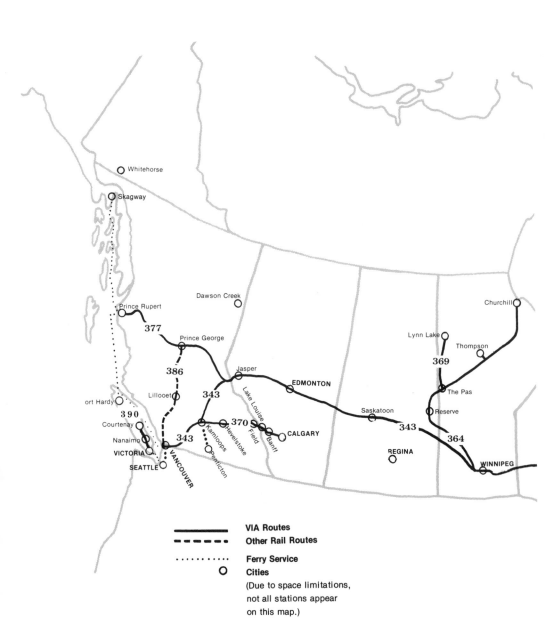

Whitehorse

Skagway

Dawson Creek

Churchill

Prince Rupert

377

Prince George

Lynn Lake

Thompson

369

386

Jasper

EDMONTON

The Pas

Lillooet

343

Lake Louise

Reserve

ort Hardy

390

Saskatoon

343

Courtenay

370

Revelstoke

Field

364

Nanaimo

343

Kamloops

Banff

CALGARY

VICTORIA

Penticton

REGINA

WINNIPEG

SEATTLE

VANCOUVER

──────── VIA Routes

── ── ── Other Rail Routes

· · · · · · · · · Ferry Service

O Cities

(Due to space limitations,
not all stations appear
on this map.)

Passenger Train
Routes in Canada

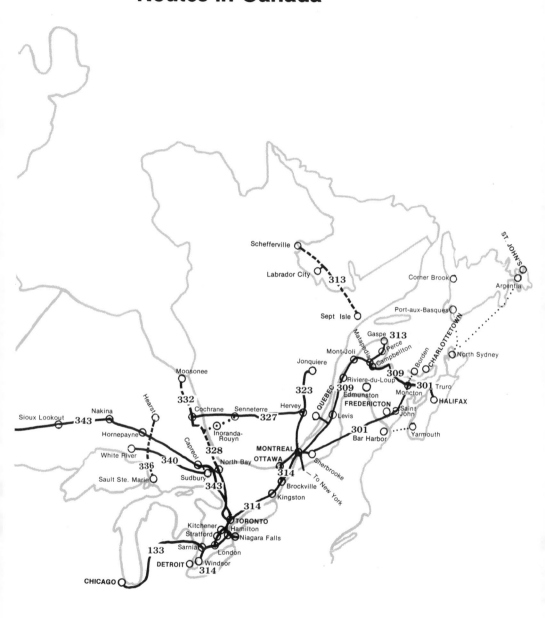

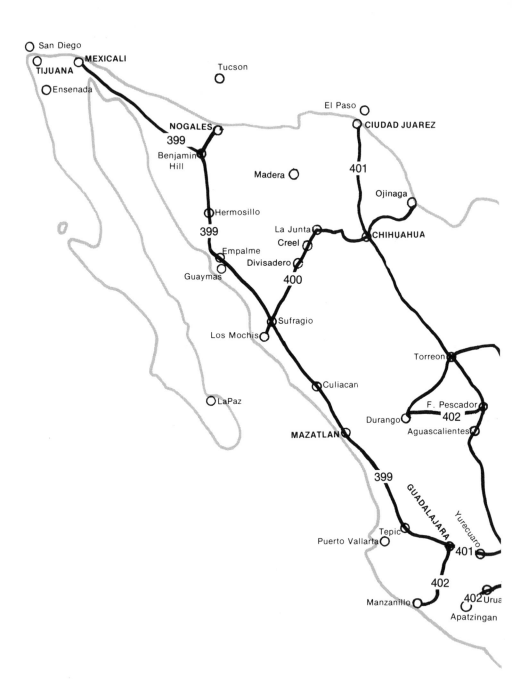

Main Passenger Train
Routes in Mexico

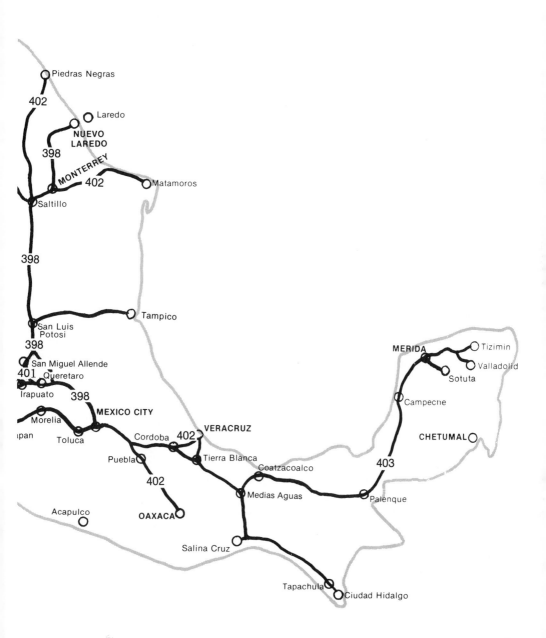

Sunset Limited

Welcome Aboard

Trains have always been something special. Their sheer impressive strength, the thunderous sounds of locomotion, iron against iron, steel against steel—all have contributed to the world's fascination with these mechanical wonders. To ride on a train has been the epitome of romantic adventure. Wonderful names such as *Empire Builder, Sunset Limited* and *California Zephyr* have added to the magic, and being immortalized in both song and legend has further assured a course bound for glory.

Today, in an age of high-tech everything, it is still these nostalgic intangibles that fuel the modern iron horse. And across the years, one aspect has remained particularly constant, an aspect which this guidebook is specifically designed to enhance: the freedom to savor the sights of our great continent without the concerns or distractions found in all other forms of travel.

Indeed, a steady stream of panoramas is limited only by our attention. There's the fastidiously sculpted woodpile, the backyard heap of time-worn appliances, the elderly couple tending their garden—scenes which convey a sense of casual acquaintanceship with so many people and places along one's journey. From the rhythmic locomotion of a determined ascent ("I think I can..."), to the heroic arrival at the station across the pass ("I knew I could..."), these are joys reserved solely for the train passenger. No other conveyance affords the opportunity to absorb so much in such a relaxed state of mind.

North America's passenger rail network is a remarkably extensive one, serving nearly every major metropolis in the United States, Canada and Mexico. One can board a train in Halifax, Nova Scotia and traverse the continent to San Diego, California without having to set foot outside a train station. Or, journey from the subarctic climes of Churchill, Manitoba to the southern tropics of Mexico, with only a short cab ride between El Paso and Juarez interrupting the rail experience.

To be sure, trains will never whisk anyone from New York to San Francisco in a fraction of a day. They will and do, however, cradle the traveler on an overnight journey between Chicago and New Orleans, and then bestow a relaxed and refreshed arrival in the very heart of the city. The ability to simply enjoy the aspect of getting there, the ease of movement in an uncrowded environment, the savoring of a meal while the countryside slips by—these are the experiences reserved exclusively for the rail traveler.

About This Guide

Traveling on a train can be an adventure filled with unlimited fun and excitement. Yet as with most pursuits, those who "know the ropes" can more readily enjoy such an experience. *Rail Ventures* wants you to have the "inside track," and is designed to better acquaint you with the special nuances inherent in rail travel. To best understand what this guide has to offer, the following comments provide an introduction to its features and format.

Finding Things in this Guide

The guide is divided into three major travel sections: The United States, Canada and Mexico. At the front of the book are national rail maps showing most major stops and all routes in each country. Each route on the map is keyed to page numbers in the text where information will be found about trains that use that particular route, sites to be viewed and cities along the routes. This is the quickest way to locate route information in the book. City information can be quickly located by using the full index at the back of the book.

How Do You Get There?

Besides comprehensive route descriptions, information for each long-distance train includes: services and accommodations on board, distance and time it takes to complete the entire route, running "logs" describing things to be seen from the train, and approximate arrival and departure times for selected cities. Arrival and departure times are not precise, but are given in general terms, such as: "Early Morning," "Late Afternoon," etc. in condensed schedules.

Obviously, when planning a trip, it is important to verify exact times. See the general information section of the appropriate country for how to obtain current schedule data.

What Can You See?

For the U.S. and Canada, *Rail Ventures* provides a running description ("route log") of points of interest to be seen along each major route. The description of each point of interest begins with the approximate elapsed time in minutes since departing the last scheduled stop in the log; i.e., 0:25 would be 25 minutes from the last scheduled stop while 1:25 would be one hour and 25 minutes. The name of each stop is shown in boldface.

In most instances, route logs are presented from east to west or north to south. To use in reverse order start at the end of the log, read the parenthetical times rather than the boldface, "right" and "left" would be just the opposite and, of course, "depart" and "arrive" should be interchanged.

These logs are written in a succinct style to allow the reader to quickly determine what is being observed, or what to watch for without distracting from the scene. We believe they will not only help plan your next train trip but also be a great travel companion—rather like adding sound to a silent movie.

Where Will You Arrive and What Should You Do?

Although all stops on logged routes are described, more than 70 major cities are covered in considerable detail. Included are some logical places to stay, some of the more interesting attractions (many within walking distance of the station), how to find other transportation (buses, cabs, rental cars, etc.), where you can obtain tourist information, where the stations are located and station services—redcaps, luggage carts, phone numbers, restaurants, etc. There are maps showing station and hotel locations and points of interest for many of these cities. Amtrak and VIA Rail Canada nationwide phone numbers for reservations and information are listed in the Appendix.

What are the Trains Like?

Since many readers have not traveled by train in recent years (if ever), an Equipment chapter is included which describes the various types of passenger equipment (e.g. Amcoaches, Superliner Sleepers, etc.) giving an insight as to what to expect after boarding.

What About Mexico?

Mexico is treated somewhat differently than the U.S. and Canada. Emphasis is placed on what to expect (or not to expect) while traveling by train through that country, how to make reservations and obtain tickets, general schedules for the better trains, station information for several cities, and a general description of several routes. A description of the famous Copper Canyon trip is also included.

Symbols

 A scheduled train stop.

 Train station services.

 Visitors information center.

 Other available transportation.

 Accommodations, usually within a mile of the train station.

 Some major attractions.

 Train enters a different time zone.

City Accommodations

The selection of hotels and motels in *Rail Ventures* is based on location, quality and reasonableness of rates—the latter, of course, being relative to each city. Large convention-oriented hotels have generally been omitted, unless they are next to a station. Location is usually within a mile of the station, particularly in cities where connections are frequently made.

If no hotels are near the station, then accommodations are included where some of the major attractions are located, usually in the central business district. Some bed and breakfasts have been shown since their popularity is growing. Also, there are an increasing number of downtown B&Bs offering reasonable alternatives to high-priced hotels.

Unless otherwise noted, the rate shown for each establishment is the rack (regular) rate for the least expensive (standard) room for two people based on weekday rates for the most recent high season prior to this guide's publication date. Canadian accommodation rates are shown in Canadian dollars which should translate into lower U.S. dollars.

It is almost always possible to avoid paying a metropolitan hotel's rack rate. Discounts are commonly given for business travel (corporate rates), seniors, AARP members, weekends (in larger cities but not for B&Bs), special promotions, etc. As a hotel manager once stated: "The more questions you ask, the lower the rate." There are also consolidator discounts, clubs, etc. And Amtrak has its own package offerings that include discounted hotel rates for train travelers.

Toll free reservation numbers (within the continental U.S.) for the following "chains" are not shown in the text and are listed here to avoid repetition:

Best Western	800-528-1234
Days Inn	800-325-2525
Hampton Inn	800-HAMPTON
Hilton Hotels	800-445-8667
Holiday Inns	800-HOLIDAY
Hyatt Corp.	800-228-9000
Howard Johnson's	800-654-2000
LaQuinta Motor Inns	800-531-5900
Quality Inns	800-228-5151
Radisson Hotels	800-228-9822
Ramada Inns	800-228-2828
Sandman	800-663-6900
Sheraton	800-325-3535
TraveLodge	800-255-3050

(These numbers will get you a reservation clerk particularly skilled at selling an establishment's higher-priced rooms, so be persistent in asking for their lowest rate, if that's what you want.)

Please Note

The train schedules, fares and routes shown in this guide are always subject to change at any time. Accommodation information is also subject to change. City maps are designed to show locations of stations, hotels, attractions, etc.; however, they are not always drawn to scale and major streets may be omitted for simplification. Commuter trains are too numerous to be included in this guide. Many flag stops appear on VIA Rail Canada's timetables, but have not been identified in the logs of those routes.

United States Rail Service

After World War II, two events almost spelled the demise of rail service in the United States—the "taking off" of the airlines and the invention of the Interstate Highway. To thwart disaster, Congress in 1971 came up with a legislative solution known as Amtrak (The National Railroad Passenger Corporation). The idea was to relieve the nation's railroads from operating their unprofitable passenger trains and to turn these trains into a viable form of transportation.

After nearly two decades of improvement and modernization, today's trains are modern, comfortable and attractive. Their timeliness record frequently excels that of the airlines, and on-board personnel are a far cry from those uniformed curmudgeons of postwar days. The food is quite good in full-service dining cars with meals, wake-up coffee and orange juice as well as newspapers included with bedroom fares. And there are even movies and bingo on the long-distance Western trains.

Reservations - Reservations can be made at any Amtrak ticket office, travel agent, or by calling Amtrak's toll-free reservation number, 800-USA-RAIL. (Local numbers may sometimes be used and are shown in the station information for certain cities.) If reservations are made by phone sufficiently in advance, Amtrak will mail tickets and bill the customer. If time is short, usually three weeks or less, you will be given a specific time within which you must purchase your tickets, either from a ticket office or authorized travel agent. If tickets are not purchased by that date, your reservations will be cancelled. A computer-furnished reservations number is assigned when reservations are made, and it is important to retain this number for future reference in obtaining tickets or changing reservations. If your travel plans change, sleeping car reservations should be cancelled at least 48 hours before train time to avoid paying a "substantial penalty."

Be sure to reserve sleeping-car accommodations early since these are frequently sold out months in advance, particularly on the more popular trains during the summer and holidays.

In addition to train reservations, Amtrak can reserve rental cars in many cities, but this does not necessarily mean that the cars or pick-up and drop-off service are available at the station. Amtrak also offers "Thruway Buses" that make train/bus connections for many off-line cities. Amtrak makes reservations for these as well as some other selected bus routes.

Payment - In addition to cash, tickets may be purchased either by credit card or personal check. Amtrak accepts American Express, Carte Blanche, Diners Club, JCB, MasterCard, Visa and Air Travel Card. These cards (except JCB and ATC) are also accepted in the dining car. Checks (in the amount of $25 or more) can only be for the amount of sale, and some form of identification is required. You may also purchase meals on long-haul dining cars and club cars in this manner. It is also possible to pay locally for tickets which are to be picked up at an Amtrak ticket office somewhere else. This can be particularly helpful when your son or daughter calls from college and hasn't funds to get home for Christmas.

Travel Agents - Authorized travel agents will be glad to make train reservations and sell tickets, and since they are paid a commission by the carrier, there is no extra charge to the customer for this service. This certainly simplifies things. The only disadvantage—once the agent issues the tickets, there may be a penalty for changing or cancelling reservations.

Timetables - Amtrak publishes system-wide timetables semiannually, coinciding with the nation's changeover to or from daylight saving time. These schedules can be obtained free of charge from any Amtrak ticket office, authorized travel agency or by calling 800-USA-RAIL. Times shown for each stop are the prevailing local times. Bear in mind that if a train is running late, stops at stations may be shorter than those indicated in the timetable. There have been instances of passengers detraining under the mistaken assumption that the train will be at a particular stop 20 or 30 minutes, only to find the train (and their luggage) gone when they return to the station area.

Times and routes are always subject to change, and timetables may not necessarily reflect current schedules.

Fares - All coach travel is one class except for Club Service and Custom Class (available on some trains in the East and Southern California) which, because of the more luxurious seating and service, have a higher price tag. Also, certain service in the Northeast Corridor is designed as Metroliner service. These trains are scheduled for fewer stops and make better time, so a premium is charged for Metroliner tickets. And, quite logically, for sleeping cars you must pay an accommodation charge over and above the basic coach fare. This additional charge ranges from as low as $57 a night for a Slumbercoach berth to $272 for a deluxe bedroom. An economy bedroom on a Superliner will run about $125. But there's a bonus. Meals are included with the price of sleeping car accommodations (except Slumbercoach).

Coach fares can range from about 16 cents to 26 cents per mile, depending on the route, but these figures are deceptively high since there are almost always special discounts available. Round-trip excursion fares offer savings and there are also family plans that allow children, ages two through eleven, to travel at half-fare if accompanied by a parent. Children under two travel free.

Senior citizens are also offered discounts of 25% off one-way fares and round trips are 150% of one way. Keep in mind that group rates are established from time to time with discounts determined by the size of the group. This may not seem important, but in the past, as few as three adults have been considered a group.

Reduced or discounted fares do not normally apply to bedroom charges. Stopovers are permitted at no extra charge unless you are traveling on a special excursion rate.

Amtrak's All Aboard America Fare is very attractive particularly when a round trip is involved. This plan divides the country into three regions—Eastern, Central and

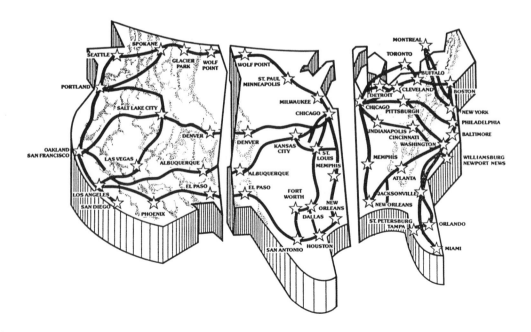

Western. The Eastern extends from the Atlantic Seaboard west to Chicago and New Orleans. The Central is that region from those two cities west to a line from Wolf Point, Montana through Denver, Albuquerque and El Paso. The Western region extends from that line to the West Coast. These fares change with the seasons, but as an example, the summer fares prior to this publication allowed a round trip within any one of these regions for $189, within two adjoining regions for $269 and anywhere in the U.S. for $309. Rates are usually lower during the winter months. One stopover is allowed each direction as well as the destination point. Perhaps the best feature is that the return can be on an entirely different route.

Amtrak sells USA Rail Passes which allow unlimited rail travel in the United States for a fixed fare and for a limited period of time. These can be used only by non-residents of the United States, and are only sold outside North America.

Amtrak Travel Packages - Amtrak offers a bevy of travel packages that amount to a discounted hotel rate when booked with Amtrak travel. Twice a year, Amtrak publishes a *Travel Planner* that lists these bargains.

These hotel rates apply only to bookings through Amtrak, and there is limited availability. If you must cancel, it should be done through Amtrak. It takes one to three working days for Amtrak to confirm hotel reservations while they check on availability.

For information, check with your travel agent or call Amtrak at 800-USA-RAIL, and ask for the tour desk.

Stations and Connections - Rail stations are frequently located in the heart of town, giving the rail traveler a city-center point of arrival or departure. It is important to keep in mind that some cities have more than one rail station, such as New York City. It would be an understatement to say that being at the right station is critical. This will also be a consideration in planning connections, if the trains involved each use a different station.

It may not be advisable to attempt connections between trains having scheduled arrival and departure times within an hour of each other. Amtrak will, however, "guarantee" connections when scheduled arrival and departure times are an hour or more apart. This guarantee means that Amtrak will make other arrangements for you to reach your destination (usually on the next train) if a late train causes a missed connection.

Dining - Most long-distance trains carry full-service dining cars that provide complete menus for three meals a day. Lighter fare will be found on other trains in cafe-type or lounge cars. Cafe service includes tray meals, such as light breakfasts, microwave sandwiches and beverages, while sandwiches, beverages and other snacks are available in lounge cars. It is also quite acceptable to bring your own lunch on board, but food should not be taken to the dining car.

Amtrak has taken a giant step forward in reducing the problem of waiting for a table during peak travel periods. Reservations are now taken early in the day at your seat, and you can select any one of three or four seatings for dinner. Dinner prices range from about six to twelve dollars, luncheons four to five dollars and breakfast three to five dollars. A typical dinner menu might include a selection of baked chicken, seafood, roast beef, New York strip steak or lasagna. Lunches may include salads and sandwiches, while breakfast may offer bacon and eggs, pancakes, French toast and hot or dry cereal. Cafe and lounge cars serve simpler fare at lower prices.

Sleeping - As mentioned above, sleeping car accommodations are available for an additional charge. (See the Equipment chapter for a description of these accommodations.) Although a bed is by far more restful for most train travelers and certainly more private, a majority of overnight travelers will prefer the coach, most because of the lower cost, some because they will reach their destination early in the morning and want the convenience of sleeping until the last possible moment—and a few who believe the point of their trip is to socialize in the lounge car all night.

If you do decide to sleep in your coach seat, pick out a seat near the center of the car to avoid noisy door action that is guaranteed to occur all night at each end of the car.

Although Amtrak provides pillows, it might also be a good idea to have a blanket or coat with you just in case the air conditioning becomes too efficient. If two are traveling together and only single seats are available, the conductor may ask someone to move so that the couple can sit together. If not, move to adjoining seats in your coach as soon as some become available, frequently at the next stop, taking the destination slips above your seats to your new location.

If you should be in a bedroom, plan to pack so that everything you may need at night is handy. Many veteran train riders will take along an extra small suitcase or bag to hold only those items they will need in their bedroom. This is particularly advisable if two people are trying to use small quarters such as an economy bedroom on a Superliner.

Lounge and **Club Cars** - Some trains carry lounge cars where passengers can smoke and obtain beverages and light snacks. Superliner lounge cars offer excellent viewing of the passing scenery, with large windows wrapping up over the top of the car. Club cars are on a few Northeastern Corridor trains (between Boston and Washington, D.C.), and offer more luxurious reserved seats with snack and beverage service at your seat. Fares are higher, of course, for club seating. (See the Equipment chapter for examples of lounge and club cars.) Also, Custom Class, with reserved deluxe coach seating and complimentary coffee, tea or juice and newspaper, is available on the San Diegans, Empire Service trains (New York state) and the Adirondack.

Smoking - You can smoke in certain designated coaches on short-haul trains and in designated sections of club-cars, lounges, and long-distance coaches—but cigarettes only. You can also smoke in your sleeping car and in the rest rooms.

Baggage - Stations at most larger cities handle checked baggage (baggage to be carried in the baggage car) permitting each passenger to check up to three pieces of baggage without charge, not exceeding 75 pounds each or 150 pounds total. Extra baggage may be checked, but it is subject to a surcharge. These should be checked at least 30 minutes prior to departure (even earlier during crowded holiday periods), and will be ready for claiming at your destination within 30 minutes after arrival. Generally, baggage can be checked through to your final destination even when making connections from one train to another at the same station. (But like the airlines, if the connection is tight, there is a risk your checked luggage may arrive the day after you do.)

Personal baggage can also be carried on board in coach, limited to two pieces per passenger when checked baggage service is available. These are stored either in racks overhead or in special storage areas of the car. Sleeping car passengers can carry on as much as can be accommodated in their rooms. But remember, some accommodations are fairly tight such as economy bedrooms on Superliners. Most leave the bulk of their luggage stowed in the luggage bins available near the entrance of the Superliner sleepers (with the disadvantage of lack of security).

There should be another luggage consideration when you plan short stopovers. If an overnight visit with a friend in a particular city along the route is planned, pack so the things you don't need for that night can be left in a locker or the baggage check room at the station rather than hauling your entire wardrobe with you. Locker rental rates (usually 75 cents) are for only 24 hours. Many stations have eliminated lockers and will hold luggage in the baggage room for a dollar an item.

Baggage should always have an I.D. tag with your name and address.

Pets - Except for guide dogs, pets are not permitted on trains.

Tipping - Tipping dining-car waiters is customary, and the same amount that one would tip in a restaurant would be appropriate. Also, many sleeping car passengers tip their car attendant for the extra services they frequently provide. Some even tip their car attendants in advance believing this will ensure the service they want throughout their trip.

Redcaps - Assistance with baggage is furnished at many stations by uniformed redcaps. This service is free, although tipping is appropriate. It is not advisable to accept service from anyone not in a redcap uniform. Redcap service is generally available only in larger cities. The station services shown in this guide for larger cities indicate whether this service is available.

Boarding - If the ticket agent has not told you your car location, ask the gate attendant as you enter the train platform. This can save a walk in the wrong direction in a city like Denver where you have to make a choice—left or right—when reaching the train.

Important - Train times shown in this section are given only in general terms (such as "Early Morning"), and are for use in planning before making reservations. Since times are not specific and schedules are always subject to change, actual times should be ascertained from the carrier or a travel agent before setting out on your trip. Fares and food prices are also subject to change.

Northeast Corridor

Amtrak's 457-mile Northeast Corridor, running between Washington and Boston, carries fully half of the national corporation's 20 million annual riders.

Apart from a short section to the north and east of New York, Amtrak owns the track and most of the stations. The corridor also includes the 62-mile New Haven-Hartford-Springfield Connecticut Valley Branch. The Northeast Corridor is electrically operated from Washington through New York to New Haven (a stretch, incidentally, which has had every grade crossing eliminated), and is diesel-operated from there to Boston and to Springfield. The frequency of departures, with trains operating 24 hours a day, is the highest in the country.

The Northeast Corridor Improvement Project, a long-term commitment to provide reliable high-speed service on the existing roadbed, has resulted in additional sections rated for speeds up to 125 miles per hour. Between New York and Washington, regular-fare conventional trains now offer the fastest schedules ever, while the premium-fare Metroliner Service trains all have less than three-hour running times making them the fastest regularly scheduled trains in the Western Hemisphere. Such service has allowed Amtrak to become the number one carrier of passengers between these two cities.

On the 231-mile New York-Boston segment, the fastest trains equal the former New Haven's highest average speeds and match the running times, when the slightly longer Hell Gate Route to and from Penn Station is taken into account.

Nearly all corridor trains carry modern high-density (84 seats) Amfleet I cars. In addition, Boston-Washington trains usually have one roomier 60-seat legrest Amfleet coach. The majority of the New York-Philadelphia "Clockers" use high-density Heritage-Fleet coaches, mainly built in the 1950s and 1960s. (Historically, Clockers were hourly Pennsylvania Railroad trains between New York and Philadelphia.)

Boston-Washington through trains carry premium-service club cars with two-and-one seating, attendants and offer free meals, wine and snacks. Pre-boarding is another convenience. One overnight train provides sleeper service with free continental breakfast served in the compartment before arrival at terminal stations. (In New York City, Washington, D.C. passengers are permitted to board or detrain from a separate sleeper at convenient early-morning or late-evening times, even though New York arrivals and departures for this train are in the middle of the night.)

Metroliner Service trains carry the rebuilt Amfleet I cars with 60-seat low-density coach seating and even roomier two-and-one club car seating. Amdinettes, cafe cars with table seating, provide food, drink and lounge service on all trains and on selected Boston-Washington runs. Otherwise, all trains carry Amcafes with snack counter take-out service. No food is provided on the Philadelphia Clockers or on the coach-equipped mail trains.

Through Springfield-New York-Washington trains and the Inland Route trains (Boston-New Haven via Springfield) provide Amfleet I, Amcafe and sometimes club car service. Other Springfield-New Haven trains carry through cars to Washington, D.C. which are added to or taken off Boston-Washington trains at New Haven.

Several Northeast Corridor stations have recently received outstanding restorations, making them worth a special detour to explore. The most notable are Baltimore Penn Station, the Wilmington, Delaware station, Newark Penn Station and Washington Union Station. Restoration projects are putting finishing touches on Philadelphia's venerable Thirtieth Street Station and reopened New Haven's station as the city's intermodal transportation center.

New York's Penn Station, Amtrak's busiest, is undergoing extensive rebuilding, and Boston's South Station has been in part restored and in part added to, creating an intermodal train, bus and subway station. Stamford and Boston's Back Bay have brand new stations and Providence's station has been relocated along a newly realigned track through downtown.

The finer points of several smaller stations are noted in the route guide.

The former New Haven's "Scenic Shoreline Route" is one of the finest corridor routes in the country. From spectacular views of the Manhattan skyline while crossing Hell Gate Bridge to mile after mile of New England coastal seascape, the Shore Line route to Boston is a veritable feast for the keenly interested sightseer.

The route log for the Corridor is divided into three sections: New York to Boston, New York to Washington, D.C., and New Haven to Springfield.

Route Log

New York to Boston—For route from New York to Washington, D.C., see page 31; New Haven to Springfield, see page 41; Philadelphia to Atlantic City, see page 42.

To enjoy it all, be sure to sit on the right-hand side of the train when leaving New York, and on the left leaving Boston.

The log shows elapsed times for trains making those stops made by most trains.

NEW YORK CITY, NY - The first reported real estate transaction in the "Big Apple" was in 1624 when Peter Minuit, the Dutch colonial governor, supposedly purchased Manhattan Island from the Indians for $24 worth of goods. This set the pattern and tone for the city. Today, New York remains not only a world center for finance and trade, but also for transportation, fashion, the performing arts and many other industries.

To the uninitiated, it may seem the conventional wisdom about this city ("a nice place to visit but I wouldn't want to live here") is backwards. While the natives seem to have everything at their fingertips, the visitor often sees the Big Apple as more of a big hassle. The secret is knowing how to cope—or maybe better stated, how to get around safely and conveniently in a town with an intimidating subway system, plodding buses, and cabbies that can't speak English. The transportation section below offers some tips that should make your visit more enjoyable.

Although New York has more than its share of problems, the town can be an exhilarating experience. That may be why more tourists come here than any other city in America.

New York City has two Amtrak stations, each serving different routes. Pennsylvania (Penn) Station serves the Northeast Corridor, while Grand Central Terminal (don't call it "Station") handles Empire Service to upper New York State as well as the Adirondack and the Maple Leaf to Montreal and Toronto respectively. Amtrak plans to consolidate all of its New York City service at Penn Station sometime in 1991.

Passengers making connections between these stations can reserve space on an Amtrak shuttle bus when reserving train space. (If New York is a stopover, you are not eligible for this service.)

For information and reservations regarding trains using both stations, call (212) 582-6875. For Metroliner Service reservations and information only, call 800-523-8720.

Additional Amtrak ticket offices

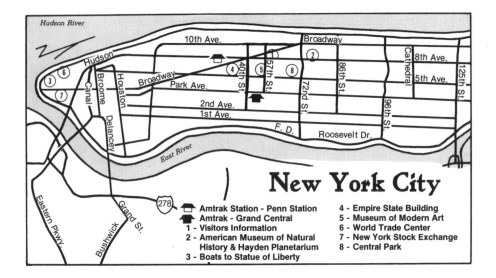

New York City

Amtrak Station - Penn Station	4 - Empire State Building
Amtrak - Grand Central	5 - Museum of Modern Art
1 - Visitors Information	6 - World Trade Center
2 - American Museum of Natural	7 - New York Stock Exchange
History & Hayden Planetarium	8 - Central Park
3 - Boats to Statue of Liberty	

are at Rockefeller Plaza, 12 West 51st St.; 1 East 59th St.; and 1 World Trade Center (Main Lobby).

Pennsylvania Station, bounded by Eighth and Seventh avenues at 31st and 33rd streets, is directly beneath Madison Square Garden. In the past, it has been considered something to be more or less endured. It's understandable why a young boy, struggling to learn the Lord's Prayer, said, "Lead us not into Penn Station." With 82 million users annually, it's no wonder the facility has been overtaxed.

Thankfully, most of the problems are now being dealt with. A $22 million (Phase I) remodeling effort has been recently completed, smoothing out pedestrian flow and improving ticket counters, waiting areas and cab stands. Phase II will further improve retail space and other amenities.

The station is multi-leveled, with all trains arriving at the Platform Level. Immediately above that is Level A which houses the Long Island Rail Road (commuter) station and subway entrance; continuing upward, Level B is the Amtrak station with escalators to the other three levels; and Level C is at street level with entrances and taxis. All levels are handicapped accessible.

There are both video monitors and display boards with arrival and departure information. And besides a refurbished waiting area, first-class ticket holders now have a separate lounge area. Redcap service is available and numerous retail outlets are here.

Grand Central Terminal, E. 42nd Street and Park Ave., is beneath the Pan Am Building. There is a hurried atmosphere here, and it is downright frantic during evening rush hours when thousands of New Yorkers head for the hundreds of commuter trains operated by Metro North. In spite of age and wear, it still maintains its architectural elegance.

All Amtrak trains arrive and depart on the main (upper) level, while Metro North commuter trains use both the main and lower levels. A subway station is also beneath the terminal. There are numerous snack bars, restaurants, stores and shops. Redcap service is available.

The Island of Manhattan is rather compact and many of its attractions can be reached by walking. When walking is not appropriate, there are several options. Perhaps the best source for how to travel in and around the city is Ted Scull's *The Carefree Getaway Guide for New Yorkers*. It not only has fascinating area trips, the appendix is an excellent source of information about New York's extensive commuter trains, subways and buses.

Cabs are what most visitors resort to, even though there is a comprehensive bus and subway system. If this is your choice, make sure the driver fully understands your destination before he starts out. There are two kinds of taxis: licensed (yellow medallion) taxis and unlicensed (gypsy) taxis. Use the licensed variety. Those that are available have their roof lights on, and some vigorous waving and shrill whistling should get their attention. Don't expect to catch one in the rush hour and never in the rain. Even evening theater time can be bad; consider taking a cab earlier to a restaurant that's near the theater so you can walk to the play during this busy period. New York cabbies uniformly expect a tip—generally 20% is acceptable.

Buses are slow, even slower than the traffic, but they are more civilized than the subway, and you can see the sights as you go. Unfortunately, they tend to come in batches and, like everywhere else, ignore schedules. But they are easy to use, and route diagrams are posted at many of the stops. The fare is one dollar and you must have the exact change or a token. There are bus route maps for each of the city's five boroughs, and these can be obtained from the Metropolitan Transit Authority by calling (212) 878-7000. It's an easy way to get cross town. Call the MTA for information, (718) 330-1234.

The **subway** is usually the fastest way to get around. Statistically, this is safer than the streets in spite of its reputation. Stick to the safer routes, sit toward the center of the train when it isn't full and travel when they're being well used. The daylight hours are the best. On the other hand, avoid the unpleasant rush hours.

The city has been improving the system's acceptability—the graffiti is gone, better schedules, etc. But stations can be sweltering and smelly. Few of the public rest rooms are open. But you haven't experienced New York if you haven't ridden the subway; just be sure you know what route to use to get to your destination. Token booths are at each station. If you plan to use the subway more than once, buy enough tokens to avoid waiting in line again. Ten-packs are sold for convenience but at no discount. They may also be used

on the city buses.

Maps are available at bookstores for about a dollar or call the MTA, (212) 878-7000. The best bet, however, is to pick up a copy of *NYC Access,* a sophisticated guidebook that has probably the best designed map of the system, particularly for the borough of Manhattan. Again, call MTA, (718) 330-1234, for information.

Commuter trains make New York City possible. Metro North has three lines that head north out of Grand Central: The Hudson Line that runs along that river to Poughkeepsie; the Harlem Line that goes farther east, through Scarsdale and north; and the New Haven Line that runs up the coast to that city, with three northerly branches to New Canaan, Danbury and Waterbury. For information, call (212) 532-4900.

The Long Island Rail Road serves virtually all of Long Island from Penn Station. Call (718) 454-5477 for information.

PATH (Port Authority Trans Hudson) offers excellent service to Hoboken, Jersey City and Newark, with connections to New Jersey Transit. PATH trains run south from 33rd Street along the Avenue of the Americas (Sixth Ave.) and also from the World Trade Center. Call (212) 732-8290.

Intercity buses operate from the Port Authority Bus Terminal at 8th Ave. and 41st St. **John F. Kennedy International Airport** (JFK) is 15 miles east of midtown, **LaGuardia Airport** is eight miles northeast, and **Newark International Airport** is 15 miles southwest.

The **automobile** is not really useful in New York City, but if you must rent one, Avis, Budget, Hertz and National all have **rental car** locations in midtown.

? **New York Convention and Visitors Bureau,** Two Columbus Circle (59th St. and Broadway), 10019; (212) 397-8222.

This is a town where a moderately priced room will run well over $100 for two people during the week. The hotels shown below are conveniently located and are more or less in that price range. Two viable alternatives to hotels are also included.

Weekend packages are common among New York hotels, and "deals" change frequently. Check with your travel agent for best weekend rates.

-Best Western Milford Plaza, 270 West 45th St., 10036; (212) 869-3600. Caters to tourists; many bargain weekend packages; small rooms. About a mile from Penn Station and four blocks from Grand Central. Just off Times Square. $110.

-Comfort Inn Murray Hill, 42 West 35th St., 10001; (212) 947-0200. Excellent location, just across from the Empire State Building. Three blocks from Penn Station, about a mile from Grand Central. $114.

-New York Penta, 401 Seventh Ave., 10001; (212) 736-5000 or 800-223-8585. Venerable, Stanford-White-designed hostelry, formerly the Statler. Its phone number (Pennsylvania 6-5000), made famous by Glenn Miller, is now longest in continuous use in the city. Hotel recently underwent $35 million remodel. Directly across from Penn Station. $150.

-Roosevelt on Madison Ave., 45 E. 45th St., 10017; (212) 661-9600 or 800-223-1870. Only one block from Grand Central. $139.

-For apartments and **Bed and Breakfasts,** call Urban Ventures, (212) 594-5650. They offer apartments throughout the city made available by New Yorkers who want extra income while they are out of the city. Like a bed and breakfast without the host or the breakfast. Prices in midtown range from $90 to $150 and usually have a three-night minimum. Bed and breakfasts are also available, usually with a two-night minimum. Prices for midtown B&Bs range from $70 to $85.

-or try sleeping beneath Penn Station (but not with the homeless) if you are arriving from, or departing for, Washington, D.C. The Executive Sleeper, which is carried by the Night Owl, arrives in Penn Station from Washington about 3 am, but is set off on a siding and you may stay on board as late as 8 am. Southbound, the sleeper departs New York about 3:45 am, but you may board and occupy your room as early as 9:30 pm. Arrival in Washington is about 8 am. A complimentary continental breakfast is served in your room. The bedroom surcharge (for two) is a bargain $77.

An indispensable tool for enjoying New York City is the **Visitors Guide and Map,** available free from the New York Convention and Visitors Bureau. This is a handy, well-designed handout that packs a lot of information on a single sheet of paper.

Perhaps the best bargain in the city is **Circle Line Sightseeing Yacht** tours around Manhattan, which let you see both the city and harbors. For a bird's-eye view, of course, both the **Empire State Building** and the **World Trade Center** observation decks are magnificent vantage points on a clear day. The one and only **New York Stock Exchange,** at 20 Broad Street, is the focal point of the world of finance and can be seen from the visitors' gallery or by guided tour. And boats to the **Statue of Liberty** are boarded at the southern tip of Manhattan.

Museums are in abundance. The **Museum of Modern Art,** 11 W. 53rd St., and the **American Museum of Natural History,** 79th and Central Park West, are national treasures. **Lincoln Center for the Performing Arts,** Broadway and 64th, is renowned for its musical virtuosos. And, of course, **New York's theaters** offer something for every taste.

To see the city's sights as a New Yorker, buy a copy of *The Carefree Getaway Guide for New Yorkers* mentioned earlier. There are some wonderfully insightful chapters on how to savor the city at very little cost—everything from riding the M-4 bus through Manhattan's diversity to taking PATH to Hoboken where one discovers a broad spectrum of ethnic restaurants.

0:00 (0:29) Departing New York's Pennsylvania Station, travel eastward under Manhattan streets and East River rising to surface on Long Island in Sunnyside section of Queens.

0:08 (0:26) To left are extensive rail yards for Amtrak and New Jersey Transit trains. All passenger equipment is cleaned, stored, serviced and provisioned here before their next trip. Tracks dropping down to right pass through mechanical washers then loop under main line into Sunnyside Yards.

0:10 (0:19) At Harold Tower interlocking,

our elevated Hell Gate Route separates from Long Island Rail Road line that continues on to Jamaica and points east.

The Hell Gate Route, once officially known as the New York Connecting Railroad and completed in 1917, joined the Pennsylvania Railroad with the New York, New Haven and Hartford, permitting for the first time, a direct, all-rail route between Washington, Philadelphia, New York, Providence and Boston.

Prior to the Hell Gate Route, the only through train, the Federal Express, used a transfer ferry to complete the missing rail link between terminals in the Bronx and the New Jersey side of the Hudson River.

The Hell Gate Route climbs through Astoria, a heavily Greek and Italian community, swinging back over the East River onto Wards and Randalls islands. On a clear day or night, the view of the Manhattan skyline is nothing less than magical, and it is worth moving temporarily to the city-side to take in the glorious spectacle.

0:18 (0:11) Down to left is Manhattan State Hospital, a grim-looking structure built just prior to World War II. To right, small vessels moored at river's edge are New York City sludge boats, popularly referred to as "honey barges." They haul treated waste out to sea for dumping about eight miles beyond Ambrose Channel light tower. Next to sanitation facility, City of New York maintains its Fire Department Training Academy. Four-story windowless brick tenement is used for simulation of real fires and can sometimes be seen erupting in flames for exercise purposes. Often a red fireboat is tied up nearby. Leaving Hell Gate Viaduct, train drops into a cut through South Bronx, a severely depressed area of New York City, then crosses Hutchinson River.

0:25 (0:04) Huge, stark Coop City apartment complex rises to left, as train crosses Pelham Bay drawbridge.

0:28 (0:01) At Shell Tower interlocking, Hell Gate Route joins Metro-North Commuter Railroad Line from Grand Central Terminal. Frequent New Haven Line trains from Grand Central operate the 72 miles to New Haven. Prior to and during early years of Amtrak operations, some Amtrak trains ran out of Grand Central to Boston in addition to those operating through Penn Station and south to Washington.

0:29 (0:00) Arrive New Rochelle.

NEW ROCHELLE, NY - This is the first high-level platform commuter station encountered northbound. High-level platforms, a phenomenon of the Northeast, allow for rapid boarding of trains without having to drop the train's steps.

0:00 (0:17) Depart New Rochelle and gather speed on four-track electrified Shore Line Route. First tree-lined suburban streets appear in Connecticut, and brief glimpses of Long Island Sound begin after Greenwich and at Cos Cob.

0:17 (0:00) Arrive Stamford.

STAMFORD, CT - At Stamford, a burgeoning city boasts one of the lowest unemployment rates in the country. Clusters of new corporate headquarters, modern office buildings and hotels surround the new transportation center. Nearly all Amtrak trains stop here to serve local communities and to allow passengers to make convenient connections with Metro-North's New Haven Line trains. An eight-mile, single-track electrified branch line runs from Stamford north to New Canaan.

0:00 (0:25) Depart Stamford.

0:10 (0:15) At South Norwalk, Metro-North trains stop to allow transfers to the 24-mile Danbury Branch, operated outside of rush hours with a single RDC (rail diesel car).

0:14 (0:11) At Westport, scenery improves substantially, and one of first wooden barn-style stations appears. Through trees, most houses seen are worth small fortunes—some even more. Tidal marshlands open up between Westport and Green's Farms.

0:19 (0:06) Southport, 49 miles from Grand Central, may be considered end of intensively used commuting stations, though some daily riders originate even farther east. Approaching Bridgeport, scenes become industrial and urban once again. On right, simple dock serves as landing for Bridgeport and Port Jefferson

25

Steamboat Company's ferry Grand Republic, operating year-round service across Sound to Port Jefferson on Long Island's North Shore. Fanciful Moorish-style building to left houses P. T. Barnum's personal and circus memorabilia collection.

0:25 (0:00) Arrive Bridgeport.

BRIDGEPORT, CT - Passengers for the Metro-North's 32-mile Waterbury Branch change here for the diesel rail car up the scenic and historic Housatonic and Naugatuck valleys.

0:00 (0:24) Departing Bridgeport, line crosses first Pequonnock then Housatonic rivers and runs through Milford, last Metro-North station stop, before skirting harbor on approach to New Haven.

0:24 (0:00) Arrive New Haven.

Seconds after coming to a stop in New Haven, the lights will go out and the air circulation will cease for about seven minutes, while the electric locomotive is traded for a diesel engine for the remainder of the trip to Boston. Trains to Hartford, Springfield and other Inland Route stations between here and Boston branch off to the north. Historic New Haven Station, which was closed for many years, is now a major transportation center for Amtrak and commuter trains as well as local and long distance buses.

NEW HAVEN, CT - This is the home of Yale University, where historic personages such as Noah Webster, Nathan Hale and William Howard Taft studied. Black Rock Fort and Fort Nathan Hale, restored Revolutionary War forts, and the Peabody Museum of Natural History, containing the world's largest natural history painting, are of particular interest.

0:00 (0:31) Depart New Haven.

Finally, when out of reach of New Haven's urban influence, the landscape becomes genuinely rural for the first time. It is this 69-mile stretch, as far as Westerly, where the Scenic Shore Line earns its name. Rocky hillocks rise out of tidal marshes laced with meandering streams. Isolated houses loom large on the tiny offshore Thimble Islands. The broad sweep of Long Island Sound is visible for long intervals while the train races fast through the Connecticut resort towns of Guilford, Madison and Clinton.

0:31 (0:00) Arrive Old Saybrook.

OLD SAYBROOK, CT - Note the handsome wooden station dating from 1873, one that has changed little in more than 100 years. Passengers leave here for the Connecticut River town of Essex and excursions on the steam-hauled Valley Railroad, a few miles to the north. It is here that the Connecticut River flows into Long Island Sound.

0:00 (0:18) Depart Old Saybrook.

0:03 (0:15) Look both ways while rumbling across drawbridge spanning Connecticut River. Until 1931, nightly steamer service plied between New York and numerous landings on river as far north as Hartford.

Between Old Saybrook and New London, the Shore Line parallels the sandy beaches at Rocky Neck State Park and along Niantic Bay, at times less than 100 feet from the lapping salt water.

0:18 (0:00) Arrive New London where elegant red-brick 1887 H. H. Richardson railroad station also houses local restaurant.

NEW LONDON, CT - New London, located on the River Thames (rhymes with James), grew up with the whaling industry and other commercial maritime pursuits to become one of the most important ports on the New England coast. Today, the Coast Guard and its Academy, the Navy and the shipyards keep the area humming to a similar salty tune. Nautilus, the world's first nuclear submarine, was launched in nearby Groton.

Virtually at the station's doorstep, three different ferry operators run boats to Fishers Island, Orient Point and Block Island (summer season only).

0:00 (0:14) Leaving New London, swing right to pass over Thames where a quick look upstream may reveal Coast Guard sail training ship Eagle. Scan both ways for nuclear submarines and other vessels downstream at General Dynamics shipyard.

0:12 (0:02) Approaching Mystic, water laps both sides of embankment. New drawbridge and track realignment are important improvements to Northeast

Yankee Clipper – Green Farms, Connecticut

Corridor, permitting higher speeds and more reliable service. Glance to either side for hundreds of moored sailing and motor yachts.

0:14 (0:00) Arrive Mystic.

MYSTIC, CT - The station built in 1905 has recently received a complete restoration. The two-tone wooden depot once served as a model for Lionel's Lionelville station. Amtrak and local community groups joined forces to reopen the building as a train information and local community center and gift shop.

Mystic is best known for its 19th-century Seaport Restoration housing a fine collection of private residences, an aquarium, a large fleet of ships and a working shipyard. In addition, Mystic offers many lived-in houses that formerly belonged to ship captains, a noted aquarium and several windjammer cruise operators.

0:00 (0:10) Depart Mystic.

0:05 (0:05) At Stonington, one of Connecticut coast's most attractive towns, look for large Victorian structure (a former hotel) next to water on right-hand side.

0:10 (0:00) Arrive Westerly.

WESTERLY, RI - This older Rhode Island city has an industrial background which provides several factory buildings facing Amtrak's brick and granite railroad station.

0:00 (0:14) Depart Westerly and head inland into extensive wooded areas of evergreen and deciduous trees. From here through Davisville train is permitted to run at 110 miles per hour, longest fast stretch of track between New York and

Boston.

0:14 (0:00) Arrive Kingston.

 KINGSTON, RI - The town's blue-gray Victorian-style wooden station is particularly attractive. An old New Haven baggage cart to one side appears to be holding up a large tree. The nearby University of Rhode Island, the resort towns of Newport, Narragansett and Jamestown are popular destinations for passengers leaving the train here.

0:00 (0:26) Depart Kingston.

0:12 (0:14) At East Greenwich, there are close-up views of Narragansett Bay and numerous yacht marinas. Some trains stop here.

Upon approaching Providence, the track has been realigned away from downtown and closer to the hillside state capitol building. Unfortunately, the new station is now less convenient for passengers connecting to buses for Cape Cod.

0:26 (0:00) Arrive Providence where Capitol comes into view. Brown University buildings can be seen on hill above and to right.

PROVIDENCE, RI - Providence is the capital of the smallest state in the nation. Closely associated with the sea during its early years, it has become one of the important commercial and financial centers of the East. Old State House, where the Rhode Island General Assembly renounced allegiance to King George III on May 4, 1776, still stands at 150 Benefit St.

0:00 (0:25) Depart Providence and scenery becomes flat and dull as train runs fast through Attleboro and Canton.

0:25 (0:00) Arrive Route 128.

ROUTE 128, MA - This suburban stop is used mostly by passengers using the Beltway which circles Boston.

0:00 (0:18) Depart Route 128.

The final approach to Boston is slow, with the impressive skyline of Back Bay off to the left.

0:15 (0:00) Arrive Boston's Back Bay Station.

BOSTON (BACK BAY), MA - This station, just three miles from our final stop, was recently reopened to better serve this area of Boston. Besides

MBTA commuter trains, this stop is also served by the Orange Line subway with direct service to Boston's North Station and the northern suburbs.

0:00 (0:05) Depart Back Bay Station, emerging slowly from below grade.

0:03 (0:02) On right, building signage modestly proclaims "Gillette World Shaving Headquarters."

0:05 (0:00) Boston's huge central post office facility appears on right upon train's arrival South station.

BOSTON, MA - First settled in 1630, Boston and the nation's history have always been closely intertwined. English Puritans endured early hardships here, including death from disease and cold, but held on through those difficult years. Its location on Boston Bay soon made it the most important port in America, with trading vessels sailing to and from all parts of the world. Its port, yet today, is one of the world's busiest.

The American Revolution had its roots in Boston when British troops fired on a gathering of citizens in 1770, killing several. The Boston Tea Party was held in 1773 and Paul Revere's historic ride started here. It was the early cultural center of the nation having such residents as Hawthorne, Emerson and Longfellow. Historically a leader in education, the city still enjoys the distinction of being a major focal point of scientific and medical research. There are a quarter of a million students attending 50 colleges and universities in the greater metropolitan area.

Boston is the largest city in New England with a metropolitan population of nearly three million. It is the capital of Massachusetts, and the city has an impressive collection of financial institutions. There is a unique blend of new and old architecture in its downtown district (the oldest part of the city) where there is a maze of twisting, narrow streets. This historic area is easily toured on foot, but a good map is a requisite.

South Station, Atlantic Ave. and Summer St., 12210. This glorious old station, constructed largely of pink marble just before the turn of the century, has been undergoing a massive rehabilitation project. Started in the 1980s, the nearly completed result is a modern-day gem of a depot.

An enormous canopy encloses a spacious and airy waiting room that houses traditional (but quite modern) benches, some very inviting lunch stands, dining tables and slick arrival and departure boards, one for Amtrak and one for commuter trains. Around the perimeter are shops and services, including ticket windows (be sure to note the elegant ceiling over the separate ticket lobby), a bank, shoe repair, a newsstand and other retail operations. Redcap service is available.

The remodeling should be completed in late 1990 which will include a direct passageway to the adjoining MBTA station (Red Line) and a parking garage to be built over the tracks.

The waiting room is open from approximately 5:30 am to midnight, while ticket window hours are slightly shorter. The baggage room is open from 7 am to 11 pm. Call (617) 482-3660 for reservations and other information.

Amtrak also has a second in-town facility, **Back Bay Station.** This station is at 145 Dartmouth St. and is served by some, but not all, of the Amtrak trains that use South Station.

Cab stand is at the station; Checker, 536-7000 and Red & White, 742-9090. **Local buses** and **subway** are in front. Also, various **commuter trains** use this station. For bus, subway and commuter train information, call MBTA, 772-3200. Commuter trains also use the North Station, 150 Causeway Street. **Greyhound** bus terminal, 10 St. James Ave.; 423-5810. **Peter Pan** bus terminal, 55 Atlantic Ave., one block from the station, 426-7838. **Rental cars** are not available at the station, but Budget will pay cab fare to their Long Wharf location, about a mile from the station. **Logan International Airport** is just across the harbor and can be reached by subway (Blue Line).

Boston Common Information Booth, Tremont Street at West Street. Also, **Boston National Historical Park Visitor Center,** 15 State Street at Devonshire St. Both of these centers are on the "Freedom Trail." Write or call Greater Boston Convention and Tourist Bureau, Prudential Tower, Box 490, 02199; (617) 536-4100. **Bostix Ticket Booth,** at Faneuil Hall, provides tickets and information for theaters and other events and attractions; (617) 723-5181. For current happenings, (617) 972-6000.

Because of Boston's ubiquitous and easy-to-use "T" (rapid transit), numerous hotels may be considered "convenient" for travelers not minding a subway ride.

-Chandler Inn, 26 Chandler St., 02116; (617) 482-3450 or 800-842-3450. A small, popular hotel, operated as a bed & breakfast. A bit out of the way, but a reasonable walk to the "T" and only three blocks from Back Bay Station. Quiet neighborhood. Twelve blocks from South Station. $79.

-57 Park Plaza Hotel (Howard Johnson), 200 Stuart St., 02116; (617) 482-1800. High rise with spacious rooms, all with balconies; in the Theater District. Five blocks from Back Bay Station and ten blocks from South Station. Four blocks from the "T" (Boylston or Arlington on Green Line). $125.

-Tremont House (Quality Inn), 275 Tremont St., 02116; (617) 426-1400. Well-maintained high rise in the Theater District (formerly The Bradford). Midway between Back Bay and South stations; about eight blocks to each. Three blocks to the "T" (Boylston on Green Line). $120.

-Lenox Hotel, 710 Boylston St. at Copley Pl., 02116; (617) 536-5300 or 800-225-7676. Recently redecorated small hotel in Back Bay. About three blocks from Back Bay Station and the "T," about two miles from South Station. $125.

-The Eliot Hotel, 370 Commonwealth Ave. (at Mass. Ave.), 02215; (617) 267-1607. Small, European-style, mostly suite hotel in Back Bay, across from the "T" (Auditorium on Green Line). About a mile from Back Bay Station and three miles from South Station. Continental breakfast included. Recently refurbished rooms $115; others $85.

-Bed and Breakfast Associates Bay Colony, Ltd., P.O. Box 57166, 02157; (617) 449-5302. Boston's oldest and largest B&B reservation service.

 Three of Boston's attractions are within two blocks of the station on

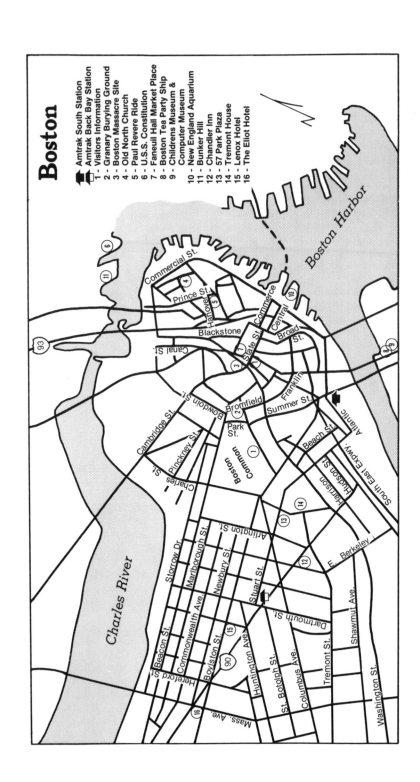

Boston

- Amtrak South Station
- Amtrak Back Bay Station
- 1 - Visitors Information
- 2 - Granary Burying Ground
- 3 - Boston Massacre Site
- 4 - Old North Church
- 5 - Paul Revere Ride
- 6 - U.S.S. Constitution
- 7 - Faneuil Hall Market Place
- 8 - Boston Tea Party Ship
- 9 - Childrens Museum &
     Computer Museum
- 10 - New England Aquarium
- 11 - Bunker Hill
- 12 - Chandler Inn
- 13 - 57 Park Plaza
- 14 - Tremont House
- 15 - Lenox Hotel
- 16 - The Eliot Hotel

Boston Harbor

Charles River

Commercial St.
Prince St.
Hanover St.
Blackstone
Canal St.
Central
Broad St.
Commerce
State St.
93
Cambridge St.
Bowdoin St.
Bromfield
Summer St.
Franklin
Pinckney St.
Charles St.
Park St.
Beach St.
Atlantic
Boston Common
South East Expwy.
Hudson St.
Harrison St.
Storrow Dr.
Marlborough St.
Arlington St.
Newbury St.
Stuart St.
E. Berkeley
Beacon St.
Commonwealth Ave.
Hereford St.
Boylston St.
Huntington Ave.
Dartmouth St.
Shawmut Ave.
Mass. Ave.
St. Botolph St.
Columbus Ave.
Tremont St.
Washington St.
90

Congress Street. The **Boston Tea Party Ship and Museum,** on the Congress Street Bridge, is a replica of the original brig "Beaver" on which the famous act of protest took place in 1773. Just beyond is the **Children's Museum,** with "hands-on" exhibits; it's one of the best such institutions and is extremely popular. Adjacent, is **The Computer Museum,** the only one of its kind, with more "hands-on" exhibits that entertain the kids as well as the grown-ups.

Most of Boston's historic points of interest are along the **Freedom Trail,** a walking route through downtown Boston marked by a red stripe along the sidewalks. Maps of the route and descriptions of the things to visit along the way may be obtained from the visitors center. Highlights of this tour include: **Faneuil Hall** and **Quincy Market,** a very large, popular collection of produce stalls, delis, shops, bakeries and restaurants; **Boston Common,** originally used as a militia training ground and pasture for cattle; **Granary Burying Ground,** with gravesites of Paul Revere, John Hancock and Samuel Adams; **Old North Church,** which is the city's oldest church and the site of the signal by lantern notifying patriots across the river whether the British were arriving by land or by sea; **Paul Revere House,** the oldest structure in Boston; the **USS Constitution** ("Old Ironsides"), launched in Boston in 1797 and fought in more than 40 engagements; and **Bunker Hill Pavilion,** 200 yards from the USS Constitution, has a film and sound show recounting the history of the battle at Bunker Hill.

For a non-history break, visit the **New England Aquarium** on Central Wharf with a coral reef, sharks and sea turtles among 2,000 aquatic creatures on exhibit.

New York to Washington, D.C.

NEW YORK, NY - See page 21.

0:00 (0:14) Depart New York's Penn Station and head westward beneath streets of Manhattan toward Hudson River. Twin tubes, sometimes called North River Tunnels, each carry single sets of tracks beneath Hudson. Tunnels were first opened in 1910 when Penn Station was completed, allowing Pennsylvania

Railroad to gain competitive presence in New York City. Until then Pennsylvania's passengers had to be ferried across Hudson from New Jersey terminal.

0:05 (0:09) Surface in North Bergen, New Jersey, some 2¾ miles from Penn Station, and curl southward toward wetlands known as Jersey Meadows.

0:08 (0:06) Off to left, familiar silhouettes of 110-story World Trade Center and legendary Empire State Building, world's second and third tallest buildings (only Chicago's 1,454-foot Sears Tower is taller), can be seen on left. These modern wonders are engineering masterpieces. Over 100,000 people populate World Trade Center's 110 stories on any given workday, a structure that can safely sway up to three feet in high winds.

0:09 (0:05) Cross Hackensack River while flood of vehicular traffic streams across same waterway on New Jersey Turnpike.

0:13 (0:00) Cross Passaic River and enter heavily industrialized outskirts of Newark.

0:14 (0:00) Arrive Newark's Pennsylvania Station.

NEWARK, NJ - Anchoring the northern end of New Jersey's industrialized core, Newark has the dubious distinction of being one of the world's most important manufacturing communities as well as the largest city in the state. Such stature has not come without serious urban problems, but Newark will undoubtedly survive and continue its role as a world producer.

The town has literally grown up in the shadow of New York City. Newark International Airport has become one of the nation's busiest because of this proximity. And Newark generates considerable business for Amtrak, with commuters transferring here to PATH trains for lower Manhattan.

0:00 (0:33) Upon departing Newark, travel on elevated track through more residential and industrial suburbs.

0:04 (0:29) Pass through Elizabeth, a manufacturing metropolis whose industrial roots date to pre-Revolutionary days— a time when Elizabeth was New Jersey's capital. Both Aaron Burr and Alexander Hamilton lived in this historic city.

0:06 (0:27) Large General Motors assembly plant spreads out on right.

0:08 (0:25) Glide into Rahway on elevated track where old brownstones line each side of right-of-way.

0:09 (0:24) Enter Metro Park, an impressive, modern business and industrial park on left.

From here to Trenton, there are large industrial complexes bearing familiar names such as Revlon, Delco, Johnson & Johnson, American Standard, Bayer Aspirin and Trans America, incongruously interspersed with farms and pastureland.

0:16 (0:17) Pass through New Brunswick, home of Rutgers University which was founded in 1776. Although a state university, it took its name from a generous donor in 1825. First intercollegiate football game was played here in 1869 with Rutgers winning over Princeton by a mighty score of 6 to 4.

0:17 (0:16) On right, beautifully landscaped Johnson & Johnson headquarters often has various waterfowl gallivanting on front lawn.

0:25 (0:08) On right, whimsical cow-shaped shrubbery makes appropriate landscaping for Walker Gordon Milk Farms.

0:26 (0:07) Pass through Princeton Junction where connections are made to trains of New Jersey Transit for Princeton University, just three miles west of here. Branch was originally built in 1865 by Camden & Amboy Rail Road Transportation Company, one of earliest railroads in America. School is nation's fifth oldest institution of higher learning.

0:33 (0:00) Arrive Trenton.

TRENTON, NJ - The capital of New Jersey is home to more than 400 industries. British and Hessian troops were housed here during the night General George Washington and his army made their famous Delaware River crossing. "The Old Barracks" have been reconstructed on their original South Willow Street site where, ironically, man-made artifacts dating to 2000 B.C. have been recently uncovered.

0:00 (0:31) Depart Trenton and cross Delaware. It was on Christmas Eve, 1776, that Washington crossed its icy waters just eight miles northwest of here to attack Trenton's Hessian Garrison. Ensuing Battle of Trenton marked first victory by Washington over German mercenaries. Off to right, beyond bridge with sign "Trenton Makes – The World Takes," can be seen glistening gold dome of New Jersey's State Capitol, built in 1792 and second oldest continually used statehouse in U.S.

0:05 (0:26) On left, numerous small boats dot picturesque inlet of Delaware River.

0:12 (0:19) Campus of Holy Family College is on right.

0:18 (0:13) On left, note Sterling Paper Company's unique clock tower.

0:20 (0:11) North Philadelphia's newly remodeled station is at right. Connie Mack Stadium, named after organizer of baseball's American League and owner and manager of renowned Philadelphia Athletics from 1901 to 1950, once loomed just beyond.

0:22 (0:09) Two-story brick structure at trackside is called Zoo Tower (Zoo for its closeness to Philadelphia's Fairmont Park). Tower oversees Corridor's most complex junction where train traffic is sifted through maze of tracks without a single crossing at grade. Corridor tracks keep to upper level.

0:26 (0:05) Cross Schuylkill River as it meanders through Fairmont Park.

0:27 (0:04) On left is skyline of downtown Philadelphia, while city's popular zoo is in foreground. Along far shore of river and immediately after zoo is Boat House Row, home to numerous racing scull clubs. Crews can frequently be seen practicing their rowing skills along this stretch of Schuylkill.

0:28 (0:03) In distance to left is Philadelphia Museum of Art, known for not only fine art but its prominence in movie "Rocky."

0:29 (0:02) To left, City Hall can be seen, topped by enduring statue of William Penn—a long-time informal height restriction for buildings in Philadelphia. Barrier was broken, however, with construction of One Liberty Place, now visible as tallest structure on skyline.

0:31 (0:00) Arrive Philadelphia beneath venerable 30th Street Station.

PHILADELPHIA, PA - William Penn's desire to form a colony for "religious minorities" and the fact the

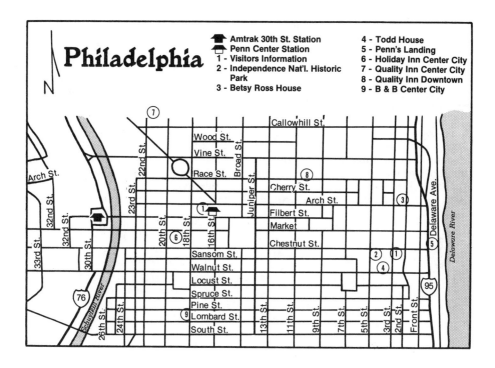

Philadelphia

- Amtrak 30th St. Station
- Penn Center Station
1 - Visitors Information
2 - Independence Nat'l. Historic Park
3 - Betsy Ross House
4 - Todd House
5 - Penn's Landing
6 - Holiday Inn Center City
7 - Quality Inn Center City
8 - Quality Inn Downtown
9 - B & B Center City

British Crown owed a debt to his father combined to give birth to Philadelphia. King Charles II gave a large parcel of land to Penn to enable him to create such a settlement in the New World, and in 1682 Penn founded the colony of Pennsylvania ("Penn's Woods") in memory of his father. He soon identified a peninsula between the Delaware and Schuylkill rivers as the site of Philadelphia, Greek for "City of Brotherly Love."

Penn's chief surveyor was asked to lay out the city in a grid pattern with five public squares to provide both sunlight and fresh air for the city's residents—the first recorded effort toward urban planning. These five public squares still exist. The city flourished both economically and culturally, becoming for awhile the second largest English-speaking city in the world.

The city's history is tightly interwoven with America's independence. The Second Continental Congress met in what is now called Independence Hall, and it was here the decision was made to prepare the Declaration of Independence. Philadelphia was the nation's capital until the year 1800.

Although the city showed signs of urban decay after World War II, the 1960s saw a great renewal effort. Today, Philadelphia is a distinctive city of nearly five million, with attractive office buildings, restored town houses and a collection of cobblestone streets illuminated by old-fashioned lampposts.

30th Street Station, on the edge of downtown at 30th and Market streets, is the main passenger train station serving Philadelphia. It is perhaps the best of the grand-style stations with everything done in excellent taste. A massive "rehabilitation" project is underway and should be completed by mid 1991.

This is Amtrak's second busiest station in passengers served (New York's Penn Station is first). There are redcaps, restaurants, snack bars, newsstands, a bookstore and other shops. The baggage room is open 24 hours Monday thru Friday, and 7 am to 11 pm, Saturday, Sunday and holidays. Pay-parking, behind the station at 30th and Arch streets, is open 24 hours. SEPTA commuter trains also operate from this station.

For arrival and departure information,

33

call 800-USA-RAIL; for reservations and other information, call (215) 824-1600. Ticket windows are open from early morning to late evening. The waiting room is open 24 hours.

Penn Center Station, 1617 John F. Kennedy Blvd. (also referred to as "Suburban Station") is located in the heart of downtown about a mile east of the 30th St. Station. It can be reached by commuter train in a few minutes from the 30th St. Station; no charge for those holding Amtrak tickets.

Cab stand is at the 30th Street entrance; Yellow Cab, 922-8400. Nearest **local bus** stop at 30th and Market streets just outside the station, 574-7800. A **subway** station is across the street at the same intersection. Hertz, Avis and American International have **car rentals** available at the station. National, Sears and Budget are located nearby. **Greyhound,** 931-4000. **Philadelphia International Airport** is approximately ten miles south of the city center.

Philadelphia Visitors Center, 16th St. and John F. Kennedy Blvd. (adjacent to Penn Center Station); (215) 636-1666 or 800-321-9563. Write Philadelphia Convention & Visitors Bureau, 1515 Market St., Suite 2020, 19102.

Holiday Inn Center City, 18th and Market streets, 19103; (215) 561-7500. Nine blocks to the 30th Street Station; three blocks from Penn Center Station. $116.

-**Quality Inn Center City,** 501 N. 22nd, 19130; (215) 568-8300. Just north of Fairmount Park, about 11 blocks from the 30th Street Station. $81.

-**Quality Inn Downtown Suites,** 1010 Race (at 10th), 19107; (215) 922-1730. Next to Chinatown; 18 blocks from 30th St. Station and 10 blocks from Penn Center Station. $74.

-**Bed and Breakfast, Center City,** 1804 Pine, 19103; (215) 735-1137. B&B that also acts as a reservation service for other downtown B&Bs. Eight blocks from Penn Center Station. $40.

For other downtown bed and breakfast reservations, **All About Town Bed & Breakfast of Philadelphia,** P.O. Box 562, Valley Forge, PA 19481; (215) 783-7838.

Philadelphia's charm is in its history. Of greatest historic significance is **Independence National Historical Park** in the area of 5th and Chestnut streets. It can be reached by Transit bus; parking is at 2nd and Sansom Street. The Park includes: **Independence Hall,** originally built between 1732 and 1756 as the Pennsylvania State House, the Declaration of Independence was adopted and U.S. Constitution was written here; **Congress Hall,** adjacent to Independence Hall, was first built as a courthouse and later used by the U.S. Congress from 1790 to 1800 and is where Washington delivered his first message to Congress; **Liberty Bell Pavilion** is the location of America's most beloved symbol of freedom, the Liberty Bell; and the **City Tavern, First Bank of the United States, Carpenters Hall,** and **Franklin Court,** all just east of Liberty Bell Pavilion. The Visitors Center, at Third Street between Chestnut and Walnut, has a film about the American Revolution which is shown every hour.

The **Betsy Ross Flag House,** 239 Arch St., was the home of Betsy Ross who is credited with making the first American flag. The **Todd House,** 4th and Walnut streets, built in 1775, was the home of Dolly Todd Madison. And **Penn's Landing,** waterfront area in the vicinity of Delaware Avenue and Chestnut Street, is where William Penn first stepped ashore. Old naval ships are anchored here, including a World War II submarine.

0:00 (0:21) Depart Philadelphia.

0:01 (0:20) On right stands University of Pennsylvania's Franklin Field.

0:02 (0:19) Pass Philadelphia Convention Center complex, on right.

0:05 (0:16) Miniature railroad is amusing exhibit fronting large General Electric plant on left.

For the next few miles, depart the industrial congestion, and venture through some of the most handsome residential neighborhoods one is apt to encounter on any route.

0:08 (0:13) Small building at trackside named "Baldwin" identifies town of Eddystone where Baldwin Locomotive Works, producer of more than 1,500 locomotives, was once major industry. Former Eddystone facility still stands on left.

0:09 (0:12) Chester, with its ancient brownstones bordering tracks, could easily pass for oldest town in Pennsylvania, which it is.

0:13 (0:08) Leave Pennsylvania and enter Delaware. Unique state boundary was formed in 1681 as section of a circle with center at spire of Old Court House in New Castle, DE. Delaware River comes into view on left. Enormous vessels traverse its wide expanse while a burgeoning maze of machinery and apparatus awaits their arrival at dockside.

0:14 (0:07) Sprawling acreage of Phoenix Steel Corporation extends for miles on right.

0:18 (0:03) Cross Brandywine Creek which flows south to meet Christina River before emptying into Delaware.

0:19 (0:02) Christina River joins on left with drawbridges every mile or so. Immediately thereafter, enter grounds of Fort Christina Park at Wilmington. Here, in 1638, a Swedish expedition, under command of Peter Minuit, came ashore and established first European settlement in Delaware. On right, note "Old Swede's Church," erected in 1698. Maintaining services to this day, church is oldest in North America still standing as originally built. Adjacent log cabin is authentic 200-year-old structure.

0:21 (0:00) Arrive Wilmington. Attractive depot, accented by old brass weather vane atop spire, is an historic 1905 structure which underwent a 10.4-million-dollar restoration in 1984.

WILMINGTON, DE - Shortly preceding the Swedish settlement, Dutch, English, and American colonists all played integral roles in Wilmington's formative development. Yet, perhaps most important, the abundant water power of the Brandywine River Valley was soon harnessed to provide an extensive gristmill industry, enabling Wilmington to emerge as an active center for trade and marketing, with easy accessibility along the Delaware River.

In 1802, Eleuthere duPont established a black-powder mill upon the banks of Brandywine Creek. From these humble beginnings, the duPont Corporation has evolved into one of the largest producers of chemicals, plastics, synthetic cloth and dyes in the U.S. It is still, today, the foundation for Wilmington's claim as "Chemical Capital of the World."

0:00 (0:42) Depart Wilmington. For next several miles, beautiful farmhouses and lush agrarian settings alternate paradoxically with expansive industrial complexes.

0:09 (0:33) On left note large Chrysler Corporation plant.

0:11 (0:31) Once through Newark, DE, cross Delaware state line into Maryland at Mason and Dixon's line, surveyed by those two Englishmen in 1776 to resolve a boundary dispute between Pennsylvania and Maryland. Bear southwest through lushly wooded landscapes and quaint residential districts, where prominent influence of Colonial architecture and platting within these beautifully preserved communities imparts a real sense of living history throughout region.

0:16 (0:26) Northeast River appears on left. Northeast, Bush, Gunpowder, and Back rivers are all inlets of Chesapeake Bay.

0:19 (0:23) Pass through Perryville on eastern bank of Susquehanna River. Delightful old brick depot stands out on left.

0:20 (0:22) Cross Susquehanna River. Large steel bridges span river on right, while multitude of sailboats adorn marinas on both banks.

0:21 (0:21) Pass through Havre de Grace. Charming bayside community is home to last working light tower on upper Chesapeake Bay.

0:23 (0:20) Pass through Aberdeen where U.S. Army Ordnance Museum exhibits array of historical military hardware, uniforms, and the like.

0:26 (0:16) Cross Bush River.

0:28 (0:14) Pass through Edgewood. Just north is birthplace of William Paca, one of fifty colonists to sign Declaration of Independence.

0:30 (0:12) Cross Gunpowder River. It was here on January 4, 1987 that Amtrak's Colonial, just out of Baltimore and traveling in excess of 100 mph, slammed into three Conrail locomotives which, in spite of cautionary and stop signals, had just pulled onto main line. It was Amtrak's worst wreck—16 fatalities and 176 injuries.

0:33 (0:09) On left, border facilities of Maryland National Guard. Martin Marietta operation is immediately adjacent.

0:35 (0:07) Back River appears on left.

0:39 (0:03) Enter city limits of Baltimore atop elevated track bed. On right, clusters of high-density brownstones are huddled along hillsides, while on left, beautiful old church presides in foreground of downtown skyline.

0:42 (0:00) Arrive Baltimore. Depot, like many other Northeastern facilities, features a fascinating combination of architectural forms, stretching many stories skyward from cobblestone walkways below. Also of interest are numerous placards and billboards touting current cultural offerings of area.

BALTIMORE, MD - Started as a harbor town in 1729, Baltimore is now a city of varied nationalities and independent neighborhoods. It has long been one of the more important shipping, financial and industrial centers for the East. Although many of the older portions of the downtown have been razed and renewed, much of our nation's early history can still be virtually seen and felt amongst the city's retained landmarks.

During the War of 1812, Francis Scott Key penned the words to the *Star Spangled Banner* while witnessing the battle of Ft. McHenry from a ship in the harbor. For a brief period during the American Revolution, Baltimore served as the nation's capital. It is also the birthplace of baseball's Babe Ruth.

Pennsylvania Station, 1515 N. Charles Street, has been finely restored to its original grandeur. The station is about a mile north of downtown, but public buses and rubber-tired "trollies" provide easy access during the day.

The station has a snack bar, a newsstand and redcap service. A manned information counter is located in the center of the station with bus schedules and other information. There is a Citibank ATM center on the premises and a Travelers Aid counter. Arrival and departure information occurs on electronic display boards and public address announcements are unusually understandable. Closest parking is a half block away on St. Paul. Covered parking is about a block on Lanvale, between Charles and St. Paul.

Call 800-USA-RAIL for reservations and other information.

Cab stand is at the station; Yellow Cab, 685-1212; and Sun Cab, 235-0300. There are direct phones to Avis and Hertz for **rental car** pick up at the station. Nearest **bus stop** for southbound buses (to downtown) is one block away on St. Paul Street; 539-5000. **"Trolley"** service to downtown is available on Charles Street in front of the station, from 11 am to 7 pm; fare is 25 cents. **Greyhound,** call 744-9311. **Subway-Metrorail** information, call 539-5000. **MARC** commuter trains use Pennsylvania Station and travel south on the Northeast Corridor tracks to Washington, D.C., then west to Gaithersburg. MARC trains also use a separate line between the downtown Camden Station and Washington. Call 800-325-RAIL for MARC information. Certain Amtrak and MARC trains stop at **Baltimore-Washington International Airport,** the quickest (about 15 minutes) and cheapest way ($4 to $6) to get from Baltimore to this airport. Although the MARC fare is somewhat cheaper, the free shuttle bus between BWI station and the terminal theoretically is only for Amtrak passengers.

Baltimore Convention and Visitors Bureau, 600 Water Street, The Brokerage, 21202; 659-7300. A visitor information center is also located at the Inner Harbor. Some information is also available at the station.

Lodging shown below is located in two desirable areas, the beautifully reclaimed Inner Harbor area and historic Fell's Point. Fell's Point and the Inner Harbor are connected by the rubber-tired trolleys, and the Inner Harbor and Penn Station are also linked by this pleasant form of transportation.

-Days Inn Baltimore Inner Harbor, 100 Hopkins Place, 21201; (301) 576-1000. Attractive high rise located downtown on the trolley route, about four blocks from the Inner Harbor and a mile from the

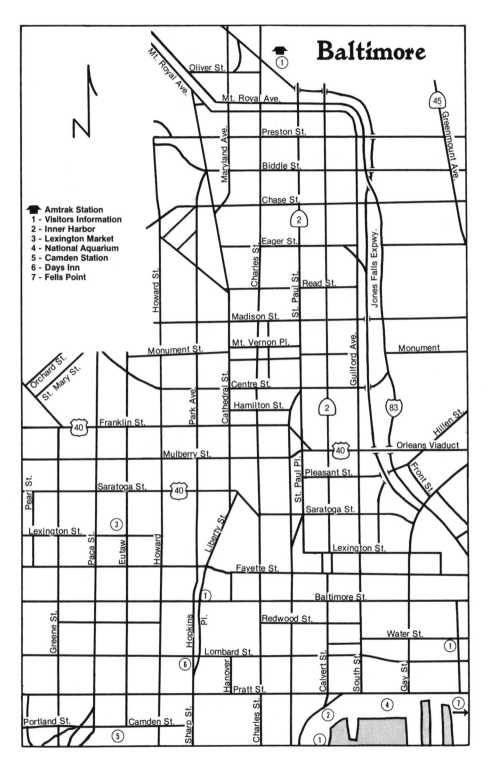

Baltimore

Amtrak Station
1 - Visitors Information
2 - Inner Harbor
3 - Lexington Market
4 - National Aquarium
5 - Camden Station
6 - Days Inn
7 - Fells Point

station. $90.

-Admiral Fell Inn, 888 S. Broadway, 21231; (301) 522-7377 or 800-292-4667. Elegantly renovated inn on the waterfront in Fell's Point. On the trolley line. Excellent restaurant. Complimentary continental breakfast. Free shuttle service throughout the city; if not available, inn will pay for cab fare from the station. $115.

-Celies Waterfront Bed and Breakfast, 1714 Thames Street, 21231; (301) 522-2323. Newly constructed B&B, overlooking the waterfront in Fell's Point. On the trolley line. $90.

The **Inner Harbor,** at Pratt and Light streets, is a waterfront showpiece in the heart of the city. Restaurants, shops, harbor tours and harbor activities are delightfully compatible in this urban setting. The **U.S. Frigate Constellation,** the world's oldest floating ship, is docked here and can be boarded.

The adjacent **U.S. Maritime Museum** is actually comprised of three vessels: the submarine U.S.S. Torsk, the Lightship Chesapeake and the U.S.C.G.C. Taney. And next door is the fine **National Aquarium in Baltimore** with aquatic exhibits, including a coral reef, sharks, eels, jellyfish, whales and a rain forest. Moving ramps carry visitors through much of this outstanding facility. For a view of the city, an **observation deck** is on the 27th floor of the World Trade Center, also at the Inner Harbor.

Fell's Point, just a mile east of the Inner Harbor and easily reached by trolley (or water shuttle in the summer), is Baltimore's old waterfront neighborhood—it's one of the oldest waterfront communities in the country. Once a tough district known for its sailor-filled bars, Fell's Point has become a mixture of Georgetown and Greenwich Village. The shipyards where the renowned Baltimore Clippers were once built are gone, but this is still a working community, and tramp steamers and harbor tugs are common sights. About half of the row houses that line its Belgian-block paved streets have been restored. Unusual shops, a public market, some offbeat eateries, old inns and fashionable bed and breakfasts make this an enjoyable place to visit.

For an entirely different look at Baltimore, **Lexington Market,** in the downtown area at Lexington and Eutaw streets, is a zesty crush of market stalls, brimming with seafoods, meats, produce, ethnic foods—and humanity.

Fort McHenry National Monument, at the foot of E. Fort Ave., southeast of the city, is the site of Baltimore's successful battle against the British during the War of 1812, and inspired Francis Scott Key to write the words of the *Star Spangled Banner.* A water shuttle from the Inner Harbor is available during the summer months.

And for those interested in trains and streetcars: The **Baltimore Streetcar Museum** is at 1901 Falls Road, where one can see the streetcar history of the city, as well as take a mile-long streetcar ride; and the **B. & O. Railroad Museum,** Pratt and Poppleton streets, is in a fine, old circular roundhouse, over 100 years old, with a world famous display of old locomotives and other rail artifacts.

0:00 (0:24) Depart Baltimore, noting old stone bridge on right. Proceed into eerily lit century-old B & P Tunnel—a dark, wet, 7,492-foot bottleneck. Emerge minutes later amidst another covey of old brownstones.

0:10 (0:14) Extensive cemetery lines route on right.

0:12 (0:12) On right pass distilleries of Calvert Whiskey.

0:18 (0:06) Baltimore-Washington International Airport is a stop for some trains where Amtrak passengers are shuttled directly to and from airport's terminal. Passing through Odenton, note interesting old hotel peeking through trees on right.

0:24 (0:00) Arrive New Carrollton.

NEW CARROLLTON, MD - This very modern station serves the northern suburbs of Washington, D.C. There is a Metro station here with subway and bus service to D.C., Virginia and Maryland.

0:00 (0:09) Depart New Carrollton and cross Maryland state line into District of Columbia.

0:00 (0:05) Cross Anacostia River.

0:04 (0:02) Approaching Washington, silhouette of Washington Monument can be

discerned in distance on right.
0:09 (0:00) Arrive Washington, D.C.

WASHINGTON, DC - The nation's first president played a guiding role in developing what would become the country's capital. Not only did he personally select the men to lay out and plan the city, Pierre Charles L'Enfant and Andrew Ellicott, he also chose the sites for both the White House and the Capitol Building.

The result of such presidential involvement is an unusually well laid-out city, with broad streets, many radiating from small parks and circles, lined by imposing marble edifices. It is handsome geometry—and one of the reasons Washington is among the most visited towns in the U.S.

The city is easy to see. Many of its attractions line the Mall—a lengthy, broad esplanade, stretching from the Capitol Building on the east to the Lincoln Memorial on the west. An extensive, modern and easy-to-use subway system makes it possible to do more venturesome exploring without a car, a real plus since heavy traffic is constant and parking is scarce.

Union Station, 50 Massachusetts Ave., NE, located on Capitol Hill, is undisputedly the nation's premier train station. Thanks to a heroic renovation effort, Union Station is no longer a national eyesore, but a gleaming showpiece of marble floors, mahogany woodwork and gold-leafed ceilings.

When Daniel Burnham's beaux-arts masterpiece was first opened in 1908, it lived up to his simple creed: "Make no little plans." It was large enough to hold the entire U.S. Army—then 50,000 in number. It reached its zenith of activity during World War II when no less than 5,000 employees worked here. Subsequently, rail travel declined and so did Union Station. Surviving a 1983 runaway train that crashed into its main concourse, a 1960 effort to demolish it, and finally the 1968 National Visitors Center fiasco, it has now undergone a triumphant resuscitation.

An electronic arrival and departure board over an information counter greets passengers entering the front doors. There are spaces for 100 retail shops, restaurants and fast-food outlets; there is even a nine-screen theater. Luggage carts and redcaps are available. (Phase II construction will be necessary to complete the remodeling, putting tracks closer to the waiting area, eliminating the temporary inconvenience getting to the tracks, and adding a lounge for holders of 1st class tickets.) A 1,400-car garage guarantees space for Amtrak passengers who can park here for $7.50 a day. Enter on H Street or Massachusetts Ave. Elevators and escalators take patrons to the station.

For Amtrak reservations and other information, call 484-7450.

Cab stand is at the station; Diamond, 387-4821. Cab fares in D.C. are based on zones, rather than being metered, and rates are somewhat higher during the evening rush hour. A Metrorail **subway** stop (red line) is at the station, as well as the nearest **local bus** stop; call 637-7000 for information. **Tourmobiles,** a convenient way to see many of the sights, also stop at the station. **Greyhound/Trailways,** call (301) 565-2662 for fare and schedule information. Both Avis and National have **rental cars** available at the station. **Washington National Airport** is just across the Potomac in Virginia and can be reached by Metrorail. **Dulles International Airport** is much farther south, about 27 miles from the station. **Baltimore-Washington International Airport** is 31 miles northeast of the station and can be reached by some Amtrak trains. A shuttle is provided for Amtrak passengers between the BWI station and the airport terminal.

Washington Convention and Visitors Association, 1212 New York Ave., 20005; (202) 789-7000. **Visitors Information Center,** 1455 Pennsylvania Ave. (between the Willard and Washington hotels).

The hotels shown here are within easy walking distance from the station and are also convenient to the Capitol, the Mall and the Metro.
-**Bellevue Hotel,** 15 E Street, NW, 20001; (202) 638-9000 or 800-327-6667. Nicely remodeled older hotel, with locally popular pub. Two short blocks from the station.

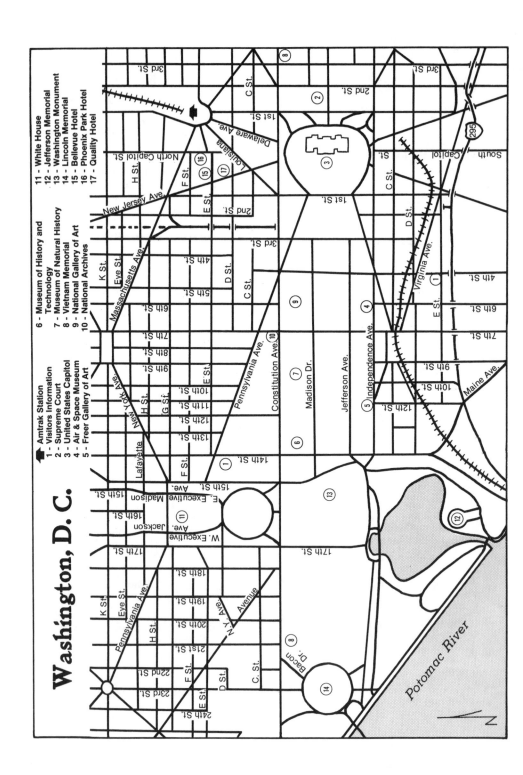

Washington, D. C.

- Amtrak Station
1 - Visitors Information
2 - Supreme Court
3 - United States Capitol
4 - Air & Space Museum
5 - Freer Gallery of Art
6 - Museum of History and Technology
7 - Museum of Natural History
8 - Vietnam Memorial
9 - National Gallery of Art
10 - National Archives
11 - White House
12 - Jefferson Memorial
13 - Washington Monument
14 - Lincoln Memorial
15 - Bellevue Hotel
16 - Phoenix Park Hotel
17 - Quality Hotel

Potomac River

Standard rate, $114. Special rate for Amtrak passengers, $89.

-Phoenix Park Hotel, 520 North Capitol Street, NW, 20001; (202) 638-6900 or 800-824-5419. Smaller hostelry with deluxe accommodations, only a block from the station. Standard rate, $147. Special rate for Amtrak passengers, $94.

-Quality Hotel Capitol Hill, 415 New Jersey Ave., NW, 20001; (202) 638-1616. Four blocks from the station. $94.

 For a reasonable fare, the popular **Tourmobile** takes passengers on a narrated tour of 18 historic sites, including Arlington Cemetery, while another route goes to historic Alexandria and Mt. Vernon. Passengers are permitted to reboard throughout the day at no extra charge.

The attractions shown below are along or near the Mall, and a healthy walker (read hiker) theoretically could reach them all on foot from the station. The Metro or a taxi, however, might be considered for those points of interest near the east end of the Mall.

The **Smithsonian Museums** are mostly spread out along the Mall. Some of the more popular ones include: The **National Air and Space Museum,** with superb displays of aircraft, from the Wright Brothers' plane to modern-day space vehicles; the **Freer Gallery of Art** with fine displays of Oriental and other art; the **National Museum of American History,** displaying aspects of the nation's history and development; and the **National Museum of Natural History** with collections including the Hope Diamond.

Some other popular points of interest along or near the Mall include: the **United States Capitol,** at the east end of the Mall, with chambers of both houses of Congress and guided tours available every 15 minutes; the **Supreme Court,** just east of the Capitol, with tours except when the court is in session; the **National Gallery of Art,** comprised of two buildings with a large collection of Western and American art; the **National Archives,** the resting place for the Constitution, the Declaration of Independence and the Bill of Rights; the **Washington Monument** with an elevator to the observation room at the top (waits can be long); and the

Lincoln Memorial anchoring the west end of the Mall.

Not far from the Mall is: the **White House** at 1600 Pennsylvania Avenue, NW, which has been the home and working office of each president since 1800 (tours are 10 am to noon, Tuesday through Saturday); and the **Jefferson Memorial** on the south bank of the Tidal Basin.

New Haven to Springfield

0:00 (0:20) Departing New Haven, Inland Route trains swing northward away from shoreline route and angle across Connecticut, directly toward Hartford.

0:20 (0:00) Arrive Wallingford.

 WALLINGFORD, CT - One of Connecticut's older cities, Wallingford is known for its silver manufacturing. Note classic old brick church with fine spire just after station on right.

0:00 (0:08) Depart Wallingford.

0:08 (0:00) Arrive Meriden.

 MERIDEN, CT - This city of nearly 60,000 is home to the world's largest producer of silverware—International Silver Company. At its main plant visitors can see Heritage House, furnished to illustrate 18th-century life in America, while silversmiths and pewters demonstrate early methods of production.

0:00 (0:10) Depart Meriden.

0:04 (0:06) Small pool on left is Beaver Pond.

0:05 (0:05) Idyllic Silver Lake stretches along tracks on right.

0:10 (0:00) Arrive Berlin.

BERLIN, CT - Here, first tinware in America was produced in early 1700s.

0:00 (0:13) Depart Berlin.

0:13 (0:00) Arriving Hartford, marble capitol building with its gold-leafed dome looms above train on right. One of Hartford's more unusual industries, gold-beating, provided the gild for this elegant structure. Some fine historical exhibits are housed within.

HARTFORD, CT - Referred to as the "Insurance Capital of the World," more insurance is underwritten in Hartford than in any other city in the United States. Other major employers include Colt Industries, makers of firearms (including the famed Colt "45") and Hueblein Industries of alcoholic beverage renown.

The town had its first permanent inhabitants in 1633 when a trading post was established by the Dutch. The nation's oldest statehouse is still preserved near the center of town.

During its development, Hartford fostered some of America's greatest intellectuals. In 1874, Mark Twain built a whimsical brick mansion (it looked more like a Mississippi riverboat), and penned Huck Finn and Tom Sawyer as well as many of his other beloved tales. Noah Webster was born in West Hartford, and although best known for creating the first comprehensive American dictionary in 1783 he authored the "Blue-Backed Speller" which was still in use during the early part of this century. Harriet Beecher Stowe ("Uncle Tom's Cabin") also lived here.

0:00 (0:14) Depart Hartford.

0:06 (0:08) First glimpse of Connecticut River, flowing southeastward toward its Atlantic mouth at Old Saybrook, is afforded on right.

0:09 (0:05) Windsor, CT, located in shade-grown tobacco country, is one of Connecticut's earliest settlements, having been founded by Plymouth colonists in 1663. This is a stop for some trains. Newly remodeled station serves buses as well as Amtrak.

0:10 (0:04) Farmington River is now crossed. This broad stream follows a 60-mile serpentine course from its Algonquin-State-Forest birthplace, only 20 miles straight west of us, to its Connecticut-River joinder just east of here.

0:14 (0:00) Arrive Windsor Locks.

WINDSOR LOCKS, CT - This New England manufacturing community also serves as the location for Hartford's airport (Bradley International Airport) which is just west of here, as well as the Bradley Air Museum which houses a collection of vintage military aircraft.

0:00 (0:24) Depart Windsor Locks and roll under Interstate 91, stretching from New Haven northward to Vermont-Quebec border.

0:03 (0:21) Across Windsor Locks Canal, on right, sign on factory proclaims "C. H. Dexter & Sons – Established 1767."

The company is an American institution. It is the oldest corporation listed on the New York Stock Exchange and quite possibly the third oldest continually operated company in America. Its specialty is the manufacture of long-fiber papers which Dexter then makes into tea bags (world's largest supplier), oil filters, surgical gowns and other paper products. Although the canal was constructed in the early 1800s to provide a shipping bypass needed to avoid a dam further upstream, it now provides fresh water (critical in paper production) to Dexter.

0:06 (0:18) Having tired of following west bank of Connecticut River, rails now cross to eastern shore.

0:11 (0:13) Rumble through Enfield where Jonathan Edwards, perhaps Colonial New England's most effective revivalist, delivered one of his greatest sermons—"Sinners in the Hands of an Angry God." Although his voice was weak and he read from manuscripts held closely to his near-sighted eyes, his logic and power were extraordinary. Edwards eventually became president of College of New Jersey—eventually known as Princeton University.

0:15 (0:09) After passing through Thompsonville, leave Connecticut and enter Massachusetts.

0:24 (0:00) Arrive Springfield.

SPRINGFIELD, MA - An important manufacturing city of the Northeast, Springfield had its start as a mere trading post in the 1630s. In 1794 the United States opened an important armory here, now the Springfield Armory Museum. Today, the Basketball Hall of Fame is located here, and the Strategic Air Command has operations at Westover Air Force Base just northeast of town.

For route between Boston and Springfield, see Lake Shore Ltd. log, page 63.

Philadelphia to Atlantic City
(Atlantic City Express)

With the meteoric rise of Atlantic City from a rather forlorn seaside resort to the nation's most visited city, Amtrak has stepped in to share in the resulting transportation bonanza. Several trains now travel daily between the Boardwalk and Philadelphia where connections are easily made to other points along the Northeast Corridor. There are also some through trains that originate in New York City and New Haven to the north, and Washington, DC to the south.

Service is provided on reserved Amfleet coaches, with sandwiches and beverages available on board. Club cars are also carried by each train. The one-way trip from Philadelphia takes about 1¼ hours.

0:00 (0:33) Depart Philadelphia's 30th Street Station northbound.

0:02 (0:31) Philadelphia Museum of Art is at right, then on far banks of Schuylkill River are handsome boat houses, home to several rowing organizations. Houses make a particularly delightful sight after dark, with each outlined by strings of lights.

0:03 (0:29) Philadelphia Zoo (America's first) slips past on right, easily identified by statuary of zoo's inhabitants.

0:04 (0:28) Cross Schuylkill River, a waterway often used by boating crews for practicing rowing skills.

0:07 (0:26) Almost every city has an area that can only be described as ugly, and tracks now pass through what must be Philadelphia's worst—depressing shells of commercial buildings and wretched-looking row houses paint a grim scene on both sides of right-of-way.

0:10 (0:23) Juniata Terminal Company, easily identified by sign at right, restores antique railroad cars for private car owners. Enormous shops (50,000 square feet) house various railroad artifacts such as Robert Kennedy's funeral car. Company usually has interesting array of rail cars parked outside in view of main line.

0:11 (0:22) Pass rail intersection known as Shore Interlocking.

0:13 (0:20) Ornate clock tower highlights facilities of Sterling Paper Company off to right.

0:16 (0:17) Cross expansive waters of Delaware River, forming boundary between Pennsylvania and New Jersey. Delaire Bridge was originally built in 1895/6 as a swing span, but was retrofitted

with a vertical lift section about 30 years ago during a widening of river's channel.

0:24 (0:09) Slicing through parking lot of Cherry Hill's Garden State Race Track, modern glass and brick betting facilities are seen just to left.

0:33 (0:00) Arriving Lindenwold, large assemblage of PATCO (Port Authority Transportation Corp.) commuter trains rest in PATCO's yards awaiting duty between here and Philadelphia.

 LINDENWOLD, NJ - This city of 18,000 is the heart of Philadelphia's easternmost "suburbs." As well as Amtrak service, PATCO trains can be ridden into the heart of that Pennsylvanian metropolis, and New Jersey transit trains can be taken to Atlantic City.

0:00 (0:43) Depart Lindenwold.

0:08 (0:35) Having slipped from heavily populated sections of New Jersey, train now courses through bucolic New Jersey forests.

0:09 (0:34) Tree nursery spreads out on left.

0:26 (0:17) As train nears ocean, terrain and architecture take on a seacoast appearance. Soil becomes sandy, then marshy, while quaint three-story, white-with-green-trim Victorian home appears on right.

0:38 (0:05) High rises of "new" Atlantic City now rise dramatically, dead ahead.

0:41 (0:02) Cross channel known as Beach Thorofare, part of Intracoastal Waterway system.

0:43 (0:00) Arrive Atlantic City's new train station. City's new convention center is to be constructed just beyond.

ATLANTIC CITY, NJ - A first impression could be: This is Las Vegas with seagulls. But it's more than this. Atlantic City is a place of memories rapidly being engulfed by the new order of legalized gambling.

The fashionable piers are gone, replaced only by a three-layered shopping arcade called Ocean One which now serves as a token of what once was an Atlantic City trademark. The famous Boardwalk with its herringbone slats is still the main beat of the sightseer, angling along the white sand beach for nearly five miles. The honky-tonk shops and arcades that have long lined this thoroughfare continue to stand their ground but are overshadowed by the ostentatious gambling palaces that now share space on this hallowed ground. A thousand years from now, this will be a suitable subject for archaeological excavation—and speculation.

There are three reasons to come to Atlantic City: to gamble, to take in shows or just to look and relax in the midst of a unique bit of Americana.

Atlantic City Rail Terminal, One Atlantic City Expressway (at Kirkman Blvd.), is one of Amtrak's newest stations. The inside has an open glass-and-steel atmosphere—efficient, practical and attractive, adorned with black steel-mesh benches. (The outside, however, has all the appeal of an aircraft hangar.)

A large electronic display board registers arrival and departure information for both Amtrak and New Jersey Transit trains that also use the station. There is a snack bar and a visitor information counter in the lobby. Train platforms are both high-level and covered. Parking is adjacent to the station. The Boardwalk is within walking distance, just five long blocks to the east. A new convention center is being built adjacent to the station and should be completed in 1992.

For Amtrak reservations and information, call 800-USA-RAIL.

Cab stand is at the station; Atlantic City Yellow Cab, 344-1221. **Jitney** service to the Boardwalk is also available for about a dollar. **Buses to all casinos** depart regularly from the station, $5 round trip. **Harrahs** has had free shuttle service for Amtrak passengers. **Municipal Bus Terminal** (the former railroad terminal) is two blocks from the station; **Greyhound,** 345-5403; New Jersey Transit, 344-8181. **Bader Field Airport** is only a few minutes from the center of town.

Convention and Visitors Bureau, 2314 Pacific Avenue (at Mississippi), 08401; (609) 348-7100 or 7130. Conveniently located between the station and the Boardwalk (behind Trump Plaza).

Caesars Atlantic City Hotel Casino, Arkansas and Pacific avenues, 08401; (609) 348-4411 or 800-257-8555. On the Boardwalk and closest hotel casino to the station; five blocks. $120.

-The Royal Inn, Pacific Ave. and Park Place, 08401; (609) 344-7021. A popular non-casino motel, only a block from the Boardwalk and seven blocks from the station. $85.

-Quality Inn, S. Carolina and Pacific avenues, 08401; (609) 345-7070. A block from the Boardwalk and a mile from the station. $65.

Casino gambling and **big-name shows** are popular ways to pass the time in this seaside resort, but there are other things to see, which can easily be accomplished in a day. The **Boardwalk,** with its strolling hordes, is remarkable in and to itself. Along this planked walkway are the sights, sounds and smells that are uniquely Atlantic City. Visit **Ocean One's** three tiers of shops, restaurants and arcades suspended out over the Atlantic. Its upper balconies provide excellent panoramas of the city. Be sure to note the memorial plaque commemorating Charles Darrow, the inventor of the game of **Monopoly,** the game that borrows heavily from the city's street names, located appropriately at the corner of Park Place and Boardwalk. Walk past (and into if construction is completed and it is open) the **Trump Taj Mahal,** a vastly overstated version of the Indian architectural wonder. Try out the elevated, covered, **moving sidewalk** that sucks patrons from the Boardwalk area and takes them on a one-way journey to the Sands and Claridge. Its walls are a nostalgic photo gallery, while the sounds of performances from days past fill the air. Lastly, for some rare Atlantic City memorabilia, visit the **Atlantic City Art Center** on Garden Pier, the northernmost spot on the Boardwalk.

Other Northeast Service

Besides Northeast Corridor trains, including those that run up the Connecticut Valley terminating at Springfield, MA, Amtrak offers Inland Service trains linking Boston and Washington, DC by way of Springfield.

Montrealer

This is one of Amtrak's two trains to Montreal. Each is as different as night and day—literally. The Montrealer is an overnight expedition through the Connecticut River Valley and Vermont with Washington, DC its southern terminus, while the Adirondack's more direct route up the Hudson and west shore of Lake Champlain is a daylight run, and with New York City its southern endpoint.

The Montrealer's slightly out-of-the-way route (it is 70 miles longer than the Adirondack's path between New York and Montreal) provides winter access to some of New England's better ski areas, while in the summer, there is some wonderfully pastoral viewing of Vermont's maple syrup country in the early-morning hours. Covered bridges and forests interspersed with small dairy farms enhance the scene.

Northbound Schedule (Condensed)
Washington, DC - Late Afternoon Departure
New York, NY - Midevening
Springfield, MA - Middle of the Night
Montpelier Jct., VT - Early Morning
Montreal, Que. - Midmorning Arrival

Southbound Schedule (Condensed)
Montreal, Que. - Late Afternoon Departure
Montpelier Jct., VT - Late Evening
Springfield, MA - Middle of the Night
New York, NY - Early Morning
Washington, DC - Midmorning Arrival

Frequency - Daily.
Seating - Heritage Fleet coaches.
Dining - Tray meals, snacks, sandwiches and beverage service.

Lounge - "Le Pub," with live entertainment.
Sleeping - Bedrooms, roomettes and Slumbercoach rooms.
Baggage - Checked baggage handled at some stations.
Reservations - All-reserved train except for local travel between Washington, DC and New York City.
Length of Trip - 1,082 miles in 16 hours.

Note that in early 1990 The Montrealer will follow a temporary routing between New London, CT and Brattleboro, VT. This more easterly course will bypass Hartford, Springfield and Northampton.

Route Log - Springfield, MA to Montreal

For route between Washington, DC and Springfield, MA, see that portion of Northeast Corridor log, pages 21 and 31.

0:00 (0:45) Depart Springfield, leaving Amtrak roadbed in favor of the Boston and Maine.
0:40 (0:00) Arrive Northampton.

NORTHAMPTON, MA - This was the very heart of the religious revivalist movement during the first half of the 18th century, and was the home of Jonathan Edwards. Later, Northampton was home to "shy, silent" Calvin Coolidge, the nation's 30th president. Besides Smith College, with its all-girl enrollment, three other colleges are nearby: University of

Massachusetts, Amherst and Mt. Holyoke.

0:00 (1:05) Depart Northampton.

0:30 (0:35) At Greenfield, Troy section of B&M tracks curves off to left.

A few miles to the west, those tracks pass under the Berkshire Hills through the 4¾-mile Hoosac Tunnel. Started in 1851, the tunnel was not completed until 1875 at a cost of 136 lives and $14,000,000. Although private companies started the project, ultimately the state of Massachusetts had to finish the job.

0:50 (0:20) Leave Massachusetts and enter Vermont.

1:10 (0:00) Arrive Brattleboro.

BRATTLEBORO, VT - Rudyard Kipling, whose stories and poetry gave heroic support to the British Empire, lived here for four years near the end of the 19th century. His wife was a Brattleboro girl. An old rail station houses the Brattleboro Museum and Art Center.

0:00 (0:34) Depart Brattleboro.

0:30 (0:00) Arrive Bellows Falls.

BELLOWS FALLS, VT - The town derives its "Falls" name from falls in the adjacent Connecticut River, which, in the early 19th century, forced construction of a canal with nine locks to raise or lower river traffic past the cascades.

0:00 (0:50) Depart Bellows Falls, and immediately cross Connecticut River into New Hampshire.

This is the only state in which Amtrak operates but makes no stops. The east bank of the river is followed until Cornish, NH where the river is crossed back into Vermont.

0:40 (0:18) Cross Connecticut River once again and enter Vermont, and then town of Windsor.

This is the birthplace of Vermont. The "Republic's" constitution was signed here July 9, 1777, and the old tavern, where this historic event took place, still stands.

1:00 (0:00) Arrive White River Junction.

WHITE RIVER JUNCTION, VT - As you would expect, this is the joinder of the White River with the Connecticut River. Historically a railroad center, this is also the point where the Boston and Maine and Central Vermont meet. While the B&M heads due north, the CV angles northwesterly, the latter being the route of the Montrealer. Hanover, NH, home to Dartmouth College, is less than five miles from here.

0:00 (1:25) Depart White River Junction and follow White River northwestward across very heart of Vermont.

0:10 (1:15) At West Hartford, cross hikers' delight—the Appalachian Trail.

0:25 (1:00) This is South Royalton. Three miles east of here is Sharon, the birthplace of Joseph Smith, founder of the Mormon Church. A 38½-foot polished granite shaft (not visible from tracks) marks spot.

0:30 (0:53) Bethel is northern end of trackage where Vermont's first passenger train made its way from White River Falls. Town has unique eight-sided library originally constructed as a school.

0:40 (0:42) Montrealer cruises through Randolph. Note unusually wide streets which were designed so that town could become state's capital, being located at geographic center of Vermont. It didn't happen, however. The Morgan horse breed, now Vermont's official state animal, started here.

0:42 (0:40) Having left Third Branch of White River, we now follow beside Dog River.

1:00 (0:15) Just before Northfield, Norwich University, nation's oldest private military institution, is on right.

1:03 (0:12) As we rumble through Northfield Falls, watch for covered bridges. Four of these picturesque structures are located within a quarter of a mile from here.

1:19 (0:00) Arrive Montpelier Junction, suburban stop for Montpelier.

MONTPELIER, VT - Vermont's capital city is home to not only the state's government, but also a large segment of the life insurance industry. Admiral George Dewey, hero of Manila Bay, was a Montpelierite, and his father founded the National Life Insurance Company located here. Rock of Ages Granite Quarry, largest in the world, is just southeast of here near Barre (rhymes with Harry).

0:00 (0:15) Depart Montpelier and proceed northwestward through Winooski River Valley.

0:14 (0:00) Arrive Waterbury.

WATERBURY, VT - This is the heart of Vermont's ski country with several slopes nearby. Stowe is only ten miles up the road.

0:00 (0:28) Depart Waterbury, continuing to trace course of Winooski and through very heart of Green Mountains.

0:03 (0:25) Off to left is 4,083-foot Camel's Hump, Vermont's third highest and most distinctive mountain. State's highest peak at 4,393 feet is Mount Mansfield which is bending point in range stretching off to right.

0:24 (0:04) July 7, 1984, one of Amtrak's worst accidents occurred on this segment of right-of-way when seven of Montrealer's thirteen cars plunged into a gulley by Winooski River Bridge.

A localized storm had plugged a stone culvert (built around 1850) and washed out the trackbed shortly before the train reached this point. Five people were killed and 133 injured.

0:28 (0:00) Arrive Essex Junction, which serves adjacent Burlington.

BURLINGTON, VT - With over 38,000 population, Burlington is Vermont's largest city. Beautifully situated on the eastern shore of Lake Champlain with the Green Mountains just to the east, it is home to the University of Vermont, the oldest such institution in the state. Ethan Allen, who helped organize The Green Mountain Boys, and led them on a raid that captured Ft. Ticonderoga from the British during the American Revolution, is buried here. John Dewey, the celebrated philosopher, was born here. Ferry service operates between Burlington and Port Kent, New York.

0:00 (0:29) Depart Essex Junction, continuing on Central Vermont, following a course due north through Vermont's dairy and sugar maple country.

0:13 (0:16) Pass through Milton at southern tip of Arrowhead Mountain Lake which is on our left. A pre-Columbian Indian flint quarry is located here.

0:29 (0:00) Arrive St. Albans, where Amtrak station is just north of Central Vermont's large, brick station.

ST. ALBANS, VT - Hardly a likely setting for a Civil War skirmish, but on October 19, 1864, the northernmost conflict of that war took place when Confederates raided three of the town's banks. During the War of 1812, smugglers used the area as a base of operations.

Today, the most excitement occurs during the Vermont Sugar Maple Festival, held here in early April with parades, fiddling contests, trips to nearby sugar houses and even rolling pin competitions.

This is also a junction point for the Central Vermont. Southbound passengers will go through U.S. Customs here.

0:00 (2:00) Depart St. Albans past Central Vermont shops.

0:30 (1:30) Just after Stanton, cruise through 4,800-acre Missisquoi National Wildlife Refuge, where most of 400-plus species that inhabit eastern half of the U.S. have been spotted at one time or another.

0:38 (1:22) Negotiate half-mile-long bridge carrying us over neck of Missisquoi Bay. Pivot span in center accommodates occasional boat traffic.

0:44 (1:16) Cross into Canada. During prohibition, this train was nicknamed "The Bootlegger" as it supposedly provided a steady stream of hooch to U.S. customers.

0:52 (1:07) Bridge Richelieu River and enter Cantic, Quebec.

Northbound passengers will either go through Canadian Customs at this point or later upon arrival at Montreal's Central Station. We are now on Canadian National track, which will transport us across flat, flat farmland on the rest of our journey, in sharp contrast to everything that has preceded us. The Richelieu is actually Lake Champlain's drainage course into the St. Lawrence River.

1:53 (0:10) After passing through St. Lambert, one of Montreal's many suburbs, ascend toward Victoria Bridge which first carries us over venerable St. Lawrence Seaway (those two concrete-lined channels below with a lock), then over river itself. Islands downstream to right were site of Expo 67. Downtown Montreal, with Mt. Royal directly behind, is forward to right. A truly impressive cityscape.

1:58 (0:06) Through large CN rail yards. In a moment we will cross attractively landscaped Lachine (pronounced luh-sheen) Canal before going underground for final two minutes of trip. Canal predates Seaway and was built to bypass Lachine Rapids in St. Lawrence River.

2:00 (0:00) Arrive Montreal's Central Station.

 MONTREAL, QUE. - See page 307.

Montreal
Albany
New York City

Adirondack

Take a trip to France by land? Absorb breathtaking mountain vistas while hugging high on the side of rocky cliffs, but without leaving the East? These seemingly incongruous questions are answered in the affirmative for travelers who ride the train from New York City to Montreal, passing through 200 years of history on nearly 400 miles of track.

For nine hours, those aboard the Adirondack are treated to a changing scene that grows more spectacular as their northbound journey progresses. The old New York Central Route (now Conrail) up the east side of the Hudson River is steeped with riverside beauty, history and New England tradition.

But the thrilling part of this journey takes place farther north as the tracks embrace the western shore of Lake Champlain. Rock cuts, lily ponds, sailboats, Victorian depots, and the Adirondacks of New York and Green Mountains of Vermont line the route. And in the fall, the color is sublime. If you think you can almost hear the salvos from the battles of Lake Champlain and Saratoga, it could be the cannons that are still fired at Ft. Ticonderoga.

Northbound Schedule (Condensed)
New York, NY (Grand Central) - Late
    Morning Departure
Albany-Rensselaer, NY - Early Afternoon
Plattsburgh, NY - Late Afternoon
Montreal, Que. - Midevening Arrival

Southbound Schedule (Condensed)*
Montreal, Que. - Early Morning Departure
Plattsburgh, NY - Late Morning

Albany-Rensselaer, NY - Late Afternoon
New York, NY (Grand Central) - Early
    Evening Arrival

*Schedule is later on Sundays.

Frequency - Daily.
Seating - RTG Turboliners. Custom Class available with coffee, tea or juice and newspapers.
Dining - Tray meals, snacks and beverages.
Baggage - No checked baggage.
Reservations - Unreserved coaches and reserved Custom Class.
Length of Trip - 385 miles in 9½ hours.

Route Log

 NEW YORK, NY - See page 21.

0:00 (0:43) Depart New York City's Grand Central Terminal through underground corridor, emerging minutes later amidst high-density neighborhoods of uptown Manhattan.
0:09 (0:34) Tall, elaborate mural adorns building-side on right.
0:13 (0:30) Cross Harlem River into borough known as "The Bronx." River was once important barge route, but now mainly accommodates sightseeing boats. Colorful rock ledges line route on right as river borders on left.
0:16 (0:27) Towering baseball bat is appropriate monument fronting famous Yankee Stadium on right.
0:22 (0:21) Athletic field of Columbia University, sodded with synthetic turf, is

on immediate left. Then, with impressive Henry Hudson Bridge looming overhead, Harlem River reaches its headwaters and intersects Hudson River. Train then proceeds along its eastern bank, as barges and freighters traverse waters of this vital inland passage. George Washington Bridge can be glimpsed back down Hudson.

0:26 (0:17) At Yonkers large, stately homes nestled along hillsides only preview what will soon become a premier attraction of this Hudson River run. Sign of the times is at right where former Otis Elevator plant is now partially used to house large Kawasaki operation.

0:32 (0:11) On right, fanciful European design highlights station at Ardsley-On-Hudson.

0:35 (0:08) Tappan-Zee Bridge on forward left is first of several dramatic structures that span Hudson River between here and Albany.

0:36 (0:07) Quaint little village of Tarrytown typifies many small communities along route whose resplendent colonial atmosphere reflects a proud historical heritage.

0:41 (0:02) At Ossining, track borders legendary Sing Sing state prison. As previously promised, line from Ossining north borders some of country's most graciously endowed estates. From Roosevelts to Vanderbilts, many of society's elite have chosen to make their homes amidst lush woodlands and verdant hills of this Hudson River Valley.

0:43 (0:00) Arrive Croton-On-Hudson.

CROTON-ON-HUDSON, NY - All trains once paused at this old Dutch community, switching from electric to diesel power. Long-standing regulation still prohibits diesel-powered transport within New York City tunnels.

Croton-On-Hudson is the site of the historic Van Cortlandt Manor, home of New York's first lieutenant governor. This magnificent estate dates back to the late 1600s, and through time has been host to many American and foreign dignitaries.

0:00 (0:38) Depart Croton-On-Hudson past further array of magnificent dwellings. Frequently, river inlets intrude on estates and provide picturesque playground for ducks and swans.

0:12 (0:26) Train glides beneath soaring Bear Mountain Bridge which carries not only vehicular traffic but hikers following Appalachian Trail.

0:18 (0:20) Across river, scenic Highland Falls tumble down cliffs, while campus of West Point Military Academy presides above. Established in 1802, nation's oldest service academy still resides on site where George Washington once stationed Revolutionary troops to thwart British maneuvers along Hudson River. Grant, Lee, Pershing, MacArthur, Patton, Eisenhower and Westmoreland were some of the Point's more illustrious graduates.

0:21 (0:17) For next few miles, hills bordering route burgeon in size, nearly assuming "mountain" classification.

0:24 (0:14) Ensconced in middle of river, Bannerman's Castle is fascinating recreation of old robber baron's stronghold. It was used by original owner as a storehouse for armaments.

0:31 (0:07) North of Chelsea, cross Wappinger River as it spills into Hudson.

0:38 (0:00) Arrive Poughkeepsie.

POUGHKEEPSIE, NY - Formerly the state's capital during the Revolutionary War, Poughkeepsie has since evolved into a thriving manufacturing center, with a diverse range of products ensuring economic stability. The city at one time became synonymous with the Smith Brothers who made their famous cough drops here.

Located nearby, the Franklin D. Roosevelt National Historic Site and Vanderbilt Mansion are much-frequented historical attractions. Also popular are the many "pick-your-own" farms and orchards surrounding the Poughkeepsie area.

0:00 (0:14) Departing Poughkeepsie, picturesque waterfalls of Fallkill Creek trickle down by trackside on right. Spanning river on left, old cantilever railroad bridge was largest of its type when constructed in 1889. A fire in early 1970s precluded its further use.

0:04 (0:10) Across river, letters "CIA," enscribed on cliffside, face nearby Culinary Institute of America where many of country's renowned chefs honed formative skills.

0:05 (0:09) Shortly after seeing huge, red-roofed house across Hudson (former estate

Adirondack – Ft. Ticonderoga, New York

of Father Vine), Franklin Delano Roosevelt's Hyde Park home will be above tracks on right and Vanderbilt Mansion shortly thereafter. Unfortunately, both are set back just far enough so that neither is visible from train.

0:14 (0:00) Arriving Rhinecliff, fine old lighthouse looms in midst of Hudson, while on opposite bank, castle-like mansions embellish scene seemingly plucked from Bavarian landscape.

RHINECLIFF, NY - Rhinecliff is the Amtrak stop for nearby Rhinebeck, a charming community nestled in the hills of the Hudson River Valley. Boasting one of the largest districts of homes on the National Register, Rhinebeck is also the site of Beekman Arms—the nation's oldest continuously operating hotel. F.D.R. chose to conclude many of his campaigns from this historic inn.

Here, too, is the famed Rhinebeck Aerodrome where, on weekends from July to October, vintage aircraft take to the skies for daredevil excitement. Its museum

of World War I aircraft is world renowned.

0:00 (0:21) Depart Rhinecliff.

0:10 (0:11) North of Tarrytown, small peninsulas jutting out in water afford unique setting for many splendid homes, with activity along Hudson River a "front-door" drama for all. Mountains flanking river are part of Catskill chain and will escort train into town of Hudson.

0:15 (0:06) Crossing scenic Roeliff River, docks on right are popular spot for senior fishermen to wile away hours.

0:19 (0:02) On left, exquisite old lighthouse still maintains watchful vigil.

0:21 (0:00) Arrive comely station at Hudson.

HUDSON, NY - Beautiful gardens grace the avenues of this picturesque town, named for Henry Hudson whose "Half Moon" docked here in 1609. Located here, the American Museum of Fire Fighting maintains one of the oldest and most complete collections of fire-fighting equipment in America. Olana, the elegant estate of acclaimed artist

51

Frederic E. Church, with its Persian-style mansion, is another attraction.

0:00 (0:25) Depart Hudson.

0:25 (0:00) Arriving Albany, downtown skyline stands out on left. Prominent 42-story skyscraper is centerpiece of Empire State Plaza. Left of tower, low-slung Cultural Education Center houses State Museum and Library, while on right, dynamic elliptical structure is Center for Performing Arts. Four smaller towers in background are also part of this ambitious billion-dollar project. Once in station (train actually stops in town of Rensselaer, just across river from Albany), inspiring domed archways of St. John the Baptist Catholic Church can be seen protruding above treetops on right.

ALBANY, NY - A small-town atmosphere with big-city prestige is the claim of Albany, New York's state capital. Replete with cosmopolitan amenities, Albany is likewise a stone's throw from the rural splendor depicted in the paintings of America's beloved Grandma Moses.

The aforementioned Empire State Plaza is the current pride and joy of downtown Albany. Nearly a city unto itself, shops, pubs and restaurants line the interconnecting walkways between the many governmental agencies located here. At the north of the complex stands the State Capitol, its fanciful French Renaissance architecture a dramatic contrast to the sleek, modern lines of the Plaza's other buildings.

As well as a bastion of state government, Albany has remained a vital inland port since the completion of the Erie Canal in 1825. Today, private operators conduct excursions along this historic waterway that recapture the spirit and grace of an earlier era.

In the adjacent town of Rensselaer, one can tour Fort Crailo, the nation's oldest fort built in 1642. Legend has it that a British surgeon wrote the famous "Yankee Doodle" tune while visiting this site.

0:00 (0:22) Depart Albany.

0:04 (0:19) Cross Hudson River. On left, ornate spires and turrets adorn magnificent State University Administration Headquarters. Originally built in 1916 as corporate offices of Delaware and Hudson Railroad, complex is actually three buildings interconnected, with Flemish facades maintaining delightful continuity throughout. Replica of Henry Hudson's "Half Moon" is highlight of weather vane perched atop main tower.

0:05 (0:17) Intriguing amalgam of modern and classical architecture is a most striking feature of Albany's city center on left.

0:06 (0:16) A familiar emblem for many years, large black and white mutt looms protectively above RCA facility on right.

0:10 (0:10) On outskirts of town, four lonesome high rises comprise State Office Building campus on left.

0:11 (0:09) Shoreline of Rensselaer Lake adjoins trackside on right.

0:18 (0:04) Approaching Schenectady, attractively landscaped parkways dissect sprawling grounds of General Electric industrial park on left. Combined GE operations in region employ nearly 23,000 people.

0:19 (0:00) Arriving Schenectady, tall, gold-domed City Hall clock tower is prominent fixture on right.

SCHENECTADY, NY - Emerging from the heart of the Industrial Revolution, Schenectady became known as "the city that lights and hauls the world." The American Locomotive Company's Schenectady Works and Thomas Edison's Machine Works were primarily responsible for this designation, the latter eventually evolving into the colossal General Electric Corporation.

Schenectady's "Stockade District" is a premier historical attraction, representing one of the country's best-preserved enclaves of early American architecture and culture. Its name stems from the original 1661 settlement which was surrounded by a stockade to guard against French and Indian attacks.

From here on the best viewing will generally be found on the right (east) side, particularly along Lake Champlain.

0:00 (0:29) Departing Schenectady, city's historic Stockade Area is off to left. Leave Amtrak's Empire Corridor and continue northward toward Montreal.

0:04 (0:25) Sprawling, old buildings on left were formerly occupied by American

Locomotive Works (Alco), one of America's premier locomotive builders. Turbines are now manufactured here by General Electric.

0:29 (0:00) Arrive Saratoga Springs where modern depot on right will be a disappointment to those anticipating more nostalgia from this historic town.

SARATOGA SPRINGS, NY - At the turn of the century, few spas rivaled Saratoga's popularity with the East's wealthy and socially elite. Stylish Old World bathhouses offered supposedly curative soaks in naturally carbonated mineral water and elegant hotels lined the town's thoroughfares. Fine gardens and even a spouting geyser added to the charm. For those seeking to try their luck, opulent casinos comparable to any in Europe offered gambling while the Saratoga Race Track presented thoroughbred racing. Notables who frequented Saratoga included the likes of Diamond Jim Brady and Lillian Russell, while the Vanderbilts and Whitneys had homes near the track.

Today, society no longer looks upon Saratoga Springs with the same fervor, but the town is still a fascinating summer resort. The fine old hotels, including the famous United States Hotel, have been replaced by newer hostelries, but the thoroughbred race track (the nation's oldest),the bathhouses with their famous mineral water and one of the most beautiful harness racing tracks in the world make for a great summer destination. Culture is also in abundance, headed up by the New York City Ballet and the Philadelphia Symphony, both making this their summer homes.

History buffs will remember that in 1777 the Revolutionary War Battle of Saratoga (actually fought several miles from here at Bemis Heights and Stillwater) brought defeat to 7,000 British troops, Hessian mercenaries and Indians led by Lt. General John Burgoyne and turned the war's momentum in the Patriot's favor. News of this American victory brought about the Franco-American Alliance.

0:00 (0:20) Depart Saratoga.

0:04 (0:16) Under I-87 which links two great cities, Montreal and New York.

0:19 (0:01) Cross back to east side of Hudson River. Scott Paper Company plant, which processes wood pulp into facial and toilet tissue, napkins and wax paper (only Scott facility that makes the latter), is clearly visible upstream, on left.

0:20 (0:00) Arrive Ft. Edward where old relic of a depot still stands at left.

FT. EDWARD, NY - This small upstate town derives its name from the fort constructed on the banks of the Hudson during the French and Indian War. In 1825, locks were constructed here, the highest point on the canal, allowing the Champlain Canal to connect to the Hudson River and creating a continuous trading waterway between the St. Lawrence and the lower Hudson. The canal is still used as part of the New York State Canal System, frequented now by barges with modern-day cargoes such as jet fuel.

This is Amtrak's access to Glens Falls and Lake George.

0:00 (0:23) Depart Ft. Edward and before long pass through pastoral settings which would make most city dwellers envious of their country cousins.

0:11 (0:12) Champlain Canal, on right, is encased by spectacularly beautiful rock cliffs as a prelude to what is yet to come as we near Lake Champlain. From here to Canadian border, scenery is spectacular as Adirondack hugs west shore of 105-mile-long Lake Champlain.

0:15 (0:08) While passing under highway bridge at Comstock, Great Meadows Correctional Facility can be glimpsed off to right.

0:23 (0:00) Arriving Whitehall, brick chimney on right once lifted smoke from Champlain Silk Mill prior to Great Depression. Former station, demolished in 1986 in spite of local historical society protestations, has been replaced by simple glass-box shelter.

WHITEHALL, NY - This is the northern terminus of the Champlain Canal, complete with locks giving barges access to and from South Bay—Lake Champlain's southernmost extension.

Although the U.S. Navy avoids designating any one place as its official birthplace, Whitehall claims the honor. It was here on May 9, 1775 that Colonists under orders from Benedict Arnold captured Skenesborough (now Whitehall) from a Loyalist, Philip Skene. Two days later, Skene's sailing ship was taken to nearby Crown Point where it was armed for war. The schooner was then used to capture the British naval ship Enterprize. These activities seem to predate other Revolutionary naval beginnings.

0:00 (0:25) Departing Whitehall, note old mansion with clock tower, above town to right on Skene Mountain. Using granite quarried from mountain, structure was built in 1875 by Italian artisans as home for New York State Supreme Court judge. In early 1900s, clock was added to cupola when timepiece was removed from weakened steeple of local Presbyterian Church. Movement is controlled by weights in basement. Building is listed in National Register of Historic Places and, not surprisingly, main floor is now a restaurant.

0:04 (0:21) Here we cross (and get our first view of) Lake Champlain (South Bay). Also, it is here that we enter Adirondack Park—an enormous acreage, much of which is wilderness, and largest state park in U.S. Sylvan lily ponds with assorted waterfowl stretch along right side of train.

0:13 (0:12) Navigational buoys are sprinkled along channel on right to guide water traffic between Lake Champlain proper and South Bay. Small pleasure craft are often in abundance. Main body of Lake Champlain, discovered by Samuel de Champlain in 1609, now comes into view.

0:20 (0:05) Shoreline on opposite side of Lake Champlain is Vermont.

0:25 (0:00) Arrive at Ft. Ticonderoga's matchbox station along highway at right. Town is two miles or so from here while actual fort, on bluffs ahead and to right, is almost as far.

FT. TICONDEROGA, NY - The nearby restored Colonial fort was originally established in 1755 by the French who sliced off the mountain's top and used the rocks found there for its construction. The fort defended the passage between Lake Champlain and the northern tip of Lake George (which are only about a mile apart) as well as the route between the colonies and Canada, making it one of the most strategic locations of the Revolution. It was first captured by the British, but then continued to change hands.

At the start of the Revolution the fort fell to Ethan Allen, Benedict Arnold and the Green Mountain Boys of Vermont without a shot being fired. They sent its guns to help break the siege of Boston. It was again captured by the British in 1777, a severe blow to the Colonists, only then to be later abandoned and burned after Burgoyne's ultimate defeat at Saratoga.

The fort has been beautifully restored and contains a fine museum with Revolutionary artifacts. During the summer, colorfully uniformed "soldiers" march through the grounds playing traditional fife and drum music, and cannons are periodically fired for added atmosphere.

0:00 (0:22) Depart Fort Ticonderoga and now get a fine view of fort itself to right forward, just before going through a short tunnel under fortification grounds.

0:09 (0:13) Enormous International Paper plant is just above tracks on left.

0:16 (0:06) Impressive Blue Ridge rises to an elevation of 2,680 feet off to left. Beyond, but out of sight, are a group of mountains, all rising to over 4,000 feet.

0:19 (0:03) Very fine view of Lake Champlain is afforded on right. Protrusion of land across water is Crown Point State Historic Site, location of ruins of two forts that once secured command of this vital waterway. First fort was built by French in 1734. Later, under British occupation, a three-and-one-half-square-mile stronghold was built—one of Britain's most ambitious military engineering projects in North America.

0:23 (0:00) Arrive at Port Henry's neat but old station, set serenely in Witherbee Park.

PORT HENRY, NY - Several architectural artifacts are worth watching for in this community, Port Henry's train station being but one. On departing, note the two brick buildings sitting above the tracks on the left. The three-story town hall could have easily been used for the movie "Psycho," while the other quaint structure, just to the right, is a former fire station (now used for a garage).

0:00 (0:18) Depart Port Henry. Site of Porter and Lewis Mills, former supplier of lumber to Benedict Arnold's fleet, stood just up draw to left near present brick structure of Niagara Mohawk Power.

0:18 (0:00) Upon arriving Westport, note very attractive geodesic home on right.

WESTPORT, NY - This scenic little shoreline village is perhaps best known for its bass fishing tournaments. But also popular is a summer theater which occupies the freight room of the old train station. This old depot, perched high above the town, is a grand vignette of the past. Still well maintained, its exterior sports a coat of green and ivory paint while the interior shelters some wonderful woodwork of yesteryear. But alas, Amtrak has been relegated to a big "phone booth" just a few feet north of the station.

0:00 (0:42) Depart Westport.

0:09 (0:33) On left, long since abandoned small stone depot of Delaware and Hudson is now overgrown by forest.

0:15 (0:27) Peaks to left reach elevations over 3,600 feet.

0:18 (0:24) Cross high over pretty Bouquet River.

0:19 (0:23) Small plant, covered with grey dust and just to left of train, refines walstonite ore which is mined nearby. Principal uses of walstonite include the manufacture of ceramics, china and paint.

0:20 (0:00) Through Willsboro, situated in region where lake trout, walleye and salmon are in abundance. New York and Vermont have undertaken a project to stock Lake Champlain with game fish and as a result, Willsboro Dam on nearby Bouquet River provides excellent fishing.

If you have not already been convinced that this is indeed a scenic ride, you might be shortly. Between here and Port Kent, a few miles up line, the route is embellished by spectacular rock cuts, many high above Lake Champlain. Twisting and turning, one view after another is afforded to those on the right side of the train. During one 4½-mile stretch alone, the train must negotiate 128 curves.

0:42 (0:00) Arrive Port Kent.

PORT KENT, NY - This is flag stop for Amtrak during the summer months. The dock for the summer ferry to Burlington, Vermont (10 miles directly across the lake) can be seen here.

0:00 (0:14) Depart Port Kent.

0:04 (0:10) Cross Ausable River which has its headwaters southwest of here at the base of 5,344-foot Mt. Marcy, highest point in New York.

0:06 (0:08) Owner of farm with white buildings next to tracks on right has his own miniature railroad, with tracks that are laid out around farmyard and then disappear into barn.

0:07 (0:07) Leave Adirondack Park. Valcour Island is on right, site of first naval battle between Britain and the Colonies.

0:09 (0:02) Huge Plattsburgh Air Force Base (home of SAC's 380th Bombardment Aerospace Wing) stretches along tracks on left.

0:14 (0:00) Arrive Plattsburgh after passing yacht basin on right.

PLATTSBURGH, NY - Military posts have been located in this area continually since colonial times. It was off these shores that the British fought and won the Battle of Lake Champlain in 1777, although the delay inflicted on the British played an important role in America's eventually winning the Revolution. And it was from here that Colonel Zebulon Pike, the discoverer of the peak by the same name, launched an unsuccessful march against what is now Toronto. Later, during the War of 1812, Plattsburgh was the site of two coordinated American victories, one on land and the other in Plattsburgh Bay where American sailors used anchors and winches to pivot their vessels 180 degrees, giving the surprised British two broadsides from each ship.

The SAC base and paper mills now shape the area's economy. A turntable for the old Delaware & Hudson shops is on the left.

0:00 (0:23) Departing Plattsburgh, eagle-crowned obelisk is Macdonough Monument, commemorating naval victory of 1814.

The terrain now becomes more agricultural and flat while the tracks move away from Lake Champlain (that has accompanied us for past two hours) and pass through miles of cornfields. This is the last opportunity to purchase liquor and cigarettes on the train since once into Canada (beyond Rouses Point) they are not available on the Adirondack.

0:15 (0:08) Apples are principal product of Chazy which boasts world's largest McIntosh orchards.

0:23 (0:00) Arrive Rouses Point.

 ROUSES POINT, NY - Huddled against the U.S.-Canadian Border, Rouses Point serves as the American Customs checkpoint for southbound passengers. The yellow building on the right is the customs house.

Here, Lake Champlain empties into the Richelieu River which in turn flows into the St. Lawrence.

0:00 (0:07) Depart Rouses Point and in a minute, Canadian flags identify Canadian-U.S. border.

0:07 (0:00) Arrive Cantic.

CANTIC, QUE. - Cantic is where northbound passengers are checked by Canadian Customs. Proof of citizenship is important. Although the ceremonies may sometimes be perfunctory, it is not unusual to be here for an hour while normal inspection procedures are carried out.

0:00 (0:38) Depart Cantic and head across southern Quebec's flat countryside toward Montreal. This is the Richelieu River Valley, where trains on Canada's first railway, the Laprairie and St. Johns, followed the Richelieu as early as 1851. Small agricultural communities with French-speaking citizenry are scattered throughout region.

0:26 (0:12) Adirondack slows down for Montreal suburb of St. Lambert, immediately across St. Lawrence from our destination. St. Lambert Lock, a lift station for St. Lawrence Seaway traffic, is here. Start ascent necessary for crossing St. Lawrence River on Victoria Bridge.

This structure was once known as the Jubilee Bridge when it was opened in 1898 to handle two sets of rails, an electric interurban line and auto traffic. It is one of the world's longest at 1¼ miles. Those two concrete-lined channels below us are the St. Lawrence Seaway and the St. Lambert Lock which is just one of many locks needed to raise or lower shipping using this waterway. The Seaway is narrow, and unfortunately cannot handle larger ships of today's maritime fleet.

0:27 (0:11) Islands to right were home to Canada's very successful 1967 world's fair—Expo 67. Geodesic dome was the U.S. Pavilion. Skyline of Montreal forms a dramatic scene forward on right.

0:32 (0:06) Leaving Victoria Bridge, we enter Montreal through Canadian National rail yards.

0:34 (0:04) Slip over nicely landscaped Lachine Canal, constructed before seaway to avoid Lachine Rapids.

0:36 (0:02) Sink underground as we near station.

0:38 (0:00) Arrive Montreal's Central Station.

 MONTREAL, QUE. - See page 307.

Toronto
Buffalo   New York

Maple Leaf

The charming Hudson River Valley, an international border crossing at Niagara Falls and the fascinating maritime activities along the western tip of Lake Ontario are just some of the scenes that await those aboard The Maple Leaf. This service, since its inception in 1971, has been the result of a joint U.S.-Canadian endeavor that links New York City with Toronto. The delightful run takes—almost regretfully—only 12 hours to complete.

Northbound Schedule (Condensed)
New York, NY (Grand Central) - Early Morning Departure
Albany-Rensselaer, NY - Late Morning
Niagara Falls, NY - Late Afternoon
Toronto, Ont. - Midevening Arrival

Southbound Schedule (Condensed)
Toronto, Ont. - Midmorning Departure
Niagara Falls, NY - Early Afternoon
Albany-Rensselaer, NY - Early Evening
New York, NY (Grand Central) - Late Evening Arrival

Frequency - Daily.
Seating - Amcoaches.
Dining - Amdinette with tray meal and beverage service.
Baggage - No checked baggage.
Reservations - Unreserved train.
Length of trip - 546 miles in 12 hours.

Route Log

For route between New York City and Schenectady, see that portion of Adirondack log, page 49. For route between Schenectady and Buffalo, see that portion of Lake Shore Ltd. log, page 65.

DEPEW, NY - This is a convenient suburban stop for the Buffalo region.
0:00 (0:10) Depart Depew.
0:05 (0:05) Speed slows considerably as train negotiates entangled maze of tracks and switches approaching Buffalo. Downtown skyline looms on forward right, while immediately right, grand clock tower presides atop stately Romanesque archways of old Buffalo Central Terminal.

The terminal, now on the National Register of Historic Places, had as its architect famed station designer Alfred Fellheimer who also created the elegant Cincinnati Union Terminal. After years of political haggling over an appropriate site for a larger New York Central station, it was completed in 1929, shortly before the Crash and the ensuing depression. In spite of such luckless timing, a poor location (two miles from downtown) and the gradual withering of rail service, Central Terminal held on for fifty years before Amtrak delivered a fatal blow with its move to Depew Station farther east.
0:10 (0:00) Arrive Buffalo (Exchange Street Station). City center on right sports interesting blend of architectural styles, though eye seems to gravitate to glistening white tower of Niagara Mohawk's "Electric Building." Modernistic complex on left houses Buffalo Evening News.

BUFFALO, NY - Situated on the eastern shores of Lake Erie, and across the Niagara River from Canada,

Maple Leaf – Bear Mountain Bridge, New York

Buffalo is New York's second largest city with a population approaching 400,000. The metropolitan region represents one of the largest manufacturing centers in the U.S. with steel, chemicals, auto parts and flour production a sampling of its major industries. Railroading is also an important facet of the Buffalo economy, with a large number of separate lines maintaining offices in the city.

Like many cities of this size, Buffalo offers a wide range of cultural opportunities. The Albright-Knox Art Gallery and Buffalo Zoo are consistently rated among the nation's finest. Buffalo, too, is an avid sports mecca, and supports major league franchises in football and hockey.

0:00 (0:34) Depart Buffalo. After traversing short tunnels, Lake Erie appears on left.

0:05 (0:29) Lake waters begin narrowing into Niagara River which flows 35 miles north before spilling into Lake Ontario. Along route, brief interruption of Niagara Falls tends to discourage conventional navigation.

0:06 (0:28) On left, Peace Bridge spans river to Fort Erie, Ontario, a major port of entry into Canada.

Water intake is curious spectacle protruding from water just north of bridge.

0:11 (0:23) Old drawbridge connects Squaw Island with mainland on left.

0:18 (0:16) Passing through Tonawanda, train departs river route temporarily. Clock tower of Tonawanda Middle School is distinctive fixture on left.

0:20 (0:14) Cross New York Barge Canal, offspring of historic Erie Canal, now only a few blocks from its western terminus.

0:27 (0:07) At town of Niagara, International Airport is situated on left, as well as adjacent Niagara Falls Air Force Base.

0:28 (0:06) As train heads westerly towards Canadian border, gravel and cement operation bares another modest crater on right.

0:32 (0:02) Assemblage of towering power stanchions on right readily conjures up images of Martian invasion. Nearby hydroelectric facilities are some of world's largest, tapping mighty resources of Niagara Falls.

0:33 (0:01) Spindly observation towers on forward left are popular vantage points for viewing falls.

0:34 (0:00) Arrive Niagara Falls, New York.

NIAGARA FALLS, NY - The breathtaking falls on the Niagara River continue to be the primary attraction that draws over 12 million tourists to this region annually.

0:00 (0:10) Depart Niagara Falls, New York.

0:08 (0:02) Cross into Canada via 1,082-foot bridge spanning Niagara River. From its lofty heights, brief glimpse of falls is afforded on left while torrent of rampaging Whirlpool Rapids is impressive spectacle on right.

0:10 (0:00) Arrive Niagara Falls, Ontario. Journey is delayed here while customs agents board for round of "customary" inquiries. (New York bound passengers are checked by U.S. customs at Niagara Falls, NY.) Amtrak crews are replaced by VIA personnel at this time.

NIAGARA FALLS, ONT. - Like its New York counterpart, the falls are the focal point of this town as well. Observation towers, riverboats, helicopters, cable cars and ground-level catwalks are among the many means available for viewing this natural wonder. Throughout time, less conventional methods have also been pursued. Maria Spelterina once traversed a cable across the falls wearing peach baskets on her feet. The Great Blondin took a more leisurely approach, pausing in the middle of his walk to cook lunch on a miniature stove.

0:00 (0:20) Depart Niagara Falls through Canadian National rail yards before emerging on rolling farmlands of southern Ontario.

0:07 (0:14) Cross Queenston Chippawa Power Canal.

0:10 (0:11) Winery on right represents a popular enterprise of region. Wire vine supports are also common sights throughout accompanying vineyards.

0:17 (0:04) Cross newest (1932) Welland Canal, an important shipping link connecting Lake Erie and Lake Ontario. Eight separate locks, like set seen below, allow vessels to negotiate 326-foot elevation differential between two lakes. Entire passage is now completed in less than eight hours, about half the time required to traverse one of older canals seen a few miles downline.

0:20 (0:00) From atop towering bridge, cross original (1842) Welland Canal before arriving St. Catharines.

ST. CATHARINES, ONT. - Situated in the heart of the Niagara fruit belt, bountiful harvests support St. Catharines' claim as the "Garden City." Wine production is important here too with tours of these facilities a popular attraction.

Also of interest is the St. Catharines Historical Museum where the significance of the Welland Canal is brought to light. Here, too, is Tivoli Miniature World, a neatly landscaped park bedecked with tiny replicas of the world's most noteworthy landmarks.

0:00 (0:16) Departing St. Catharines, rolling hills become more pronounced with streams meandering picturesquely through their midst. Bountiful orchards embellish landscape and provide a basic economic staple of area.

0:05 (0:11) Approaching Jordan, cross Sixteen Mile Creek. On western edge of town, Lake Ontario can be seen on right while crossing Jordan Harbour.

0:16 (0:00) Arrive "doll-house" station at Grimsby. Grocery and delicatessen are added attractions of this charming facility.

GRIMSBY, ONT. - Another hub of fruit and wine production, Grimsby was the site of Canada's first municipal government, established at a town meeting back in 1790.

0:00 (0:19) Depart Grimsby.

0:09 (0:12) Rural environs are soon displaced by industrial sprawl approaching Hamilton. A most notable feature of city is its seeming lack of centrality with clusters of high rises dispersed through every region. Area that curls around western tip of Lake Ontario is known as The Golden Horseshoe due to its industrial and agricultural productivity.

0:15 (0:04) Ivor Wynne Stadium on left is home field for Canadian Football League's Hamilton Tigercats.

0:19 (0:00) Arrive Hamilton.

HAMILTON, ONT. - Set atop ledges overlooking scenic Lake Ontario, Hamilton is Canada's third largest port and caters to a flourishing manufacturing trade. Known as the nation's "Steel Capital," tours of these modern foundries are among the city's foremost attractions.

Complementing this progressive industrial climate are a host of cultural offerings. One such diversion is the widely acclaimed Royal Botanical Gardens with over 2,000 acres of exquisite floral displays. Here, too, is the magnificent Dundurn Castle, its splendid furnishings and appointments reflecting the opulent lifestyle of its mid-19th century inhabitants. Of particular interest to sports fans is the Canadian Football Hall of Fame where over 100 years of gridiron history is brought to life through a variety of electronic exhibits.

0:00 (0:12) Departing Hamilton, emerge on shoreline of Hamilton Harbour, a scenic inlet of Lake Ontario. Countless high rises line harbor's edge, overlooking menagerie of commercial and pleasure boats alike. Train winds about waterfront, eventually settling on northeastern tack towards Toronto.

0:12 (0:00) Arrive Burlington.

BURLINGTON, ONT. - Primarily a lakefront residential community, Burlington is the home of the Joseph Brant Museum, where historical memoirs and personal effects of this famous Mohawk Chieftain are preserved in a replica of his last home. Also of interest is the Village Square, a downtown block of vintage homes that now house an array of comely shops and restaurants.

0:00 (0:10) Depart Burlington through attractive residential districts. Colonial flavor pervades early stretch, while northeastern outskirts feature more contemporary motifs.

0:08 (0:02) Industrial area surrounding Oakville bears profusion of refineries and other petro-related operations.

0:10 (0:00) Cross another Sixteen Mile Creek arriving Oakville.

OAKVILLE, ONT. - In the mid-19th century, a host of city-dwellers chose this scenic locale as the site of their summer homes. Most of these lavish retreats have been immaculately preserved, and today are the focal point of a well-documented walking tour. Another interesting attraction is the Gairlock Gardens Gallery, maintained in a 1920s mansion along the lake. Its wild bird sanctuary is a further highlight.

For golfing enthusiasts, the Glen Abbey links, designed by Jack Nicklaus, is of true championship caliber. Its clubhouse was once a monastery, and now is home to the Canadian Golf Hall of Fame.

0:00 (0:23) Depart Oakville.

0:02 (0:21) Ford auto plant on left operates private trains for touring this sprawling complex.

0:08 (0:16) At Port Credit, cross Credit River as it flows into Lake Ontario on right.

0:11 (0:13) Cross Etobicoke River.

0:12 (0:12) Giant hippopotamus whimsically adorns facade of Hippo Oil Company on right.

0:15 (0:09) Approaching Toronto, cross Humber River as it, too, empties into lake. On forward right, downtown skyline boasts a fascinating array of unconventional designs, with dynamic CN Tower a most distinctive landmark.

0:16 (0:18) On right, amphitheater poised on lake's edge is handsome attraction of Ontario Place—a cultural, recreational and entertainment complex built atop three man-made islands.

0:17 (0:07) Elaborate facilities on right are annual home of National Exhibition, the Canadian equivalent of American state fairs.

0:20 (0:05) Historic Fort York Park on right features restored British garrison from War of 1812.

0:23 (0:02) Bulbous SkyDome, on right, overshadows all else. Built in 1989 at a cost of $400 million to house baseball's Toronto Blue Jays, it has roof that can be retracted on nicer days.

0:24 (0:01) On right, Canadian National train is appropriate focal point of mural on walls of CN Tower.

0:25 (0:00) Arrive Toronto.

 TORONTO, ONT. - See page 316.

Lake Shore Limited

The historic "Water Level Route" of the old New York Central System is now the path of the Lake Shore Limited, one of Amtrak's three New York-Chicago trains. The trip, which traces through some of this country's very beginnings, might well serve as a refresher course in America's struggle for her political and economic independence.

From New York City, the tracks head northward up the eastern shore of the stately Hudson River until reaching Albany where they veer westward across upper New York State following the Mohawk Valley and the Erie Canal. Upon reaching Buffalo, the route borders the south shore of Lake Erie (hence the name Lake Shore Limited) before slicing across northern Indiana to reach Chicago. Although Boston passengers miss the Hudson River trip, they have the soft, rolling Berkshires of western Massachusetts as a substitute.

The Lake Shore Limited started as an experiment when Congress authorized its tentative start-up in 1975. The train immediately became a permanent and important part of Amtrak's service. Its 18½-hour schedule doesn't equal the 16-hour sprints performed in the late thirties by those 20th Century Limiteds powered by Henry Dreyfuss-streamlined 4-6-4 Hudson steam locomotives, but, on the other hand, those heroic trains of yore didn't have to contend with as many intermediate stops or regulatory-imposed speed limits. Nor does the Lake Shore offer a "Barber, Fresh Salt Baths, Valet, Ladies' Maid, Manicurist and Stenographer" as advertised by the New York Central for its "Centuries" as early as 1912 on what was then touted as the "fastest train in the world." Today's Lake Shore is no slacker, however, whisking you from a New York City evening to a Chicago lunch in more comfort than that offered by any other mode of transport.

Westbound Schedule (Condensed)
New York, NY (Grand Central) - Midevening Departure
Boston, MA* - Late Afternoon Departure
Albany-Rensselaer, NY - Late Evening
Buffalo, NY - Middle of the Night
Cleveland, OH - Early Morning
Toledo, OH - Early Morning
Chicago, IL - Early Afternoon Arrival

Eastbound Schedule (Condensed)
Chicago, IL - Early Evening Departure
Toledo, OH - Late Evening
Cleveland, OH - Middle of the Night
Buffalo, NY - Early Morning
Albany-Rensselaer, NY - Midmorning
Boston, MA* - Midafternoon Arrival
New York, NY (Grand Central) - Early Afternoon Arrival

*By separate section between Boston and Albany-Rensselaer.

Frequency - Daily.
Seating - Heritage Fleet coaches.
Dining - Complete meal and beverage service between New York and Chicago. Tray meals between Boston and Albany. Lounge between New York and Chicago.
Sleeping - Heritage Fleet with roomettes

and bedrooms. Slumbercoach with economy sleeping rooms between New York and Chicago.

Baggage - Handled at most stations.

Reservations - Reservations required, except for local travel between Albany and New York.

Length of Trip - 960 miles in 18½ hours (New York to Chicago).

Route Log

For route between New York City and Albany-Rensselaer, see that portion of Adirondack log, page 49.

 BOSTON, MA - See page 28.

0:00 (0:05) Depart Boston's South Station and head westerly toward the Back Bay section of Boston.

0:05 (0:00) Arrive Back Bay Station.

 BOSTON (BACK BAY), MA - This station serves Boston's rather elegant Back Bay and surroundings. At one time, much of this area was covered by water from the Charles River, forming vast mud flats. Long thought to be a liability, the land was eventually reclaimed to become a very viable part of the city.

0:00 (0:28) Depart Back Bay Station. Skyline of downtown can still be seen for brief time as train continues westward.

0:15 (0:14) Leave last of Boston's sprawling suburbs and enter rural Massachusetts, liberally splotched with pine forests and towns.

0:28 (0:00) Arrive Framingham.

 FRAMINGHAM, MA - Long a manufacturing community. A General Motors assembly plant employs a large segment of today's populace.

0:00 (0:28) Depart Framingham.

0:12 (0:16) Under Interstate 495 which skirts western edge of Boston metropolitan area.

0:25 (0:03) Approaching Worcester, glimpse of Quinsigamund Lake is afforded on right.

0:28 (0:00) Arrive downtown Worcester.

 WORCESTER, MA - One of the larger manufacturing cities in the Northeast, this city rightfully has considerable community pride in both its past and present. Isaiah Thomas, one of the outstanding printers of the 18th century, lived in Worcester. Old Sturbridge Village, a reconstructed 19th century village, is nearby.

0:00 (1:15) Depart Worcester and cross gentle, rolling countryside of central Massachusetts.

0:47 (0:28) Train accompanies Quaboag River on right for several miles.

0:55 (0:20) Frothy falls in Chicopee River on right add to countryside charm.

1:15 (0:00) Arrive Springfield's grey brick depot, named one of Amtrak's four worst stations in 1972. Fortunately, 1973 remodeling raised it from that lowly classification.

 SPRINGFIELD, MA - Another important manufacturing city of the Northeast, Springfield had its start as a mere trading post in the 1630s. In 1794 the United States opened an important armory here, now the Springfield Armory Museum. Today, the Basketball Hall of Fame is located here, and the Strategic Air Command has operations at Westover Air Force Base just northeast of town.

0:00 (1:15) Depart Springfield.

0:03 (1:12) Crossing broad Connecticut River, note grand stone-arched Memorial Bridge paralleling tracks off to left.

0:06 (1:09) Train rattles through Conrail freight yards in West Springfield.

0:41 (0:34) Deciduous trees of Chester Blanford State Forest and Westfield River combine for idyllic western Massachusetts scenery.

0:44 (0:31) Immense, abandoned roundhouse on left is nostalgic glimpse of railroad's former dominant presence in this locale.

0:49 (0:26) "S" curves, rock cuts and abandoned stone bridges continue to embellish scenery.

1:09 (0:06) Cross famous Appalachian Trail as train approaches Pittsfield.

1:15 (0:00) Arrive Pittsfield.

PITTSFIELD, MA - This is the very heart of New England's ski country. More than 40 ski areas, most with floodlights and ski-making equipment, saturate western Massachusetts. In addition to the attraction of skiing—golf courses, lakes, cultural events and spectacular fall colors make Pittsfield a year-round resort area. Herman Melville wrote his monumental novel "Moby Dick" while living here. The Boston Symphony performs during the summer months at beautiful Tanglewood.

0:00 (1:05) Depart Pittsfield.

0:07 (0:58) Richmond Pond immediately on left is one of many scenic Berkshire lakes in region.

0:17 (0:48) Enter New York and leave Massachusetts as train winds its way through Taconic Range.

0:19 (0:46) Darkness pervades while passing through short tunnel, then train descends through New York countryside.

1:05 (0:00) Arriving Albany, downtown skyline stands out on left. Prominent 42-story skyscraper is centerpiece of Empire State Plaza. Left of tower, low-slung Cultural Education Center houses State Museum and Library, while on right, dynamic elliptical structure is Center for Performing Arts. Four smaller towers in background are also part of this ambitious billion-dollar project. Once in station (train actually stops in town of Rensselaer just across river from Albany), inspiring domed archways of St. John the Baptist Catholic Church can be seen protruding above treetops on right.

For route between New York City and Albany, see that portion of Adirondack log, page 49.

ALBANY, NY - A small-town atmosphere with big-city prestige is the claim of Albany, New York's state capital. Replete with cosmopolitan amenities, Albany is likewise a stone's throw from the rural splendor depicted in the paintings of America's beloved Grandma Moses.

The aforementioned Empire State Plaza is the current pride and joy of downtown Albany. Nearly a city unto itself, shops, pubs and restaurants line the interconnecting walkways between the many governmental agencies located here. At the north end of the complex stands the State Capitol, its fanciful French Renaissance architecture a dramatic contrast to the sleek, modern lines of the Plaza's other buildings.

As well as a bastion of state government, Albany has remained a vital inland port since the completion of the Erie Canal in 1825. Today, private operators conduct excursions along this historic waterway that recapture the spirit and grace of an earlier era. And then, too, this has long been an important railroading town. Fortunately, an important piece of this past was preserved when Albany's decaying Union Station, where New York Central and Delaware & Hudson trains once arrived on different levels, was saved from the wrecking ball and restored to its original elegance by Norstar, a bank holding company.

In the adjacent town of Rensselaer, one can tour Fort Crailo, the nation's oldest fort built in 1642. Legend has it that a British surgeon wrote the famous "Yankee Doodle" tune while visiting this site.

0:00 (0:22) Departing Albany, reassume westerly tack that will essentially follow route of historic Erie Canal.

0:04 (0:19) Cross Hudson River. On left, ornate spires and turrets adorn magnificent State University Administration Headquarters. Originally built in 1916 as corporate offices of Delaware & Hudson Railroad, complex is actually three buildings interconnected, with Flemish facades maintaining delightful continuity throughout. Replica of Henry Hudson's "Half Moon" is highlight of weather vane perched atop main tower.

0:05 (0:17) Intriguing amalgam of modern and classical architecture is a most striking feature of Albany's city center on left.

0:06 (0:16) A familiar emblem for many years, large black and white mutt looms protectively above RCA facility on right.

0:07 (0:15) August 9, 1831, one of North America's earliest steam locomotives made its inaugural run between Albany and Schenectady when Mohawk & Hudson's De Witt Clinton, pulling three stagecoach-appearing cars, chugged up this grade—steepest on Water Level Route. Mohawk & Hudson was first railroad chartered in United States.

0:10 (0:10) On outskirts of town, four

64

lonesome high rises comprise State Office Building campus on left.

0:11 (0:09) Shoreline of Rensselaer Lake adjoins trackside on right.

0:18 (0:04) Approaching Schenectady, attractively landscaped parkways dissect sprawling grounds of General Electric industrial park on left. Number of people employed by regional GE operations is about equal to one-third of Schenectady's population.

0:19 (0:00) Arriving Schenectady where tall, gold-domed City Hall clock tower is prominent fixture on right.

SCHENECTADY, NY - Emerging from the heart of the Industrial Revolution, Schenectady became known as "the city that lights and hauls the world." The American Locomotive Company's Schenectady Works and Thomas Edison's Machine Works were primarily responsible for this designation, the latter eventually evolving into the colossal General Electric Corporation.

Schenectady's "Stockade District" is a premier historical attraction, representing one of the country's best-preserved enclaves of early-American architecture and culture. Its name stems from the original 1661 settlement which was surrounded by a stockade to guard against French and Indian attacks.

0:00 (1:11) Departing Schenectady, elevated track bed now affords encompassing view of one of nation's oldest communities.

0:01 (1:10) Cross Mohawk River.

0:08 (1:03) Marker buoys bob conspicuously in midst of Erie Canal which joins on left and follows intermittently to Rochester. In early days, freight and passenger vessels were drawn along this scenic passage by teams of horses, tugging from paths alongside canal.

The Erie Canal was once the major trade passage between the Atlantic Ocean and the Great Lakes, handling a continuous stream of staples such as grain, lumber and coal, and the westward migration of thousands of Americans. Many called it the Eighth Wonder of the World. But like most things, the canal has been changed by time. The railroads, the New York State Throughway and the St. Lawrence Seaway have reduced the canal

Rohr Turboliner – Albany-Rensselaer Station

to more of an historic artifact than a vital trade artery. Today, only an occasional barge load of molasses, asphalt or gasoline can be seen floating through one of the locks, while each year 120,000 pleasure boats take advantage of its no-fee-for-use policy.

New York State spends 115 million dollars a year to keep its present-day barge canal system going, a system made up of the Erie, Oswego, Champlain and Cayuga Seneca canals. Critics contend the canals have outlived their usefulness as instruments of commerce, but so far, preservationists and other supporters have prevailed, arguing that their historic value is worth the expense, not to mention the canals' roles in irrigation, flood control, domestic water supply and tourism.

Even in 1817 when the Erie's construction had just begun, it had its detractors. No less than Thomas Jefferson called it "little short of madness" to start such a project in America's infancy. Jefferson was probably right. America had virtually no workers familiar with canal building, and worse, precious few engineers. If it hadn't been for an American engineer by the name of Canvass White who walked 2,000 miles of British canals and persuaded an Irish construction engineer named J. J. McShane to come to New York to help, the canal might well have failed.

On October 26, 1825, the impossible project was finished. A 353-mile-long ditch, 40 feet wide at the top, 28 feet wide at the bottom, and four feet deep had been dug from Albany on the Hudson to Buffalo on Lake Erie. Eighty-three locks were necessary to raise traffic from Albany's elevation to Lake Erie, some 571 feet higher. A six-week trip from New York to Buffalo had just been shortened to a ten-day excursion by "fast packet boat." The impact would be immense. A trade route had been created that would make New York the financial center of the world and its port the largest on the East Coast. (And Buffalo would quickly grow from a village to a city of 18,000.)

Amidst great ceremony, Governor Dewitt Clinton, whose dream was now a reality, opened the canal at Buffalo. Cannons had been placed at 10-mile intervals along the entire route between Buffalo and New York City to relay the good news of completion (telegraphy was still a few years away). At 10 a.m. the first salvo was fired and by 11:30 that same morning the last of the cannons was fired, announcing to New Yorkers that the Erie Canal was complete.

Most of what can be seen today, however, is not the original Erie Canal. The original was enlarged in the mid-1800s, widening it to 70 feet and deepening it to 7½ feet, an improvement that allowed for 240-ton-capacity barges—an eight-fold increase. This followed the original route, except at Schoharie Crossing. But the biggest change came between 1905 and 1918 when the canal was modernized as part of the State Barge Canal System. Techniques had been developed to control the currents of the Mohawk River. Its channel was deepened to 12 feet and the river virtually became the canal. This resulted in a near-total abandonment of the first waterway, which generally followed the river's edge. Only remnants of the original Erie can occasionally be spotted from the train.

0:09 (1:02) Pass through Hoffmans where Mohawk River ferry crossing was established in late 1700s.

0:12 (0:59) On left, shipping locks spanning canal are first of several sets seen along route. Across river, grand window arches highlight old, intriguing Adirondack Power and Light facility.

0:15 (0:55) Passing through Amsterdam, architectural devotees will discover veritable bonanza in variety of classic dwellings, here in another cradle of early Americana.

Amsterdam owes much to the Johnson family who early on cultivated the friendship of the native Indians. This alliance proved most fortuitous in combating attacks during the French and Indian War. Without this support, the Mohawk Valley today might well be a French Canadian province.

On the west edge of town, Guy Park is on the left with a mansion built by Sir William Johnson for his daughter Molly. It was Sir William who organized the Iroquois to fight for the British during the

French and Indian War.

0:17 (0:54) Lock Eleven, adjacent to Guy Park and just beyond Johnson Mansion, lifts and lowers vessels a total of 12 feet. Bridge-like structure is used to lift sections of dam to control water level in summer and prevent freeze damage during canal's winter-month closures. To right of tracks, note red Volkswagen precariously perched atop brick chimney, somehow placed there to tout body shop below.

0:18 (0:53) Just beyond stone fence on right is red-shuttered Georgian-style "Fort Johnson," built in 1749 and first home of Sir William. Although no battles were fought here, thick walls contained 18 guns ports—just in case. Besides serving as a military post, it sheltered important Indian council meetings in late 1750s. Sir William's family remained Loyalists, however, and fled to Canada when Revolutionary War threatened their freedom.

Located nearby is the famed Auriesville Shrine which commemorates the martyrdom of three French missionaries who were persecuted, then slain while attempting to convert the Indians in the mid-1600s. A large coliseum was erected here in 1931 to accommodate the many worshippers who gather here.

After Amsterdam, idyllic farms and dairylands are scenically interwoven into a lush, pastoral tapestry with quaint little communities interspersed throughout.

0:19 (0:52) Schoharie Creek, which drains into Mohawk from south, once created slackwater that posed problems for early "canalers." Solution, in 1841, was to build a stone aqueduct which carried boats above creek. Roman aqueduct-appearing ruins can be glimpsed on left.

0:22 (0:49) On right, picturesque creek meanders through splendid dairy farm. Statue of gleaming white steed stands proudly in foreground of adjacent horse farm.

0:39 (0:32) Passing through Nelliston, impressive row of Italianate homes on right has been enshrined in National Register of Historic Places. Immediately thereafter stone marker across river commemorates stronghold of Fort Plain, once valley headquarters for Revolutionary Army.

0:41 (0:30) On right, charming Old Palatine Church sits amidst fairy-tale setting along banks of Caroga Creek. Built in 1770, church was spared during Revolutionary raids with Tory parishioners purportedly bearing influence on its survival. Today, Palatine remains only pre-Revolutionary church standing west of Schenectady and stands as "the shrine of Lutheranism in the Mohawk Valley."

0:44 (0:27) Just before St. Johnsville, decaying remnants of 18th-century tavern can be spotted on right.

0:52 (0:19) Old mill town of Little Falls is location of Lock 17, highest "single locking" on New York's Barge Canal System—a 40-foot lift.

0:53 (0:18) West of Little Falls, industrial operations begin intruding on landscape. Although many beautiful vistas remain, scenery never quite recaptures sublime enchantment of earlier route.

1:00 (0:11) Just beyond Herkimer, through trees on right, used hearse dealer's sales lot is bizarre scene.

1:07 (0:04) Approaching Utica, cross over Erie Canal and elaborate set of shipping locks.

1:11 (0:00) Arrive Utica through industrial district of which General Electric plant is most prominent member. Half-million-dollar preservation effort was expended at station in 1988 to maintain this once-glorious structure. Marble floors and columns enhance interior of one of America's finest depots.

UTICA, NY - Transcending generations from the original immigrant settlers, Uticans still pride themselves on a strong work ethic that remains the backbone of a vibrant industrial economy. A proud respect for history pervades the community as well, and is reflected in several of Utica's oldest institutions that have been preserved and adapted to modern uses. One such landmark is the Utica Steam Engine and Boiler Works, an 1831 industrial plant that has been converted into a workshop for American and European sculptors. Another example is "The Stanley," a grand old movie palace refurbished to house Utica's Center for the Performing Arts.

0:00 (0:43) Depart Utica.

0:10 (0:33) Obelisk atop hill at left commemorates one of bloodiest Revolutionary

Lake Shore Ltd. – near Peekskill, New York

War encounters, the Battle of Oriskany. Here, a column of 900 patriots under General Herkimer, trying to reach a besieged Fort Stanwix, engaged General St. Ledger's Army of 1,700 British and Indians. Although Herkimer's forces eventually retreated, arrival of reinforcements and survival of Ft. Stanwix resulted in ultimate withdrawal of St. Ledger to Canada. Two months later, General Burgoyne's forces, surrounded and cut off at Saratoga, and failing to receive help from St. Ledger, surrendered to General Horatio Gates.

0:14 (0:29) Entering Rome, sculpture atop Paul Revere brass factory on right portrays "midnight ride" of this famous patriot.

Not only presently noted for its prolific copper production, Rome, too, boasts a fascinating historical heritage. Fort Stanwix, reconstructed on its original site in the downtown district, commemorates the Battle of Oriskany. Legend maintains that the "Stars and Stripes" were first unfurled in battle during this critical engagement. Inspired by these events, the "Pledge of Allegiance" was later penned by local resident Francis Bellamy. On July 4, 1817, Rome was assured further recognition when ground was broken here, commencing construction of the Erie Canal.

After leaving Rome, Erie Canal makes another brief appearance on right.

0:37 (0:06) In downtown Canastota, Canal Town Museum on right has most extensive collection of Erie Canal memorabilia. First motion picture machine was developed in Canastota by Harry Marvin and Herman Casler, inventors of Wurtoscope once seen in every penny arcade in America.

0:38 (0:05) Just a mile or so south of here is Chittenango, birthplace of Lyman Frank Baum, author of "The Wonderful Wizard of Oz." Also, meagre limestone, a cement which hardens under water, was uncovered near here by Erie Canal builder Canvass White. Discovery was important to successful completion of canal.

0:43 (0:00) Arriving Syracuse, nice residential area on left overlooks bustling activity of Conrail yards.

 SYRACUSE, NY - Long known as "Salt City," Syracuse traces its industrial roots to one Simon LeMoyne, a French missionary who, in the mid-1600s, noted the peculiar taste in the waters of Onondaga Lake. Although Indians attributed this to evil spirits, it was only a matter of time before the majority of American table salt was produced from this region. Early production techniques are demonstrated at the Salt Museum located here.

Another fascinating attraction is the Canal Museum. Housed in an 1849 "weighlock," the building is equipped with scales that formerly determined tariffs for passage on the Erie Canal.

0:00 (1:24) Depart Syracuse.

0:03 (1:19) Buildings of LeMoyne College are silhouetted atop bluffs on left.

0:06 (1:17) On left, staid neighborhood of older homes surrounds extensive cemetery.

0:08 (1:15) Pass MacArthur Stadium on right, home of minor league baseball's Syracuse Chiefs.

0:09 (1:14) Shores of Onondaga Lake come briefly into view on right.

0:14 (1:09) Race track is most notable feature of New York State Fairgrounds on right.

0:31 (0:52) Just west of Weedsport, canal rejoins on right.

0:33 (0:50) Cross canal, first of several times, as train re-emerges on rolling farmlands. Apple orchards are also seen frequently along this stretch. Area was one of more trying stretches for canal workers who labored in waist-deep, malaria-infested waters of Montezuma Swamp.

0:39 (0:44) Colonial splendor of Clyde is quickly reminiscent of earlier delights. West of town, small cemetery sits tranquilly along banks of canal.

0:58 (0:25) At East Palmyra, dairy farm and small church are poised together in picture-postcard setting atop knoll on left.

1:01 (0:22) Pass through Palmyra. Just four miles south is Hill of Cumorah where, according to Mormon theology, Moroni, last survivor of a great American civilization, buried a set of gold plates recording history of the peoples. As an angel, he delivered these plates to Joseph Smith who, in 1827, translated them into the Book of Mormon. Smith's former farmstead is just southeast of town.

1:12 (0:11) Farmlands quickly give way to industrial climes entering Rochester. Chickering and Sons is famous piano manufacturer on left.

1:18 (0:05) Approaching downtown hub, verdigris-topped clock tower on left is named in honor of Hiram Sibley, founder of Western Union.

1:23 (0:00) Arrive modernistic Rochester station. Tall, distinguished building on right houses international headquarters of Eastman Kodak, world-renowned manufacturer of cameras and film. A multitude of Kodak facilities dispersed throughout city employ over 50,000 people.

ROCHESTER, NY - Set on the banks of the lovely Genesee River, Rochester has come to be known as the "Picture City"—a reference to the illustrious Eastman Kodak Company which was founded here in 1880. Kodak still maintains its international headquarters here, and together with associated operations, comprises an important mainstay of the local economy.

One of Rochester's premier attractions is the George Eastman House, home of Kodak's founding father. This magnificent Georgian mansion now houses the International Museum of Photography. Here, the evolution of photography is explained through fascinating exhibits of prints and equipment. Specialty collections are also maintained for scrutiny by serious scholars.

Rochester is also home of the National Technical Institute for the Deaf, one of two such colleges in the nation. Its on-campus theater offers many "signed" productions throughout the year.

0:00 (0:54) Depart Rochester across Genesee River. Wing-like protrusions atop Times Square Building on left reflect contemporary trend of recent downtown development.

0:05 (0:49) Endeavors of General Railway Signal Company on left are important facet of safe and timely journeys. Immediately thereafter, cross Erie Canal before skirting atop colossal crater of Limestone Dolomite mining operation on right.

0:24 (0:30) A few miles west of Bergen,

woodlands begin thinning and hills dissipate into relatively flat agricultural terrain.

0:37 (0:17) Batavia has two claims to historic fame. One of America's biggest land deals occurred in 1791 when Robert Morris (a signer of the Declaration of Independence) purchased a four-million-acre "farm" (it was most of what is now western New York) from Massachusetts for $333,333.33. Later six Dutch bankers purchased most of that land with an eye to re-selling it to pioneers, a tract that became known as The Holland Purchase. A museum in Batavia now preserves artifacts from that time. Then, along these tracks in May of 1893, a world speed record was set by a steam-powered passenger train which reached 112.5 miles per hour. Never before had humans traveled in excess of 100 miles per hour.

0:45 (0:09) At Lancaster, prison on left and guard shacks on right comprise facilities of Alden Penitentiary.

0:48 (0:06) Airplane sculpted from old garbage cans is amusing attraction of Lancaster Air Park on right.

0:54 (0:00) Arrive Buffalo (Depew Station).

BUFFALO, NY - Situated on the eastern shores of Lake Erie, and across the Niagara River from Canada, Buffalo is New York's second largest city with a population approaching 400,000. The metropolitan region represents one of the largest manufacturing centers in the U.S. with steel, chemicals, auto parts and flour production a sampling of its major industries. Railroading is also an important facet of the Buffalo economy, with a large number of separate lines maintaining offices in the city.

Although frequently the butt of cruel jokes—"There are two seasons in Buffalo, winter and the 4th of July," or to quote from *A Chorus Line,* "Suicide in Buffalo is redundant"—Buffalo offers a wide range of cultural opportunities. The Albright-Knox Art Gallery and Buffalo Zoo are consistently rated among the nation's finest. Buffalo, too, is an avid sports mecca, and supports major-league franchises in football and hockey.

0:00 (1:30) Depart Buffalo.

1:00 (0:30) Rumble through Brocton, birthplace of George Pullman whose name is synonymous with sleeping cars. Having made considerable money moving houses when Erie Canal was first widened, he went on to create an enterprise which became world's foremost producer and operator of sleeping cars.

1:15 (0:15) Enter Pennsylvania and leave New York. Darkness usually prevails during passage through Pennsylvania wine country. Out there somewhere lurk thousands of acres of vineyards. Nearby wineries include Penn Shore Winery, Presque Isle Wine Cellar, Heritage Wine Cellars and Mazza Winery, all located here in Erie County.

1:30 (0:00) Arrive Erie.

ERIE, PA - Located in the narrow neck of northwestern Pennsylvania, Erie is the state's only port on the lake by the same name. Freighters from around the world arrive and depart here daily, providing the city with its most important industry. This port was used by the American Navy as early as the War of 1812. Today, the Flagship Niagara, at the foot of State Street, recalls the stirring victory of Captain Perry over the British in 1813.

0:00 (1:28) Depart Erie.

0:22 (1:06) Enter Ohio and leave Pennsylvania.

0:27 (1:01) Former New York Central depot on left, another structure on National Register of Historic Places, now houses Connaught Historical Railroad Museum. Nickle Plate Road 2-8-4 Steam locomotive, hopper car and caboose repose just east of station.

1:28 (0:00) Arrive Cleveland.

CLEVELAND, OH - It is difficult to envision Cleveland as the capital of "Western Connecticut," but that was the plan in the late 1700s when Moses Cleveland was commissioned to chart the Connecticut Western Reserve, part of a land grant made by King Charles II. Today, Cleveland is the largest city in Ohio (nearly 2,000,000), with a higher concentration of "Fortune 1,000" corporations headquartered here, per capita, than any other U.S. city.

The city has had both the economic

ability and the foresight to create a living environment that is to the city's credit. Myriad parks surround the city; the Cleveland Orchestra is one of the finest; and The Cleveland Museum of Art has one of the more outstanding collections of fine art in the world.

Amtrak Lakefront Station, 200 Cleveland Memorial Shoreway, is located on the edge of downtown and next to Lakefront Stadium. There are storage lockers, food and beverage vending machines, luggage carts and free parking adjacent to the station.

For arrival and departure information, call (216) 696-5115. For reservations and other information, call (216) 861-0105. Waiting room and ticket windows open midnight to 5:30 pm, Monday through Saturday; midnight to 8:45 am, Sundays and holidays.

Cab stand at the station; Yellow and Zone Cab, 623-1500. **Loop bus** to downtown is one block from the station. **Rapid transit lines** (light rail service) extend from Terminal Tower downtown to: **Cleveland Hopkins Airport,** approximately ten miles from the downtown area; Windemere Station in East Cleveland; and Shaker Heights. **Local buses** also serve Greater Cleveland. For information, call Regional Transit Authority, 621-9500. **Greyhound** terminal, 781-1400.

Convention and Visitors Bureau of Greater Cleveland, 3100 Terminal Tower, 44113. Call (216) 621-4110.

Holiday Inn Lakeside, 1111 Lakeside Ave., 44114; (216) 241-5100. Three blocks from the station. $77.

Numerous attractions near the station include: **Port of Cleveland,** at the foot of West Third Street, where lake and oceangoing vessels load and unload 30 million tons of cargo each year; **Lakefront Stadium,** immediately behind station, home of the Cleveland Brown's football team and baseball's Cleveland Indians; and **USS Cod,** a World War II submarine which sank 50 times her own weight in enemy shipping.

The Mall, between Lakeside and St. Clair avenues across from the station, is Cleveland's major downtown public space;

The Arcade, 401 Euclid Ave., a multistoried enclosed mall in a unique architectural surrounding, is Cleveland's first shopping center (built in 1890), offering over 100 individual shops and spectacular views from ironwork balconies.

The **Cleveland Museum of Art,** 11150 East Boulevard, has some of the finest and best endowed art in the world.

0:00 (0:30) Depart Cleveland. Municipal Stadium looms immediately on right while downtown is on left where pointed, 52-story Terminal Tower is clearly visible.

0:01 (0:29) Cross Cuyahoga River having dubious distinction of catching on fire before America became pollution conscious.

0:11 (0:20) Goodyear plant on left and Cleveland's busy airport, Cleveland-Hopkins Field, is on right as surroundings become mostly residential.

0:16 (0:15) Finally depart Cleveland's suburbs and return to rural Ohio.

0:33 (0:00) Arrive Elyria.

ELYRIA, OH - Named for Herman Ely who founded this city in 1817, Elyria has become one of the many industrially oriented communities of northern Ohio.

0:00 (0:35) Depart Elyria.

0:07 (0:28) Train zips through Amherst, allowing glimpse of two old coaches and caboose on exhibit by station at left. Former New York Central depot is nicely preserved and is also on National Register of Historic Places.

0:13 (0:22) Cross Vermilion River where water tower greets visitors with words "Vermilion Sailors"—the name used by sports teams in this city that still has a commercial fishing fleet. Great Lakes Historical Society Museum is located on lakefront and has fine collection of Great Lakes shipping memorabilia.

0:19 (0:16) Glimpses of Lake Erie are afforded through trees on right.

0:23 (0:13) While in Huron County cross Huron River in town of Huron.

0:35 (0:00) Arrive Sandusky.

SANDUSKY, OH - Because of its fine Sandusky Bay, the city is one of Ohio's most important ports. This, too, is wine country where large quantities of grapes are grown locally.

0:00 (0:47) Depart Sandusky and pass through industrial area where such familiar names as Chrysler and Litton appear.
0:07 (0:40) Instead of skirting Sandusky Bay, tracks turn north to cross water before returning to a westward tack.
0:14 (0:33) Lake Erie makes its finale in distance on right.
0:18 (0:29) Davis-Bessie Nuclear Power Plant in far distance on right gives off massive steam plume.
0:28 (0:19) On right, enormous mounds of light grey material almost engulf town of Clay Center. These are mountains of screenings from White Rock Quarry that has been in operation since 1880s. Dolomite limestone is unearthed here and shipped throughout U.S. in sizes ranging from four-ton slabs to mere dust particles.
0:39 (0:08) Cross Maumee River as a myriad of industrial plants mark outer reaches of Toledo. Skyline is silhouetted behind bright blue suspension bridge on right.
0:47 (0:00) Arrive Toledo.

TOLEDO, OH - With a 35-mile-long harbor on Lake Erie, it is easy to understand why Michigan and Ohio both claimed this city in the early 19th century. It took presidential action by Andrew Jackson to finally settle the dispute—in Ohio's favor. (However, Michigan received its Wisconsin-connected Upper Peninsula as recompense.) Today, the city lays easy claim to being the world's leading producer of glass and glass products. A world-renowned collection of ancient and modern glassware is on display at the Toledo Museum of Art.
0:00 (0:53) Depart Toledo.
0:03 (0:50) Steeple-adorned, small brick church on right gives brightness to older residential neighborhoods.
0:13 (0:40) Holland, Ohio marks the end of Toledo's western suburbs. Landscape takes on more definite pastoral flavor as prosperous-appearing farms begin to dot countryside.
0:53 (0:00) Arrive Bryan.

BRYAN, OH - This northwestern Ohio rural distribution center was at one time known as "The Fountain City" because of an abundance of artesian wells, some of which still flow. It also boasts the world's first solar-powered radio station, WQTC, which uses 33,600 photovoltaic cells and storage batteries to maintain a constant supply of power to the station's transmitter.
0:00 (1:11) Depart Bryan.
0:09 (1:02) Cross St. Joseph River.
0:16 (0:55) Enter Indiana and leave Ohio. Terrain soon becomes rolling for the first time since leaving New York State.
0:48 (0:23) Train crosses, then follows meandering Elkhart River, forming a Currier and Ives setting.
1:11 (0:00) Arrive Elkhart.

ELKHART, IN - More band instruments and mobile homes have been produced here than anywhere else in the world. Miles Laboratories (Alka-Seltzer) was founded here and the city remains the headquarters for this pharmaceutical giant. Elkhart County contains a large Amish and Mennonite population, and the Mennonite Historical Library at nearby Goshen boasts the world's largest collection of historical books and reference works pertaining to this Christian denomination. One of the Midwest's outstanding houses is Ruthmere, built circa 1909 by one of the founders of Miles Laboratories.
0:00 (0:20) Depart Elkhart.
0:18 (0:02) Stretching for blocks on left is former Studebaker automobile plant where subsequent occupants have manufactured such diverse products as toys, postal vehicles, tools, auto bodies and hand-built Avanti motor cars.
0:20 (0:00) Arrive South Bend.

SOUTH BEND, IN - Located on one of the southernmost bends of the St. Joseph River (hence the name), South Bend is a major Indiana manufacturing city. But most notably, it is the location of the 1,700-acre campus of Notre Dame University. In mid-September, there is a Sweet Sorghum Celebration with folk dancing, turn-of-the-century working implements, music, apple pie, and a Civil War re-enactment of "The Battle of St. Patrick's Landing."
0:00 (0:56) Depart South Bend. On right is original Bendix plant where that giant manufacturer of auto and aircraft parts got its start.

Gain one hour as train passes from Eastern to Central Time. Set your watch back (forward if eastbound) one hour.

0:27 (0:29) In small town of Porter, tracks joining from right are route of International and Pere Marquette.

0:33 (0:23) Midwest Steel Corporation facility appears on right.

0:38 (0:18) Tracks and catenary of legendary Chicago South Shore and South Bend run parallel to our Conrail right-of-way, off to left.

0:43 (0:13) Where Gary began, enormous U.S. Steel Gary Works stretch along tracks at right beyond rail yards.

0:51 (0:06) Inland Steel plants straddle tracks, Plant Number One on left and Plant Number Two on right. Then cross drawbridge spanning Indiana Harbor Canal that links Lake Michigan with Calumet River.

0:52 (0:04) Standard Oil Company of Indiana refinery creates apparatus jungle at left. Lake Michigan is now only 100 feet or so to right.

0:56 (0:00) Arrive Hammond-Whiting.

HAMMOND-WHITING, IN - Most of Amtrak's trains connecting to points east from Chicago make this their suburban Chicago stop. The simple station on the right was built in 1982 at a cost of three million dollars.

0:00 (0:24) Depart Hammond-Whiting.

0:02 (0:22) Cross huge, black steel bridge over Calumet River. To left, Chicago Skyway reaches its peak over river, as around us huge bridges, grain elevators, and ships and boats of all sizes create a rugged industrial landscape.

0:04 (0:20) Roll along a wide right-of-way from which most of tracks have been removed.

0:05 (0:19) Skyway now rises on its steel supports beside us on left.

0:06 (0:18) Pass piggyback yards. Then, on right is foundation of demolished Englewood Station, from which, years ago, Pennsylvania and New York Central engineers raced each other away toward New York in a graphic symbol of their lines' competition.

0:07 (0:17) At right, spectacular view of Chicago skyline is afforded, including Sears Tower, world's tallest building, and John Hancock Building. Now roll across Dan Ryan Expressway (I-90/94) before ducking under Chicago's famous rapid transit—the "El."

0:12 (0:12) To our immediate right is Comiskey Park, historic home of American Baseball League's Chicago White Sox.

0:14 (0:10) In Conrail piggyback yard at left, it's possible to see large cranes loading semitrailers from almost every major railroad in America onto flatcars.

0:16 (0:08) Cross South Branch of Chicago River before passing under Dan Ryan Expressway.

0:18 (0:06) To left, it's possible to see an entire train gliding slowly through Amtrak's washer building.

0:20 (0:04) Enter clean, modern Amtrak yards.

At right sit examples of nearly every kind of equipment Amtrak owns—coaches and cafes; diners and domes; sleepers, slumbercoaches, and Superliners; P30CH's and F40PH's—all being readied to equip Amtrak trains that roll across America from the Atlantic to the Pacific and from Lake Superior to the Gulf of Mexico. To the left, the Burlington Northern yards are home to a fleet of big green E-9 locomotives, refurbished relics of streamliner days, that now power silver, double-decker Regional Transportation Authority commuter cars between Chicago and the suburb of Aurora.

0:24 (0:00) Leave daylight as we lumber beneath Chicago's huge post office building just before arrival at Union Station.

CHICAGO, IL - See page 116.

Other New York State Service

Various unreserved turboliner and Amfleet trains run on segments of the route between New York City and Niagara Falls, NY, with tray meals and snacks available. Checked baggage is not handled on these trains, but hand baggage may be carried on board. Several trains offer Custom Class seating.

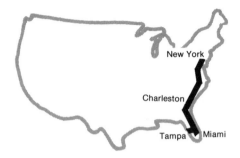

Silver Meteor

The Eastern Seaboard, where much of this country's richest heritage will be found, is visited almost from "top to bottom" by The Silver Meteor. Philadelphia, Washington, Richmond, Charleston, SC and Savannah are just some of the historic salients of this trip through eastern America.

As early as 1939, the railroads recognized Florida as a strong market for Easterners wanting to enjoy warmer winters. In February of that year, The Silver Meteor was born when Seaboard Air Line commenced its streamliner service between New York and Miami. Later that same year, the competing Champion commenced service between the same two cities. (Ironically, today's Meteor follows the old Champion's tracks more closely than it does the route of original Meteor.)

And Florida has become one of Amtrak's best markets. There are now three daily trains between New York and Florida— The Silver Star, like the Meteor, also going to both Miami and Tampa, but taking a somewhat different course, and The Palmetto terminating at Jacksonville, Florida. This comparative abundance of service makes it possible to travel the entire distance without having to ride the train overnight, even though it takes more than 24 hours to get from New York to Miami. Unlike other Amtrak long-distance routes, it's possible to stop at, say, Charleston or Savannah in the evening, stay a night or two in one of those delightful cities, then continue on with a morning departure.

The entire trip between New York City and Miami, Amtrak's southernmost point, takes 26 hours. Tampa is served by a separate Meteor section between that city and Kissimmee, Florida.

Southbound Schedule (Condensed)
New York, NY (Penn Station) - Late Afternoon Departure
Washington, DC - Late Evening
Richmond, VA - Late Evening
Charleston, SC - Early Morning
Savannah, GA - Early Morning
Jacksonville, FL - Midmorning
Tampa, FL - Midafternoon Arrival*
Miami, FL - Early Evening Arrival

Northbound Schedule (Condensed)
Miami, FL - Early Morning Departure
Tampa, FL - Late Morning Departure*
Jacksonville, FL - Late Afternoon
Savannah, GA - Midevening
Charleston, SC - Late Evening
Richmond, VA - Middle of the Night
Washington, DC - Early Morning
New York, NY (Penn Station) - Late Morning Arrival

*By separate section between Kissimmee and Tampa.

Frequency - Daily.
Seating - Amfleet II coaches.
Dining - Buffet-style dining service offered between New York and Miami. (Orlando to Tampa, sandwiches and beverages.) Lounge service between New York and Miami.
Sleeping - Heritage Fleet sleepers with bedrooms and roomettes. Slumber coach

with economy bedrooms between New York and Miami.

Baggage - Checked baggage handled at most stations.

Reservations - All-reserved train.

Length of Trip - 1,407 miles in 26 hours (New York/Miami).

Route Log

For route between New York City and Washington, DC, see that portion of Northeast Corridor log, page 31.

 WASHINGTON, DC- See page 39.

0:00 (0:17) Depart Washington southbound through regions whose roots trace back to earliest periods of American history.

0:02 (0:15) Emerge from tunnel after passing under Mall. Glimpses of Capitol and oldest Smithsonian structure ("The Castle") can be caught through various federal buildings on right.

0:07 (0:10) Perhaps Washington's most charming monument, Monticello-shaped Jefferson Memorial, resides among cherry trees of Tidal Basin, on right.

0:09 (0:08) Cross Potomac River paralleling 14th Street bridge. Washington National Airport is directly downstream to left. Back on right, Washington Monument, world's tallest masonry structure at 555.5 feet, punctuates horizon. Capitol's dome can still be seen toward rear on left.

0:10 (0:07) The Pentagon, headquarters for America's military establishment, is off to right, now mostly hidden by newer buildings.

0:12 (0:05) Glass high rises of Crystal City flaunt their starkness on right. Expansive RF&P rail yards are on left.

0:17 (0:00) Arrive Alexandria.

ALEXANDRIA, VA - This historic Washington suburb sits six miles south of the nation's capital, along the west bank of the Potomac River. Most noted for its outstanding examples of early American architecture, the Alexandria area is also replete with numerous national landmarks. Mount Vernon, beloved home and estate of George Washington from 1754 until his death in 1799, is just a few miles down the Potomac.

0:00 (1:34) Depart Alexandria.

0:01 (1:33) George Washington National Masonic Memorial, with museum of Washington memorabilia, dominates skyline on right.

0:09 (1:25) On right, Amtrak's northern Auto Train terminal handles Florida passengers who want to take their cars along—but not drive them until they get there.

0:10 (1:24) Cross inlet of Potomac River where barges can frequently be seen on right and various small boats on left. Numerous Potomac inlets and coves can be seen on left for next 20 minutes.

0:26 (1:08) Virginia Electric Power Company's huge Possum Point generating station stands on far shore at left. Enter facilities of Quantico Marine Base (a flag stop for The Palmetto).

0:27 (1:07) Quantico Airfield can be seen on left.

0:29 (1:05) Leave Quantico Marine Base.

0:30 (1:04) Broad expanse of Potomac now stretches into distance to left.

0:31 (1:03) Cross small cove with final look at Potomac before becoming immersed in rolling, wooded interior of Virginia.

0:42 (0:52) Enter Falmouth where industrial and newer residential areas appear on northern outskirts of Fredericksburg.

0:44 (0:50) Cross Rappahannock River (the one George Washington supposedly threw a silver dollar across) and enter historic Fredericksburg (a stop for The Palmetto and The Silver Star).

The history of this city spans the better part of three centuries. John Smith visited here in 1608, George Washington grew up on a nearby farm, Thomas Jefferson and Patrick Henry met here with Washington to plan the nation's future, and three quarters of a million Civil War soldiers battled here. Of particular interest is the James Monroe Museum and Fredericksburg Battlefield.

0:47 (0:47) Twenty-foot-high stone pyramid on left commemorates "The Federal Breakthrough," one of many Civil War battles fought in this region. In December 1862, Union forces commanded by General Meade broke through Confederate lines, only to be repelled. Formerly known as Meade Pyramid, it is now more appropriately called "A Southern Memorial."

0:58 (0:36) Small white frame house on left with U.S. flag and large grassy area in front is Jackson Shrine, where Stonewall Jackson died on May 10, 1863 after being accidentally wounded by his own troops at Chancellorsville, some 27 miles away. His death would be a devastating blow to Lee's forces.

1:08 (0:26) Cross Mattaponi River.

1:21 (0:13) Cross small stream called Pamunkey River.

1:26 (0:08) Enter Ashland and experience a charming encounter with a small Virginia town. Train seems out of place as it glides through lovely old residential area while literally touching very doorstep of Randolph-Macon College on left. College was founded by Methodists in 1830 as a men's school, some 61 years before its sister institution, Randolph-Macon Woman's College, was started in Lynchburg.

1:29 (0:05) Decaying Forest Lodge Hotel, with its four stories of bleached lapboard and ornate balconies, stands on right as forlorn monument to one man's unrealized dream. Constructed after Civil War by John Cussons, English adventurer and Confederate scout, this "luxury hotel" failed to capture imagination of rail travelers. Now largely abandoned and half original size, it once featured lakes, gardens and game preserve on 1,000 acres.

1:34 (0:00) Arrive Richmond, where very attractive modern station greets passengers on northern edge of city.

RICHMOND, VA - Overlooking the James River against a backdrop of rolling countryside, Richmond is truly a cradle of Americana infancy. Setting out from the first English settlement at Jamestown in 1607, Captains John Smith and Christopher Newport traveled up river and claimed the site of Richmond in the name of the Crown. The historical legacy that followed is vast.

In 1775, a convention met to determine delegates to the Second Continental Congress. The state capital was moved to Richmond in 1779 and remains here today. In 1781, Benedict Arnold turned traitor and attacked the town, forcing Governor Thomas Jefferson to flee to safer environs. Chief Justice John Marshall presided over the treason trial of Aaron Burr here in 1807.

In 1861, Richmond was established as the Capital of the Confederacy. Later, after learning of imminent attack, Confederate President Jefferson Davis would evacuate the city and have it burned, lest it fall intact into enemy hands.

Today, Richmond is still dedicated to the preservation of its illustrious heritage. It is said to have more monuments and museums than any other city in the South. Although tobacco has long been the basic economic staple, Richmond boasts a wide variety of industrial and manufacturing operations, producing the likes of chemicals, metals, and pharmaceuticals.

0:00 (0:33) Depart Richmond's station and proceed south through city.

0:08 (0:25) Large Richmond rail yards border main line.

0:14 (0:19) Cross high above James River on venerable Belt Line Bridge, as Interstate 95 spans river on right.

0:18 (0:15) Leave southern suburbs of Richmond.

0:23 (0:10) For next mile or two, acres of brick warehouses and assorted paraphernalia of Defense Central Supply Center line left side of track.

0:33 (0:00) Arrive Petersburg (Ettrick). Note nicely landscaped home made from converted rail car on left.

PETERSBURG, VA - Settled along the banks of the Appomattox River, Petersburg today is a flourishing mecca of tobacco and livestock trade. Yet less than 120 years ago, this lush countryside was blighted beneath one of the Civil War's longest and bloodiest sieges.

For ten months, Lee and Grant struggled over this strategic rail hub. When Union forces eventually prevailed, Lee's surrender at Appomattox followed within weeks.

0:00 (1:23) Depart Petersburg (Ettrick).

0:01 (1:22) Virginia State University can be seen perched atop hill in far distance to left.

0:02 (1:21) Cross Appomattox River. Waters originate some 75 miles west of here near Appomattox Courthouse, where one of America's most somber dramas occurred on Palm Sunday in 1865—Lee's surrender to Grant, concluding the Civil War. Upon crossing river, leave Ettrick which serves as stop for Petersburg, and enter Petersburg itself. Now cross high over line of Norfolk & Western Railroad.

0:06 (1:17) Clatter through CSX rail yards.

0:14 (1:09) Huge Enfield peanut operations are on right.

0:30 (0:53) Through Emporia and cross Meherrin River. It was along this stretch of track that, in December 1864, Warren's Corps attempted to permanently cut rail service to Confederate forces in Petersburg, disassembling miles of track and burning ties.

0:38 (0:45) Leave Virginia and enter North Carolina, America's leading tobacco producer. Plywood plant of Georgia Pacific, on left, marks border.

0:46 (0:37) Cruise high above Roanoke River. Stream has its origin in Blue Ridge Mountains of Virginia and, almost 400 miles later, drains into North Carolina's Albermarle Sound. Then over an intersecting freight line at Weldon (outskirts of Roanoke Rapids) linking Norfolk with Durham. This was at one time an important shipping point, freight being transferred between rail and oceangoing vessels which could navigate inland to this point. Note former station located on line below.

0:52 (0:31) One of South's principal products becomes apparent as cottonfields can be spotted along route.

1:22 (0:01) Cross Tar River. During a particularly fierce Civil War battle, Confederate troops from other states retreated, leaving North Carolinians to go it alone. Later, those that had remained to fight allowed that next time they would put tar on the heels of their faltering comrades so they would "stick better." North Carolinians are now known as Tar Heels.

1:23 (0:00) Rumble along "Main Street" upon arrival at Rocky Mount where old, picturesque three-story brick depot awaits those detraining on right.

ROCKY MOUNT, NC - Established in 1816, Rocky Mount has developed into one of the world's largest bright-leaf tobacco markets. Cotton and peanuts are also important crops that, together with a broad industrial base, ensure the city's status as a commercial core of the coastal plains.

0:00 (1:25) Depart Rocky Mount.

0:02 (1:23) For next several minutes, pass by sprawling rail yards on left.

0:20 (1:05) Through Wilson, where tobacco warehouses seem to be everywhere. Another bright-leaf tobacco center, its annual auction dubbed "The Greatest Show in Tobaccoland" provides a most unique tourist attraction. This is a stop for Amtrak's Palmetto.

0:35 (0:50) Tall, skinny sheds dotting the landscape, some with little chimneys jutting out from their tops, are tobacco curing barns.

0:44 (0:41) Through Selma. This small agricultural center is another stop for The Palmetto.

1:11 (0:14) One of area's larger cotton fields spreads out along route on left.

1:16 (0:09) Agriculture continues its dominance, as soybean fields now appear on both sides of tracks.

1:25 (0:00) Arrive Fayetteville, where 11-story Wachovia Bank Building on right (city's highest structure) anchors downtown. Region's tobacco barns apparently influenced architecture of depot on left.

FAYETTEVILLE, NC - Established by Highland Scots in 1739, Fayetteville is now a thriving tobacco, cotton and livestock trade center. During the Revolutionary War, Fayetteville served as a headquarters for Tory sympathizers. Fort Bragg military installation is located here.

0:00 (1:21) Depart Fayetteville.

0:05 (1:16) Pigs are major "crop" of agrarian operation on left.

0:23 (0:58) Farming heartland of North Carolina produces cotton, tobacco, soybeans and corn, all in evidence in this region surrounding Buie.

0:36 (0:45) Just after passing through Rowland, leave North Carolina and enter South Carolina, the Palmetto State. (Nickname derives from large number of Palmetto trees growing within state's borders —a palm-like tree looking somewhat like Southern California's joshua trees.) Watch for enormous, gaily decorated Mexican hat perched on tower of motel complex at "South of the Border." Here, impatient North Carolina couples take advantage of South Carolina's less stringent marital laws allowing them to tie the knot without red tape.

0:45 (0:36) Through Dillon, another stop for The Palmetto.

1:06 (0:15) Cross Great Pee Dee River.
1:21 (0:00) Arrive Florence amidst large CSX rail yards.

FLORENCE, SC - Cutting its teeth as a railroad town in the 1850s, Florence developed into a transportation center for goods and troops during the Civil War. It is still an important railroad center, functioning as a division point for the CSX.

And teeth are still important to Florence. The town claims to be the denture capital of the world, with three clinics offering one-day service for false teeth, turning out 40,000 sets a year at about half the price found elsewhere.

0:00 (0:32) After departing Florence, watch for preserved steam locomotive on right, a minute or so from station.
0:08 (0:24) Cross Lynches River.
0:13 (0:19) Tobacco barns continue to be centerpieces of many fields that checker region.
0:16 (0:16) Prim little church facing tracks on left is nicely adorned by free-standing bell tower.
0:32 (0:00) Arrive Kingstree where well-patronized restaurant occupies portion of train station.

KINGSTREE, SC - This agricultural center of 4,500 persons is the hometown of Dr. Joseph Goldstein, winner of the 1987 Nobel Prize for Medicine.

0:00 (0:50) Depart Kingstree, then cross over Black River.
0:14 (0:36) Cross Santee River, which traces northern border of Francis Marion Forest, almost 750 square miles of it. Forest lies on left side of tracks for next 10 or 15 minutes and stretches eastward across coastal plains until reaching Atlantic Ocean. It was named for an American Revolutionary War general whose quick-striking raids from Carolina's marshes earned him nickname of "Swamp Fox."
0:25 (0:25) Monolithic levee on left holds back waters of Lake Moultrie which in turn collects waters of larger Lake Marion.
0:29 (0:21) Cross broad Cooper River, an outlet for Lake Moultrie. Note coal-fired generating plant on right.
0:50 (0:00) Arrive at Charleston's rail station—actually in North Charleston, some distance from downtown.

CHARLESTON, SC - Dating back to the earliest days of Colonial settlement, Charleston has been deeply involved in the preservation of its abundant historical tradition. Set picturesquely at the confluence of the Ashley and Cooper rivers, quaint doll-house neighborhoods and exquisite gardens grace the avenues of this stately Southern seaport. Ironically, its post-Civil-War poverty prevented replacement of the city's old buildings which now bestow Charleston with both charm and elegance.

Founded in 1670 to offset Spanish intrusions further south, and named for King Charles II, Charleston was once regarded as the richest city in the South, combining an extensive Indian trade with a thriving export business of rice and indigo. Today the city remains an important manufacturing center for such diverse goods as fertilizer, paint, and clothing.

In the early 1800s, Charleston stood at the forefront of a pioneering railroad industry. The "Best Friend of Charleston" became the first American steam locomotive in regular service, commencing operations here in 1830.

Fort Sumter, located on the city's waterfront, became an historical landmark when it was fired upon in 1861, thus marking the start of the Civil War. The Citadel (the Military College of South Carolina), one of the last three state-operated military colleges in the nation, is located here. And Charleston's naval base is the third largest in the United States.

The intersection of Broad and Meeting streets brings together a most unlikely combination of City Hall, County Court House, U.S. Courthouse and St. Michaels Church; thus, appropriately dubbed "Four Corners of Law."

0:00 (0:46) Depart Charleston, pass beneath U.S. 52 and 78, then curve sharply to right avoiding spur that leads to downtown Charleston.
0:02 (0:44) Roll through Charleston's expansive rail yards for two or three minutes, then cross Ashley River. Ashley and Cooper (crossed earlier) discharge into Atlantic at Charleston, forming one of East Coast's finest harbors.
0:12 (0:34) Tidal lands of South Carolina's seaboard stretch out on left. For

next several miles, numerous rivers and streams cluster together as they approach their final destination.

0:26 (0:20) Cross Edisto River.

0:30 (0:16) Then cross Ashepoo River.

0:42 (0:04) And finally, cross Combahee River.

0:46 (0:00) Arrive Yemassee.

YEMASSEE, SC - This small community is named after the Yemassee Indian tribe that once populated this region. While tilling soil, farmers frequently discover arrowheads and pottery relics.

0:00 (0:46) Depart Yemassee.

0:04 (0:39) Under Interstate 95 which traverses entire East Coast, from Houlton, Maine on Canadian border to Miami.

0:31 (0:12) Pass across very impressive Savannah River as we near city of same name—and "where Georgia began."

0:46 (0:00) Arrive Savannah's rail station, located in western suburbs, about a 15-minute cab ride from downtown.

SAVANNAH, GA - Richly steeped in its colonial heritage, Savannah remains a city of grandeur and elegance as envisioned by its founding father, General James Edward Oglethorpe. It was established in 1733 by the English as a buffer between the northern colonies and the Spanish in Florida.

Early efforts at raising silk proved a disappointment, but cotton and tobacco soon gave Savannah vitality. Oglethorpe tried to forbid "drinkers, slaves, Catholics and lawyers" from his new community, but it didn't matter—he got them all.

Today, ships from all over the world sail out of the Savannah River, many to retrace the route of the S.S. Savannah which departed here in 1819 to become the first steamship to cross any ocean.

Since its fall to General Sherman in 1864, preservation and restoration have been the bywords of this proud city, and the flavor of its colorful past is reflected at every turn.

Savannah's **Amtrak station** is about six miles from downtown at 2611 Seaboard Coastline Drive. There are no nearby hotels, and cabs are the only way to reach downtown. There are luggage carts, food and beverage vending machines and free parking.

For arrival and departure information, call (912) 234-2611. For reservations and other information, call 800-USA-RAIL.

There is a **cab stand** at the station, but no nearby **local bus** service. Direct phone lines reach Avis, Hertz and National for **rental cars. Greyhound,** 233-7723. **Travis Field,** Savannah's airport, is about six miles from the station.

Visitors Center, 301 W. Broad Street, is located in what was once a Georgia Central railroad station on the edge of downtown. Write Savannah Convention & Visitors Bureau, 222 W. Oglethorpe Ave., 31499. Call (912) 233-6651.

Days Inn Downtown, 201 W. Bay St., 31401; (912) 236-4440. Adjacent to the riverfront and historic districts. $53.

-**Best Western Riverfront Inn,** 412 West Bay St., 31401; (912) 233-1011. On the riverfront next to the historic district. $58.

-**Quality Inn of Savannah,** 300 W. Bay St., 31401; (912) 236-6321. Adjacent to the riverfront and historic districts. $53.

-**Liberty Inn,** 128 W. Liberty St., 31401; (912) 233-1007. A restored colonial home in the historic district. $95.

-For information and reservations at several historic inns and guest houses, call 800-262-4667.

The **National Historic Landmark District** has more than 1,200 restored buildings, many of which were grand colonial homes, now renovated to provide lodging. This area comprises much of Savannah's downtown and near-downtown.

The **Riverfront Plaza,** composite of restaurants, pubs, and shops imaginatively housed in restored cotton warehouses, is in the heart of downtown.

One of the best ways to see Savannah is by **city tour,** offered by various operators. Inquire at your hotel or the Visitors Center.

0:00 (0:50) Depart Savannah southbound into tall, densely wooded forests of southeastern Georgia.

0:06 (0:44) On left, skirt grounds of Hunter Army Airfield.

0:12 (0:38) Cross Ogeechee River, which flows into Atlantic Ocean about ten miles east of here.

0:13 (0:37) Pass through Richmond Hill. Nearby Fort McAllister was key to Savannah's fortifications during Civil War, fending off nine naval assaults before finally succumbing in Sherman's march to the sea. Also located here is Richmond Hill Plantation, a seasonal home built by Henry Ford during 1930s.

0:46 (0:04) Cross Altamaha River. Half-sunken houseboat is curious sight on right when re-crossing river about a half-mile downline.

0:50 (0:00) Arrive Jesup.

JESUP, GA - Founded in 1870, the town was named in honor of Morris K. Jessup, a New York financier who personally subsidized the construction of a local railroad. The route would subsequently be incorporated into the Seaboard Coast Line and now the CSX.

Today, Jesup is an important distribution hub, centrally located among such large industrial meccas as Jacksonville, Savannah and Atlanta. Nearby popular tourist destinations include Brunswick and the Georgia Sea Islands. The Dogwood Festival, an annual springtime celebration, features songfests, concerts and crafts exhibitions.

0:00 (1:14) Departing Jesup, pass Wayne County Court House on left. Built in 1903, spire-topped clock tower crowns this quaint structure. On outskirts of town, logging and milling operations become frequent sights, bordering route into central Florida.

0:17 (0:57) Woodland beauty abounds as train crosses Big Satilla Creek.

0:20 (0:54) Cross Satilla River.

0:45 (0:29) Pass through Folkston, one of three points of access to primeval wilderness area known as Okefenokee Swamp.

0:47 (0:27) Crossing St. Mary's River into Florida, Colonial environs of past 1,000 miles are slowly supplanted by Spanish influence of an even earlier period.

1:14 (0:00) Arrive Jacksonville.

JACKSONVILLE, FL - Unlike many other Floridian cities, Jacksonville is not a tourist resort. Rather, it has grown to become the state's leading industrial center, with a population nearing 750,000.

Although lying a few miles west of the Atlantic Ocean, Jacksonville is still an important seaport, with an interconnecting passage along the St. Johns River. Three beautiful beaches, directly east of town, provide a weekend haven for city dwellers.

0:00 (1:01) Depart Jacksonville.

0:03 (0:53) For five minutes, train slips through large Jacksonville rail yards. After a sharp curve to right, downtown skyline will be just to left. Steel bridge on left carries auto traffic over St. Johns River.

0:10 (0:51) On immediate left, two modest churches display some fine stained glass windows.

0:11 (0:50) Under Interstate 10.

0:14 (0:47) On left, expanse of modern red-brick buildings houses Florida Junior College at Jacksonville.

0:18 (0:43) After crossing Ortega River, dramatic view of downtown Jacksonville presents itself on left, just across St. Johns River. Note innumerable fishing and pleasure craft docked on north bank of Ortega River, both sides of train.

0:21 (0:40) Armed Forces Reserve Center is at hand on left while U.S. Naval Air Station (Jacksonville) is just beyond.

0:30 (0:31) Through trees on left, glimpses are afforded of very attractive waterfront homes.

0:38 (0:23) St. Johns River appears again, briefly, on left.

0:40 (0:21) One of Florida's larger dairy farms, with hundreds of grazing black and white Holsteins, appears on right.

0:51 (0:10) Blueberry lovers will be enticed by "U-Pick" sign for blueberry plantation on right.

0:53 (0:08) Twin cooling towers dramatize coal-burning power plant on left.

0:56 (0:05) Cross tributary of St. Johns River. On right, highway bridge spanning that broad waterway carries U.S. 17 traffic between Jacksonville and Orlando.

1:01 (0:00) Arrive at Palatka's finely restored depot.

PALATKA, FL - The town gets its name from a Seminole Indian word meaning "crossing over" or "cow's crossing." Palatka is one of Florida's older cities, dating back to 1820. During the Civil War its St. Johns River location

Jacksonville, Florida Station

worked to its disadvantage, permitting federal gunboats to rake the town with cannon fire. Today, that same river is a boon to tourism, providing fishermen an ideal place to catch trophy widemouth bass and other game fish.

An annual Azalea Festival is held in the Ravine Gardens State Park, when more than 100,000 plantings of azaleas burst into springtime splendor the first two weeks in March.

0:00 (0:46) Depart Palatka.

0:06 (0:40) Drawbridge now carries train across a curl of St. Johns River.

0:13 (0:33) Passing through Park Crescent, brief look at 13-mile-long Crescent Lake is caught through trees on right.

0:24 (0:22) Just beyond small lakes on left, but out of view, is Lake George—actually an enormous widening of St. Johns River. Watch for nursery stock (shrouded from direct sunlight by black netting) for next several miles, and, of course—citrus orchards.

0:38 (0:08) Typical citrus packing plant is next to tracks on left.

0:46 (0:00) Arrive Deland.

DELAND, FL - Deland has experienced a rather checkered history. First signs of known civilization are the remains of an old sugar mill just north of town, believed to be English or Spanish, and dating back to 1570. Later, in 1587, in the area now known as Daytona Beach, a group of Franciscan missionaries established a settlement but were driven out by the Indians and English. Then, in the late 1700s, the British operated plantations here but left when Florida was ceded to Spain. Permanent settlement finally occurred in 1870 by Mathias Pay of Ohio.

Today, Deland is the home of Stetson University, named in 1886 in honor of the famous hat-maker. Houseboat tours on the St. Johns River are a popular attraction.

0:00 (0:18) Depart Deland.

0:12 (0:06) Cross St. Johns River, once again on a drawbridge.

0:18 (0:00) Arrive Sanford, southern terminus of Amtrak's Auto Train. Facilities for loading and unloading autos can be seen on left, while graveyard for interesting array of old passenger cars blights landscape on right. Diesel locomotive shops can also be seen.

SANFORD, FL - In 1870, General Henry Sanford, who had been the U.S. minister to Belgium, purchased over 12,000 acres and laid out the town that now bears his name. In 1880, President U. S. Grant was present at ceremonies here, marking the beginning of the construction of the South Florida Railroad which, by 1884, linked Jacksonville with this central Florida community.

Sanford is host to the unique "Golden Age Games" held during the second week of each November. People age 55 and older from throughout the U.S. and foreign countries compete in a broad spectrum of sporting events.

0:00 (0:21) Depart Sanford.

0:20 (0:01) Area becomes more arid, more urbanized as we enter Orlando's metropolitan area. Just one of area's many fine golf courses is on left.

0:21 (0:00) Arrive Winter Park where beautiful downtown park, complete with swaying palms, provides most attractive station setting.

WINTER PARK, FL - The first building was erected in Winter Park in 1881—a depot. In 1885, Rollins College, today a four-year liberal arts college, offered the first courses of higher learning in Florida. The Cornell Fine Arts Center is one of the finest university museums in the state. The Maltbie Museum, displaying shells from around the world, is also on this campus.

Visitors to Winter Park can enjoy Scenic Boat Tours with 12-mile cruises through Chain-of-Lakes and canals, and Genius Drive, a winding road through a private estate with more than 100 peacocks wandering freely on this beautiful acreage. This is one of the prettiest towns in Florida, with lush foliage and winding brick streets, many lined with vine-draped oaks.

0:00 (0:13) Depart Winter Park.

0:05 (0:08) Passengers are now "treated" to an unusual trip through a hospital.

Buildings of Florida Hospital line both sides of track with a walkway connection directly overhead.

0:08 (0:05) Note unusually attractive white power plant of Orlando Utilities on left upon entering heart of Orlando.

0:11 (0:02) Just before reaching Orlando's present train station, old Church Street Station is on immediate left. Note 0-6-0 steam engine now on permanent display.

0:13 (0:00) Arrive Orlando.

ORLANDO, FL - Originally a sleepy agricultural town dependent on the citrus industry, Orlando has experienced growth in the last three decades that is now legendary. Tourism, due to the area's mild year-round climate, and particularly the proximity to Disney World and its newer offshoots, largely accounts for its recent surge.

It claims to be the world's number one vacation destination. The fact that a half million rental cars cruise central Florida's highways backs this boast.

It's a city where Disney has set the standard. Other local industries seem to pick up on the young, neat, well-trained and highly organized theme—a theme that Disney has perfected.

Amtrak Station, 1400 Sligh Blvd., an attractive Spanish-style depot, is situated just to the south of Orlando's central business district. There are food and beverage vending machines, luggage carts and redcap service. Ample free parking is adjacent to the station.

Call 843-7611 for arrival and departure information. Call 800-USA-RAIL for reservations and other information.

Cab stand is at the station; Yellow Cab, 699-9999, and Gray Line Taxi, 422-5550. Nearest **local bus** stop is at Orange Ave., three blocks east of the station; call 841-2279 for information. **Greyhound** bus terminal; 843-7720. Several **rental car** companies service the station: Air Rail Rent-A-Car, (407) 649-9283 or 4150, has cars at the station; National and Avis both provide shuttle service between the station and their downtown locations. **Orlando International Airport** is approximately nine miles south of the station.

 Orlando Orange County Visitors Bureau, 7208 Sand Lake

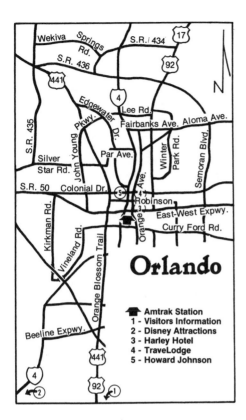

Orlando

🚂 Amtrak Station
1 - Visitors Information
2 - Disney Attractions
3 - Harley Hotel
4 - TraveLodge
5 - Howard Johnson

Rd., Suite 300, 32819; (407) 363-5871. Or visit the Visitors Center at 8445 International Drive, 32819.

TraveLodge Orlando Downtown, 409 North Magnolia (at Livingston), 32801; (407) 423-1671. Well-managed downtown bargain. About two miles from the station. $45.

-**Harley Hotel of Orlando,** 151 E. Washington St. (at Rosalind), 32801; (407) 841-3220 or 800-321-2323. A Helmsley hotel. Downtown, overlooking Lake Eola. Spacious, attractive rooms. Two miles from the station. $75.

-For reservations in one of seven hotels in **Walt Disney World,** write Walt Disney World Co., Central Reservations, Box 10, 100 Lake Buena Vista, FL, 32830, or call (407) 824-8000.

Walt Disney World, Epcot Center and **Disney MGM Studio** are several miles from Orlando. These are the major reasons people come to Orlando. Unfortunately, there is no bus service between Orlando and these attractions. A car is about the only practical way to see most of Orlando's attractions. (Several hotels near Disney World, however, offer free shuttle service to Disney.)

Kennedy Space Center, 60 minutes east of Orlando, provides tours of launch pads and other facilities. **Cypress Gardens,** 55 minutes southwest of Orlando, has acres of gardens and cypress trees which can be seen from foot paths and electric boats.

0:00 (0:20) Depart Orlando. Upon leaving metropolitan area, landscape is still dominated by now familiar citrus groves.

0:20 (0:00) Arrive Kissimmee.

KISSIMMEE, FL - Kissimmee is the closest rail station to Disney World and Epcot Center. South of town is Reedy Creek Overlook reached by a boardwalk that winds through Spanish moss and a cypress forest. Merry "D" Wildlife Sanctuary is in the same area.

0:00 (1:08) Departing Kissimmee, Monument of States can be seen on left, a 70-foot-high pyramid comprised of thousands of rocks (and other items) collected from all states and some foreign countries.

0:38 (0:30) This is Auburndale, a major intersection for two routes of the historic Seaboard Coast Line. In rail vernacular, this is known as "The Auburn Diamond." Here, The Silver Meteor's Miami and Tampa sections split when southbound and join when northbound. Expect at least a 15-minute delay to accommodate this switching, backing and coupling. Although it is not really important to understand what's happening, it is important to be in the right section of the train at this point.

For Miami section, see Silver Star Log, starting Winter Haven, at page 89.

1:08 (0:00) Arrive at Lakeland's immaculate white-brick station.

LAKELAND, FL - This is the very heart of citrus country. A fifth of all citrus grown in the United States comes from this immediate area—that's a lot of orange juice. Lakeland is also the marketing center for Florida's entire crop. But one other product is as important as oranges and grapefruit. Most of the world's phosphate is mined nearby, almost all of it going into agricultural fertilizers.

Florida Southern College is located here where students study amidst the largest assemblage of buildings designed by Frank Lloyd Wright. The Detroit Tigers have enjoyed spring training here for years. This is also Amtrak's closest stop to Cypress Gardens (at Winter Haven).

0:00 (0:32) Depart Lakeland.

0:07 (0:25) Train slows to 35 mph while coursing through heart of Plant City, spring training camp of Cincinnati Reds.

0:20 (0:12) Cross Tampa By-Pass Canal.

0:32 (0:00) Arrive Tampa, where station is backdropped by Tampa's glassy sky-scrapers.

TAMPA, FL - The first adventurers to reach Tampa were Panfilo Narvez in 1528 and DeSoto in 1539. The area was soon abandoned by the white man, however, and it was not until 284 years later in 1823 that the first settler gave Tampa some semblance of permanence. The following year Ft. Brooke was established when four companies of the U.S. Army sailed into the bay from Pensacola.

The railroad reached Tampa in 1883 which helped bring about the development of Tampa's large fishing industry. In 1885, V. M. Ybor was persuaded to bring his cigar-making operations from Key West to the Tampa area, and Ybor City was laid out northeast of Tampa to accommodate this new industry. Tampa's first famous cigars were thus manufactured in 1886.

Teddy Roosevelt set up headquarters in the Tampa Bay Hotel in 1892 with 30,000 soldiers camped nearby for training during the Spanish American War, and Tampa became the major embarkation point for troops headed for Cuba. The first regularly scheduled commercial airline flight ever flown landed here, arriving from nearby St. Petersburg.

Today, Tampa is the industrial center of western Florida, with fishing and citrus processing being mainstays. Its mild climate has made it not only a major tourist area but also a favorite retirement

Silver Meteor – Tampa, Florida

84

center.

🚂 **Tampa Amtrak Station,** 601 Nebraska Ave. at Twiggs Street, is a modern, efficient, "temporary" structure immediately behind Union Station. The latter was built in 1912 in Italian Renaissance style, and has been boarded up for some time pending possible restoration.

There are snack vending machines, luggage carts and redcap service. There is limited free parking in front of the station. Pay-parking is at the Twiggs Street Parking Garage.

Ticket window and waiting room hours are 8:30 am to 8:15 pm. For arrival and departure information, call 221-7600; for reservations, call 800-USA-RAIL.

🚌 **Cab** stand at the station; United Cab, 253-2424 and Yellow Cab, 253-0121. **Local bus** information, call 254-HART. **Greyhound,** 610 Polk, five blocks from the station; 229-1501. **Amtrak Thruway Buses** to Clearwater, Clearwater Beach, St. Petersburg, Treasure Island, Bradenton, Sarasota and Winter Haven. Avis, 221-1666, will pick up **rental car** customers at the station and cars can be dropped off at the station. **Tampa International Airport** is approximately six miles west of the station.

❓ **Tampa/Hillsborough Visitor Information Center,** 100 South Ashley, Suite 850, 33602; (813) 223-1111 or 800-826-8358.

🛏 **Days Inn Convention Center,** 515 Cass E., 33602; (813) 229-6431. Nicely maintained, spacious rooms, non-smoking floors, covered parking. On the edge of the central business district, seven blocks from the station. $42.

-Holiday Inn Downtown, 111 W. Fortune, 33602; (813) 223-1351. About a mile from the station, on the edge of the central business district. $64.

✳ Tampa's downtown is focused on the **Franklin Street Mall,** a pleasant urban stretch of stores, restaurants and services. The south end of the Mall is anchored by the smartly landscaped City Hall Plaza, surrounded by hotels, offices and popular bistros. And on the southern edge of the Plaza, a people mover transports pedestrians to **Harbor Island,** an array of specialty shops, restaurants

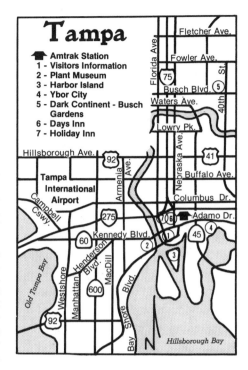

Tampa

🚂 Amtrak Station
1 - Visitors Information
2 - Plant Museum
3 - Harbor Island
4 - Ybor City
5 - Dark Continent - Busch Gardens
6 - Days Inn
7 - Holiday Inn

and quick-service eateries.

Ybor City, just a few blocks east of the station, bounded roughly by 5th and 11th avenues and 12th and 22nd streets, is Tampa's Latin Quarter. What was the beginning of Tampa's cigar industry is now filled with many historic sites, as well as **Ybor Square** which is a fine collection of shops and restaurants featuring fine Spanish cuisine.

Busch Gardens, north of downtown in the area of Busch Blvd. and 40th St., features seven adventure lands, with wild animals, thrill rides, tropical landscaping, restaurants and other entertainment. The **Henry B. Plant Museum,** 401 West Kennedy Blvd., across the river from downtown, contains art treasures from around the world. It was named after an entrepreneur who brought the railroad to Tampa.

New York

Columbia

Tampa   Miami

Silver Star

The Silver Star travels the Eastern Seaboard following a trail somewhat similar to The Silver Meteor, but keeps farther inland through most of the Carolinas. And just as its sister train does, the Star also takes in much of America's most historic environs, in this case locales such as Philadelphia, Washington, Richmond, Raleigh, Columbia, SC and Savannah.

At Jacksonville, Florida, the Star splits, with the Miami section taking the interior route through Ocala, while the Tampa section takes a more easterly course through Orlando.

Southbound Schedule (Condensed)
New York, NY (Penn Station) - Midmorning Departure
Washington, DC - Early Afternoon
Richmond, VA - Late Afternoon
Raleigh, NC - Early Evening
Columbia, SC - Late Evening
Savannah, GA - Middle of the Night
Jacksonville, FL - Middle of the Night
Tampa, FL - Midmorning Arrival*
Miami, FL - Late Morning Arrival

Northbound Schedule (Condensed)
Miami, FL - Late Afternoon Departure
Tampa, FL - Midevening Departure*
Jacksonville, FL - Middle of the Night
Savannah, GA - Middle of the Night
Columbia, SC - Early Morning
Raleigh, NC - Midmorning
Richmond, VA - Early Afternoon
Washington, DC - Midafternoon
New York, NY (Penn Station) - Midevening Arrival

*By separate section between Tampa and Jacksonville.

Frequency - Daily.
Seating - Amfleet II coaches.
Dining - Complete meals offered with buffet-style service between New York and Miami. (Jacksonville to Tampa, sandwiches and beverages.) Lounge service between New York and Miami.
Sleeping - Heritage Fleet roomettes and bedrooms. Slumbercoach between New York and Miami.
Baggage - Checked baggage handled at most stations.
Reservations - All-reserved train.
Length of Trip - 1,449 miles in 26 hours (New York/Miami).

Route Log

For route between New York and Rocky Mount, see that portion of Silver Meteor log, page 75.

0:00 (1:20) Depart Rocky Mount.
0:02 (1:18) For next several minutes, pass by sprawling CSX rail yards on left.
0:20 (1:00) Through Wilson, another bright-leaf tobacco center, where tobacco warehouses seem to be everywhere. Its annual auction, dubbed "The Greatest Show in Tobaccoland," provides a most unique tourist attraction. (This is a stop for Amtrak's Palmetto.)
0:35 (0:45) Tall, skinny sheds dotting the landscape, some with little chimneys jutting out from their tops, are tobacco curing barns.
0:44 (0:36) Through Selma, a small agricultural center, and point where our route now swings back toward Raleigh, depart-

ing from the southbound CSX tracks followed by The Silver Meteor and The Palmetto. (This is another stop for The Palmetto.)

1:20 (0:00) Arrive at Raleigh's attractive Georgian-style station.

RALEIGH, NC - Capital of North Carolina (named for Sir Walter who never saw the area) and the fastest growing city in North Carolina, Raleigh is a neat-appearing community with over 300 parks, plazas and "green spaces." A heavy emphasis has been placed on education with nine institutions of higher learning located in the metropolitan area, including North Carolina State University with an enrollment in excess of 20,000.

Of particular interest are Andrew Johnson's birthplace (our 17th president), the North Carolina Museum of Art, and the North Carolina Museum of History.

0:00 (1:06) Depart Raleigh.

0:07 (0:59) Brick fortress-appearing buildings on left comprise North Carolina Central Prison.

0:08 (0:58) Attractive campus of North Carolina State University lies immediately on left.

0:13 (0:53) Leaving Raleigh's suburbs, two barn-like brick buildings on right house veterinarian school of North Carolina State.

1:06 (0:00) Arrive Southern Pines (Pinehurst).

SOUTHERN PINES, NC - This is the heart of the "Sandhills" of North Carolina where rolling green hills forested with pines (having needles up to 16 inches long) make this one of the most popular recreational areas in the U.S. Within a 15-mile radius there are: 27 golf courses (that's 91.03 miles of golf); 131 tennis courts; 6½ miles of race tracks; and 3,460 acres of lakes and ponds. The World Golf Hall of Fame overlooks the fifth tee of the famed Pinehurst No. 2 Course.

0:00 (0:31) Depart Southern Pines.

0:31 (0:00) Arrive Hamlet.

HAMLET, NC - Founded in the late 1800s when John Shortridge established a woolen mill here, the town soon became an important seaboard rail hub. Today, the rail industry still dominates the economy with the Southeast's largest electronic rail yard located here. An old opera house still stands where such notable performers as Caruso once brought culture of the highest level to this small town during its early prosperity. The quasi-Victorian rail station is on the National Register of Historic Places and houses a fine collection of Seaboard Airline Railway memorabilia.

0:00 (1:08) Depart Hamlet.

0:08 (1:00) Leave North Carolina and enter South Carolina.

0:46 (0:22) Through Bethune, a small agricultural community claiming title of Nation's Egg Capital.

1:08 (0:00) Arrive Camden.

CAMDEN, SC - This is the oldest inland city in South Carolina, having been established in 1732. A major British garrison under General Cornwallis was located here, and the battles of Hobkirk Hill and Camden, as well as 12 other Revolutionary War battles, took place in this vicinity. Today, one can visit Historic Camden, a reconstructed colonial village where the British army spent a demoralizing winter.

The world-famous "Colonial Cup," one of the nation's richest steeplechase races, is held here each November.

0:00 (0:33) Depart Camden.

0:33 (0:00) Arrive Columbia.

COLUMBIA, SC - One of the first planned cities, it was established in 1786 to be the state's capital and has held that distinction ever since. Some local attractions include: Woodrow Wilson's boyhood home where the nation's 28th president lived as a youth while his father taught at Columbia Theological Seminary; the State House which still shows scars on its outer walls from cannon fire during one of Sherman's campaigns; and State Farmers Market with tempting fresh produce available daily—largest in the Southeast.

0:00 (0:55) Depart Columbia.

0:55 (0:00) Arrive Denmark.

DENMARK, SC - This community was born out of the intersecting of the Southbound Railroad Company and the South Carolina Railroad which occurred in 1891. At one time cotton was Denmark's most important

Silver Star – Randolph-Macon College, Ashland, Virginia

product, but in 1921 the boll weevil appeared, causing such destruction that cotton is no longer grown here. Today, the soybean is king.

Oddly enough, Denmark has played two important roles in man's war against the mosquito. In 1927, a nearby swampy mill pond was the first ever to be sprayed by air in an effort to kill mosquito larvae. In 1901, a resident of Denmark, James Hanberry, served as one of 14 volunteer "guinea pigs" in Dr. Walter Reed's famous experiment in Havana, Cuba, to find the cause of yellow fever. On February 6th of that year, "Mosquito No. 13" that had sucked blood from fever patients stung Hanberry and proved that the female mosquito carried the dreaded germ.

0:00 (1:19) Depart Denmark.
0:55 (0:24) Leave South Carolina and enter Georgia.
1:19 (0:00) Arrive Savannah.

 SAVANNAH, GA - See page 79.

0:00 (2:14) Depart Savannah.
1:41 (0:39) Leave Georgia and enter Florida.
2:14 (0:00) Arrive Jacksonville.

JACKSONVILLE, FL - Unlike many other Floridian cities, Jacksonville is not a tourist resort. Rather, it has grown to become the state's leading industrial center, with a population nearing 750,000.

Although lying a few miles west of the Atlantic Ocean, Jacksonville is still an important seaport, with an interconnecting passage along the St. Johns River. Three beautiful beaches provide a weekend haven for many city dwellers.

Here, at Jacksonville, the Miami and Tampa sections of The Silver Star split with the Miami section going through Ocala and Wildwood and the Tampa section going through Deland and Orlando. This route log traces the Miami section.

For Tampa section, see page 80.

0:00 (0:59) Depart Jacksonville. As train embarks on sweeping U-turn, tall steel bridges spanning St. Johns River are focal point of city scene on left.

Proceeding south, the diverse landscape of the Florida interior provides an ever-changing spectacle for the sightseer. Dense regions of tall pines and majestic palms stand admist an occasional marsh, but just as quickly give way to the rolling terrain of ranchlands and dairy farms.

0:44 (0:15) On right, Eastern cowpokes show their stuff at Bradford Roping Club Arena.

0:59 (0:00) Arrive Waldo.

 WALDO, FL - This stop affords access to the Gainesville area and University of Florida.

0:00 (0:45) Depart Waldo.

0:22 (0:23) Passing through Lochloosa, Lake Lochloosa can be seen on right.

0:30 (0:15) Thoroughbred horse farm on right features well-kept grounds and "official-size" track.

0:45 (0:00) Arrive Ocala.

 OCALA, FL - As well as an agricultural community, the Ocala region boasts some of the nation's top thoroughbred concerns, with many facilities open to the public.

0:00 (0:25) Depart Ocala.

0:23 (0:02) Container Corporation of America plant is prominent on left.

0:25 (0:00) Arrive Wildwood.

 WILDWOOD, FL - Throughout much of year, fresh fruit is displayed atop old baggage carts at trackside, available for purchase by passengers.

0:00 (1:23) Depart Wildwood.

0:23 (1:00) Witness more densely wooded terrain over next few miles as train borders fringe of Withlacoochee State Forest.

1:08 (0:15) Through Lakeland.

This is the very heart of citrus country. A fifth of all citrus grown in the United States comes from this immediate area— that's a lot of orange juice. Lakeland is also the marketing center for Florida's entire crop. But one other product is as important as oranges and grapefruit. Most of the world's phosphate is mined nearby, almost all of it going into agricultural fertilizers.

Florida Southern College is located here where students study amidst the largest assemblage of buildings designed by Frank Lloyd Wright. The Detroit Tigers have enjoyed spring training here for years. (This is a stop for the Tampa sections of The Silver Star and The Silver Meteor.)

1:23 (0:00) Arrive Winter Haven. Once in station, note large juicing operation on left.

 WINTER HAVEN, FL - This is an excellent debarkation point to a multitude of family-oriented attractions, including Cypress Gardens, Walt Disney World, Sea World, Busch Gardens and more.

0:00 (0:34) Departing Winter Haven, cross canal that feeds Lake Ship on right— part of Chain-of-Lakes system surrounding Winter Haven region. Emerge now into heartland of citrus groves, with trees at times within picking distance of train.

0:33 (0:01) Beautiful estates come right down to shoreline of Lake Jackson on right.

0:34 (0:00) Arrive Sebring.

 SEBRING, FL - Founded in 1912, Sebring is situated at the geographical center of Florida. The encompassing fertile terrain has nurtured a thriving agricultural economy.

0:00 (1:23) Depart Sebring.

1:15 (1:08) Lake Istokpoga makes brief appearance on right. Sebring auto track, famous for its course of flat curves laid out on a former World War II airfield, stretches in distance on left.

0:28 (0:55) Cross Kissimmee River.

0:38 (0:45) Pass through Okeechobee, an Indian word meaning "plenty big water." Lake Okeechobee, largest in southern U.S., lies three miles south and is most important source of fresh water for Miami area. (This is a stop for The Silver Meteor.)

0:58 (0:25) Passing through Indiantown, cross Okeechobee waterway.

1:05 (0:18) On right, Pratt and Whitney plant is noted manufacturer of aircraft engines.

With the southeast coastline looming just ahead, the wide-open spaces of the last several hours are quickly displaced by the bustling activity of renowned beachfront resorts.

1:23 (0:00) Arrive West Palm Beach. While sitting in station, note numerous high rises dotting shores of Clear Lake on right.

 WEST PALM BEACH, FL - One of many popular retreats of southern Florida.

0:00 (0:29) Depart West Palm Beach.

0:03 (0:26) Palm Beach airport can be seen on right.

0:07 (0:22) Departure from Palm Beach area is highlighted by scenic canals interweaving throughout attractive residential property.

0:19 (0:10) Through Delray Beach (a stop for The Silver Meteor).

0:23 (0:06) Boca Raton airport borders route on left.

0:29 (0:00) Arrive Deerfield Beach.

 DEERFIELD BEACH, FL - Another vacation haven of Florida's southern coast.

0:00 (0:16) Depart Deerfield Beach.

0:05 (0:11) On right, note Pompano Beach Race Track.

0:16 (0:00) Arrive Ft. Lauderdale.

 FT. LAUDERDALE, FL - A fort established during the Seminole Wars of 1830s gave its name to this now much-frequented seaside resort. The old Gold Coast Railroad Station and Museum are located here.

0:00 (0:12) Depart Ft. Lauderdale.

0:04 (0:08) On left, pass Ft. Lauderdale-Hollywood International Airport.

Cross numerous navigable canals over the next few miles. This area is often called the Venice of America.

0:12 (0:00) Arrive Hollywood.

 HOLLYWOOD, FL - Real estate entrepreneur Joseph Young helped this town blossom in the early 1920s by maintaining a fleet of buses to help bring in prospective investors. Nearby is Okalee Village Seminole Indian Reservation.

0:00 (0:19) Depart Hollywood.

0:04 (0:15) Tall resort hotels of Miami Beach vicinity jut above horizon on left.

0:19 (0:00) Arrive Miami, Amtrak's southernmost destination.

MIAMI, FL - There's always a perceptual reaction at the mere mention of the town's name—cops and cocaine, palms and plush. Miami is a soup that is often brought to a boil, a stew that is often called a modern Casablanca. *Newsweek* described it as "a jazzy, hectic mix of ethnicity, newfangled prosperity and foreign intrigue."

Miami has struggled with its problems and its image. And sometimes it's not always clear just who is winning. But there are still its Miami Beach resorts,

particularly the Deco District hotels, its weather and its proximity to the mysterious Everglades and that stretch of tropical islands called The Keys. These endearments make it a place to visit, and tourism is still a dominant force here.

Miami got its start as a citrus-growing area in the 1890s after killing frosts had ruined much of the orange crops in central Florida. However, its start would not have been possible without Henry Flagler extending his railroad from central Florida into the Miami area. Then in the early 1920s, real estate development began to spur the city's growth.

The city is a major international transfer point, having a steady stream of foreign visitors passing through the city each year. Its southern location has contributed to a large Latin population giving the city a strong bilingual character.

 Amtrak Station, 8303 NW 37th Ave., is located a considerable distance north of downtown in an industrial area of Hialeah. This is a very modern, attractive facility—incongruous in its environment. There is a large parking lot that is never utilized to any degree, since overnight parking is definitely not recommended.

Even Tri-Rail, the regional commuter rail experiment between Miami and West Palm Beach, doesn't acknowledge the station but breezes past, preferring to stop a few blocks to the south where it intersects with Miami's Metrorail (an elevated, sleek rail system that has yet to live up to expectations).

The station has food and beverage machines, storage lockers, luggage carts and redcap service. The adjacent parking is free. Waiting room and ticket window hours are 6:30 am to 7:30 pm. For arrival and departure information, call 835-1221; for reservations and other information, call 800-USA-RAIL.

Cab stand is at the station; Metro Taxi, 888-8888. **Local buses** stop at the station, Route L, which runs to Miami Beach via the 79th St. causeway with connections to **Metrorail** and **Tri-Rail** just south of the station at 79th Street. For local bus, Metrorail and Tri-Rail information, call 638-6700. **Greyhound,** 374-7222. **Rental cars** are at

Miami International Airport, six miles (about a $10 cab ride) southwest of the station.

? Convention and Visitors Bureau, 701 Brickell Ave., Suite 2700, 33131; (305) 539-3000 or 800-283-2707.

There are no hotels or motels very near the station, nor would it be likely anyone would stay there if there were. Logical accommodations for a single overnight are in the airport area where the nearest rental cars will also be found. As mentioned above, the cab ride to the airport is about $10.

-Hampton Inn Miami Airport, 5125 NW 36th St., Miami Springs, 33166; (305) 887-2153. Adjacent to airport, continental breakfast included. $46.

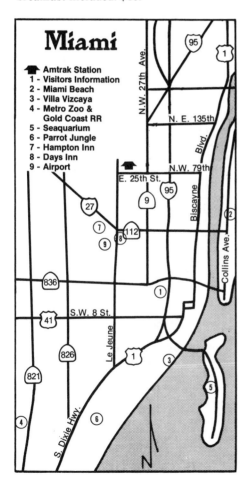

Miami

🚂 Amtrak Station
1 - Visitors Information
2 - Miami Beach
3 - Villa Vizcaya
4 - Metro Zoo & Gold Coast RR
5 - Seaquarium
6 - Parrot Jungle
7 - Hampton Inn
8 - Days Inn
9 - Airport

-Days Inn Airport, 3401 NW Je Jeune Rd., 33142; (305) 871-4221. Restaurant and free airport shuttle. $50.

The **Miami Beach** area, with its white sand beaches and handsomely restored Deco District, is an enjoyable place for a stroll or a week-long stay. For animal, fish and bird fanciers, consider these: **Metrozoo,** 124th Ave. and SW 152nd St., a newer zoo with unusually realistic environments for the various species on exhibit; **Miami Seaquarium,** southeast of downtown on Rickenbacher Causeway, the world's largest tropical oceanarium; and **Parrot Jungle & Gardens,** 11000 S. Red Road (57th Ave.) with exotic birds in a walk-thru tropical setting.

For those interested in 17th-century Italian architecture, there is **Villa Vizcaya,** 3251 South Miami Ave., a spectacular palace re-created by the late James Deering of International Harvester fame at a cost of $20 million, with European antiques, formal gardens, marble fountains and crystal pools.

And there's more unique architecture at **The Old Spanish Monastery Cloisters,** 16711 W. Dixie Highway, North Miami Beach. Originally constructed in Spain circa 1141, it was used by an order of Monks. In 1925 Wm. Randolph Hearst purchased the structure and had it dismantled and shipped to the U.S. It ultimately found its way to Florida and was reconstructed in 1925, and now houses various objects of art.

The **Gold Coast Railroad Museum,** 12450 SW 152nd St., houses a good collection of historic railroad cars, including the Ferdinand Magellan—Franklin D. Roosevelt's private car and later used by presidents Truman, Eisenhower and Reagan—and the observation lounge, Silver Crescent, from the old California Zephyr. Steam train excursions are also available.

Boston
Richmond
Newport News

Colonial

The Colonial is Amtrak's access to Newport News, Norfolk, Virginia Beach, and Colonial Williamsburg. Originally, it was thought that this train would carry mostly service personnel to and from the large naval base at Norfolk; however, nearly as many passengers now detrain at Williamsburg as they do at the base. The Colonial has its northern terminus at Boston and follows the Northeast Corridor and the route of The Silver Meteor between Boston and Richmond. It then takes CSX tracks between Richmond and Newport News.

Although it follows the course of the James River, it is generally too far north to allow passengers to see the many magnificent plantations that border the shore of this historic stream. But the history of the region can be felt. McClelland used Berkeley on the James River as his headquarters in the summer of 1862. The trip through Williamsburg, passing within view of the historic section of America's colonial capital, is exciting, even if one does not plan to disembark here. Jamestown, the first English settlement in the New World, is just a few minutes away. Then, still further downline, The Colonial passes near Yorktown, where America literally won her independence on the battlefield.

Southbound Schedule (Condensed)
Boston, MA - Early Morning Departure
New York, NY - Early Afternoon
Washington, DC - Late Afternoon
Richmond, VA - Early Evening
Newport News, VA - Midevening Arrival

Northbound Schedule (Condensed)
Newport News, VA - Early Morning Departure
Richmond, VA - Midmorning
Washington, DC - Early Afternoon
New York, NY - Late Afternoon
Boston, MA - Late Evening

Frequency - Daily. (Note that Sunday's northbound Colonial originates at Richmond instead of Newport News. However, The Tidewater, a northbound Sunday-only train, departs Newport News mid-afternoon and terminates at New York City late that evening.)
Seating - Amcoaches.
Dining - Tray meals (except on Tidewater), snacks and beverages.
Baggage - No checked baggage.
Reservations - Reserved train, except for travel locally between Boston and Washington.
Length of Trip - 871 miles in 12 hours.

Route Log

For route between Boston and Washington, DC, see Northeast Corridor log, page 21, and from Washington to Richmond, The Silver Meteor log, page 75.

0:00 (1:05) Departing Richmond's Staples Mills Road station, head south into older section of downtown Richmond.
0:09 (0:56) Off to right a few blocks, granite building with oxidized copper-

looking dome is Science Museum of Virginia. This former Seaboard Coast Line station bears a resemblance to Washington, DC's Jefferson Memorial, perhaps because John Russel Pope designed both structures.

0:16 (0:49) Pass through Brown Street rail yards, then 17th Street rail yards.

0:19 (0:46) Foreboding and vacant Main Street Station has, to date, successfully resisted restoration efforts. Downtown Richmond is immediately beyond.

0:20 (0:45) Tobacco is important to Richmond's economy, although not as dominant as in years past. Weathered sign on enormous old brick building at left indicates that Lucky Strikes have been produced here.

0:21 (0:44) Just before crossing old drawbridge across S.R. Canal, James River can be seen briefly on right.

Further downstream (to the southeast) some of the finest plantations and homes ever to grace the South still can be visited along the northern shore between Richmond and Williamsburg. Unfortunately, these great estates cannot be seen from The Colonial since they are about 10 miles south of the tracks. The most famous of these is Berkeley, the ancestral home of two U.S. presidents, William "Tippecanoe" Harrison and Benjamin Harrison, and where General Butterfield composed "Taps" while attached to McClelland's forces headquartered there in 1862. Jamestown, where America was born in 1607, is also along the northern shore of this historic river.

0:23 (0:42) Pass through CSX Fulton Yards located in Richmond's eastern industrial suburbs.

0:28 (0:37) Acres and acres of new railroad ties are stored on immediate left.

0:29 (0:36) Modernistic Nabisco bakery on right churns out $150 million worth of cookies, crackers and pretzels annually. The plant produces "high volume" products, including Ritz Crackers, Oreo Cookies and Premium Saltines. "Almost Home" brand products have also been produced here.

0:31 (0:34) Runways and terminal facilities of Richard Evelyn Byrd International Airport are visible to left. Virginia Army National Guard helicopters are also frequently seen here.

0:37 (0:28) Evidence that we are entering Virginia's low-lying region appears in form of swamplands during next few miles, mostly on right.

0:44 (0:21) Derelict, but picturesque, old Providence Forge station on right is structural clone of beautifully restored depot further downline at Lee Hall.

0:46 (0:19) Symmetrical rows of thousands of pine trees distinguish New Kent Forestry Center on right.

Operated by the Virginia Division of Forestry, this is the second largest producer of forest tree seedlings in the nation. Up to 60 million pine seedlings are started each year and sold primarily to the lumber industry. The loblolly pine is the Center's principal product. Efforts toward producing a genetically superior tree are being made here with assistance from the University of North Carolina. Watch for deer, quail and other wild creatures since this is also a wildlife preserve.

0:50 (0:15) Sailboats and other small craft can often be seen on broad expanse of Chickanominy River (a tributary of the James further south) which curls up to tracks on right.

1:05 (0:00) Arrive at Williamsburg, where station is just three blocks from this colonial capital's historic area.

WILLIAMSBURG, VA - Williamsburg was the capital of colonial Virginia for 81 years—from 1699 to 1780. Like Washington, D.C., it was originally planned and constructed with its governmental role in mind. A carefully planned restoration and preservation effort was started in 1926, and today, Colonial Williamsburg is a marvelous collection of historic structures, crafts, homes, gardens and tree-shaded streets. During the day, artisans work their historic crafts dressed in colonial attire for viewing by the public.

If you come here, plan to spend at least a day to take in the stores, shops, restaurants and perhaps an overnight stay in one of the historic hotels. Although there is no charge to stroll through the Historic Area, an admission ticket is necessary to gain entrance to artisan shops. Your ticket also entitles you to use the buses which make frequent trips between the Historic

Area and the Visitors Center about a mile away. Tickets are available at the Visitors Center and the Information Booth on the edge of the Historic Area.

Williamsburg Transportation Center, 468 North Boundary St., is only three blocks from the historic district. There are storage lockers, luggage carts, food and beverage machines and free parking.

For information and reservations, call 800-USA-RAIL. Ticket windows and the waiting room are open from early morning to midafternoon Monday thru Saturday.

Cab stand is at the station; Colonial Cab, 561-1240. There is a **public bus** between the historic area and the Visitors Center. **Greyhound,** 887-2626, is at the station. **Patrick Henry International Airport** is 15 miles from the station.

The Colonial Williamsburg Information Center is on the edge of Williamsburg. Write Williamsburg Area Convention & Visitors Bureau, Box GB, 23187, or call (804) 253-0192. The Information Center should be visited prior to touring Colonial Williamsburg itself.

Governor's Inn, 506 N. Henry St., 23185; 800-HISTORY. Near the Historic Area and only three blocks from the station. $55.

-**Williamsburg Inn,** Francis St. (on the edge of the Historic Area), Box B, 23187; 800-HISTORY. Rooms in hotel or colonial houses. Pricey and unique; 1½ miles from the station. $185.

There are also numerous Holiday Inns, Quality Inns, Best Westerns, etc. in the area. Call 800-446-9244 for reservations.

Colonial Williamsburg is a village full of 18th-century buildings and peopled with actors in attire of that era. Don't miss the Governor's Palace, the Capitol, Burton Parish Church, Raleigh Tavern, the Magazine and Guardhouse, to name but a few. Be sure to obtain an Official Guidebook and map when you purchase your ticket.

0:00 (0:10) Departing Williamsburg, a glimpse can be caught of Palace of Governors (topped by a small tower and flanked by two chimneys) just beyond brick wall on right which is boundary of historic district. This has served as residence of seven royal governors as well as first two governors of Virginia.

0:06 (0:04) Parking for Busch Gardens is on immediate right—a 360-acre "theme" amusement park.

0:10 (0:00) Arrive at Lee Hall's attractively restored depot, a dolled-up twin to one seen at Providence Forge.

LEE HALL, VA - This is a suburban stop for Newport News and serves nearby Fort Eustis on Mulberry Island, headquarters of the U.S. Army Transportation Center.

0:00 (0:10) Depart Lee Hall.

0:02 (0:08) Cross what appears to be a river but is actually an arm of City Reservoir.

0:12 (0:00) Arrive Newport News station, still some distance from downtown area.

NEWPORT NEWS, VA - Here at the mouth of the James River, four cities cluster around the water's edge and make the absolute most of their coastal status. Newport News, Norfolk, Portsmouth and Hampton share one of the finest harbors in the world. The bay is over 14 miles long and 40 feet deep.

Maritime activities run the gamut. Newport News Shipbuilding and Dry Dock Company is the world's largest shipbuilder, with the luxury liner United States and the nuclear aircraft carrier Enterprise both to its credit. It employs 25,000 workers when the yards are in full swing. Nearby Norfolk boasts the world's largest naval base, being the home port for over 100 vessels of the Atlantic and Mediterranean fleets. And maritime commerce is immense. Huge tonnages of coal, tobacco and other goods pass through the harbor facilities each year.

Even though this is an industrial center, there is much to interest visitors. Waterfront restaurants with fine seafood menus; Virginia Beach, a short bus ride away, with resort hotels, boardwalks and arcades; and harbor tours are all quite popular. History buffs will definitely want to visit Yorktown where the most decisive battle of the American Revolution was fought. And if naval warfare is of interest, be sure to take in Fort Monroe. Had you been at this site on March 9, 1862 you would have had a front row seat for that mighty, but inconclusive, battle between the iron clads, Monitor and Merrimack. (The Merrimack was actually called the "Virginia" by the South after they raised this scuttled Union frigate and encased her wooden sides in armor.) And, understandably, the finest collection of ship models to be found anywhere is housed in the Mariner's Museum which is located in Newport News.

Other Mid-Atlantic & Florida Service

The **Palmetto** is a daily reserved train between New York City and Jacksonville, Florida, following the route of the Silver Meteor but making more stops. Both southbound and northbound trains depart early morning and arrive at their final destinations late that evening. The train has Amcoaches and an Amdinette with tray meals, sandwiches, snacks and beverages. (Northbound passengers be sure to secure a table in the cafe car for the evening meal before commuters board at Washington, DC.) Checked baggage is handled at most stations.

The **Virginian** is daily direct service between New York City and Richmond, leaving New York midafternoon and arriving Richmond late evening and departing Richmond early morning and arriving New York early afternoon. Reserved train; sandwiches and beverages. The train does not run northbound on Sundays.

Auto Train is Amtrak's unique service for those who want to travel by train between Washington, DC and central Florida—and take their cars along. The train leaves each end point in the late afternoon and arrives at the other in the early morning the next day. Lorton, VA (south of DC) is the northern terminal, while Sanford, FL (one-half hour from Disney World), is the southern end.

The train provides a buffet-style dinner, a continental breakfast, dome cars, lounge service, bedrooms and roomettes, and entertainment consisting of feature-length motion pictures. It is an all-reserved train, and although no checked baggage is handled, extra bags can be stored in your car (with no access during the trip). Only passengers with autos are permitted and should arrive two hours early for boarding. Autos must have four inches of ground clearance and cannot be higher than 65 inches.

New York
Atlanta
New Orleans

Crescent

The Crescent provides direct, no-change service between New York City and New Orleans. The route follows the Northeast Corridor between New York's Pennsylvania Station and Washington, DC, then takes the tracks of the Southern Railway through Atlanta and Birmingham before finally reaching New Orleans.

This train has a distinct case of dual personalities. The northern facet is the bustling, urbanized Northeast Corridor, predominated by New York City, Philadelphia, Baltimore and Washington, DC, while the southern and longest segment leaves one with the relaxed impressions of the rural Deep South. Darkness covers the Carolinas when The Crescent crosses these two states.

The most unique aspect of the trip occurs during the approach to New Orleans, when The Crescent slowly glides for ten minutes or so just above the surface of Lake Pontchartrain. Here, the feeling is more of an ocean liner than a passenger train.

Southbound Schedule (Condensed)
New York, NY (Penn Station) - Early Afternoon Departure
Washington, DC - Early Evening
Charlotte, NC - Middle of the Night
Atlanta, GA - Early Morning
Birmingham, AL - Late Morning
New Orleans, LA - Early Evening Arrival

Northbound Schedule (Condensed)
New Orleans, LA - Early Morning Departure

Birmingham, AL - Early Afternoon
Atlanta, GA - Early Evening
Charlotte, NC - Middle of the Night
Washington, DC - Early Morning
New York, NY (Penn Station) - Early Afternoon Arrival

Frequency - Daily.
Seating - Heritage Fleet coaches.
Dining - Complete meal service, sandwiches, snacks and beverages. Lounge service is also available.
Sleeping - Heritage Fleet roomettes and bedrooms. Slumbercoach between New York and Atlanta.
Baggage - Checked baggage at most stops.
Reservations - All-reserved train.
Length of Trip - 1,380 miles in 29 hours.

Route Log

For route between New York City and Washington, DC, see that portion of Northeast Corridor log, page 31.

 WASHINGTON, DC - See page 39.

0:00 (0:17) Depart Washington southbound through regions whose roots trace back to earliest periods of American history.

0:02 (0:15) Emerge from tunnel after passing under Mall. Glimpses of Capitol and oldest Smithsonian structure ("The Castle") can be caught through various federal buildings on right.

0:07 (0:10) Perhaps Washington's most

charming monument, Monticello-shaped Jefferson Memorial, resides among cherry trees of Tidal Basin on right.

0:09 (0:08) Cross Potomac River paralleling 14th Street bridge. Washington National Airport is directly downstream to left. Back on right, Washington Monument, world's tallest masonry structure at 555.5 feet, punctuates horizon. Capitol's dome can still be seen toward rear on left.

0:10 (0:07) The Pentagon, headquarters for America's military establishment, is off to right, now mostly hidden by newer buildings.

0:12 (0:05) Glass high rises of Crystal City flaunt their starkness on right. Expansive RF&P rail yards are on left.

0:17 (0:00) Arrive Alexandria.

 ALEXANDRIA, VA - This historic Washington suburb sits six miles south of the nation's capital, along the west bank of the Potomac River. Most noted for its outstanding examples of early American architecture, the Alexandria area is also replete with numerous national landmarks. Mount Vernon, beloved home and estate of George Washington from 1754 until his death in 1799, is just a few miles down the Potomac.

0:00 (0:30) Depart Alexandria.

0:01 (0:29) George Washington National Masonic Memorial, with museum of Washington memorabilia, dominates skyline on right. Metro subway station on left provides commuters with quick, easy access to downtown Washington.

0:30 (0:00) Arrive Manassas.

 MANASSAS, VA - This was the site of intense fighting during the Civil War. The town was burned several times by both Yankees and Confederates, generally in an effort to cut supply lines to fighting troops. The two Battles of Manassas (Bull Run) were fought in July of 1861 and August of 1862 just northeast of town, and are now commemorated by the 5,000-acre Manassas National Battlefield Park. The quaint rail station was built circa 1915.

0:00 (0:32) Depart Manassas.

0:32 (0:00) Arrive Culpeper.

 CULPEPER, VA - The Culpeper Minute Men were the very first to respond in 1775 to Patrick Henry's call-to-arms. Then, during the Civil War, the area saw heavy fighting and the town served as headquarters for both sides. George Washington described this area as a "high and pleasant situation," when he surveyed the county, and the town still prides itself on its fresh water supply and clean air.

Flour milling, furniture, wire rope and automotive parts are now important products. History buffs should enjoy the Culpeper Cavalry Museum.

0:00 (0:49) Depart Culpeper.

0:49 (0:00) Arrive Charlottesville.

 CHARLOTTESVILLE, VA - "These mountains are the Eden of the United States." Thomas Jefferson wrote these flattering words in describing the area in and around Charlottesville. As the county seat of Albemarle, the town was a veritable treasure trove of talent and wisdom—Jefferson, James Madison and James Monroe were all part of the local scene. In more recent times, William Faulkner, Lady Astor and William McGuffey all called Albemarle County their home during some point in their lives.

Of particular interest to visitors is Jefferson's beautiful and cleverly designed home (Monticello) and the estate of James Monroe (Ash Lawn). These two men were close friends, and Jefferson personally selected the Monroe house site, donating his own gardeners to help start orchards at Ash Lawn. Jefferson also founded the University of Virginia which is located here and designed many of its original structures.

0:00 (1:06) Depart Charlottesville. Campus of University of Virginia will be on right.

1:06 (0:00) Arrive Monroe.

 MONROE, VA - This small Virginia town is located on the very edge of Lynchburg, and serves as a stop for nearby Sweet Briar College.

0:00 (0:12) Depart Monroe.

0:12 (0:00) Arrive Lynchburg.

 LYNCHBURG, VA - A young Quaker by the name of John Lynch established a ferry here in the 1750s, opening up a trade route to Richmond and beyond. Soon, tobacco warehouses were built which established the town's economic foundation. As a matter of fact, tobacco became so important that, just prior to the Civil War, Lynchburg became the second wealthiest town in the country on a per capita basis. After the war, however, the tobacco industry began to move south and other endeavors gradually took its place.

0:00 (1:09) Depart Lynchburg.
1:09 (0:00) Arrive Danville.

DANVILLE, VA - This colorful tobacco auction center was the last capital of The Confederacy. Near the end of the Civil War, Jefferson Davis and his cabinet settled here for about a week after being forced from Richmond, then fled southward again after the surrender at Appomattox.

0:00 (1:00) Depart Danville.
1:00 (0:00) Arrive Greensboro.

GREENSBORO, NC - This is not just golf country—it is the very heart of golf country. No less than eighteen courses in the immediate area offer stiff challenges to any level of player. One of the top PGA tournaments, The Greater Greensboro Open, draws more than 180,000 spectators annually and has a purse in excess of a quarter million dollars.

Of historical interest is Guilford Courthouse National Military Park, where England's General Cornwallis won a costly victory over America's General Nathaniel Greene in March of 1781. The battle, however, so weakened the English troops that they surrendered at Yorktown later that year.

0:00 (0:18) Depart Greensboro.
0:18 (0:00) Arrive High Point.

HIGH POINT, NC - It was a railroad surveyor, marking this location as the "high point" on the route between Goldsboro and Charlotte, who was responsible for giving the city a name which would stick. High Point can easily lay claim to being the nation's furniture capital with 85 furniture factories, including the 15 largest manufacturers in the world, located near here. In the 1950s it replaced Chicago as the nation's largest

wholesale furniture market. But the manufacture of another product is equally as impressive. With 14 mills capable of turning out nearly a million pairs of stockings a day, High Point has the distinction of being the largest hosiery producer in the world.

0:00 (0:38) Depart High Point.
0:38 (0:00) Arrive Salisbury.

SALISBURY, NC - This attractive community is the center for Rowan County, with a widely diversified manufacturing base as well as agriculture consisting mostly of livestock and small grains. Salisbury was hometown to at least two notables, frontiersman Daniel Boone and former Secretary of Transportation Elizabeth Dole.

0:00 (0:47) Depart Salisbury.
0:47 (0:00) Arrive Charlotte.

CHARLOTTE, NC - Located on the North Carolina/South Carolina border, Charlotte is the largest city visited by The Crescent between Washington, DC and Atlanta. This thriving city is a center for commerce, industry, finance and communications. Two of its banks boast assets outranking all others in the Southeast. Charlotte also bears the unlikely distinction of being the site of the first authenticated gold discovery in the U.S. The famous Charlotte Motor Speedway holds stockcar and motorcycle races, drawing thousands each year. Its enormous stockcar stadium incorporates forty luxury condominiums overlooking the first turn.

0:00 (0:28) Depart Charlotte.
0:28 (0:00) Arrive Gastonia.

GASTONIA, NC - The Crescent makes a jog in its southerly course to stop at this textile-oriented city, some 28 miles west of Charlotte, before heading into South Carolina.

0:00 (0:57) Depart Gastonia.
0:07 (0:50) Enter South Carolina and leave North Carolina.
0:57 (0:00) Arrive Spartanburg.

SPARTANBURG, SC - Having experienced two decades of industrial boom, Spartanburg has become a truly "international" city with the influx of persons of various nationalities. The county lays claim to being the most prolific

peach producer in South Carolina.
0:00 (0:39) Depart Spartanburg.
0:39 (0:00) Arrive Greenville.

GREENVILLE, SC - The numerous textile manufacturing plants located here give rise to Greenville's title, "Textile Center of the World." Outlet shops of these many factories are favorites of both local and visiting bargain hunters. The city has also been home to some well-known religious figures. Rev. Jesse Jackson was born here, and in 1927 evangelist Dr. Bob Jones chose this location when he founded Bob Jones University.
0:00 (0:35) Depart Greenville.
0:35 (0:00) Arrive Clemson.

CLEMSON, SC - This charming college town was known as Calhoun, named for the political giant John Calhoun. In 1943 the name was changed to that of the university located here. Clemson University, with an enrollment of almost 10,000, allows visitors to tour their unusual greenhouses and gardens, featuring over 2,200 varieties of plants. Also, Clemson's famous ice cream and blue cheese are favorites of dairy product connoisseurs.
0:00 (0:35) Depart Clemson.
0:35 (0:00) Arrive Toccoa.

TOCCOA, GA - Toccoa is the home of Toccoa Falls Bible College which features the spectacular 186-foot Toccoa Falls on its campus.
0:00 (0:41) Depart Toccoa.
0:41 (0:00) Arrive Gainesville.

GAINESVILLE, GA - This agricultural community of northeastern Georgia is situated near the northern end of Georgia's largest body of water, Lake Sydney Lanier, featuring a 1,200-acre family recreation resort on the Lake Lanier Islands.
0:00 (0:55) Depart Gainesville.
0:27 (0:28) Surroundings become more forested as train moves deeper into The South.
0:35 (0:20) Industrial and commercial developments begin to proliferate near Atlanta.
0:45 (0:10) Medieval-appearing buildings of Oglethorpe University are just to right.
0:47 (0:08) Inviting fairways and greens

of Standard Golf Club stretch out on left.
0:51 (0:04) Atlanta's modern skyline is forward on left.
0:55 (0:00) Arrive at Atlanta's suburban Peachtree Station.

ATLANTA, GA - Atlanta grew quickly from its founding as a railhead in the early 1800s to become a major manufacturing center of the South. During the Civil War it served as an arms marshalling point and the intersection of four railroads until General Sherman almost totally destroyed the city during his march-to-the-sea campaign.

The city made a quick recovery, however, becoming the center of the Reconstruction process following the war. Later, it became the capital of Georgia.

Today, with a metropolitan population in excess of 2,000,000, it is the financial, industrial and transportation center of the South. Its MARTA urban rail system is one of the finest transit operations in the country. For many, Atlanta is also a vacation destination, offering numerous options for both fun and leisure. Major league sports, a symphony, numerous historic sites and fine shopping are all found here.

Brookwood (Peachtree) Station, 1688 Peachtree St., N.W., is located approximately four miles north of the center of downtown in a bustling neighborhood. The station actually straddles the main line of the Southern. There are storage lockers, food and beverage vending machines and parking across the street at the Masonic Temple. Advance arrangements must be made for long-term parking; (404) 874-8514. Redcaps are available at night.

Call 800-USA-RAIL for information and reservations.

Cabs are usually at the station at train time; Yellow Cab, 521-0200. **Buses** are one block away at the corner of Peachtree and 26th streets. Take the #23 bus south to the nearest MARTA commuter rail station (Arts Center); for MARTA rail and bus information call 848-4711. **Greyhound** bus terminal, 81 International Blvd., N.W.; (404) 522-6300. Both Budget and National **rental cars** will pay cab fare from the station to their

Atlanta

- Amtrak Station
1 - Visitors Information &
    Peachtree Center
2 - Underground Atlanta
3 - Martin Luther King
    Historic District
4 - TraveLodge

borhood. One block from the station. $39.

-Bed & Breakfast Atlanta, 1801 Piedmont Ave., N.E., Suite 208, 30324, is a reservation service for B&Bs in homes or inns in the Atlanta area, including close-in locations. All accommodations have private baths. Several locations are convenient to the Amtrak station. $32 to $70.

On the southern edge of the central business district is **Underground Atlanta.** Rather ominous sounding, it's actually a six-block labyrinth of eclectic shops and restaurants, albeit devoid of sunlight. Nearly abandoned when the city built a system of viaducts that covered the area, a $140 million rejuvenation has turned it into one of Atlanta's "in" places. It is served by MARTA's rail system (Five Points station).

In the heart of downtown, **Peachtree Center** is the focal point of downtown shopping, hotels and restaurants, all in an urban indoor environment. The **Martin Luther King, Jr. Historic District,** on the edge of the central business district, includes the birthplace of that civil rights leader, his gravesite and Ebenezer Baptist Church where he preached. Take MARTA rail to King Memorial station.

For the professional consumer, the really power shopper, there's Lenox Square, reached by MARTA rail, located in upscale **Buckhead.** Stores include Saks, Neiman-Marcus, Lord and Taylor, Abercrombie and Fitch, and Macy's.

And on Saturdays, **The New Georgia Railroad** either runs along an eighteen-mile loop through some of the city's historic neighborhoods using restored antique passenger cars pulled by a steam locomotive, or it chugs out to **Georgia's Stone Mountain Park** where the world's largest bas-relief sculpture has been carved into a mountain of granite. A dinner train operates on Thursday, Friday and Saturday nights. Call (404) 656-0769 for New Georgia RR schedules and information.

0:00 (2:15) Depart Atlanta and immediately cross busy Interstate 75.
0:13 (2:02) Cross Chattahoochee River as train proceeds through industrialized area of Atlanta.
0:14 (2:01) Cross under Interstate 285.
0:15 (2:00) Leave Atlanta's suburbs and

downtown locations. **Hartsfield Atlanta International Airport** is nine miles south of the station and can be reached by MARTA commuter rail.

ACVB Visitor Information Center, Peachtree Center Mall. Write or call: Atlanta Convention and Visitors Bureau, 233 Peachtree St., N.E., Suite 2000, Atlanta, GA 30303; (404) 521-6688. Information centers are also located at Lenox Square (north) and at the airport.

TraveLodge Atlanta Peachtree, 1641 Peachtree St., N.W.; (404) 873-5731. Well maintained, in a good neigh-

return to rolling forests of Georgia.

0:41 (1:34) Large-leafed vines that are so prolific along right-of-way are kudzu. Brought here from Japan many years ago to control erosion, plant is now bane of southern agriculture, enveloping everything it encounters. House on left is completely covered by the stuff.

1:20 (0:55) Attractive course on left provides sport for golfers of Tallapoosa.

1:30 (0:45) Cross Tallapoosa River—just one of many streams between Atlanta and New Orleans.

1:31 (0:44) Leave Georgia and enter Alabama.

 Gain one hour as train passes from Eastern to Central Time. Set your watch back (forward if eastbound) one hour.

1:45 (0:30) Train crosses over U.S. Highway 78 and plunges into woods of Talladega National Forest.

2:15 (0:00) Arrive Anniston.

 ANNISTON, AL - Anniston is an industrial hub of eastern Alabama. Numerous industries include the enormous Anniston Army Depot just west of the city.

0:00 (1:30) Depart Anniston.

0:09 (1:21) For next four minutes pass sprawling Anniston Army Depot on right, nation's largest military storage depot. Tanks and other miscellaneous vehicles and equipment can be found here.

0:11 (1:19) Four World War II Sherman tanks stand guard over depot complex.

0:28 (1:02) Northern tip of beautiful Logan Martin Lake touches tracks on left.

0:42 (0:48) No train trip would be complete without a tunnel. Pass through only one on today's run, Chula Vista Mountain Tunnel.

1:07 (0:23) Two lofty bridges carry us across Gahaba River.

1:08 (0:22) Fancifully painted sculpture on right suggests iron city of Birmingham is near.

1:13 (0:17) Industrial suburbs of Birmingham commence, contrasting sharply with miles of forest lands just traversed.

1:24 (0:06) One of Birmingham's many steel mills is on immediate right.

1:26 (0:04) Vulcan, world's largest cast iron statue, keeps watch over city from atop Red Mountain on left. Vulcan was Roman god of fire and patron of metal workers. In recent times, Birmingham has used it as a safety symbol, displaying a red light when a traffic fatality has occurred and a green light on fatality-free days.

1:30 (0:00) Arrive Birmingham. University of Alabama's sprawling Medical Center, employing 11,000 people, can be seen to left of station.

 BIRMINGHAM, AL - Although this is the very heart of Alabama's coal and steel production, the city has experienced an economic rebirth fostered by biomedical and other high-tech industries. An outstanding downtown shopping area, parks, tree-lined streets, theaters, museums and various festivals all greatly enhance Birmingham's lifestyle. This is the hometown of Nat King Cole, Phil Harris and Willie Mays.

0:00 (1:03) Depart Birmingham.

0:05 (0:58) As we leave through southwestern residential suburbs of Birmingham, take a last look at Vulcan, still visible on horizon to left.

0:12 (0:51) Former Pullman-Standard factory, which once produced over 3,000 boxcars a year, now stands in disuse on right.

0:39 (0:24) Road sign on hill on right directs traffic to "Bama Scenic Rock Gardens"—a fine collection of native plants, complete with nature trails.

1:00 (0:03) Campus of perennial football powerhouse University of Alabama (The Crimson Tide) can be seen on right as train nears downtown Tuscaloosa.

1:03 (0:00) Arrive at Tuscaloosa's old but nice-appearing station.

 TUSCALOOSA, AL - Once the capital of Alabama, the city is now primarily a vibrant university town. Of particular interest is "The Old Tavern," a museum with numerous historical artifacts, originally built as a tavern in 1827.

0:00 (1:35) Depart Tuscaloosa.

0:12 (1:23) Train slips through swamps of southern Tuscaloosa County.

0:15 (1:20) Prehistoric Indian mounds flash by quickly on right as train passes Mound State Monument.

The mounds in this area, several of which are visible from the train, were constructed about 800 years ago by Indians that inhabited this area. Three thousand were estimated to have lived here between 1200 and 1500 A.D. The mounds closest to the tracks originally had homes on them which were used by nobility. The far-distant mounds were ceremonial structures. The tallest mound, back to the right in the trees, now has a reconstructed temple at the top and was thought to have been the central ceremonial area.

0:16 (1:19) Fuzzy white cotton fields appear on both sides of train as "The Deep South" gets deeper.

0:17 (1:18) About here, northbound Crescent should zip by on its way back to Atlanta and points north.

0:29 (1:06) Cross over muddy, still waters of Black Warrior River.

0:57 (0:38) Cross large Tombigbee River, a link in an ambitious government waterway project (Tenn-Tom) to create an alternative to traditional Mississippi River route between Mississippi's upper tributaries and Gulf of Mexico.

1:12 (0:23) On right, quaint storefronts of York watch train go by from other side of "Main Street."

1:19 (0:16) Enter Mississippi and leave Alabama.

1:29 (0:06) On right, exquisite brick farmhouse, with white colonnades reflecting typical southern architecture, faces charming little pond.

1:35 (0:00) Arrive Meridian.

MERIDIAN, MS - Founded in 1860 at the junction of two railroads, Meridian is now a trade center serving an area with almost 70,000 people. Jimmy Rogers, father of country music and first name to be entered in Nashville's Country Music Hall of Fame, was born here in 1897. The Jimmy Rogers Museum has exhibits including a steam locomotive that pay tribute to this "Singing Brakeman's" life. Also, Merrehope, a twenty-room antebellum mansion of Greek Revival architecture, was one of five Meridian buildings to escape General Sherman's torch during his march to the sea.

0:00 (0:55) Depart Meridian.

0:07 (0:48) Key Field, on right, has interesting mixture of clientele, including sleek private aircraft close to tracks as well as more pugnacious jets of Mississippi Air National Guard parked on apron in distance.

0:19 (0:36) Cross curiously named Chunky Creek.

0:23 (0:32) Large natural gas pumping facility is on left.

0:55 (0:00) Arrive Laurel.

LAUREL, MS - This agricultural and trade center boasts an unusually fine art museum for a community its size. The Lauren Rogers Library and Museum not only has a national reputation for its collection of 19th century American and European art, but also maintains an excellent collection of Georgian silver and Indian baskets. Laurel was the birthplace of Metropolitan opera star Leontyne Price.

0:00 (0:31) Depart Laurel, and literally look right through modern downtown shopping mall on right.

0:30 (0:01) Cross Leaf River which will someday play an important role in a newly planned waterway.

0:31 (0:00) Arrive at Hattiesburg where a steam engine and rail passenger cars stand on display adjacent to station.

HATTIESBURG, MS - Referred to as the "Hub City" and "Gateway to the Gulf South," this progressive community was among the first in the state to qualify for the All Merit Community Award. The 11,000-student University of Southern Mississippi is located here, as well as smaller Carey College, with its well-known School of Music. The city hosts the Magnolia Classic, the only PGA tournament in Mississippi. An annual Heritage Tour in March emphasizes the city's railroading and lumbering roots.

0:00 (1:02) Depart Hattiesburg.

0:14 (0:48) Futuristic-looking facility on right, with tall, stack-like tower, is part of R.D. Morrow Generating Plant using the latest in generating technology. Cooling water is obtained from five nearby wells and coal from southeastern Kentucky to produce 400,000 kilowatts of power with minimal environmental impact.

0:26 (0:36) Complex on right is Purvis Refinery of Amerada Hess.

0:40 (0:22) Through Poplarville, the birthplace of Senator Theodore Gilmore Bilbo,

New Orleans Union Passenger Terminal

a highly controversial U.S. senator (1934-40) who was also the first to serve two terms as governor of Mississippi.

The agricultural research center located here is attempting to find a replacement for tung oil (tung tree farms were destroyed by Hurricane Camille in 1969), and also improve the production of blueberries (often called huckleberries) that are indigenous to the Southeast.

1:02 (0:00) Arrive Picayune.

PICAYUNE, MS - This Mississippi border town of 10,000 is The Crescent's last stop in Mississippi. The terrain now starts to flatten out upon approaching Louisiana.

0:00 (0:17) Depart Picayune.

0:07 (0:10) Enter Louisiana and leave Mississippi as train crosses over Pearl River.

0:15 (0:02) Note Albertson's new 6.2-million-dollar shopping center resembling early-day depot located within easy view of tracks.

0:17 (0:00) Arrive Slidell.

SLIDELL, LA - Slidell is actually a bedroom community for New Orleans, just across the eastern tip of Lake Pontchartrain. Because of its healthful air, this side of the lake is happily called the "Ozone Belt."

0:00 (0:53) Depart Slidell.

0:07 (0:46) Now, start an unusual, watery journey as train appears to paddle its way across eastern end of 610-square-mile Lake Pontchartrain on an incredible 6.2-mile-long wooden rail bridge only a few feet above water's surface. Glorious "ocean" sunsets are afforded when sun and train schedules cooperate.

0:17 (0:36) Pick up speed as train reaches terra firma and race past scores of stilted fishing huts along shore.

0:26 (0:27) Tracks and Lake Pontchartrain now part company.

0:33 (0:20) Skyline of downtown New Orleans, our destination, is now clearly visible on left as train takes a roundabout approach in getting there. University of New Orleans Field House drifts by on right, then buildings of University of Tulane Dental School appear on left.

0:51 (---) Stop, and back final few hundred yards to station.

0:56 (0:04) Massive egg-like Superdome is just to right.

1:01 (0:00) Arrive New Orleans.

NEW ORLEANS, LA - Thoughts of New Orleans stir a swirl of color in the mind. Images of excellent restaurants, the French Quarter, jazz, Mardi Gras and, for trolley aficionados, the St. Charles Streetcar line are some of the visions conjured up at the mere mention of this unique city. It is quite understandably one of the nation's more popular places to visit.

New Orleans has existed under four different flags since it was founded in 1723 by Jean Baptiste Le Moyne, Sieur Bienville. It was first ruled by the French and was the capital of French Louisiana. The Spanish succeeded the French some 40 years later. New Orleans became an American city in 1803 with the Louisiana Purchase, and during the Civil War was a Confederate City. Today, it is Louisiana's largest metropolis with an area population in excess of 1,200,000.

Union Passenger Terminal (also known as the Transit Center), 1001 Loyola Ave., is one of Amtrak's newer and more attractive facilities. Modern and efficient, it not only accommodates Amtrak, but it also serves as the Greyhound bus terminal. There are ample storage lockers, pay-luggage carts, a restaurant, food and beverage vending machines and a gift shop. Pay-parking is in front of the station.

Ticket window hours are 6 am to 8:30 pm; the waiting room is open 24 hours. For arrival and departure information, call 528-1610; for reservations and other information, 800-USA-RAIL.

Cab stand is at the station; Yellow Checker Cab, 943-2411. Nearest **local bus** stop is across the street; 569-2700. Convention Loop bus shuttles passengers between the Superdome and the French Quarter for a modest charge. **Greyhound** is at the station; 525-9371. **Airport Limousine** service is available at the station, call Rhodes Limo, 943-6621. **New Orleans (Moisant) International Airport** is 12 miles west of downtown.

? French Quarter Information Center, 916 N. Peters Street. Write or call Greater New Orleans Tourist & Convention Commission, 1520 Sugar Bowl Drive, 70112; (504) 566-5011.

Two hotel choices, about midway between the French Quarter and the station, would be:

-Le Pavillon Hotel, 833 Poydras Plaza, 70140; (504) 581-3111 or 800-535-9095. Very nice accommodations. Seven blocks from the station. $69.

-The Warwick, 1315 Gravier St., 70112; (504) 586-0100 or 800-535-9141. Well maintained hostelry. $56.

For French Quarter accommodations, be sure to reserve well in advance. Two possibilities are:

-French Quarter Maisonnettes, 1130 Chartres St., 70116; (504) 524-9918. Very unusual hotel in quiet section of French Quarter. Seven units, some with two rooms. Small, spotless, excellent value. No children under 12 and no credit cards. Parking is one block away, $5 per day. Make reservations several months in advance. Closed July. $39-$45.

-Le Richelieu, 1234 Chartres St., 70116; (504) 535-2492 or 800-535-9653. Small,

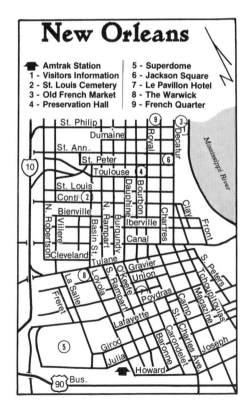

New Orleans

⬛ Amtrak Station	5 - Superdome
1 - Visitors Information	6 - Jackson Square
2 - St. Louis Cemetery	7 - Le Pavillon Hotel
3 - Old French Market	8 - The Warwick
4 - Preservation Hall	9 - French Quarter

charming hotel; one of the city's best. $80.

The **French Quarter** is the core of New Orleans magnetism; 66 blocks of the old city with restaurants, jazz, shops, small hostelries with ironwork-decorated balconies—and, of course, raucous Bourbon Street. Free tours of the area are offered by the Park Service.

Be sure to take the **St. Charles Streetcar** through neighborhoods of fine old homes. This is also a good way to reach New Orleans **Audubon Park** and the fine **Zoological Gardens.** The **Riverfront Streetcars,** inaugurated in 1988, now tour 1½ miles of Mississippi waterfront. Also, in the 800 to 1000 block of Decatur Street, is the **Old French Market,** with shops and cafes, and a fascinating farmers market.

Gulf Breeze

In the fall of 1989, Amtrak expanded its Alabama service to include Montgomery and Mobile. The Gulf Breeze, which is combined with the Crescent between Birmingham and New York City, runs as a separate train between Birmingham and Mobile.

The route is through Alabama's pastoral countryside, with scattered forests and cottonfields lining the right-of-way. Highlights of this six-hour trip include a stop in the heart of Montgomery's restored downtown and a Mobile arrival that slips along that historic city's waterfront.

Southbound Schedule (Condensed)
Birmingham, AL - Late Morning Departure
Montgomery, AL - Early Afternoon
Mobile, AL - Late Afternoon Arrival

Northbound Schedule (Condensed)
Mobile, AL - Early Morning Departure
Montgomery, AL - Midmorning
Birmingham, AL - Early Afternoon Arrival

Frequency - Daily.
Seating - Amfleet II and Heritage Fleet coaches.
Sleeping - Heritage Fleet sleepers with bedrooms and roomettes.
Dining - Complete meal and beverage service as well as lighter fare.
Baggage - Carry-on baggage only.
Reservations - All-reserved train.

Route Log

For route from New York to Birmingham, see pages 31 and 96.

0:00 (2:20) Depart Birmingham and for next several minutes, wend southward through many of city's more industrial scenes.

0:25 (1:55) Cross Cahaba River.

0:50 (1:30) At southern edge of Calera, tan building, assorted cabooses and locomotives comprise Heart of Dixie Railroad Museum, just off to left.

1:10 (1:10) After passing through Thorsby, large plant on right is Union Camp Corporation's veneer board operation. Timber in yard is moved by huge contraption looking more like a scorpion than a log snatcher.

1:20 (1:00) Passing through Clanton, newly built mall is centerpiece of downtown, just to left.

1:55 (0:25) After Deatsville, Draper Correctional Center is imposing facility off to left.

2:09 (0:11) Natural gas pumping paraphernalia of Southern Gas Company is on left.

2:15 (0:05) Cross Alabama River which flows south into Gulf of Mexico. Its nine-foot channel allows navigation to Great Lakes by way of controversial Tennessee-Tombigbee Waterway. Fort Jackson, when built in 1814 just upstream at junction of Coosa and Tallapoosa rivers, marked end of Creek Indian War.

2:20 (0:00) Pure white dome of State Capitol Building, one of just a few capitols to be designated a National Historic Landmark, can be seen off to left upon arrival Montgomery's station platform. Old grain elevators on immediate right may someday become Amtrak depot.

MONTGOMERY, AL - In 1540, Hernando de Soto visited this location and symbolically drove a Spanish flag into the banks of the Alabama River. But it was almost two centuries later before the French created the first permanent white settlements, East Alabama and New Philadelphia, which later merged to become the city of Montgomery.

Montgomery, named for a Revolutionary War hero, became Alabama's fourth capital after the seat of government was moved here from Tuscaloosa in 1846. Jefferson Davis was sworn in as president of the Confederacy on the capitol steps in 1861, and Montgomery served as the first capital of the Confederacy from February 8 to May 21, 1861.

This is the birthplace of the civil rights movement. In 1955, a black seamstress, Rosa Parks, was arrested for refusing to give up her seat on a city bus to a white man, and a year-long bus boycott by blacks ensued. Ten years later, protesting discriminatory voter laws, Martin Luther King led a 50-mile march from Selma to the steps of the State Capitol, only a block from his first ministry, the Dexter Avenue Baptist Church. Today, the Civil Rights Memorial, completed here in 1989, has become one of Montgomery's top attractions. The memorial was designed by Maya Lin, the same artist who created the Vietnam Memorial in Washington, DC.

Montgomery has paid considerable attention to its heritage. Commerce Street, an early-day mixture of commercial and residential buildings, and later home to elaborate warehouses, has been the object of a remarkable restoration effort that began in the 1970s. This handsome thoroughfare, just south of the station, can easily be seen from the train. The street goes directly beneath the tracks and served as a passageway for wagon loads of cotton on their way to riverboats that once docked on the shores of the Alabama River, just north of the station. The area is now Riverfront Park. And the nation's first electric trolley system, known as the "Lightning Route," is still remembered in the form of trolley tour buses called "Lightning Trolleys" that carry tourists through the city's historic areas.

0:00 (0:55) Departing Montgomery, Commerce Street is dazzling scene of immaculate storefronts, back to left. On immediate left, Montgomery's wonderful old Union Station now houses a bank, bakery and restaurant. Colorful stained glass panels adorn peaks of 1897 train shed. Over 40 passenger trains a day stopped here at the time of its construction.

0:48 (0:07) Over two centuries ago, naturalist and botanist William Bartram followed Indian trails through this region while studying plants, birds, insects and fish.

0:55 (0:00) Arrive Greenville.

GREENVILLE, AL - This town of 8,000 is the trading center of Butler County and is the halfway point between Birmingham and Mobile.

0:00 (0:40) Depart Greenville.

0:15 (0:25) On left, huge lumber mill of Union Camp Corporation transforms locally grown trees into sheets of plywood.

0:40 (0:00) Arrive Evergreen.

EVERGREEN, AL - Amtrak has utilized the old depot here, but only a small part. The long, grey frame structure in the center of town now houses a small waiting room, a small market and the local chamber of commerce.

0:00 (0:53) Depart Evergreen.

0:08 (0:45) Cotton fields continue to appear from time to time, forming soft, white blankets laid helter skelter throughout countryside.

0:11 (0:42) Through town of Castleberry, dilapidated and abandoned older portion of town is forlorn sight on left.

0:27 (0:26) Just south of Brewton, large Container Corporation of America facility turns out myriad paper container products.

0:34 (0:19) This wide-spot-in-the-tracks is called Pollard. Established at juncture of Alabama & Florida and Mobile & Great Northern railroads, it was named for Charles T. Pollard, builder of Alabama & Florida Railroad. One of Confederacy's largest military training camps and a huge stores depot were here and suffered considerable devastation during Federal raids of December, 1864 and March, 1865.

0:53 (0:00) Arrive Atmore where "station" on left is roof and fence, about large enough to accommodate a picnic bench.

ATMORE, AL — The community believes in centralized community services. Beyond the jet trainer in the park adjacent to the tracks is the City

Hall, Fire Department, Chamber of Commerce and YMCA, all in a neat-appearing light-brick structure.

0:00 (0:50) Depart Atmore and immediately pass under Burlington Northern Railroad bridge.

0:04 (0:46) Atmore Country Club and golf course are just across highway to left.

0:25 (0:25) Entering town of Bay Minnette, recently closed Reichold Chemical plant is on left. Plant had been in operation for nearly 60 years, producing coatings and resins, then 1989 closure dealt economic blow to community. Town is home to University of South Alabama Baldwin County.

0:34 (0:16) Cross Tensano River.

0:41 (0:09) Cross Mobile River.

0:45 (0:05) On left, Mobile River now accompanies train approaching Mobile. Skyline is forward right.

0:48 (0:02) Trundle through freight yards. Alabama state docks, capable of handling 34 ocean-going vessels at one time, are seen on immediate left. Land on other side of Mobile River is Blakely Island situated in Polecat Bay, a northern extension of Mobile Bay. Freighters and other maritime vessels are usually prominent sights here. Battleship U.S.S. Alabama, permanently moored in harbor, is just beyond structures at left, but not visible from tracks.

0:50 (0:00) Arrive Mobile's CSX-Amtrak station. In middle of Government Street on right, statue of Admiral Raphael Semmes, who was commander of Confederate States Steamer Alabama, seemingly welcomes Amtrak passengers to Mobile.

MOBILE, AL - A handful of modern skyscrapers alongside Mobile Bay punctuates the skyline of Alabama's only seaport, in sharp contrast to the collection of handsome Old-South neighborhoods that make Mobile a city of charm and grace. Mobile is at its best in the spring when the city's 35-mile Azalea Trail, comprised of several streets lined with those showy flowers, is in full bloom.

Like Texas, Mobile has lived under six flags: French, British, Spanish, the State of Alabama, Confederate and U.S. It was the last Southern stronghold to surrender to Union Forces during the Civil War after being completely blockaded by the Union Navy. (It was during this blockade that Admiral Farragut supposedly exclaimed: "Damn the torpedoes! Full steam ahead!") The Bay remains important to Mobile, whose maritime trade and shipbuilding are still vital to the city's economy.

Amtrak Station, Government and Water streets, occupies a portion of the former CSX station, conveniently wedged between the compact central business district and the Mobile River. The station opened in October 1989 when Amtrak service commenced here on a permanent basis, with a lobby that was small, simple and had limited amenities.

For reservations, call 800-USA-RAIL.

Write or call **Mobile Convention & Visitors Bureau,** One St. Louis Centre, Suite 2002, 36602; (205) 433-5100 or 800-666-6282. Visit the Information Center at historic Fort Conde; 434-7304.

Yellow **Cab,** 432-7711; **local buses,** 344-5656. **Greyhound,** two blocks from the station, 432-1861 (or 433-6762 for New Orleans service). Budget **rental cars,** 633-0660, offer pick up and delivery in the downtown area. **Mobile Municipal Airport** is on the west edge of the city.

Oak Tree Inn, 255 Church St., 36602; (205) 433-6923. Large motel in attractive setting next to central business district and convenient to visitors center. Five blocks from the station. $36.

-**Radisson Admiral Semmes Hotel,** 251 Government St., 36602; (205) 432-8000. Very attractively maintained older high rise, three blocks from the station. $68.

-**Stouffer's Riverview Plaza,** 64 Water St., 36602; (205) 438-4000 or 800-468-3571. Modern high rise with large, bright rooms. Very attractive AARP rates. Second floor dining room overlooks tracks. Immediately across intersection from station. $95.

Grayline of Mobile has **city tours** which provide an excellent way to sample this historic city when time is limited. Two of the area's outstanding examples of early Southern living are: **Bellingrath Gardens and Home,** a few miles south of the city, with 65 acres of gardens and landscaping where one can enjoy breakfast or lunch in an Old South setting; and **Oakleigh Mansion,** nearer to downtown, a Greek Revival mansion noted for its graceful lines and beautiful gardens.

Near the station is **Waterfront Park,** a small open space next to the station, providing a view of Mobile's waterfront activity. Two blocks away is Fort Conde Historic French Fort, a reconstruction of the original built circa 1724-36 and serves as the city's information center.

The **Battleship Alabama Memorial Park** is the permanent anchorage for that World War II battle wagon, the submarine USS Drum and a B-52 bomber. The highlight of the Park is the tour of the Alabama herself.

Broadway Limited

From New York City to Chicago, The Broadway Limited traces much of the route traveled by its famed predecessor of the same appellation. That Broadway Limited (named for the formerly wide, multi-tracked roadbeds of the Pennsylvania Railroad—now a part of Conrail) began in 1902 and was the arch rival of the New York Central's 20th Century Limited which started the same year. In the 1920s the trains captured the imagination of the traveling public with their celebrated "speed wars" between New York and Chicago—speeds that approached 130 mph. They were among the world's premier trains. The old Broadway was finally discontinued in 1967, America's last all-pullman service, after suffering a terminal decline in ridership. Today's Broadway Limited takes a course along the busy Northeast Corridor between New York and Philadelphia before it turns westward. After Philadelphia, the train passes through Pennsylvania's rolling Amish countryside into the Alleghenies where it climbs around the famous Horseshoe Curve, on into Pittsburgh and finally across northern Ohio and Indiana before reaching its western terminus, Chicago.

Westbound Schedule (Condensed)
New York, NY (Penn Station) - Early Afternoon Departure
Philadelphia, PA - Late Afternoon
Harrisburg, PA - Early Evening
Pittsburgh, PA - Late Evening
Fort Wayne, IN - Early Morning
Chicago, IL - Early Morning Arrival

Eastbound Schedule (Condensed)
Chicago, IL - Midevening Departure
Fort Wayne, IN - Middle of the Night
Pittsburgh, PA - Early Morning
Harrisburg PA - Early Afternoon
Philadelphia, PA - Early Afternoon
New York, NY (Penn Station) - Late Afternoon Arrival

Frequency - Daily.
Seating - Heritage Fleet coaches.
Dining - Complete meal and beverage service, as well as lighter fare. Lounge service is also available.
Sleeping - Heritage Fleet with bedrooms, roomettes and Slumbercoach.
Baggage - Checked baggage at most stops.
Reservations - All-reserved train.
Length of Trip - 911 miles in 19 hours.

Route Log

(The route of the Broadway Limited between Chicago and Pittsburgh may be rerouted through Youngstown and Akron, bypassing Ft. Wayne and Lima.)

For route between New York and Philadelphia, see that portion of the Northeast Corridor log, page 31.

0:00 (0:25) Depart Philadelphia's 30th St. Station with city clearly visible back to right.
The course is now due west toward Harrisburg and Pittsburgh. The Philadelphia suburbs dominate for about 30

minutes until the train departs Paoli, where the pastoral scenes of central Pennsylvania farmland begin.

This nicely engineered section of trackage between Philadelphia and Harrisburg is Amtrak's Keystone Corridor. Although it has been electrified since 1938, The Broadway Limited retains its diesel units for this run.

0:01 (0:24) To right, City Hall can be seen, topped by enduring statue of William Penn—a long-time informal height restriction for buildings in Philadelphia. Barrier was broken, however, with construction of One Liberty Place, now visible as tallest structure on skyline. Also, in foreground on right, just across Schuylkill, is Philadelphia Museum of Art known for not only fine art, but its prominence in movie "Rocky."

0:02 (0:23) Buildings of Boat House Row, home to numerous racing scull clubs, is on far shore of river. Crews can frequently be seen practicing their rowing skills along this stretch of Schuylkill.

0:19 (0:06) Passing through Strafford, note commuter station which is architectural jewel. Originally built for Philadelphia's American Centennial Celebration in 1876, it was later moved to this site.

0:25 (0:00) Arrive Paoli.

PAOLI, PA - This stop, named after a revolutionary in Corsica, is the western edge of the densely populated Eastern Seaboard. Historic Valley Forge, where General George Washington and his Revolutionary Army suffered through a trying winter, is just two miles to the north of here.

0:00 (0:42) Depart Paoli.

After leaving Paoli, our route passes through Coatesville and then into the fascinating "Pennsylvania Dutch" country. Beautiful farms, set in these rolling Pennsylvania hills, have been operated by the Amish with little change in lifestyle in the last 300 years. Watch for black-attired farmers in their horse-drawn buggies sharing the roads with more modern conveyances.

0:42 (0:00) Arrive Lancaster.

LANCASTER, PA - The train halts briefly in this city which produced arms for the American Revolution, and where the first Woolworth store was opened in 1879. The nation's oldest iron mine is but a few miles north at Cornwall and The Pennsylvania Rifle (misnamed The Kentucky Rifle according to Pennsylvanians) was developed here during the 1700s. The city is now the commercial center and heart of Amish farming country. Several of the country's finest farmers' markets are in this area. The Pennsylvania Farm Museum, north of town on State 272, and the Pennsylvania Railroad Museum at Strasburg are local attractions. Also at Strasburg is the ever-popular Strasburg Railroad, America's oldest short-line railroad.

0:00 (0:36) Depart Lancaster.

0:08 (0:26) Through Mt. Joy, where manufacturing plants of familiar names such as National Standard, NCR and AMP are in evidence.

0:14 (0:22) First commercial telegraph lines in U.S. were strung along this railroad right-of-way between Lancaster and Harrisburg. In 1846 first message was transmitted and logically asked, "Why didn't you write, you rascals?"

0:22 (0:14) Four spectre-like cooling towers in distance, to left, each rising 372 feet from its base, belong to infamous Three Mile Island nuclear power plant, which came close to a meltdown in March 1979. Cleanup is still continuing in spite of staggering costs.

0:33 (0:03) Large bridge on left carries forerunner of interstate highways across Susquehanna River—the Pennsylvania Turnpike. Pennsylvania State University's attractive Harrisburg campus lies just beyond highway on right. Less attractive Bethlehem Steel rail and expanded pipe facility will soon dominate scene.

0:36 (0:00) Arrive Harrisburg's finely remodeled intermodal Amtrak station. Handsome #4859 GG-1 electric locomotive stands on permanent display between train and depot.

HARRISBURG, PA - This city of 55,000 is now over 200 years old. In 1812 it became the state capital and subsequently one of the finest capitol buildings in the nation was built here—just beyond the station. Built in 1906 at a cost of $10 million, the capitol's interior marble was shipped from the Pyrenees Mountains in Italy. Its exquisite dome was patterned after St. Peter's Basilica in Rome. The unusual William Penn Memorial Museum, which houses an historic treasure trove, and Archives Building are also particularly noteworthy.

0:00 (1:12) Depart Harrisburg and immediately on left is State Capitol Building just described.

0:04 (1:08) Cross over Susquehanna River on Rockville Bridge, four miles north of Harrisburg. Structure is world's longest and widest stone-arch bridge and contains 48 arches made of Pennsylvania white sandstone. It is 3,820 feet in length, has a 52-foot roadbed and is 42 feet above Susquehanna. First train crossed this bridge in 1902 on Easter Sunday.

0:22 (0:50) Pass through Duncannon, leave Susquehanna River, and enter easternmost hills of Allegheny Mountains. From here to Altoona, tracks accompany Juniata River. Line was originally built to compete with Erie Canal and is still a busy freight road as will be noted from numerous Conrail freight trains.

1:06 (0:00) Arrive Lewistown.

LEWISTOWN, PA - This industrial town is in the very heart of Pennsylvania. The Frank McCoy House, former home of General Frank Ross McCoy, will be of interest to historians.

0:00 (0:39) Depart Lewistown.

0:23 (0:16) Blue Mountain on left and Jack's Mountain on right are prominent Allegheny ridges stretching along each horizon.

0:39 (0:00) Arrive Huntingdon.

HUNTINGDON, PA - A small industrial town, Huntingdon is attractively situated along the Juniata River. The popular Raystown Lake recreational area lies just to the south. This is home to Juniata College.

0:00 (0:44) Depart Huntingdon. Immediately on right is large Owens-Corning Fiberglass plant which melts small fiberglass marbles into large tanks which are sometimes visible next to plant.

0:12 (0:32) Cross Spruce Creek, a fine trout fishing stream which at one time provided sport for former president Jimmy Carter. Enter Spruce Creek Tunnel for a sudden but brief period of darkness.

Broadway Limited – Rockville Bridge

0:44 (0:00) Arriving Altoona, Broadway Ltd. slips through enormous Altoona rail yards, and then past Railroaders Memorial Museum, on left, where numerous rail cars and locomotives can be seen, including Raymond Loewy-designed GG-1 electric locomotive. Famous K-4, 234-ton steam locomotive, a design that dates back to 1914, is also here. Engine was formerly on display at nearby Horseshoe Curve. At one time, Pennsylvania Railroad had 400 of these, which served as standard passenger engines on this line until World War II. On opposite (right) side of train, predominant structure is Cathedral of Blessed Sacrament. Station is very efficient intermodal transit center.

ALTOONA, PA - A supply point for building the Pennsylvania Railroad, Altoona now has one of the world's largest assemblages of rail maintenance facilities.

0:00 (1:01) Depart Altoona and commence a steep climb toward Gallitzin Summit. Ascending grades will now range from 1.75% to 1.85%, forcing most westbound freights to add helper engines at Alto, just west of Altoona.

0:11 (0:50) Reservoirs below on left are part of Altoona's domestic water storage system.

0:12 (0:48) Horseshoe Curve (the Pennsylvania Railroad spelled horseshoe as two words), a beautiful hairpin turn, nearly a half-mile long, is one of railroading's most notable landmarks.

Eastbound passengers can view the entire side of the train by looking out of the right side while rounding this extremely sharp curve. Westbound passengers, however, looking to the left will get a view of lights only, except during the longest of days. The Curve permits a tolerable 1.73% grade through this section of mountains which will allow 6 diesels to pull 125 fully loaded freight cars around its perimeter. A short cut across valley's mouth would have produced a 4.37% grade, but those same diesels would then handle only 43 cars. At one time four sets of track rounded the curve, but one set was removed in 1981 as an economy move. Pennsylvania Railroad diesel Number 7048 is now displayed on the inside of the Curve.

0:19 (0:43) On right, secluded in heart of Alleghenies, is skinny two-story brick structure known as MG Tower, once described by a rail writer as "remote and mysterious." Built to control crossovers and signals in this area, it is now closed— another victim of modern centralized dispatching.

0:21 (0:40) Pass through one of three tunnels, as route handily crests Alleghenies. Allegheny and Gallitzin tunnels, each over a mile in length, usually handle westbound traffic while shorter New Portage Tunnel takes eastbound trains that must descend a 2.27% grade.

At one time, though, it was not so easy. Just three miles to the south, from 1834 to 1855, the Allegheny Portage Railroad, with its system of canals, trains and incline railroads, ingeniously lifted sectionalized canal boats (people, cargo and all) over these mountains on a series of inclined planes and level stretches, allowing continuous transportation between Philadelphia and Pittsburgh. However, construction of the Horseshoe Curve provided a direct rail link and ended operations for one of America's most unique transportation systems.

1:01 (0:00) Arrive Johnstown.

JOHNSTOWN, PA - In 1889, the nation's most disastrous flood devastated this city of steel mills. An overly enlarged dam, 14 miles east of here on the Conemaugh River, formed a reservoir some two miles long. The lake was the centerpiece of the South Fork Fishing and Hunting Club, a secretive retreat for many of Pittsburgh's wealthy and socially elite. Two excursion steamers plied the waters in the summer months. On May 31 of that year, after a day of drenching rain, the poorly maintained dam began to give way. Warnings earlier in the day were ignored by the populous—citizens who had heard similar warnings almost every spring. At 4:07 in the afternoon the inhabitants heard a "roar like thunder," then were suddenly engulfed by a 36-foot wall of water. Over 2,200 people died and hundreds more were never accounted for.

Johnstown's history of flooding has continued. In 1936, 25 lives were lost and in 1977, 85 persons died.

Bethlehem Steel is still the principal

employer, but the town's economy has been less than vibrant. In 1983, when the steel market hit bottom, Johnstown had the highest unemployment in the U.S.

0:00 (0:54) Depart Johnstown. Incline on slope behind station is a people conveyor providing unusual access to community atop hill.

0:02 (0:52) Sign painted on brick building, "Conemaugh & Black Lick Railroad Company" touts former Bethlehem Steel operated railroad.

0:48 (0:08) Pass through Latrobe, home to past training camps of formidable Pittsburgh Steelers—and Arnold Palmer's well-oiled tractor.

0:52 (0:00) Arrive Greensburg.

GREENSBURG, PA - Near this western Pennsylvania town is Bushy Run Battlefield where Colonel Henry Bouquet defeated hostile Indians in 1763.

0:00 (0:44) Depart Greensburg.

0:44 (0:00) Arrive Pittsburgh.

PITTSBURGH, PA - Once known for its steel mills and smoke, Pittsburgh now exemplifies what can be done with urban renewal when the determination (and money) to do so exists. The city now has clean air, shiny skyscrapers and beautiful parks as a result of a massive effort undertaken in recent years. With a metropolitan population in excess of two million and located in the "Golden Triangle," where the Allegheny and the Monongahela rivers join to form the Ohio River, the city is one of the nation's primary industrial centers.

Amtrak Station, Liberty Avenue at Grant Street, is located near the heart of downtown. The station will soon move next door into newly remodeled quarters in what was once Penn Central Station. There are storage lockers and food and beverage vending machines. Pay-parking is one block away at the Greyhound terminal.

For reservations and information, call (412) 621-4850. Ticket windows are open 10 pm to 6:45 am, 8:30 am to 1 pm and 2 pm to 5:15 pm. The waiting room is open 24 hours.

Yellow Cab, 665-8100. Nearest **local bus** stop, half block from the station. **Greyhound,** (412) 391-2300; across the street from the station. **Greater Pittsburgh International Airport** is 20 miles west of the city.

Visitor Information Center, Gateway Center, Downtown Pittsburgh, (412) 281-9222. Write Pittsburgh Convention and Visitors Bureau, 4 Gateway Center, 15222. Call 800-821-1888 (or 800-255-0855 in Pennsylvania).

Hotels in the downtown Golden Triangle area are fairly expensive; one is included since it is close to the station. The other two accommodations shown are a few minutes cab ride from downtown and are logical alternatives.

-**Westin William Penn,** 530 William Penn Place, 15230; (412) 281-7100 and 800-228-3000. Four blocks from the station. $150.

-**The Priory,** 614 Pressley St., 15212; (412) 231-3338. A bed and breakfast on the North Side about a half mile from the station (but not very walkable). Free shuttle in the mornings. Prices range from $65 to $130 with most rooms at $88.

-**Hampton Inn Greentree,** 555 Trumbull Dr., 15205; (412) 922-0100. Continental breakfast included. Between downtown and the airport, about three miles from the station. $60.

Point State Park is at the confluence of the Allegheny and Monongahela rivers, where one will find the only local remnant of the French and Indian War, the Fort Pitt Blockhouse. Also located here are a large fountain, the Fort Pitt Museum with historic exhibits, and military drills held during the summer months.

Station Square, just across the Smithfield Bridge from downtown, includes shops, restaurants, a marina and the Industrial Transportation Museum with restored antique railroad cars, trolleys and locomotives. This area also contains the historic buildings of the P&LE Railroad.

Inclines to the top of Mount Washington can be ridden from their lower stations, either just west of the Smithfield Bridge or west of the Fort Pitt Bridge, both on West Carson Street. Observation platforms are at the top of each, and a restaurant is at the summit of the western-

Pittsburgh

- Amtrak Station
- 1 - Visitors Information
- 2 - Station Square
- 3 - Inclines
- 4 - Point State Park
- 5 - The Priory
- 6 - Westin William Penn

most incline.

The **Carnegie Institute,** at 4400 Forbes Ave. in the eastern section of Pittsburgh, contains two fine museums: The **Museum of Art** has an outstanding permanent collection of European paintings and sculpture, as well as American works; the **Museum of Natural History** has various exhibits of plant life, current and prehistoric wildlife, as well as other exhibits.

0:00 (2:04) Depart Pittsburgh.

After leaving Pittsburgh, the tracks lead out of the Allegheny Mountains and into farming and industrial regions of Ohio and Indiana, traversing these environs during the night.

2:04 (0:00) Arrive Canton.

CANTON, OH - This is one of the more heavily industrialized cities in Ohio. Today, it is probably best known for its Pro Football Hall of Fame, with exhibits of football memorabilia from the 1890s to the present.

0:00 (1:40) Depart Canton.

1:40 (0:00) Arrive Crestline.

CRESTLINE, OH - A railroad junction point, Crestline receives its name from its location on the drainage divide between the Ohio River and Lake Erie.

0:00 (1:17) Depart Crestline.

1:17 (0:00) Arrive Lima.

LIMA, OH - Named after Lima, Peru, this city is perhaps best known for its former prowess in manufacture of steam locomotives. The Lincoln Park Railway Exhibit has the last steam locomotive built in Lima, as well as an 1883 private car and an 1882 caboose.

0:00 (1:01) Depart Lima.
1:01 (0:00) Arrive Fort Wayne.

FORT WAYNE, IN - An industrial city, whose economy depends heavily on plants such as General Electric and International Telephone and Telegraph Co., Fort Wayne boasts of being the home of the first night baseball game and the first gasoline pump. Historic Fort Wayne, a reconstructed military post, and The Fort Wayne Children's Zoo, one of country's finest, are both located here.

0:00 (0:39) Depart Fort Wayne.
0:36 (0:03) Large lake on left at southeastern edge of Warsaw is Winona Lake, Middle West Chautauqua headquarters. Many summer camps are located on its shores, as is former home of evangelist Billy Sunday. Quaint, rambling old frame structure looking out on its waters is Billy Sunday Tabernacle. Somewhat smaller structure is Winona Hotel.
0:38 (0:01) Now in Warsaw, shortly after crossing an intersection with another Conrail line, fine example of a Victorian home stands on left, beautiful in its black and white coats of paint.
0:39 (0:00) Arrive Warsaw.

WARSAW, IN - Evangelist Billy Sunday's home is now a museum and is open to the public during the summer months. The Billy Sunday Tabernacle and the Winona Hotel, focal points of the religious community that was formed where he lived, are open only during special events.

0:00 (1:03) Depart Warsaw.
0:26 (0:37) This is Plymouth, with a population of 7,600. Note another Victorian home, below on left, loaded with gingerbread trim.

Just six-and-one-half miles southwest of here, at Twin Lakes, one of the sadder events involving this country's treatment of Indians took place. In 1838, Potawatomi Chief Menominee, in vain, resisted the efforts of white soldiers sent secretly by the governor of Indiana to move the Indians west. They were marched across Indiana, Illinois and Missouri into the Kansas

prairie on a "Trail of Death" with graves marking each encampment along the 900-mile route.

0:56 (0:07) Face of famous popcorn king, Orville Redenbacher, looks across from sign by his plant on right.

Gain one hour as train passes from Eastern to Central Time Zone. Set your watch back (forward if eastbound) one hour.

1:03 (0:00) Arrive Valparaiso.

VALPARAISO, IN - Valparaiso is an agrarian stronghold with myriad agricultural products, including, of course, popcorn. The city is home of Valparaiso University with an enrollment of 5,000 students, located on the southeast edge of town. Also, Valparaiso Technical Institute of Electronics (VIT&E), with a 400-student enrollment, will be visible immediately after our departure.

0:00 (0:34) Depart Valparaiso.
0:21 (0:13) Through Gary, Indiana, one of America's largest steel-producing communities, with USX, Bethlehem and Inland all having facilities here.
0:29 (0:05) Inland Steel plants straddle tracks, Plant Number One on left and Two on right. Then cross drawbridge spanning canal that links Lake Michigan with Calumet River.
0:31 (0:03) Amoco refinery creates boggling apparatus forest at left. Lake Michigan is now only 100 feet or so to right.
0:34 (0:00) Arrive Hammond-Whiting.

For route description from here to Chicago, see that portion of Lake Shore Ltd. log, page 73.

CHICAGO, IL - Rail passengers traveling across the U.S. funnel through Chicago like sands through the neck of an hourglass. A quick look at a map of the United States tells why Chicago has grown up to become the nation's major transportation hub, where much of America's east-west traffic has to converge. Lake Michigan, cutting strategically into the heart of the Midwest, provided early-day shipping access to a developing frontier. With the coming of the railroad, tracks soon radiated from The Windy City in almost every direction, a pattern that is still followed today.

Oddly, in spite of heavy volumes of traffic, trains don't go through Chicago—just their passengers do. All thru passengers must change trains. It's always been this way, and it's unlikely to be otherwise in the foreseeable future. So everyone arriving in Chicago on Amtrak gets off here, at least for a little while. This phenomenon, along with 160-or-so commuter trains a day, makes Chicago Union Station a very busy place.

The 1926 depot has not handled the crush well. However, help is on the way in the form of a major remodeling project aimed, in part, at improving the interior's efficiency. Two 24-story office towers are also planned. Of course, while all of this takes place, passengers will have to tolerate the inevitable disruptions that come with this sort of progress.

Amtrak Station
1 - Visitors Information
2 - Chicago Board of Trade
3 - Adler Planetarium
4 - Museum of Science and
    Industry
5 - Sears Tower
6 - Field Museum of Natural
    History
7 - Art Institute of Chicago
8 - John G. Shedd Aquarium
9 - Bismark Hotel
10 - Quality Inn Downtown
11 - Midland Hotel

Union Station, 210 S. Canal St. (at Adams St.), is in the heart of downtown. Many of the city's commuter trains also use the station, giving it a stampede-like atmosphere during the afternoon rush hour. Its cavernous, marble-pillared waiting room still contains the original hardwood benches. Some of the shops that were in the station have been closed during the remodeling mentioned above. There are a cafeteria, a restaurant, and snack bars in the station, and several restaurants are within easy walking distance. There are no lockers; the baggage checkroom is open 8 am to 8:30 pm. Luggage carts are obtained by inserting four quarters into cart dispensers. There is no free parking; parking garages and lots are nearby.

For reservations and other information, call 558-1075 or 800-USA-RAIL.

Cab stand at the station and it is usually well supplied; Yellow, 892-4222 and Checker, 421-1300. **Greyhound** is about a mile from the station, 781-2900. **Local buses** are just outside the station; for bus and commuter train information, call 836-7000 (suburbs, 800-972-7000). Train to **O'Hare International Airport,** 19 miles northwest of downtown, is two blocks away at Clinton and Congress. **Midway Airport** is nine miles southwest of downtown.

Visitor Information Center, located in the old pumping station across from the Water Tower, 163 E. Pearson; (312) 280-5740. The State of Illinois also has a center in the Sears Tower with some Chicago information. Or write Chicago Tourism Council, 806 North Michigan Ave., 60611.

Bismark Hotel, 171 W. Randolph St. (at Wells), 60601; (312) 236-0123 or 800-643-1500. Fine old hostelry, well maintained and managed. Seven blocks from the station. $85.

-Quality Inn Downtown, One Mid City Plaza (Madison at Halstead); (312) 829-5000. West of downtown, off the Kennedy Expressway. Five blocks from the station, but not a nice walk. $85.

-Midland Hotel, 172 W. Adams (at LaSalle), 60603; (312) 332-1200 or 800-621-2360. Excellent hotel, only four blocks from the station. $125.

-The Palmer House, 17 E. Monroe, 60603; (312) 726-7500 or 800-HILTONS. Long-time favorite of visitors. Amtrak package, $92. Eight blocks from the station. $140.

"The Loop," bounded by Van Buren, Wells, Lake and Wabash, has some of the best shopping in the city, particularly along State Street. The **Magnificent Mile** on North Michigan Ave. is home to an assemblage of Rodeo-Drive-class stores, including Saks, Bloomingdales, Neiman-Marcus and Marshall Field's. The **Sears Tower,** Wacker Drive and Jackson, is the world's tallest building at 110 stories. It's just two blocks east of the station and has an observation deck for the best view in town. The **Chicago Board of Trade,** 141 West Jackson, is the largest commodities futures market, with several tours during the day, five blocks from the station.

Also downtown, but somewhat farther away: the **Field Museum of Natural History,** Roosevelt Rd. and S. Lake Shore Dr., is one of the nation's finest; the adjacent **Shedd Aquarium** has an outstanding collection of marine life; and just east of these two attractions is the **Adler Planetarium** with daily multimedia shows that display much of the heavens.

Two of Chicago's major attractions are out of the downtown area: the **Museum of Science and Industry,** 57th St. and South Lake Shore Dr., with acres of outstanding technological exhibits, is one of the best such museums in the world; and the **Brookfield Zoo,** 1st Ave. and 31st St., in Brookfield, is one of the largest zoos in the nation.

Other Pennsylvania Service

The **Pennsylvanian** links New York City with Pittsburgh by way of Philadelphia. Daily New York departures are early morning with late afternoon arrivals in Pittsburgh. Pittsburgh departures are midmorning (early afternoon on Sundays) and New York is reached nine hours later.

It is likely this train's route will be extended from Pittsburgh to Cleveland.

Harrisburg is served by numerous other trains to and from Philadelphia.

Capitol Limited

The Capitol Limited operates over CSX tracks from Washington, DC to Pittsburgh, where it then takes the route of The Broadway Limited (on Conrail) to Chicago. Following roughly the Maryland-West Virginia boundary (the Potomac River), it passes through historic Harpers Ferry and Cumberland before twisting through the very scenic valleys and mountains of southwestern Pennsylvania to reach Pittsburgh. From there, it makes a trek across northern Ohio and Indiana, following the route of The Broadway Limited to reach Chicago. More interesting scenery can be seen traveling eastbound, since much of western Pennsylvania is traveled at night when westbound.

Westbound Schedule (Condensed)
Washington, DC - Late Afternoon Departure
Cumberland, MD - Late Evening
Pittsburgh, PA - Middle of the Night
Fort Wayne, IN - Early Morning
Chicago, IL - Midmorning Arrival

Eastbound Schedule (Condensed)
Chicago, IL - Early Evening Departure
Fort Wayne, IN - Late Evening
Pittsburgh, PA - Early Morning
Cumberland, MD - Midmorning
Washington, DC - Early Afternoon Arrival

Frequency - Daily.
Seating - Heritage Fleet coaches and dome car.
Dining - Complete meal and beverage service. Lounge service is also available.
Sleeping - Heritage Fleet with bedrooms and roomettes.

Baggage - Checked baggage handled at most stops.
Reservations - All-reserved train.
Length of Trip - 766 miles in 17 hours.

Route Log

(The route of the Capitol Limited between Chicago and Pittsburgh may be rerouted through Cleveland.)

 WASHINGTON, DC - See page 39.
0:00 (0:20) Depart Washington.
0:02 (0:18) Familiar obelisk of Washington Monument can be seen back on left.
0:03 (0:17) Streamlined "Metros" on above-ground portions of Washington's subway zip to and from downtown on immediate left.
0:07 (0:13) Beautiful white building on left with dazzling blue and gold tiled dome is National Shrine of the Immaculate Conception—largest Catholic church in United States and seventh largest church in world.
0:13 (0:07) Suburbs momentarily give way to a few wooded hills before modern office parks and shopping centers of Rockville appear.
0:20 (0:00) Arrive Rockville.

ROCKVILLE, MD - First settled in the early 1700s, it was frequented by travelers on a "great road" between Georgetown and Frederick. Rockville is now one of Washington's larger suburbs.

0:00 (0:42) Depart Rockville.

Leave more populous fringes of Washington and settle back to enjoy Potomac countryside, punctuated by an occasional rural community.

0:04 (0:38) At trackside in Gaithersburg, small, charming depot still serves D.C. commuters.

0:19 (0:23) Cross Monocacy River which empties into Potomac half-mile to left.

0:21 (0:21) On left, broad Potomac River flows placidly toward Washington. Long-since-abandoned Chesapeake and Ohio Canal, now overgrown with shrubs and trees, is still visible between tracks and river.

Quaint rock bridges spanning this historic canal can be seen from time to time. Opened in 1850 shortly after the completion of the B&O Railroad, this 184-mile waterway connected Cumberland with tidewater at Georgetown following the course of the Potomac. It took about a week for freight-laden canal boats to make the entire trip.

Locks, stone aqueducts and the 3,080-foot Paw Paw Tunnel contributed to its hefty $22 million cost. Operations finally ceased in 1924. Today, canoes in its placid waters and bicycles along its towpath are common sights.

0:26 (0:16) At Point of Rocks, MD, church-like station, complete with steeple, is another fascinating elderly depot, now serving commuter passengers.

0:41 (0:01) Cross Potomac into West Virginia where Shenandoah River confluence can be seen just to left, and enter Harpers Ferry.

0:42 (0:00) Arrive Harpers Ferry. Note unusual signal on station roof.

 HARPERS FERRY, WV - Originally a ferrying point in 1733, the town gained prominence in the 1790s when a national armory was established here. As early as 1836, a railroad bridge linked Maryland with West Virginia by crossing the Potomac at this point.

The first wooden trestle had an unlikely "Y" junction in the middle—branching off to the Shenandoah Valley on the left. This bridge and its many successors were subsequently destroyed by war or flood, including being dismantled by John Brown

who hoped to incite a slave uprising with his infamous raid on the armory. Today, Harpers Ferry is a National Historical Park.

0:00 (0:20) Depart Harpers Ferry.

0:01 (0:19) Small hydroelectric plant of an earlier era is on right.

0:04 (0:16) Low dam, which formerly funneled water from Potomac into aqueduct leading to power plant just described, appears on right.

0:20 (0:00) Arrive Martinsburg.

 MARTINSBURG, WV - Since 1941, when the B&O Railroad first reached here, Martinsburg has been closely tied to railroading—for better or for worse. In 1849, shops and roundhouses were built with extraordinary workmanship and architectural detail, only to be later destroyed during the Civil War. The present station was the only survivor. Fortunately, outstanding roundhouses and most of the other buildings were rebuilt in 1866. Then in 1877, workers of the B&O went on strike, which developed into the largest railroad strike in the nation's history. A plaque commemorating this event is on the left, next to the old five-story brick station.

0:00 (1:25) Depart Martinsburg. Two outstanding brick roundhouses described above are on right.

0:13 (1:12) Fine panorama of distant mountains comes into view on right. These distant scenes start to diminish as terrain gradually becomes more confining.

0:15 (1:10) Potomac is visible once again on right.

0:30 (0:55) Passengers now are afforded an excellent look at serene Potomac back to right.

0:51 (0:34) Enter very short tunnel.

0:53 (0:32) Enter lengthy tunnel that blots out daylight for about one minute.

0:54 (0:31) Make a quick trip into Maryland and then back into West Virginia as train crosses Potomac twice in rapid succession. More short tunnels are encountered.

1:16 (0:09) Bid final farewell to West Virginia and Potomac as train crosses that stately river for last time and enters Cumberland, Maryland.

1:25 (0:00) Arrive Cumberland.

 CUMBERLAND, MD - At one time, Cumberland was known as

Capitol Limited – Harpers Ferry, West Virginia

"Washington Town" (George Washington's military career started and ended here) and also "Mills Creek," but it was finally christened "Cumberland" after the fort by the same name. The fort was located here during the French and Indian War (1756-1763). Both Colonel Washington and General Braddock left from here on expeditions against the French.

In June of 1755, Braddock led a force of 2,300 men, 200 wagons and 600 horses from Ft. Cumberland to a point near Ft. Dusquesne, now Pittsburgh, where he and nearly a thousand others were killed in what has been considered by most historians as a series of tactical blunders. It was this engagement that triggered the war with the French and Indians when the British disputed France's attempt to control the Mississippi and Ohio river valleys.

Today, Washington's headquarters, a small log cabin, is all that remains of the fort.

0:00 (2:20) Depart Cumberland. (From here to Pittsburgh, best viewing will be on left.)

0:03 (2:16) Pass through "The Narrows" where Wills Creek cuts through Allegheny Mountains. Originally a trading route, it was later a military wagon road. Some believe General Braddock came through here on his ill-fated march to Ft. Dusquesne. Road finally became first federally financed U.S. highway (The National Pike —now U.S. 40). This was also passage for America's first east-west railroad.

0:04 (2:15) Stone quarries are on immediate right.

0:09 (2:11) Leave Maryland and enter Pennsylvania.

0:26 (1:54) Wills Creek begins to narrow, and countryside becomes more mountainous as tracks climb toward summit at Sandpatch.

0:28 (1:52) Brief trip through Falls Cut Tunnel.

0:32 (1:48) Pass through village of Glencoe with its colorful array of quaint frame stores and houses.

0:41 (1:39) Rushing waters of Wills Creek, on left, are favorite of trout fishermen in early spring.

0:45 (1:35) Enter Sandpatch Tunnel, nearly a mile long and consuming two minutes before emerging at other end; it is longest of trip.

0:47 (1:34) Crest summit of Alleghenies at Sandpatch. Marker on right places elevation at 2,258 feet.

0:50 (1:31) Pass beneath curving bridge of Western Maryland Railroad where trains loaded with bituminous coal from nearby mines cross regularly.

0:55 (1:26) Pass through Meyersdale which is destination of special trains from Pittsburgh carrying syrup lovers to maple syrup festival held here each spring.

1:01 (1:22) At Blue Lick, pass beneath intriguing, abandoned rail bridge of Western Maryland Railroad. Watch for Belgian draft horses cavorting in field in front of barn on left. Ridge forming backdrop is abandoned strip mine.

1:04 (1:19) Those sitting on left should be able to spot two huge stone grain-grinding wheels, long since abandoned in Casselman River next to tracks.

1:05 (1:18) Serpentine trails etched on hillside across river on left are roads for logging trucks.

1:06 (1:17) Unusual series of "caves," just to right, were once former rock quarry.

1:11 (1:11) At Rockwood, another rail bridge, carrying branch north to Johnstown, crosses over Casselman River.

1:20 (1:01) Quaint log home across Casselman River on left is one of many spots where deer can frequently be spotted from train.

1:24 (0:58) Pass through Pinkerton Tunnel for 20 seconds and emerge on single set of tracks, where traffic is now controlled by operator at nearby Confluence.

1:25 (0:57) Pass through Shoefly Tunnel and return to luxury of two sets of tracks.

1:29 (0:52) Enter darkness for about one minute as train negotiates Brook Tunnel. Train normally saves three miles by taking "highline" at this point, while "lowline" branches off to left following more leisurely river route.

1:36 (0:45) We are rejoined by "lowline" and Youghiogheny (pronounced yawk-a-haney) River on left. Pass through Confluence and cross sleepy Laurel Creek.

1:43 (0:37) High ridge of Sugar Loaf Mountain can be seen on right, while fallen trees near river below show evidence of hard-working beavers. Watch for canoes which frequent this popular river in summertime.

1:49 (0:31) Enter Ohiopyle, where Ohiopyle Falls are located (just out of view and beyond town on left). Laurel Highlands

Trail leaves town on right, taking energetic hikers to Johnstown, some 45 miles "as a crow flies."

Between here and Connellsville, watch for fishermen trying their luck for elusive perch, pike, trout, walleye, and bass, all stocked in the Youghiogheny. Kayaks and rafts can frequently be seen in the summer. Maple trees combine to produce a color spectacular in the fall, making this a favorite sightseeing run at that time of year. Evergreens are mostly hemlock.

1:58 (0:21) Road across river on left, zig-zagging up through trees, is used to bring rafts up from stream after float trips from Ohiopyle. Derelict boxcar in river below on left is from wreck occurring more than 20 years ago.

2:03 (0:14) Cross Indian Creek spanned by small stone-arch bridge—one of few remaining. Summer youth camp, just across river on left, is located in heart of state game lands. Abandoned rail right-of-way across river is now a popular hiking trail.

2:15 (0:00) Arrive Connellsville.

CONNELLSVILLE, PA - In the late 1700s, vast coal deposits were discovered in the immediate area, but were thought to have no value because of their soft and crumbly character. However, it was later discovered that by roasting this coal in ordinary "beehive" coke ovens for two or three days, it made outstanding metallurgical fuel and became known as the famous pearl-grey Connellsville Coke. Always a railroad town (it is still a division point with a large classification yard), during World War II the "Connellsville Canteen," consisting of 800 women volunteers, served meals to more than 600,000 servicemen that came through on troop trains in a two-year period!

0:00 (0:59) Depart Connellsville, and in a moment, cross under a towering railroad trestle that also spans river on left.

0:06 (0:53) Forsaken structures just to left are ghostly remains of whiskey distillery.

0:23 (0:36) Enormous black slag heaps are first evidence that Pittsburgh is near.

0:24 (0:35) Pass far beneath another railroad bridge.

0:28 (0:31) Pass under Interstate 70.

122

0:54 (0:05) Enter heavily populated suburbs of Pittsburgh as train can't make up its mind as to which side of Youghiogheny River it should follow.

0:59 (0:00) Arrive McKeesport.

 MCKEESPORT, PA - This is a heavily industrialized suburb of Pittsburgh, where the Youghiogheny flows into the Monongahela River.

0:00 (0:30) Depart McKeesport and pass series of impressive steel mills, mostly belonging to industrial giant U.S. Steel.

0:11 (0:19) Skyline, featuring many new high rises, is discernible forward to left.

0:13 (0:17) University of Pittsburgh's Cathedral of Learning soars majestically skyward on hill to left. Carnegie Mellon University is on right. Enter Schenley Tunnel as train leaves Oakland and enters Pittsburgh.

0:30 (0:00) Arrive Pittsburgh.

PITTSBURGH, PA - See page 114.

For route between Pittsburgh and Chicago, see that portion of Broadway Ltd. log, page 115.

Chicago

New York

Cincinnati

Washington, DC

Cardinal

The Cardinal makes a thrice-weekly trek between New York City and Chicago by way of Charleston, WV, Cincinnati and Indianapolis. With stops at several small towns, it is perhaps the last of America's full-service locals.

The route is a particular treat through West Virginia's spectacular New River Gorge. In the fall, the color is sublime. Eastbound passengers can also view much of the Ohio River scenes during daylight hours across northern Kentucky. During the summer months on Friday and Sundays, interpretive guides ride a portion of the route and explain points of interest between Charleston, WV and White Sulphur Springs.

Westbound Schedule (Condensed)
New York, NY - Early Morning Departure (Sunday, Tuesday, Friday)
Washington, DC - Early Afternoon
Charleston, WV - Late Evening
Cincinnati, OH - Middle of the Night
Indianapolis, IN - Early Morning
Chicago, IL - Midmorning Arrival (Monday, Wednesday, Saturday)

Eastbound Schedule (Condensed)
Chicago, IL - Early Evening Departure (Tuesday, Thursday, Saturday)
Indianapolis, IN - Late Evening
Cincinnati, OH - Middle of the Night
Charleston, WV - Midmorning
Washington, DC - Early Evening
New York, NY - Late Evening Arrival (Wednesday, Friday, Sunday)

Frequency - Tri-weekly, see above.
Seating - Heritage Fleet coaches.

Dining - Complete meal and beverage service, as well as lounge service.
Sleeping - Roomettes and bedrooms and slumbercoach with single and double rooms.
Baggage - Checked baggage handled at most larger cities.
Reservations - All-reserved train.
Length of Trip - 1,149 miles in 26½ hours.

Route Log

For route between New York and Washington, see that portion of the Northeast Corridor log, page 31.

 WASHINGTON, DC - See page 39.

0:00 (0:17) Depart Washington southbound through regions whose roots trace back to earliest periods of American history.

0:02 (0:15) Emerge from tunnel after passing under Mall. Glimpses of Capitol and oldest Smithsonian structure ("The Castle") can be caught through various federal buildings on right.

0:07 (0:10) Perhaps Washington's most charming monument, Monticello-shaped Jefferson Memorial, resides among cherry trees of Tidal Basin on right.

0:09 (0:08) Cross Potomac River paralleling 14th Street bridge. Washington National Airport is directly downstream to left. Back on right, Washington Monument, world's tallest masonry structure at 555.5 feet, punctuates horizon. Capitol's dome can still be seen toward rear on left.

0:10 (0:07) The Pentagon, headquarters for America's military establishment, is off to right, now mostly hidden by newer buildings.

0:12 (0:05) Glass high rises of Crystal City flaunt their starkness on right. Expansive RF&P rail yards are on left.

0:17 (0:00) Arrive Alexandria.

ALEXANDRIA, VA - This historic Washington suburb sits six miles south of the nation's capital, along the west bank of the Potomac River. Most noted for its outstanding examples of early-American architecture, the Alexandria area is also replete with numerous national landmarks. Mount Vernon, beloved home and estate of George Washington from 1754 until his death in 1799, is just a few miles down the Potomac.

0:00 (0:32) Depart Alexandria.

0:01 (0:29) George Washington National Masonic Memorial, with museum of Washington memorabilia, dominates skyline on right. Metro subway station on left provides commuters with quick, easy access to downtown Washington.

0:32 (0:00) Arrive Manassas.

MANASSAS, VA - This was the site of intense fighting during the Civil War. The town was burned several times by both Yankees and Confederates, generally in an effort to cut supply lines to fighting troops. The two Battles of Manassas (Bull Run) were fought in July of 1861 and August of 1862 just northeast of town, and are now commemorated by the 5,000-acre Manassas National Battlefield Park. The quaint rail station was built circa 1915.

0:00 (0:32) Depart Manassas.

0:32 (0:00) Arrive Culpeper.

CULPEPER, VA - The Culpeper Minute Men were the very first to respond in 1775 to Patrick Henry's call-to-arms. Then, during the Civil War, the area saw heavy fighting and the town served as headquarters for both sides. George Washington described this area as a "high and pleasant situation" when he surveyed the county, and the town still prides itself on its fresh water supply and clean air.

Flour milling, furniture, wire rope and automotive parts are now important products. History buffs should enjoy the Culpeper Cavalry Museum.

0:00 (1:00) Depart Culpeper.

1:00 (0:00) Arrive Charlottesville.

CHARLOTTESVILLE, VA - "These mountains are the Eden of the United States." Thomas Jefferson wrote these flattering words in describing the area in and around Charlottesville. As the county seat of Albemarle, the town was a veritable treasure trove of talent and wisdom—Jefferson, James Madison and James Monroe were all part of the local scene. In more recent times, William Faulkner, Lady Astor and William McGuffey all called Albemarle County their home during some point in their lives.

Of particular interest to visitors are Jefferson's beautiful and cleverly designed home (Monticello) and the estate of James Monroe (Ash Lawn). These two men were close friends, and Jefferson personally selected the Monroe house site, donating his own gardeners to help start orchards at Ash Lawn. Jefferson also founded the University of Virginia which is located here and designed many of its original structures.

0:00 (0:58) Depart Charlottesville. Campus of University of Virginia will be on right.

0:05 (0:56) Off to right, ridge of mountains holds beautiful Shenandoah National Park and spectacular Skyline Drive, extending northward from Waynesboro.

0:35 (0:23) Pastoral valley, serene and green, makes great viewing off to left as we ascend renowned Blue Ridge Mountains. Cardinal ducks into tunnel for full minute before regaining daylight.

0:58 (0:00) Arrive Staunton.

STAUNTON, VA - Located in Augusta County which, when formed in 1738, extended as far as the Mississippi and the Great Lakes, Staunton is distinguished by being the birthplace of both Woodrow Wilson and the McCormick reaper. The town is also recognized as having the largest remaining collection of 19th-century architecture in Virginia. Scenery is abundant, and just east of here is the junction of two of the nation's more

Cardinal – New River Gorge, West Virginia

scenic roadways: Skyline Drive and Blue Ridge Parkway.

The unique Museum of American Frontier Culture, opened in 1988, consists of four different farms, each representing major cultures who settled the American frontier.

0:00 (1:10) Depart Staunton.

0:17 (0:53) Elliott Knob rises to elevation of 4,458 feet above sea level, back to right.

0:34 (0:36) Through two short tunnels; there will be many more as we progress westward and into West Virginia mountains.

1:06 (0:04) Extensive CSX rail yards begin on approach to Clifton Forge.

126

1:10 (0:00) Arrive Clifton Forge.

CLIFTON FORGE, VA - This is the very heart of western Virginia's vacationland. The surrounding area has such points of interest as: Humpback Bridge, a covered bridge of unusual architecture; Fort Young, built during the French and Indian War; Falling Spring, a 200-foot waterfall; and the Allegheny Central Railroad, Virginia's only "scenic" railroad.

0:00 (0:49) Depart Clifton Forge and continue through CSX yards.

0:10 (0:39) Pretty Covington, below to right, has idyllic setting beneath mountain backdrop.

0:25 (0:24) Picturesque covered bridge stretches across small stream below on left.

0:38 (0:11) Steep, deep valley to left now provides truly breathtaking view.

0:49 (0:00) Arrive White Sulphur Springs.

WHITE SULPHUR SPRINGS, WV - This is home to one of the world's renowned spas, Greenbriar Resort. The station is at the very doorstep of this elegant playground; note the entrance just across the road to the right of train.

0:00 (1:01) Depart White Sulphur Springs.

0:31 (0:30) Through flag stop of Alderson where gaggle of two-story, light-brick buildings enclosed by barbed wire, to left above, is federal prison for women.

0:49 (0:13) Stream that has been following on right is Greenbriar River.

0:59 (0:03) At juncture of two streams, join New River and start through what is probably highlight of trip—dramatic New River Gorge. Large dam upstream, about a quarter of a mile to left, retains enormous Bluestone Lake.

1:01 (0:00) Arrive Hinton where rambling, decrepit brick station, on right, greets Cardinal.

HINTON, WV - This small town is in the shadow of Bluestone Lake, a very popular West Virginia recreational area. Historically a railroad town, Hinton now boasts a population of 4,600 and is the county seat.

0:00 (0:30) Depart Hinton.

0:04 (0:26) Bass Lake, a typical early-day mountain resort village, composed mostly of small cabins, is in trees on right.

0:08 (0:22) Small but dazzling falls momentarily interrupt river on left.

0:11 (0:19) New I-64 bridge crosses above.

0:30 (0:00) Arrive Prince.

 PRINCE, WV - This small mountain community rests at the east end of the New River Gorge.

0:00 (1:04) As we depart Prince, New River will become increasingly rock-strewn and the scenery more spectacular.

Paradoxically, the New River, formed during the Mesozoic Period, is one of the oldest streams in the world. The gorge it has created has its own ecosystem, supporting over a thousand species of plants and more than 150 species of birds. And during a time now past, as many as 14 passenger trains a day thundered along its tracks.

0:15 (0:50) Through community of Thurmond, another Cardinal flag stop.

0:35 (0:30) Look forward—above and to left.

The magnificent New River Gorge Bridge spans the entire valley carrying auto traffic from one rim to the other, some 876 feet above the river! The main span is 1,700 feet long making it the world's longest steel arch span. It is the nation's second highest bridge (only Colorado's Royal Gorge Bridge is higher), and it weighs a total of 88 million pounds.

On "Bridge Day," the second Saturday in October, hundreds of thrill-seekers gather here to go over the railing and parachute to the gorge floor below. This is the only day jumping from the span is legal. The bridge accounts for most of such BASE jumps in the U.S.

0:52 (0:13) Cascading waterfalls of merging stream, on right, are unusual in that they seem to be flowing away from river.

1:04 (0:00) Arrive Montgomery.

MONTGOMERY, WV - This stop is home to West Virginia Institute of Technology. School stretches out along left side of tracks, readily visible from station.

0:00 (0:30) Depart Montgomery.

0:04 (0:26) London hydroelectric plant and dam are on right.

0:09 (0:21) Another electricity producer,

Kanawha Power Plant, is on shores of Kanawha River at right.

0:10 (0:20) Rusty flotilla of ancient barges reposes on far shore of river.

0:28 (0:02) As we enter Charleston, state government office complex, with gold-domed capitol building as centerpiece, is off to right.

0:30 (0:00) Arrive Charleston, with downtown just across river to right. Far shore, beautifully landscaped, sets off striking skyline.

 CHARLESTON, WV - The Kanawha River cuts deeply through the Appalachians at this point, carving out a steep valley setting for Charleston, the state's capital. The capitol building is generally considered to be the most beautiful in the nation, featuring a 300-foot dome supported by Roman porticos and colonnades. Designed by internationally recognized architect Cass Gilbert, the capitol is open for tours enabling visitors to see its ornate rotunda and elegant legislative chambers. Adjacent to the capitol is the newly built Science and Cultural Center. Also of interest is Sunrise, the name given to two grand mansions situated on 16 landscaped acres atop a hill overlooking the city. These mansions now house a children's museum and an art gallery. Several fine glass factories in this area are special attractions.

0:00 (0:58) Depart Charleston and proceed through a region heavily concentrated with chemical plants and other industrial operations.

0:10 (0:48) This is Institute. Sprawling facility, looking somewhat like a refinery with myriad pipes and towers, is Union Carbide's methyl isocyanate plant—the only location where this chemical is manufactured in the United States. Similar facility in Bhopal, India, in December 1984, created the world's worst industrial accident when a deadly gas leak killed over 2,500 persons.

0:58 (0:00) Arrive Huntington's modern, white-brick station on left.

HUNTINGTON, WV - Situated on the banks of the Ohio River, where West Virginia, Ohio and Kentucky all converge, Huntington has long been an important railroading town. Today, visitors can experience a bit of earlier times by visiting Heritage Village which is in a restored B&O rail yard. Only a few miles north of here, where the Kanawha flows into the Ohio River, is the site of the first battle of the American Revolution—the Battle of Point Pleasant.

0:00 (0:18) Depart Huntington; downtown area is off to right.

0:13 (0:05) Trundle across Big Sandy River Bridge and enter Kentucky.

0:18 (0:00) Arrive Catlettsburg.

CATLETTSBURG, KY - This stop also serves Kenova, WV and Ashland, KY.

0:00 (1:00) Depart Catlettsburg.

From here to Cincinnati, The Cardinal follows along the scenic Kentucky shoreline of the Ohio River. Today, the Ohio is still heavily utilized as a means of transportation, with tugs and barges continually plying this stretch of the river. It's the numerous dams and locks, easily visible from the train, that make this waterway navigable. Industrial scenes, such as electric power plants, dot the shores; and one can frequently spot stately homes on the Ohio bluffs across the river. All of these combine to make this one of the more enjoyable segments of "training" in the U.S. Unfortunately, westbound passengers normally miss this segment because of darkness.

0:08 (0:52) Twin highway bridges span Ohio on right. On left is Ashland, seventh largest city in Kentucky. Note one home, apparently sitting above all, on forested ridge behind city. Both steel production and oil refining are important industries here. Charcoal furnaces dating back to 1800s can still be found nearby.

0:12 (0:48) Pass by two monstrous, rust-bathed Armco steel mills on immediate right.

0:16 (0:38) Grind to an unadvertised stop for fuel and water in midst of huge CSX rail yards at Russel. This "recharging" takes about eight minutes or so.

0:44 (0:12) Off to right is Greenup Dam and Lock. Portion of lock is visible, just this side of river.

Nineteen navigational locks dot the Ohio River between Pittsburgh, PA and Cairo, IL, with the Greenup Lock being number nine upstream. Built in 1959 by the Army

128

Corps of Engineers, it is 340 miles below Pittsburgh and 641 miles above Cairo. Port of Huntington, which we passed through earlier, generates more tonnage (mostly coal) than any other inland waterport in the nation—18 million tons annually.

0:57 (0:00) Arrive South Portsmouth.

 SOUTH PORTSMOUTH, KY - This is a stop for Portsmouth, Ohio just across the river.

0:00 (0:49) Depart South Portsmouth.

0:42 (0:07) Large conveyor system travels over train and down to river where quarried material is then loaded onto river vessels.

0:47 (0:02) Impressive suspension bridge, on right, carries Highway U.S. 62, one of few bridges that link Kentucky with Ohio.

0:49 (0:00) Arrive at Maysville's very attractive small station.

MAYSVILLE, KY - This charming pioneer river gateway was first settled in 1784. Fifteen French-style houses from the 1800s are nicely maintained in an area called "Little New Orleans," while several other colorful frame houses can be seen on the hillside above on the left. The world's second largest loose-leaf tobacco market features burley auctions December through February.

0:00 (1:19) Depart Maysville. Back on right, excellent view is afforded of coal-fired power plant, sizeable enough to require four stacks. Just to south, between here and Lexington, lies thorough-bred heaven—Kentucky's lush bluegrass country.

0:25 (0:54) Captain Anthony Meldahl Dam with its shipping locks creates brief pause in river's westward flow.

0:29 (0:50) Train literally passes through operating limestone quarry.

0:31 (0:48) Telltale cooling tower of nuclear power plant rises dramatically from opposite shoreline. This is Wm. H. Zimmer Nuclear Power Station which, when and if ever completed, would provide 810 megawatts of power to region. Initially estimated to cost $240 million, actual costs have exceeded $1.6 billion. Total completion cost could be $3 billion.

0:42 (0:37) Train traverses flood plain where houses on right rest on stilts to avoid river's potential overflow.

0:44 (0:35) Magnificent homes line bluffs across river.

0:49 (0:30) Pass beneath Interstate 275 which spans river on right.

1:04 (0:15) Cross Licking River where Cincinnati's skyline is now visible in distance on right. Saucer-like Riverfront Stadium, home of football's Bengals and baseball's Reds, rests imposingly on far shore.

1:06 (0:13) Leave Covington, Kentucky and enter Cincinnati, Ohio as we cross Ohio River. Large bridge to right is aptly named Suspension Bridge, while Brent Spence Bridge, carrying interstates 75 and 71, is off to left. Fine view of stadium and city's skyline, to right, is afforded from center of river. Lesser structure beyond stadium is Coliseum. Delta Queen riverboat is frequently berthed just below Coliseum.

1:12 (0:07) Now, close your eyes while train creeps through what must be one of world's longest scrap heaps.

1:19 (0:00) Arrive at Cincinnati's surprisingly small station, located about a mile from downtown. (Eastbound passengers to Washington, DC, note that best viewing will be on left side of train.)

CINCINNATI, OH - Cincinnati is one of America's most attractively situated midwestern cities. Located in the Ohio River Valley just across from northern Kentucky, its business and industrial areas occupy separate terraces above the river, while these, in turn, are dominated by seven residential-studded hills forming a sweeping arc around the downtown area.

The city's beginning can be traced to its convenient river location, and early days saw a busy river trade carried on by picturesque paddle-wheeler riverboats plying the Ohio. Early-day Cincinnati was marked by a small town appearance with its large population being strung out along the shores of the river; it was perhaps this atmosphere that caused many notables to refer to the city as one of the most appealing in America.

Among those attracted by its charm was Alphonso Taft who moved here from Connecticut in 1883. He raised a family which included a son, William Howard Taft, who would become the nation's twenty-seventh president.

Amtrak Station, 1901 River Road, is a suburban-type station, about 1½ miles from downtown. The station has storage lockers, luggage carts and food and beverage vending machines. Free adjacent parking (unattended). Nearest pay-parking is downtown.

For arrival and departure information, call 921-4172. For reservations and other information, call 579-8506. Waiting room and ticket window hours are 9:30 am to 5 pm, Monday through Friday, and 11 pm to 6:30 am Tuesday through Sunday.

There has been much talk about Amtrak moving back downtown into the splendid old Union Terminal. Such a move would greatly improve Amtrak's presence in Cincinnati.

Cab stand at the station; Yellow Cab, 241-2106. Nearest **local bus** stop (for downtown) is three blocks from the station on the 8th Street Viaduct (station personnel do not recommend walking to the bus stop, particularly at night). **Greyhound,** (512) 352-6000. **Greater Cincinnati Airport** is approximately 11 miles southwest of the rail station.

Visitor Information Center at 5th and Vine at Fountain Square. Write Cincinnati Convention and Visitors Bureau, 300 W. 6th St. (at Plum Street), 45202. Call (513) 621-2142.

Terrace Hilton, 15 W. 6th St., 45202; (513) 381-4000. One-and-one-half miles from the station. $102.

-**Holiday Inn Queens Gate,** 800 West 8th Street (at Linn), 45203; (513) 241-8660. Five blocks from the station. $69.

Downtown attractions include: **Fountain Square,** with an 1871 bronze statue purchased in Munich, Germany; **Fourth Street Art Colony,** at Fourth and Elm, with galleries and shops; **Public Landing,** near the Riverfront Stadium, which is the home port for the Delta Queen and Mississippi Queen; **Carew Tower Observation Deck,** Fifth and Vine, offers a 48-story-high view of the city; and the **Fire Department Historical Museum,** 311 W. Court St., has both modern and vintage fire equipment on display.

The **William Howard Taft Historic Site,** 2038 Auburn Ave., was the boyhood home of William Howard Taft.

0:00 (1:05) Depart Cincinnati, retracing our route backward through same scrap yard and out over middle of river, then proceed northward through industrial areas of city, including plants of Carthage Mills, Kroger and Mosier Company.
0:39 (0:26) Sign on left welcoming us to Wyoming refers to town—not state.
0:48 (0:17) Under Interstate 275.
1:05 (0:00) Arrive at Hamilton's rather ancient brick station.

HAMILTON, OH - One of southern Ohio's larger cities, Hamilton is located on the northern fringes of Cincinnati.
0:00 (2:30) Depart Hamilton.
2:30 (0:00) Arrive Indianapolis, where Union Station has been made focal point of major downtown development.

INDIANAPOLIS, IN - It was in 1820 that Indianapolis was chosen to be the Indiana capital, principally because of its location as the geographic center of the state. Much like Washington, DC, the layout of the city was made after deciding to make it a governmental home using a wheel and spoke design for the streets. At the very hub of the city is Monument Circle with the Soldiers and Sailors Monument serving as an axle.

But Indianapolis' claim to national fame has to be The Indianapolis 500—that dazzling spectacle of color, motion and sound that takes place every Memorial Day. The city is jammed with people for this renowned event, including the two weeks preceding. If you are planning to attend the big race, or any of the other festivities, make reservations and be sure to make them early.

Union Station, 350 South Illinois, P.O. Box 1485, 46225. A beautifully restored Romanesque-Revival structure, America's oldest Union railway depot (1888), now has over 100 shops, restaurants, nightspots—and a Holiday Inn (without direct access from the station) where guests can stay in actual Pullmans.

For arrival and departure information, call 263-0550. For reservations and other information call 632-1905.

Cabs are usually available at train times; Yellow Cab, 637-5421. **Greyhound and Southeastern Trailways** have a combined terminal a half mile from the station; 635-4501. **City buses** at the station, 635-3344. Hertz has a **rental car** location in the Hyatt Regency, about five blocks from the station, 634-6464. **Weir Cook Airport** is approximately five miles from the station.

Indianapolis Convention & Visitors Association, One Hoosier Dome, 46225; (317) 639-4282.

Holiday Inn Union Station, 123 W. Louisiana; (317) 631-2221 or 800-465-4329. Adjacent to the station. $96. (Pullman rooms, $125.)

-**Ramada Inn,** 501 W. Washington (at West), 46204; (317) 635-4443. Seven blocks from the station. $85.

Union Station, with its shops and restaurants, has become an attraction itself. The new **Indianapolis Zoo** is located on the west edge of downtown in White River State Park.

Farther out, the **Speedway,** with its 2½-mile oval and museum, can be visited throughout the year.

0:00 (0:54) Depart historic Union Station. Immediately, bulbous Hoosier Dome fills our windows to right. Beyond that modern structure, downtown Indianapolis, with attractive capitol as its centerpiece, comes into view.

0:20 (0:35) Pass through Brownsburg and enter more rural surroundings.

0:24 (0:30) Roll through Pittsboro. A few minutes later, I-74 comes into view on our right, just before Cardinal rolls through Raintown.

0:33 (0:21) I-74 stays visible for several miles as we pass through Lizton, Jamestown and New Ross in midst of typical Indiana flatlands.

0:54 (0:00) Curve sharply to right at Conrail's Ames Tower, now just a modern shack, as train transfers off Conrail onto Seaboard System (former Louisville & Nashville, former Monon Railroad) tracks before we arrive at Crawfordsville.

CRAWFORDSVILLE, IN - A small glass shack serves as the Amtrak station here, next to a red-brick depot bearing the Seaboard System logo.

Wabash College, founded in 1832, is located here.

0:00 (0:31) Depart Crawfordsville. Cross high above Cherry Creek as it winds its way prettily through woods; then slide under I-74.

0:10 (0:21) Roll through Cherry Grove, then under U.S. 231 and through village of Linden, where we cross Norfolk & Western (N&W) tracks. To left, large grain elevator sports its own white center-cab switcher locomotive.

0:23 (0:08) Pass along a classically scenic stream, meandering through woods and valleys to our left. Soon, cross stream in one of prettiest areas of journey.

0:31 (0:00) At Lafayette, move slowly under stone bridge and through backyards of homes almost close enough to touch. Tippecanoe County Courthouse, a beautifully ornate-domed building, painted white with brown trim, comes into view as our tracks run down center of Fifth Street (as they have since early Monon days). We pull to a stop squarely in middle of Fifth Street at one of Amtrak's unique stations: the Potpourri Gift Shop. (Plans have been made to re-route trains to avoid this down-the-street course by moving over west two blocks.)

LAFAYETTE, IN - Purdue University is located here. Each fall more than 4,500 members of 18th-century reenactment groups—military units, traders, crafts people and merchants, as well as voyageurs and most of the midwest's fife and drum corps—gather for two days along the Wabash River southwest of here at Fort Ouiatenon. This is known as the Feast of the Hunters' Moon, commemorating the French and Indian gatherings of the 1700s, when the voyageurs arrived from Canada in their 40-foot canoes filled with goods to trade. More than 50,000 spectators annually witness the event.

0:00 (1:32) Depart the "station," passing on left old depot still bearing its Monon Route insignia.

0:03 (1:29) Stop briefly in Seaboard Yards to change train crews. Famous Lafayette Shops are above us on hill to right.

In the 1888 football game between Wabash College and Purdue University, Wabash, after seeing the immense size of some of their opponents, accused Purdue of adding boilermakers from the Monon Shops to their team. The name stuck. Today, Purdue teams are still called the Boilermakers.

0:07 (1:25) Roll under U.S. 52, then cross broad Wabash River a couple minutes later. Shortly thereafter, pass under I-65, main Indianapolis-Chicago freeway.

0:11 (1:21) Sign, on left, marks Tippecanoe Battlefield State Memorial, where General William Henry Harrison defeated Indians led by Prophet, brother of Tecumseh. Then pass through town of Battle Ground, and leave Wabash River Valley for flat Indiana farmland which we'll trundle across almost entire way to Chicago.

0:17 (1:15) Pass through Brookston, a pretty tree-lined town, then travel due North through Chalmers.

0:26 (1:06) At Reynolds cross tracks of old TP&W—Toledo, Peoria & Western—now merged into the Santa Fe.

0:31 (1:01) Sign on left, picturing a semi-trailer truck, welcomes us to "Monon, a community built by the transportation industry and Home of the Monon Trailer." It doesn't mention the old Monon Railroad.

0:35 (0:57) Vulcan Materials Company quarry opens rocky ground to left.

Gain one hour as train passes from Eastern to Central Time. Set your watch back (forward if eastbound) one hour.

0:40 (0:52) Soon, light-blue Monon water tower comes into view and train curves sharply left past red-brick Monon depot on our right. Between train and northbound tracks to Michigan City, IN sits an old Monon caboose.

0:52 (0:40) Roll through Pleasant Ridge, then through Rensselaer; a stop for The Hoosier State but not The Cardinal. St. Joseph College is here.

1:02 (0:30) Pass through town of Fair Oaks before ducking again under I-65.

1:12 (0:20) Cross Kankakee River into Shelby. A few minutes later, roll through Lowell and then Creston.

1:22 (0:10) To our left we see Cedar Lake, and then through city of same name.

1:32 (0:00) After passing through St. John and under U.S. 41, enter residential tree-lined outskirts of Dyer, where a child's little treehouse sits in yard before train's arrival at station.

DYER, IN - Another glass-shack station, functional but without aesthetic value, serves southeastern suburbs here.

0:00 (0:51) Depart Dyer. Minutes later, approach a large rail junction where train curves left off Seaboard tracks onto Conrail. Cross I-80/94.

0:20 (0:25) In next few minutes, clatter across several important rail junctions. At Chippewa Avenue, intersect South Shore with its catenary—overhead wire, to power its electric locomotives.

0:30 (0:21) On right, Eggers Woods Forest Preserve seems out of place in industrial jungle, but nice.

0:35 (0:16) Curve left and roll under Chicago Skyway where we join Conrail tracks from the right. We are approximately five minutes northwest of Amtrak's Hammond-Whiting, IN station.

For route description from here to Chicago, see that portion of Lake Shore Ltd. log, page 73.

Toronto
Lansing
Chicago

International

As its name implies, The International travels in two countries, providing direct passage between Toronto and Chicago. Amtrak and VIA Rail Canada run this train as a joint venture with personnel changes at the border. The path heads west out of Toronto, gliding across southeastern Ontario's flat farmscapes until it crosses into Michigan at Port Huron. From there, it makes a rainbow descent across Michigan to the top of Lake Michigan before proceeding into Chicago.

The International has been a popular way for citizens of Toronto to conveniently visit Chicago, and for Chicagoans to take in Canada's second largest city. The train is heavily used by Michigan State University students, particularly at school break periods, traveling to and from Lansing.

Westbound Schedule (Condensed)*
Toronto, Ont. - Early Morning Departure
Port Huron, MI - Early Afternoon
East Lansing, MI - Midafternoon
Chicago, IL - Early Evening Arrival

Eastbound Schedule (Condensed)*
Chicago, IL - Midmorning Departure
East Lansing, MI - Midafternoon
Port Huron, MI - Late Afternoon
Toronto, Ont. - Late Evening Arrival

*Departures are later on Sundays.

Frequency - Daily.
Seating - LRC-1 coaches.
Dining - Tray meals, snacks and beverages.
Baggage - No checked baggage.
Reservations - Unreserved train.
Length of Trip - 491 miles in 10 hours.

Route Log

(Note: The International may be re-routed through Stratford between Toronto and London. That routing appears on page 322.)

 TORONTO, ONT. - See page 316.

0:00 (0:23) Depart Toronto's Union Station on CN trackage. In about 60 seconds, emerge from beneath terminal's canopy and CN Tower soars skyward directly in front of us on left.

0:02 (0:21) After passing CN Tower, $400-million SkyDome, on left, overshadows all else. This bulbous edifice, completed in 1989, was built to house baseball's Toronto Blue Jays, shops, restaurants and a 350-room hotel. On nicer days, roof can be shifted from a closed to an open position in 30 minutes to put 90% of its spectators in sunshine. While passing this structure, be sure to look up to see whimsical groupings of spectators protruding from building like modern-day gargoyles.

0:04 (0:19) Tops of brick buildings and sign on grassy knoll are all that can be seen of Historic Fort York Park on left. Park features restored British garrison from War of 1812.

0:06 (0:17) Elaborate facilities on left are annual home of Canadian Exhibition, Canadian equivalent of American state fairs.

0:07 (0:16) Lake Ontario comes into clear view off to left. Amphitheater poised on lake's edge is handsome attraction of Ontario Place—a cultural, recreational and entertainment complex built atop three man-made islands.

0:08 (0:15) Note High Park and lake on right and then cross Humber River and marshes as train traces alongside Highway 2 and curls up and around Humber Bay on left. Fine view of Toronto's skyline is seen back to right.

0:09 (0:14) Cross Mimico Creek which drains into Lake Ontario, as do all other streams of this region.

0:10 (0:13) Through rail yards where, on left, VIA Rail has shops and various equipment standing ready for use. Sleek-looking yellow trains are LRCs (light, rapid, comfortable, with tilting capabilities for rounding curves at high speeds) and newer LRC-1s. "GO Trains" (Government of Ontario) are green and white, double-decked equipment parked on right awaiting call for Toronto commuter service and which can be seen along our route until International's first stop, Oakville.

0:12 (0:11) Cross Etobicoke Creek.

0:15 (0:08) At Port Credit, cross Credit River.

0:20 (0:02) On right, sprawling Ontario Ford truck plant actually operates private trains for touring its facilities.

0:22 (0:01) Observation car of former Florida East Coast Railway has undoubtedly been rescued by rail buff and stands on siding at left.

0:23 (0:00) Arrive Oakville's very attractive, modernistic station.

OAKVILLE, ONT. - In the mid-19th century, a host of city-dwellers chose this scenic locale as the site of their summer homes. Most of these lavish retreats have been immaculately preserved, and today are the focal point of a well-documented walking tour. Another interesting attraction is the Gairlock Gardens Gallery, maintained in a 1920s mansion along the lake. Its wild bird sanctuary is a further highlight.

For golfing enthusiasts, the Glen Abbey links, designed by Jack Nicklaus, is of true championship caliber. Its clubhouse was once a monastery, and now is home to the Canadian Golf Hall of Fame.

0:00 (0:10) Depart Oakville and immediately sail high over Sixteen Mile Creek. Original settlement of Oakville was started near the mouth of this local landmark, sometimes called Oakville Creek.

0:04 (0:06) Industrial area surrounding Oakville bears profusion of refineries and other petroleum-related operations.

0:05 (0:05) Cross Bronte Creek at Bronte.

0:10 (0:00) Arrive Burlington West. (East-bound International does not stop here.)

BURLINGTON WEST, ONT. - Here, The International stops for the metropolitan area of Burlington, primarily a lakefront residential community.

0:00 (0:11) Depart Burlington West.

0:03 (0:09) On left, brick-domed structure is Halton Ceramics, Ltd.

0:05 (0:07) At Bay View, quick but startling view of Hamilton Harbour is offered with its profusion of both commercial and pleasure boats. Momentarily, note tracks that cut off to left; these carry The Maple Leaf to Niagara Falls and ultimately to New York City.

0:13 (0:00) Arrive Dundas, with town proper lying far below grade on left. (Eastbound International does not stop here.)

DUNDAS, ONT. - This is a suburb of Hamilton, Canada's steel capital and third largest port. Tours of Hamilton's steel mills are major attractions. Here, too, at Hamilton, is the magnificent Dundurn Castle with splendid furnishings and appointments reflecting the opulent lifestyle of its mid-19th century inhabitants.

0:00 (0:18) Depart Dundas.

0:02 (0:17) Note fairways of Dundas' Golf Course below on left.

0:07 (0:12) Countryside begins to appear increasingly agricultural as fields of corn, wheat and other crops become more in evidence.

0:16 (0:03) Tall, spindly structure off to left is Bell communications tower.

0:17 (0:02) On eastern edge of Brantford, huge building complex, immediately left of tracks, is former Massey Ferguson farm equipment plant which ceased operations in 1980s. Brantford has been considered "Combine Capital of Canada" and factory's closure was severe blow to city.

0:19 (0:00) Arriving Brantford, glimpses of downtown and town hall's tower can be had to left. Fine old station on the left, a brick beauty adorned with a stately square tower, is further enhanced by a semaphore at trackside. Station dates back to 1904.

BRANTFORD, ONT. - The city was named for the Indian chief Joseph Brandt who brought his group known as Six Nations Indians from Upper New York State to this site.

This is where Alexander Graham Bell invented the telephone and "placed" the first long distance call which was to Paris, Ontario, a distance of ten miles. Brantford is now constructing a museum which will display some of the world's most sophisticated telecommunications equipment, including a NORAD control system, and should open in 1991.

0:00 (0:24) Depart Brantford.

0:01 (0:23) Fine old three-story brick home sports elegant white gingerbread trim on right. Home and grounds known as Glenhurst Gardens are on left.

0:06 (0:18) Trestle carries International high over Grand River at Paris where three attractive churches predominate cityscape. After crossing river, note wonderful old stone mansion, now converted to retirement facility, on right.

0:24 (0:00) Arrive Woodstock where grey, almost Victorian in style, 1853 station greets us on left. (Eastbound International does not stop here.)

WOODSTOCK, ONT. - This charming, well-preserved town, with many residences dating to the mid-1800s, was named for Woodstock in Oxfordshire, England in honor of the Duke of Marlborough whose estate was near there.

0:00 (0:10) Depart Woodstock.

0:03 (0:07) At milepost 52, countryside takes on a pastoral ambience as we course through a delightful valley, complete with meandering brook on left and especially attractive homes on hillside at right.

0:07 (0:03) Huge excavation on left is result of extensive quarrying operations. Kilns and other paraphernalia are part of operation.

0:10 (0:00) Arrive Ingersoll. (Eastbound International does not stop here.)

INGERSOLL, ONT. - This was the birthplace of Canada's cheese industry, with the first factory built in 1864, and still is famous for the manufacture of this dairy product. There is a Cheese Factory Museum where antique cheese-making tools are on display, and a nine-day wine and cheese festival in mid-September.

0:00 (0:18) Depart Ingersoll.

0:02 (0:16) Be sure to note palatial Landfair Stables horse farm, just to right, with its colonial-style home, handsome landscaping and neatly painted fences and outbuildings.

0:07 (0:11) Focal point of Dorchester is ornate single-spired church on left at milepost 68.

0:13 (0:03) Pass through sprawling CN rail yards with shops on left as we enter London's eastern suburbs.

0:18 (0:00) Arrive at London's very busy VIA station, where two major VIA routes intersect and connections can be made for Windsor to the southwest and Stratford to the northeast.

LONDON, ONT. - Located on the River Thames, many of London's streets are named for those of its English namesake. This is one of southeastern Ontario's busier industrial centers. A large air show, featuring aircraft from five countries, is held here the first weekend in June.

0:00 (0:19) Departing London, many of town's earliest three- and four-story buildings, one block to right, are in vivid contrast with London's newer downtown.

0:02 (0:17) Cross Thames River.

0:03 (0:16) Cross Thames River one more time.

0:17 (0:02) Tobacco-curing kilns, those skinny red barns with multiple doors, dot fields on either side of tracks.

0:19 (0:00) Arrive Strathroy.

STRATHROY, ONT. - This community of 9,000 boasts a lovely Victorian mansion built in 1871, known as "Murray House." The home now houses the Strathroy Middlesex Museum with some rare pioneer artifacts.

0:00 (0:36) Depart Strathroy.

0:20 (0:16) Through small town of Wyoming, not named for the state, but an Indian word meaning "on the great plain."

0:31 (0:05) Entering Sarnia, industrial sights dominate, with numerous manufacturing and refinery complexes surrounding this seaport at the mouth of Lake Huron.

This is the customs checkpoint for the eastbound International heading into Canada.

0:36 (0:00) Arrive Sarnia.

SARNIA, ONT. - As you may have already inferred from the numerous refineries in evidence, this is Ontario's major oil-refining and petrochemical center. It is also a Canadian port-of-entry, where auto traffic is carried over the St. Claire River to and from Port Huron, MI by the Blue Water Bridge. Trains, however, will pass beneath the river.

0:00 (0:10) Depart Sarnia.

0:04 (0:02) We literally sink out of sight for about four minutes as train glides into opening of Grand Trunk's St. Claire Tunnel, built in 1886, passing beneath St. Claire River.

The St. Claire River connects Lake Huron (to the north) with Lake St. Claire (to the south) and is the artery for all shipping out of Lake Superior and Lake Huron heading for Detroit and other points east through the St. Lawrence Seaway. At midway through the tube we leave Canada and enter the United States. We haven't escaped customs, however; that detail takes place at our next stop, Port Huron. Customs forms handed out by the conductor earlier will be collected here. Although the stop can be quite perfunctory, waits up to an hour can occur.

0:10 (0:00) Arrive Port Huron.

PORT HURON, MI - This city of 34,000 has been a significant Great Lakes port and is home to the Fort Gratiot lighthouse, the oldest on the lakes.

This is also the eastern terminus of the Grand Trunk Western, and the boyhood home of Thomas Edison. Edison worked as a "news butcher" on the Grand Trunk, selling sandwiches and candy on the trains. This job was short-lived, however, when phosphorous he was experimenting with in the baggage car burst into flames and ignited the car. He also printed a paper on the train called the *Weekly Herald,* the first printed on a moving train.

0:00 (0:45) Having finished with U.S. customs procedures, depart Port Huron.

0:04 (0:41) Entering Grand Trunk Western's Tunnel Yard, old roundhouse stands on left.

0:30 (0:15) On left, in front of Champion assembly plant, rows of white Ford cabs

and chassis await transformation into motor homes.

0:45 (0:00) Arrive Lapeer.

 LAPEER, MI - This is a small agricultural community of 6,000.

0:00 (0:20) Depart Lapeer.

0:02 (0:18) Brick buildings behind chain link fence on right belong to Oakdale Center, a mental health institution.

0:11 (0:09) Landing strip, complete with assemblage of small planes, parallels tracks on left.

0:16 (0:04) AC Spark Plug off to right is easily identified by white and orange initials on silver standpipes.

0:30 (0:00) Arrive Flint.

FLINT, MI - Second only to Detroit in U.S. auto production, Flint produces Chevrolets, Buicks and GM car bodies. General Motors supplies 40% of Grand Trunk railroad's business. With a population of 160,000, Flint is the third largest city in Michigan.

0:00 (0:20) Depart Flint.

0:03 (0:17) GM truck plant on left produces Blazers and GM buses.

0:04 (0:16) Further back on left, grey buildings house another GM plant producing parts and truck assemblies, while hundreds of auto transport cars are parked on sidings awaiting new-vehicle shipments.

0:20 (0:00) Arrive at Durand's enormous grey stone 1905 depot, on left. Train stops on a major intersection of Grand Trunk.

DURAND, MI - This is the hub of the Grand Trunk's rail operations, and is also served by the Ann Arbor Railroad. Although no longer the railroad center of seventy years ago when residents could count an incredible 42 passenger trains, 22 mail trains and 78 freight trains per day, 75% of the Grand Trunk's carloadings still pass through Durand. A fine Railroad History Museum, three blocks from the depot, focuses on train crews, depots, famous train wrecks, track maintenance and workers.

0:00 (0:26) Depart Durand.

0:25 (0:03) High rises of Michigan State University come into view as we enter East Lansing. Stadium, one of college football's largest, is off to right. Now pass directly through campus.

0:28 (0:00) Arrive East Lansing where

unusual bell tower can be observed off to right.

EAST LANSING, MI - Adjacent to the capital city of Lansing, East Lansing is home to Michigan State University which is known for its research capabilities—and 44,000 students. The metropolitan area has a population of 250,000, and has origins dating back to the beginning of the century when R. E. Olds produced and sold one of the first automobiles.

0:00 (0:50) Depart East Lansing.

0:03 (0:43) Cross Grand River and glimpse State Capitol Building at right. Structure has a high rise center with an antenna-like pole on top.

0:06 (0:44) Snake through power plant and then past Oldsmobile plant on right.

0:07 (0:43) The broad Grand River, on left, provides recreational opportunities during the summer months, including water-skiing.

0:11 (0:39) Meijer grocery chain's huge automated facility covers several acres on right.

0:12 (0:38) Past large Delta Power Plant.

0:22 (0:28) Windmill fancier obviously lives in farmstead at right where three miniature wind pumps serve as lawn embellishments.

0:23 (0:27) Green and white piles in front of Owens- Illinois plant are made up of glass waiting to be recycled into bottles.

0:28 (0:22) In spring, watch for pails hanging from maple trees to collect syrup throughout this area.

0:35 (0:15) Cross Battle Creek, so named because of an Indian skirmish that took place on its banks in 1825.

0:37 (0:13) At left, built into hillside by tracks are long-abandoned brick ovens.

0:44 (0:04) Now enter Battle Creek through Grand Trunk Western's rail yards where derelict steam locomotive and two tenders can be spotted at left. Shops are grey buildings across yards to left. Then past five-story, red-brick Post cereal plant (next to new windowless addition).

0:50 (0:00) Arrive Battle Creek's ultra-modern, intermodal station on immediate right. Station features unusual seating and imaginative use of brick and glass. Both Greyhound and city buses share this facility with Amtrak.

This is the end of the Grand Trunk tracks. From here to Niles, we will follow Amtrak rails, then Conrail into Chicago.

BATTLE CREEK, MI - Literally built on the cereal industry, both Kellogg and Post have two enormous facilities here, the largest of their type anywhere.

0:00 (0:26) Depart Battle Creek, and pass Ralston Purina plant on left.

0:05 (0:21) Sprawling vacant complex on left was once operated by Clark Equipment Co., builders of materials handling machinery.

0:13 (0:13) Pilots (with lots of nerve) can land their small crafts on strip cut from forest on left.

0:20 (0:06) Motorists in need of domestic legal services might be persuaded to stop at lawyer's office with sign displaying scales of justice and "Divorce" written in bold print, on left.

0:25 (0:01) Cross Kalamazoo River as we enter city of same name. Note some streets are still paved with brick.

0:26 (0:00) Arrive Kalamazoo where elongated station on left greets passengers with bars on windows and an informative sign that welcomes passengers to Kalamazoo while announcing Chicago is 138 miles away and Detroit is 142.

KALAMAZOO, MI - The city with the funny name that everyone has heard of gets its name from the river we just crossed. Kalamazoo is an Indian word roughly translated as "where the water boils in the pot." This town of 80,000 has a diverse industry base, and is home to Western Michigan University with an enrollment of 19,000 students.

0:00 (0:42) Departing Kalamazoo, note fine collection of older homes with classic pillared front porches on left.

0:02 (0:40) Campus and stadium of aforementioned Western Michigan University are now on immediate left.

0:13 (0:29) Watch for vineyards on both sides of tracks. This is wine country.

0:16 (0:26) Besides wine, grapes are also made into juice and jellies. Note Welch plant on right which processes grapes grown in this area. Escaping steam makes plant easy to spot.

0:30 (0:12) Through Dowagiac where

steel furnaces were at one time produced. One of those factories is on right.

0:41 (0:01) Large factory of venerable Simplicity Pattern Co., world-wide suppliers of sewing patterns, is on left.

0:42 (0:00) Arrive Niles, with old Michigan Central depot and clock tower on right. This classic 1892 Romanesque station was restored in 1988, and has appeared in several movies, including *Continental Divide* and *Midnight Run.*

NILES, MI - This railroad and agricultural town of 13,000 is the last stop before leaving Michigan. The Indiana border is just five miles straight south.

0:00 (1:13) Depart Niles.

0:02 (1:11) Cross St. Joseph River which flows northwest and into Lake Michigan.

0:05 (1:08) Vineyards continue, intermixed with fruit orchards.

0:22 (0:51) Lake Michigan's waters come into view. A marina with hundreds of pleasure craft is at right as we near Grand Beach.

0:25 (0:48) Enter Indiana and leave Michigan.

Gain one hour as train passes from Eastern to Central Time. Set your watch back (forward if eastbound) one hour.

0:32 (0:41) Cross a lift bridge at Michigan City, with another marina at right.

0:44 (0:29) In small town of Porter, join route of Lake Shore Limited into Chicago.

0:50 (0:23) Midwest Steel Corporation facility appears on right.

0:55 (0:18) Tracks and catenary of legendary Chicago South Shore and South Bend run parallel to our Conrail right-of-way, off to left.

0:57 (0:13) Where Gary began, enormous U.S. Steel Gary Works stretch along tracks at right beyond rail yards.

1:07 (0:06) Inland Steel plants straddle tracks, Plant Number One on left and Plant Number Two on right. Then cross drawbridge spanning Indiana Harbor Canal that links Lake Michigan with Calumet River.

1:09 (0:04) Standard Oil Company of Indiana refinery creates apparatus jungle at left. Lake Michigan is now only 100 feet or so to right.

1:13 (0:00) Arrive Hammond-Whiting.

For route description from here to Chicago, see that portion of Lake Shore Ltd. log, page 73.

Detroit
Toledo
Chicago

Lake Cities

The Lake Cities is a 1980 extension of one of Amtrak's Chicago-Detroit trains to Toledo, OH, where it provides guaranteed connections with The Lake Shore Limited to and from points east, such as Cleveland, Albany, Boston and New York.

The Chicago-Detroit route, Amtrak's "Michigan Corridor," was once the pride of the Michigan Central. Its deterioration began under the New York Central, and became total under the bankrupt Penn Central. The State of Michigan and Amtrak have refurbished old and built new stations, and Conrail and Amtrak have rebuilt the track into a smooth and fast raceway again for the Detroit-Chicago trains.

Westbound Schedule (Condensed)
Toledo, OH - Midmorning Departure
Detroit, MI - Late Morning
Battle Creek, MI - Early Afternoon
Chicago, IL - Late Afternoon Arrival

Eastbound Schedule (Condensed)
Chicago, IL - Midafternoon Departure
Battle Creek, MI - Early Evening
Detroit, MI - Late Evening
Toledo, OH - Late Evening Arrival

Frequency - Daily.
Seating - Unreserved coach seats, usually Amfleet.
Food Service - Sandwiches, snacks, and beverages.
Baggage - Carry on. No checked baggage service available.
Length of Trip - 337 miles in 7½ hours.

Route Log

TOLEDO, OH - With a 35-mile-long harbor on Lake Erie, it is easy to understand why Michigan and Ohio both claimed this city in the early 19th century. It took presidential action by Andrew Jackson to finally settle the dispute—in Ohio's favor. Today, the city lays easy claim to being the world's leading producer of glass and glass products. A world-renowned collection of ancient and modern glassware is on display at the Toledo Museum of Art. Considerable other attractions are in Toledo, including the Port of Toledo Observation Deck and the Waterfront Electric Railway offering old-fashioned trolley trips.

0:00 (1:40) Depart Toledo's yellow brick and glass Central Union Terminal, crossing Swan Creek and passing tower to Airline Junction Yard, where route of The Lake Shore splits away to left.

0:09 (1:31) Curve sharply left, roll across I-75, pass a large American Motors plant on left, then pass under I-75 as it loops back to northeast.

0:20 (1:20) Cross Chessie System tracks at Alexis Tower. Lights of Raceway Park are visible on left upon arrival in Toledo at night. Pass under State Highway 184 and cross Silver Creek less than a mile south of Michigan border.

0:23 (1:17) Now in Michigan, cross Halfway Creek and run parallel to tracks of Grand Trunk Western (GT) Railroad at right.

0:36 (1:04) To left, large open quarry ringed by huge boulders lies just south of Monroe, where we cross River Raisin on its way to Lake Erie. Only battle in Michigan between regular forces occurred near here during War of 1812. Massacre of wounded Americans after their surrender gave rise to battle cry, "Remember the Raisin." General George A. Custer was raised in Monroe, and Lazy Boy, famous recliner manufacturer, also claims this as its home town.

0:41 (0:59) Cross I-75 on its way to Detroit, then parallel an overgrown, but still visible, abandoned railroad right-of-way on left.

0:55 (0:45) Roll through Newport, then South Rockwood, across Huron River, and then through Rockwood.

1:08 (0:32) In Gibralter pass a large Chrysler plant and slip under Fort Road, State Highway 85.

1:13 (0:27) After FN Tower, where we intersect again with GT, huge McClouth Steel Products Corporation's Trenton Plant occupies several blocks on right. Proceed slowly through Riverview and Wyandotte, just two of several suburban communities which have passed ordinances limiting train speeds.

1:22 (0:18) Between Wyandotte and Ecorse cross South Branch of Ecorse River. Evidence of decline of nation's steel industry looms on left—abandoned facilities of Michigan Steel Works.

1:24 (0:16) Roll through Conrail's River Rouge Yard, then cross river into city of Detroit.

1:37 (0:03) Pass West Detroit Tower, rattle through main plant of General Motors' Cadillac Division, then cross I-75. Ambassador Bridge, a beautiful sight at night, connects Detroit with Windsor, Ontario on right.

Oddly enough, as we look toward Canada out the right side of the train, we are looking almost due south at "our neighbors to the north."

1:40 (0:00) Roll past new Southwest Detroit Hospital and arrive at temporary depot that has replaced Detroit's huge Michigan Central Terminal.

DETROIT, MI - In 1701, the French colonist Antoine de la Mothe Cadillac landed on what is today's riverfront area of Detroit and established Fort Pontchartrain, later the site of battles during the French and Indian Wars. In 1805 the settlement burned to the ground from an accidental fire. It was rebuilt following, to some extent, the layout of the streets in Washington, D.C. Detroit ultimately became "Motor City" largely because of the imagination and determination of people like Henry Ford, good transportation facilities and an available work force at the time the auto industry was being born.

In the 1970s, Detroit, led by Henry Ford II, made a heroic effort to put a new shine on the city's rusting image in the form of a massive ($350 million) urban development project called the Renaissance Center—"RenCen" for short. Quadruplet 39-story glass office towers surrounding a nearly twice-as-high core hotel were built on the banks of the Detroit River to revitalize the city's downtown. The result was certainly architecturally striking.

But there is debate over the success of the project. Although RenCen's office space has been virtually 100% occupied, its retail impact has been meager. And there has been another curious problem. People continually get lost in RenCen's legendary maze-like confines—so much so that a $27-million remodeling was undertaken in the late 1980s to make the place more "user friendly."

Amtrak Station, 2601 Rose St. (Michigan Ave. and 17th St.), is a one-story structure which Amtrak moved into after the historic Michigan Central Station (next door) was finally closed in early 1988. (Many Detroit Amtrak passengers use the Dearborn station in western Detroit.) There are snack and drink vending machines, a newsstand and adjacent free parking.

For arrival and departure information, call 964-5336; for reservations and other information, 963-7396. Ticket windows are open 6:30 am to 11 pm while the waiting room is open 6:30 am to 1 am.

Cab stand at the station; Checker Cab, 963-7000. **Greyhound,** (313) 963-9840. Detroit's major airport is **Metropolitan Airport,** 16 miles southwest of downtown. Closer-in **City Airport** is served by Southwest Airlines. Detroit's **People Mover,** elevated and fully automatic trains, snakes counter-clockwise around the downtown area. Trains are one or two cars in length, arrive at any of the 13 stops every 3 or 4 minutes, and take approximately 15 minutes to make the entire loop. **Detroit Trolley** is another way to see the downtown, running from Washington Blvd. to Jefferson Ave.

? Visitor Information Center, 2 East Jefferson Ave., 48226; (313) 567-1170. Open seven days a week.

International Plaza Inn, 111 E. Larned, 48226; (313) 968-0050. Very reasonable accommodations in the center of downtown. $58.

-**Days Inn Downtown,** Washington Blvd. at Michigan Ave., 48226; (313) 967-4646. Located in the heart of downtown, adjacent to a People Mover station. $90.

While downtown, be sure to ride the **People Mover** and **Trolley,** both mentioned above. The **Renaissance Center,** also mentioned above, has numerous shops and is an adventure to explore. **Greektown,** a small enclave near downtown, has some great Greek restaurants and numerous small shops anchored by Trapper's Alley, a fashionably converted five-story warehouse with its own collection of boutiques and cafes.

Detroit's most popular attraction is out in Dearborn. The **Henry Ford Museum** and adjacent **Greenfield Village** are seen by well over a million visitors each year. The Museum has four acres of floor space devoted to displaying the industrialization of America, including a newly developed Automobile-in-American-Life exhibit, complete with a 1940s Texaco station and a 1946 diner. Greenfield Village has over 100 buildings on 240 acres, with the likes of the Wright Brothers home and cycle shop, Edison's Menlo Park Laboratory and rides on an 18th-century steam train.

0:00 (0:16) Depart Detroit by backing out of station.

0:08 (0:08) Continue backwards deep into yards of Cadillac plant before stopping and pulling forward alongside loading docks holding auto carriers from many different railroads. Pass West Detroit Tower again, where tracks to Toledo curve away to left.

1:12 (0:03) Slip through a large Conrail

yard. Off to left, Ford Motor Company's huge River Rouge Plant is an impressive sight. Cross I-94.

1:14 (0:00) Arrive at handsome Dearborn station, built in 1978 to serve Detroit's western suburbs.

DEARBORN, MI - This is the birthplace of Henry Ford. The 12-acre Henry Ford Museum is here, and adjacent is the 240-acre Greenfield Village, a wonderful collection of historical American buildings and artifacts.

0:00 (0:30) Depart Dearborn with Ford Motor's Central Office Building appearing at right. Cross over Southfield Freeway, then over River Rouge for an excellent view on left of Henry Ford Museum and Greenfield Village complex.

0:10 (0:20) Roll past Wayne Tower and Junction and enter another set of rail yards, then pass under I-275.

0:20 (0:12) Enter Willow Run Yard, and then Ypsilanti, site of Eastern Michigan University. Ancient depot on left now holds a farmers' market.

0:23 (0:07) Make first of an incredible 11 crossings of meandering Huron River as it twists and turns through and between "Ypsi" and western edge of Ann Arbor.

0:28 (0:02) Cross Huron River a fifth time, as a dam appears on right. Route then follows river along a beautiful parkway on both sides of tracks.

0:30 (0:00) Run past University of Michigan Hospital high above to left, then follow Huron as it curves right. Pass famous Gandy Dancer Restaurant located in fine Michigan Central depot on left as train arrives at new orange brick Ann Arbor station on opposite side of Plymouth Road viaduct.

ANN ARBOR, MI - The University of Michigan is located here, making this a major stop on the corridor. An interesting station feature is the new stairway to Plymouth Road with the Amtrak name and logo engraved into the concrete.

0:00 (0:37) Depart Ann Arbor, and immediately resume Huron River crossings.

0:10 (0:27) Final crossing of Huron places river on right as it meanders through a wooded park. Then cruise through Dexter, with interesting mill and dam on left.

0:15 (0:22) This is crossroads community of Four Mile. A bit later, Chelsea is reached, a pretty little town of old homes and tree-lined streets.

0:25 (0:12) At Grass Lake, just before passing burned-out stone depot, look left for an old fire truck a collector keeps in his back yard. A few minutes later rumble through Leoni and then Michigan Center.

0:37 (0:00) After sliding through Conrail's Jackson Yard, arrive at old red brick Jackson station on our right, oldest of the Michigan Corridor's stations, built in 1876 and restored between 1976 and 1978.

JACKSON, MI - Named after Andrew Jackson, the town was founded in 1829 by travelers over the Territorial Road (now roughly paralleled by I-94). It was first called Jacksonopolis and later Jacksonburgh. Several years later, on July 6, 1854, 1,500 Michigan residents assembled here and organized a new political group named the Republican Party. Today, Jackson is home to Michigan's oldest and largest state prison.

0:00 (0:24) Depart Jackson as its downtown rises on right, then past Jackson's airport a few minutes later. Then continue journey through countryside.

0:21 (0:03) After Parma, Kalamazoo River flows serenely through a farm pasture and marshy area immediately to left, just beyond an abandoned railroad bed.

0:24 (0:00) Arrive at Albion.

ALBION, MI - Albion is home to Albion College, which was passed on our right as we rolled into town.

0:00 (0:30) Depart Albion and, a few minutes later, pass Marengo and continue along Kalamazoo River, wending its way through marshes below to left.

0:14 (0:16) After Marshall, cross I-69 a few minutes later and follow river through Caresco.

0:25 (0:05) After crossing I-94, enter "Cereal City"—Battle Creek—with Kellogg's huge plant and Tony the Tiger in its front yard on right. A quick succession of Battle Creek sights parade past. Just beyond to left, an old GT steam engine sits on silent display. Then Post plant looms up suddenly on left. Old Grand Trunk depot comes into view on right, and GT tracks to Lansing and Port Huron, used by Amtrak and VIA's International, curve to right behind us.

0:30 (0:00) Arrive at New Battle Creek Transportation Center, built to accommodate all public area transportation systems.

For route between Battle Creek and Chicago, see that portion of International Log, page 137.

Grand Rapids

Chicago

Pere Marquette

The Pere Marquette, one of Amtrak's newest trains, began service August 5, 1984 between Grand Rapids, MI and Chicago, IL over the tracks of the Chessie System's Chesapeake & Ohio Railroad. The route hadn't had passenger train service since Amtrak took over in 1971 and discontinued the old Pere Marquette, namesake of the railroad incorporated into the C&O in 1947 and a French missionary explorer of the Great Lakes.

The train provides a daily round trip between Grand Rapids and Chicago, leaving the Michigan metropolis early in the morning and returning later that evening.

Westbound Schedule (Condensed)*
Grand Rapids, MI - Early Morning Departure
Chicago, IL - Midmorning Arrival

Eastbound Schedule (Condensed)
Chicago, IL - Early Evening Departure
Grand Rapids, MI- Late Evening Arrival

*Two hours later on Sundays.

Frequency - Daily.
Seating - Unreserved coaches, usually Amfleet.
Food Service - Sandwiches, snacks, and beverages.
Baggage - Carry on. No checked baggage service.
Length of Trip - 181 miles in 3¾ hours.

Route Log

GRAND RAPIDS, MI - After Detroit, this is Michigan's largest city, with a population of 181,000, famous for its manufacture of home and office furniture since early in its history. The Gerald R. Ford Museum is here in the former president's home town. The newly developed Grand Center features modern convention facilities with the five-star-rated Amway Grand Plaza Hotel, downtown's only major hotel, nearby. Most of the "chain" hotels are several miles south along 28th Street.

0:00 (0:38) Depart Grand Rapids' attractive, new wood-sided depot south of downtown at the corner of Market and Wealthy. (A depot on a more grandiose scale was demolished some years ago to make way for an interstate highway.) Swing sharply right and roll through Chessie's Lamar Yard.

0:12 (0:26) Pass through mixed residential-industrial suburb of Grandville, then under I-196 and finally pick up speed.

0:20 (0:18) Enter Hudsonville, with its fairgrounds and greenhouses, followed by flat, fertile vegetable fields.

0:27 (0:11) Zeeland, where seventy percent of all U.S.-produced grandfather clocks are made, is easily identified by city water tower.

0:38 (0:00) Lake Macatawa lies at right upon arrival at Holland. Depot, surrounded by a tulip-filled park, sits unused as passengers occupy a small adjacent shelter.

HOLLAND, MI - Each May witnesses the famous Tulip Time Festival when this area celebrates its Dutch heritage with parades, dancing and a lavish display of millions of tulips.

0:00 (0:36) Depart Holland past buildings of Hope College, then re-enter agricultural land while crossing I-196.

0:09 (0:25) Quickly through hamlet of East Saugatuck and curve left across a pleasant little stream. Then ride high above it and surrounding woods in valley to left.

0:13 (0:23) Stream again comes into view at left. Sway through New Richmond and, a couple minutes later, cross Kalamazoo River on its way to Lake Michigan ten miles west.

0:22 (0:14) Breeze through Fennville, where Pere Marquette sometimes makes a special stop in mid-October for town's annual Goose Festival. Now, after scenic areas of rivers, ravines and ridges, terrain flattens out again.

0:26 (0:10) In next several minutes, roll through towns called Pearl, Bravo and Pullman, and finally reach Grand Junction, where several tracks connect with ours. Orchards are in abundance in this region.

0:36 (0:00) Cross Black River and arrive at Bangor.

 BANGOR, MI - The old depot, just outside our window on the right, now houses the "Bangor Train Factory, Manufacturer of the Kalamazoo Toy Train."

0:00 (0:35) Depart Bangor, continuing journey through apple orchards of western Michigan.

0:08 (0:27) Cross Paw Paw River upon reaching Hartford, where Fruit Exchange's wooden skids and boxes lie at left.

0:17 (0:18) After passing grey wooden Watervliet depot, and crossing Paw Paw River again, Pere Marquette rambles through downtown Coloma. A few minutes later, duck under I-196 and then cut through Riverside.

0:25 (0:10) A large electric power station looms at right. At left Paw Paw appears again as it meanders through trees in search of a marsh beyond.

0:30 (0:05) Curve sharply left approaching a drawbridge over St. Joseph River between Benton Harbor and St. Joseph. Train slows to a mere 15 miles per hour on bridge, giving a longer look at Lake Michigan and lighthouse guarding river's mouth.

0:35 (0:00) Curve left and arrive at an old, grey stucco depot. At left, just north of station, a stairway up bluff begins under a concrete arch engraved "St. Joseph, Michigan."

 ST. JOSEPH-BENTON HARBOR, MI - Michigan's Twin Cities join 28 other southwestern Michigan communities each spring as sponsors of the Blossomtime Festival in anticipation of the coming fruit harvest. The Benton Harbor Fruit Market is said to be the largest of its kind in the nation.

0:00 (0:28) Depart St. Joseph-Benton Harbor as a bluff looms on left and Lake is visible on right. After gradual ascent to top of bluff, Lake Michigan now spreads out on right until view is obliterated by a clutch of factories as Pere Marquette moves farther inland.

0:06 (0:22) Through fields of grapes, then pass under I-94 and cut quickly through downtown Stevensville.

0:11 (0:17) Here, at Bridgman depot on our right is milepost 100. Cross Galien River.

0:14 (0:14) Paralleling highway on right is I-94. A barn inscribed "Dunes View Farm" is a reminder that distant hills are actually stabilized sand dunes from Lake Michigan and nearby Warren Dunes State Park.

0:19 (0:09) Pass through Sawyer, and again roll under I-94.

0:26 (0:02) Cross another stream and follow it for a moment. Then cross handsome set of tracks of Amtrak's Chicago/Detroit Corridor.

0:28 (0:00) Arrive at a glass bus shelter that serves as New Buffalo's train station.

 NEW BUFFALO, MI - Michigan's largest marina is located here on Lake Michigan.

0:00 (0:48) Depart New Buffalo.

0:08 (0:40) Terrain becomes more urbanized upon approaching Michigan City, IN.

0:24 (0:24) Sign at right proclaims "Indiana Dunes Recreational Area." Pass under I-94 and Chesterton water tower comes into view on left.

0:29 (0:19) Approach white and green Porter Tower, on right, where our Chessie tracks meet Conrail at left and Amtrak's Michigan line at right. Our speed limit is now 79 mph. South Shore Line and its clutter of catenary—overhead wire to power electric locomotives—is on left.

 Gain one hour as train passes from Eastern to Central Time. Set your watch back (forward if eastbound) one hour.

0:37 (0:11) Pass the huge Gary Works plant of U.S. Steel.

0:45 (0:03) Take several minutes to pass through heart of Inland Steel complex, then continue with Lake Michigan in view on right.

0:48 (0:00) Arrive at Amtrak's 1982 Hammond-Whiting, IN depot.

For route description from here to Chicago, see that portion of Lake Shore Ltd. log, page 73.

Other Michigan Service

The **Wolverine** and **Twilight Ltd.** provide service between Detroit and Chicago, in addition to the Lake Cities. There is daily service in the morning westbound and in the evening, eastbound. In addition, there is Friday, Saturday and Sunday service eastbound in the morning and westbound in the evening.

Chicago

Memphis

New Orleans

City of New Orleans

Until 1981, this overnight train between Chicago and New Orleans was called the Panama Limited. A curious name until one realizes that Midwesterners once set sail for the Orient from New Orleans rather than make the arduous trip across the Rocky Mountains to reach San Francisco. The train was inaugurated at the time the Panama Canal was built.

There was a City of New Orleans, however, but it made a daylight run between these two great towns, carrying some of America's most colorful travelers —gamblers, migrant workers, jazz musicians, to name but a few. "Don't you know me, I'm your native son?" asked Arlo Guthrie.

But one train between Chicago and New Orleans was all Amtrak could afford, and the Panama Limited survived. It kept that name until a New Orleans mayor persuaded Amtrak to re-name the train for its southern destination—a much more appropriate appellation.

"The City" travels a direct route between Chicago and New Orleans through Memphis and Jackson. The train passes through eastern Illinois, the western edges of Kentucky and Tennessee, and then through the very heart of Mississippi. The Kansas City to New Orleans train, The River Cities, is a section of this train between Centralia and New Orleans.

Southbound Schedule (Condensed)
Chicago, IL - Early Evening Departure
Champaign-Urbana, IL - Late Evening
Carbondale, IL - Middle of the Night

Memphis, TN - Early Morning
Jackson, MS - Early Morning
New Orleans, LA - Early Afternoon Arrival

Northbound Schedule (Condensed)
New Orleans, LA - Midafternoon Departure
Jackson, MS - Early Evening
Memphis, TN - Late Evening
Carbondale, IL - Middle of the Night
Champaign-Urbana, IL - Early Morning
Chicago, IL - Midmorning Arrival

Frequency - Daily.
Seating - Amcoaches and dome car.
Dining - Tray meals, sandwiches and beverage service. Lounge service.
Sleeping - Heritage Fleet roomettes and bedrooms.
Baggage - Checked baggage at larger cities.
Reservations - All-reserved train.
Length of Trip - 924 miles in 18 hours.

Route Log

 CHICAGO, IL - See page 116.

0:00 (0:41) Depart Chicago Union Station, backing southbound from beneath Chicago's main post office terminal.
0:03 (0:39) Still in reverse, slip past Amtrak's coach yards and car-washing facility.
0:04 (0:37) Route of California Zephyr and Southwest Chief swings away to west on tracks of Burlington Northern.
0:05 (0:36) Cross South Chicago River.
0:07 (0:34) Train finally ends its back-

ward ways and starts forward, curling slowly right (east) onto Illinois Central tracks, following historic St. Charles Air Line right-of-way. Illinois Central was nation's first major land grant railroad (two-and-a-half-million acres for 7% of its gross revenues), and boasts the likes of Casey Jones, Abraham Lincoln and Mark Twain as employee alumni.

0:09 (0:32) Chinatown's colorful storefronts are just off to right.

0:12 (0:29) Amtrak's best offering of Chicago's spectacular skyline holds forth at left. Dominant building with twin antenna is famous Sears Tower, nation's tallest skyscraper, while slope-sided John Hancock Building (also with two antennae) is also apparent. Tallest white monolith, closer to Lake Michigan, is marble-faced Standard Oil Building that may receive a $30 million face lift due to problems related to its weighty facade.

0:13 (0:28) No major U.S. city train departure would be complete without a display of artistic graffiti, now below on left.

0:14 (0:27) Curling south, giant Soldier Field, home of NFL's Chicago Bears, is just off to left, while Field Museum can be seen beyond. Shortly, dome of Adler Planetarium can be discerned back left along lakefront.

0:18 (0:23) Pass beneath entrance to McCormick Place and McCormick Hotel. Black, flat Exposition Center is quite visible back to left after returning to daylight.

0:20 (0:21) Now, waters of Lake Michigan lap against Burnham Park paralleling Lake Shore Drive on left.

0:22 (0:19) Architecturally interesting collection of older buildings faces tracks on left. Jackson Park with its world renowned Museum of Science and Industry lies beyond. Campus of University of Chicago stretches off to right.

0:24 (0:17) Rumble beneath Chicago Skyway and tracks of Conrail at aptly named Grand Crossing.

0:27 (0:14) Buildings of Chicago State University border tracks on right.

0:34 (0:07) Cross Little Calumet River.

0:38 (0:03) Expansive Markham Yards of Illinois Central now stretch along route on left. Black IC switchers can be spotted shuffling long consists of freight cars among various tracks.

0:41 (0:00) Arrive at attractive community of Homewood.

 HOMEWOOD, IL - Giant oak and pine trees surround this well-to-do Chicago suburb. Homewood's per capita income places it amongst 200 most affluent American cities.

0:00 (0:30) Depart Homewood.

0:30 (0:00) Arrive Kankakee.

 KANKAKEE, IL - Set along the banks of the Kankakee River, many vestiges of Kankakee's early French influence still pervade this city. Renowned for its abundant gladiola harvests, unusual rock formations surround the many limestone and sand quarries that are noteworthy here as well.

0:00 (0:52) Depart Kankakee and cross Kankakee River.

0:26 (0:27) This is Gilman, IL, a stop northbound only. Besides an agrarian focal point for Iroquois County, Gilman has been a modest rail center and division point for the Illinois Central.

0:50 (0:00) Arrive Rantoul.

RANTOUL, IL - The Rantoul stop affords easy access to Chanute Field, one of the largest technical training centers of the U.S. Air Force. Aircraft and missile exhibits are the focus of its on-base museum.

0:00 (0:14) Depart Rantoul.

0:14 (0:00) Arrive Champaign-Urbana.

CHAMPAIGN-URBANA, IL - Defying consolidation since the mid-19th century, Illinois' "Twin Cities" still maintain separate identities. Champaign has evolved into a commercial and industrial center, while Urbana is more collegiate-oriented with the University of Illinois campus lying primarily within its boundaries.

Boasting a one-of-a-kind campus facility, the University's Krannert Center for the Performing Arts is similar in concept to New York's Lincoln Center where separate theaters have been specifically designed for different types of productions. Also of interest is the Wilber Mansion, a turn-of-the-century Victorian home restored as the Champaign County Historical Museum.

0:00 (0:38) Depart Champaign-Urbana.
0:38 (0:00) Arrive Mattoon.

MATTOON, IL - An industrial community and service center for the surrounding farmlands, Mattoon is a convenient stop for students attending Eastern Illinois University in Charleston. Also nearby is the Lincoln Log Cabin State Park where the modest home of our nation's 16th president has been restored atop its original foundation.

0:00 (0:25) Depart Mattoon.
0:25 (0:00) Arrive Effingham.

EFFINGHAM, IL - As well as a service center for smaller agricultural communities, Effingham supports an active manufacturing industry with products spanning the gamut from church furniture to golf clubs.

0:00 (0:44) Depart Effingham.
0:44 (0:00) Arrive Centralia.

CENTRALIA, IL - Centralia, one of three cities comprising this metropolitan area, is an industrial-oriented community with railroad shops and yards providing major employment for the region. This is where The River Cities joins the southbound City of New Orleans.

0:00 (0:54) Depart Centralia.
0:54 (0:00) Arrive Carbondale.

CARBONDALE, IL - As its name implies, Carbondale sits in the midst of extensive coalfields which provide the basic industrial staple of this community. The home of Southern Illinois University, Carbondale is but a short distance from the Crab Orchard National Wildlife Refuge, a haven of outdoor recreation and a popular winter haunt for thousands of Canadian geese. Here, too, is Bald Knob, a high point in the Ozarks overlooking three states. Each Easter, sunrise services are held beneath the cross at its summit.

0:00 (1:48) Depart Carbondale.
0:58 (0:50) Through the town of Cairo.

Situated at the confluence of the mighty Ohio and Mississippi rivers, Cairo was the early Civil War headquarters of General Grant, affording him complete command of operations along these waterways. Today, bridges across three rivers connect the states of Missouri, Kentucky and Illinois. Locals have dubbed this portion of Southern Illinois as "Little Egypt" (not to be confused with the dancer) because of its resemblance to the flat silt banks of the Nile River Valley.

0:59 (0:49) Cross Ohio River and enter Kentucky.

Shortly, the train crosses a geologic feature known as the New Madrid Fault which caused North America's strongest earthquake (probably an incredible 8.7 on the Richter scale) during the winter of 1811-12. Nearby, the Mississippi actually changed direction and, as far away as Boston, church bells were clanging from the shock. Experts say the fault, more than 500 million years old, is building up pressure and might some day trigger the nation's worst natural disaster.

1:48 (0:00) Arrive Fulton.

FULTON, KY - Until recently, the majority of banana shipments from Latin America stopped in Fulton while refrigerator cars were re-iced, and the fruit was prepared for distribution. Although this practice has since been discontinued, the town's International Banana Festival remains a popular summer event, with Latin American music, crafts and food highlighting the festivities.

0:00 (0:51) Depart Fulton.
0:51 (0:00) Arrive Dyersburg.

DYERSBURG, TN - Founded in 1821, the city was named in honor of Colonel William Henry Dyer who served under General Andrew Jackson during the War of 1812. Today, bountiful crops of cotton and fruit are processed by local industry.

0:00 (1:34) Depart Dyersburg.
1:32 (0:02) Dawn is usually breaking on approach to Memphis. On right, Hernando-Desoto Bridge, with lights aglow, spans Mississippi River carrying Interstate 40 traffic between Memphis and Little Rock. Mud Island, home to a park focusing on Mississippi River history and geography, is separated from shore by Wolf River. Once a muddy trap for river vessels, its reclamation has turned it into a Memphis showplace. Venerable Peabody Hotel, on left, is easily identified by rooftop neon sign.

1:34 (0:00) Arrive Memphis.

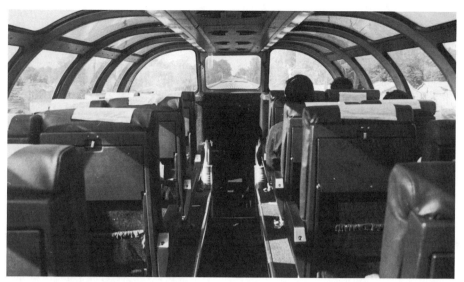

City of New Orleans Dome Car

MEMPHIS, TN - Memphis was born in 1819 when Andrew Jackson, yet to be elected president, laid out a town on the Chickasaw Bluffs overlooking the Mississippi River. This unusually high location above the Mississippi turned out to be fortuitous, since many towns established along the banks of that great river were ultimately washed away or abandoned due to recurring flooding.

Although severely decimated by several yellow fever epidemics in the 1800s, the city not only came back, it is now the largest city on the Mississippi between St. Louis and New Orleans. Memphis has laid claim to numerous distinctions, including: the "Hardwood Center of the World"; the world's largest mule-trading market; the "Birthplace of Blues"; four times winner of the nation's "cleanest city" award; the home of W. C. Handy and Elvis Presley; and the home of the first Welcome Wagon.

Central Station, 545 South Main St., is a terminally (no pun intended) forlorn structure in one of the worst areas of town, an area where passengers should not walk at night. Fortunately, there are plans to improve Amtrak's situation by relocating the station to the Mud Island parking garage near the center of town. The present station has storage lockers and adjacent free parking (no security).

For reservations and ticket information, call 800-USA-RAIL. For arrival and departure information, 526-0052.

Cab stand at the station; Yellow Cab, 577-7777. **Local buses** stop in front of the station, 274-6282. **Greyhound,** 523-7676. **Memphis International Airport** is approximately eight miles southeast of the station.

Visitor Information Center, 207 Beale, 38103; (901) 526-4880. Information may also be obtained from Memphis Convention and Visitors Bureau, Morgan Keegan Tower, 50 N. Front St., Suite 450, 38103; (901) 576-8181.

Days Inn Downtown, 164 Union Ave., 38103; (901) 527-4100. Located downtown, about two miles from Central Station. $45.

-The Peabody, 149 Union, 38103; (901) 529-4000 or 800-732-2639. Venerable landmark, located downtown, about two miles from the station. $130.

Wilson Inn, 2705 Cherry Road, 38118; (901) 366-9300 or 800-333-9457. Near the airport, across from the mall of Memphis. Not downtown, but one of the best values in the city. $39.41.

Memphis and the Mississippi River are inseparable. Recognizing this, the City of Memphis has spent over $60 million developing **Mud Island,** just offshore of the downtown area. The Island is a showcase for all aspects of the River—recreational, educational, cultural, historic and scientific. There are boat rides, a river museum, restaurants and other attractions, all set along a five-block river walk that is actually a flowing model of the entire Mississippi River Basin.

Some of the city's past can be savored in **Victorian Village,** downtown in the area of 680 Adams Street, where various historic buildings have been restored. Some of these are open to the public.

Nightlife and blues, a Memphis tradition, can be found downtown along **Beale Street** where W. C. Handy lived and wrote much of his beloved music. **Overton Square,** at Madison and Cooper, comprises three blocks of shops, nightclubs and unique restaurants.

The best-known tourist attraction in town is still **Graceland,** the showplace home of Elvis Presley, where visitors can get a firsthand look at "The King's" lifestyle. The estate is south of downtown at 3717 Elvis Presley Blvd.

And the legendary **Peabody ducks** are mandatory for anyone visiting Memphis for the first time. At 11 am each day, the hotel's ducks that reside in a rooftop penthouse are herded into an elevator and brought to the lobby for their ritualistic feeding.

0:00 (1:13) Depart Memphis.
0:48 (0:25) Cross Coldwater River.
0:50 (0:23) Entering town of Coldwater, cotton gin with yellow cotton wagons is on right.
1:08 (0:05) Cross Tallahatchie River.
1:13 (0:00) Arrive Batesville. Because of train's length and platform's brevity, "City" usually makes a second "spot" stop for convenience of passengers.

 BATESVILLE, MS - Set admist an array of colorful and fragrant flowers, Batesville is the home of the highly regarded "Art-Mart," a midsummer festival drawing craftsmen and artisans from across the South. Nearby Enid and Sardis lakes are also popular attractions, offering a multitude of recreational possibilities.

0:00 (0:41) Depart Batesville.
0:41 (0:00) Cross Yalobusha River immediately preceding arrival at Grenada.

GRENADA, MS - Originally established as two separate towns, it became one community early on with a celebration that was highlighted by a wedding of a groom who hailed from one township and a bride who resided in the other.

At once a vital mecca of cotton production, Grenada caters as well to a growing tourist trade, lured primarily by the nearby Grenada Lake recreation resort.

0:00 (0:21) Depart Grenada across rolling farmlands and forests of the Deep South. Of many agricultural products, cotton is by far most prevalent. Cotton wagons and ginning plants are as common to this region as tractors and grain elevators are to Midwest. Boxcars brimming with fresh-cut hardwood are also a frequent sight, indicative of another flourishing industry.
0:04 (0:17) Railroad is principal customer of lumber mill on right where thousands of cross ties await shipment.
0:21 (0:00) Arrive Winona. Across from station on left stands time-honored Wisteria Hotel, its rooms now rented as apartments.

WINONA, MS - On January 31, 1860, a ceremonial spike was driven just south of Winona, linking the Great Lakes region with the Gulf of Mexico. This was a major boon to Winona farmers who previously depended on oxcarts for distribution of their crops. Since completion of the rail line, Winona has maintained an active agricultural and industrial economy.

Still scattered throughout this area are a number of resplendent antebellum homes, several of which are open to the public.

0:00 (0:25) Departing Winona, beautifully preserved white mansion stands distinctively on left.
0:17 (0:08) Flat, swampy wetlands, now most apparent, are commonplace between Memphis and New Orleans.
0:25 (0:00) Arriving Durant, quaint gazebo on right would seem popular spot for officiating town festivities.

DURANT, MS - Another agricultural service community, Durant is surrounded by a number of Indian reservations. These include tribes who originally inhabited the region when it was first explored by DeSoto in 1541.

0:00 (0:30) Depart Durant.

0:02 (0:28) Two dozen or so dangling silver gourds serve as birdhouses in yard on right.

0:12 (0:18) Surrounded by extensive cotton fields, pass through appropriately named town of Pickens. A few miles downline, note woodlands on left that have been ravaged by fire.

0:18 (0:12) Pass through small town of Vaughan that was site of famous "Casey Jones" wreck.

Trying to make up lost time, an unsuspecting Casey ran his speeding train into a derailed freight just north of town. He died in the wreck and was supposedly found with one hand on the throttle and the other on the brake. Chronicles of this legendary engineer, as well as other railroad memorabilia, are housed here in a restored depot museum.

0:19 (0:11) Cross Big Black River.

0:30 (0:00) Madison County Court House on left immediately precedes arrival at Canton station.

CANTON, MS - Primarily a manufacturing hub of textiles and lumber products, Canton's modest population is swelled by 20,000 each May and October during the nationally acclaimed Canton Flea Markets.

0:00 (0:32) Depart Canton.

0:03 (0:28) Flourishing pecan groves on left represent another agricultural staple of this state.

0:19 (0:15) Intersect Natchez Trace Parkway at Ridgeland.

The Natchez Trace was an early Indian and trappers' trail that extended from Natchez northeastward into Kentucky. Before steam power made it practical to navigate upstream, boatsmen who brought goods and people from the Ohio River Valley down the Mississippi River would often terminate their southward journey at Natchez. Here, having no further use for their boats, they would sell them for lumber, then return home by the cheapest means—on foot along the Natchez Trace. Unfortunately, robbers frequently helped themselves to the rivermen's profits.

0:23 (0:12) Plant of Presto Corporation, well-known cookware manufacturer, can

be seen on right approaching Jackson.

0:28 (0:08) On left, Memorial Stadium is scene of fierce gridiron rivalries between "Ole Miss" and Mississippi State University. For rest of season, field is home to Jackson State University and Millsaps College.

University of Mississippi Medical Center is situated just south of stadium.

0:34 (0:02) Downtown Jackson skyline appears on forward left, with broad dome of "new" Capitol Building predominant. Built in 1903, golden eagle (flying south, of course) is proudly perched atop this grand structure.

0:36 (0:00) Arrive Jackson. Former Hotel King Edward, once an important Jackson landmark, now stands empty and in utter disrepair, forward on left.

JACKSON, MS - Crossroads of the South, capital of and largest city (over 300,000 population) in Mississippi, Jackson had its humble beginnings as a trading settlement on the banks of the Pearl River. This outpost grew to prominence, only to be burned to the ground by General Sherman during the Civil War. The city recovered mightily, and is now the trading and transportation center of the state. History buffs will find much to occupy them throughout this region.

0:00 (0:30) Depart Jackson. Mississippi Arts Center and Planetarium are housed within white-domed complex on left.

0:25 (0:06) Pass through Crystal Springs whose bountiful tomato harvests of early 1900s prompted its designation as "Tomatopolis of the World."

0:30 (0:00) Arrive Hazelhurst past comely residential district on right.

HAZELHURST, MS - Set deep in the heart of farm country, Hazelhurst serves a region devoted primarily to the production of cotton and livestock.

0:00 (0:21) Depart Hazelhurst. On immediate left is Royal Maid Association for the Blind, employing blind workers to manufacture plastic flatware, mops, brooms and other products.

0:14 (0:07) Passing through Wesson, note historic Wesson Hotel on left. During railroad's heyday, a gambling casino was maintained in hotel's attic, and proved a popular diversion for awaiting passengers.

Building is presently enshrined in National Register. Adjacent to hotel is campus of Copiah-Lincoln Junior College.

0:20 (0:01) Small Southern mansion on left is appropriate home for Magnolia Manor Antiques.

0:21 (0:00) Arriving Brookhaven, regal magnolia trees line walkways of station. Small monument on right offers brief account of town's historical highlights.

 BROOKHAVEN, MS - A recruiting and hospital center during the Civil War, Brookhaven has likewise flourished since completion of the railroad. Today, industrial development is focused around the region's natural resources of petroleum, wood pulp and clay, and provides an attractive balance for Brookhaven's strong agricultural economy.

0:00 (0:21) Departing Brookhaven, fanciful Victorian homes enhance neighborhood on left.

0:03 (0:15) Bogue Chitto River makes first of several brief appearances on left.

0:19 (0:02) Outstanding composition of lake and rural homes, on right, produces one of more attractive scenes along route.

0:21 (0:00) Arrive McComb.

MCCOMB, MS - This southern Mississippi town was named in honor of Colonel H. S. McComb who spearheaded reconstruction of the railroad following its destruction during the Civil War.

McComb is presently renowned as the home of the "Lighted Azalea Trail," an enchanting Easter-time spectacle fashioned by local residents who pin tiny lights around the delicate pink and white blossoms of their azalea bushes.

0:00 (0:53) Depart McComb.

0:10 (0:43) At Magnolia, two outstanding Colonial mansions can be seen on right. Splendid magnolia trees grace yard of larger home.

0:13 (0:40) Cross Tangipahoa River which then follows intermittently on left.

0:19 (0:34) At southern edge of Osyka, cross Mississippi state line into Louisiana.

0:28 (0:26) A few miles south of Kentwood, pass Camp Moore Confederate Cemetery on left. Once a major training camp for Confederate Army, museum of Civil War relics now stands amidst graves of over 500 soldiers.

0:31 (0:22) Wetland homes are often elevated a foot or two above ground for obvious reasons. Builder of house at left was expecting the worst.

0:32 (0:21) Beautiful estates grace landscape on right, just south of Tangipahoa.

0:39 (0:14) Early vestiges of French influence can be detected in curlicues and trelliswork adorning homes of Amite. On left, colossal old bell is enshrined in front of fire station. Standpipe on left proclaims Amite as "The Friendly City—500,000 Gallon Capacity."

0:47 (0:06) On southern outskirts of Independence, note intriguing cemetery on right. Tombs are positioned above ground in deference to saturated soil that would otherwise seep into graves. This is a fairly common spectacle throughout pervading wetlands of southern Louisiana.

0:49 (0:04) Supporting town's claim as one of world's "Strawberry Capitals," copious fields of this delectable fruit line route into Hammond.

0:53 (0:00) Arrive Hammond, where station, on right, sports eye-catching brown tile roof.

HAMMOND, LA - As well as those aforementioned strawberries, Hammond is also the home of the Tally-Ho Railroad Museum. Here, a fine collection of steam locomotives and vintage passenger cars is poised alongside a delightful old train station.

0:00 (1:01) Depart Hammond.

0:09 (0:52) Passing through Ponchatoula, old 2-8-0 narrow-gauge steam locomotive of Louisiana Express can be seen on left.

Now venture forth amidst the haunting beauty of the Louisiana swamplands. From the dark recesses of the encompassing bog, the contorted silhouettes of moss-laden cypress can easily conjure up menacing, untamed images. Yet at once, this primitive wilderness has nurtured the lifeblood and soul around which an entire Acadian culture has evolved.

0:12 (0:50) On right, Interstate 55 sits atop concrete piers, impressively fixed into forbidding landscape below. Grey-green material hanging from trees is Spanish moss, a harmless non-parasite, and one of nature's more attractive embellishments.

0:17 (0:46) Cross Pass-Manchac water-way that connects Lake Maurepas on right with Lake Pontchartrain on left.

0:26 (0:38) Approaching suburbs of New Orleans, train skirts shoreline of Lake Pontchartrain on left. Once inland, de-lightful sights of this exciting city are unfortunately denied along a rather non-descript route into station.

0:34 (0:31) Duck under I-10 which then follows on left.

0:43 (0:22) On left, Moisant Field is New Orleans International Airport.

0:52 (0:13) Famed Huey P. Long Bridge, carrying both automobile and rail traffic across Mississippi River, is visible on horizon at right.

1:00 (0:05) After crossing beneath major highway interchange, campus of Xavier University can be seen on right.

1:03 (0:03) To forward left, Superdome is an imposing structure in foreground of New Orleans skyline. Sports facility is home of National Football League's Saints. Adjacent to east is modernistic Hyatt Regency Hotel.

1:07 (0:02) Engage in U-turn around pub-lishing headquarters of Picayune States-Item Times. Train then backs into New Orleans station. Elephantine Superdome stands at immediate left.

1:14 (0:00) Arrive New Orleans.

 NEW ORLEANS, LA - See page 104.

Empire Builder

It was James J. Hill, a rugged empire-building tycoon in the finest sense, who constructed his Great Northern Railway around the turn of the century, creating a transcontinental link between St. Paul and the Pacific Northwest. The railroad brought farmers and ranchers to the prairies of North Dakota and Montana, miners to the mineral rich mountains of western Montana and lumberjacks to Washington's forests. And virtually overnight, an international trade with the Orient developed through Seattle's natural harbor, Puget Sound.

In 1929 Hill's Great Northern inaugurated the passenger train called the Empire Builder—a train which became one of the few of that era to have its name live on. Now, The Empire Builder makes this same jaunt across the northern tier of states, but starts in Chicago, following the Milwaukee Road to St. Paul before trekking across the old Great Northern route (now the Burlington Northern) to Seattle. This is America's northernmost passage.

Ken Wescott Jones, a British rail travel authority, described today's "Builder" as "the most comfortable, all-class, non-supplementary-fare train in the world." Add to this proclaimed contentment some of this country's most attractive countryside and the trip becomes an enticement that is hard to refuse. America's fruited plains, her purple mountain majesties, her gleaming shores—they are all on display. The pastoral environs of the upper Mississippi River and the vast expanses of the northern plains contrast sharply with the mountains of Glacier National Park and the Cascades of Washington, a contrast that can only be fully absorbed and enjoyed while traveling on a train.

The Portland section breaks off at Spokane and offers its own attractions with a cruise along the northern shore of the majestic Columbia River, including a memorable trip through the verdant-cliffed Columbia Gorge.

Westbound Schedule (Condensed)
Chicago, IL - Midafternoon Departure
Milwaukee, WI - Late Afternoon
St. Paul/Minneapolis, MN - Late Evening
Fargo, ND - Middle of the Night (2nd Day)
Havre, MT - Midafternoon (2nd Day)
Belton—West Glacier, MT - Midevening (2nd Day)
Spokane, WA - Middle of the Night (3rd Day)
Portland, OR* - Midmorning Arrival (3rd Day)
Seattle, WA - Midmorning Arrival (3rd Day)

Eastbound Schedule (Condensed)
Seattle, WA - Late Afternoon Departure
Portland, OR* - Midafternoon Departure
Spokane, WA - Late Evening
Belton—West Glacier, MT - Early Morning (2nd Day)
Havre, MT - Late Morning (2nd Day)
Fargo, ND - Middle of the Night (3rd Day)
St. Paul/Minneapolis, MN - Early Morning (3rd Day)
Milwaukee, WI - Early Afternoon (3rd Day)
Chicago, IL - Late Afternoon Arrival (3rd Day)

*By separate section between Spokane and Portland.

Frequency - Daily.
Seating - Superliner coaches.
Dining - Complete meal and beverage service as well as lighter fare. Lounge service available, with movies.
Sleeping - Superliner sleepers with deluxe, family, economy and special bedrooms.
Baggage - Checked baggage handled at most stations.
Reservations - All-reserved train.
Length of Trip - To Seattle: 2,206 miles in 45½ hours. To Portland: 2,257 miles in 45 hours.

Route Log

 CHICAGO, IL - See page 116.

0:00 (0:26) Depart Chicago's Union Station beneath streets of Chicago, emerging amidst some of city's most notable landmarks. On immediate right, Marina City's twin cylindrical towers are an architectural eye-catcher, while on forward right, Merchandise Mart is stoutly entrenched on banks of Chicago River.
0:03 (0:20) Following a quick turn west, smartly tapering design of Hancock Building is readily distinguishable back on right. Multi-tiered Sears Tower, currently world's tallest building at 1,353 feet, dominates skyline back on left.

For the next several miles, elevated trackbed affords encompassing views of Chicago's older north side. Multi-domed and multi-spired churches are impressive fixtures throughout this neighborhood.
0:23 (0:00) Arrive Glenview.

 GLENVIEW, IL - Glenview is a convenient suburban stop for the northern Chicago region.
0:00 (1:03) Depart Glenview north through a comely residential district. Between here and Milwaukee, landscape bares an interesting mix of older farms and modern industrial complexes. Underwriter's Laboratories, Fiat, Sara Lee, American Motors and AC are but a few of the corporate strongholds seen throughout this stretch.

0:02 (1:01) On left, skirt grounds of Glenview Naval Air Station where numerous helicopters, fixed-wing craft and a star-spangled water tower can be observed.
0:20 (0:43) Passing through Gurnee, Marriott's popular Great American Amusement Park can be seen on left.
0:23 (0:40) At Wadsworth, Des Plaines River follows infrequently on left. A couple miles hence, cross Illinois state line into Wisconsin.
0:38 (0:25) Old hotel at Sturtevant, on right, is interesting curiosity with its turret-adorned corners.
0:54 (0:09) On right is General Mitchell Field, Milwaukee's airport.
0:58 (0:05) With Milwaukee's skyline coming into full view, note two architecturally outstanding and historical churches to left. St. Josaphat's Basilica distinguished by its inspiring verdigris dome (modeled after St. Peter's in Rome) was built at turn of the century by poor immigrant parishioners using materials salvaged from Chicago's Federal Building. It was first Polish basilica in North America.

St. Stanislaus Cathedral, readily identified by its twin golden-domed spires, was nation's third Polish church at time of its construction. Colorfully faceted glasswork and sculptured marble bedeck interior of this magnificent structure.
0:59 (0:04) On left, Allen Bradley clock tower is stately landmark in foreground of downtown.
1:03 (0:00) Arrive Milwaukee station, crossing confluence of Menomonee and Milwaukee rivers. Watch for collection of private vintage rail cars sometimes parked at left.

 MILWAUKEE, WI - Milwaukee, an Indian word meaning "beautiful meeting place by the waters," is the largest city in Wisconsin with a metropolitan population of 1,400,000. It is also one of the nation's leading industrial centers, as well as being an important inland seaport on the Great Lakes.

Of course, a major industry is the brewing of beer—so important that Milwaukee is oft referred to as "beer town." The brewery image should not be misleading. Milwaukee, located on a beautiful bay of Lake Michigan, is one of America's most attractive cities.

Union Station, 433 W. St. Paul Ave., is on the edge of downtown. The station has a large waiting room, redcaps, a restaurant, a newsstand, a Hertz counter and pay-parking across the street.

For arrival and departure information and for reservations, call (414) 933-3081. Ticket window and waiting room hours are 6 am to 9 pm, Monday thru Friday; 7:30 am to 9 pm, Saturday and Sunday.

Cab stand at the station; Yellow Cab, 271-1800. Hertz **rental cars** are available at the station. **Local bus** stop is at the front door. **Greyhound,** (414) 272-8900. **Wis-Mich Trailways** and Lamers Bus Lines stop at the station. **Milwaukee Airport** (General Mitchell Field) is six miles south of the station.

Milwaukee Visitors Bureau, 756 N. Milwaukee St., 53202; (414) 273-3950.

Ramada Inn Downtown, 633 W. Michigan St., 53203; (414) 272-8410. Attractive and convenient. Three blocks from the station. $60.

-**Marc Plaza Hotel,** 509 W. Wisconsin Ave.; (414) 271-7250 or 800-558-7708. A Milwaukee landmark. Three blocks from the station. $95.

-**Howard Johnson Plaza Hotel,** 611 W. Wisconsin Ave.; (414) 273-2950. Four blocks from the station. $61.

Milwaukee is one of several cities that has a **Skywalk** system, permitting weatherproof strolling and shopping. Nearest access is W. Michigan and 4th, three blocks from the station. Spirit of Milwaukee Theatre, on Wisconsin Avenue, between 1st and 2nd streets in the Grand Ave. Mall, has a **multimedia show** giving a Milwaukee overview, four blocks from the station. **First Wisconsin Center,** 11 blocks east of the station, is the state's highest building; the 41st floor has a superb view. **Milwaukee Public Museum,** 800 W. Wells St. and eight blocks from the station, is the nation's fourth largest natural history museum. **Mitchell Park Conservatory,** 524 Layton Blvd., houses horticultural exhibits from around the world in three massive glass domes. **Milwaukee County Zoo** is one of the finest in the world.

0:00 (1:14) Depart Milwaukee.

0:05 (1:09) On left, three unusual glass domes house Mitchell Park Horticultural Conservatory (world's largest curved-glass horticultural structures). Botanical displays representing the world's three climatic conditions—arid, temperate and tropical—are cultivated here in buildings that simulate their native environs.

0:09 (1:05) Milwaukee County Stadium, home of baseball's "Brewers," can be seen on left.

0:10 (1:04) "If you've got the time, Miller's got the beer"—on right. This brewery is just one of many for which Milwaukee is famous. Immediately thereafter, cross Menomonee River.

0:21 (0:53) Passing through handsome suburb of Elm Grove, campus-like complex on right is Notre Dame Health Care Center, a facility for elderly nuns.

0:30 (0:44) Border edge of Pewaukee Lake on left, with town of same name encircling shoreline.

0:38 (0:36) At Okauchee, Ocono Lake appears on left. Quick glimpse of Okauchee Lake is afforded on right.

With the vestiges of urban influence slowly waning, embark across the open spaces that are America's heartland. Thomas Jefferson once exhorted that we be "a nation of yeoman farmers." To that end, the rustic farmsteads set amidst rolling fields of grain are picturesque reminders that this early American ideal still flourishes.

0:46 (0:28) On eastern outskirts of Ixonia, cross Rock River.

0:56 (0:18) Approaching Watertown, cross Rock River twice again, noting attractive homes lining banks. Proceeding through town, tall spire of St. Bernard's Catholic Church protrudes noticeably above treetops on right. Immediately thereafter, campus and stadium of Maranatha College can also be seen on right.

1:14 (0:00) Cross Crawfish River arriving Columbus. Once in station, note interesting design of 125-year-old Zion Evangelical Lutheran Church on left. Large bell mounted beneath its steeple was gift from Emperor of Germany, cast from pieces of French cannon captured during Franco-Prussian War.

Immediately adjacent to church, fanciful clock tower sits atop 1892 Columbus City Hall.

COLUMBUS, WI - Famed for its springtime regalia of redbud blossoms, Columbus is also a convenient stop for students attending the University of Wisconsin in nearby Madison.

0:00 (0:28) Depart Columbus.

0:39 (0:03) While passing through Wyocena, don't miss "Santa's Super Rocket." Looking capable of interplanetary travel, this cosmic contraption was surely the highlight of many Christmases past. Regrettably, it has since been put out to pasture, and today ages gracefully in back lots of a Wyocena salvage yard on right.

0:43 (0:00) Arrive Portage.

PORTAGE, WI - Situated on a narrow strip of land between the Fox and Wisconsin rivers, Portage is a prosperous commercial hub of the surrounding farmlands. As its name implies, the town was once a popular stopover for traders and settlers who had to "portage" their gear from one river to the other.

0:00 (0:25) Depart Portage.

0:13 (0:12) Wisconsin River joins on left. A couple miles downline, American Baptist Indian Church and cemetery are scenically isolated atop bluff on right.

0:20 (0:00) Arriving Wisconsin Dells, magnificent canyon cut by river can be seen on left. Throughout much of year, boats and rafts traverse its scenic course, providing feature attraction of this popular tourist haven. Area is also highlighted by a host of man-made amusements, several of which surround station site.

WISCONSIN DELLS, WI - From airplane rides to water slides, an amusement-park atmosphere pervades this renowned Midwestern resort. Yet, as previously noted, the natural beauty and drama surrounding "The Dells" is still the mainstay around which the town has flourished.

0:00 (0:56) Depart Wisconsin Dells across Wisconsin River.

0:02 (0:54) On right, miniature train winds through midst of old-time railroad village.

0:18 (0:31) Built in 1902, multi-spired St. Patrick's Catholic Church on right is prominent feature of "midtown" route through Mauston. On western edge of town, train skirts shoreline of Lake Decorah on right, formed by dam across Lemonweir River.

0:28 (0:18) Fascinating rock formations are an unexpected delight of Camp Douglas area. Once in town, Camp Douglas Village Hall is a most impressive structure on left.

0:40 (0:00) Arriving Tomah, well-preserved Pullman car of Milwaukee Road houses Chamber of Commerce on left.

TOMAH, WI - In a tribute to its agricultural roots, Tomah is host each July to the Wisconsin Dairyland Grand National Tractor Pull—a grueling test of skill and equipment, attracting hundreds of farmers from across the Midwest and Canada. From "souped up" rigs to stock models, contestants hauling weighted sleds vie for over $100,000 in prize money while an impassioned throng of spectators cheers on its favorites.

Tomah is also noted as the boyhood home of Frank King, creator of the famed comic strip "Gasoline Alley." Many of King's drawings and cartoons are preserved throughout the town. Walt and Skeezix can be seen holding up the sign in front of the Chamber of Commerce office next to the station.

0:00 (0:54) Depart Tomah.

0:01 (0:53) On left, pass Tomah Lake.

0:07 (0:46) Brief intrusion of alpine-like terrain highlights geography surrounding Tunnel City. Quick trip through tunnel appropriately follows.

0:17 (0:33) On right, pass small Sparta airport. At same time, begin following La Crosse River to its juncture with Mississippi River twenty miles west.

0:29 (0:18) In Bangor, distinctive Village Hall stands out on right.

0:41 (0:04) Cross La Crosse River.

0:44 (0:00) Two beautiful churches on right preview arrival at La Crosse.

LA CROSSE, WI - An old Indian game that the French dubbed "lacrosse" gave its name to this picturesque community, set at the confluence of the Black, La Crosse and Mississippi rivers. Agricultural, industrial and commercial enterprises all contribute to the town's well-balanced economy.

0:00 (0:45) Departing La Crosse, cross Mississippi River into Minnesota. Islands in middle of this historic waterway divide river into three channels here. Once on western bank, pass through "apple capital" of La Crescent and begin a northerly tack that generally parallels river through Richard J. Dorer Memorial Hardwood State Forest. Oak, birch, maple and walnut are but a sampling of hardwood trees that thrive in these parts.

The ensuing 125 miles is one of the most scenic legs of The Empire Builder route. Quaint little townships, elegant in their simplicity, are splendidly well-preserved along these riverbanks. At their doorstep, barges and riverboats leisurely traverse the waters of the mighty Mississippi. To the west, the lush farmlands and forests of this fertile river valley provide a serene backdrop for a setting that has assuredly inspired many an artist or photographer.

0:10 (0:33) On right, note Number 7 dam and locks.

0:22 (0:18) On right, note Number 6 dam and locks.

0:35 (0:01) Towering 500 feet above the river, Sugar Loaf Mountain is a renowned landmark of Winona on left. According to Indian legend, silhouette of famous Sioux Chief Wa-Pa-Sha was once prominent feature of mountain prior to quarrying operations of late 1800s.

0:36 (0:00) Another "midtown" route into station avails intriguing insights into this hardy Midwestern community upon arriving Winona. Cozy chalet-style depot greets passengers on left.

 WINONA, MN - Since construction of the first sawmills here in the early 1850s, Winona has grown from a one-industry town into a bustling manufacturing center. Essential throughout its development, the influence of the Mississippi riverboat remains an important aspect of the town's present-day charm.

Winona is also a popular connection for passengers traveling to the famed Mayo Clinic in nearby Rochester.

0:00 (1:26) Depart Winona.

0:03 (1:23) Large cluster of grain elevators on right evidences major distribution port.

0:15 (1:08) On right, note Number 5 dam and locks.

0:20 (1:01) Numerous fishing camps flourish about Weaver, supporting area's claim as "White Bass Capital of the World." Passing through town, stately structure perched atop bluffs on left was formerly grandiose hotel. Recognized in National Register, building was recently remodeled to house studio of local artist.

0:37 (0:39) Comely Wabasha is home of Anderson House Hotel, Minnesota's oldest operating inn since 1856. As special amenities, complimentary shoeshines are provided, as well as hot bricks to warm the feet in winter. For lonesome travelers, house cats are also available upon request.

0:38 (0:38) Mississippi River widens considerably to accommodate waters of Chippewa River flowing in from east. Waterskiing is said to have originated here in resultant expanse known as Lake Pepin.

0:56 (0:15) Pass through beautiful little town of Frontenac whose roots trace back to original French fort established here in 1723.

0:57 (0:13) On left, T-bar lift ascends slopes of Mt. Frontenac Ski Area.

1:01 (0:08) Antique rooster weather vane sits proudly atop barn of beautiful farm on left.

1:03 (0:05) On right, nostalgic advertisement for Beechnut chewing tobacco weathers picturesquely on side of barn.

1:04 (0:04) Approaching Red Wing, Minnesota State Training School is easily recognized on left by its lofty tower, with Minnesota and U.S. flags fronting property. Internationally acclaimed for success of its "Positive Peer Group" therapy, facility was originally established in 1891, and modeled after castle on Rhine River.

1:08 (0:00) Arrive Red Wing. Just south of station, historic St. James Hotel can be seen on left. Its 41 rooms are adorned in Victorian splendor, and each named for a famous riverboat that once plied waters of Mississippi. Built in 1875, Red Wing Shoe Company saved it from decay in late 1970s with an ambitious restoration program. Prior to invention of dining cars, trains stopped here to feed passengers in hotel's well-regarded restaurant.

 RED WING, MN - This lovely riverside community takes its name from generations of Sioux Chieftains who chose as their emblem a swan's wing dyed scarlet. Long known for its manufacture of shoes and pottery, tourists are presently discovering a wealth of recreational opportunities in the hills, forests and rivers surrounding Red Wing.

0:00 (1:10) Depart Red Wing.

0:06 (1:06) Cross Cannon River.

0:09 (1:01) On right, note Number 3 dam and locks.

0:21 (0:49) Cross Vermillion River into Hastings. Domed Dakota County Courthouse, built in 1871, can be seen on left.

0:25 (0:45) Cross Mississippi River, its lakes and inlets bordering on left into St. Paul/Minneapolis.

0:33 (0:37) On left, pass large 3-M Plant. Based here in St. Paul/Minneapolis, "Scotch Tape" is one of more well-known products of this diverse corporation.

0:47 (0:23) On left, St. Paul Downtown Airport can be seen across river. At same time, city skyline juts imposingly above horizon in distance.

0:51 (0:19) Central fixtures of downtown hub preside atop palisades on right, overlooking succession of bridges spanning Mississippi River.

0:53 (0:17) On left, old sternwheelers are frequently moored alongside Harriet Island. From May through September, nostalgic riverboat excursions to nearby Ft. Snelling are popular tourist attraction.

0:54 (0:16) Modeled after St. Peter's in Rome, magnificent St. Paul Cathedral on right is readily identified by its verdigris domes and outstanding classical architecture.

0:59 (0:11) Whimsical castle-like facilities on left are home of Schmidt Brewery.

1:10 (0:00) Arrive modernistic St. Paul station. Access to Minneapolis is also afforded by this stop.

MINNEAPOLIS-ST. PAUL, MN - After Lt. Zebulon M. Pike explored the region, Ft. Snelling was established in 1819 approximately five miles from the current site of St. Paul. Its location as the northernmost navigable portion of the Mississippi River made the region a natural port and trade center. St. Paul received its start as a trading post while Minneapolis was born somewhat later when flour and lumber mills were started on the other side of the river.

Today, those industries are still important to the area's economy, and the "Twin Cities" are the financial, cultural and industrial focal point of the upper Midwest. Their combined population is well over two million and St. Paul is the capital of Minnesota. Companies like General Mills, Control Data and Dayton Hudson are headquartered here. Clean, modern, young and growing are first impressions, and an elaborate pedestrian "skyway" system throughout downtown makes legendary winters more tolerable.

Midway Station, 730 Transfer Road, St. Paul, MN 55114, is literally "midway" between the two downtown areas of Minneapolis and St. Paul, being approximately four miles from each. Storage lockers, luggage carts and food and beverage machines are available at the station. Free parking is adjacent to the station.

For information and reservations, call (612) 339-2382.

Cab stand at the station; Yellow Cab (direct line in station), 824-4444. Budget **rental cars** are located downtown and Budget will pick up and drop off customers at the station. **Local buses** to either city at University and Transfer Rd., one "long" block south; call 827-7733. **Greyhound** bus terminal, 371-3311. **Minneapolis-St. Paul International Airport,** seven miles south of station.

Minneapolis Convention and Visitors Assn., 1219 Marquette Ave., 55403; (612) 348-4313.

Twins Motor Inn, 1975 University Ave., 55104; (612) 645-0311. Two blocks from the station. $37.95.

The nation's longest shopping plaza, **Nicollet Mall,** stretches along Nicollet Ave. in downtown Minneapolis. The **IDS** center's 57-story, architecturally renowned skyscraper has an observation deck for a commanding view of the region, and **Loring Park** (and lake) is a great place to relax in the heart of the city. The **Walker Art Center** has one of the finest collections in the country. **St. Anthony Main/Riverplace** has a collection of shops and restaurants near

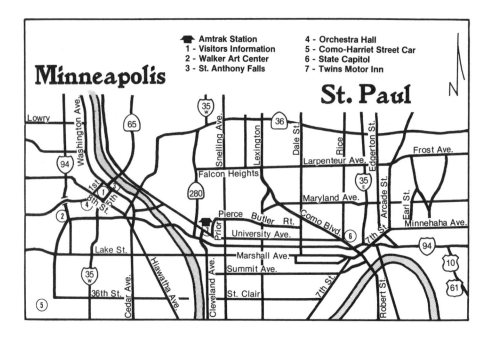

Minneapolis

St. Paul

N

- Amtrak Station
1 - Visitors Information
2 - Walker Art Center
3 - St. Anthony Falls
4 - Orchestra Hall
5 - Como-Harriet Street Car
6 - State Capitol
7 - Twins Motor Inn

the Mississippi River's St. Anthony Falls.

The **Como-Harriet Streetcar Line and Minnesota Transportation Museum** can be reached by driving south on Interstate 35W, then west on W. 36th St., then left at Richfield Road. There is a 1908 streetcar transporting riders from Lake Como to Lake Harriet and rail equipment in various phases of reconstruction.

0:00 (1:32) Departing St. Paul, Minneapolis can be viewed in distance left, where 57-story I.D.S. Tower is prominent landmark of downtown area.
1:32 (0:00) Arrive St. Cloud.

ST. CLOUD, MN - Set scenically along the banks of the Mississippi River, St. Cloud is noted for its numerous granite quarries which have supplied stone for many venerable structures throughout the country. In recognition of this vital industry, Anthony Caponi's sculpture of "The Granite Trio" is the centerpiece of St. Cloud's downtown mall.
0:00 (0:59) Depart St. Cloud.
0:59 (0:00) Arrive Staples.

STAPLES, MN - Once a dying railroad town, Staples' fortunes improved dramatically when its Voca-

tional Training Institute was established in 1960. Enrolling hundreds of students, its on-the-job curriculum encompassed many local projects, and at the same time, prepared a work-ready labor force that continues to attract new industry to the region.
0:00 (0:54) Depart Staples.
0:54 (0:00) Arrive Detroit Lakes.

DETROIT LAKES, MN - Surrounded by no fewer than 412 lakes, Detroit Lakes is the hub of a vast recreation haven. Although outdoor adventure is nearly limitless, fishing is still king, with walleye, bass and sunfish the most frequent catches.

Prior to road improvements of the 1930s, steamboats were a popular transport between the immediately surrounding lakes, and also serviced the railroad depot where 14 passenger trains arrived daily.
0:00 (0:56) Depart Detroit Lakes.
0:56 (0:00) Arrive Fargo.

FARGO, ND - Lying in the heart of the fertile Red River Valley, Fargo is North Dakota's largest city and is a vital commercial and livestock center for a vast region. Ten thousand years earlier, the Fargo townsite was submerged beneath 200 feet of water, dammed by the continental glacier to the north.

Named for the founder of the Wells Fargo Express Company, Fargo is a convenient stop for students attending North Dakota State University located here.

0:00 (1:11) Depart Fargo.

1:00 (0:00) Arrive West Grand Forks, a western suburb of Grand Forks.

GRAND FORKS, ND - As suggested by its name, Grand Forks is situated at the confluence of the Red Lake River and the Red River of the North. Located here, the University of North Dakota lends a collegiate atmosphere to this agriculturally oriented community. A 1980s study named Grand Forks and State College, PA the least stressful cities in America.

Both Greyhound and Amtrak Thruway buses between Grand Forks and Winnipeg, Manitoba are available daily, making this a feasible Amtrak-VIA transfer point.

0:00 (1:25) Depart West Grand Forks.

1:23 (0:00) Arrive Devils Lake.

DEVILS LAKE, ND - Settled along the shores of North Dakota's largest natural lake, Devils Lake is a sportsman's paradise, and acclaimed in particular as the goose- and duck-hunting capital of North America. Not always held in such high esteem, Sioux and Chippewa Indians originally named the lake in deference to the evil spirits that once overturned their canoes in the midst of a fierce inter-tribal battle.

0:00 (1:02) Depart Devils Lake.

1:02 (0:00) Arrive Rugby.

RUGBY, ND - As well as an agricultural stronghold, Rugby is noted as the geographical center of North America. Located a half-mile south of town, a towering stone monument pays tribute to this distinction. Rugby is also less than 50 miles from the U.S.-Canadian border where the beautiful International Peace Garden commemorates the many years of friendship between these two countries.

0:00 (1:08) Depart Rugby.

1:10 (0:00) Arrive Minot.

MINOT, ND - Once a desolate frontier outpost, Minot has blossomed into a flourishing industrial mecca, due in large part to its abundant natural resources of oil and coal. Set along the House River that frequently floods the town, Minot is also host to numerous military installations that further supplement a booming economy.

0:00 (0:50) Depart Minot.

0:50 (0:00) Arrive Stanley.

STANLEY, ND - Grain and livestock production are the foremost concerns of this small agricultural community. A prominent focal point of the town is the resplendent Montrail County Courthouse, located just north of the train station.

0:00 (1:05) Depart Stanley.

1:05 (0:00) Arrive Williston.

WILLISTON, ND - Since completion of the Garrison Dam Project along the adjacent Missouri River, Williston has maintained a dependable agricultural and livestock trade, virtually free from threat of drought that frequently plagued the region. Yet, like Minot, oil discoveries have played an important part in Williston's development.

Just west of Williston are two important historical sites: Fort Union which in its heyday was one of the most active trading posts in the West and Fort Buford where Chief Sitting Bull surrendered following the Battle of Little Bighorn.

0:00 (1:28) Departing Williston, Missouri River joins on left and follows intermittently for next 60 miles.

0:24 (1:04) Cross North Dakota state line into Montana and proceed through one of world's largest grain production belts. Along route, many small communities service needs of this expansive agricultural region. County fairgrounds are a popular adjunct of these remote rural outposts.

Gain one hour as train passes from Central to Mountain Time. Set your watch back (forward if eastbound) one hour.

0:52 (0:36) Just west of Culbertson, enter grounds of Fort Peck Indian Reservation that extends nearly ninety miles west to Nashua.

1:12 (0:16) Cross Poplar River.

1:28 (0:00) Arrive Wolf Point.

WOLF POINT, MT - Once a popular haunt of wolf trappers, Wolf Point is host each July to the "Wild Horse Stampede," acclaimed statewide as the "granddaddy of Montana rodeos."

0:00 (0:45) Depart Wolf Point.

0:40 (0:04) Approaching Glasgow, beautiful farmstead is nestled admist wooded glen on left. Bordering property is Milk River which train follows and crosses periodically to Havre.

0:45 (0:00) Letter "G" inscribed on hillside at right denotes arrival at Glasgow.

GLASGOW, MT - Lying in the heart of the Great Northern Wheat Belt, Glasgow has flourished in earnest since construction of the Fort Peck Dam just south of town. The resultant expanse of Fort Peck Lake continues to generate a healthy tourist trade attracted by its many recreational opportunities.

Glasgow is also renowned as a haven for fossil hunters. Exhibits at the Fort Peck Museum display the many varieties of dinosaur bones that have been found in the region.

0:00 (0:59) Depart Glasgow.

0:10 (0:49) On right, lovely home and outbuildings are attractive highlight of Tampico.

0:37 (0:22) Large bell atop Methodist church on right summons parishioners from many miles around Saco.

0:50 (0:08) Cross arm of Lake Bowdoin. Abundance of waterfowl denotes success of nearby Bowdoin National Wildlife Refuge.

0:59 (0:00) Arrive Malta.

MALTA, MT - Once the center of a great cattle empire, the region surrounding Malta was also the inspirational setting for many works of the famous artist Charles Russell whose paintings so vividly captured the unbridled spirit of the Western frontier.

0:00 (1:13) Depart Malta.

0:09 (1:04) Here in Wagner, at turn of the century, Butch Cassidy and The Sundance Kid carried out one of their many successful train robberies, escaping with nearly $70,000.

0:17 (0:56) Between Dodson and Harlem, traverse northern border of Fort Belknap Indian Reservation. At this time, Bear Paw Mountains can be seen forward on left.

0:30 (0:43) Passing through Savoy, note quaint old country schoolhouse on right. Built in 1916, drought and crop failures of early '70s precipitated a rapid decline in enrollment. School had only four students left when finally closed in 1974.

0:45 (0:28) In Zurich, another venerable schoolhouse stands proudly on right.

A few miles south of town lies historic Chief Joseph Battleground of the Bear's Paw. In 1877, after a 1,700-mile retreat through some of the most rugged country in the West, a disheartened Chief Joseph surrendered proclaiming, "From where the sun now stands, I will fight no more forever."

1:13 (0:00) Finely preserved S-2 steam locomotive of Great Northern Railway previews arrival at Havre station on left.

HAVRE, MT - At once the commercial hub of a sprawling agricultural region, Havre's attention in more recent times has focused on discoveries of natural gas.

Of Havre's many interesting attractions, the H. Earl Clark Museum, with its famous "Buffalo Jump Site," is one of the most popular. Here beneath precipitous cliffs are the skeletal remains of buffalo herds driven to a death plunge by Indian hunters.

0:00 (1:35) Depart Havre.

0:04 (1:31) On right, Milk River departs north for brief tour of Canada before returning to its source amidst Montana's Glacier National Park.

1:35 (0:00) Arrive Shelby. "Hot wire" draped across station roof helps melt snow in winter.

SHELBY, MT - Although oil and farming are the principal concerns here, Shelby is most remembered as the unlikely site of the 1923 world heavyweight championship fight between Jack Dempsey and Tommy Gibbons.

Remembering Dempsey after his death in 1983, a *Time* magazine writer opined that Shelby had a fight "the way Johnstown had a flood." The town of 2,000 constructed a 40,000-seat arena but then had trouble raising the guaranteed purse. While 24,000 attended the Fourth of July bout, only 7,000 bothered to pay; the rest crashed the gates. Dempsey won on points, the promoter skipped town, two banks

failed and the town was left insolvent.
0:00 (0:29) Depart Shelby.
0:29 (0:00) Arrive Cut Bank.

CUT BANK, MT - Another bastion of agriculture, livestock and oil production, Cut Bank often has the unglorious distinction of recording the nation's coldest midwinter temperatures.
0:00 (0:33) Depart Cut Bank across high trestle spanning Cut Bank Creek. Dramatic panorama of Rocky Mountain peaks begins to jut above the horizon, becoming more and more dynamic as train approaches Glacier National Park. Enroute, pass through territory of Blackfeet Indian Reservation.
0:22 (0:11) On left, small obelisk alongside highway commemorates northernmost explorations of Lewis and Clark when searching for passage through Rocky Mountains.
0:33 (0:00) Arrive Browning.

BROWNING, MT - A seasonal winter stop, Browning lies in the heart of the Blackfeet Indian Reservation, and is a popular shopping haunt for Native American goods. Here, too, is the Museum of the Plains Indian, featuring a permanent exhibit of historic arts from eleven Northern Plains tribes.
0:00 (0:22) Depart Browning.
0:16 (0:06) Dilapidated, yet character-laden fixtures of an early farming settlement are picturesquely poised at base of mountains on outskirts of East Glacier.
0:22 (0:00) Arriving Glacier Park Station, cross Two Medicine River from atop lofty trestle. In early 1900s, Great Northern Railway transported timber in from Washington and Oregon to construct spacious Glacier Park Lodge on right, as well as other hotel facilities within Park. Development not only promoted rail travel along their line, but as well enlightened tourists to a previously untapped vacation haven. Today, lodges are popular "base camps" for multitude of outdoor enthusiasts who flock here each summer.

GLACIER PARK STATION, MT - This seasonal summer stop is the gateway to untold adventure admist the breathtaking beauty of Glacier National Park. Established by Congress in 1910, hundreds of miles of hiking trails now lead to the rich forests, shimmering lakes and flower-blanketed meadows of this Rocky Mountain retreat. As reflected in its name, the Park is also home to 50 "living" glaciers, among the few in the U.S. considered relatively accessible.

Another of Glacier's foremost attractions is the Going-to-the-Sun highway, a spectacular mid-park route across the Continental Divide. Open from early summer through mid-October, this 50-mile drive is a popular alternative to backcountry exploration.
0:00 (1:32) Departing Glacier Park Station, begin ascent of Marias Pass and Continental Divide just south of Glacier National Park. Within minutes, rolling terrain of last 1,500 miles gives way to jagged intrusions of Rocky Mountains. On western slopes of pass, scenery is even more dramatic as train winds past waterfalls, river gorges and other wondrous spectacles of this diverse alpine geography. Additionally, trackside signposts identify names and altitudes of monumental peaks that encompass these majestic environs.
0:20 (1:15) Arriving 5,213-foot summit of Marias Pass (lowest Rocky Mountain rail crossing in U.S.), tall monument seen on left is commemorative to Theodore Roosevelt for whom adjacent highway is named. Markers proclaiming explorations of John Stevens are stationed on right.

Although reputedly traversed by Indians during inter-tribal raids, abortive and inaccurate attempts at charting this area gave rise to its original designation as "Mystery Pass." It was only when the railroad hired Stevens in 1889 that this elusive passage was at last established as a permanent route through the northern Rockies.
0:53 (0:46) Middle Fork of Flathead River joins on left.
0:56 (0:43) From high atop dramatic trestle, cross Flathead River which then proceeds to follow on right.
1:03 (0:35) Small village of Essex features impressive Izaak Walton Hotel on right. This is a flag stop for The Builder.
1:43 (0:00) Arrive Belton amidst cluster of rustic cabins surrounding station.

BELTON, MT - This stop affords access to the western reaches of Glacier National Park.

163

0:00 (0:31) Depart Belton.

0:10 (0:20) Cross Flathead River which is soon joined by South Fork approaching from left.

0:17 (0:13) Large Anaconda aluminum plant on right is one industrial stronghold of Columbia Falls. Once in midst of town, note old steam locomotive preserved on left.

0:31 (0:00) Old Bavarian-style station is a handsome sight on left arriving Whitefish.

WHITEFISH, MT - Set amidst a picturesque valley of the Flathead National Forest, Whitefish is another gateway to outdoor recreation. Besides its proximity to Glacier National Park, Whitefish is only 25 miles from Flathead Lake, the largest natural freshwater lake west of the Mississippi. Closer to home, Whitefish Lake borders the town to the north, and is a noteworthy attraction in its own right.

Activity flourishes here in wintertime as well with vacationers flocking to the slopes of nearby Big Mountain, one of the nation's foremost ski resorts.

0:00 (1:54) Depart Whitefish.

0:44 (1:05) Penetrate seven-mile-long Flathead Tunnel, third longest in North America.

1:45 (0:00) Arrive Libby.

LIBBY, MT - From its formative development as a gold-mining town, Libby is now the center of an active logging industry, with tours of its sawmills and processing plants an interesting attraction. The region is also rich in vermiculite, mined for its use as a horticultural rooting agent.

Situated in the midst of the Kootenai National Forest, Libby is a favorite retreat for sportsmen who cherish the hunting and fishing opportunities of the surrounding wilderness.

0:00 (1:50) Depart Libby.

Gain one hour as train passes from Mountain to Pacific Time. Set your watch back (forward if eastbound) one hour.

1:50 (0:00) Arrive Sandpoint.

SANDPOINT, ID - Set along the shores of beautiful Lake Pend Oreille (a seemingly bottomless lake which produces occasional "sightings" of its own sea monster), Sandpoint is rapidly emerging as one of the most popular vacation resorts of the Northwest. While lakeside activities highlight the summer season, winter's prime attraction is the nearby Schweitzer Ski Area where the view from the summit is equally as enthralling as the powder-laden slopes.

0:00 (1:13) Depart Sandpoint and cross mouth of Pend Oreille River on ultra-long (8,000-foot) deck bridge.

1:25 (0:00) Arrive Spokane.

SPOKANE, WA - From its humble beginnings as a sawmill town, Spokane has emerged as one of the most vibrant cities of the Northwest, set alongside the thundering falls of the Spokane River. Dubbing itself "Monarch of an Inland Empire," Spokane is surrounded by a wealth of natural resources and fertile farmlands that, for more than 100 years, have been the mainstays of its dynamic prosperity. An important rail center as well, the Great Northern Clock Tower (that formerly presided atop one of the nation's finest train stations) remains a cherished landmark of the downtown district.

As a celebration of its good fortunes, Spokane was host to the 1974 World's Fair, its facilities built around the site of the town's original sawmill. Several of the Fair's most prominent attractions are now preserved amidst the beautifully landscaped acreage of Riverfront Park.

Highlighting an impressive list of cultural endowments, Spokane's Museum of Native American Cultures is recognized as one of the most comprehensive collections of Indian art and artifacts in existence. Another interesting diversion is Gonzaga University's Crosby Library where a nostalgic array of Bing Crosby memorabilia pays tribute to one of the school's most distinguished alumni.

Also of interest is Spokane's Old Flour Mill, recently refurbished as a delightful setting for cozy shops and restaurants. Further shopping adventures are also in store along the city's Skywalk, a ten-block enclave of retail merchants, interconnected by glass-enclosed walkways suspended above the downtown streets.

Empire Builder – West Portal, Cascade Tunnel

(At Spokane, the Portland and Seattle sections of The Builder divide. Spokane to Seattle route appears first below.)

For route from Spokane to Portland, see page 167.

0:00 (2:05) Depart Spokane.
2:05 (0:00) Arrive Ephrata.

EPHRATA, WA - A town of 5,000, it is in the heart of irrigated farmland with water coming from the Columbia River Basin irrigation project.
0:00 (1:00) Depart Ephrata.
0:50 (0:42) Pass Rock Island Dam, stretching across Columbia River, on left.

0:55 (0:46) Cut sharply to left and cross Columbia, then roll high above its west bank into Wenatchee. If you haven't already done so, wake your friends—a morning of spectacular sightseeing has begun.
1:10 (0:00) Arrive Wenatchee. Note new glass-box depot in place of more traditional one still standing nearby that once served ill-fated North Coast Hiawatha which used this route until its discontinuance in October 1979.

WENATCHEE, WA - Another of the world's "Apple Capitals," Wenatchee is nestled in the scenic foothills of the Cascade Mountains that provide the ideal climes for its abundant orchards. Here, too, is the North Central Washington Museum where live demonstrations (butter-churning, bread-making, etc.) enhance one's appreciation of pioneer domestic life. The nearby Ohme Gardens and Mission Ridge Ski Resort are also much-frequented attractions.

0:00 (2:55) Depart Wenatchee, rolling past warehouses surrounded by piles of skids and apple crates with Wenatchee River to left. Evidence of area's two major industries, logging and apples, appear on both sides of train. For first hour westbound from Wenatchee, best scenery occurs on left.

0:20 (2:35) Pass through Cashmere, also with stacks of apple crates and warehouses.

0:22 (2:33) Curving right, squeeze between rocks and Wenatchee River. Train crosses river three times in next five minutes while approaching Cascades, with mountains beginning to appear at left.

0:30 (2:25) Begin gradual climb out of river valley and pass through Bavarianesque Leavenworth with apple orchards still visible.

0:34 (2:20) Scenic mountains on left offer preview of what is to come.

In the next several minutes, The Builder passes through a beautiful valley dotted with houses, barns and horses, and then enters the first of several tunnels built to establish this incredible route through the Cascades.

0:44 (2:10) Soon after first tunnel, again cross Wenatchee River with beautiful scenery to both sides, then through another tunnel. Soon after emerging, join U.S. Highway 2 at its milepost 82 and railroad milepost 1689 (measured from St. Paul along old Great Northern Railway).

0:59 (1:55) At Merritt, an old wooden water tower is visible to right as train slows for its charge through mountains.

1:01 (1:52) River crossings continue and mountain vistas become more dramatic.

1:05 (1:48) From here, best scenery (westbound) is to right. Roll across trestle over a beautiful canyon, move through another tunnel, and emerge with tumbling river on right which is followed to Cascade Tunnel.

1:14 (1:40) Enter Cascade Tunnel, 2,247 feet above sea level, a 7.8-mile bore beneath forbidding Stevens Pass.

It takes approximately 15 minutes to traverse the tunnel, time enough to check your film for the scenic run through the Cascades and down Puget Sound to Seattle. Completed in 1929, tunnel is the second longest in North America, exceeded only by the 9.1-mile-long MacDonald Tunnel through the Canadian Rockies.

1:29 (1:25) Emerge from Cascade Tunnel, soon passing sign at right indicating that our location is appropriately named "Scenic" as Builder rolls high above a beautiful valley to right.

1:34 (1:20) Cross roaring South Skykomish River which will be followed to Everett north of Seattle.

1:37 (1:15) Between mileposts 1721 and 1722, a rushing stream and small waterfall appear to left of train. Better scenery from here to Seattle will be to right with tall trees, huge granite rocks, ravines and streams, with our train curving through this landscape and crossing Skykomish on high steel trestles.

1:47 (1:05) Curve to right across a spectacular steel trestle high above fast-moving Foss River on its way to join Skykomish.

1:52 (1:00) Pass Mt. Baker-Snoqualmie National Forest Ranger Station on right.

1:55 (0:57) Roll through village of Skykomish, an old railroad town with several interesting buildings. Skykomish Hotel, across street on right, has been social hub of community since its completion in 1904. Train crews still park their engines in front and go in for hearty lunch. On left, multi-storied concrete structure with broken windows once was power plant that furnished electricity for railroad when 71-mile section from here through Cascade Tunnel was electrified. Diesels, however, ultimately took over in 1956. Old Great Northern depot also still stands.

1:58 (0:54) Pass unusual concrete sculpture on left.

2:09 (0:45) Roll past Sunset Falls, actually more a steep rapids than a true waterfall, on left. Vertical cliffs and spectacular finger-like Mt. Index rise above valley floor beyond river.

2:11 (0:43) Cross river again at village of Index, on right. Large boardinghouse-like building at southwest corner of town, partially hidden by trees, is historic Bush House, a 1904 hostelry which once accommodated such notables as Calvin Coolidge, Teddy Roosevelt, William Howard Taft and William Jennings Bryan.

2:23 (0:31) Two more crossings of river bring us into Gold Bar.

2:33 (0:21) Gradually leave Cascades behind for flatter terrain, and enter Monroe where huge smokestack rises from supermarket parking lot to right. Old depot reposes about 30 yards to right where it appears there are no longer any tracks.

2:55 (0:00) Arrive Everett.

EVERETT, WA - Noted foremost for its lumber production and airplane manufacture, Everett's location along a natural landlocked harbor is likewise tailor-made for a shipping and fishing industry that continues to flourish. One of the city's most popular attractions is tours of Boeing's 747/767 assembly plant, located here within the world's largest (by volume) building.

0:00 (0:23) Depart Everett southbound, skirting shoreline of Puget Sound. Whidbey Island can be seen directly right, while peaks of Olympic Range loom majestically in distance.

0:23 (0:00) Arriving Edmonds, state ferries shuttling to and from Olympic Peninsula can be observed on right.

EDMONDS, WA - Self-proclaimed as the "Gem of the Puget Sound," Edmonds is a gracious residential suburb, only 15 miles north of Seattle's city center. Here, the Edmonds Museum provides a reflective glance at the town's short but colorful history. Also of interest is the Old Milltown shopping arcade, imaginatively housed in a turn-of-the-century Ford garage.

0:00 (0:31) Depart Edmonds.

0:04 (0:27) Large refinery and dockside facilities are entrenched along waterfront at Point Wells.

0:10 (0:21) Approaching Seattle, colonies of sailboats are a picturesque backyard spectacle for a host of elegant homes, perched atop colorfully foliated sea cliffs on left.

0:14 (0:17) Statue of Leif Ericson maintains vigil over hundreds of boats tethered at Shilshole Bay Moorage on right. Across water lies Bainbridge Island.

0:16 (0:15) Temporarily depart coastline route, crossing Salmon Bay inlet of Puget Sound. In middle of bridge, note elaborate Chittenden Locks on left, affording access to more easterly ports along Lake Washington. To forward left, another throng of sailboats surrounds Salmon Bay Terminal.

0:21 (0:10) Travel through grounds of U.S. Naval Reservation before emerging amidst Seattle's colorful waterfront district.

0:23 (0:08) On right, Pier 70 is largest wooden building to be restored in America. In its heyday, warehouse was chock full of teas and spices arriving from Orient. Today, over 40 imaginative shops and restaurants are tucked within this historic structure. At adjacent Pier 69, "Princess Marguerite" departs daily for excursions to Victoria, British Columbia.

On left, Seattle's towering "Space Needle" was architectural centerpiece of 1962 World's Fair. In foreground, delicate arches front grounds of Pacific Science Center.

0:30 (0:01) Enter tunnel, emerging minutes later beneath shadows of two prominent towers on right. White castle-like Smith Tower was tallest building west of Mississippi River when constructed in 1914. Fanciful clock tower to its left rises above King Street Station, the western terminus of Empire Builder route.

0:31 (0:00) Arrive Seattle.

 SEATTLE, WA - See page 256.

Route Log for Spokane to Portland

0:00 (2:46) Depart Spokane.

2:46 (0:00) Arrive Pasco.

PASCO, WA - A city of 18,000, Pasco is heavily involved in agriculture, an industry which has been helped considerably by the Columbia Basin irrigation project. The community also has been closely linked to transportation, with rail lines radiating in all directions, as well as river freight transfers due to its location at the confluence of the Columbia and Snake rivers. This is the Columbia's farthest navigable point for sizeable ships.

0:00 (1:55) Depart Pasco.

1:12 (0:43) Now Columbia River makes its dramatic appearance at left. This 1,210-mile giant produces more than one-third of America's hydroelectric power! Bluffs on other side are northern edge of Oregon's landscape. River traffic, mostly consisting of tugs pushing barges, will be quite heavy between here and Vancouver.

1:19 (0:36) This is Roosevelt with grain-loading facilities between tracks and river.

1:25 (0:30) An unusual orchard "oasis," surrounded by slender poplar trees, is above to right.

1:32 (0:23) River begins to look more gorge-like as train moves closer to Pacific Ocean.

1:39 (0:16) Bridge on far side of Columbia carries auto traffic on Interstate 84 across mouth of John Day River.

1:40 (0:15) Impressive John Day Dam backs up Columbia, on left. Navigational lock is on this side of river and handles eight million tons of commercial traffic each year. With 113 feet maximum lift, it is one of world's highest single lift locks. Dam's 16 generating units can produce enough electricity to handle needs of two Seattles. Four more units are planned.

1:45 (0:10) Bridge spanning Columbia is U.S. 97. Maryhill Museum is located here; originally built as a mansion, it was dedicated as a museum by Queen of Romania in 1920s and now houses an extensive collection of rare art. Above tracks is Stonehenge, built as a memorial to World War I dead by railroad entrepreneur Sam Hill, and is a replica of its namesake in England.

1:52 (0:03) Through a brief tunnel, one of thirteen between Pasco and Vancouver.

1:55 (0:00) Arrive at rail yards of Wishram.

WISHRAM, WA - This is primarily a stop for railroad workers, with one of the last railroad-operated "beaneries" in the country.

0:00 (0:29) Depart Wishram.

0:01 (0:28) Rail bridge crossing Columbia is Burlington Northern line to Klamath Falls in southern Oregon. The Pioneer, Amtrak's Salt Lake to Seattle section of The California Zephyr, travels the other side of Columbia on Union Pacific tracks.

0:10 (0:19) The Dalles Dam (pronounced dals) staggers across Columbia, making a two-mile-long Z.

The powerhouse, located in the portion of the dam which runs parallel to the tracks, is a half-mile long and contains 22 generators. The dam also has two fish ladders and a navigational lock on the Washington shore. The town of The Dalles, a French word meaning trough and derived from the cut the river makes, can be seen on the Oregon shore. The white building above the shore on a bluff is a unique electric rectifer, changing AC to DC for transmission to Los Angeles.

0:23 (0:06) On clear days, Mount Hood, the highest peak in Oregon at 11,235 feet and continually snow-capped, can be seen rising like a pyramidal spectre in far distance to left.

0:29 (0:00) Arrive Bingen-White Salmon.

BINGEN-WHITE SALMON, WA - This is orchard country. From here west, foliage will become more abundant as the Columbia Gorge, with its high annual rainfall, is entered.

0:00 (1:13) Depart Bingen-White Salmon.

0:07 (1:06) Venerable Hood River Hotel can be spotted across river, with waterfalls higher up.

0:13 (1:00) More falls cascading down the cliffs can be seen across river. Now enter Columbia Gorge, first explored by Lewis and Clark.

0:16 (0:57) Empire Builder slows to a crawl and now crosses geographic fault that is so active tracks must be realigned almost monthly, with tracks being monitored daily.

0:23 (0:50) Enter a rain forest, having left near-desert country just a few minutes ago.

0:30 (0:43) Bridge of the Gods is forward and to left. This magnificent web of steel crosses Columbia on exact spot where legendary natural stone bridge of Indians supposedly fell into river when nearby volcanic peaks argued, causing ground to tremble. Town of Cascade Locks is on far shore.

0:33 (0:40) Bonneville Dam backs up Columbia, forming 48-mile-long Lake Bonneville. Dam utilizes two islands in mid-stream to help close off river's flow. This was earliest of Columbia River dams.

168

Elaborate fish ladders are popular with salmon watchers.

0:38 (0:35) Sheer-walled, 800-foot monolith on right is Beacon Rock, proclaimed to be largest such formation in U.S. and second only to Gibraltar.

0:40 (0:33) Most spectacular of waterfalls on far side is 620-foot Multnomah Falls, second highest in nation. Its downward plunge ends in a beautiful tree-lined pool.

0:46 (0:27) Longest tunnel of day is 2,369 feet in length and penetrates Cape Horn on western edge of Cascades as we exit Columbia Gorge.

1:13 (0:00) Arrive Vancouver where delightful chalet-style depot greets passengers. From here to Portland, Empire Builder follows route of The Coast Starlight.

 VANCOUVER, WA - Strategically placed on the Columbia River, where ocean, air, rail and highway transportation converge, Vancouver has become a major shipping hub of the Northwest. Its lengthy history (it is the oldest non-Indian settlement in Washington) saw the likes of a trading outpost of the Hudson's Bay Company, the construction of Fort Vancouver, and the presence of Ulysses S. Grant when he was but a mere lieutenant in the Army. Both Fort Vancouver and the U. S. Grant Museum are open to the public.

0:00 (0:19) Depart Vancouver, crossing Columbia River (and Washington/Oregon state line) into Portland. In midst of river, traverse Hayden Island while vessels and dockside facilities of fast shipping industry abound on both banks.

0:13 (0:06) Cross Willamette River which then follows on left into Portland station. Willamette is another important shipping channel, as evidenced by heavy concentration of industry along its banks. Dramatic bridges span this waterway, with downtown Portland skyline silhouetted in background.

0:18 (0:01) On left, grand old steamboat now provides nostalgic atmosphere for River Queen Restaurant.

0:19 (0:00) Arrive Portland beneath stately clock tower of Union Station.

 PORTLAND, OR - See page 260.

California Zephyr

Named after a gentle west wind, The California Zephyr breezes along one of Amtrak's most delightful routes. Not so long ago, in the fifties and sixties, its predecessor by the same name was considered the West's premier train. Today's Zephyr unquestionably vies for that same honor, revealing much of America's finest scenery to passengers riding comfortably in state-of-the-art Superliner equipment. The verdant croplands of northern Illinois and southern Iowa, a splendid excursion through the heart of the Colorado Rockies, and finally a trek over magnificent Donner Pass of the Sierra Nevadas are highlights of this two-day adventure.

This trip is also a visit to some very historic moments in U.S. railroading. The first generation of diesel streamliners, the Pioneer Zephyr, made much of its inaugural run along these tracks in 1934, blazing a dawn-to-dusk nonstop dash from Denver to Chicago in just over 13 hours—a stellar accomplishment, even by today's standards. And in the West, today's train follows much of the route established when the race was on to build America's first transcontinental railroad—the successful construction of which stands as one of the world's greatest railroading achievements.

This blend of beauty and history makes The California Zephyr a very special train, and riding it a very special event. American poet Joaquin Miller brought things into perspective when he pointed out there is "more poetry in the rush of a single railroad train across the continent" than there is in all of the "story of burning Troy."

Two other trains are joined with The California Zephyr between Chicago and Salt Lake City. West of Salt Lake, however, The Pioneer and The Desert Wind split off from the Zephyr and follow separate paths to Seattle and Los Angeles, respectively. These three trains provide Amtrak's longest runs.

Westbound Schedule (Condensed)
Chicago, IL - Midafternoon Departure
Omaha, NE - Late Evening
Denver, CO - Early Morning (2nd Day)
Salt Lake City, UT - Late Evening (2nd Day)
Reno, NV - Early Morning (3rd Day)
Oakland, CA - Midafternoon (3rd Day)
San Francisco, CA - Late Afternoon Arrival (3rd Day)

Eastbound Schedule (Condensed)
San Francisco, LA - Late Morning Departure
Oakland, CA - Early Afternoon
Reno, NV - Early Evening
Salt Lake City, UT - Early Morning (2nd Day)
Denver, CO - Late Evening (2nd Day)
Omaha, NE - Early Morning (3rd Day)
Chicago, IL - Late Afternoon Arrival (3rd Day)

Frequency - Daily.
Seating - Superliner coaches.
Dining - Complete meal and beverage service as well as lighter fare. Lounge service also available, with movies.
Sleeping - Superliner sleepers with deluxe, family, economy and special

bedrooms.

Baggage - Checked baggage handled at larger cities.

Reservations - All-reserved train.

Length of Trip - 2,423 miles in 51 hours.

Route Log

 CHICAGO, IL - See page 116.

0:00 (0:35) Depart Chicago.

After emerging from beneath Chicago's huge post office, slowly pull through Amtrak's coach yards, then, picking up speed, take a westward course through lighter industrial areas, with familiar names such as Ryerson Steel, Kroehler, Burlington Northern and Nabisco in evidence. Numerous commuter stops, such as Berwyn, La Grange, Western Springs and Hinsdale, are mere blurs as "Windy City's" majestic skyline, dominated by twin-spiked Sears Tower, slowly narrows on eastern horizon.

0:07 (0:28) Westbound and eastbound Zephyrs meet about now, if each is on time.

0:35 (0:00) Arrive Naperville.

NAPERVILLE, IL - This attractive town has replaced Aurora as Chicago's western suburban stop. Connections are made here to commuter trains serving towns along the Burlington Northern between Chicago's Union Station and Aurora, including Downer's Grove, Hinsdale, La Grange and Cicero, among others.

0:00 (1:06) Depart Naperville.

0:09 (0:57) Upon entering Aurora, note dilapidated stone roundhouse on right. This relic of bygone days is the oldest such structure still standing in U.S. Adjacent buildings are Burlington shops where Vistadome cars and early dining cars were first designed. The Chicago, Burlington and Quincy Railroad got its start here in 1844. Aurora also claims the distinction of being the first city in Illinois to install electric street lights.

Double-decked silvery trains parked on left are BN commuter trains awaiting call to service. Green and white diesel units make it a rather colorful scene.

0:11 (0:55) Cross Fox River.

0:14 (0:52) Sea of yellow earth-moving equipment on right is produced by adjacent Caterpillar plant.

0:53 (0:13) Two small "mountains" in distance to left are mine tailings which mark spot of one of nation's worst coal mine disasters. In 1909 a fire ignited, resulting in the deaths of over 200 miners.

1:06 (0:00) Upon arriving at Princeton, note quaint community picnic shelter, at left.

PRINCETON, IL - Founded in 1833, this fine old town interestingly claims to be the world's pig capital, while at the same time takes on the motto "where tradition meets progress." Famed abolitionist Owen Lovejoy lived just east of here where he maintained an important station on the Underground Railroad.

0:00 (0:49) Depart Princeton.

0:21 (0:28) On left, Hyster-brand heavy equipment is stored between tracks and manufacturing facility.

0:23 (0:26) Passing through Kewanee, historic Kewanee Boiler Corporation's old brick buildings face tracks on right.

0:30 (0:19) Hog farming is not limited to the Princeton area, but is prevalent throughout Illinois and Iowa. Small A-frame buildings on left are typical shelters for porkers.

0:38 (0:11) When passing through Oneida, be sure to look to left at what must be world's smallest high school—it's about five-foot square and not much higher, with "High School" written over the door.

0:49 (0:00) Arrive at Galesburg's handsome new South Seminary Street Station. (North Broad street station, used by Southwest Chief, is some distance across town from here.) Locomotive 3006, a 4-6-4 Hudson class, donated by Burlington Northern to city of Galesburg, stands next to station on right.

GALESBURG, IL - Reverend George Washington Gale chose this spot for a ministers' college after searching westward on behalf of a fundamentalist Presbyterian group located in Oneida, New York. Famed American poet Carl Sandburg was raised here, and this was the site of a Lincoln-Douglas Debate in 1858. Olmstead Ferris, a "Galesburgite" (and a relative of George Washington

Ferris, inventor of the Ferris wheel), was an important experimenter with popcorn—one of the area's important products. This was such a novelty in those days that Ferris gave a corn-popping command performance before England's Queen Victoria and Prince Albert.

0:00 (0:44) Depart Galesburg through Burlington Northern freight yards, then watch on right for Knox College, site of 1858 Lincoln-Douglas debate and identified by bell-topped building.

0:09 (0:35) Pass beneath main line of Santa Fe. This is route once used by legendary Super Chief between Chicago and Los Angeles, and now traveled by Amtrak's Southwest Chief.

0:18 (0:25) Cruise through Monmouth, birthplace of Wyatt Earp—one of West's most famous lawmen. Event is memorialized on a 15,000-pound block of granite hauled in by former Minneapolis and St. Louis Railroad.

0:41 (0:02) Zephyr now crosses mighty Mississippi River, where splendid views of river and town of Burlington are afforded from a 2,002-foot-long bridge. At midstream, enter Iowa and leave Illinois. From its source to its Gulf-of-Mexico outlet, this great river travels 2,350 miles and drains an area equal to two-fifths of U.S.

0:44 (0:00) Arrive Burlington, where steam engine #3003 is enclosed by fence just beyond station on left.

BURLINGTON, IA - The Indians considered this neutral territory since it was one of the few locations in the region where important flint could be acquired for tools and weapons. Burlington holds the distinction of having served as a temporary capital of two territories—Wisconsin in 1837 and Iowa from 1838 to 1841—when its river location gave it considerable prominence. Later, the convergence of three railroads made it a major rail hub as the river's dominance waned. Much of the research in developing George Westinghouse's air brake occurred on West Burlington Hill—perhaps one of the most significant advancements in railroading technology. Ripley dubbed one of the town's thoroughfares "crookedest street in the world." Built with curves to moderate a horse's descent, residents now refer to it as "Snake Alley."

0:00 (0:30) Depart Burlington and slip through older portion of downtown, nearly touching some of buildings that virtually enshroud tracks.

0:04 (0:26) Cheery sign on left identifies former quarters of Embalming Burial Case Company.

0:08 (0:22) Burlington shops are on immediate right.

0:12 (0:18) Facility on left is Iowa Army Ammunition Plant—presumably *U.S.* Army in Iowa.

0:30 (0:00) Arrive at attractive little town of Mt. Pleasant with typical Midwest-style frame homes and tree-lined streets.

MT. PLEASANT, IA - Originally accessed by three toll roads which were protected from the elements by plank surfaces, Mt. Pleasant was eventually reached by railroad, putting the expensive toll roads out of business (they charged two cents a mile). Today, the Midwest Old Settlers and Threshers Association holds an annual reunion for five days ending each Labor Day. This event began with a few farmers trying to preserve Midwest frontier heritage, and has grown to become internationally famous—the largest of its kind in the U.S. Each year, more than 200,000 visitors visit this festivity involving antique farm machinery, autos, crafts, "old thresher meals" and much more.

0:00 (0:39) Depart Mt. Pleasant. Historic Iowa Wesleyan College will be on right in just a moment. School was founded in 1842, making it oldest collegiate institution west of Mississippi River.

0:01 (0:38) Acres and acres of yellow school buses and other vehicles are results of assembly plant on immediate left.

0:05 (0:34) Cross curiously named Skunk River.

0:16 (0:23) Entrance to Fairfield is easily identified by golf course and small lake to right of tracks at east edge of town.

Fairfield has the distinction of being home to Maharishi International University, partially visible off to the right, the only school in the U.S. to make transcendental meditation basic to its curriculum. Started in Santa Barbara in 1973 by Maharishi Mahesh Yogi, the university moved here in 1974 and occupies the 260-

acre campus of now-defunct Parson's College. Fully accredited and offering traditional courses ranging from management to physics at both undergraduate and graduate levels, it has 800 students coming from over 50 countries and nearly every state. Two gold domes are twice-daily meditating places for the entire student body.

0:30 (0:09) White stone letters on right, reading "Chief Wapello," commemorate former Indian leader whose grave is nearby.

0:39 (0:00) Arriving Ottumwa, John Deere plant and Hormel meat-packing facility on left are typical of industries which have been foundation of community's past.

OTTUMWA, IA - Located on the banks of the Des Moines River, which was one of the many obstacles for westward-bound pioneers, the city is now a major trading center of southeastern Iowa. In the category of fame: "Radar O'Reilly" of TV's M*A*S*H has a pig farm nearby, and the city council proclaimed Ottumwa as the "Video Gaming Capital of the World" when the first American video championships were held here in 1983.

Nearby Blakesburg hosts an unusual antique aircraft convention the week prior to Labor Day when the skies become an apparition of aviation's past. The elegantly stark house which served as a backdrop for Grant Wood's classic painting "American Gothic" is at nearby Eldon.

0:00 (1:15) Depart Ottumwa and for several minutes remain in confines of Des Moines River Valley.

0:05 (1:10) Cross Des Moines River, a serene tributary of Mississippi River.

0:08 (1:07) In Chillicothe, birdhouses fill front yard of feathered creatures' friend, on left.

0:10 (1:05) Off to right, smokestack and coal conveyors identify one of newer Iowa Southern power plants.

1:15 (0:00) Arrive Osceola.

OSCEOLA, IA - The first settlers arrived here in the mid-1800s and named their settlement in honor of a Seminole Indian chief. Supposedly the first Delicious apple tree was discovered

30 miles from here, becoming the ancestor of some eight million fruit trees.

0:00 (0:30) Depart Osceola.

0:02 (0:28) Note large carved bust of Osceola himself, at shopping center on left.

0:16 (0:14) Cross Thompson River.

0:30 (0:00) Arrive Creston.

CRESTON, IA - Creston has long been a railroad town and at one time sported large rail yards, a roundhouse and shops. One of the early-day engineers gained renown by noisily roasting two ears of corn for lunch each day using his engine's steam whistle. The town's historic three-story depot, with its green trim and tile roof, now houses a museum just to the right of the tracks.

0:00 (1:42) Depart Creston.

0:03 (1:39) Metal grain storage units have replaced many of Midwest's picturesque silos. Papa-, mama- and baby-bear units are seen on left.

0:22 (1:20) Community of Corning, on left, is birthplace of comedian Johnny Carson.

0:39 (1:03) Whimsical water tower, on right, is enormous coffeepot (640,000 cups!) in honor of Mrs. Olson of TV coffee-commercial fame, who learned her mountain-grown coffee secrets right here in Stanton. Not surprisingly, town considers itself "Swedish Capital of Iowa."

0:46 (0:56) In Red Oak, on right, grand old brick Montgomery County Courthouse is centerpiece for town, crowned with a clock tower complete with flagstaff. Red Oak is home to Murphy Calendar Company, originator of art calendars.

1:00 (0:42) Excellent example of terracing, a conservation practice that both controls erosion and retains moisture, can be seen on hillside at left.

1:12 (0:30) At Pacific Junction, clatter through rail yards of Burlington Northern and cross north-south BN line that follows eastern shore of Missouri River.

1:13 (0:29) Intersect Interstate 29, connecting Omaha and Kansas City.

1:17 (0:25) Enter Nebraska and leave Iowa as Missouri River is crossed. Note large natural gas pipeline also spanning waters at right.

A note about the Missouri. Over 100 years ago steamboats plied these waters between Omaha, just 20 miles north of here, and St. Louis, almost 500 miles downstream. Although often thought of as a river that drains southerly, it actually flows east twice as far as it does to the south. Its headwaters are in the mountainous regions of western Montana where three rivers, the Gallatin, Jefferson and Madison, converge almost simultaneously at Three Forks. The river then starts its long north and east trek through Montana, swings southeastward through North and South Dakota, slips between Iowa and Nebraska, and finally flows eastward across Missouri, joining the Mississippi River at St. Louis.

1:15 (0:27) Red caboose on display at left in Plattsmouth is just one of what must now be hundreds of these artifacts on display across America.

1:24 (0:18) Zephyr bridges Platte River, once described by a James Michener character as "the sorriest river in America." However, its surface waters and underflow provide vital irrigation to large portions of Nebraska, Colorado and Wyoming. Although too shallow to navigate, its flat valley floor has been an excellent east-west route for trails, highways and railroads crossing Nebraska.

1:29 (0:13) Nearing Omaha, cruise through Bellevue, oldest continuous settlement in Nebraska. Of greater note, however, is Offutt Air Force Base, partially visible off to left, which is headquarters for nation's Strategic Air Command.

1:42 (0:00) Arrive Omaha.

OMAHA, NE - Located on the mighty, muddy Missouri River at the eastern terminus of the Union Pacific Railroad, Omaha has risen from its pioneer beginning on the plains to become both a transportation hub and the major cattle and grain market of the Prairie States. It is also the headquarters and global control center for the U.S. Air Force.

Amtrak Station, 1003 South 9th Street, is about a mile south of the downtown shopping area. This relatively new and attractive station is almost too small. There are candy bar and beverage vending machines, handcarts and adjacent free parking. (There is only one pay phone inside, often in use, but there is one outside by the tracks that is usually unnoticed.)

For arrival and departure information and reservations, call 800-USA-RAIL. The station is open daily from 10:30 pm to 7:30 am, and also weekdays from 7:30 am to 3:30 pm (with an hour lunch-break closure).

Cab stand at the station; Yellow, Happy and Checker have common dispatch, 341-9000. Avis is closest **rental car** agency (about a mile) and will reimburse cab fare to pick up car; returns can be made at the station; (402) 348-0621. Nearest **local bus** stop is at 10th and Pacific, one block away; Metro Area Transit, 341-0800. **Greyhound** bus terminal, (402) 341-1900. **Eppley Airfield** is four miles northeast of station.

Greater Omaha Convention & Visitors Bureau, 1819 Farnam St., Suite 1200, 68183; (402) 444-4660 or 800-332-1819. Events Hotline, 444-6800.

Red Lion Inn, 1616 Dodge St., 68102; (402) 346-7600 or 800-547-8010. Ten blocks from the station. $98.

-**Days Inn of Omaha,** 3001 Chicago Street, 68131; (402) 345-2222 or 800-325-2525. Complimentary breakfast. Two miles from the station. $56.

Union Pacific Historical Museum, at 12th and Dodge streets, has a large collection of railroad memorabilia, housed in the national headquarters of the Union Pacific. **Omaha History Museum** now occupies the old Union Station, 10th and Marcy streets, three blocks from the present Amtrak station. **Joslyn Art Museum,** 2200 Dodge St., is one of the major fine arts museums in the central U.S. **Boys Town,** on the west edge of Omaha, is the best-known home and school for underprivileged boys; formed by Father Flanagan in 1917. **Strategic Air Command Museum** is south of town in Bellevue, at 2510 Clay Street, with "Red Alert" Theater simulations and several aircraft and missiles on display. A good way to spend an evening waiting for the westbound train is to take in a production at the **Omaha Community Playhouse**—nation's largest with 11,000 members. Henry Fonda made his debut here. 69th and Cass, four miles west of downtown.

0:00 (1:00) Depart Omaha.

Current scheduling takes the Zephyr through Nebraska at night making most of the state unviewable from the train.

1:00 (0:00) Arrive Lincoln.

LINCOLN, NE - Lincoln's rather subdued skyline is dominated by the State Capitol, a 400-foot "Tower of the Plains" which is an early-20th-century architectural masterpiece. Art work and mosaics, both inside and out, depict pioneer life. The only unicameral (one house) legislature in the nation occupies this structure.

Lincoln is also home of the University of Nebraska, a perennial Big Eight football powerhouse. Nebraskans would have you believe the bronze statue atop the capitol dome is of the University's football coach, however, when the building was constructed in 1932, it was supposed to be "The Sower," casting grain upon the plains.

William Jennings Bryan, the "silver-tongued orator from the Platte" and thrice-defeated presidential candidate, once lived in Lincoln.

0:00 (1:23) Depart Lincoln.
1:29 (0:00) Arrive Hastings.

HASTINGS, NE - Hastings, together with its nearby rival cities, Grand Island and Kearney, combine to form the major trade and manufacturing hub for this central Nebraska region. Farm machinery and irrigation equipment are just some of the principal products. Of particular interest is "The House of Yesterday," a museum which offers a planetarium and extensive exhibits of both pioneer and natural history.

0:00 (0:51) Depart Hastings.

The rolling-to-flat fertile farmlands that have prevailed since leaving Chicago start to disappear as the more arid plains of the West begin to dominate. If one were to draw a line perpendicular through the United States at this point, this same change would occur no matter where the line is crossed. Irrigated cropland slowly gives way to more arid cattle country, except for the heavily farmed river valleys. And we start to climb—nearly nine feet per mile between here and Denver.

0:15 (0:36) Pass through Kenesaw and cross historic Oregon Trail that was used by hundreds of westward-bound wagon trains.

0:30 (0:21) Breeze through Minden, where renowned Pioneer Village, re-creating early prairie life, can be glimpsed.

0:47 (0:00) Arrive Holdrege.

HOLDREGE, NE - Holdrege is an agricultural trading center for this region, with much of its population being of Swedish extraction. The community was named for George W. Holdrege, a former general manager of the Chicago, Burlington and Quincy—one more instance of a railroad leaving its imprint beyond the tracks that it laid.

0:00 (1:03) Depart Holdrege.
0:07 (0:56) Pass through Atlanta, which was a detention center during World War II, and located far from more sensitive wartime areas.

1:13 (0:00) Arrive McCook.

MCCOOK, NE - Founded as a division point on the railroad in 1882, McCook still enjoys this status. Reclamation projects and oil have added much to the town's economy. Of interest is the Senator Norris Home, a finely restored structure where the father of the Tennessee Valley Authority once lived.

0:00 (2:27) Depart McCook.
0:23 (2:04) Off to left is Massacre Canyon where last battle between Pawnee and Sioux occurred in 1873.

0:31 (1:56) Swanson Reservoir on left, resulting from Trenton Dam on Republican River, furnishes important irrigation water and flood control, as well as recreational opportunities.

Gain one hour as train passes from Central to Mountain Time. Set your watch back (forward if eastbound) one hour.

1:11 (1:16) Enter Colorado and leave Nebraska.

1:15 (1:12) Republican River Valley continues to provide a gentle route for tracks. North Fork of Republican is on right.

1:18 (1:09) It was along these tracks that history-making Pioneer Zephyr reached its top speed of 112.5 m.p.h. during its Denver to Chicago sprint in 1934. Today's California Zephyr cruises closer to 80 m.p.h. through here.

1:30 (0:57) Giant irrigation sprinkler on right is typical of those which sweep from a center pivot, creating green circles of crops a quarter-mile across. Water is pumped from enormous but vastly overused Ogallala Aquifer.

1:52 (0:35) If dawn has broken, westbound passengers should now see for miles in all directions as train rumbles through eastern Colorado on its way to Mile High City—Denver. This was formerly domain of buffalo, sodbusters and Pony Express riders.

1:56 (0:31) Rocking arms of pumps on right draw oil from one of many isolated "pools" found throughout region.

1:58 (0:29) This is Akron, trading center for an area rich in wheat and ranchland as well as oil production.

2:15 (0:12) Fortunately, train's environment is insulated from aroma of large feedlot on right, where thousands of unsuspecting cattle munch placidly on locally produced crops.

2:18 (0:09) Broad valley off to right has been formed by shallow but wide South Platte River. River originates in central Colorado Rockies and flows northeastward to combine with North Platte River in western Nebraska (where names North and South are dropped).

2:27 (0:00) Arrive Ft. Morgan.

FT. MORGAN, CO - This city was named for a fort built here in 1864 to protect westbound pioneers from Indian attacks. Later an Overland Stage stop was established, which served the route to Denver. Sugar beets, cattle sorghums and oil all make Ft. Morgan one of eastern Colorado's more prosperous cities.

0:00 (1:25) Depart Ft. Morgan.

0:09 (1:16) Off to right a few miles is Orchard, where much of television's "Centennial" was filmed.

0:20 (1:05) Westbound passengers, weather permitting, receive first glimpse of Front Range of Rockies, on right—some eighty miles distant.

0:23 (1:02) Pikes Peak, 14,110 feet high, can be discerned far off to left as a mere bump on horizon—but only on clearest of days.

0:50 (0:35) Another cattle feedlot, a famil-iar sight throughout eastern Colorado, is on right.

0:52 (0:33) Vast acreage of U.S. Army's Rocky Mountain Arsenal spreads out on left, where controversial nerve gas was manufactured and stored for many years. Massive, expensive cleanup efforts are now underway.

1:05 (0:20) Industrial sights of aptly named Commerce City, a northeast Denver suburb, now prevail.

1:11 (0:14) On right, sign for Riverside Cemetery, founded in 1876, proclaims graveyard as Denver's "pioneer cemetery."

1:13 (0:12) Formerly bustling stockyards area is now largely unused. National Western Stock Show, held here each January, is largest event of its kind, and draws exhibitors from throughout western U.S. and Canada. On left, with its enormous curved roof, Coliseum is focus of those activities. Pass beneath Interstate 70. Denver's newly shaped skyline now dominates on left.

1:22 (---) Front of train is now clearly visible on right as train makes a giant curl northward while Zephyr prepares to back into station. (Train will depart northbound retracing, for a short distance, tracks on which it has just arrived.)

1:31 (0:00) Arrive Denver's Union Station, built in 1881. Generally there is time to get out and stretch here, but verify this with a crew member first.

DENVER, CO - Compared to most cities its size, Denver's history is relatively short, having been founded in 1858 during the gold rush to the mountains. The gold played out, but Denver's climate, its proximity to the mountains and its institutions born of those early years assured Denver's destiny as the trading, financial and tourism center of the Rocky Mountain region.

First-time visitors are often surprised to find a mile-high city not in the mountains, just near them, and a ski-oriented community that gets only 16 inches of moisture per year. Its once modest downtown is now a maze of glassy skyscrapers which sprouted in the 80s—largely the result of an energy boom that later went bust.

The town is still a pretty city and a logical point from which to start a Rocky Mountain vacation. Its Civic Center, presided over by the golden-domed state capitol, is a jewel; Denver's parks are some of the finest anywhere; its tree-lined boulevards in east Denver are delights to drive; and its downtown area is easy to shop with free transit up and down the 16th Street Mall.

 Union Station, 17th and Wynkoop streets, anchors the revitalized end of downtown. When it was completed in 1881, it was said to be the largest single structure in the West. An 1894 fire destroyed much of the original center section, but the rebuilding produced an even finer appearance. There has been talk of moving Amtrak out of this splendid location, but only time will tell. Its classic waiting room still has the old high-backed wooden benches, and surrounding this area are a large gift shop, a food counter and a "Grandpa's Depot"—the latter selling a large assortment of railroad-related merchandise. The station also has storage lockers, luggage carts and adjacent pay-parking. There are direct phone lines to several hotels and three rental car companies.

Ticket window hours, 7 am to 9:45 pm; waiting room hours, 6:30 am to 10:30 pm. For information and reservations, call (303) 893-3911.

Cab stand at the station; Yellow Cab, 892-1212. Direct phones to

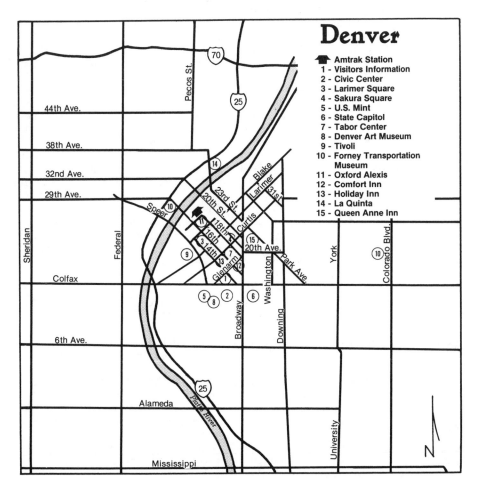

Denver

- ⬛ Amtrak Station
- 1 - Visitors Information
- 2 - Civic Center
- 3 - Larimer Square
- 4 - Sakura Square
- 5 - U.S. Mint
- 6 - State Capitol
- 7 - Tabor Center
- 8 - Denver Art Museum
- 9 - Tivoli
- 10 - Forney Transportation Museum
- 11 - Oxford Alexis
- 12 - Comfort Inn
- 13 - Holiday Inn
- 14 - La Quinta
- 15 - Queen Anne Inn

Hertz and Budget **rental cars,** with limited hours pick up and drop off at the station. **Local bus** stop is across the street; main terminal is two blocks away; call RTD, 778-6000; schedules and maps available at the station. **Greyhound** bus terminal at 19th and Curtis streets, seven blocks from the station; (303) 292-6111. **Stapleton International Airport** seven miles east of downtown.

? **Denver Metro Convention and Visitors Bureau,** 225 W. Colfax, 80202; (303) 892-1112.

Downtown accommodations are still a bargain in Denver, but prices have been firming up a bit as the city's economy recovers.

-**Comfort Inn,** 401-17th St., 80202; (303) 296-0400. Small but luxurious rooms at the uptown end of 17th Street in what was once the "new" annex of Denver's Brown Palace Hotel. Breakfast included. One of the best values in downtown. Thirteen "short" blocks from the station. $53.

-**Holiday Inn Denver Downtown,** 1450 Glenarm Place, 80202; (303) 573-1450. Very nicely maintained, conveniently located. Can usually offer shuttle service to and from the station (about a mile) in the am. $80.

-**Oxford Alexis Hotel,** 1600-17th St., 80202; (303) 628-5400. Marvelously restored old hotel with some good weekend packages. Half block from the station. $110.

-**LaQuinta Inn-Denver Center,** 3500 Fox, 80216; (303) 458-1222. At I-25 and West 38th, it is not within walking distance but a good bet for an "overnight." Rail fans might like its near-trackside location. Free shuttle to and from nearby station, and special Amtrak passenger rate of $43.

-**Queen Anne Inn,** 2417 Tremont Place, 80205; (303) 296-6666. A bed and breakfast in historic district on the edge of downtown. Beautifully restored Victorian home. Just what every bed and breakfast should be. Mile and a half from the station. $84.

Downtown attractions include: the **U.S. Mint,** across from the visitors center; **Civic Center,** a handsomely landscaped set of state and city buildings, near Colfax and Broadway; **Denver Art Museum,** 100 West 14th Parkway; **shopping** at Larimer Square, Sakura Square, Tabor Center, The Tivoli (all in lower downtown), and the 16th Street Mall with free shuttle buses. If you like antiques, Stuart Buchanan, 1625 Wazee, is probably the largest such store west of the Mississippi, and Wazee Deco, 1701 Wazee, has items bordering on the bizarre. Both stores are handy to the station.

Near downtown is the **Forney Transportation Museum,** 1416 Platte St., and near Golden is the **Colorado Railroad Museum,** 17155 W. 44th Ave.

For something different, tour **Coors Brewery** (largest in the world) in Golden and enjoy a meal at **Casa Bonita** (sort of a combination Taco Bell and Disneyland), 6715 West Colfax.

0:00 (1:57) Depart Denver along route of former Denver and Salt Lake Railroad.

We bid farewell to the Burlington and take to the rails of the highly scenic Denver and Rio Grande Western, exploring the very heart of the Colorado Rockies. The pace is slow. Grinding up laborious grades and negotiating never-ending twists and turns, it takes more than seven hours to reach Grand Junction, 273 rail miles to the west—a less-than-blazing 38 miles per hour.

But this is the Rio Grande. The railroad cut its teeth on narrow-gauge tracks (3 feet between the rails, in this case, rather than 4 feet, 8¼ inches) which allowed it to snake up canyons and cling to cliffs while reaching almost every remote mining camp in the state. This "baby railroad" could "curve around the brim of a sombrero," so it was said. Mark Twain once wondered why the Rio Grande even bothered to use cowcatchers since their trains couldn't outrun the beasts.

Although the Rio Grande converted to standard gauge long ago, trains on this line still take their time. And that's perfect for seeing the Rockies.

0:02 (1:55) Cross usually placid South Platte River. Denver was born just a few hundred yards upstream when gold was discovered in 1858.

0:05 (1:52) Slip through extensive freight yards of Rio Grande, as sights of Denver's industrial aspects continue.

0:13 (1:39) Angling through Arvada, a large northwestern Denver suburb, Front Range of Rockies looms directly ahead. Tallest peak in distance to right (north) is 14,255-foot Longs Peak. Immediately to left is 14,264-foot Mt. Evans.

0:22 (1:33) Small complex of buildings and curious tower-like structures, on right, were once used to explore various shale oil extraction techniques.

0:32 (1:19) At Rocky, train reaches formidable foothills, and a giant "S" curve (called "Big Ten" in reference to degrees of curvature) is negotiated while struggling to gain necessary altitude. On inside of upper curve weathered hopper cars filled with sand are permanently anchored to protect trains from fierce west winds which occasionally reach velocities in excess of 100 miles per hour. Grade is a demanding two percent as route steadily ascends across face of foothills before turning westward directly into mountains.

0:40 (1:12) Rumble through first of 28 tunnels between here and six-mile-long Moffat Tunnel.

0:45 (1:10) This area is referred to as Plainview—understandably, as plains of eastern Colorado seem to stretch out forever. Back on right, Denver's entire metropolitan area is now visible. Industrial complex in foreground is Rocky Flats, nation's only processor of plutonium, which is an occasional target of pacifist protests. Plant has a reputation of being one of the "dirtiest" in nuke industry, and faces possible closure. Forward on right is city of Boulder and University of Colorado with its red-tiled roofs.

0:51 (1:06) After having enjoyed sweeping panoramas of plains while train gained altitude along eastern face of Rockies, we now head up South Boulder Canyon into very heart of mountains. This is where eastbound passengers first get one of Amtrak's most breathtaking views—looking down on evening lights of Denver's metroplex. Lounge car lights are usually dimmed for added drama.

0:59 (0:58) Gross Reservoir, one of Denver's many important water storage facilities, is below on right. This collection unit supplies billions of gallons each year to a city which receives only 16 inches of

California Zephyr – Front Range, Colorado Rockies

precipitation annually.

1:20 (0:37) Old wooden barn-like structure on left once provided storage for ice cut from adjacent lake in winter. Ice was used in boxcars until modern refrigeration methods made this technique obsolete.

1:35 (0:23) Fine views are afforded of towering Continental Divide directly ahead as train enters Roosevelt National Forest. Watch for deer and elk on slopes above tracks.

1:42 (0:15) At last, plunge into historic Moffat Tunnel where total darkness prevails for nine minutes as train passes beneath Continental Divide.

The construction of the Moffat Tunnel was considered a Colorado need. An efficient east-west railroad directly through the mountains was critical, otherwise the flow of commerce would entirely bypass the state by following routes already established through Wyoming to the north and New Mexico to the south. David Moffat's Denver and Salt Lake Railroad (it never really made it to Salt Lake) had not proven to be the answer. That line's arduous negotiation of Rollins Pass was not only slow, but winters at that elevation turned schedules into shambles. (The original route over the top can still be seen above and to the right before entering the tunnel westbound.) The tunnel was deemed so important that money was raised through a special improvement district which issued bonds and then retired them by levying taxes on virtually all Colorado real estate within earshot of the train's whistle.

When it was finished in 1927, the Moffat Tunnel was 6.2 miles long, the longest rail tunnel in North America. (It was subsequently bettered by the 1929 Cascade Tunnel in Washington and a recently completed Canadian Pacific tunnel.) The feat was of such moment that President Calvin Coolidge pushed a button from the White House triggering the holing-through blast. It took one thousand men digging from both ends, and using 2.5 million pounds of dynamite, nearly four years to complete the task. The main bore is 24 feet by 18 feet, while a smaller 8-foot-diameter bore supplies Denver with West Slope water.

It is now a mere nine-minute trundle through 13,260-foot-high James Peak instead of a five-hour ordeal over the top. Somewhere in the tunnel's innards the rails reach their apex—9,239 feet above sea level, and the highest point anywhere for Amtrak.

1:48 (0:06) We are suddenly awash in brilliant daylight as train pops out of Moffat Tunnel into land where all water now flows westward. Immediately on left is Winter Park ski area—one of City of Denver's many mountain parks.

1:53 (0:00) Arrive Winter Park.

WINTER PARK, CO - This popular ski destination, particularly for Denverites, is in a section of the Rockies composed of mountains and meadowlands called Middle Park, where ranching and tourism are of primary importance. A favorite fishing retreat of former president Dwight Eisenhower was in the mountains off to the left. The depot is actually in the small town of Fraser, adjacent to the Winter Park ski area. For years, Fraser often recorded the coldest wintertime temperatures in the nation, but the situation was finally alleviated when the town's weather station was removed.

0:00 (0:22) Depart Winter Park.

0:10 (0:05) Sparkling trout-filled Fraser River escorts train through remote canyon.

0:25 (0:00) Arrive Granby.

GRANBY, CO - This is a trading center for Middle Park and popular stopping point for travelers. Beautiful Grand Lake and Rocky Mountain National Park are just to the north (right) of here. Incomparable Trail Ridge Road—highest continuous auto road in the world—traverses the Continental Divide through the center of the Park.

0:00 (2:57) Depart Granby.

0:02 (2:53) Here we join Colorado River near its headwaters, and follow its winding course for next 238 miles.

0:13 (2:44) Small mountain community of Hot Sulphur Springs derives its names from local geothermal springs. Indoor swimming pool, on right, capitalizes on this free source of heated water.

0:14 (2:43) Enter Byers Canyon where invincible rocky-spired cliffs tower high above roadbed. Highway on left is U.S. 40.

0:22 (2:35) Emerge from Byers Canyon and for first time since Denver pick up considerable speed as train heads for Kremmling in heart of some of Colorado's best cattle country. Large herds of deer can often be seen along right-of-way, particularly in winter.

0:36 (2:22) Roll through Kremmling. Lofty peaks to left belong to Gore Range and reach elevations in excess of 13,000 feet.

0:41 (2:18) Enter awesome Gore Canyon, where sheer rock sides of this rugged gorge hover menacingly overhead, and where not even an auto road has dared to invade.

0:52 (2:08) Emerge from Gore Canyon. Small meadows and ranches will continue to fleck landscape as we journey westward through middle of Rockies.

0:57 (2:03) Enter Little Gore Canyon, not as exciting as Gore but still impressive.

1:00 (2:00) Hole in canyon wall at about water level on left was to be intake of ambitious irrigation tunnel, but project was abandoned circa 1913.

1:02 (1:58) Exit Little Gore Canyon.

1:25 (1:36) Remains of historic State Bridge (it preceded railroad) and its modern replacement are just to left.

1:31 (1:21) Curl through the old railroad town of Bond, with its handful of rundown buildings. On right, a Rio Grande branch line can be seen angling above, making its way to Steamboat Springs and Craig, Colorado. This was former line of Moffat's Denver & Salt Lake. Zephyr follows Dotsero Cutoff, a 38-mile link completed in 1934 connecting to the Rio Grande's Royal Gorge route. Cutoff and Moffat Tunnel now provide a route that is 176 miles shorter than Rio Grande's first Denver-to-Salt-Lake-City route, which required a southern Colorado excursion through Royal Gorge. (Rail junction just before Bond was Orestod—Dotsero spelled backwards—and eastern end of Dotsero Cutoff.)

1:36 (1:18) Giant waterwheel on left, looking more like an incongruous Ferris wheel, scoops water from river and empties into irrigation ditch.

1:37 (1:17) Enter Red Canyon, where sur-prisingly red cliffs offer an almost refreshing change from dramatic scenery behind. Eroded rocks play fanciful tricks on imagination—note pilgrims' "Mayflower" resting at anchor just to right.

2:05 (0:52) Spread on right bears pessimistic title, "Rancho Starvo."

2:24 (0:34) Train rolls through Dotsero where Eagle River, from left, now adds to Colorado River's flow. It was from this point that an early Colorado River survey was commenced and marked ".0" or "dot zero." Rails also join Rio Grande's Royal Gorge route which threads its way back through mountains to Pueblo.

2:29 (0:29) Enter Glenwood Canyon where the grandeur of these great cliffs is said to have inspired creation of Vista-domes.

In July of 1944, the general manager of GM's Electro-motive Division was riding through the canyon in the cab of a Rio Grande diesel locomotive when he first visualized glass-canopied rail cars. Five years later they were in service on The California Zephyr. The tracks twist and turn, lazily following the river through this truly beautiful gorge for nearly half an hour.

2:32 (0:26) Across river, construction of controversial Interstate 70 proceeds in spite of early environmental protests. To modify concerns, rock cuts and concrete structures are stained to blend with canyon walls. A paved pathway, designed to withstand occasional flooding, will take hikers and bicyclers along river's edge.

2:39 (0:19) Dam diverts water into underground penstocks that carry water to power plant farther downstream. At times Colorado River is nearly dry between here and plant.

2:43 (0:15) On right, Public Service Company of Colorado's Shoshone hydroelectric generating plant is outlet for water diverted upstream. Plant is small, producing a relatively modest 15 megawatts. Below this point, river rafters are frequent sight.

2:52 (0:05) Just before emerging from canyon, handful of houses on right comprise thoughtfully monikered community of "No Name."

2:57 (0:00) Arrive Glenwood Springs at western mouth of Glenwood Canyon. Be sure to note picturesque stone and brick

California Zephyr – Battlement Mesa, Colorado

station on left.

GLENWOOD SPRINGS, CO - Ultra-posh Aspen is just up the Roaring Fork Valley from Glenwood Springs, making this a busy skier stop for The California Zephyr. But many who come to Glenwood are not interested in Aspen—they come here because of the world's largest outdoor hot-water swimming pool. This attraction is just to the right and across the river from the station, and is always filled with swimmers—even in the dead of winter. Water is supplied by the adjacent Yampa Hot Springs.

Beyond the pool can be seen the venerable Hotel Colorado, opened in 1893. Built of sandstone and trimmed with Roman brick, it was patterned after the Medici Hotel in Florence, Italy. This hostelry has accommodated numerous well-known personages over the years, including Teddy Roosevelt to name but one.

That famous gunslinger, Doc Holliday, once lived in Glenwood and is buried in the town's cemetery.

0:00 (1:40) Departing Glenwood Springs, majestic Mt. Sopris dominates Roaring Fork River Valley on left.

0:08 (1:32) Train wends its way through Colorado River Valley encased by red stratified mountains which typify this region of Rockies.

0:18 (1:22) Near New Castle, black slash on left identifies former Wheeler coal mine, long ago abandoned due to persistent fires. Two catastrophic explosions, one in late 1800s and one in early 1900s, resulted in 91 deaths.

0:30 (1:10) This is Rifle. Historically a ranching community, a few years ago it experienced a rather short-lived boom based on prospects of developing vast Colorado shale oil reserves which lie north and west of here. Some of these deposits are visible high up on cliffs, just to right and forward of train.

0:36 (1:03) Anvil Points Oil Shale pilot plant is at base of cliffs on right.

0:42 (0:56) Oil shale town of Parachute received severe economic shock in early 1982 when Exxon withdrew local shale research and development.

1:01 (0:37) Enter Debeque Canyon which easily could have been setting for Zane Grey novel.

1:11 (0:26) Colorado River (once known as "Grand River") is momentarily held back by ornate Grand River Diversion Dam, built by U.S. Bureau of Reclamation for irrigation purposes.

1:15 (0:22) Buffalo in field at left are unusual twentieth-century sight.

1:16 (0:21) Coal mine, across river on left, taps some of region's vast coal reserves to fuel power plant on right. Coal is transported via impressive conveyor spanning river.

1:23 (0:14) Emerge from Debeque Canyon and enter famed fruit-growing region of Colorado's Western Slope. Peaches, harvested here at end of summer, are outstanding.

1:28 (0:12) Huge plateau on left is Grand Mesa. Reaching an elevation of more than 10,000 feet, it is reputedly world's largest flat-top mountain.

1:33 (0:07) Unusual variegated palisades on right are known as Book Cliffs.

1:40 (0:00) Arrive Grand Junction where 1905 station on right not only records elevation as 4,578 feet, but population as a seemingly permanent 28,000.

GRAND JUNCTION, CO - This is western Colorado's largest community. Overlooked by white men long after the rest of the state was overrun by fur trappers, it finally saw "civilized" settlement in 1881 when settlers were permitted to stake claims shortly after the Northern Ute Indians were removed to Utah. Five men, including George A. Crawford, a former governor of Kansas who had a reputation of establishing a new town "every decade or so," staked a townsite here. It was first named Ute, then West Denver, and finally Grand Junction because the Colorado (remember it used to be the Grand) and the Gunnison rivers joined here.

Grand Junction's economy was once heavily linked to railroading, but energy-related industries eventually became the dominant force. The fickleness of energy development over the years, however, has now forced the community to work toward broadening the town's economic base beyond coal, oil shale and uranium.

Of particular interest to visitors are nearby Colorado National Monument with its free-standing rock monoliths, Grand Mesa's beautiful forests and lakes, and a unique museum with life-size dinosaurs that growl and snap at visitors.

0:00 (1:18) Departing Grand Junction, broken red cliffs of Colorado National Monument border route on left.

0:12 (1:06) Passing through Fruita, imposing tyrannosaurus rex greets patrons of shops on right. Region was once heavily populated by dinosaurs, and important skeletal remains have been unearthed here.

0:20 (0:58) Refinery on left has processed gilsonite, a hard black asphalt rarely found in usable quantity but readily available in this region.

0:22 (0:56) Mack was former eastern terminus of narrow-gauge Uintah Railroad which hauled gilsonite from eastern Utah until line was abandoned in 1939.

0:23 (0:55) West of Mack, emerge from short tunnel and follow Colorado River's graceful meanders through spectacular gorges of Ruby Canyon. Twenty-mile stretch is being considered for possible wild and scenic designation.

0:36 (0:41) On right, markings enscribed on canyon wall denote Utah-Colorado boundary.

0:38 (0:39) After a 238-mile joint venture, Colorado River now departs tracks at Westwater and heads for Arizona. A little farther downstream, river tumbles through Westwater Canyon, a popular run for white-water enthusiasts.

With the departure of the Colorado River, canyonlands are quickly displaced by a vast expanse of desert terrain. Over the next 150 miles, stark mesa tops of the Roan Cliffs stand stoicly on the right as the trains weaves through cuts and gullies across this barren landscape. What sometimes appears to be sparkling snow in the heat of the summer is only surface alkalie.

Someone once said that horses graze at 40 miles per hour in this country just to stay alive.

0:52 (0:25) On left at Cisco, one of town's many weather-beaten buildings is surprising site of elaborate mural, depicting scenic wonders of Colorado River canyon.

1:15 (0:00) Arriving Thompson, La Sal Mountains are an imposing sight in distance on left. Henry Mountains are prominent lump on horizon left forward.

THOMPSON, UT - Thompson is a stop for nearby Moab, hub of southeastern Utah's vast, scenic wonderlands. Surrounding Moab are such spectacular settings as Canyonlands National Park, Arches National Park, Dead Horse Point and Monument Valley. Since Thompson is a flag stop, Zephyr will pass right on through unless someone is boarding or detraining.

0:00 (1:40) Departing Thompson, note intriguing Desert Moon Hotel on left. Sign touts it as also a retirement home and trailer park.

0:13 (1:27) Rocky debris of eroding mesas is an interesting sight on right, as Roan Cliffs loom closer between Thompson and Green River.

0:25 (1:16) Cross Green River, then through town of same name. At an altitude of 4,080 feet, river crossing lies at lowest point along this section of Rio Grande line. Although dry-farming concerns are foremost here, town is best known for its cantaloupes and watermelons, nurtured by Green's waters.

0:27 (1:12) From tobacco and cigars to candy and ice cream, old billiard hall on right seems to offer something for everyone.

0:54 (0:49) Cross Price River which will subsequently rejoin in Helper.

1:37 (0:10) Re-emergence of agriculture and ranching spreads around Price signals gradual departure from desert climes.

1:40 (0:00) Arrive Helper.

HELPER, UT - As evidenced by the congestion of this busy rail terminal, Helper is a vital distribution outlet for a region replete with abundant coal resources. So rich are these deposits that they alone could supply the U.S. for 300 years. When founded in 1882, the town was named in deference to "helper" locomotives which were coupled here onto westbound freights for the arduous ascent up Soldier Summit.

0:00 (1:53) Departing Helper, historic Western flavor pervades downtown area on left. Nostalgia buffs should delight in old hand-painted Coca Cola advertisement, weathering gracefully on north side of Main Street apartments.

0:03 (1:50) At Martin, on left, substantial brick building ensconced on hillside houses operating headquarters of Utah Railway Company. Railway is a short-line hauler, collecting coal along 23 miles of company-owned track, then delivering it to Provo using "trackage rights" and "paired trackage agreements" along route of D&RGW.

0:05 (1:46) Balanced Rock perched high above tracks on right has seen numerous attempts to top it with Old Glory. Three valiant efforts in 1929 met with successive defeats. First, a canvas flag was blown from its mast after two months of fluttering, then a silk one lasted but eight days, and finally a 16-gauge steel "flag" snapped off after 48 hours of gusts. Not wanting to see an unfestooned flag pole, citizenry hoisted a 100-pound grease drum as ultimate solution.

As Price River rejoins on left, enter Wasatch Mountains and proceed up 2.4 percent twisting grade to Soldier Summit. Photo possibilities are nearly limitless, as train winds dramatically through scenic environs of Price River Canyon.

0:08 (1:46) On right, pass entangled maze of machinery and apparatus at Castle Gate Preparation Plant. Situated in midst of extensive coal beds, this sprawling operation serves as a "washing" facility for loads from nearby Price River Coal Company. Sign affixed to main gate proudly proclaims, "The best men in the world work here."

0:10 (1:44) Castle Gate Rock is renowned landmark of this stretch, protruding like prow of ship above trackside on right.

0:40 (1:13) Breaking out onto flat terrain denotes arrival at Soldier Summit—7,440 feet in elevation. Name of pass commemorates Union soldiers buried here in 1860. Train now descends into Spanish

Fork River Canyon.

0:49 (0:55) Across next six minutes, Zephyr bends around two giant reversing horseshoe curves to resolve dilemma of steep terrain.

1:25 (0:33) On both sides, recesses carved in sandstone cliffs shelter towering rock spires, poised like chess pieces in their midst.

1:32 (0:24) Enter Thistle Tunnel.

During the heavy spring rains and snow runoff of 1983, the town of Thistle met an untimely end. An enormous mud slide engulfed the bottom of Spanish Fork Canyon on April 14, permanently damming the river and forming what became known as Lake Thistle. The small town was completely submerged under 200 feet of water, as was the highway and the main line of the Rio Grande. Ultimately the Rio Grande tunneled above and to the east of the lake, through Billies Mountain. The tunnel is 3,100 feet long and is laid on a 4-degree curve. The lake was subsequently drained, but the new track and tunnel remain. When we exit the tunnel, the slide area will be quite apparent on the left.

1:49 (0:07) At Springville, attractive two-story Colonial building on right was town's schoolhouse from 1900 until 1967. Recently it was converted into office quarters.

1:52 (0:04) Pacific States Cast Iron Pipe Company on left is predominant fixture of industrial region approaching Provo.

1:56 (0:00) Arrive Provo.

PROVO, UT - Nestled between the Wasatch Mountains to the east, and Utah Lake to the west, Provo has flourished since it was first founded by Mormons in 1849. Of particular importance has been the influx of large industry into the region, attracted in particular by the area's abundant mineral wealth, and a labor force whose strong work ethic is a longstanding tradition of Mormon culture. Provo, too, is the home of Brigham Young University, the largest privately owned college in America. All 50 states and 70 foreign countries are represented amongst its 27,000-member student body. And Mormons Donnie and Marie Osmond have a recording studio in Provo.

As well as the recreational opportunities afforded by Utah Lake, Provo is also a convenient gateway to the highly acclaimed ski resorts of Sundance and Park City. Both lie a short distance up the magnificent Provo Canyon, which is also the scenic locale of the Bridal Veil Falls aerial tramway and the Heber Creeper steam railroad.

0:00 (0:50) Depart Provo.

0:02 (0:48) Cross Provo River.

0:07 (0:43) Mounds of coal surround furnaces of U.S. Steel Geneva complex on right.

0:10 (0:40) Shoreline of fresh-water Utah Lake borders on left, while Tintic Mountains hover in distance. Mount Timpanagos soars to 11,975 feet on right.

0:16 (0:34) At Lehi, rustic wooden stadium on left bears "Welcome" banner for fans of Lehi Roundup Rodeo.

0:26 (0:24) Across valley on left, cavities of famed Kennecott open-pit copper mine are just beyond lengthy strand of tailings stretched along hilltops.

0:33 (0:17) Highway turnoff on right at Midvale represents only half-hour trek to internationally renowned ski resorts of Alta and Snowbird.

0:45 (0:05) Approaching Salt Lake City, copper-domed Capitol Building and spires of Salt Lake Temple are both readily distinguishable landmarks of downtown skyline on forward right.

0:50 (0:00) Train now glides to stop beside D&RGW's 1910 station, concluding one of railroading's most sublime adventures.

SALT LAKE CITY, UT - Although Jim Bridger first discovered the Great Salt Lake in 1824, it was not until 1847 that a group of Mormons, led by Brigham Young, arrived at the current site of Salt Lake City and decided to settle here. An industrious people, they planted crops on the day of their arrival.

Today, Utah is still predominantly Mormon, the name given to members of The Church of Jesus Christ of Latter-day Saints. The church is well known for its stance against consumption of alcohol, but, interestingly, Brigham Young imbibed and Utah voted to repeal prohibition. The state is not dry and, even more interestingly, owns and operates (near Temple Square) one of the finest wine stores in the U.S.

Two or three years ago, Utah changed their already-puzzling drinking laws to make them nearly incomprehensible. Suffice it to say, it became possible to have a mixed drink served with a meal at a restaurant—but you had to empty the mini-bottle of booze into the setup yourself. Then in 1990, new legislation finally made it possible to serve drinks already mixed but with less alcohol than in the mini-bottle.

The city, which is the capital of Utah and has a metropolitan population (including Ogden) of nearly one million, is laid out in a grid with wide streets, and, to many, has a rather confusing street indexing system with names such as Second South Street and addresses such as 90 South 500 East. Nonetheless, after studying this system, there is a logic to it that is actually quite helpful. The city is clean, modern and architecturally both interesting and attractive.

D&RGW Station, 3rd South & Rio Grande St., is a handsomely remodeled depot of classical architecture, with Amtrak occupying the south wing. A fine Mexican restaurant in the north wing has a unique trackside patio that is a summertime favorite for lunch. There are snack vending machines and a food vending truck at trainside in the morn-

ings. A museum occupies the central portion of the building.

Ticket windows are open at various intervals, including train times, Mon. thru Fri., and 4:15 pm to midnight on Sundays. Call 800-USA-RAIL for information and reservations.

Cab stand at the station; Yellow Cab, 521-2100. **Local buses** are approximately four blocks east of the station on West Temple; 263-3737. **Greyhound** bus terminal, 160 West South Temple, is about a mile from the station. There is no rental car service at the station, but cars are available 24 hours at the airport. **Salt Lake City International Airport** is only six miles west of the station.

Salt Lake Valley Convention & Visitors Bureau, 180 South West Temple (next to the Salt Palace), 84101; (801) 521-2868.

Peery Hotel, 110 West Broadway (Third South), 84101; (801) 521-4300. An elegantly restored small hotel. Free Amtrak shuttle service. Four blocks from the station. $69.

-Hornes Howard Johnson, 122 West South Temple, 84101; (801) 521-0130. Very sharp hotel in an excellent location. Seven blocks from the station. $58.

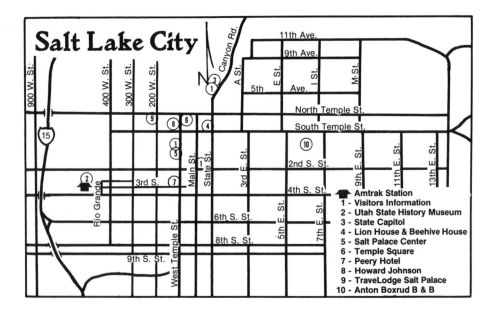

-TraveLodge Salt Palace, 215 W. North Temple, 84103; (801) 532-1000. Nice motel in a good location. Seven blocks from the station. $40.

-Anton Boxrud Bed and Breakfast, 57 South 600 East, 84102; (801) 363-8035. Lovely Victorian on a quiet residential street, close to downtown. Shared and private baths. Well managed. Free Amtrak shuttle service. Thirteen blocks from the station. $45-$55.

In the downtown area, **Temple Square,** South Temple and Main, is the heart of The Church of Jesus Christ of Latter-day Saints. A magnificent six-spired Temple and the near-acoustically perfect Tabernacle are the highlights; beautifully landscaped grounds. Free tours of the Tabernacle and Visitor Center are offered daily. The **Mormon Tabernacle Choir** rehearsals on Thursdays, 8 pm, are open to the public. Also, their broadcasts on Sunday morning are public, and visitors should be seated no later than 9:15 am. Free 30-minute **organ recitals** are held at noon on weekdays and at 4 pm on weekends. The **Lion House** and **Beehive House,** South Temple and State streets, were residences of Brigham Young. The latter building is open for tours. Downtown **shopping** malls are at 50 South Main (Crossroads) and 45 South Main (ZCMI). Near-downtown Trolley Square is another popular shopping complex. The **Utah State History Museum** is located at the D&RGW depot (Amtrak).

And, of course, the **Great Salt Lake,** with its high salt content, tempts swimmers to try their buoyancy, now somewhat lessened because of unusual wet weather in the early 1980s. It lies west of downtown along Interstate 80.

0:00 (4:37) Depart Salt Lake City, skirting southern tip of Great Salt Lake on tracks of Union Pacific, formerly of Western Pacific acquired by UP in 1982.

Since the lake has risen in recent years due to abnormally high rain and snowfalls in the Utah mountains, water now stands to the south of the tracks as well as the north, giving the appearance that the line is built across the lake. Like other lakes in the Great Basin, the Great Salt Lake does not drain, but relies on evaporation to keep from overflowing. Unfortunately,

the high levels of precipitation combined with cool, damp summers have produced serious floodings of low-lying properties. In 1979, the situation became so bad that the state legislature, in an effort to get nature's attention, passed a law forbidding the lake from rising any higher. The legislation proved ineffective, however.

The railroad took a more positive approach. In order to put the tracks out of harm's way, it spent several million dollars to raise its roadbed—a roadbed that was thought to be quite safe when it was constructed in 1902. Until late 1983, Amtrak used the Southern Pacific tracks through Ogden which literally crossed the northern portion of the lake, but frequent closures forced today's more southerly routing.

Amtrak's scheduling is such that darkness usually prevails between Salt Lake City and Winnemucca, Nevada—a desert stretch that, in any event, offers little to see during the daytime.

Gain one hour as train passes from Mountain to Pacific Time. Set your watch back (forward if eastbound) one hour.

4:12 (0:00) Arrive Elko, completing Amtrak's longest run without a scheduled stop.

ELKO, NV - Once an important wagon-train stop along the Humboldt River Overland Trail, Elko has emerged as the commercial hub of a vast ranching domain. Incessant squabbles between cattlemen and sheepherders have punctuated its relatively short but lively history.

Two popular events are held in Elko each year, both drawing from the traditions of ancient cultures. The World Championship Chariot Races are a favorite springtime spectacle, while age-old contests of strength and agility are the highlight of July's National Basque Festival.

0:00 (1:50) Depart Elko.
1:50 (0:00) Arrive Winnemucca.

WINNEMUCCA, NV - Winnemucca traces its roots to an 1850s trading post, established at a point where westbound wagons would cross the Humboldt River. Its formative name of French Ford was eventually changed to honor the last great Paiute chief whose people inhabited the region.

Winnemucca was also visited by the notorious Butch Cassidy gang who, in 1900, successfully robbed the First National Bank, despite the efforts of a determined posse who tracked them all the way into central Wyoming.

0:00 (2:48) Depart Winnemucca on Southern Pacific tracks which will carry California Zephyr to its final destination.

0:15 (2:33) Low, soft mountains rise from desert floor everywhere, presenting pleasing surrealistic scene to early-morning risers on westbound Zephyr.

1:55 (0:53) Alkalie-coated dry lake bed on right is typical of region.

Most of Utah and portions of surrounding states lie in what is known as the Great Basin, a large expanse of desert where all lakes and streams stay within the Basin's boundaries. Rivers either disappear beneath the earth's surface or flow into lakes and evaporate. Sinks (depressions that hold water) occur throughout the region, the Great Salt Lake being the largest. The tracks follow the Humboldt River through this portion of Nevada, one of the many streams that are eventually absorbed back into the ground.

2:22 (0:31) At Fernley, Truckee River joins on right. Numerous crossings occur as train traces river to its source atop High Sierras. Hillside scars seen in distance on left are result of limestone mining operations.

2:41 (0:11) Across river on left, what could pass for just another motel is notorious Mustang Ranch, easily identified by its large parking lot, iron fence and guard tower.

2:53 (0:00) Arrive Sparks.

SPARKS, NV - Predominantly a railroad town, Sparks is rapidly becoming a major distribution center for western markets, due to Nevada's tax-free warehousing. The Zephyr is also serviced here at this large Southern Pacific division point.

Only 30 miles north of town, the inspiring expanse of Pyramid Lake is a popular recreation haven, and important bird sanctuary as well. The pyramid-like rock formations protruding from its midst comprise a setting of mysterious beauty,

used frequently as a backdrop for motion picture productions.

0:00 (0:09) Departing Sparks, elaborate hotels and casinos are off to right, while industrial ticky-tacky best describes rest of scene.

0:07 (0:02) Approaching Reno, massive MGM Grand Hotel is a prominent fixture on left, set a short distance east of downtown hub.

0:09 (0:00) Arrive Reno. Arched windows and tile roof highlight Spanish design of station.

RENO, NV - In many respects, Reno has never departed from its illustrious frontier heritage—it's just better lighted than it used to be. Although best known as one of the nation's foremost gambling resorts, Reno is also a gateway to the untold beauty and year-round recreation of nearby Lake Tahoe, nestled in the High Sierras only 35 miles southwest of town. It is also a convenient stop for students attending the University of Nevada.

Amtrak Station, 135 E. Commercial Row, is in the heart of downtown. For reservations and other information, call 800-USA-RAIL.

Cab stand at the station; Yellow Cab, 331-7171. **Greyhound,** 322-4511. Budget **rental cars** are about a mile from the station, 444 N. Center, and will pick up and deliver Amtrak passengers during business hours; (702) 785-2880. **Reno Cannon International Airport** is just southeast of town.

Reno-Sparks Convention and Visitors Authority, 4590 South Virginia. Call 800-FOR-RENO or write to P.O. Box 837, 89504.

Numerous hotels are within a few blocks of the station. Those shown below are some of the closest. Like Las Vegas, weekend rates are higher and are the second figures shown.

-Harrahs, 210 N Carter St., at 2nd St., 89504; (702) 786-3232 or 800-648-3773. Posh and close. Half block from the station. $69-$85.

-Holiday Hotel Casino, 111 Mill St., 89501; (702) 329-0411 or 800-648-5431. Comfortable facilities at reasonable rates. Three blocks from the station. $46-$60.

-Eldorado Hotel and Casino, 4th and

Virginia streets, 89505; (702) 786-5700 or 800-648-5966. Amtrak package, $31 to $61. Two blocks from the station. $55-$68.

As well as the glitzy hotels and **casinos** for which this city is most renowned, a host of additional attractions enhance Reno's stature as one of the nation's foremost gambling resorts. Headlining a long list is **Harrah's Automobile Collection** with its magnificent array of antique and classic cars, a perennial favorite of nostalgia and auto buffs alike. The **gun collection** at Harold's, **antique slot machines** at the Liberty Belle Saloon and **gold exhibit** at Carson City are also popular diversions.

0:00 (0:52) Depart Reno. On left, archway spanning breadth of famous Virginia Street welcomes visitors to "The Biggest Little City in the World." At night, street is ablaze in neon psychedelia, as hotels and casinos vie for attention of potential patrons.

0:03 (0:49) Elegant, multi-domed St. Thomas Aquinas Catholic Church, in distance on left, seems an oasis of temperament admist encompassing hullabaloo and hype.

0:10 (0:42) Attractive ranching spreads surround handsome River Inn Mineral Spa on left.

As train emerges in Tahoe National Forest, proceed across the Sierra Nevadas, retracing the route of the early "Gold Rush" enthusiasts. Still a marvel of railroad engineering, this magnificent mountain passage remains a lasting tribute to the thousands of Chinese and Irish laborers who miraculously hand-cut much of the current railbed 120 years earlier—the route of America's first transcontinental railroad.

0:18 (0:32) Small hydroelectric plant at Verdi takes water from flume above on left.

0:21 (0:29) Cross Nevada state line into California. On left, wooden flumes clinging to cliffside are nostalgic remnant of mining era. Troughs would originate upstream and transport water to mill sites that were often much higher than adjacent riverbed.

0:28 (0:22) Beautiful yellow mansion stands out on left at small town of Floriston.

0:41 (0:12) Spillway of Boca Reservoir is visible on right.

0:53 (0:00) Arriving Truckee, horses are about only thing missing admist delightfully preserved Main Street of "Old West."

TRUCKEE, CA - Set along the banks of the lovely Truckee River, this rustic Western town has grown from a small logging concern into a bustling vacation retreat. Winter activities are foremost, however, due to Truckee's proximity to a number of California's finest ski resorts.

0:00 (2:09) Depart Truckee past magnificent grouping of Victorian homes before embarking on ascent of Donner Pass. A scenic wonderland, snow-capped peaks still provide an all-too-vivid reminder of ill-fated "Donner Expedition," many of whose members froze or starved to death during unrelenting winter blizzards of 1846.

The route today still remains one of the snowiest in the world. The small town of Norden, elevation 6,963 feet and near the summit, averages over 34 feet of snowfall each winter. Yet sophisticated equipment quickly clears the track for safe and timely travel, with line closures less frequent than those of the adjoining Interstate. It once took 40 miles of snowsheds to protect this right-of-way, but today less than three miles of track are covered by these structures.

0:16 (1:49) Attractive vacation homes and lodges dot shoreline of Donner Lake on right, flanked by picture-postcard backdrop of High Sierra peaks.

0:25 (1:46) Westbound line now passes beneath eastbound, as train enters tunnel that carries westbound traffic under Mt. Judah. Inside, Zephyr reaches highest point in Sierra Nevadas—approximately 7,000 feet.

0:29 (1:42) Exiting tunnel, slopes of Sugar Bowl ski area appear, as chairlift passes directly overhead. Start careful descent of what is known as "The Hill."

0:33 (1:38) With a lot of speed, and a good insurance policy, skiers at Royal Gorge resort on left can practically schuss to cozy confines of Ski Inn Lodge on right.

0:54 (1:17) It was here, near Yuba Gap,

that an ill-fated City of San Francisco, with its crew and passengers, became snowbound for four harrowing days in January, 1952.

0:56 (1:15) Interstate 80 passes overhead at Emigrant Gap. Strange-looking green cubicle on stilts, off to right, is fire watchtower.

1:01 (1:09) Unbounded alpine beauty surrounds shimmering blue waters of Spaulding Lake on right.

1:18 (0:52) Pass through quaint old mining community of Blue Canon. Like other small towns seen along western slope, Blue Canon was once a bustling mecca of activity and excitement when "gold fever" ran rampant through its burgeoning population.

1:30 (0:48) Continue tour of this historic region as train winds slowly along cliffs of spectacular American River Canyon.

1:39 (0:29) Natty red fire station stands proudly on right at small town of Alta.

1:47 (0:21) On left, old frame post office is nostalgic fixture at Gold Run.

2:03 (0:05) High steel trestle known as Long Ravine Bridge affords excellent view of encompassing mountainscapes.

2:08 (0:00) Arriving Colfax, clapboard storefronts on right and turn-of-the-century hotel on left are enduring reminders of town's colorful frontier legacy.

COLFAX, CA - Noted today for its bountiful harvests of Bartlett pears, Hungarian prunes and Tokay grapes, Colfax rose to prominence during the Gold Rush era when goods were transferred here to mule train for transport to remote mountain camps.

0:00 (0:45) Departing Colfax, east and westbound lines take separate routes for next 35-mile stretch into Rocklin. Scenery is essentially same for both, except in Auburn where distinctions are made for each train.

Subtle geographic changes can now be detected as train proceeds down western side of Sierra Nevadas.

0:33 (0:23) Emerge upon charming little community of Auburn. Founded in days of Gold Rush, town was an important communication and supply link for surrounding mining camps. Today, countless landmarks preserve colorful heritage of this historic boomtown.

For westbound trains, pass steepled Firehouse #1 on right. This 1888 structure houses a hand-pulled hook-and-ladder truck, and boasts oldest volunteer fire department this side of Boston. Fire bell fixed atop adjacent stanchion still bears 1869 San Francisco inscription.

0:35 (0:21) Still in Auburn, westbound passengers can look to right and spot gold-domed Placer County Courthouse standing on grounds that were once site of public hangings.

Eastbound travelers can also view courthouse on right, as well as adjacent structures of Auburn's "Old Town." Red and white bell tower of Firehouse #2 is a distinctive focal point of this historic district. Departing town, note picturesque Auburn Cemetery perched atop hillside on right.

As the descent continues, golden hills slowly displace mountainous terrain. Tucked within their midst are some of the most beautiful ranchlands one is likely to find in any part of the country. A little further downline, abundant orchards and agricultural fields reflect the fertile environs of the Sacramento River Valley.

0:48 (0:18) Royal palms and prickly pear cacti on right are assurances we are approaching warmer climes.

0:53 (0:13) On right, enormous cedar logs are cut, split and resplit until they become mere pieces of firewood.

0:56 (0:10) Approaching Rocklin, intriguing antique store on right is housed in old stone building that assuredly qualifies as an antique in itself.

0:57 (0:09) East and westbound routes rejoin, and together travel through attractive residential neighborhoods of Rocklin. Bohemia Brewery stands next to tracks at left.

1:06 (0:00) Arrive Roseville.

ROSEVILLE, CA - Roseville started as a railroad town and, as will be noted upon departure, the community still relies heavily on this activity. The Coast Starlight, which links Los Angeles to Seattle, joins the route of The California Zephyr at this point and uses the same Southern Pacific tracks between here and Oakland.

0:00 (0:24) Depart Roseville and negotiate miles of switches and tracks through vast

Southern Pacific classification yards. Shortly, boxcar rehabilitation shops will appear on right and locomotive shops ("Pride of the Sierras") will be on left.

0:11 (0:14) Approaching Sacramento, pass facilities of McClellan Air Force Base on right, while Haggin Oaks golf course borders on left.

0:16 (0:09) On left, modernistic "Cal Expo" center is September site of lively State Fair. Harness racing is also popular attraction at park throughout summer.

0:18 (0:07) Cross American River.

0:23 (0:02) Travel directly through midst of sprawling Blue Diamond Almond Company. Frequent tours enable visitors to observe procedures involved in processing one of region's most important agricultural products.

0:29 (0:00) Arriving Sacramento, gracious Spanish architecture highlights many buildings of downtown district on left. Ornamental domed tower is City Hall, whose weighty bronze doors require at least two strong men to open for business each morning.

SACRAMENTO, CA - To describe Sacramento as a treasure chest of Western historical lore would still be something of an understatement. Consider first that the famous California "Gold Rush" began here when nuggets were discovered at Sutter's Mill in 1848. Only 12 years later, the Pony Express was welcomed into town at the completion of its first historic run. And in 1863, a group of Sacramento visionaries began charting a route across the Sierra Nevadas that would eventually become the most ambitious link in the nation's first transcontinental railroad.

Such monumental distinctions would seemingly be hard to surpass, although Sacramento's current role as one of the world's largest food production centers assures it a status of increasingly vital importance. The city, too, maintains statewide prestige as the capital of California.

As might be expected, historical highlights are the emphasis of Sacramento's major attractions, from the reconstructed facilities of Sutter's Fort to the splendid array of Victorian homes preserved throughout the city. Of particular interest to train buffs is the California State

Railroad Museum, located only one block from the Amtrak station. Here, sound effects and even simulated motion are used to re-create the romantic atmosphere surrounding the glory years of the railroad.

0:00 (0:20) Departing Sacramento, stately Capitol Building can be seen on left. Built in 1869, gilded globe still remains atop dome, despite protestations of original architect who described it as "simply ridiculous and abominable—a slur on our tastes forever." During 1906 remodeling, "modern" conveniences replaced 45 fireplaces that once heated building. Iron hitching posts surrounding carriage entrance were also lost at that time.

On immediate left is aforementioned California State Railroad Museum, while Sacramento Locomotive Works are on right.

0:02 (0:17) Proceed across Sacramento River, noting on left riverboats along shore and interesting drawbridge a few blocks downstream.

0:10 (0:06) At considerable expense, railroad and highway have been elevated for several miles permitting underlying lands to be flooded for rice farming. On left, over 4,000 columns hold road above muddy croplands.

0:20 (0:00) Arrive Davis. Spanish motif of this handsome station is popular style of depots throughout Southern California.

DAVIS, CA - Long known for its prolific production of agricultural crops, Davis is noted more recently for its pioneering attitude in the field of energy conservation. In 1975, the City Council enacted the nation's first energy conservation building code, setting standards for all new houses and apartments. A citywide recycling program is also highly successful. Most impressive, however, is Davis' claim that its many miles of scenic bicycle paths account for as much as 25% of the city's total vehicle traffic.

0:00 (0:26) Departing Davis, border University of California at Davis campus on right. Grapevines are part of school's renowned wine research program.

0:08 (0:18) Elongated ancient shed at left sags with age, but still provides shelter for several hundred sheep.

0:24 (0:00) Arriving Suisun-Fairfield, stately, white-pillared Solano County

Courthouse stands distinctively on right at terminus of palm-lined Union Avenue.

SUISUN-FAIRFIELD, CA - At once another agricultural stronghold, this "twin-city" stop also affords access to the nearby facilities of Travis Air Force Base.

0:00 (0:20) Depart Suisun-Fairfield, shortly emerging upon waters of Suisun Bay.

0:10 (0:10) On immediate left, hundreds of Merchant Marine vessels are clustered in storage along shoreline, readily conjuring up images of Normandy invasion. Ships are awaiting tow to Sacramento where they will be unceremoniously cut into scrap. Meanwhile, invasion of different sort is evidenced on forward left, where docks are often overflowing with thousands of Japanese auto imports. Last ship before bridge is fabled Glomar Explorer, easily identified by helicopter pad on stern. Although ostensibly a research vessel, it has performed such feats as raising a sunken German submarine during World War II.

0:16 (0:04) Cross drawbridge spanning Suisun Bay. Prior to its construction in 1930, train was broken down into sections and ferried across water. Once on southern shore, entangled maze of refinery apparatus escorts train into Martinez.

0:22 (0:00) Arrive Martinez. While in station, Martinez Museum can be seen in old frame house on left.

MARTINEZ, CA - This important commercial and military port was also the home of John Muir, one of the nation's earliest and most outspoken conservationists. His house is now preserved as a National Historic Site. Joe Dimaggio Drive is on the right side of the train, honoring the renowned "Yankee Clipper" who was raised here.

0:00 (0:30) Depart Martinez along Carquinez Strait, connecting Suisun and San Pablo bays. Carquinez Bridge looms impressively in foreground right, while on left, famed golden hills are subtly encroaching upon landscape.

0:09 (0:20) With town of Crockett huddled on hillside left, travel directly through midst of C&H sugar refinery. Immediately thereafter, train bears south along shores of San Pablo Bay.

0:29 (0:00) Arrive Richmond.

RICHMOND, CA - Richmond's popularity as a convenient suburban stop is enhanced by its trackside connections with BART, a rapid transit system servicing many outlying regions throughout the Bay Area.

0:00 (0:12) Departure from Richmond affords first view of dramatic San Francisco skyline across bay. Golden Gate Bridge can be seen north of city, while Bay Bridge connects with Oakland to the south. Alcatraz Island is also visible below Golden Gate Bridge.

0:05 (0:07) On right, pass Golden Gate Race Track.

0:07 (0:05) Intimidating "jumps" provide challenge for waterskiers at Aquatic Park on right.

0:12 (0:00) Arrive Oakland, Zephyr's final destination. Amtrak buses are waiting at the station for passengers enroute to San Francisco.

OAKLAND, CA - Oakland, California's fifth largest city, is situated across the bay from San Francisco. The California Zephyr never actually gets to San Francisco, but terminates in Oakland where passengers are then bused across the bay to San Francisco's Transbay Terminal. This is not necessarily a disadvantage, however, since many travelers looking for a San Francisco vacation are finding Oakland an economic alternative as a base of operations.

Amtrak Station, 16th & Wood streets, 94607, is in a poorer section of the city. Its once beautiful interior still bears fascinating ceiling lights and two grand murals at each end of the waiting room, but has otherwise grown rather shabby. Consideration is being given to relocating Amtrak to the Jack London Square area.

After the October 1989 earthquake, the interior of the station was closed pending determination of the station's future.

For reservations and other information, call 800-USA-RAIL.

Cab stand at the station; Bay Area Cab Co., 536-3066. **Local buses** are at the station; #88 to Oakland city center and 12th St. Bart station. For bus information, call 839-2881; for BART, call

465-BART; **Greyhound,** (415) 834-3070. **Oakland International Airport** is ten miles south of the station.

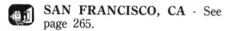 **Oakland Convention and Visitors Bureau,** 1000 Broadway, Suite 200, 94607; (415) 839-9000. Events line, (415) 835-ARTS.

The following hotels are in the Jack London Square area, a few-minutes cab ride from the station:

-Best Western Boatel, 88 Jack London Square, 94607; (415) 836-3800. On the wharf with waterfront views. $73.

-Thunderbird Lodge, 233 Broadway, 94607; (415) 452-4565. One block from Jack London Square. $66.

The following hotel is at Embarcadero Cove, a yacht basin one mile east of Jack London Square:

-Apple Inn Embarcadero, 1801 Embarcadero, 94606; (415) 436-0103 or 800-323-8622. Shuttle service to and from the station; free breakfast. $55 ($59 wharfside).

Lake Merritt, in heart of downtown, has boat rentals, a sightseeing launch, parks, a Japanese Garden and a special "Children's Fairyland" (with child-size buildings, animals and puppet show). **Jack London Square,** Broadway and Alice, on the waterfront, has many restaurants, specialty and import shops; Oakland's leading tourist attraction.

SAN FRANCISCO, CA - See page 265.

Pioneer

The feature attraction of this Salt Lake City-to-Seattle excursion is The Pioneer's "cruise" along the dramatic Columbia River, following the same route taken by those earlier pioneers that once braved the Oregon Trail. After traversing southern Idaho in darkness, passengers are treated to all the spectacular grandeur of the Columbia Gorge in broad daylight. After Portland, the train courses northward through western Washington to Seattle, its ultimate destination.

Through coaches and sleepers provide direct service to and from Chicago by way of The California Zephyr with connections being made at Salt Lake City.

Westbound Schedule (Condensed)
Salt Lake City, UT - Late Evening Departure
Boise, ID - Early Morning (2nd Day)
Portland, OR - Late Afternoon (2nd Day)
Seattle, WA - Early Morning Arrival (2nd Day)

Eastbound Schedule (Condensed)
Seattle, WA - Early Morning Departure
Portland, OR - Midmorning
Boise, ID - Late Evening
Salt Lake City, UT - Early Morning Arrival (2nd Day)

Frequency - Daily.
Seating - Superliner coaches.
Dining - Complete meals, snacks, sandwiches, beverages and lounge service.
Sleeping - Deluxe, economy, family and special bedrooms.
Baggage - Checked baggage handled at larger cities.

Reservations - All-reserved train.
Length of Trip - 1,081 miles in 21½ hours.

Route Log

See The California Zephyr for route log from Chicago to Salt Lake City, page 171.

 SALT LAKE CITY, UT - See page 185.

0:00 (0:53) Depart Salt Lake City.
(The route between Salt Lake City, UT and Boise, ID is traveled during the night.)
0:53 (0:00) Arrive Ogden.

OGDEN, UT - Railroading history was made near Ogden when the Union Pacific and Central Pacific railroads met at Promontory just north of the Great Salt Lake in 1869. This meeting was ceremoniously climaxed on May 10th of that year when a golden spike was driven completing a rail route between both oceans. Immediately after completion of this transcontinental line, Ogden was chosen by the Union Pacific as a major junction point, assuring the city's future growth and prominence.

The Golden Spike National Historic Site, northwest of here, has exact replicas of the engines used in the original ceremonies when the golden spike was driven linking the Atlantic and Pacific. A fine railroad museum in the Ogden Amtrak station has audiovisual displays depicting functions of steam locomotives, historic engines and a rail history relief map. Browning Museum, also in the station, has the definitive gun collection of the world's foremost firearms inventor for whom the museum was named.

0:00 (2:25) Depart Ogden.
2:25 (0:00) Arrive Pocatello.

POCATELLO, ID - It was the Portneuf Valley which provided a transportation corridor to the western Montana mines in the 1860s that gave birth to Pocatello. Now this city of nearly 50,000 is a vibrant trade center and home of 5,000-student Idaho State University. Enjoying both a mild climate and a proximity to many rivers and lakes, recreational opportunities abound, including several popular geothermal pools.

0:00 (1:30) Depart Pocatello.
1:30 (0:00) Arrive Shoshone.

SHOSHONE, ID - Shoshone is a small southern Idaho trading center situated in one of the more arid regions of the state, receiving 10.3 inches of precipitation annually. Of interest are nearby Shoshone Ice and Mammoth caves.

0:00 (2:05) Depart Shoshone.
2:05 (0:00) Arrive Boise. Situated on a pleasantly landscaped hilltop setting, commanding a fine view of the city, station boasts a handsome clock tower and an unusually attractive waiting room, topped by a high beamed ceiling.

BOISE, ID - Although the Oregon Trail passed through here, so did most of those using it—that is, until gold was discovered near here in 1861. Then a fort was established by the federal government to thwart Indian raids along the trail which not only assured Boise protection but also eventual economic success. The railroad brought more activity to the region in 1865—but to the disappointment of the citizenry, bypassed Boise in favor of nearby Nampa when a dispute developed between the Oregon Short Line Railroad and the Boise city fathers. Finally, in 1887 a stub line was completed, giving Boise direct rail access to the rest of the country. Today, Boise boasts capital city status as well as being home to several national corporations, including Morrison Knudsen, Boise Cascade and J R Simplot.

0:00 (0:35) Depart Boise.
0:14 (0:21) Train moves gingerly along "Boise Cutoff" connecting Boise to main line of Union Pacific at Nampa.
0:35 (0:00) Arrive Nampa.

NAMPA, ID - In 1886 several settlers began to build here, naming their new town after a legendary Shoshone Chief—Nampuh (Bigfoot), supposedly being of "huge proportions." The town has had its share of setbacks, most notably in 1903 when an untimely fire burned much of the business district, just when wooden water mains were being replaced that left the town with no water. A "silver-plated" pumper truck was quickly hauled in by special train from Boise, making the harrowing trip in only 20 minutes.

Today, this is the heart of a desert-area-turned-Eden due to the resourceful use of irrigation from deep wells and the Snake River. Of interest is the museum in the restored U.P. Depot and pictographs 20 miles from town, including one of the largest Indian rock drawings on record.

0:00 (0:36) Depart Nampa on main line of Union Pacific.
0:05 (0:31) Mountains on right form a special backdrop for irrigated farmlands.
0:27 (0:09) Enter Oregon and leave Idaho. Metal-superstructured bridge carries us over Snake River on its way toward one of Western Hemisphere's deepest gorges, just 90 miles north of here—Hells Canyon.
0:36 (0:00) Arrive Ontario.

ONTARIO, OR - Located on the beautiful Snake River which divides Oregon and Idaho, Ontario serves as a trade center for eastern Oregon's extensive ranch country.

0:00 (1:50) Depart Ontario and immediately cross twisting course of Snake, as Pioneer pays one last visit to state of Idaho.
0:07 (1:43) Cross Payette River where myriad of bird species can often be spotted along its shores.
0:08 (1:42) Through Payette, birthplace of Minnesota Twins' baseball great, Harmon Killebrew.
0:18 (1:32) Broad waters of Snake River on left continue northward flow until eventually reaching Columbia River at

Boise, Idaho Station

Pasco, Washington.

0:24 (1:26) On right, unusual sand dunes stretch lazily for almost half mile.

0:25 (1:25) At Farewell Bend, note campground across river. Here, Oregon Trail made its final contact with Snake River after following it, off and on, for 350 miles. Pioneers camped at this site 100 years ago, including explorer John C. Fremont. Train now enters one of many canyons of Snake, as bordering mountains rise to almost 1,000 feet above roadbed.

0:31 (1:09) Exit canyon and recross Snake River, as Pioneer enters Oregon and leaves Idaho.

Gain one hour as train passes from Mountain to Pacific Time. Set your watch back (forward if eastbound) one hour.

0:34 (1:16) Stop in Union Pacific yards at Huntington for crew change only.

0:36 (1:14) Depart Huntington and enter broadening Burnt River Valley as train slants across northeastern Oregon.

0:44 (1:06) Limestone from mine on right has only short distance to go to reach cement plant, also on right.

0:53 (0:57) Tunnel's darkness interrupts scenery for about half minute.

1:03 (0:47) Another cement plant, on left, takes advantage of area's prevalent limestone.

1:31 (0:20) Having climbed out of Burnt River drainage, crest summit at 3,998-foot elevation and descend toward Powder River Valley. To left is 5,392-foot Dooley Mountain.

1:50 (0:00) Arrive Baker.

BAKER, OR - In 1861, Baker experienced its own gold rush when exaggerated stories of fantastic gold-laden streams lured miners here in droves. Now encircled by ghost towns that were once flourishing mining communities, Baker is the center for wheat farming and ranching. Recreationalists are drawn here by excellent fishing and trips to Snake River country. The dominant white structure in the center of town is the historic Antler Hotel, built in 1912. Of interest is an incredible 80-ounce gold nugget on display in the lobby of a local bank.

0:00 (1:00) Depart Baker.

0:07 (0:53) Train follows a route bordered by forested Eagle Cap Wilderness Area in Wallowa Mountains on right and Elkhorn Ridge in Wallowa Whitman Forest on left.

0:11 (0:49) On right in Haines, green-roofed building houses town's therapeutic springs.

0:45 (0:15) In small town of Union, circle of pioneer-planted trees was once used to contain sheep during shearing, on right. Hot springs can also be glimpsed off to right.

0:55 (0:05) Anchoring north end of moun-tain range on right is 6,725-foot Mt. Prominence.

1:00 (0:00) Arrive LaGrande.

LAGRANDE, OR - Farming and ranching, made possible by the fertile lands of the Grande Ronde River Valley, give LaGrande a rich Western flavor. The scenery and outdoor recreational opportunities of the Wallowa and Blue mountains make this a sportsman's paradise.

0:00 (2:05) Depart LaGrande and start a grinding ascent taking us over ridge of Blue Mountains directly ahead.

0:08 (1:57) Train slips beneath old arched concrete structure which once carried highway traffic prior to Interstate 84.

0:47 (1:18) Train finally crests 4,205-foot summit of lovely forested Blue Mountains at Kamela and starts its downward roll toward Pendleton, a 2.2% grade—steepest of route.

0:58 (1:07) Train follows sweeping reverse curves to right which someday will be eliminated to enhance coal train traffic.

1:47 (0:18) Cross Umatilla River and return to flatter environs of farm and ranch country.

2:04 (0:01) On right, Pioneer slips past one of several world-renowned Pendleton Mills. This particular factory specializes in producing blankets.

2:05 (0:00) Arrive Pendleton.

PENDLETON, OR - This Western town (ruts of the Oregon Trail can still be seen at the edge of the city) hosts the renowned Pendleton Round-up during the second full week of each September. The main attraction is one of the nation's most important rodeos, including unusual trick riding and stagecoach races, as well as the standard rodeo fare. Another highlight is the Happy Canyon Pageant when regional Indian tribes compete in age-old ceremonial dances.

0:00 (0:35) Depart Pendleton, following meandering Umatilla River to Pioneer's next stop, Hinkle.

0:35 (0:00) Arrive Hinkle.

HINKLE, OR - Here, a very small station serves the Hermiston area. If each train is punctual, eastbound and westbound Pioneers will meet here.

0:00 (1:25) Depart Hinkle, and continue

to roll through northeastern Oregon's farm and ranch country as route approaches Columbia River.

0:12 (1:13) Suddenly, broad waters of Columbia River are off to right. This 1,210-mile giant produces more than a third of nation's hydroelectric power! Bluffs on far side are in state of Washington.

0:18 (1:07) Hundreds of earthen mounds on right house ammunition of Umatilla Army Ordnance Depot.

1:01 (0:24) Cross 300-mile-long John Day River, named after former Western scout.

1:03 (0:22) Wind generators on far side of river are $4-million (each) experimental contraptions of Department of Energy.

1:04 (0:21) On right, John Day Dam momentarily interrupts Columbia's westward flow. Navigational lock is on far side of river and handles eight million tons of commercial traffic annually. With 113 feet maximum lift, it is one of world's highest single-lift locks. Dam's 16 generating units can produce enough electricity to handle needs of two Seattles.

1:08 (0:17) On far side of river, just to right of bridge supporting U.S. 97, are mysterious-looking ruins of Stonehenge, a memorial to World War I dead, built by railroad entrepreneur Sam Hill.

1:09 (0:16) Just to left of that same bridge, set in a small grove of trees on far side, is Maryhill Museum. Originally built as a mansion, it was dedicated as a museum by Queen of Romania in 1920s and now houses very diverse collections of art.

1:14 (0:11) Deschutes River crosses beneath tracks just before it flows into Columbia.

1:23 (0:02) Mount Hood, like some pyramidal spectre, rises to an elevation of 11,235 feet almost directly ahead, visible now on right.

1:24 (0:01) The Dalles Dam stretches impressively across Columbia on right. Dam's hydroelectric capacity gives it a top-ten ranking in free world. Powerhouse is located in dam and is half-mile long, containing 22 generators. There are two fish ladders and a navigational lock along Washington shore.

1:25 (0:00) Arrive The Dalles.

 THE DALLES, OR - This was the terminus of the Oregon Trail,

and a basalt memorial in a city park marks the spot where it actually ended. Now, The Dalles has become a major shipping point, and, in season, wheat-laden barges and other traffic can be seen headed down-river from here. The Dalles Dam, where visitors can see the power-house and a fish-counting station, can be reached by a free passenger train leaving Seufert Park. Also of interest, St. Peter's Catholic Church with 36 stained glass windows donated by pioneer families and an old pipe organ built from rare tigerwood.

0:00 (0:26) Depart The Dalles.

0:26 (0:00) Cross Hood River and arrive at town of same name.

HOOD RIVER, OR - This area was probably first visited by white men in 1805 when Lewis and Clark camped in this locale. Hood River is the gateway city to Mt. Hood with its year-round recreational opportunities, including one of the continent's longest ski runs. Sailboarding is popular throughout the Columbia Gorge due to its smooth waters and prevalent winds. Annually, sailboarders from around the world compete in the Gorge Pro-Am. Fruits and berries thrive here, and packing can be observed in October—or perhaps better yet, wine made from these products can be sipped at a local winery.

0:00 (1:13) Depart Hood River and catch glimpse of majestic Mt. Adams on right. Sadly, Mt. St. Helens is no longer viewable from here since its spectacular 1980 eruption.

0:01 (1:12) Columbia Gorge now begins to take on more dramatic proportions as river cuts through a gap in Cascades while foliage of heavy rain forests blankets southern shore. Farming and ranching of western Oregon are now scenes left behind.

0:05 (1:08) Logging flume on far side of Columbia is last being used in U.S.

0:29 (0:44) At Cascade Locks, Columbia River boat docks and river cruise boats can be seen on right.

This is the site of the historic Cascade Locks built in 1896 to bypass what were then the Cascade Rapids. The town is the beginning of several trails in the gorge as well as the beautiful Pacific Crest Trail.

0:30 (0:43) Bridge on right is "Bridge of

the Gods" which now crosses river on exact spot where legendary natural stone bridge of Indians supposedly fell into river when nearby volcanic peaks caused ground to tremble by arguing amongst themselves.

0:33 (0:40) Venerable Bonneville Dam, first federal hydroelectric dam on Columbia, is on right. Built in 1933 at a cost of $88 million, it is now but one of nine on entire river. Shipping lock is able to raise or lower vessels 70 feet in 15 minutes, a process that uses 40 million gallons of water. Visitors can watch salmon and steelhead trout find their way up giant fish ladders.

0:36 (0:37) Into total darkness for 15 seconds as Pioneer rumbles through one of longer tunnels on route.

0:38 (0:35) Sheer-walled, 800-foot monolith across river is Beacon Rock, proclaimed to be largest such formation in U.S., and second only to Gibraltar.

0:39 (0:34) Appropriately named Horsetail Falls can be glimpsed at left.

0:42 (0:31) Mostly hidden by trees at left is 620-foot Multnomah Falls. It's high, but still dwarfed by California's 1,430-foot Yosemite and 1,612-foot Ribbon falls.

0:48 (0:25) Rooster Rock, the tall black spire on right, stands watchful guard over river as it makes its way to Pacific Ocean.

0:49 (0:24) Final tunnel before reaching Portland plunges train into momentary darkness for last time.

1:07 (0:06) Interstate 84 (Banfield Freeway) escorts train along a winding course through eastern Portland.

1:11 (0:02) Now in heart of Portland, cross over navigable waters of Willamette River on Steel Bridge. Oceangoing vessels can usually be spotted on either side of train.

1:13 (0:00) Arrive Portland.

 PORTLAND, OR - See page 260.

For route between Portland and Seattle, see The Coast Starlight log, page 257.

Desert Wind

Ample portions of desert landscape are served passengers on board the aptly named Desert Wind as it crosses some of the most arid regions of Utah, Nevada and California. Darkness usually prevails between Salt Lake City and Las Vegas, but beyond, travel is during daylight hours allowing for fine desert viewing. The unusual rock formations of Cajon Pass are particularly intriguing.

Between Chicago and Salt Lake, the Wind is combined with The California Zephyr and The Pioneer, where all three operate as a single train. A three-way split occurs at Salt Lake City, however, and The Desert Wind strikes out on its own to Los Angeles, tracing the route formerly traveled by The City of Los Angeles, the once-proud flagship of the Union Pacific.

Westbound Schedule (Condensed)
Chicago, IL - Midafternoon Departure
Omaha, NE - Late Evening
Denver, CO - Early Morning (2nd Day)
Salt Lake City, UT - Late Evening (2nd Day)
Las Vegas, NV - Early Morning (3rd Day)
Los Angeles, CA - Early Afternoon Arrival (3rd Day)

Eastbound Schedule (Condensed)
Los Angeles, CA - Early Afternoon Departure
Las Vegas, NV - Midevening
Salt Lake City, UT - Early Morning (2nd Day)
Denver, CO - Late Evening (2nd Day)
Omaha, NE - Early Morning (3rd Day)
Chicago, IL - Late Afternoon Arrival (3rd Day)

Frequency - Daily.
Seating - Superliner coaches.
Dining - Complete meal and beverage service as well as lighter fare and lounge service. (Movies between Chicago and Salt Lake City.)
Sleeping - Superliner sleepers with deluxe, family, economy and special bedrooms.
Baggage - Checked baggage handled at larger cities.
Reservations - All-reserved train.
Length of Trip - 2,397 miles in 48 hours.

Route Log

See The California Zephyr for route log from Chicago to Salt Lake City, page 171.

 SALT LAKE CITY, UT - See page 185.

0:00 (3:05) Depart Salt Lake City, following Union Pacific rails until we reach Daggett, California.

2:10 (0:55) Pass through Delta, Utah, a farming community of 2,000, situated in Utah's western desert country.

2:57 (0:05) In distance, off to left, cluster of lights pinpoints Milford geothermal power plant of Utah Power and Light Company. Electricity is produced from steam generators which are powered by tapping into underground reservoir of 500-degree-Fahrenheit water. Although output is a modest 20,000 kilowatts, it is first sizeable facility of its kind outside of California.

3:02 (0:00) Arrive Milford.

MILFORD, UT - Predominantly a railroad town for more than a hundred years, a new wave of excitement now surrounds Milford's geothermal developments. Possibilities, such as the nearby geothermal power plant, rouse expectations for new employment and lower energy costs.

Aside from the industrial boon, Milford remains a popular gateway to unlimited outdoor adventure. Within a day's drive and return are six national parks and three national monuments, as well as the recreation resorts of Lake Powell and Glen Canyon. Milford, too, is a paradise for rock hounds, boasting one of the world's most extensive deposits of opalized material. Also found here is the rare snowflake obsidian, once used by the Indians for arrowheads.

0:00 (2:05) Depart Milford.

Gain one hour as train passes from Mountain to Pacific Time. Set your watch back (forward if eastbound) one hour.

1:53 (0:00) Arrive Caliente. Old Union Pacific depot houses city offices, police department, an art display and Amtrak's waiting room.

CALIENTE, NV - As reflected in its name, Caliente (Spanish, for "hot") is blessed with an abundance of geothermal energy. Its hot springs and mud baths were a welcome respite for railroad workers who founded the town at the turn of the century. Today, studies are under way directed at encouraging resort development which could capitalize on this valuable resource.

As well as its geothermal attractions, Caliente offers convenient access to three state parks, including the magnificent Cathedral Gorge 15 miles north of town with dynamic sandstone formations sculpted through time to resemble spires and turrets of a grand cathedral. Also of interest is the nearby ghost town of Delamar, where over 75 million dollars in gold was mined between 1891 and 1909.

0:00 (2:19) Departing Caliente, enter Meadow Valley Wash. Lovely Rainbow Canyon is contained within but unfortunately Desert Wind's schedule calls for traversing this scenic stretch mostly at night—eastbound and westbound. During longest days of year, eastbound passengers might get a view at dusk, and a late-running westbound might offer early morning viewing.

2:19 (0:00) Arrive Las Vegas. Station is located downtown in Union Plaza Hotel. Just beyond Plaza's front door lies dazzling neon maelstrom of world-renowned Fremont Street.

LAS VEGAS, NV - From its humble beginning, first as a Mormon settlement and then a railroad town, the city has grown to become famous as a world gambling mecca and "Showtown, U.S.A." Casinos and posh hotels line "The Strip" from one end of town to the other. Even the Amtrak station is located in one of the many high-rise hotels. Nevada's legalized gambling, the city's warm and dry desert climate, and its proximity to populous Southern California combine to account for Las Vegas' uniqueness.

Amtrak Station, 1 Main St., is located in the Union Plaza Hotel. The station itself is quite spartan, with limited seating and some snack and drink vending machines. But down the hall is another world, the Union Plaza's lobby, restaurants and casino.

For information and reservations, call 800-USA-RAIL.

Cab stand at the station; Yellow Cab, 873-2227. **Local buses** (Las Vegas Transit System, 384-3540) in front of the station at Fremont and Main. **Greyhound** bus terminal, 382-2640. **McCarran International Airport** is just three miles south of town.

Las Vegas Convention and Visitors Authority, Convention Center, 3150 Paradise Rd., 89109; (702) 733-2471.

Because this is Las Vegas, there is an abundance of reasonably priced hotels throughout the city. The hotels shown below are within a block of the station. Weekend rates are higher, the second figures shown.

-Union Plaza Hotel and Casino, 1 Main St., 89101; (702) 386-2110 or 800-634-6575. $30-$50.

-Las Vegas Club, 18 E. Fremont, 89101; (702) 385-1664 or 800-634-6532. $40-$50.

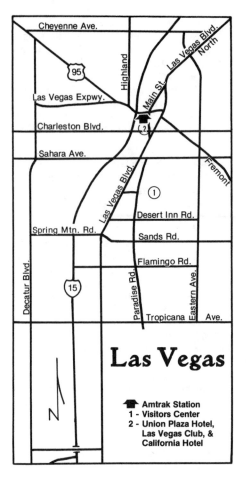

Las Vegas

🚂 Amtrak Station
1 - Visitors Center
2 - Union Plaza Hotel,
    Las Vegas Club, &
    California Hotel

-California Hotel and Casino, 12 Ogden Ave., 89101; (702) 385-1222 or 800-634-6255. $40-$50.

⭐ **Gambling,** of course, is the chief attraction for millions of visitors each year. Casinos abound and most will be found along "The Strip" (Las Vegas Boulevard). **Shows and Reviews** at the larger hotels are true spectaculars in every sense of the word. Complete listings of these can be obtained from the Chamber of Commerce. Reservations for shows should be made directly with the hotels.

Hoover Dam and the Lake Mead National Recreation Area are located 32 miles southeast on U.S. 93. The dam, built before Las Vegas developed, was an engineering marvel of its time, and still remains so today. Standing 726 feet tall in the Black Canyon of the Colorado River, it is one of the world's tallest.

0:00 (2:54) Depart Las Vegas past lavish hotels and casinos of city's illustrious "Strip" district on left. Train then proceeds southwest across parched landscape of Mojave Desert.

0:25 (2:29) Back on left, Las Vegas now spreads out across valley floor presenting a spectacular sight for eastbound evening passengers.

0:51 (2:03) Whiskey Pete's casino, at right, offering Californians their first chance at Nevada gambling, clearly defines California-Nevada border.

2:39 (0:15) At Yermo, travel through expansive Union Pacific yards.

2:40 (0:14) Vast array of military equipment is stockpiled alongside warehouses of Marine Logistics Base Annex on right. Main facilities are located in nearby Barstow.

2:41 (0:13) Water-filled tower on right is focus of hundreds of huge mirrors which continually track sun, creating steam for nation's first solar electric facility.

2:42 (0:12) Calico Ghost Town, snuggled against hillside on right, surrounds site of richest silver strike in California history. Veins were so productive that "nuggets" frequently tipped the scales at a mere half ton or more. Today, flavor of "Old West" is recaptured amidst authentically restored fixtures of this historic boomtown.

Also of interest is nearby Calico Dig. In 1968, a limestone hearth was unearthed, suggesting evidence of prehistoric man over 50,000 years earlier. Area has subsequently become one of North America's most important archaeological sites.

2:44 (0:10) Passing through Daggett, note two historic structures on right. Venerable 1880s Stone Hotel, soon to become Daggett Museum, was home-away-from-home for Death Valley Scotty, who continuously reserved room #7 (with private entrance) for his personal use. Adjacent Scott's Market was popular spot for miners to convert "high grade" into spendable currency. Destroyed by fire in 1908, reconstructed market became first fireproof building in desert, using cement freighted in from the East. Here, we leave Union Pacific and enter upon tracks of Santa Fe.

2:48 (0:06) Marine Corps Logistics Base

Desert Wind – Las Vegas, Nevada

on left is largest of two such facilities in country. Operation's main concern is procurement, maintenance and disbursement of all classes of military equipment. It is presently Barstow's largest employer.

2:50 (0:04) On left, McDonald's restaurant and host of shops are imaginatively housed within refurbished railroad cars.

2:54 (0:00) Arrive Barstow.

On the right, "Casa del Desierto" (House of the Desert) is appropriately enscribed across the facade of a grandiose structure next to the station. This old building was originally a Harvey House—just one of a chain of elegant eateries and hotels that once stretched along the Santa Fe. Fred Harvey's restaurants became legendary for good food—many thought it the best in the country—and pretty waitresses, in what was an otherwise wild and woolly West.

Prior to 1876, the year Harvey opened his first restaurant in Florence, Kansas, rail passengers were forced to endure inedible meals foisted on them by the railroad at trackside greasy spoons. (Dining cars were yet to come!) Seeing what he thought was a great opportunity, Harvey sold his idea of fine food in a

pleasant atmosphere to the Santa Fe and acquired exclusive rights to establish diners along their entire line. Both parties prospered as passengers soon chose to ride the Santa Fe because of Fred Harvey's restaurants.

BARSTOW, CA - Originally founded as a way station along the old Santa Fe Trail, Barstow has emerged as an important distribution lifeline, strategically located at the crossroads of two major Interstates and railroads. Large military installations and a healthy tourist trade further bolster the city's burgeoning economy.

Barstow, too, enjoys a share in technology. Located here is NASA's Goldstone Tracking Station, a vital communications link for orbiting satellites and deep space probes.

An interesting attraction is the Barstow Way Station, with exhibits emphasizing the ecological aspects of the high desert. As well, visitors have an opportunity to sample native plants once used by the Indians for food and medicine.

0:00 (1:42) Depart Barstow through awesome sprawl of Santa Fe's classification yards. Over next several miles, onset of hillier terrain previews approach into San Bernardino Mountains.

0:21 (1:21) Just beyond peaks of Kramer Range on right lies Edwards Air Force Base, primary landing site of NASA's space shuttle.

0:25 (1:17) Elaborate maze of fences and paddocks is home to fine-looking horses on left.

0:29 (1:13) At Oro Grande, well-preserved steam locomotive is enshrined in town park on left.

0:33 (1:09) Towering facility crowding tracks on left is Victorville cement plant.

0:35 (1:07) Sudden rock outcroppings form scenic little canyon as train crosses Mojave River into Victorville. Once through town, begin ascent of Cajon Pass which will lift us out of the Mojave Desert. Noble joshua tree cactus is a prominent feature of northern climb, while spectacular rock formations line descent into San Bernardino.

(Amtrak has plans to make Victorville a scheduled stop.)

0:42 (1:00) Another cement plant borders on right.

0:56 (0:46) Nearing Cajon summit, San Gabriel Mountains are prominent features to right, with San Bernardino Mountains off to left.

0:58 (0:44) Bid farewell to unconfining spaces of West and start dramatic descent of Cajon Pass into Los Angeles Basin.

Since 1885 when Santa Fe's predecessor, the California Southern, pushed the first rails over the 3,811-foot top, Cajon Pass has been one of railroading's more fascinating artifacts.

Three sets of tracks now descend Cajon. To the right is the Southern Pacific, the middle set is Santa Fe's steeper North Track, while on the left is Santa Fe's gentler but two-mile-longer South Track. Since a third railroad, the Union Pacific, has Cajon trackage rights on the Santa Fe, this can become a very busy place.

Westbound traffic on the Santa Fe will normally descend the three percent grade of the South Track (unless weight dictates the more moderate routing), while eastbound Santa Fe traffic will climb the "casual" 2.2% North Track.

1:05 (0:36) White flatiron-like Mormon Rocks are most prominent geographic feature on right. Infamous San Andreas Fault is nearby.

--- (0:31) Eastbound trains now curl through horseshoe turn known as Sullivan's Curve, named after early-day railroad photographer.

1:16 (0:24) Two Santa Fe routes now become one again. Highway on left is Interstate 15, linking Los Angeles and Las Vegas.

1:22 (0:17) Entanglement of wire and steel bars, looking like a World War II beach defense, serves as breakwater to protect tracks from creek's occasional floodwaters.

1:26 (0:13) Passage beneath I-15 marks finish of Cajon Pass adventure.

1:37 (0:02) Approaching San Bernardino, lush woodlands, colorful shrubbery and majestic palms represent radical departure from desert environs of last 750 miles.

1:39 (0:00) Arrive San Bernardino. Railroad equipment is maintained within large Santa Fe shops on right while on left nicely landscaped grounds encircle vine-covered station.

SAN BERNARDINO, CA - Lying in the heart of fertile citrus country, San Bernardino was first settled in the mid-19th century by a group of Mormons who modeled the town after their former home of Salt Lake City. Adjoining San Bernardino is the inspiring Rim o' the World Highway, a splendid mountain drive leading to such popular vacation retreats as Lake Arrowhead and Big Bear Lake.

0:00 (1:03) Depart San Bernardino and traverse Riverside/Fullerton branch of Santa Fe.

0:09 (0:54) At Colton, elderly sheds of California Citrus Pulp operation line tracks on right.

0:17 (0:46) Through Riverside, home to March Air Force Base. Boarded up Santa Fe station on right is nostalgic relic of earlier years.

0:42 (0:21) Cross northern end of Santa Ana Mountains, and descend into congestion of southeastern Los Angeles. One last glimpse of San Gabriels is afforded to right where 10,064-foot Mt. San Antonio stands above all.

0:56 (0:07) At Orange Growers Association on left, seedling orange trees await transplantation.

1:00 (0:03) Clusters of attractive industrial parks comingled with residential areas precede arrival at Fullerton.

1:03 (0:00) Arrive Fullerton. Home of well-known Donald Duck citrus juices appears on right next to station. Santa Fe depot is a delight. Its pink stucco facade topped with a dark, red-tile roof is further enhanced by unusually large, arch-shaped windows and fine grill work.

For route from Fullerton to Los Angeles, see San Diegan log, page 276.

Southwest Chief

When the Atchison, Topeka and Santa Fe ran its Super Chief between Chicago and Los Angeles, ladies received boutonnieres of fresh flowers, gentlemen were given alligator wallets and it was possible to have your hair cut in the train's barbershop. Movie stars and other important personages were commonplace among the train's passengers.

The Southwest Chief, Amtrak's direct descendant of the Super Chief, still travels those same historic rails, and still provides luxurious accommodations and carries a fascinating clientele. Haircuts are not available and Amtrak doesn't give away wallets, but passengers are treated to the likes of movies in the evening and bingo in the afternoon. There is even an Indian guide who travels the segment between Albuquerque and Gallup, describing some of the scenes and historical aspects of that fascinating area.

Originally conceived to intersect northbound cattle drives coming up from Texas and Oklahoma (which it successfully did for 20 years), "The Santa Fe" follows much of the old Santa Fe Trail. This is the shortest and quickest route of the three used by Amtrak between Chicago and Los Angeles. Major stops include Kansas City, Albuquerque and Flagstaff. Ironically, the main line of the Santa Fe does not go through the town by the same name. Passengers destined for Santa Fe, New Mexico detrain at nearby Lamy and complete their trip by van.

Westbound Schedule (Condensed)
Chicago, IL - Late Afternoon Departure
Kansas City, MO - Middle of the Night
LaJunta, CO - Early Morning (2nd Day)
Albuquerque, NM - Late Afternoon (2nd Day)
Flagstaff, AZ (Grand Canyon) - Late Evening (2nd Day)
Los Angeles, CA - Early Morning Arrival (3rd Day)

Eastbound Schedule (Condensed)
Los Angeles, CA - Midevening Departure
Flagstaff, AZ (Grand Canyon) - Early Morning (2nd Day)
Albuquerque, NM - Early Afternoon (2nd Day)
LaJunta, CO - Midevening (2nd Day)
Kansas City, MO - Early Morning (3rd Day)
Chicago, IL - Midafternoon Arrival (3rd Day)

Frequency - Daily.
Seating - Superliner coaches.
Dining - Complete meal and beverage service as well as lighter fare. Lounge service with movies. Dinner is served on eastbound train upon departing Los Angeles.
Sleeping - Superliner sleepers with deluxe, family, economy and special bedrooms.
Baggage - Checked baggage handled at most stations.
Reservations - All-reserved train.
Length of Trip - 2,245 miles in 37 hours.

Route Log

 CHICAGO, IL - See page 116.

0:00 (0:55) Depart Chicago's venerable Union Station and emerge from beneath huge Chicago Post Office.

0:04 (0:51) Amtrak coach yards, on right, offer interesting variety of modern-day Amtrak equipment. At Union Tower Junction, continue southward on Santa Fe tracks.

0:10 (0:45) Cross South Chicago River.

For the next 1½ hours, the sights of some of Chicago's more industrial environs will pass by as The Southwest Chief traverses through rail yards, along shipping canals and past power plants, refineries and assorted manufacturing facilities before finally entering rural Illinois.

0:12 (0:38) Chicago's dynamic skyline is now clearly visible back on right. Sears Tower, with its twin antennae, is world's tallest skyscraper with 110 stories.

0:15 (0:29) On left, busy Stevenson Expressway briefly accompanies tracks.

0:38 (0:13) Cross Chicago Sanitary and Ship Canal at Lemont where, on right, former flagstone quarry was accessed through tunnel beneath road.

0:47 (0:03) Somber walls of Illinois State Prison can be seen on left.

0:50 (0:00) Arrive Joliet.

JOLIET, IL - Joliet's economy is dominated by manufacturing and refining, largely developed due to its strategic rail and waterways location. Also, extensive limestone deposits are quarried in this region.

0:00 (0:45) Depart Joliet where industrialization continues with enormous coal-powered generating plants and oil refineries appearing on either side of tracks.

0:14 (0:41) Cross Kankakee River, just one of many tributaries of Illinois River.

0:45 (0:00) Arrive Streator.

STREATOR, IL - Manufacturing of glass containers gives Streator an unusual industrial base. Containers were hand-blown in early days, but mechanization has now supplanted that older art form.

0:00 (0:35) Depart Streator and cross Vermilion River. Typical Illinois farming scenes now prevail throughout this flat, fertile land.

0:34 (0:01) Cross Illinois River whose waters flow 420 miles from Indiana to Mississippi River.

0:35 (0:00) Arrive Chillicothe.

CHILLICOTHE, IL - Just 18 miles upstream from Peoria, this grain-processing community has a delightful setting on the west bank of the Illinois River.

0:00 (0:45) Depart Chillicothe.

0:45 (0:00) Arrive at Galesburg's North Broad Street station.

GALESBURG, IL - Reverend George Washington Gale chose this spot for a ministers' college after searching westward on behalf of a fundamentalist Presbyterian group in Oneida, New York. Famed American poet Carl Sandburg was raised here, and this was the site of a Lincoln-Douglas Debate in 1858. Olstead Ferris, a "Galesburgite" (and a relative of George Washington Ferris, inventor of the Ferris wheel), was an important experimenter with popcorn—one of the area's important products. This was such a novelty in those days that Ferris gave a corn-popping command performance before England's Queen Victoria and Prince Albert.

0:00 (0:54) Depart Galesburg.

0:38 (0:16) After passing through Lomax, Southwest Chief is escorted on right by America's mightiest of rivers—the Mississippi. This 2,350-mile giant drains an area equivalent to two-fifths of U.S.

0:49 (0:05) Turn westward and cross Mississippi on bridge with world's largest double-track, double-deck swing span, handling both trains and vehicles. At midpoint, cross Illinois state line and enter Iowa.

0:50 (0:04) On left, retired Santa Fe steam locomotive stands on display while old Santa Fe depot now serves as museum of local history.

0:54 (0:00) Arrive Fort Madison, only Iowa stop on route.

FORT MADISON, IA - Built on the site of historic Fort Madison (1808-1813) which protected an early trading post, the city is now a community that is dependent on light manufacturing. The Atchison, Topeka and Santa Fe had planned to take its line through the more southerly Iowa town of Keokuk, but Fort Madison, recognizing the railroad's economic importance, outbid its neighbor, persuading the Santa Fe to build farther north.

0:00 (1:03) Depart Fort Madison, with final view of Mississippi River Valley afforded back on left.

0:12 (0:51) Traverse Des Moines River, and at mid-point, cross Iowa state line and enter Missouri.

1:03 (0:00) Arrive LaPlata.

LAPLATA, MO - This small farming community of 1,400 also serves as a stop for its much larger northern neighbor, Kirksville. America's oldest school of osteopathic medicine was founded there in 1892.

0:00 (0:34) Depart LaPlata.

0:34 (0:00) Arrive Marceline.

MARCELINE, MO - This pleasant little Missouri community was the boyhood home of the now legendary Walt Disney. Walsworth Press, one of the country's largest book printers, is Marceline's major employer.

0:00 (1:39) Depart Marceline.

0:05 (1:34) Swampy environs on right are edge of wetlands comprising Swan Lake Refuge, a way station for hundreds of thousands of migrating waterfowl.

0:11 (1:28) Cross Grand River.

1:39 (0:00) Arrive Kansas City, some 450 miles from Chicago. Santa Fe originally constructed this entire stretch in only nine months.

KANSAS CITY, MO - This second largest city in Missouri (1,350,000 people) has long been one of America's most important rail centers. This would in part account for why the city's Union Station, which also served Kansas City, Kansas, was once the third largest rail passenger station in the nation.

Today, everything **is** up-to-date in Kansas City—with the nation's first and perhaps finest shopping center (Country Club Plaza), a futuristic new airport, and the $500 million Crown Center, about a block from the station, with 85 acres of new office buildings, apartments, and other facilities.

Amtrak Station, 2200 Main St., is located in the downtown area. This is a very modern, new station, constructed adjacent to the much older Union Station. It's somewhat small, but quite functional. There are storage lockers, redcaps, a newsstand, a gift shop and pay-parking.

For arrival and departure information, call 421-3622. For reservations and other information, call 421-4725. Ticket windows and the waiting room are open 24 hours.

Cab stand at the station; Yellow Cab, 471-5000. Hertz, Avis, National and Budget have downtown **rental-car** locations with station pick up and drop off. **Greyhound,** 698-0080. **Kansas City International Airport** is 15 miles north of the station.

Convention and Visitors Bureau, City Center Square, 1100 Main, Suite 2550, 64105. Call (816) 221-5242.

The Westin Crown Center, Kansas City, One Pershing Road, 64108; (816) 474-4400 or 800-228-3000. Luxurious high-rise hotel, 1½ blocks from the station. $144.

-**The Embassy on the Park,** 1215 Wyandotte, 64105; (816) 471-1333 or 800-821-5714. Thirteen blocks from the station. Breakfast and evening cocktails included. $78.

-**Radisson Suite Hotel,** 106 W. 12th, 64105; (816) 221-7000. Ten blocks from the station. $89.

Crown Center, near the station at Grande and Pershing, has retail stores, restaurants and theaters.

The **Harry S. Truman Library and Museum,** in Independence, has documents, art objects and other memorabilia of the life of this former U.S. president. **Country Club Plaza,** some distance south of downtown, is a highly attractive shopping center, with tile-roofed buildings modeled after Seville, Spain. And the **zoo** in Swope Park is quite nice with special children's exhibits.

0:00 (0:45) Depart Kansas City, Missouri and cross state line into Kansas City, Kansas.

0:45 (0:00) Arrive Lawrence.

LAWRENCE, KS - In 1854, abolitionists established the town of Lawrence only to have it become a focal point of pro-slavery attacks—Quantrill's raid in 1863 being the bloodiest. Lawrence changed, and the University of Kansas was founded here only three years after that infamous incident.

0:00 (0:28) Depart Lawrence.
0:28 (0:00) Arrive Topeka.

TOPEKA, KS - The capital of Kansas is also the location of the world-renowned Menninger Foundation. This institution offers the finest in education, research and treatment of mental illness, and has one of the largest collections of Sigmund Freud's papers in America.

0:00 (1:05) Depart Topeka.
0:32 (0:33) Through Burlingame where in 1863, with most men away fighting with Union forces, womenfolk erected a stone fort from which they successfully defended themselves against Quantrill's raiders.
1:05 (0:00) Arrive Emporia.

EMPORIA, KS - This is where editor and publisher William Allen White wrote and printed his famed *Emporia Gazette.* Turning down opportunities to write for larger newspapers, White chose to stay in Emporia and wrote some of the most important editorials of his time. The paper is still published by members of his family, and a library on the campus of Emporia State University contains many of his mementos.

0:00 (0:12) Depart Emporia.
1:12 (0:00) Arrive Newton.

NEWTON, KS - In 1872, Russian Mennonites immigrated here and brought with them Turkey Red hard winter wheat. Ironically, this Russian wheat import led to Kansas becoming the "Breadbasket of the World." The area is now one of the largest Mennonite settlements in the country.

The Santa Fe intersected the historic Chisholm Trail at this point, a trace that extended as far south as Corpus Christi, Texas.

0:00 (0:34) Depart Newton.
0:34 (0:00) Arrive Hutchinson.

HUTCHINSON, KS - Wheat and salt are Hutchinson's staples. This is the largest prime wheat market in the world, and over 50 elevators handle this commodity, including one structure that holds 18 million bushels and stretches for nearly a half mile! Large salt evaporation plants of Carey, Morton and Barton process rock salt from one of the world's largest salt mines.

0:00 (1:33) Depart Hutchinson.
0:04 (1:29) Forest of white pipes "growing" out of ground on right identifies just one of Kansas' many gas fields.
0:45 (0:48) Profusion of black rocking-arm pumps, on both sides of tracks, pull oil from far beneath ground. These are a common sight throughout oil-productive Kansas.
1:04 (0:29) Passing through Kinsley, note large sign near park on right proclaiming its geographic claim to fame—halfway between New York and San Francisco, 1,561 miles from each. Pioneer sod house and steam locomotive are both restored and on exhibit in park.
1:32 (0:01) Chief glides through Santa Fe rail yards on outskirts of Dodge City.
1:33 (0:00) Arriving Dodge City, note two white sundials made of stones on right and next to station, one representing Central Time, the other Mountain. Curiously, actual time zone boundary is some 60 miles west of here.

DODGE CITY, KS - Although it had early beginnings as an army outpost and later a fort, it was not really established as a town until 1872 when the Santa Fe Railroad arrived. Then, millions of Texas longhorns were driven for loading and Dodge City became "Cowboy Capital of the World."

The law was slow to arrive, however, and its nickname soon changed to "Wickedest Little City in America." It is said the term "Red Light District" was first used in Dodge. Headlights on locomotives were fair game for a rowdy citizenry, and train crews departing at night would not light them until the trains were safely out of town. Conditions were once so bad that the Army asked the State to spend money protecting its troops from "the meaner element." Both Bat Masterson and Wyatt

Earp served as sheriff here, and Boot Hill became famous as the gunfighter's final resting place.

0:00 (0:42) Departing Dodge City, on right, exterior of First National Bank and Trust Co. sports giant mural depicting a stagecoach being drawn by six horses—just in case there's any question about what part of the world you are in. Then, town's rebuilt Front Street is on other side of fence, on right, catering to tourists anxious to sense part of the Old West.

0:12 (0:30) Here on right, about five miles east of Cimarron, can be seen snake-like mounds of Soule Canal which are all that remain of an early-day attempt at irrigation. A sixty-mile, hand-dug ditch was started to carry water from nearby Arkansas River to Spearville east of Dodge City, but was ultimately abandoned.

0:16 (0:26) Through Cimarron where Santa Fe Trail made its crossing of Arkansas River. Much of our route follows this historic way west.

0:17 (0:25) On right, handsome Warren Ranch raises Herefords, adding to nation's supply of beef. Note large concrete-lined pits beyond highway which store insulage. Tree-lined Arkansas River is off to left.

0:21 (0:21) More evidence that this is cattle country is seen on right where Ingalls Feed Lots are positioned on slopes that permit important drainage. Several thousand head are fed here each year.

0:42 (0:00) Arrive Garden City.

GARDEN CITY, KS - A lot of "largests" are in this small Kansas community. One of the world's largest natural gas fields and Kansas' largest buffalo herd are near here. An annual Industry, Irrigation and Implement Show in late June and a concrete municipal swimming pool both claim to be the largest of their kinds in the world.

In 1929, before nighttime flying was commonplace, Garden City played an important role in an imaginative coast-to-coast travel option offered by three transportation companies. Passengers could travel by rail between New York and Cleveland on the New York Central's Southwestern Ltd., by plane from Cleveland to Garden City on Universal Air, and by train between Garden City and Los Angeles aboard the Santa Fe's California Ltd. The trip took three nights and two days.

0:00 (1:13) Depart Garden City.

0:06 (1:07) Holcomb is easily identified by city standpipe decorated with horns of longhorn steer, an animal that could endure arid southwestern ranges and was foundation of U.S. cattle industry in 1800s. This is also locale for murders Truman Capote described in his book *In Cold Blood.*

0:31 (0:42) Watch for fields of sunflowers in this part of The Sunflower State. No longer considered a pesky weed, plants are grown for their seeds and also used as cattle feed.

0:50 (0:23) Leave Kansas and enter Colorado.

The State of Kansas had guaranteed the Santa Fe a grant of three million acres, comprised of all odd-numbered sections ten miles either side of its tracks, if Colorado was reached by March 1, 1873. The Santa Fe almost lost this valuable asset when, in December 1872, construction crews mistakenly stopped four miles east of here thinking they had reached the border. When a government surveyor pointed out the mistake, the crews hurriedly pulled up four miles of sidings for the necessary materials and finished the job.

0:56 (0:17) Cross Arkansas River.

This portion of the stream once formed the boundary between Mexico and the United States. Its headwaters are high in the Colorado Rockies near Leadville. From there it flows through the Royal Gorge, out of the mountains at Pueblo, across southeastern Colorado and southwestern Kansas, then through Tulsa, Oklahoma and Little Rock, Arkansas before joining the Mississippi River—a 1,450-mile trip. The river is actually named for a tribe of Indians, rather than the state.

1:13 (0:00) Arrive Lamar where statue known as The Madonna of the Trail commemorates pioneer mothers of the covered wagon days, on left.

In the 1920s, a Daughter of the American Revolution and Harry Truman, then a Missouri county judge, jointly petitioned Congress for an endorsement that would commemorate America's well-known pioneer trails. The National Old Trails Road designation was the outcome, and included such routes as the National Pike and the Santa Fe Trail. Twelve identical statues were commissioned to honor the pioneer women who faced the trails' hardships and were placed at appropriate spots along the Old Trails Road. Lamar was one of those honored places.

The monuments were cast by sculptor August Leimbach of St. Louis, and contain granules of marble, granite and lead ore which give the statues a subdued texture. The mother holds an infant in her left arm, a rifle barrel in her right hand while another child clutches at her skirts.

LAMAR, CO - Ravaged by sand and dust storms in the early thirties, careful conservation efforts have allowed Lamar to become the trading center of southeastern Colorado with cattle and grain important to its economy. Large, shallow lakes nearby make it the "Goose Hunting Capital of America."

The major employer in Lamar is Neoplan, a German-owned bus manufacturing firm. The plant can produce up to four buses per day, and is the tallest building in town. It can be seen some distance to the north (right) of the tracks.

0:00 (0:43) Depart Lamar.

0:09 (0:34) John Martin Dam, on right, backs up Arkansas, creating John Martin Reservoir. Dam was constructed during the 1930s as a flood control and irrigation project by Army Corps of Engineers. Firm that contracted for this work was same one that built Panama Canal's locks. Watch for herons, cranes and other waterfowl.

0:21 (0:22) Brick buildings clustered amidst trees, on right, are Fort Lyon Veterans Administration Hospital and National Cemetery. Old Fort Lyon housed a regiment of soldiers whose job was to protect trappers and traders from Indian attacks. Kit Carson died at Fort Lyon in 1868 due to complications from an arrow wound in his shoulder.

0:22 (0:21) Cross Purgatoire River, so-named by French, but earlier called El Rio de las Animas Perdidas (River of Lost Souls) by Spanish. American frontiersmen, however, cared for neither title and

called in Picketwire.

0:32 (0:11) If you look sharply, you may be able to spot Bent's Old Fort just across the river, back to right and through trees. It's hard to see though.

The fort controlled the mountain fur trade in the early 1800s, and served wagon traffic along the Santa Fe Trail. As many as 60 persons worked at the fort during its peak.

When the fort's owner William Bent tried to sell it to the Government, the U.S. wouldn't meet his purchase price of $16,000 and he blew it up. Later the remains became a stop for Barlow and Sanders stages. Today it is a near-perfect replica of the original fort, having been meticulously restored by the National Park Service.

0:43 (0:00) Arrive LaJunta (pronounced LaHunta).

LAJUNTA, CO - Kit Carson once lived in this southern Colorado town that now serves as divisional headquarters for the Santa Fe Railroad. Situated in the fertile Arkansas River Valley, numerous fruit, melon and vegetable crops are grown in the area—perhaps best-known is the famous Rocky Ford cantaloupe.

Highly regarded Koshare Indian dancers, who are really not Indians but local Explorer Scouts, have preserved Koshare dances throughout the years and have given performances from coast to coast.

0:00 (1:15) Depart LaJunta and leave river valley, swinging southwestward through a patchwork of buttes and prairies called Comanche National Grassland. Santa Fe's Pueblo branch forks off to right, following Arkansas River.

0:02 (1:13) Another preserved steam locomotive is in park-like setting on left, this time Number 1024.

1:00 (0:15) Prominent twin summits of West and East Spanish Peaks of Colorado Rockies can be seen on right. Indians once referred to these two mountains as "Breasts of the World."

1:15 (0:00) Arrive Trinidad.

TRINIDAD, CO - Established in 1859 at the base of the Culebra Range and on the Purgatoire River, Trinidad witnessed a period of unrest between

Spanish and non-Hispanic settlers which finally reached a climax in the "Battle of Trinidad" on Christmas Day in 1867. After four days of skirmishing, Federal troops arrived and put an end to the open hostilities. The Old Baca House and Pioneer Museum have fine collections of frontier artifacts and antiques.

0:00 (1:04) Depart Trinidad and commence a climb of 1,563 feet within next 10 miles as Southwest Chief traverses scenic Raton Pass. Interstate 25 will now accompany train off and on until Albuquerque.

0:15 (0:49) Coal mines on right once furnished coal to both railroad and steel mills in Pueblo.

0:33 (0:31) Wootton Ranch buildings are on right, as well as portion of original Santa Fe Trail.

Richens Lacey "Uncle Dick" Wootton was a Virginian-turned-Westerner who once hunted buffalo with Kit Carson for provisioning Bent's Fort. However, like Lucien Maxwell, he made part of his fortune by driving several thousand sheep (thought to be descended from a small band brought here by Coronado) to California's hungry Forty Niners in the Sacramento Valley.

He settled here and built a hotel and a 27-mile toll road over Raton Pass as part of the Santa Fe Trail, a venture that did quite well. All had to pay except Indians, Mexicans and posses chasing horse thieves. When the Santa Fe came through, he rejected the railroad's offer of $50,000 for his operation and asked only for a lifetime pass for his family and $25 per month in groceries.

0:38 (0:21) Train crests Raton Pass at an elevation of 7,588 feet—highest point on route between Chicago and Los Angeles. Cross Colorado state line and enter New Mexico by way of one-and-a-half-mile tunnel.

1:04 (0:00) Arrive at Raton at southern base of Raton Pass. On right, Spanish-style station with its pink-and-turquoise color scheme greets detraining passengers.

RATON, NM - Once known as Willow Springs, Raton was founded in the foothills of the Sangre de Cristo (Blood of Christ) Mountains and grew because of coal and the railroad. Livestock is now its economic mainstay.

0:00 (1:53) Depart Raton, then follow southeast boundary of historic Maxwell Land Grant for 62 miles.

The Maxwell Land Grant was huge—roughly three times the size of Rhode Island. To be precise, the grant totaled 1,714,764.94 acres, a holding that stretched from Springer, New Mexico well into southern Colorado.

Mexico originally granted the property to Carloz Beaubien and Guadalupe Miranda, but in 1864, Lucien Benjamin Maxwell, a frontier tycoon of sorts who had accumulated considerable wealth through shrewd and fortuitous dealings, bought the property, only to later lose it when gold was found on his land. Unable to keep the discovery a secret, and tired of fighting off claim jumpers, he sold it all, invested the proceeds in a railroad and bank—and lost everything.

0:41 (1:12) At Springer depart from Canadian River and cross Cimarron River. High mountain to right is 12,440-foot Baldy Peak.

1:02 (0:51) Small town of Wagon Mound is named for landmark butte of Santa Fe Trail off to left.

1:31 (0:21) Pass through canyon country where willows and cottonwoods, along with stubby pinon pines, embroider creek bottoms. Just before Watrous, watch for ruins of Fort Union on hillside on left. This historic outpost once guarded old Santa Fe Trail and easier-but-more-Indian-exposed Cimarron cutoff.

1:43 (0:10) Just six miles north of here is Montezuma.

In 1879, Jesse James spent a month there at the Old Adobe House hotel while inquiring about the sheep business and other opportunities. Soon afterwards, The Santa Fe put a spur to the property and erected a luxurious hostelry called Montezuma Hot Springs Hotel and Sanitarium. The 268-room Queen Anne-style castle pampered railroad-traveling tourists for years before finally declining into disuse. In 1982, no less than England's Prince Charles and financier Armand Hammer transformed the former spa into a unique half-high school, half-college with students from around the world. Known as the United World of the American West, it teaches appreciation and tolerance of cultures and political differences of others.

1:47 (0:06) Forward on right, at some distance, are higher peaks of Sangre de Cristos.

1:53 (0:00) Arrive Las Vegas. Note Castaneda Hotel just before station on right. This building, with its tiled roof and arched facade, was part of original Harvey House system of hotels and restaurants along the Santa Fe.

Harvey, himself, was dining here one evening in 1883, when a band of drunken cowhands rode their horses into the dining room and began shooting bottles on display behind the bar, swearing loudly and demanding food. Calmly, Harvey stood up and in a cool but authoritarian voice said, "Gentlemen, ladies are dining here. No swearing or foul language is permitted. You must leave quietly at once." They did just that. Fred Harvey later bought them all lunches, but insisted they wear jackets (which the hotel was always prepared to offer if their guests could not furnish their own).

In 1899, Colonel Theodore Roosevelt arrived by train to rejoin his Rough Riders for their first reunion which was held in this hostelry. This also served as a setting for the movie *Red Dawn* in 1983.

 LAS VEGAS, NM - Although in the 1830s a Mexican land grant gave rise to the first permanent settlement of Las Vegas, Coronado probably first visited this region in 1541. The Santa Fe Trail made Las Vegas important regionally, but with the arrival of the railroad in 1879, the town became the major shipping point for the entire Southwest.

0:00 (1:47) Upon departing Las Vegas, an interesting railroad roundhouse appears momentarily on right.

0:02 (1:45) On left, large "H" etched in hillside is for New Mexico Highlands University.

0:29 (1:18) Off to left and forward, Starvation Peak, appearing like a miniature volcano, is site of a supposed tragedy years ago. Supposedly 30 or 40 Spanish settlers, pursued by Navajos, climbed the peak and held off their attackers with rocks. Stories differ whether they then starved to death at the top, or descended because of lack of food, only to be massacred by their Indian foes. Fact or myth? Sign on left identifies its location as 2½ miles away.

0:38 (1:07) Dramatic double-S curve allows marvelous photo opportunities for those hoping to get shots of entire train, fore and aft.

0:50 (0:57) Cross Pecos River where old Spanish mission of San Miguel can be seen on left.

1:16 (0:31) At Rowe, Pecos National Monu-

Southwest Chief – Raton Pass

ment is off to right, containing ruins of one of largest pueblos. Known as Cicuye, it had two four-story apartments, with each floor containing 500 rooms. These and other buildings, including a four-towered cathedral built after arrival of Spanish missionaries, supported a population of 20,000. By 1840 only 17 inhabitants were left. Plague and war, including revolt against Spanish, had decimated their people.

1:19 (0:28) Pinon, scrub oak and juniper contrast vividly with red-rock canyons in and around Glorieta. Twisting route through these dry washes offers more opportunities to view entire train.

1:25 (0:22) Glorieta is easily identified by Baptist Assembly's huge retreat building on right. One of West's few Civil War conflicts occurred at Glorieta Pass when Colorado Volunteers confronted Texas Confederates.

1:42 (0:05) Southwest Chief seems to miss rocks by only foot or so while snaking through spectacular Apache Canyon, one of trip's highlights.

1:47 (0:00) Arriving Lamy, note Legal Tender saloon and restaurant on right, oldest structure (1881) in Lamy.

Restaurant is one of best in Santa Fe area, and has a fine collection of period American paintings and prints, including two works by renowned artist Thomas Moran. Hand-carved cherry wood bar was imported from Germany by first owner who operated premises as a saloon and general store. Building sports National Register of Historic Places plaque—and, supposedly, at least three ghosts.

LAMY, NM (SANTA FE) - Named for the first archbishop of Santa Fe, Lamy serves as Amtrak's stop for Santa Fe, 15 miles to the north. Originally, Santa Fe was supposed to be on the railroad's main line (after all, it was first called the Atchison, Topeka and Santa Fe Rail Road), but by the time the railroad reached New Mexico, Santa Fe had declined in importance as a trade center, and reaching it other than by a spur would pose difficult and expensive construction problems. Coal and timber availability were other reasons for placing the main line farther south. So only a branch was

built in 1880 to the town that is the railroad's principal appellation. Sante Fe was the western terminus of the Santa Fe Trail and the railroad's arrival meant the trail would soon fade from scene.

A connecting shuttle van operates between here and Santa Fe, including stops at major hotels. This can be booked when train reservations are made.

SANTA FE, NM - Santa Fe epitomizes what many search for in the Southwest—charming Spanish architecture, Indians selling beautifully crafted silver and turquoise on the Plaza, splendid art galleries, wonderful restaurants, and a special sort of relaxed atmosphere.

In about 20 years, Santa Fe will celebrate its 400th birthday. Coronado first explored New Mexico in 1540/42, and in 1610—ten years before the landing of Pilgrims at Plymouth Rock—Spain established Santa Fe as its Colonial Capital. The Palace of the Governors was the original place of government and is still in use today as a public building—the nation's oldest public structure.

Except for a brief period when an Indian uprising forced them to leave, the Spanish were in control until 1824. Santa Fe then came under Mexican jurisdiction until, in 1846, the Army of the West entered Santa Fe and claimed it (and New Mexico) for the United States.

Santa Fe's uniqueness is owed in large part to its architecture that reflects the city's roots. A strict building code was enacted in 1957 to assure its preservation.

It wasn't until the turn of the century that Santa Fe started to grow as an artists' colony. That trend continues even today, and the town is now second only to New York City in art dollars traded. Tourists flock to the galleries that are sequestered in almost every nook along the town's twisting, shaded streets.

A connecting **Amtrak shuttle van** operates between Santa Fe and Lamy, a stop for the Southwest Chief. Reservations are preferred and can be made when making train reservations, or by calling (505) 982-8829, or writing Lamy Shuttle Service, 1476 Miracerros Loop N., Santa Fe, NM, 87501. The fare is $9 and stops can be provided at Santa Fe hotels.

For Capital City **Cab,** call 989-8888 (includes service to Lamy for $22.50). **Greyhound,** 471-0008. The "Chile Line" provides some **local bus** service along four "tour routes" throughout Santa Fe during the day with its "hub" being at Sanbasco shopping area at the Old Train Yard Mall, Guadalupe and Montezuma streets; 989-8595. **Albuquerque International Airport,** which services Santa Fe, is about an hour's drive.

Santa Fe Convention and Visitors Bureau, 201 W. Marcy, Box 909, 87504; (505) 984-6760 or 800-777-CITY.

Most visitors to Santa Fe prefer to stay in a hotel that's near the Plaza. As a result, those accommodations tend to be more expensive than those outlying such as along the very commercial Cerrillos Rd. The TraveLodge shown below is within walking distance of the Plaza and a good compromise for those not seeking atmosphere. The other hostelries all exude Santa Fe charm.

-**TraveLodge Santa Fe,** 646 Cerrillos Rd., 87501; (505) 982-3551. One of Santa Fe's better motel bargains. Six blocks from the Plaza. $42.

-**Hotel St. Francis,** 210 Don Gaspar, 87501; (505) 983-5700 or 800-666-5700. Comfortably renovated landmark, with antique furnishings. National Register of Historic Places. Afternoon tea in the lobby, excellent dining room. Just 1½ blocks from the Plaza. $75.

-**LaFonda,** 100 E. San Francisco, 87504; (505) 982-5511 or 800-523-5002. Literally "The Inn at the End of the Santa Fe Trail." Historic Santa Fe centerpiece; the only hotel on the Plaza. $105.

-**LaPosada de Santa Fe,** 330 E. Palace Ave., 87501; (505) 986-0000 or 800-727-5276. Individual casitas throughout six acres of landscaping. Many rooms with Spanish fireplaces. Both indoor and outdoor dining. Two long blocks from the Plaza. Some rooms as low as $75.

-**Grant Corner Inn,** 122 Grant Ave., 87501; (505) 983-6678. One of Santa Fe's most popular bed and breakfasts, well-managed and attractively furnished. About three blocks from the Plaza (also, condo units farther out). As low as $70.

Santa Fe is the mecca of **Southwestern art.** Galleries are throughout the city, many clustered in the center of town near the Plaza while the greatest number line nearby Canyon Road. Perhaps the best known art market in Santa Fe takes place under the canopy in front of the Palace of the Governors where Indian artisans spread their silver and turquoise jewelry on the public sidewalk.

Southwestern food is served in a variety of styles, depending on the restaurant you choose—hot, mild, spicy, not-so-spicy—for almost any palate. Ask locally for guidance.

Several fine museums are in Santa Fe. Two of the best are on the Plaza: the **Museum of Fine Arts** with changing exhibits of contemporary and historic art, both Southwest and American; and the **Palace of the Governors,** housing exhibits of New Mexico history.

Three outstanding museums are grouped together in the southeast suburbs: the **Museum of International Folk Art,** boasting the world's largest collection of international folk art; the **Museum of Indian Arts & Culture,** highlighting the traditions and culture of regional Native Americans: and the **Wheelwright Museum of the American Indian Cultures.**

Several old churches and missions are near the center of the city, including: **San Miguel Chapel,** originally constructed in the 1600s, but rebuilt in 1710; **Santuario de Guadalupe,** an 18th-century mission; **Loretto Chapel;** and **St. Francis Cathedral.**

0:00 (1:03) Depart Lamy.

0:06 (0:57) Final look at Sangre de Cristo Mountains is afforded, back on right. Former ranch of folk singer Burl Ives is off to left.

0:07 (0:56) Los Cerrillos, freshly painted in 1988 for Hollywood's film *Young Guns,* passes by.

0:27 (0:36) Note front of Santa Domingo Trading Post, on right, attractively adorned with Indian designs.

0:29 (0:34) Santa Domingo Pueblo, where beehive-shaped ovens are apparent, is at right. Pueblo dates back to 16th century.

0:36 (0:27) Pass by Pueblo of San Filipe Indian Reservation. Here, vivid mural adorning side of church, on right, presents a startling visual contrast with its colorless surroundings.

0:50 (0:13) Sandia Peak, rising to 10,768 feet on left, is eastward buttress of Rio Grande Valley as train approaches Albuquerque.

1:03 (0:00) Arriving Albuquerque, golden globe perched atop tower of Federal Office Building is distinctive feature of downtown skyline on right. Also, University of New Mexico dormitories can be seen on left.

ALBUQUERQUE, NM - Located in the fertile Rio Grande Valley and protected from severe weather by the Sandia Peaks to the east, Albuquerque enjoys a pleasant year-round climate with an ample quantity of sunshine during the winter months.

Albuquerque rightfully claims to be one of America's oldest inland cities. It was in 1706, seventy years before the American Revolution, that a handful of Spanish settled in what is now called "Old Town."

Paradoxically, most of the city's growth has been new. It is the trading and industrial center of New Mexico with industries ranging from nuclear research to the large Santa Fe railroad shops.

Amtrak Station, 314 First St. SW (at First and Lead) is an attractive small station of "Southwestern" architecture on the edge of the downtown area. There are snack vending machines and adjacent long-term pay-parking. Covered pay-parking is three blocks from the station. Indian artisans usually sell jewelry at trainside (but be sure to ask where the jewelry was made).

The waiting room and ticket windows are open 6:30 am to 6 pm. For reservations and information, call 800-USA-RAIL.

Cab stand is at the station; Yellow Cab, 247-8888. Budget offers pickup and drop-off service at the station for **rental car** customers, (505) 881-6324. **Local buses** through downtown, two blocks from the station at Third and Gold; call Sun Tran, 843-9200. **Greyhound/ Trailways** terminal, 300 Second St. SW, is immediately across the street from the station; 243-4435. **Albuquerque International Airport** is three miles south of the city.

Albuquerque Convention and Visitors Bureau, Box 26866, 625 Silver Ave. SW, 87125; (505) 243-3696.

LaPosada de Albuquerque, 125 2nd St. NW, 87102; (505) 242-9090 or 800-621-7231. Popular, comfortable Southwestern-style hotel. Conveniently located on the edge of the central business district, just four blocks from the station. $72.

-El Centro Plaza Hotel, 717 Central Ave. NW, 87102; (505) 247-1501. Former Quality Inn on the edge of the central business district. Free shuttle to and from the station which is about one mile. $35.

-The American Inn, 4501 Central Ave. NE, 87108; (505) 262-1681 or 800-343-2597. Motel located four or five miles east of the station, but provides free shuttle service to and from the station. $28.

Downtown Albuquerque, with many shops and restaurants, is at the station's doorstep.

An alternative to the standardized stores and restaurants of downtown, **Old Town** is about two miles from the downtown area. This was the first settlement of Albuquerque. Shops and restaurants around a gas-lit plaza offer unique shopping and dining. San Felipe de Neri Church was built in 1793; mass has been held here on an uninterrupted basis since its completion.

The **Museum of Albuquerque** has exhibits of science, history and art; about three blocks northeast of Old Town Plaza, between Mountain Road and Old Town Road. It can be easily reached by walking from the plaza.

Indian Pueblo Cultural Center, 2401 12th NW, is owned and operated by the 19 Indian Pueblos of New Mexico. There are shops with arts and crafts, a museum, a restaurant and dancers. A **visitors center** is also located here.

The **National Atomic Museum,** located on the grounds of Kirtland Air Force Base, has exhibits, movies and tours that focus on the Manhattan Project. This highly secretive development of the first atomic bomb was centered in New Mexico.

Sandia Peak Aerial Tram, the world's longest at 2.7 miles, takes visitors to the top of 10,378-foot Sandia Peak in 20 minutes, where expansive views of Albu-

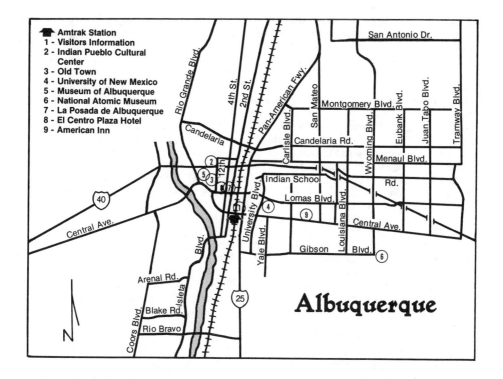

Amtrak Station
1 - Visitors Information
2 - Indian Pueblo Cultural
    Center
3 - Old Town
4 - University of New Mexico
5 - Museum of Albuquerque
6 - National Atomic Museum
7 - La Posada de Albuquerque
8 - El Centro Plaza Hotel
9 - American Inn

Albuquerque

querque and the Rio Grande Valley are afforded. Restaurants are at both the base and the summit.

In early October, Albuquerque is host to its biggest event, the renowned **International Balloon Fiesta.** Over 500 hot-air balloons from around the world take part for this nine-day extravaganza. If you plan to attend, make hotel reservations early.

0:00 (2:20) Departing Albuquerque, farmlands of Rio Grande Valley soon give way to arid terrain of Southwestern desert.

0:02 (2:18) On left, pass University of New Mexico's sports stadium.

0:04 (2:16) Grounds of Rio Grande Park and Zoo are visible in distance on right.

0:09 (2:11) Manzano Mountains protrude above horizon on left, while Ladron Peak (9,176 feet) is most prominent member of Ladron Mountains on right. New Mexican ranges represent subclassification of much larger range known as Rocky Mountains.

0:13 (2:07) Cross Rio Grande River.

0:14 (2:06) Handsome mission stands proudly amidst Isleta Indian Reservation on left.

0:26 (1:54) At railroad junction of Dalies, train intersects with "main line," and proceeds westerly across desert landscape, its mystic beauty now further enhanced by a dramatic intrusion of mesas and buttes. An early cradle of Western civilization, area has spawned a vast historical legacy with elements of Indian, Spanish and Frontier cultures all colorfully assimilated into lifestyles and livelihoods of modern-day New Mexicans.

0:28 (1:52) Peak seen in distance on right is Mt. Taylor, named for President Zachary Taylor and nobly presiding at 11,301 feet.

0:34 (1:46) Cross Rio Puerco which flows into Rio Grande a few miles downstream. Also at this time, embark on a gradual 3,000-foot ascent that culminates atop Continental Divide outside Thoreau.

0:48 (1:32) Pass under wooden trestle that supports historic "Route 66."

0:51 (1:29) "Kneeling Nuns," who appear to be praying before a stone altar, is appropriate title of rock formation on right.

0:54 (1:26) Stark gypsum cliffs border on right as train passes through grounds of

Mesita Pueblo. Some primitive buildings seen here on left have been inhabited by as many as five generations of same family.

0:55 (1:25) Join small San Jose River on left which train crosses several times over next few miles.

0:58 (1:22) Pass through Laguna Pueblo. As in other pueblos, anthill pilings are frequently spread across rooftops of these adobe structures in deference to their unique watershedding capabilities.

1:02 (1:18) Venerable mission of Acoma Indians is most prominent fixture of Acomita Pueblo, on left.

1:08 (1:12) Picturesquely poised atop bluff on left, resplendent two-centuries-old mission at McCartys Pueblo is reputedly built upon foundation of earlier Franciscan mission. Mission is part of Acoma Indian Reservation.

1:11 (1:09) Exposed lava beds lining trackside on left reflect early volcanic nature of aforementioned Mt. Taylor.

1:20 (1:00) At Grants, importance of uranium mining is evidenced by profusion of gouged hillsides surrounding community.

1:23 (0:57) On right, note large Anaconda uranium smelter.

1:52 (0:28) Imperceptibly, cross Campbell's "Pass" and Continental Divide where waters behind us flow to Atlantic and waters ahead run to Pacific.

2:12 (0:08) Pyramid Rock and spire-crowned Church Rock appear on right.

2:14 (0:06) Cliffs on right are part of Red Rock State Park, site of annual Gallup Intertribal Indian Ceremonial where tribes from around the country gather each August for ceremonial dancing and rodeo competition.

2:18 (0:01) About four blocks east of Gallup's station is venerable El Rancho Hotel, on left. Built in 1937 by movie magnate D. W. Griffith to house actors for Westerns (frequently filmed in region), its guests included John Wayne, Humphrey Bogart, Lucille Ball, Tom Mix and Ronald Reagan. After slipping into bankruptcy in 1987, it was restored and reopened the following year.

2:20 (0:00) Arrive Gallup's inter-modal train station, remodeled in 1988 at a cost of 1.6 million dollars.

GALLUP, NM - Hopi, Navajo and Zuni Indians all live in and around Gallup, and these native Americans comprise more than half of the town's population. Here, visitors can find beautiful silver jewelry, baskets, rugs and pottery in numerous large trading posts, and just east a few miles, the famous Intertribal Ceremonial is held at Red Rock State Park.

Gallup is also a gateway to the Four Corners region (where New Mexico, Arizona, Colorado and Utah make a unique four-state convergence) and Mesa Verde National Park, 150 miles to the north, where ancient Anasazi cliff dwellings can be visited.

0:00 (1:41) Depart Gallup.

0:20 (1:21) Pass beneath I-40, and enter Arizona and southern protrusion of Navajo Indian Reservation.

At Arizona border, enter Pacific Time Zone. Since Arizona does not observe daylight saving time, set your watch back (forward if eastbound) one hour, if rest of country is currently on daylight saving time.

0:32 (1:09) At Sanders, tracks exit Navajo Indian Reservation.

0:56 (0:45) Cross through neck of hourglass-shaped Petrified Forest National Park. This stark country was heavily wooded 150 million years ago. Now, giant agatized logs and smaller fragments lie scattered throughout area forming world's largest and most colorful concentration of petrified wood. Colorful soils of Painted Desert lend added drama to landscape, particularly when sun is near horizon.

1:14 (0:27) Through Holbrook, one of northern Arizona's larger ranching and trading centers, and former important "gas stop" on legendary Route 66. Little Colorado River follows on left until just before Winslow, when stream swings northwest toward its juncture with Colorado River at eastern end of Grand Canyon.

1:22 (0:19) Electric generating station at right consumes about four carloads of coal each hour to keep much of Southwest supplied with energy.

1:41 (0:00) Arrive Winslow.

WINSLOW, AZ - Another trading center for Navajos and Hopis, Winslow sometimes goes by the nickname "Meteor City." Twenty miles west of town is Meteor Crater, a 4,000-foot-wide,

600-foot-deep hole created when an enormous meteorite, traveling at incredible speed, struck the earth 20,000 years ago.
0:00 (1:02) Depart Winslow.
0:29 (0:33) Cross Canyon Diablo on 560-foot steel bridge, 225 feet above creek's bed. This was one of railroad's major hurdles in its march westward. Original bridge took 15 months to construct and was started on site long before tracks reached this mini-gorge, bridge sections being freighted from railhead using mule power.
0:53 (0:10) San Francisco Peaks, tall mountains right forward, rise to 12,670 feet above sea level and are home to the Hopi, Kachinas and Snow Bowl ski area.
1:02 (0:00) Arrive Flagstaff.

FLAGSTAFF, AZ - On the nation's 100th birthday, celebrants stripped a pine tree of its branches so that it could serve as a flagstaff for the country's flag. The site was near a spring and frequently served as a camping spot for California-bound travelers—who soon began to refer to it by its present name. This is the stop for Amtrak passengers visiting the Grand Canyon, with bus connections to and from the station. (Buses leave Flagstaff early in the morning and return late that evening.) Other major attractions include nearby Oak Creek Canyon, Lowell Observatory (responsible for the discovery of the planet Pluto), skiing (Flagstaff's elevation is 6,900 feet) and the fine Museum of Northern Arizona, with its many Indian artifacts and books about the Southwest.

Amtrak Thruway Bus service is available between Flagstaff and the Grand Canyon as well as Sedona and Phoenix.
0:00 (2:56) Depart Flagstaff.
0:44 (2:12) Rumble across intersection with Grand Canyon Railway, just north of Williams from where seasonal steam train excursion service to Grand Canyon is available.
1:37 (1:39) Through Seligman, established in 1882 at the junction of the Santa Fe's main line and a line to Prescott.

Seligman still gets much of its support from railroad facilities. Tourism is important because of the town's strategic location on Interstate 40 and its Grand Canyon

proximity. Cattle ranches provide a wide trading market. Expansion of U.S. Lime Company's mine, 25 miles west, has given the town additional stimulus.
2:56 (0:00) Arrive Kingman.

KINGMAN, AZ - Like Seligman, Kingman was established in 1882 along the Santa Fe's main line. Throughout the sparsely settled West, towns had a propensity to sprout along the tracks, quite unlike the East where railroads were built to serve existing population centers.
0:00 (1:01) Depart Kingman.

Pass from Mountain to Pacific Time as train crosses Colorado River and Arizona state line into California. Since Arizona does not observe daylight saving time, set watch back (forward if eastbound) one hour only if rest of country is not currently on daylight saving time.
1:01 (0:00) Arrive Needles.

NEEDLES, CA - California's easternmost city is located in the arid Mojave Desert, where temperatures frequently are the highest in the nation. Named for a group of nearby rock pinnacles, Needles was first a railroad way station, then a mining town, and finally a city of pipeline companies and tourist industries. Fred Harvey once broke with tradition and used male waiters at Needles Harvey House, since he felt town too bawdy for his prim and proper waitresses.
0:00 (2:31) Depart Needles.
2:31 (0:00) Arrive Barstow.

On the right, "Casa del Desierto" (House of the Desert) is appropriately enscribed across the facade of a grandiose structure next to the station. This old building was originally a Harvey House—just one of a chain of elegant eateries and hotels that once stretched along the Santa Fe. Fred Harvey's restaurants became legendary for good food—many thought it the best in the country—and pretty waitresses, in what was an otherwise wild and wooly West.

Prior to 1876, the year Harvey opened his first restaurant in Florence, Kansas, rail passengers were forced to endure inedible meals foisted on them by the railroad at trackside greasy spoons. (Dining cars were yet to come!) Seeing what he thought was a great opportunity, Harvey sold his idea of fine food in a pleasant atmosphere to the Santa Fe and acquired exclusive rights to establish diners along their entire line. Both parties prospered as passengers soon chose to ride the Santa Fe because of Fred Harvey's restaurants.

BARSTOW, CA - Originally founded as a way station along the old Santa Fe Trail, Barstow has emerged as an important distribution lifeline, strategically located at the crossroads of two major Interstates and railroads. Large military installations and a healthy tourist trade further bolster the city's burgeoning economy.

Barstow, too, enjoys a share in technology. Located here is NASA's Goldstone Tracking Station, a vital communications link for orbiting satellites and deep space probes.

An interesting attraction is the Barstow Way Station, with exhibits emphasizing the ecological aspects of the high desert. As well, visitors have an opportunity to sample native plants once used by the Indians for food and medicine.

0:00 (1:42) Depart Barstow through awesome sprawl of Santa Fe's classification yards. Over next several miles onset of hillier terrain previews approach into San Bernardino Mountains.

0:21 (1:21) Just beyond peaks of Kramer Range on right lies Edwards Air Force Base, primary landing site of NASA's space shuttle.

0:25 (1:17) Elaborate maze of fences and paddocks is home to fine-looking horses on left.

0:29 (1:13) At Oro Grande, well-preserved steam locomotive is enshrined in town park on left.

0:33 (1:09) Towering facility crowding tracks on left is Victorville cement plant.

0:35 (1:07) Sudden rock outcroppings form scenic little canyon as train crosses Mojave River into Victorville. Once through town, begin ascent of Cajon Pass which will lift us out of the Mojave Desert. Noble joshua tree cactus is a prominent feature on northern climb, while spectacular rock formations line descent into San Bernardino.

(Amtrak has plans to make Victorville a scheduled stop.)

0:42 (1:00) Another cement plant borders on right.

0:56 (0:46) Nearing Cajon summit, San Gabriel Mountains are prominent features to right, with San Bernardino Mountains off to left.

0:58 (0:44) Bid farewell to unconfining spaces of West and start dramatic descent of Cajon Pass into Los Angeles Basin.

Since 1885 when Santa Fe's predecessor, the California Southern, pushed the first rails over the 3,811-foot top, Cajon Pass has been one of railroading's more fascinating artifacts.

Three sets of tracks now descend Cajon. To the right is the Southern Pacific, the middle set is Santa Fe's steeper North Track, while on the left is Santa Fe's gentler but two-mile-longer South Track. Since a third railroad, the Union Pacific, has Cajon trackage rights on the Santa Fe, this can become a very busy place.

Westbound traffic on the Santa Fe will normally descend the three percent grade of the South Track (unless weight dictates the more moderate routing), while eastbound Santa Fe traffic will climb the "casual" 2.2% North Track.

1:05 (0:36) White flatiron-like Mormon Rocks are most prominent geographic feature on right. Infamous San Andreas Fault is nearby.

--- (0:31) Eastbound trains now curl through turn known as Sullivan's Curve, named after early-day railroad photographer.

1:16 (0:24) Two Santa Fe routes now become one again. Highway on left is Interstate 15, linking Los Angeles and Las Vegas.

1:22 (0:17) Entanglement of wire and steel bars, looking like a World War II beach defense, serves as breakwater to protect tracks from creek's occasional floodwaters.

1:26 (1:13) Passage beneath I-15 marks finish of Cajon Pass adventure.

1:37 (0:02) Approaching San Bernardino, lush woodlands, colorful shrubbery and majestic palms represent radical departure from desert environs of last 750 miles.

1:39 (0:00) Arrive San Bernardino. Railroad equipment is maintained within large

Santa Fe shops on right while on left nicely landscaped grounds encircle vine-covered station.

SAN BERNARDINO, CA - Lying in the heart of fertile citrus country, San Bernardino was first settled in the mid-19th century by a group of Mormons who modeled the town after their former home of Salt Lake City. Adjoining San Bernardino is the inspiring Rim o' the World Highway, a splendid mountain drive leading to such popular vacation retreats as Lake Arrowhead and Big Bear Lake.

Big Mac connoisseurs should know that McDonald's opened its first outlet in San Bernardino.

0:00 (0:35) Departing San Bernardino, journey into bustle and congestion of Southern California's sprawling megalopolis.

0:17 (0:18) A few miles west of Fontana, pass huge steel plant originally built by Kaiser, but later operated as a multi-national consortium, on left. Adjacent mounds of sand are by-product of operation and are subsequently sold to railroad for trackbed construction.

0:25 (0:10) Nostalgic advertisements are a delightful, yet time-worn adornment of vine-covered Cucamonga depot on left.

0:35 (0:00) Arrive Pomona's North Garey Avenue station. (Note that Sunset Ltd. uses Commercial Street station.)

POMONA, CA - In 1875, Solomon Gates was awarded a free lot for naming Pomona after the Roman goddess of fruit. The name remains appropriate to this day, reflecting the city's prominence as a mecca of citrus production. Pomona is also the noted autumn host of the Los Angeles County Fair, boasting the largest attendance of any such fair in the U.S. Nearby, too, is the resort of Mt. Baldy, whose ski slopes, trout streams and scenic campgrounds provide a haven of year-round recreation.

0:00 (0:31) Depart Pomona as San Gabriel Mountains border on right.

0:02 (0:29) Futuristic fabric-covered building on right houses gymnasium and theater of La Verne College. Students affectionately refer to facility as "The Supertent."

0:08 (0:23) Passing through Glendora, attractive homes cling to hillsides, both right and left.

0:11 (0:20) At Azusa, train travels past extensive acreage of Monrovia Nursery on right. Established in 1926, operation was subsequently moved from Monrovia to its present locale, and today is recognized as world's largest distributor of ornamental plants and trees.

0:14 (0:17) West of Azusa, pass Miller brewery on left.

0:16 (0:15) Cross often-dry San Gabriel River.

0:19 (0:12) At Monrovia, note quaint old depot on right. Its Spanish Colonial architecture is popular style of many stations in Southern California. A short distance downline, handsome mission-style church on right is further evidence of Spanish influence.

0:22 (0:09) Emerge upon median of Interstate 210, and dart indifferently past traffic snarl of envious commuters. State and County Arboretum, on left, has been setting for various Hollywood jungle flicks.

0:24 (0:07) Approaching Pasadena, train passes Colorado Boulevard on left. This legendary thoroughfare is noted primarily as annual Tournament of Roses Parade site.

0:26 (0:05) Another resplendent mission-style church stands at foot of San Gabriel Mountains on right.

0:30 (0:01) Descend from "freeway route" into tunnel, emerging moments later in heart of downtown Pasadena. On left, red-domed City Hall is one of country's most distinctive government enclaves, its classical Renaissance design inspired by 16th-century Italian architect Andrea Palladio.

0:31 (0:00) Arriving Pasadena, old railroad building on right is presently owned by antique fancier. "Case Eagle" perched atop its roof is a sampling of treasures contained within. Building is further identified by its lengthy German inscription, "PASADENANTIKSPIELENBAHNHOP-PLATZ," meaning "Antique Playhouse at the Train Station." Also noteworthy here is gracious old Green Hotel, its mission-like towers and decorative balconies looming above treetops on right. Since its construction nearly a hundred years ago, hotel has been host to many luminaries, including President Harrison in 1891. Recently converted into apartments, building remains enshrined in National Register of Historic Places.

 PASADENA, CA - Nestled amidst a lush and colorful valley of the San Gabriel Mountains, Pasadena has flourished since its formative development as a vacation resort for winter-weary Easterners. Today, the city is recognized not only as a premier cultural center, but a cradle of modern technology as well.

Located here is the highly acclaimed California Institute of Technology, whose pioneering programs in research and development have lured many prominent industries to the region, including NASA's Jet Propulsion Laboratories. Since its formal founding in 1920, numerous Nobel Prizes and National Medals of Science have been awarded to alumni and faculty members of this prestigious school. The school also owns the famed 200-inch telescope atop Mt. Palomar.

The name Pasadena is still associated foremost with the Tournament of Roses Parade and Rose Bowl game, hosted here each New Year's Day. Originally conceived as a promotion for Pasadena's mild winter climate, the first parade was held in 1890, and featured a modest procession of colorfully flowered buggies and tallyhos. Since then, the event has burgeoned to epic proportions, its pageantry now encompassing a myriad of floats, marching bands and equestrians.

In 1902, another tradition was established when football teams from Stanford and Michigan met in the first Rose Bowl. Now, each New Year's Day, teams from the Big-Ten and Pac-Ten square off in one of the nation's most heated rivalries.

0:00 (0:25) Departing Pasadena, note old AT&SF steam locomotive consist preserved on left.

0:10 (0:15) Colorful flowers and shrubbery accent comely neighborhoods as train turns south through Highland Park.

0:12 (0:13) Tower protruding atop cliffsides on right is part of Southwest Museum, acclaimed for its fascinating collection of Indian and Spanish artifacts.

0:18 (0:07) Cross concrete channel that sometimes becomes Los Angeles River.

On forward right, prominent tower of downtown Los Angeles skyline is City Hall, while double-domed building in foreground houses Post Office annex.

0:22 (0:03) Back atop bluffs on right can be seen lights and bleacher tops of Dodger Stadium, home of Major League Baseball's 1988 champions.

0:25 (0:00) Pass County Jail on left before arriving Los Angeles Union Passenger Terminal.

 LOS ANGELES, CA - See page 273.

Chicago
St. Louis
San Antonio Dallas
Houston

Texas Eagle

From Chicago, The Texas Eagle travels to St. Louis through Abe Lincoln's central Illinois, on through the Ozarks to Little Rock, across eastern Texas to Dallas and Ft. Worth, then a final southward thrust to San Antonio. There is also a separate section that splits off at Dallas to serve Houston. Through coaches and sleepers are available to and from Los Angeles, by way of The Sunset Limited.

When traveling from Chicago to Los Angeles, there is a four-hour layover at San Antonio in the middle of the night. Traveling from Los Angeles to Chicago the layover is one hour in the early morning.

Southbound Schedule (Condensed)
Chicago, IL - Midafternoon Departure
St. Louis, MO - Late Evening
Little Rock, AR - Middle of the Night (2nd Day)
Dallas, TX - Early Afternoon (2nd Day)
San Antonio, TX - Late Evening Arrival (2nd Day)
Houston, TX - Late Evening Arrival (2nd Day)*

Northbound Schedule (Condensed)
Houston, TX - Early Morning Departure*
San Antonio, TX - Early Morning Departure
Dallas, TX - Midafternoon
Little Rock, AR - Late Evening
St. Louis, MO - Early Morning (2nd Day)
Springfield, IL - Midmorning (2nd Day)
Chicago, IL - Early Afternoon Arrival (2nd Day)

*By separate section to and from Dallas.

Frequency - Daily.
Seating - Superliner coaches.
Dining - Complete meal and beverage service as well as lighter fare. Lounge service with movies, games and hospitality hour, Chicago-Houston. Sandwiches and snacks, Dallas-Houston.
Sleeping - Superliner sleepers with deluxe, family, economy and special bedrooms.
Baggage - Checked baggage handled at larger cities.
Reservations - All-reserved train.
Length of Trip - 1,308 miles in 30 hours (Chicago-San Antonio).

Route Log

 CHICAGO, IL - See page 116.

0:00 (0:43) Depart Chicago's venerable Union Station and emerge from beneath huge Chicago Post Office.
0:04 (0:51) Amtrak coach yards on right offer interesting variety of modern-day Amtrak equipment.

For forty minutes the sights of some of Chicago's more industrial environs will pass by as The Texas Eagle traverses through rail yards and past power plants, refineries and assorted manufacturing facilities, before finally entering rural Illinois.
0:06 (0:35) Cross South Branch Chicago River, then turn west following Sanitary Ship Canal out of city. Illinois has more active miles of canals than any other state. Stevenson Expressway briefly ac-

companies tracks on left.

0:15 (0:28) Chicago's dynamic skyline is now clearly visible back on right.

0:21 (0:22) Illinois Central freight yards stretch along route on left.

0:28 (0:15) Rumble over Calumet Sag Canal connecting Chicago Sanitary Ship Canal with Lake Michigan—an engineering feat that reversed flow of Chicago River so that it now flows out of Lake Michigan.

0:37 (0:06) Note towpath along banks of Illinois and Michigan Canal, on right.

0:40 (0:03) On left are dreary walls of Joliet Correctional Center.

0:43 (0:00) Arrive Joliet.

JOLIET, IL - Joliet's economy is dominated largely by manufacturing and refining, developed largely due to its strategic rail and waterway location.

0:00 (0:50) Depart Joliet.

0:06 (0:44) Size of cavernous limestone quarry on left is brought into perspective by focusing on huge trucks at bottom.

0:13 (0:37) Earthen mounds (in distance through trees) are actually munitions storage bunkers of U.S. Army Arsenal.

0:17 (0:33) Cross Kankakee River.

0:22 (0:28) Large windowless structure with two enormous "silos" is Commonwealth Edison's Briarwood Nuclear Power Station. Golf course on left rests on reclaimed coal strip mine.

0:34 (0:16) As train enters Dwight, small white church with spire-like steeple is Pioneer Gothic Church where Prince of Wales attended services in 1860. Travel down Main Street of Dwight where rambling old depot on right dates back to 1892. Designed by Henry Ives Cobbs, designer of first buildings of University of Illinois, it was considered finest between Chicago and St. Louis. Just beyond, across West Main Street, is one-story brick structure with clock on top. This is one of three banks designed by Frank Lloyd Wright, and only one still standing. Two doors to right of that is a state hospital, originally a fine hotel. Its lights were first turned on by Teddy Roosevelt while making a brief stop here in 1903. Then on left, magnificent windmill, built in 1896 to supply water to a private estate, is Dwight's pride. Tower houses an 88-barrel cypress tank, while 3,000-pound fan wheel

was constructed in Argentina to replace original which was broken by a 1975 storm.

0:50 (0:00) Arrive Pontiac.

PONTIAC, IL - Pontiac is primarily an agriculturally oriented trading and distribution center.

0:00 (0:31) Depart Pontiac. (Northbound Texas Eagle does not stop here.)

0:25 (0:06) Pass under Interstate 55 and enter outskirts of Normal. Archaic, institutional buildings off to right once housed Illinois Soldiers' and Sailors' Children's School, but now stand vacant.

0:27 (0:04) Watterson Towers, impressive twin high rises on right, are dormitories of Illinois State University; campus lies just beyond.

0:31 (0:00) Arrive Bloomington.

BLOOMINGTON, IL - This is the birthplace of former vice president Adlai E. Stevenson and the site of Abraham Lincoln's "Lost Speech" which launched him toward the presidency. Once dependent on coal mining, the Bloomington-Normal area now has a much broader based economy, boasting facilities of several well-known companies, including the corporate headquarters of State Farm Insurance. This is also the home of Illinois State University, with an enrollment of 1,900—the state's first public institution of higher learning. Illinois Wesleyan University also provides courses for 1,650 students. Of interest is the Hudelson Museum of Agriculture and The Original American Passion Play presented each spring.

0:00 (0:30) Depart Bloomington.

0:27 (0:00) Arrive Lincoln.

LINCOLN, IL - First town to be named in honor of Abraham Lincoln, an historical marker in the shape of a watermelon on the grounds of the Lincoln Depot, just to the left, marks the spot where he christened the city "Lincoln" in 1853—with watermelon juice. Domed building, a block to the left, is Logan County Courthouse where Lincoln once practiced law.

0:00 (0:30) Depart Lincoln.

0:32 (0:00) Arrive Springfield where the capitol complex is dominated by the awesome State Capitol Building directly to the right. Ground was broken for construction in 1886 where its massive dome and rotunda now rest on bedrock. Multicolumned building midway between train and Capitol is State Supreme Court Building.

SPRINGFIELD, IL - In 1837, the state capital moved to Springfield, and simultaneously a circuit-riding Abraham Lincoln decided to settle here and opened his law office. Also, the only home he ever owned is about five blocks east of the tracks. The Lincoln Depot, where he delivered his famous "Farewell Address" before departing for Washington in 1861, is also a few blocks east of the present Amtrak route. Also of interest is the Old State Capitol, a painstakingly restored Greek Revival structure where the legislature met when the capital was first moved to Springfield. Lincoln delivered his "House Divided" speech here. The current capitol building is also open to visitors and has regular tours.

0:00 (0:37) Depart Springfield.
0:08 (0:29) Cross tip of beautiful Lake Springfield where attractive homes of Springfield's more affluent suburbanites can be seen nestled in trees on left.
0:21 (0:16) Pretty little Virden golf course adjoins tracks on left.
0:37 (0:00) Arrive Carlinville. Southbound stop only.

CARLINVILLE, IL - At one time this agricultural center had aspirations of becoming the state capital. It was hoped the silver-spired Greek Revival county courthouse (off to the left about three blocks) would house the state's young legislature, but Carlinville was never selected, and extreme cost overruns infuriated the citizenry.

But the town lays claim to something of a more lasting consequence—the largest assemblage of Sears Roebuck mail order homes. Between 1909 and 1937 Sears sold 100,000 precut houses that arrived by train, ready for assembly, even including the fixtures. Segments arrived to coincide with construction schedules with the paint arriving last. These "HonorBilt" homes ranged in price from a mere $595 to $5,000, depending on the degree of simplicity or amount of "elegance."

One hundred fifty-six of these were erected in Carlinsville's Standard Addition, a subdivision built by Indiana Standard for their coal miners. Today, nearly all are occupied and lovingly maintained.
0:00 (0:30) Depart Carlinville.
0:05 (0:25) Terrain becomes momentarily rolling and forested, suggesting the Mississippi River could be near.
0:30 (0:00) Arrive Alton.

ALTON, IL - Located on the mighty Mississippi River, across from St. Louis, this historic area was first visited by white men when, in 1673, Marquette and Joliet recorded a description of a bird-like monster painted on the river's cliffs below the present townsite. Lewis and Clark built their first camp and spent the winter here before making their great Northwest expedition.

In 1858, the seventh and last of the Lincoln-Douglas debates was held in Alton. During the Civil War this was a main supply point for the Union Army. The first Illinois state penitentiary was located here, and the world's tallest man, at eight feet eleven inches, was born, educated and buried in Alton. Two of the nation's corporate giants, Owens-Illinois, Inc. and The Olin Corporation, started here.

0:00 (0:40) Depart Alton.
0:07 (0:33) Cross Cahokia Diversion Canal whose banks have been built up to contain sometimes high waters of Mississippi.
0:10 (0:30) At Lenoe, parallel route of former "Wabash Cannonball," which ran from St. Louis to Detroit.
0:17 (0:23) Factory of renowned candymaker, Nestle, is on left.
0:18 (0:22) Industrialization, including foundries and other heavy industry, becomes more apparent as we near St. Louis.
0:23 (0:17) Train curls slowly to right as it prepares to cross great Mississippi River.
0:24 (0:16) Now high over Mississippi an excellent view of St. Louis is afforded on left. Soaring Gateway Arch is clearly visible. At midstream we enter Missouri and leave Illinois.
0:27 (0:13) As train turns southward again, square brick spire of antique water tower still stands on hill to right.
0:32 (0:08) Gateway Arch and skyline

forward on right create exciting approach into city.

0:34 (0:06) Pass under Martin Luther King Memorial Bridge and then Eads Bridge with fascinating steelwork. Bridge was completed in 1874 and designed by a self-educated engineer James Eads. Its spans were largest ever constructed at that time.

0:36 (0:04) Mississippi River sternwheeler can often be seen docked on left.

0:37 (0:03) Imposing Busch Memorial Stadium, home of baseball's Cardinals, is just to right.

0:40 (0:00) Arrive St. Louis.

ST. LOUIS, MO - Founded in 1764 by two French fur traders as a trading post, St. Louis grew rapidly into one of the most important cities in the Frontier West. Due to its location at the confluence of the Mississippi and Missouri rivers, it was readily accessible for river boat travel and farther exploration to the west. Lewis and Clark began their two-year expedition from this point. Railroad construction after the Civil War made St. Louis an even more dominant factor in the nation's development.

Today, the view of this metropolis of 2,400,000 is dramatized by perhaps one of the most striking and imaginative structures to be built in any American city, the Gateway Arch.

Amtrak Station, 550 South 16th Street. A small "temporary" (1978) facility located in an industrial area near downtown, between 15th and 16th, two blocks south of Clark (and a few blocks from the old Union Station). There are storage lockers and food and beverage vending machines. Free parking is adjacent to the station.

For arrival and departure information, call (314) 331-3300. For reservations and other information, call (314) 241-8806. Ticket windows and the waiting room are open from early morning to midnight.

Cab stand is at the station; Yellow Cab, 361-2345. Both Budget and Hertz have downtown **rental car** locations and will pick up and drop off customers at the station. Nearest **local bus** stop is four blocks from the station on Market Street. **Greyhound,** 231-7800.

Lambert St. Louis International Airport, 16 miles northwest of the station.

Convention and Visitors Commission, 10 S. Broadway, 63102; (312) 421-1023 or 800-247-9791. Funphone, call 421-2100.

All of the accommodations below are in the downtown or near-downtown area.

-**Hyatt Regency St. Louis,** St. Louis Union Station, 1820 Market; (314) 241-6664 or 800-228-9000. A luxury hotel located in the original Union Station. Five blocks from the Amtrak station. $150.

-**Holiday Inn Riverfront,** 200 N. 4th St.; (314) 621-8200. Near Gateway Arch, 17 blocks from the station. $99.

-**Thrifty Inn,** 1100 N. 3rd St., 63102; (314) 421-6556. North of Martin Luther King Bridge, near the river. About two miles from the station. $50.

Gateway Arch, 11 North 4th Street, a magnificent 630-foot-high monument, the nation's highest. This fourth most attended man-made attraction in the world has trams at each of the two bases to carry passengers to an observation deck with an incredible view of the metropolitan area. Obtain tickets early to avoid being disappointed, since sellouts are frequent.

-**Museum of Westward Expansion,** underground beneath Gateway Arch, portrays early pioneering efforts.

-**St. Louis Union Station,** 1820 Market St., has been beautifully restored to accommodate shops, restaurants, and the Hyatt Regency Hotel. It's five blocks from the station.

-**Forest Park,** seven miles west of downtown, on U.S. 40, has several attractions, including: **St. Louis Zoological Park** with more than 2,500 animals and exhibits; **St. Louis Art Museum,** with 70 galleries containing more than 15,000 art objects, is one of the nation's finest.

The **National Museum of Transport,** 3015 Barret Station Rd., exhibits the history and technology of both transportation and communication. Included are airplanes, autos, locomotives, rail cars, buses and horse-drawn vehicles. The **Missouri Botanical Gardens,** 4334 Shaw Boulevard, is a National Historic Landmark and considered to be one of the

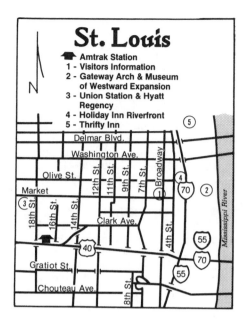

St. Louis

🚂 Amtrak Station
1 - Visitors Information
2 - Gateway Arch & Museum
    of Westward Expansion
3 - Union Station & Hyatt
    Regency
4 - Holiday Inn Riverfront
5 - Thrifty Inn

most beautiful botanical displays in the nation. There are 79 acres of gardens in the heart of the city, including the largest Japanese garden in the U.S.

0:00 (3:45) Depart St. Louis.
0:35 (3:10) St. Louis Ship Co. shipyards are on left.
0:40 (3:05) Through Jefferson Barracks, site of historic 18th-century military post.
3:45 (0:00) Arrive Poplar Bluff.

POPLAR BLUFF, MO - This winner of an All American City Award has the undulating Ozarks for recreation while the nearby fertile lands of southeast Missouri produce an abundance of cotton, rice, corn, soybeans, beef and hogs. Local manufacturers turn out such varied products as custom kitchen cabinets, Christmas ornaments, shoes and living room furniture. Nearby Wappapello Lake, with its rugged shoreline, offers fine bass fishing and water sports.
0:00 (0:52) Depart Poplar Bluff.
0:18 (0:34) Enter Arkansas and leave Missouri.
0:52 (0:00) Arrive Walnut Ridge.

WALNUT RIDGE, AR - Several points of interest are near this northeastern Arkansas trading center.

Old Davidsonville State Park is the site of one of Arkansas' earliest settlements, and Lake Charles State Park has superb camping on the shores of its 645-acre lake.
0:00 (0:34) Depart Walnut Ridge.
0:34 (0:00) Arrive Newport.

NEWPORT, AR - Had it not been for the resistance of steamboat men and townspeople of nearby Jacksonport, the railroad (then the Cairo and Fulton) would have gone through that upstream community instead of Newport. Steamboating on the navigable White River faded around the turn of the century and Newport, with its rail service, prospered. The Old Jacksonport Courthouse has memorabilia from Civil War times when the town was a major mustering point for Confederate troops.
0:00 (1:20) Depart Newport.
1:19 (0:01) Cross Arkansas River separating North Little Rock from Little Rock.
1:20 (0:00) Arrive Little Rock's old multistoried brick station on left, topped by intriguing clock tower.

LITTLE ROCK, AR - The capital of Arkansas and largest city in the state, Little Rock is attractively situated on tree-covered Ozark bluffs overlooking the Arkansas River. Its history runs the gamut from frontier trading post, to a Union-occupied Confederate city, to today's bustling central Arkansas metropolis.

Union Station, Union Station Square, Markham and Victory streets, two miles west of downtown. There are storage lockers, luggage carts, food and beverage vending machines and two restaurants. There is free parking by the station.

For arrival and departure information, call (501) 372-6841. For reservations and other information, call 800-USA-RAIL.

Cab stand is at the station; Black and White, 374-0333. Nearest **local bus** stop is one block at 3rd & Victory. **Greyhound,** 372-1861. **Adams Field Municipal Airport** is three miles east of the city.

Little Rock Convention & Visitors Bureau, Statehouse Convention Center, Markham and Main, Box 3232, 72203; (501) 376-4781.

Camelot Hotel, 111 W. Markham, 72201; (501) 372-4371 or 800-643-6938. Seven blocks from the station. $61.

-Holiday Inn City Center, 617 S. Broadway, 72201; (501) 376-2071. In the heart of the financial district. One mile from the station. $59.

The Old State House, 300 W. Markham, is one of three historical capitol buildings that can be found here; free programs. **State Capitol Building,** Woodlawn and Capitol streets, houses the current state legislature. **Arkansas Arts Center,** MacArthur and Park, has many fine exhibits, and **Burns Park** has a scenic covered bridge. **Quapaw Quarter** has several stately Victorian homes open to the public. The very popular **Zoo of Arkansas** attracts visitors from all over the nation.

0:00 (0:45) Departing Little Rock, on left, size of State Capitol Building makes it appear much closer than three city blocks. At night, floodlights on its Batesville granite walls produce surrealistic, white brilliance. Massive dome, reaching 230 feet above ground, is clad in 16-carat gold leaf.

0:09 (0:36) Under Interstate 30 as light industrial scene now changes to residential.

0:16 (0:29) Texas Eagle seems to have left civilization behind as landscape becomes heavily forested with pines and hardwoods.

0:20 (0:25) Small, colorfully eroded hillside has become a "mini-Bryce Canyon" on left.

0:27 (0:18) Through Benton where bauxite is king. Ninety-eight percent of aluminum in U.S. comes from this region. Town even has a home built with this clay-like substance.

0:28 (0:17) Cross Saline River on southern edge of Benton.

0:45 (0:00) Arrive Malvern.

MALVERN, AR - This stop serves the spa city of Hot Springs and Hot Springs National Park, just 23 miles from here. Nestled in the lovely Ouachita Mountains and featuring 47 thermal springs, the resort is the most visited spot in Arkansas. The Park is one of the nation's oldest, and its "Bathhouse Row" displays the finest group of historic bathhouses remaining in the U.S.

0:00 (0:22) Depart Malvern.

0:06 (0:16) Note large ponds with numerous waterfowl on right.

0:21 (0:01) At left, large plant in distance with silver standpipe is Fafnir Bearing, manufacturer of ball bearings.

0:22 (0:00) Arriving Arkadelphia, cross Ouachita River. Large plant on right with green standpipe is Reynolds Metal aluminum plant. Town itself is actually off to right beyond trees.

ARKADELPHIA, AR - Aluminum is important now, but in earlier times, steamboats once docked here after steaming up the Ouachita River.

0:00 (1:10) Depart Arkadelphia.

0:18 (0:52) Cross Little Missouri River.

0:24 (0:46) Rather neat depot, on right, with red tile roof is distinguishing feature of downtown Prescott as train chugs along "Main Street."

0:28 (0:42) Some Southern-style ranching is carried on in this part of state with typical herds being Brahma crosses. Watch for rodeo variety bulls on right.

0:36 (0:34) On right, fine old smokestack of brick factory helps pinpoint Hope, Arkansas. Watermelon lovers will be interested to know that world's largest grow here—a record 200-pounder having been harvested in 1979.

0:49 (0:21) Cross 1,300-mile-long Red River which originates in northern Texas, creating a portion of Texas-Oklahoma border. Continuing southward (to left), it joins Mississippi River near Alexandria, Louisiana. Sometimes tinted red by its high silt content, this stream drains 90,000 square miles of land. Natural gas pipeline is suspended over water beyond highway bridge to left.

1:02 (0:08) Texarkana Municipal Airport is on immediate left.

1:10 (0:00) Arrive at Texarkana's ugly old station located at the Texas-Arkansas state line, where front of train comes to rest in Texas and rear portion stops in Arkansas.

TEXARKANA, AR/TX - This city lies carefully balanced on the Arkansas-Texas border and even boasts a

Dallas Union Station

post office straddling the state line—the only federal building in the U.S. sitting in two states. Of particular interest is the Texarkana Museum with exhibits emphasizing the city's history. The beautifully restored Perot Theatre features shows, ballets, concerts and film festivals. Numerous lakes make this area a fisherman's paradise.

0:00 (1:15) Depart Texarkana on trackage of Texas and Pacific, an affiliate of Missouri Pacific, and enter Texas heading due south along Lone Star State's eastern border.

0:06 (1:09) Enormous rail tie manufacturing and storage operation stretches for almost a mile along right side of tracks.

0:23 (0:52) Through Atlanta, Texas. Nearby, over 25 sites of prehistoric Caddo Indian villages have been found.

1:15 (0:00) Arrive Marshall where rail station, looking more like an old brick mansion, greets train's departees on left.

 MARSHALL, TX - This northeastern Texas town is located amidst cypress-fringed bayous and pine forests. Both its natural beauty and mild climate make it a popular tourist area, while oil, agriculture, lignite processing and manufacturing are economic mainstays. During the Civil War, saddles, harnesses and ammunition were produced here for the Confederacy, and it became the wartime capital of Missouri. This is also the birthplace of Lady Bird Johnson.

0:00 (0:28) Depart Marshall. For some time now, Eagle will slip past one industrial operation after another, most turning out the stuff for which Texas is best known. Oil equipment manufacturers and other petroleum-related industries dominate the flat landscape.

0:28 (0:00) Arrive Longview.

LONGVIEW, TX - This industrialized community is heavily oil

229

oriented with refineries, oil equipment manufacturing and the loading end of the famous "Big Inch" pipeline. Oil isn't the only industry in Longview, however; Schlitz turns out 4½ million barrels of beer a year from Texas' largest brewery. The R. G. LeTourneau Museum with early earthmoving equipment on display and the Caddo Indian Museum with artifacts from that prehistoric culture are both located here.

0:00 (2:33) Depart Longview.

0:17 (2:16) Through Gladwater and the very heart of famed East Texas oilfield, one of nation's biggest producers.

0:25 (2:08) On right, white board fence looks like it belongs on a Kentucky horse farm, but actually encloses Ambassador College, founded by Garner Ted Armstrong and his brother Herbert.

0:31 (2:02) Jarvis Christian College is just to right.

1:39 (0:54) Under Interstate 20 connecting Dallas with Atlanta, Georgia.

1:51 (0:42) Enter Dallas' fastest growing suburb, Mesquite (pronounced meskeet), named for that scraggly, thorny shrub that thrives in Southwestern U.S. and northern Mexico. Whimsical smiling pink elephant, on left, adorns wall of Blue Bell ice cream plant.

1:57 (0:36) In far distance to right, top of Ferris wheel identifies location of Texas State Fair Grounds, where Texans hold what they claim is biggest fair in nation.

2:00 (0:33) Dallas cityscape is now clearly visible on right.

2:32 (0:01) Flat-roofed Reunion Arena sports complex, home to Dallas Maverick basketball, is on left.

2:33 (0:00) Arrive Dallas. White marbled Union Station is on right while spectacular

glass facades of Hyatt Regency Hotel and spherically domed Reunion Tower rise abruptly above us on left. Station and hotel complex are conveniently connected beneath train by an attractive underground concourse.

DALLAS, TX - Dallas began in 1841 as a trading post which was started by a Tennessee lawyer, John Neely Bryan, who named the post after "his friend Dallas." Although no one today knows who that "Dallas" was, the County of Dallas was eventually named after George Mifflin Dallas, Vice President of the United States under James Polk.

As is true with so many western cities, early growth was due to the arrival of the railroad. In the early 1870s, rail lines extended both to the east and to the north making the city an important distribution center. Today, with a metropolitan population (including Ft. Worth) of 3,000,000, Dallas is one of the Southwest's leading financial, industrial and transportation centers, and entertains more than two million tourists annually.

Union Station, 400 South Houston St. This beautifully renovated marble structure, included in the National Register of Historic Places, is located on the edge of downtown. There are a variety of restaurants (on the 2nd floor), a gift shop and a florist in this popular setting. Luggage carts and adjacent pay-parking are available. Luggage can be stored at the baggage counter. A visitors information counter is also located in the station. An underground walkway connects to Hyatt Regency Hotel and the Reunion Tower (observation deck and restaurant).

For arrival and departure information, call (214) 651-8341. For reservations and other information, call 800-USA-RAIL. The ticket office is open 10 am to 5:30 pm.

Cab stand at the station; Yellow Cab, 426-6262 and Executive Cab, 554-1212. Avis **rental cars** are available on the premises. Nearest **local bus** stop is in front of the station. **Greyhound** is at Commerce and Lamar, five blocks from the station, 655-7000. **Dallas-Ft. Worth Regional Airport** is 17 miles west of the city; call Super Shuttle (817) 329-2000 (local but dial area code) for transporta-

tion to and from D/FW. Closer in, but less used, **Love Field** can be reached by bus #39 from downtown.

Visitor Information Center, in Union Station. Write Dallas Convention and Visitors Bureau, 1507 Pacific Ave., 75201. Call (214) 954-1111.

Bradford Plaza, 302 S. Houston St., 75202; (214) 761-9090 or 800-822-2500. Very well maintained, comfortable and just one block from the station. Complimentary breakfast and evening cocktail. $70.

-**Hyatt Regency Dallas,** 300 Reunion Blvd., 75207; (214) 651-1234. Dazzling architecture. Connected to the station by block-long concourse. $170.

-**Holiday Inn Downtown,** 1015 Elm, 75202; (214) 748-9951. Six blocks from the station. $82.

Dealey Plaza and the **Texas Book Depository,** site of President Kennedy's assassination, are but three blocks north of the station on Houston St. **Reunion Tower** has an observation deck and a revolving restaurant with commanding views of the city, across tracks from the station and reached by an underground concourse. **West End MarketPlace,** a former cracker factory, has several floors of unusual shopping and eating, about a mile north of the station at 603 Munger. **Neiman Marcus,** at Ervay and Commerce, seven blocks from the station, is regal king of the nation's department stores. And two miles of **subterranean** and elevated **pedestrian-ways** with over 200 shops and restaurants, connect various downtown hotels, retailers and financial institutions.

0:00 (1:05) Depart Dallas and head westward through solid development which has made Dallas and Ft. Worth almost appear as one city.

0:01 (1:04) Look back on left for a fine view of Hyatt Regency Hotel and Reunion Tower. Texas Book Depository, which played such an important role in President Kennedy's assassination, is off to right.

0:04 (1:00) Top of Dallas Cowboys' Texas Stadium is in far distance to right.

0:09 (0:56) Good view of Dallas' modern skyline back on right.

0:17 (0:48) Literally pass through a construction engineer's nightmare as train simultaneously crosses above and below massive highway bridges.

0:25 (0:40) Hensley Field and Texas National Guard aircraft are on left.

0:27 (0:38) Jets and helicopters of Dallas Naval Air Station are parked on left.

0:29 (0:36) Vaught complex, longtime military aircraft manufacturer, is just to left.

0:31 (0:34) Pass through Grand Prairie. Located here because of railroad, town boomed with defense plants during World War II.

0:36 (0:29) Unusual tower in distance to right belongs to Six Flags Over Texas, a huge entertainment park—one of Texas' most popular attractions.

0:37 (0:28) Enter Arlington. University of Texas at Arlington is on right while Arlington Stadium is about a mile in distance.

0:47 (0:18) Off to left, it is possible to catch a glimpse of 2,275-acre Arlington Lake, owned by city of Arlington and popular with boaters and fishermen.

1:00 (0:05) Ft. Worth skyline is now on right. Train stops, then backs into Ft. Worth station.

1:05 (0:00) Arrive Ft. Worth.

FT. WORTH, TX - This city began as a military camp during the war with Mexico and then became a major shipping point for cattle after the Civil War. Now one of Texas' major cities, it has a wide assortment of industries including aviation plants of General Dynamics and Bell Helicopter. An impressive downtown convention complex covers 14 blocks and features an unusual "Water Garden" of fountains and ponds.

A culturally conscious city, Ft. Worth offers musicals, concerts, ballets, theater performances and numerous outstanding museums to satisfy almost any taste. The Amon G. Carter Museum of Western Art has permanent collections of both Remington and Russell. The Kimbell Art Museum has works that span from prehistoric to Picasso. The domed Casa Mana Theatre is one of the nation's most notable theaters-in-the-round. Pate Museum of Transportation has an antique railroad car, vintage autos, military aircraft and a minesweeper on exhibit.

0:00 (0:38) Depart Ft. Worth.

0:06 (0:32) Last look at downtown Ft. Worth is afforded back on right.

0:17 (0:21) Numerous small aircraft dot the edge of interestingly named Luck Field on right.

0:36 (0:02) On left, enormous rail shops of Santa Fe Railroad are largest construction and repair shops in Texas.

0:38 (0:00) Arrive Cleburne.

CLEBURNE, TX - Named in honor of Confederate General Pat Cleburne, the city is the trading center for an area featuring farming, dairying and livestock.

0:00 (1:02) Depart Cleburne.

0:15 (0:59) Train now imperceptibly crosses Balcones Fault where flat prairies quickly turn to more hilly terrain.

0:18 (0:44) Cross legendary Brazos River. Off to left is 15,760-acre Lake Whitney, formed by damming Brazos River. This 45-mile-long reservoir is one of nation's most popular water recreation areas with four million visitors annually.

0:30 (0:32) Train passes white fields of fuzzy cotton which are a trademark of nation's southern tier of states.

0:35 (0:27) Cross Bosque River which winds its way along our route for next 30 minutes.

0:51 (0:13) Climb up out of Bosque River Valley and cut through unusually rocky terrain.

1:02 (0:00) Arrive McGregor.

MCGREGOR, TX - This community serves as a stop for its much larger neighbor 19 miles to the west—Waco. At one time, Waco was referred to as "Six Shooter Junction" when cattle drives along the Chisholm Trail frequented the town. Now, the city relies on five "Cs" for its support—cattle, cotton, corn, collegians and culture. It is the home of Baylor University as well as several other institutions of higher learning. The Old Suspension Bridge, still used to cross the Brazos, was the largest in the nation when built in 1870 and was used as a pattern for the Brooklyn Bridge.

0:00 (0:28) Depart McGregor.

0:28 (0:00) Arrive Temple where train is greeted by an attractive brick station whose familiar emblems are a reminder that we have been on Santa Fe tracks since Ft. Worth.

TEMPLE, TX - Since its inception in 1880, Temple has always been closely tied with railroading when it grew along the Gulf, Colorado and Santa Fe Railroad, and the Missouri, Kansas and Texas lines. Railroad shops are still located here. Temple is one of the Southwest's leading medical centers, whose facilities include King's Daughters Hospital, Scott-White Hospital and Clinic, and (quite aptly) the Santa Fe Hospital.

0:00 (0:50) Depart Temple.

0:12 (0:38) Rolling, forested hills provide a most aesthetic backdrop for area's ranches.

0:37 (0:13) Cross San Gabriel River.

0:50 (0:00) Arrive Taylor.

TAYLOR, TX - Having been on the Missouri, Kansas, Texas tracks since Temple, we now change to Missouri Pacific trackage, which leads to San Antonio. Taylor is a railroad junction point and retail center for the surrounding farm and ranch country.

0:00 (0:41) Depart Taylor.

0:22 (0:19) Large cement plant on left is just one of many between here and San Antonio.

0:26 (0:15) Enter suburbs of Austin.

0:34 (0:07) Train passes between Camp Mabry on right and Texas Blind, Deaf and Orphan School on left.

0:38 (0:03) Pass under an immense highway interchange as train nears center of Austin.

0:41 (0:00) Arrive at Austin's station, somewhat west of downtown.

AUSTIN, TX - In 1839 a site was chosen on the north shore of the Colorado River (not the one of Grand Canyon fame) to become the capital of the Republic of Texas. The site was well-chosen, as Austin has grown to be a hub city of Texas, with healthy industries, numerous colleges and universities, and is still the seat of government. The University of Texas at Austin, the state's largest university, is located here. Of particular interest: the State Capitol Complex; the Elisabet Ney Museum, with many works of this prominent 19th-century sculptor; the home of O. Henry,

where this short-story writer (William Sydney Porter) once lived; and the Lyndon B. Johnson Library and Museum, with artifacts from his presidency.

0:00 (0:38) Depart Austin.

0:03 (0:35) Ornate dome of capitol, constructed of Texas pink marble, is off to left. Train makes a curve to right and crosses Colorado River.

0:06 (0:32) Last view of Austin's skyline and capitol dome back on left.

0:21 (0:17) On right, quaint little storefronts in town of Buda seem to stare at train as it zips past.

0:37 (0:01) On outskirts of San Marcos, train slips through scenic campus of Southwest Texas State University—alma mater of Lyndon B. Johnson, the nation's 36th president.

0:38 (0:00) Arrive San Marcos.

SAN MARCOS, TX - Besides Southwest Texas State University, San Marcos is the site of the Republic of Texas Chilympiad (state chili cooking contest), held each September, with the winner going to the World Chili Cook-off each November at Terlingua, Texas. For eight days in June, the Texas Water Safari is celebrated here—one of the world's toughest canoe races. Entrants must canoe down hundreds of miles of rivers and saltwater bays, traveling from San Marcos to Seadrift.

0:00 (1:31) Depart San Marcos.

0:02 (1:29) Tower, off to right, was once used to train World War II paratroopers.

0:15 (1:16) Cross Guadalupe River.

0:20 (1:11) Enter German community of New Braunfels, famous for sausages, breads and pastries. This small town was once fourth largest city in Texas.

0:48 (0:43) San Antonio International Airport is on right.

0:51 (0:40) Enter outskirts of San Antonio with Alamo Cement Plant on left, then pass directly through Olmos Basin Golf Course.

1:08 (0:23) Interstate 10 stretches on left, directly toward San Antonio's skyline.

1:19 (0:12) Lone Star Beer brewery is on immediate right. Skyline is dominated by 750-foot Tower of the Americas, built for HemisFair held in 1968.

1:21 (0:10) Cross San Antonio River.

1:31 (0:00) Arrive San Antonio.

(Note - Trains northbound from San Antonio take a slightly different route on departure, going to Craig Junction where main line is rejoined. This adds 19 miles, but eliminates reversing trains in San Antonio.)

SAN ANTONIO, TX - San Antonio, a city now in excess of one million, was named by Captain Domingo Teran who was exploring the region for Spain in 1691 and arrived in the area on the feast day of Saint Anthony of Padua. However, a permanent settlement was not established until 27 years later when the Mission of San Antonio de Valero was built, later to become known as the Alamo.

San Antonio has the distinction of having been under six different flags since its beginning: French, Spanish, Mexican, Republic of Texas, Confederate and American. It was the scene of one of the most historic and dramatic battles in our nation's history, when 188 Texans defended the Alamo against the Mexican Army led by General Santa Anna, falling on March 6, 1836 after all of its defenders were killed. Later that year, Texas successfully ended Mexican rule and became a Republic.

Today, with its rich past intermixed with the new and modern, San Antonio is clearly one of the more fascinating cities in the United States. The restoration of its charming river-front area is one of the major urban-renewal achievements of our time.

Amtrak Station, 1174 E. Commerce St., is an appealing Spanish-style structure. Although the exterior still wears an overly thin coat of pink and brown paint, the interior has been restored to its original stateliness. A grand staircase beneath a vivid stained-glass window and an arched baroque ceiling give the interior a feeling of opulence rarely found in American train stations. The station still has storage lockers, and food and beverage vending machines are curiously located in the entryway to the ladies rest room. Free parking is adjacent to the station.

For arrival and departure information, call (512) 223-3226. For reservations and other information, call 800-USA-RAIL.

Cab stand at the station; Yellow Cab, 226-4242. Nearest **local bus** stop is in front of the station; call 227-2020. **Greyhound** terminal, 270-5800. **San Antonio International Airport** is eight miles north of the city center.

Visitors Information Center, 317 Alamo Plaza, immediately across from the Alamo. Write the San Antonio Convention & Visitors Bureau, P.O. Box 2277, 78298; call (512) 299-8155.

Menger Hotel and Motor Inn, 204 Alamo Plaza, 78205; (512) 223-4361 or 800-345-9285. This venerable landmark is still an excellent place to absorb San Antonio's relaxed Southwest charm. Five blocks from the station. $78.

-**La Quinta Convention Center,** 1001 E. Commerce, 78205; (512) 222-9181. Closest hotel to the station and convenient to downtown. Three blocks from the station. $68.

The Amtrak station is approximately five blocks from the downtown area reached by traveling west on E. Commerce Street. The heart of San Antonio's appeal is Paseo del Rio, nearly two miles of cobblestone walkways with bridges, tropical foliage, fine shops, restaurants and nightclubs set along the river. Boat rides offer a unique way to see much of this area. **The Alamo,** at Alamo Plaza, is one of the most famous shrines in the country. Tours, a museum, slides and a movie about the battle help re-create the struggle that took the lives of its 188 defenders. **HemisFair Plaza,** which was the site of the 1968 HemisFair, now contains the Convention Center and several attractions including the **Tower of Americas** topped by an observation deck and revolving restaurant.

Rivercenter is San Antonio's new downtown shopping arcade featuring 125 shops and cafes, an I-MAX theater and a Marriott. And for an unforgettable dining experience, ride **The Texan** dinner train departing every evening from the Amtrak station.

La Villita, at Villita and South Alamo, is a restored portion of the city which houses craft shops, art galleries and boutiques. And just west of the central business district is colorful **Market**

San Antonio

1 - Visitors Information
2 - La Villita
3 - Market Square
4 - The Alamo
5 - HemisFair Plaza
6 - Paseo del Rio
7 - Menger Hotel
8 - La Quinta Convention Center

Amtrak Station

Square where farmers' produce is sold in the early morning.

Route Log for Dallas to Houston

0:00 (1:25) Depart Dallas, slipping past Reunion Tower and Reunion Arena sports facility on right, then past modernistic home of *Dallas Morning News* on left.

0:05 (1:20) Multi-storied Sears warehousing and distribution facility dwarfs all else on left.

0:07 (1:14) At Tower 19, northbound Texas Eagle swings to east, then stops and backs up into Dallas so cars are in proper position to be joined with San Antonio section before continuing to Chicago.

0:10 (1:11) White refinery-like structure at left is Proctor and Gamble soap factory.

0:15 (1:06) Traverse long bridge spanning Trinity River. This stream that bisects Dallas was once thought to be capable of handling shipping traffic, but waterway plans were ultimately abandoned as impractical.

0:17 (1:04) Through Southern Pacific's Miller Yard where SP locomotives and other rolling stock are in evidence.

0:24 (0:57) Concrete bridges above carry I-20 and I-635 traffic.

0:41 (0:40) Cleverly designed rest stop along I-45 sports miniature lake and other attractive ornamentations, on left.

0:44 (0:37) Round-steepled First Baptist Church in Palmer, on right, was built around turn of century. Before its construction, members were sometimes baptized across street in small pond. Nation's new "Super Collider," world's largest atom smasher, is being constructed just west of Palmer, its outer edge to be a mere mile or so from town.

0:48 (0:33) Rolling fields and cattle-filled pastures of Texas' ranching country continue to afford lovely pastoral scenes. In spring, blankets of bluebonnets (they're blue, of course) and black-eyed Susans (they're yellow) add a feathery softness to the countryside.

0:55 (0:26) Large facility of Ennis Business Forms is on left. Firm is a major manufacturer of business forms, most being customized to customers' specifications, and is headquartered here in Ennis, TX.

1:03 (0:18) Stacks of black plastic pipe on left at Alma conjure up images of huge licorice sticks.

1:21 (0:00) Arrive Corsicana.

 CORSICANA, TX - The roots of Corsicana go back to 1849, but it wasn't until 1894, when the city drilled for water and struck oil, that the town began to bloom. Petroleum is still important, with refineries and other oil-related companies located in this city of 22,000.

World-renowned Corsicana Fruit Cakes are produced here, the only such bakery product to receive New York's prestigious Gourmet Society Culinary Merit Award. Several hundred thousand of these "Deluxe" brand delights are sold through the mail each year, utilizing nearly a half million pounds of Texas pecans. The bakery is about two blocks from the station, but can't be seen from the train.

Navarro College is here with Texas' most outstanding collection of arrowheads. This is also the home town of Country-and-Western singer Lefty Frizzell.

0:00 (2:10) Depart Corsicana.

0:02 (2:08) K mart distribution center occupies huge, windowless building on left.

0:26 (1:44) Through attractive little community of Mexia, named for Mexican general who served under Santa Ana before finally leading an unsuccessful rebellion against the dictator and losing his life. Town was named for him after his family donated townsite.

0:33 (1:37) Cross Navasota River.

1:30 (0:40) Entering rail yards at Hearne, excellent look at railroad turntable is afforded on left.

2:08 (0:02) Clock tower is centerpiece of main entrance to Texas A & M University on right.

2:09 (0:01) Kyle Field, University's football stadium, hugs tracks on left while school's fine baseball stadium is on right of campus bisected by tracks. (Chancellor of University would like to see tracks tunnel beneath campus, but railroad has not been receptive to this rather costly concept.)

2:10 (0:00) Arrive College Station.

 COLLEGE STATION, TX - This is home to Texas' first institution of higher learning, Texas A & M University. The school is renowned for its ROTC and military Cadet Corps programs.

Northbound passengers might well consider going to the lounge car at this time. The Brazoria Bakery, located here in College Station, often puts complimentary Bohemian pastries on board, and it's first-come first-served when the announcement is made shortly after departure. They're delicious!

0:00 (1:55) Depart College Station.

0:22 (1:33) Again, cross Navasota River.

0:26 (1:29) Through historic town of Navasota, which in 1822 had Anglo-American settlers, some of first in Texas. Note interesting architecture of some of older limestone buildings on left.

1:00 (0:55) Highway signage at both edges of Waller alerts motorists that Waller is "Not just another Texas small town."

1:23 (0:32) Ranchlands slowly give way to citified outer limits of Houston megalopolis.

1:55 (0:00) With almost futuristic-looking skyline on right, arrive Houston.

 HOUSTON, TX - See page 244.

Other Chicago Area Service

The **Calumet** departs Chicago late afternoon and arrives in Valparaiso early evening. Valparaiso departures are early morning and Chicago arrivals are also early morning.

The **Illini** provides daily service between Chicago and Carbondale with runs each direction late in the day.

Chicago-Milwaukee has several trains each way, each day, including The Empire Builder.

The **Illinois Zephyr** carries passengers from West Quincy, MO (sic) to Chicago early in the day and returns in the evening, daily. The route is the same as The California Zephyr between Chicago and Galesburg, but between the latter and W. Quincy, this train forges its own route through Macomb and Quincy, IL. It is the only Amtrak service to these two communities. Macomb, IL, named in honor of Alexander Macomb, a U.S. General during the War of 1812, is home to Western Illinois University. Quincy is a town of 42,000, and a century ago, was the second largest city in Illinois. Its importance declined along with the steamboat.

The **State House** leaves Chicago mid-afternoon and takes the route of The Eagle to St. Louis, arriving there late evening. St. Louis departures are late afternoon with late evening Chicago arrivals. This daily train is unreserved, has sandwiches and beverages and no checked baggage.

The **Ann Rutledge** links Chicago with Kansas City through St. Louis. Daily unreserved service leaves Chicago late morning, arriving in Kansas City late evening. Northbound trains leave Kansas City early morning and arrive in Chicago late evening. Tray meals, snacks and beverages, no checked baggage.

The **Loop** links Chicago and Springfield with morning service to Springfield and late afternoon service to Chicago, except Sundays. Snacks and beverages.

The **Hoosier State,** in addition to The Cardinal, provides Chicago-Indianapolis service with runs to Chicago in the morning and to Indianapolis in the evening.

River Cities

The River Cities cuts across the very heart of Missouri, carrying passengers between Kansas City and St. Louis through undulating farmlands and forests along the Missouri River. It also provides same-car travel to and from New Orleans. The New Orleans leg is made as a part of The City of New Orleans, connecting at Centralia, Illinois.

Between St. Louis and Kansas City, this train is also known as either the Kansas City Mule or the St. Louis Mule, depending on which city it is bound for.

Southbound Schedule (Condensed)
Kansas City, MO - Midafternoon Departure
Jefferson City, MO - Early Evening
St. Louis, MO - Late Evening
Memphis, TN - Early Morning
New Orleans, LA - Early Afternoon Arrival

Northbound Schedule (Condensed)
New Orleans, LA - Midafternoon Departure
Memphis, TN - Late Evening
St. Louis, MO - Early Morning
Jefferson City, MO - Midmorning
Kansas City, MO - Early Afternoon Arrival

Frequency - Daily.
Seating - Amfleet coaches.
Dining - Tray meal service as well as sandwiches, snacks and beverages.
Baggage - No checked baggage.
Reservations - All-reserved train.
Length of Trip - 1,014 miles in 21 hours.

Route Log

 KANSAS CITY, MO - See page 208.

0:00 (0:19) Depart Kansas City, heading due east and somewhat below grade. Shortly, pass beneath Interstate 70 which stretches from Baltimore to western Utah, and then under Interstate 435 that carries traffic through eastern suburbs of city.
0:08 (0:11) Cemetery with tombstone forest on hillside left obviously has "no vacancies."
0:19 (0:00) Arrive Independence.

INDEPENDENCE, MO - This large Kansas City suburb was the home of former president Harry S. Truman who came into office when Franklin Roosevelt died April 12, 1945. He served until 1953. Not long after becoming president, he made one of the most difficult decisions ever made—the approval to drop an atomic bomb on Japan.

But Independence's historical importance commenced much sooner when it was an important way station for the Santa Fe, California and Oregon trails. Among those who stopped here were Mormons who left a considerable imprint on the city. Independence is now the world headquarters of the Reorganized Church of Jesus Christ of Latter-Day Saints.

Just north of here is Liberty, where

Jesse James got his start by robbing his first bank.

0:00 (0:16) Depart Independence.

0:05 (0:11) On left, Truman High School bears name of town's favorite son.

0:16 (0:00) Arrive Lee's Summit where old red-brick depot is no longer used.

LEE'S SUMMIT, MO - This metropolitan suburb was once the domain of the Osage Indians until they were forced off their land in 1825. Lewis and Clark passed through the county shortly before they spotted their first bison in nearby Kansas. It was the Missouri Pacific Railroad that finally assured the town's future, however, when in 1846 the town became one of the largest shipping points between Kansas City and St. Louis.

0:00 (0:40) Depart Lee's Summit.

0:38 (0:02) Rumble across branch of Black-water River.

0:40 (0:00) Arriving Warrensburg, about three blocks before station, as tracks curve slightly to the right, across street on left was "Warrensburg Brewery Cave" (now boarded up), formerly used to store beer in its cool environs. This use came to a sudden end in 1873, however, when Carrie Nation of Temperance League fame burned it out. Today, only a small house marks the site.

WARRENSBURG, MO - Few towns have had as interesting a past as Warrensburg.

On the south edge of town are Pertle Springs, at one time having its waters shipped to every state in the Union because of their "curative" powers. A renowned resort area surrounded the springs with as many as 10,000 attending camp meetings. The Democratic National Convention was held there in 1895. The land was eventually purchased by Central Missouri State College.

Just a block south of the station was the old Estes Hotel which, in 1899, served as a depot for a small steam train that made eight runs daily to the Pertle Springs Hotel.

The first business area of the town was just a block to the left (north) of here, but an 1866 Christmas Eve fire destroyed most of the buildings. A few of the original facades can still be seen, however. Carrie Nation attended the State Normal School here, now Central Missouri's State University just three blocks south.

The old courthouse was the site of perhaps the most famous of legal trials involving canines. In 1870, Leonidas Hornsby was found guilty of killing his brother-in-law's dog, but it was the eloquent eulogy given the dog Drum by the plaintiff's lawyer that apparently swayed the jury.

Be sure to note the old Missouri Pacific depot with Richardsonian Romanesque architecture, built in 1890 of Warrensburg sandstone.

0:00 (0:30) Depart Warrensburg.

0:24 (0:16) Limestone quarry forms large excavation at left.

0:30 (0:00) Arrive Sedalia's modern brick station on left.

SEDALIA, MO - Founded in 1857, Sedalia owes its beginnings to the railroad, serving as a provisioning point and later a military post during the Civil War. One of America's best-known composers, Scott Joplin, composed the "Maple Leaf Rag" in a local saloon known as the Maple Leaf Club. It was this song that first brought him both fame and success. Now, if you're here in mid-August, all the excitement is about the state fair.

0:00 (1:04) Departing Sedalia, note monument to aforementioned Scott Joplin and Maple Leaf Club.

0:02 (1:02) Through Missouri Pacific rail yards where seemingly thousands of red cabooses stand in storage at left.

1:02 (0:02) Entering Jefferson City, broad Missouri River comes into view on left. Highway bridge spanning this great river carries auto traffic north to Columbia, home of University of Missouri, and to Fulton, home of Westminster College. (It was on campus of latter that Winston Churchill delivered his famous "Iron Curtain" speech in 1946.) Then, perched above and to right, is Missouri's sparkling white state capitol. Built in 1917 of Missouri limestone, its Renaissance dome towers 260 feet above ground.

1:04 (0:00) Arrive Jefferson City where Amtrak now occupies first level of former Union Hotel, circa 1855.

Ann Rutledge, near Herman, Missouri

 JEFFERSON CITY, MO - Named for Thomas Jefferson, the site of this city was chosen as the state capital in 1821. Its location on the Missouri River, halfway between St. Louis and Kansas City, made it a logical choice. Today, "Jeff City" has a population of 35,000.

0:00 (1:41) Depart Jefferson City, following Missouri River until just east of Washington, approximately 80 miles downstream.

0:07 (1:34) Neat-appearing buildings with silver water tank on hillside to left are Missouri Department of Corrections minimum security prison.

0:10 (1:31) Train slows as it carefully crosses Osage River.

0:14 (1:27) Note houses on each side of river perched on stilts to avoid Missouri overflows.

0:29 (1:12) Huge form of electric generating facility (reminiscent of Three Mile Island) dominates horizon on left.

0:37 (1:04) Cross Casconade River.

0:45 (0:56) Pass through historic town of Hermann. Some Bavarian-like architecture can be spotted here and there, looking uphill to right. This small town, with strong German heritage, is home to two wineries, one of which can be seen at right, just east of bridge.

1:13 (0:28) Tracks bid farewell to Missouri River and start a gradual ascent towards St. Louis.

1:15 (0:26) Briefly encounter darkness while passing through tunnel for five seconds.

1:17 (0:24) Turquoise buildings with white roofs comprise Purina Poultry Research Center, which is a reminder that Ralston Purina makes farm feeds as well as breakfast foods.

1:18 (0:23) Through one more short tunnel.

1:36 (0:05) Three venerable steam locomotives, long since retired from duty, stand in forlorn deterioration at left.

1:39 (0:02) Over Interstate 270, then past attractive fairways of Greenbriar Country Club on left.

1:41 (0:00) Arrive downtown Kirkwood. Be sure to take note of quaint Kirkwood depot with its swooping roof lines and circular tower.

 KIRKWOOD, MO - This is a western suburb of St. Louis, and the last stop before that city.

0:00 (0:20) Depart Kirkwood.

0:03 (0:16) Two more country clubs pass by on left, first Westborough, then Algonquin.

0:19 (0:01) On left, restored St. Louis Union Station, with its marvelous old train shed, now houses shops, a beer garden and a luxury hotel. Also, various privately owned rail cars can frequently be seen parked there. In its heyday, Union Station handled as many as 276 trains daily. Unfortunately, Amtrak does not stop here, but rolls on to its temporary depot opened in 1978!

0:20 (0:00) Arrive St. Louis.

 ST. LOUIS, MO - See page 226.

0:00 (0:30) Depart St. Louis.

Busch Memorial Stadium will soon be impressive sight on left, home to baseball's St. Louis Cardinals. Then an even more impressive sight will come into view—the 630-foot, stainless steel Gateway Arch, America's tallest monument. Soon thereafter, cross the Mississippi River on the MacArthur Bridge and then head across Illinois to Centralia.

0:30 (0:00) Arrive Belleville.

 BELLEVILLE, IL - This city of 40,000 serves as the easternmost suburb of St. Louis, as well as having its own industrial base of manufacturing and coal mining. Scott Air Force Base is just east of here.

0:00 (0:45) Depart Belleville.

0:45 (0:00) Arrive Centralia.

Note - Westbound passengers boarding at Centralia should be aware that the station is not open, there is no nearby restaurant that is open, and food service on board will not be available until St. Louis.

For route between Centralia and New Orleans, see City of New Orleans log, page 148.

Sunset Limited

The Sunset Limited is Amtrak's most southern transcontinental train. Three times a week it connects New Orleans and Los Angeles, traveling through the swampy bayous of Louisiana and along the Mexican border across the desert Southwest.

It was in February 1883 that the first through trains, then known as the Pacific Express and the Atlantic Express (depending on which direction they were headed), traveled these rails. But in 1894, The Sunset Limited title was bestowed on this service, appropriate enough since passengers from New Orleans to Los Angeles head into two sunsets before reaching the end of the line—a line which surprisingly reaches an elevation of nearly a mile at 5,074-foot Paisano Pass, Texas and sinks to 202 feet below sea level near Salton, California.

There are through coaches and sleepers between Chicago and Los Angeles by a connection with The Texas Eagle at San Antonio.

Westbound Schedule (Condensed)
New Orleans, LA - Early Afternoon Departure
Houston, TX - Late Evening
San Antonio, TX - Middle of the Night (2nd Day)
El Paso, TX - Early Afternoon (2nd Day)
Tucson, AZ - Midevening (2nd Day)
Phoenix, AZ - Late Evening (2nd Day)
Los Angeles, CA - Early Morning Arrival (3rd Day)

Eastbound Schedule (Condensed)
Los Angeles, CA - Late Evening Departure
Phoenix, AZ - Early Morning (2nd Day)
Tucson, AZ - Midmorning (2nd Day)
El Paso, TX - Late Afternoon (2nd Day)
San Antonio, TX - Early Morning (3rd Day)
Houston, TX - Late Morning (3rd Day)
New Orleans, LA - Midevening Arrival (3rd Day)

Frequency - Departs New Orleans Monday, Wednesday and Saturday, and arrives in Los Angeles two days later on Wednesday, Friday and Monday. Departs Los Angeles Sunday, Tuesday and Friday, and arrives in New Orleans two days later on Tuesday, Thursday and Sunday.
Seating - Superliner coaches.
Dining - Complete meal and beverage service as well as lighter fare. Lounge service is also available with movies. Dinner is not served upon departure from Los Angeles.
Sleeping - Superliner sleepers with deluxe, family, economy and special bedrooms.
Baggage - Checked baggage handled at larger cities.
Reservations - All-reserved train.
Length of Trip - 2,033 miles in 43 hours.

Route Log

 NEW ORLEANS, LA - See page 104.

0:00 (1:25) Departing New Orleans, imposing Superdome structure can be seen directly on right. This multi-purpose sports complex is home of National Football League's Saints. Adjacent to east is modernistic Hyatt Regency Hotel.

0:04 (1:18) On left, train winds around publishing facilities of *Picayune States-Item Times*.

0:05 (1:17) Just prior to major highway interchange, campus of Xavier University can be seen on left.

0:14 (1:08) On forward left, magnificent 4.4-mile-long Huey P. Long Bridge comes into view. Within minutes train will ascend its lofty heights, affording "airliner" view of encompassing sights. On right lie industrial parks of Jefferson Parish while, on left, New Orleans skyline is silhouetted against rolling Louisiana landscape. And below, barges and freighters ply waters of mighty Mississippi River at one of nation's busiest ports. Avondale Shipyards occupy shoreline at right.

0:25 (0:57) Gradually descend from bridge into swamplands of famous "Bayou Country." Here, admist haunting imagery of this forbidding wilderness, lies heartland of Cajun culture.

0:30 (0:52) At Harahan, intriguing "above-ground" cemetery on right is typical of many such cemeteries in southern Louisiana where saturated soil discourages conventional burials.

0:37 (0:45) On right, vast grain loading facilities are entrenched along banks of Mississippi River.

0:39 (0:43) Highway 90 joins on left, and follows for nearly 1,100 miles to El Paso, Texas.

0:41 (0:41) On right, first of many refineries reflects abundant petroleum resources of this area. In distance, another dramatic bridge spans Mississippi River.

0:49 (0:33) Cross Bayou Des Allemands. ("Bayou" is common Southern colloquialism for slow-moving river.)

0:55 (0:27) Sugarcane crop on left represents an important staple of state's agricultural economy.

1:06 (0:06) At town of Lafourche, cross bayou of same name.

1:10 (0:02) In distance on right is campus of Nichols State University.

1:12 (0:00) Cross Bayou Blue and arrive Schriever station.

SCHRIEVER, LA - An industrial oriented town of southern Louisiana, Schriever has become home for offshore-drilling related industries.

0:00 (1:23) Depart Schriever.

0:14 (1:09) Gargantuan equipment of offshore-drilling rigs is assembled at McDermott plant on left.

0:17 (1:06) Pontooned helicopters, seen on left, play an important role in offshore industry. Immediately thereafter, cross Bayou Chene whose banks are clustered with maze of freighting apparatus.

0:22 (1:01) Approaching Morgan City, miles of pipe border tracks on right, soon to tap depths beneath ocean floor.

0:26 (0:57) Intracoastal Waterway on left affords convenient access to miles of inland industries which line its banks.

0:27 (0:56) At eastern edge of Morgan City, cross Atchafalaya River that, too, is a scene of bustling dockside activity.

0:38 (0:45) East of Patterson, cross large outlet of Grand Lake.

0:43 (0:40) At Garden City, beautiful plantation estate can be seen on right.

0:52 (0:31) A few miles east of Franklin, cross outlet of Bayou Teche.

1:06 (0:17) Attractive church on right, and ornate "above-ground" cemetery on left highlight journey through Jeanerette.

1:22 (0:01) On right, stately colonial mansions accent gracious neighborhood of New Iberia. Immediately adjacent can be seen lofty domed towers of St. Peter's Catholic Church.

1:23 (0:00) Arrive New Iberia.

NEW IBERIA, LA - A blend of France and Spain in a semi-tropical setting gives New Iberia a special sort of charm. Several attractions draw tourists to this modern business community, including: Shadows on the Teche, an antebellum plantation and museum; Mintmere and the Armand Broussard House, two more antebellum plantation homes; and Jungle Gardens on Avery Island, where a bird sanctuary exists on 200 landscaped acres, and Tabasco Sauce is manufactured.

0:00 (0:22) Depart New Iberia.

0:04 (0:18) Nice homes and large lake through trees on right make for attractive Louisiana scene.

0:10 (0:12) Sugarcane, one of state's predominant crops, is grown in field on left.

0:19 (0:03) Lafayette Municipal Airport is immediately across U.S. 90 on right.

Cross Vermilion River.
0:22 (0:00) Arrive Lafayette.

LAFAYETTE, LA - This fast-growing city is in the very heart of "Cajun" country. Many oil-related firms have located here, and it is home for the University of Southwestern Louisiana. Longfellow described this country as "The Eden of Louisiana" in his poem "Evangeline"—and it is indeed, with soft-flowing bayous, verdant, moss-covered forests and flowers blooming year-round. Each fall, "Festivals Acadiens" is held here, featuring Acadian culture with Cajun food, music and crafts.
0:00 (1:25) Depart Lafayette.
0:37 (1:00) Cross Mermentau River which connects Lake Arthur, Lake Charles and Intracoastal Waterway—the latter being a series of connecting bodies of water that extend from Brownsville, Texas along the Gulf and then up the Atlantic coast until it reaches Boston—the world's longest such waterway.
1:25 (0:00) Arrive Lake Charles.

LAKE CHARLES, LA - A deep-water port with access to the Gulf of Mexico has made this the industrial center of southwestern Louisiana. Oil, cement and chemicals are just some of the varied products that are produced or processed here. Of interest is the Imperial Cacasien Museum with a 300-year-old Sallier Oak still offering protective shade.
0:00 (1:25) Depart Lake Charles.
0:38 (0:47) As we cross Sabine River, bid farewell to Louisiana and welcome to Texas, largest of the 48 contiguous states. Don't expect to see the open ranges quite yet, as countryside is still heavily agricultural, with rice fields and sorghums more dominant than herefords and angus.
1:18 (0:07) Cross a shipping channel as we near Beaumont; downtown will be off to right. Here, terrain starts to open up a bit, as Texas begins to look a bit more like Texas.
1:25 (0:00) Arrive Beaumont.

BEAUMONT, TX - Although settled much earlier by French and Spanish fur trappers, Beaumont was truly born in 1901 when the world's greatest oil well, the Lucas Gusher of Spindletop fame, blew in and started a new era. Besides being an industrial giant, it is both a major port and an agricultural center. Beaumont has a tradition of producing fine athletes. Numerous professional football players have been produced by local high schools, and Babe Didrikson Zaharias, perhaps the world's greatest woman athlete, called this her home.
0:00 (1:37) Depart Beaumont.
0:14 (1:23) Small Beaumont Municipal Airport on right handles private craft with commercial aircraft using airport southeast of town.
0:25 (1:12) On right, some of area's rice fields, which use flood irrigation during growing season, appear just before Nome, TX.
0:47 (0:50) Cross Trinity River about two miles west of Liberty, TX.
1:08 (0:29) Cross large San Jacinto River which flows into Galveston Bay just south of here.
1:09 (0:28) Just before Sheldon, St. Regis Paper mill is clearly visible through trees on right.
1:12 (0:25) Far in distance, across enormous pipe storage yard on left, it is possible to pick out 570-foot-high San Jacinto Monument—looking like a small smokestack on the horizon. It was here that Texas finally won its independence from Mexico with Santa Ana's capture by Sam Houston's Texas army in 1836.
1:18 (0:19) Small campus of Southern Bible College is on left as we near Houston.
1:22 (0:15) Sprawling Southern Pacific yards are adjacent on left.
1:26 (0:11) Note considerable rail freight containers awaiting use on left and railroad tie manufacturing operation on right.
1:37 (0:00) Arrive Houston where, to left and beyond station, America's most dramatic skyline of modern architecture should impress any visitor. Although basic structures withstood hurricane of 1983, storm broke thousands of windows and filled streets with six inches of glass.

HOUSTON, TX - Houston, the largest city in Texas with a metropolitan population of nearly three million, grew for two reasons: its excellent port facilities, enhanced by the construction of a ship canal to Galveston, and the discovery of oil in the immediate area.

In the late 1970s and early 1980s, spurred by a then-booming oil industry, Houston's skyline grew into a compacted maze of geometric patterns and reflections. A resurgence in the American skyscraper occurred here, creating a look that is the epitome of modernism.

Amtrak Station, 902 Washington Ave., 77002, is a small, efficient structure located on the edge of the downtown area. There are storage lockers, luggage carts, food and beverage vending machines and ample adjacent free parking.

For arrival and departure information, call (713) 224-1577; for reservations and other information, call 800-USA-RAIL.

Cabs are usually available at train times. United Cab, 699-0000. Avis and Budget will pick up **rental car** customers at the station. Nearest **local bus** stop is two blocks from the station, 635-4000. **Greyhound,** 2121 Main, 759-6500. **Houston International Airport** (to the north) and **William P. Hobby Airport** (to the south) are both considerable distances from downtown.

Greater Houston Convention and Visitors Council, 3300 Main St., 77002. Call (713) 523-5050.

Holiday Inn Downtown, 801 Calhoun St. (at Milam), 77002; (713) 659-2222. Located on the southern fringe of Houston's downtown. Free shuttle to and from the station, about two miles. $68.

-Doubletree Hotel at Allen Center, 400 Dallas Street, 77002; (713) 759-0202. Across from Sam Houston Park. About a mile from the station with free shuttle. $129.

-Hyatt Regency Houston, 1200 Louisiana St., 77002; (713) 558-1234. Amtrak package, $84. A block from the Allen Center, one mile from the station. $161.

Downtown has a four-mile **underground pedestrian-way,** lined with shops and restaurants, with maps for self help. Inquire at the visitors center or your hotel. Also downtown is **Sam Houston Park,** 1100 Bagby, near the Allen Center, with a collection of historical buildings that can be toured. The **Houston Civic and Cultural Center** covers 16 blocks and contains performing arts facilities.

Houston's biggest attractions, however, are not downtown. NASA's **Johnson Space Center** is 30 minutes southeast of town with two-hour, self-guided tours. The **Port of Houston** has two-hour boat tours of the nation's third largest port. And **San Jacinto Battleground,** where Texas won its independence and current mooring place of Battleship Texas, is east of downtown, off Hwy. 225 and Farm Road.

0:00 (4:08) Depart Houston.

0:26 (3:42) Impressive skyline of Bellaire, a Houston suburb, is off to right.

0:43 (3:25) Plant of Imperial Sugar Company is on right in aptly named Sugarland, TX.

0:45 (3:23) White and tan buildings, about one-fourth mile distant on right, are facilities of Central State Farm, Department of Corrections.

0:53 (3:15) Cross huge Brazos River just before entering Richmond. Note elegant old frame depot on right.

1:15 (2:53) Cotton and soybeans, growing on both sides of tracks, are typical crops of southern Texas. Rice fields are also prevalent along this stretch.

1:24 (2:44) Silo-like elevators on right marked "Rice Industries" are for storing and shipping local rice crops.

1:48 (2:20) Cross a Colorado River—not of Grand Canyon fame, but smaller river that drains an enormous section of west-central Texas plains before emptying into Gulf of Mexico.

1:49 (2:19) In Columbus, be sure to note stylish old courthouse on left, complete with clock-embedded dome.

2:03 (2:05) At Weimar, former rail station on left now serves as attractive community library.

3:35 (0:33) Nearing San Antonio, runways of Randolph Air Force Base are off to left.

4:02 (0:06) East Yards of Southern Pacific are on left as Sunset Ltd. nears center of San Antonio.

4:08 (0:00) Arrive San Antonio where nicely renovated station on right is but a stone's throw from heart of downtown. Tower of Americas, constructed for 1968 HemisFair, bolts skyward.

SAN ANTONIO, TX - See page 234.

0:00 (3:04) Depart San Antonio.

As the train now proceeds across the vast expanse of the west Texas prairie, sage, yucca and cactus periodically punctuate this otherwise arid landscape.

2:56 (0:08) Approaching Del Rio, pass grounds of Laughlin Air Force Base on left.

3:04 (0:00) Cross series of finely landscaped canals arriving Del Rio.

DEL RIO, TX - This "Queen City of the Rio Grande" is the largest city between San Antonio and El Paso. Sheep and Angora goat production is the prevalent industry, giving rise to the town's claim of "Wool and Mohair Capital of the World." The Mexican border is just to the south where Ciudad Acuna, a city of 40,000, offers night spots and shops for those wanting a taste of Old Mexico.

0:00 (2:24) Departing Del Rio, Mexican city of Acuna can be seen atop bluffs on left. This is only recognized port of entry between here and El Paso. Rio Grande, obscured at this time, represents border between U.S. and Mexico.

0:11 (2:13) Rio Grande now joins on left.

0:16 (2:08) Cross waters of Amistad Reservoir. Constructed just below confluence of Rio Grande and Devil's River, Amistad was joint project of U.S. and Mexico, with Spanish word for "friendship" reflected in its name.

For the next 200 miles, a perceptive eye can detect subtle changes in the desert vegetation, as the train climbs nearly 3,500 feet to the high prairies surrounding Alpine.

0:48 (1:36) Suddenly, train embarks across Pecos High Bridge spanning magnificent canyon cut by Pecos River 321 feet below. This awesome spectacle, certainly one of trip's scenic highlights, was perhaps not so endearing to early pioneers who had to cross by wagon without benefit of bridges. High Bridge was completed in 1892. After original was replaced in 1944, it was cut into numbered sections and shipped to Guatemala where it now serves as a highway bridge.

We are in the western end of the state and it will take The Sunset Limited nearly

seven more hours to reach El Paso. This is mercurial, however, compared with those historic Butterfield Stages that took more than two full days to cover the same route.

1:04 (1:20) It was near here, on a trestle high over Deadman's Gulch, that a silver spike was driven in January 1888, completing a New Orleans-San Francisco route—nation's second transcontinental rail line. (Actual section of track was abandoned when Pecos High Bridge went into service.)

1:06 (1:18) Pass by Langtry on left where Judge Roy Bean once enforced his own brand of "law west of the Pecos." Visitors' center is replete with memorabilia of this legendary "lawman."

A monumental airlift took place here in 1954 when devastating storms, spawned by Hurricane Alice, left an eastbound Sunset Limited stranded, unable to travel in either direction due to washed out track. Some 200 passengers had to be evacuated by helicopter.

1:26 (0:58) Sunset route was especially vulnerable to outlaws who could easily retreat across nearby Mexican border. In 1912, last attempted train robbery in these parts took place at Baxter's Curve, just west of Val Verde and Terrell county line. Two desperados, one of whom had ridden with Butch Cassidy and The Sundance Kid, boarded a westbound train from their galloping horses, only to have their villainous effort end in failure when they were shot to death during the incident.

2:09 (0:15) Ruins of wall built by U.S. Infantry to defend against Pancho Villa in 1916 still stand near tracks.

2:24 (0:00) Arriving Sanderson, old caboose is central fixture of town park on right.

SANDERSON, TX - Now a railroad shipping point for this sparsely settled ranching country, Sanderson was once the lair of renegades, outlaws, cattle rustlers and general ne'er-do-wells. Judge Roy Bean operated a saloon here as well as one in Langtry, Texas.

0:00 (1:40) Departing Sanderson, crumbling brick walls of Sanderson Wool Commission on right are a time-worn testimonial to an industry that, to this day, remains a vital economic mainstay of region.

0:05 (1:35) At right, cave and earthen mound were used by Apaches for shelter and cooking, respectively.

0:32 (1:09) Glass Mountains can now be discerned in distance, both directions. Throughout Texas and New Mexico, mountain ranges represent subclassifications of much larger range known as Rocky Mountains.

0:57 (0:44) On forward right and left, Davis Mountains are now interposed upon horizon.

1:38 (0:02) Approaching Alpine, large "SR" enscribed on hillside right identifies campus of Sul Ross State University. Students from over 20 countries attend this school perhaps best known for its rodeo teams.

1:40 (0:00) Handsome Spanish-style station greets passengers arriving Alpine.

ALPINE, TX - This is the trading center and county seat of Brewster County—Texas' biggest county and larger than the state of Connecticut. Its mild winter climate, together with Big Bend National Park 80 miles to the south, have made Alpine a favorite tourist stop.

0:00 (3:25) Small "canyonlands" are a temporary delight departing Alpine.

0:15 (3:10) At Paisano Pass, Sunset Limited reaches 5,074 feet, highest point on route.

0:18 (3:07) On forward left, Chinati Peak (7,730 feet) is most prominent member of Cuesto del Burro Range.

0:28 (2:57) Passing through Marfa, watch for sailplanes which frequent updrafts above nearby mesas. Palatial domed building seen on right houses Presidio County Courthouse. Although dome was formerly crowned by "Scales of Justice," ornament was displaced by rifle blast from a disgruntled prisoner who apparently felt that justice had not been served.

0:30 (2:55) On western outskirts of town, Mitre Peak (6,100 feet) stands out back on right. White domes of University of Texas' McDonald Observatory are on southern prominence of Davis Mountains in far distance right. At base, Ft. Davis is highest town in Texas at 5,050 feet. Town's courthouse reputedly has turnstiles to keep stray cattle from appearing in court.

0:44 (2:41) Antelope herds are a frequent sight throughout this particular region.

0:54 (2:31) Re-emergence of agricultural fields outside Valentine reflects gradual descent off high plains. Sierra Vieja Mountains border on left, while peaks of Van Horns approach on forward right. A scene from movie *Giant* was filmed near old windmill on left.

1:22 (2:03) Highway 90, trackside companion of last 24 hours, now departs north.

Gain one hour as train passes from Central to Mountain Time. Set your watch back (forward if eastbound) one hour.

1:32 (1:53) On left, Sierra Vieja Mountains give way to Quitman Range.

1:55 (1:30) At Sierra Blanca, mountains of same name hover in distance on right, while Quitmans are now dwarfed by Mexican Hueso Range on left. Town has only adobe courthouse still in use in Texas.

2:22 (1:03) Pass through McNary where gas station/museum makes curious combination on left.

2:26 (0:59) Remnants of old fort, which once guarded U.S. mail, can be seen on right at Fort Hancock.

2:39 (0:46) Cotton fields and pecan groves are suddenly popular sights of Rio Grande Valley.

2:47 (0:38) South of Fabens, colorful decorations adorn graves of Hispanic cemetery on right. Once in town, nice mission-style church is notable on left, while large facility on right gins and bundles area's cotton crop.

3:14 (0:11) Approach El Paso through industrial district of which Mobil refinery and Nichols Copper operations are predominant. Ahead north, Franklin Mountains encircle city. Supposedly, if light is right (and imagination vivid), silhouette of Ben Franklin can be discerned in their midst.

3:22 (0:03) On right, pass campus of religiously founded Laredo Academy.

3:23 (0:02) On left, note publishing facilities of *El Paso Herald Post and Times.*

3:25 (0:00) Arrive El Paso. Station, styled in early mission architecture, with pieces of Mexican pottery displayed atop surrounding walls, was completed in 1905 and designed by firm of Daniel H. Burnham, designers of Washington, D.C.'s Union Station. Back on left, unusual sweeping shell encloses Civic Auditorium and Theatre.

EL PASO, TX - This is the largest U.S. city on the Mexican border, and its southerly neighbor Juarez is likewise the largest Mexican border city. Their combined populations approach one million. Cradled in an ancient mountain pass (hence the name "El Paso"), it is surrounded by mountains over one mile in elevation. Its excellent climate has also made it a popular winter resort. This is Amtrak's gateway to Carlsbad Caverns National Park, 145 miles northeast of here, and is the closest Amtrak comes to connecting with the National Railways of Mexico which can be boarded in Juarez.

0:00 (1:16) Departing El Paso, Mexican sister-city of Juarez can be seen on left atop palisades of Rio Grande.

0:02 (1:14) On right, pass campus of University of Texas at El Paso.

0:03 (1:13) Floodlight banks protrude above university's "Sun Bowl" stadium, carved within hillsides on right.

0:04 (1:12) On forward left, massive monument of Christ on cross is ensconced atop Sierra de Cristo Rey. On last Sunday in October, thousands of pilgrims trek four miles to summit to celebrate "Feast of Christ the King." Shrine also represents point where Texas, New Mexico and Mexico all meet.

0:06 (1:10) Sprawling Southwestern Portland Cement Company on right, and Asarco refinery on left, greet train as it crosses Rio Grande from Texas into New Mexico. Proceed along through dramatic outcroppings and rock formations before finally settling back atop parched landscape of Southwestern desert.

0:07 (1:09) Sunland Park Race Track can be seen on right.

0:10 (1:06) White post on immediate left identifies international border, only 30 feet away and Amtrak's closest encounter with Mexico.

0:20 (0:56) Mountains now extending both on right and left are known as the Portillos.

1:00 (0:16) Florida Peak (7,295 feet) prevails amidst Florida Mountains on left, while Cooke's Peak (8,408 feet) is mainstay of Cooke's Range on right. In Florida Range, mountain with hole through it is Window Peak.

1:12 (0:02) On eastern outskirts of Deming, cross Mimbres River.

1:16 (0:00) Arriving Deming, distinctive clock tower of Luna County Courthouse juts prominently above town on left.

DEMING, NM - Situated in a beautiful agricultural area of 70,000 irrigated acres, Deming farmers raise cotton, peanuts, pecans, beans and grain sorghums in abundance. This is a rock hound's delight, and a state park has been established just for their needs— appropriately named "Rock Hound State Park." A warm winter climate, with an average snowfall of only 2.7 inches, makes this a popular spot for retirees.

0:00 (0:50) Depart Deming.

0:24 (0:26) Crest Continental Divide at 4,584 feet, Amtrak's lowest crossing of nation's rooftop.

0:50 (0:00) Arrive Lordsburg.

LORDSBURG, NM - As with so many Western towns, Lordsburg was established with the arrival of the railroad. It is situated near the eastern edge of The Gadsden Purchase, a strip of land acquired by the United States from Mexico in 1854 that permitted the railroad to continue its march westward to the Pacific Ocean.

Nestled between the Burro and Pyramid mountain ranges, this area was once controlled by Cochise, greatest of the Apache chiefs. Now a desert community of 4,250, serving as the trade center for southwestern New Mexico, it enjoys 350 days of sunshine and a typically mild southern New Mexico climate. As was the case in Deming, Lordsburg's weather makes this another appealing retirement area.

Phelps Dodge has recently constructed a large smelter near here to process ore from copper deposits found throughout the region.

0:00 (1:50) Depart Lordsburg.

0:11 (1:39) Large, dry lake bed on right frequently produces deceiving mirage that creates acres of "water" glimmering across its barren sands.

0:19 (1:31) On left, as Sunset crests a

248

ridge, adobe ruins and some live-in shacks mark site of camp where thousands of Chinese laborers were once housed during construction of Southern Pacific.

0:23 (1:27) Reddish-brown water tank on right sits in New Mexico while windmill on left is in Arizona as Sunset crosses states' boundary.

0:34 (1:16) At left are Chiricahua Mountains which rise to a maximum height of 9,795 feet. Face of Indian warrior Cochise can be clearly distinguished at top of ridge staring skyward as he lies atop "his mountains." Peloncillo Mountains are off to right.

1:05 (0:45) Breeze through Willcox, AZ, home of former Western movie star Rex Allen. To right, just before enormous old depot, bright red rail car houses Peking Express Restaurant, dispensers of Mandarin food.

Our elevation is now 4,167 feet above sea level, but by the time we reach Phoenix, we will have descended 3,075 feet to an elevation of only 1,092 feet.

1:11 (0:39) Tracks now stretch across broad flats called Willcox Playa. Although much of surface is covered with brown stagnant water, much more is host to clear imaginary water of one of country's more deceiving mirages. Dragoon Mountains, on left, are clearly reflected in this "non lake." Cochise electric power plant is also off to left.

1:47 (0:03) Small airport on left serves Benson, AZ, our next stop.

1:49 (0:01) Cross San Pedro River whose waters flow north and west into Gila River, and eventually join Colorado River at Yuma, AZ.

It was along this stretch of the San Pedro, in 1540, that Coronado and his expedition, up from Mexico, first entered the present United States in their search for the legendary Seven Cities of Cibola—cities thought to have streets lined with goldsmith shops and doorways studded with emeralds and turquoise. No such cities were ever found, but the horses left behind, and the teachings of Spanish

Sunset Limited, Tucson, Arizona

priests, forever changed the lives of the Indians of the Southwest.

1:50 (0:00) Arrive Benson where small shelter on left pretends to be a rail station.

BENSON, AZ - As early as 1860, Benson served as a stop for the old Butterfield Stage. Then in 1880, with the arrival of the railroad, it became a shipping point for the mines around Tombstone. In recent times, ranching and explosives manufacturing have become more important.

0:00 (1:10) Departing Benson, Rincon Mountains form familiar desert horizon on right.

0:07 (1:03) Hillside on left has profusion of yuccas—those plants with clusters of spear-like leaves out of which tall shafts spurt upwards, culminating in tops of clustered whitish blossoms. Resourceful Indians of Southwest made a variety of products from this decorative bush, including sandals, baskets, edible fruit and even soap.

0:09 (1:01) Lonely, abandoned movie set for *Flash Point,* filmed in 1983, can be glimpsed about a mile off to right. Except during stormy weather, radar surveillance blimp can be seen hovering above Ft. Huachuca in distance to left. Idea is to spot planes bringing in drugs from Mexico.

0:25 (0:45) Through this stretch, eastbound and westbound tracks are often separated by a half-mile distance or so, with a more curving route on eastbound trackage, permitting an easier uphill grade. Eastbound tracks can be seen some distance off to left.

0:31 (0:39) Precariously perched atop peak on right is "castle" built by Duane Durant, a petroleum entrepreneur who obviously prefers mountaintop opulence to more mundane flatland setting.

0:32 (0:38) Just ahead lie two overlapping rail bridges, westbound traffic taking the higher route and eastbound the lower. Highway bridge also crosses eastbound tracks.

0:38 (0:32) Snaking downward through Texas Canyon, excellent views of front of train are frequently offered.

0:41 (0:29) On right, pink Catholic church, with century-plant landscaping, is Shrine of Santa Rita in the Desert.

The church was dedicated in 1935 to the memory of a Japanese scientist, Dr. Jokichi Takamine, who built the first superphosphate works in Tokyo. His widow's second husband, a local rancher by the name of Beach, had a church constructed in honor of Takamine. Built around stained glass windows of a dismantled Methodist church, the interior contains a black marble font designed in Italy and a hand-carved crucifix from Bavaria.

0:53 (0:17) Tall tail fins of mothballed military aircraft can be seen on right at Davis Monthan Air Force Base. Nearly 5,000 planes are stored here for salvage.

0:54 (0:16) Numerous World War II aircraft are huddled together at Pima Air Museum, on right, including presidential plane used by Lyndon B. Johnson.

0:57 (0:13) On right, Tucson Electric Power Co. generating facility provides electricity to much of Tucson's metropolitan area.

0:58 (0:12) Parked in yards of Rail Passenger Services, on right, fascinating assortment of vintage rail passenger cars are in various stages of restoration.

0:59 (0:11) Last glimpse of Davis Monthan Air Force Base on right. Olive twin-beamed aircraft are Air Force A-10 attack planes, built with heavy emphasis on survivability.

1:03 (0:07) Southern Pacific rail yards extend along route as train enters Tucson.

1:06 (0:04) University of Arizona campus, distinguished by stadium, is off to right, while Santa Rita Mountains hunker down on horizon to left.

1:10 (0:00) Arrive Tucson where stretched out mission-style station awaits on left.

TUCSON, AZ - Very possibly the oldest continually inhabited city in North America, Tucson has lived under four flags in the last 300 years: Spanish, Mexican, Confederate, and American. It was first visited by Father Kino, a Jesuit missionary, in the late 17th century. The Spanish Army later chose the site for a frontier fortress, constructing a walled "Presidio" near what is now the center of Tucson. The site of the original Presidio can still be visited, along with many other old structures in the historic area of the city.

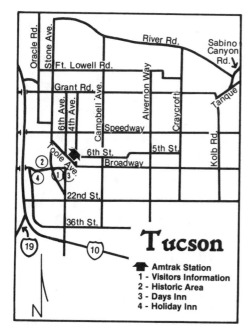

Tucson

- Amtrak Station
1 - Visitors Information
2 - Historic Area
3 - Days Inn
4 - Holiday Inn

N

A sunny and dry climate contributes to the popularity of Tucson as both a retirement and a tourist community. It has a metropolitan population of 550,000, with a casual, desert style of living predominating. It is also a gateway to Mexico, with the international border just 67 miles to the south at Nogales.

Amtrak Station, 400 E. Toole Ave., 85701. This fine old Spanish-style station is located on the eastern edge of Tucson's small but vital downtown. There are storage lockers and vending machines. There is metered parking in front and a pay-parking lot one block away on Toole Ave.

For reservations and information, call 800-USA-RAIL. Ticket and waiting room hours: Sun., Mon. and Thur., 8:15 am to 9:15 pm; Tues. and Wed., 1:45 pm to 9:15 pm; Fri. and Sat., 8:15 am to 3:45 pm.

Cab stand at the station; Yellow Cab, 624-6611. **Local bus** information, 792-9222; Transit Center is one block west of the station; **Greyhound/Trailways,** two blocks from station at 2 South 4th Ave., 792-0972. Budget **rental cars** are closest to the station and offer pick up and drop off for Amtrak passen-

gers, 623-5743. **Tucson International Airport** is 11 miles south of the station.

Tucson Convention & Visitors Bureau, 130 S. Scott Ave., 85701; (602) 624-1817.

Holiday Inn Broadway, 181 W. Broadway, 85701; (602) 624-8711. A very popular downtown hotel, five blocks from the station. $56.

-Days Inn Tucson Downtown, 88 East Broadway, 85701; (602) 622-4000. Former Santa Rita Hotel, a long-time Tucson landmark, has been nicely maintained by Days Inn. Only three blocks from the station. $50.

"Historic" Tucson, the original town, is within walking distance, just west of the station in an area bounded roughly by 6th Ave., Kennedy, Main and Toole. This area includes many old buildings and sites of historic interest including the El Presidio Park which occupies a portion of the original "Presidio" and the Tucson Museum of Art. A brochure describing this entire area with a walking tour map is available from the Visitors Bureau.

Not in the downtown area, but a must, is the **Arizona-Sonora Desert Museum,** 16 miles west of Tucson, with a fine collection of desert animals and plants. Drive west and southwest on Speedway, then follow the signs, or west on Ajo and right at Kinney Rd. Also popular, but rather "touristy," is **Old Tucson,** 14 miles southwest of Tucson, which has been used as a set for various Western movies. Shops and gunfights. Near the Desert Museum.

The **Mission San Xavier Del Bac** (the White Dove of the Desert), nine miles south of Tucson, is perhaps the most beautiful mission in the Southwest. Its white structure stands out vividly against the brown desert sand. The **Saguaro National Monument** is in two sections, one east and one west of Tucson. The eastern section is perhaps a bit more impressive and has dense stands of Saguaro cactus. **Kitt Peak National Observatory,** 45 miles west of Tucson, is one of nation's top observatories; tours weekends and holidays. The **Pima Air Museum** has an excellent collection of Air Force planes, dating from the 1940s.

The **Sierra Madre Express of Tucson** offers deluxe passenger train tour service to Mexico's Copper Canyon; (602) 747-0346 or 800-666-0346.

0:00 (1:50) Departing Tucson, small but showy downtown skyline appears on immediate left.

0:09 (1:41) Santa Catalina Mountains, off to right, rise to a height of 9,157 feet at summit of Mt. Lemmon and contain Tucson's closest ski area.

0:17 (1:33) Facility of Arizona Portland Cement Company is just beyond Interstate 10 on left.

0:33 (1:17) Marana Air Base in distance to left has world-wide clientele for restoration of aircraft. On right, Arizona Public Service Company plant has enormous oil storage capacity for fuel, while supply tank cars are frequently at siding on right farther downline.

0:34 (1:16) Sprawling pecan orchards provide sudden change of scenery on right. Besides pecans and cotton, truck farming is prevalent between here and Phoenix, raising the likes of cauliflower, broccoli and cabbage.

0:38 (1:12) On left, Picacho Peak juts dramatically from Arizona desert. Westernmost conflict of Civil War was fought 12 miles south of here. Fine stands of saguaro cactus stud hills on both sides and continue on left for several miles, offering finest stands to be viewed on Amtrak.

0:45 (1:05) Bid farewell to Interstate 10 as tracks curve away to right.

0:46 (1:04) On left, warehouses with adjoining storage yard of yellow cubes are Federal Compress, where bales of cotton are received from nearby gins to have them compressed, stored and then sold. Larger yellow blocks are uncompressed bales while smaller ones are sans air. Crops are harvested in March and October but bales are marketed throughout year.

0:56 (0:54) Facility on left, with enormous piles of scrap metal along tracks, is recycling plant of Proler International Corp., where scrap is shredded and then melted down into ingots of nearly pure tin.

0:57 (0:53) Small community at left of tracks is Randolph, with all streets named after black activists and others who have played important roles in black advancement—names such as Cleaver, Malcolm X, King and Kennedy.

1:03 (0:47) Through Coolidge, future Amtrak stop.

1:04 (0:46) About a mile or so to left is enormous canopy protecting a smaller structure beneath it. This is Casa Grande Ruins National Monument. The protected building was constructed almost 650 years ago out of unreinforced coursed caliche—a desert soil with a high lime content. Main structure was centerpiece of a Hohokam Indian village, but its exact use and purpose is still unknown. Recent studies, however, suggest possible astrological use.

1:17 (0:33) Sprawling H and G Feedlots on left fatten cattle while large shades above pens provide protection from desert sun.

1:19 (0:31) Note grape vineyard on left—just one more crop raised in this fertile area.

1:22 (0:28) Arizona Boys Ranch, where disadvantaged youth are offered a better chance, is immediately adjacent to route on left.

1:25 (0:25) Jets, barracks and aircraft hangers of Williams Air Force Base are off to right.

1:33 (0:17) Agricultural surroundings now give way to industrialized suburbs of Phoenix.

1:47 (0:03) Arizona State University is on right as we enter Tempe. Sports stadium is site of annual Fiesta Bowl football game, while circular building is school's music hall designed by Frank Lloyd Wright.

1:50 (0:00) Arrive Tempe where Amtrak shares depot with Mexican restaurant.

TEMPE, AZ - A part of the Phoenix metroplex, Tempe is home to Arizona State University with 40,000 students. The school is Arizona's largest and oldest institution of higher learning.

0:00 (0:15) Depart Tempe.

0:02 (0:13) Sunset Limited crosses Salt River which has its sources in Sierra Anchor and White mountains to east, providing water for massive irrigation projects throughout south central Arizona.

0:07 (0:10) Sky Harbor Airport, serving Phoenix, is just to left with major east-west runway paralleling tracks.

0:12 (0:03) Downtown Phoenix stands on right—dominating glass-sided skyscraper houses headquarters of Valley National Bank; brown 24-story structure with disk-like revolving restaurant on top is Hyatt Regency.

0:15 (0:00) Arrive Phoenix.

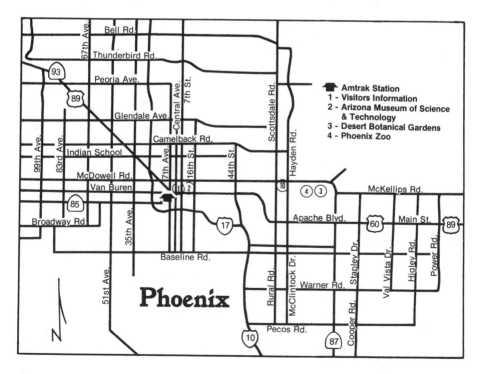 **PHOENIX, AZ** - The capital of Arizona and one of America's fastest growing cities, Phoenix began in 1860 as a small settlement on the banks of the Salt River. As with so many other towns, its first real growth came when the railroad arrived in 1887.

The name "Phoenix" comes from the mythical Phoenix bird which supposedly burns itself on its own funeral pyre every 500 years, and then mysteriously rises from its own ashes. The city was predicted to eventually rise from the ancient Indian ruins found nearby—thus the name.

Although hot in the summer, its mild winter climate has accounted for its popularity as a winter destination for tourists from colder climes. Its Southwestern architecture in a desert setting lends further appeal. Besides tourism, manufacturing and agriculture (cotton and citrus) are other leading industries.

Amtrak Station, 401 West Harrison St., 85003; (on 4th Ave. seven blocks south of Van Buren St.) is a recently renovated structure located in a marginal downtown area. There are storage lockers and very limited free parking.

For arrival and departure information and reservations, call 800-USA-RAIL.

Cab stand at the station; Yellow Cab, 252-5252 and Checker, 257-1818. **Local buses** are three and four blocks north of the station on Jefferson and Washington streets; 253-5000. **Greyhound,** (602) 248-4060. Nearby **rental car** locations are Dollar in the Sheraton, 257-1557 and Southwest Car Rental in the Hyatt, 258-1918. **Sky Harbor International Airport** is four miles east of the station.

Phoenix and Valley of the Sun Convention & Visitors Bureau, 404 N. Second St., Suite 300, 85004; (602) 254-6500. A second center is located at the Hyatt Regency, 2nd St. and Adams.

While the metropolis seems to enjoy (or suffer) a never-ending expansion, downtown Phoenix has remained compact and, by most standards, under-

Amtrak Station
1 - Visitors Information
2 - Arizona Museum of Science & Technology
3 - Desert Botanical Gardens
4 - Phoenix Zoo

Phoenix

developed. A few new high-rise offices and hotels crowd the convention center, while the rest of the inner city tries to fight off urban shabbiness. Unless convention-bound, most visitors tend to find accommodations and attractions farther out. The following hotels are reasonably convenient to the station and are in good downtown locations:

-EconoLodge Convention Center, 401 N. 1st St. (at Polk), 85004; (602) 258-3411 or 800-446-6900. Formerly Heritage Hotel, completely renovated in 1988. Eleven blocks from the station. $46.95.

-Days Inn San Carlos, 202 N. Central Ave., 85004; (602) 253-4121. Former Hotel San Carlos, built in 1927, now operated by Days Inn. Ten blocks from the station. $50.

-Sheraton Phoenix, 111 N. Central Ave., 85004; (602) 257-1525. Large, convention-oriented hotel. Amtrak package, $73. Nine blocks from the station. $134.

There are few downtown attractions in Phoenix. One would be the **Arizona Museum of Science & Technology,** 80 N. 2nd Street (its temporary location until the permanent home is built in Heritage and Science Park), which has numerous "hands-on" science exhibits. For an outstanding **view of the city,** enjoy a meal in the revolving restaurant at the top of the Hyatt Regency, 2nd St. and Adams.

Phoenix's major attraction, however, is its winter sun and warmth. To better appreciate this desert environment, the **Desert Botanical Garden** in Papago Park, 1201 N. Galvin Parkway, has pathways through unusual cacti and other desert plants, and the **Phoenix Zoo,** 5810 E. Van Bureau, has over 1,000 animals, many representative of the Arizona-Sonora region.

0:00 (3:20) Depart Phoenix. Darkness usually prevails on stretch between Phoenix and Pomona.
3:20 (0:00) Arrive Yuma.

YUMA, AZ - Yuma does quite well in this southwestern Arizona setting. Irrigation from the Colorado River has turned much of its sand into productive farmland and its climate has made it a popular resort center. Just outside of town is the site of the infamous Yuma Territorial Prison which is now a State Historical Park. Built by convicts, it was nearly escape proof and was considered to be the most secure prison in the West.
0:00 (1:45) Depart Yuma.

Pass from Mountain to Pacific Time as train crosses Arizona state line into California. Since Arizona does not observe daylight saving time, set watch back (forward if eastbound) one hour, only if rest of country is not on daylight saving time.
1:10 (0:35) As Sunset cruises near California's Salton Sea, lowest point on route is touched—202 feet below sea level.
1:45 (0:00) Arrive Indio.

INDIO, CA - Indio had a typical beginning in 1894 when it was a minor stop on the Southern Pacific, and the depot served as the town's social center. Climate and irrigation, however, led to Indio's eventually becoming "The Date Capital of the World," with this tasty fruit being feted each February during the National Date Festival. Just to the south is California's largest inland body of water, the Salton Sea. This recreational lake was formed at the turn of the century when the Colorado River broke through levies and flooded into a depression for two years. Indio also serves as Amtrak's stop for nearby Palm Springs.
0:00 (1:50) Depart Indio.

As the train now emerges upon the Southern California megalopolis, the small farms and dairies which have dotted the landscape since daybreak are suddenly engulfed in the imposing shadows of mammoth industrial operations and the ever-encroaching suburban sprawl.
1:26 (0:24) Coming into Colton, cross concrete-lined Santa Ana River. San Gabriel Mountains now border on right into Los Angeles.
1:42 (0:08) Extensive vineyards surround Brookside Winery on right. Facility is oldest commercial winery in California.
1:43 (0:07) On left, pass Ontario International Airport. (Amtrak plans to make Ontario a scheduled stop in near future.)
1:50 (0:00) Arrive Pomona Commercial Street station. (Southwest Chief uses Garey Ave. station.) Agricultural theme highlights colorful mural across from

station on left. (Amtrak plans to replace this stop with Ontario, mentioned just above.)

 POMONA, CA - In 1875, Solomon Gates was awarded a free lot for naming Pomona after the Roman goddess of fruit. The name remains appropriate to this day, reflecting the city's prominence as a mecca of citrus production. Pomona is also the noted autumn host of the Los Angeles County Fair, boasting the largest attendance of any such fair in the U.S. Nearby, too, is the resort of Mt. Baldy whose ski slopes, trout streams and scenic campgrounds provide a haven of year-round recreation.

0:00 (0:45) Departing Pomona, St. Joseph's Catholic Church is attractive fixture on left. A short distance downtown, St. Paul's Episcopal Church is easily recognized on right by its distinctive mission-style architecture.

0:03 (0:42) On right, skirt campus of California Polytechnic University at Pomona.

0:12 (0:33) At La Puente, massive building complex ensconced atop bluffs on right is Indian Hills Convention and Golf Center.

0:16 (0:28) Between La Puente and El Monte, cross oft-dry San Gabriel River.

0:18 (0:26) Pass El Monte airport on right, then proceed across concrete riverbed of Rio Hondo.

0:23 (0:22) Emerging from brief tunnel at Temple City, train travels briskly down median of Interstate 10 past an envious stream of congestion-bound commuters.

0:30 (0:14) Just prior to departing "freeway route," campus of California State University at Los Angeles can be seen on right.

0:36 (0:09) On right, cluster of tall buildings is Los Angeles County Hospital which operates in conjunction with University of Southern California.

0:39 (0:05) Concrete channel, which sometimes becomes Los Angeles River, joins and follows on left. Perched atop bluffs on forward left is Dodger Stadium, home of one of baseball's powerhouses.

0:44 (0:01) Engage in U-turn across Los Angeles River and slip past County Jail on left. On forward right, City Hall is predominant tower of downtown Los Angeles skyline, while double-domed building in foreground houses Post Office annex.

0:45 (0:00) Arrive Los Angeles.

 LOS ANGELES, CA - See page 273.

' Coast Starlight

Those well populated West Coast megalopolises of Seattle, San Francisco and Los Angeles are all ports of call for Amtrak's Coast Starlight. With numerous intermediate stops that include such popular destinations as Portland, Sacramento, San Luis Obispo and Santa Barbara, the Starlight is now one of America's most patronized trains. Make your reservations early.

A cavalcade of aesthetic delights makes this trip worth taking just for the experience of being there. A grand trek through the Cascades of Oregon, a maritime excursion along San Francisco Bay, a delightful amble over Cuesta Grade and a 113-mile daylight traverse along California's frothy shoreline north of Ventura (much of it only accessible by train) are just some of high points of a trip that offers one fascinating glimpse after another.

Although called The Coast Starlight, fortunately most of the route is traveled during the daylight, leaving only northern California's scenes obscured in darkness.

Southbound Schedule (Condensed)
Seattle, WA - Late Morning Departure
Portland, OR - Midafternoon
Eugene, OR - Late Afternoon
Oakland, CA - Early Morning (2nd Day) (Trainside motor coach service to and from San Francisco's Transbay Terminal and Caltrain/SP Station)
San Jose, CA - Midmorning (2nd Day)
Santa Barbara, CA - Late Afternoon (2nd Day)
Los Angeles, CA - Early Evening Arrival (2nd Day)

Northbound Schedule (Condensed)
Los Angeles, CA - Midmorning Departure
Santa Barbara, CA - Early Afternoon
San Jose, CA - Early Evening
Oakland, CA - Late Evening (Motor coach service to and from San Francisco's Transbay Terminal and Caltrain/SP Station)
Eugene, OR - Midmorning (2nd Day)
Portland, OR - Early Afternoon (2nd Day)
Seattle, WA - Early Evening Arrival (2nd Day)

Frequency - Daily.
Seating - Superliner coaches.
Dining - Complete meal and beverage service, as well as lighter fare. Lounge service also available, with movies.
Sleeping - Superliner sleepers with deluxe, family, economy and special bedrooms.
Baggage - Checked baggage handled at most stations. Baggage checked through, to or from points south of Los Angeles, subject to delay. Those passengers taking the connecting Vancouver bus in Seattle should carry their own luggage on board the train.
Reservations - All-reserved train.
Length of Trip - 1,390 miles in 33 hours.

Route Log

SEATTLE, WA - Seattle lies on the eastern shores of Puget Sound and is flanked by two beautiful ranges of mountains, the Olympics to the west and the Cascades to the east. Although situated relatively far north, its proximity to the Pacific Ocean, warmed by the Japan Current, gives it a very temperate climate year-round.

Founded in the mid-nineteenth century, the city grew to importance largely because of its excellent natural harbor—even though it is more than 100 miles from the open sea. It developed rapidly in the 1870s during the Alaska gold rush, and more recently as a leader in aircraft and space technology.

King Street Station, 3rd and South Jackson streets, is located on the south edge of the downtown area next to the Kingdome. The station has vending machines, a snack bar, a newsstand, redcaps, luggage carts and pay-parking.

For arrival and departure information, call (206) 382-4125; for other information and reservations, (206) 464-1930 or 800-USA-RAIL. Ticket window hours are 5:15 am to 5:30 pm; waiting room, 5:15 am to 10:30 pm.

Cab stand at the station; Yellow Cab, 622-6500. **Local buses** are one block from station; free bus rides within the downtown area; call 555-1212. **Greyhound,** (206) 624-3456. **Monorail** (to the Space Needle) terminal, 5th Ave. and Virginia, 1½ miles from the station. **Washington State Ferries** to various Puget Sound destinations, 464-6400. B.C. Stena Line has cruises between Seattle and Victoria, B.C.; 800-962-5984. There is a connecting **Vancouver bus** between the King Street Station and the Sandman Hotel in downtown Vancouver, B.C. **Seattle Tacoma International Airport** is 12 miles south of the station.

By June 1990, **Waterfront Streetcar** service will be extended to the International District next to King Street Station, with trolley service to the waterfront, and later, connections to the downtown transit (bus) tunnel.

Seattle-King County Convention and Visitors Bureau, 666 Stewart Street; (206) 461-5840; or write them at 520 Pike Ave., 98101.

Hotel Seattle, 315 Seneca, 98101; (206) 623-5110 or 800-426-2439. Moderately priced older hotel, remodeled in the 1980s; ¾ mile from the station. $54.

-Town Center Days Inn, 2205 7th Ave., 98121; (206) 448-3434. On the northern edge of downtown, about 1½ miles from the station. $55.

For those interested in touring sports facilities, **the Kingdome,** home to three of Seattle's major league teams, is next to the station. The **Chinatown, International District,** with shops and restaurants, is located approximately three blocks east of the station, in the area of 6th Ave. and South Main Street. **Pioneer Square,** in the area of James St. and First Avenue, features shops, restaurants and "underground tours" of an historic downtown area, much of which was covered over after a fire in 1889; includes underground abandoned stores and store fronts. It's approximately five blocks from the station.

Of course, in Seattle, **seafood dinners** are a major attraction, in and of themselves. Some find seafood restaurants are located along the waterfront between Union and Madison streets. Other sealife, not for eating, can be viewed at the **Seattle Aquarium** at Pier 59. **Tours of the harbor** are available at Pier 57.

The **Space Needle** has a great observation deck and a nice restaurant (revolving, of course) at the top. This can be reached from downtown by taking the monorail.

0:00 (0:54) Depart Seattle. Back on right, peaks of Olympic Range hover majestically in distance, while in foreground, castle-like Smith Tower was once tallest building west of Mississippi River. King Street Station's stately clock tower is another impressive fixture of Seattle skyline.

Directly on right is "Kingdome" sports complex, home of baseball's Mariners, basketball's Supersonics and football's Seahawks. Adjacent to Kingdome, small grassy square enshrines old Northern Pacific caboose.

For the next several miles, pass by the grounds of such recognizable corporations as Westinghouse, Sears, Nabisco, Ford and Zellerbach. Even in the midst of these industrial climes, one is immediately impressed by the general cleanliness pervading this entire Northwestern region.

0:05 (0:49) Silhouettes of steel superstructures on right evidence major dockside activity at Elliott Bay.

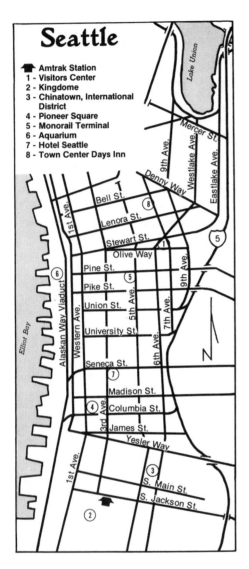

Seattle

- **Amtrak Station**
- **1 - Visitors Center**
- **2 - Kingdome**
- **3 - Chinatown, International District**
- **4 - Pioneer Square**
- **5 - Monorail Terminal**
- **6 - Aquarium**
- **7 - Hotel Seattle**
- **8 - Town Center Days Inn**

Lake Union

Mercer St.

9th Ave.

Westlake Ave.

Eastlake Ave.

Denny Way

Bell St.

1st Ave.

Lenora St.

Stewart St.

Olive Way

Pine St.

Alaskan Way Viaduct

Western Ave.

5th Ave.

9th Ave.

Pike St.

Union St.

University St.

7th Ave.

6th Ave.

Seneca St.

Madison St.

Columbia St.

3rd Ave.

James St.

Yesler Way

1st Ave.

S. Main St.

S. Jackson St.

Elliot Bay

0:09 (0:45) On right is sprawling expanse of Boeing Aircraft plant, largest employer in Seattle area. Foreign markings on many planes indicate diverse clientele of this huge corporation.

0:14 (0:40) Green River joins on right as it lazily winds through residential district of Tukwila.

0:16 (0:38) Nicely landscaped grounds of Longacres Race Track can be seen on left.

0:19 (0:35) Pass through another large industrial district with Reynolds and

Goodyear plants predominant on left, and General Electric on right.

0:22 (0:32) At tidy community of Kent, note charming gazebo on left in midst of town park. Quaint old depot is also noteworthy on left.

0:25 (0:29) Cross Green River.

As the urban congestion begins to thin, small farms and dairy operations become a more frequent sight. These pleasant pastoral environs are enwrapped in an endless blanket of greenery, nurtured by the abundant moisture so common to this part of the country.

0:31 (0:23) Another modest Boeing operation can be seen on right.

0:32 (0:22) Cross White River. Soon thereafter, train engages in a broad right turn that eventually settles on a northwesterly tack towards Tacoma.

0:36 (0:18) Cross Puyallup River. Old concrete bridge parallels on right.

0:41 (0:13) Travel directly through downtown streets of Puyallup. Distinguished older buildings now rival for recognition in shadows of more modern intrusions. Wide variety of flowers and shrubs accent attractive neighborhoods on west end of town.

0:43 (0:11) Cross Clark's Creek.

0:47 (0:07) Broad, arching treetops seemingly create tunnel through forest. Splendid covered bridge, crossing overhead, tops off this short but delightful stretch.

0:49 (0:05) Puyallup River joins momentarily on right.

0:51 (0:03) Downtown Tacoma comes into view, perched atop lofty bluff on forward right.

0:52 (0:02) City Waterway joins on right. This inlet of Commencement Bay is central hub of Tacoma's vast shipping industry.

0:54 (0:00) Arrive Tacoma station, whose sweeping arches and verdigris dome are strikingly reminiscent of an ancient temple or observatory.

TACOMA, WA - The need for lumber in the 1850s gave birth to Tacoma when the first sawmill was established here. Today, two giants of this industry, Weyerhaeuser and St. Regis Paper, produce thousands of wood products. Shipbuilding is also a major industry, and Tacoma has become the second largest seaport on Puget Sound. The world's largest collection of octopi can be seen here, as well as one of the world's tallest totem poles. A week-long Daffodil Festival each spring culminates in the nation's third largest floral parade.

0:00 (0:43) Depart Tacoma, once again traversing banks of City Waterway. Here, shipping, logging and refinery operations share spotlight with bevy of comely shops and restaurants, cleverly housed in renovated wharf facilities.

0:04 (0:39) Looming above cliff walls on left is ornate clock tower of Tacoma's Old City Hall. Originally constructed in 1893, building is enshrined in National Register of Historic Places, and now accommodates host of specialty shops, restaurants and office suites. Rounded tower, seen immediately adjacent to Old City Hall, presides atop general offices of Northern Pacific Railroad.

0:08 (0:35) In a near overstatement of ecological consciousness, note manicured gardens throughout sewage plant on left.

0:10 (0:33) Enter tunnel in midst of which train heads back south before finally emerging on shoreline of Puget Sound inlet. Impressive suspension bridge connects Tacoma with Olympic Peninsula on right.

For the next several miles, clusters of pleasure craft and secluded fishing coves are nicely interwoven along the rocky coastline of the Puget Sound. A magnificent array of gracious homes are ensconced atop the seacliffs, with this picturesque panorama an everyday spectacle.

0:16 (0:27) Fox Island can be seen directly on right, with McNeil Island lying a short distance south.

0:25 (0:18) Continue along seaside route, with Ketron Island now seen in midst of Sound.

0:32 (0:11) Train heads inland now, as farmlands, forests and rolling hills quickly displace nautical environs of last several miles.

0:34 (0:09) Cross Nisqually River.

0:40 (0:03) Cross Lake St. Clair with attractive homes along surrounding shoreline.

0:43 (0:00) Arrive East Olympia.

 EAST OLYMPIA, WA - This is as close as the Starlight gets to Washington's capital city, Olympia, just seven miles off to the right and situated at the southern end of Puget Sound.

0:00 (0:18) Depart East Olympia.

0:02 (0:16) Cross Deschutes River.

0:12 (0:06) Just south of Bucoda, cross Skookumchuck River.

0:18 (0:00) Cobblestone walkways front grounds of handsome brick station as train arrives Centralia. Large white building, situated atop bluffs on left, is Centralia Armory.

 CENTRALIA, WA - Founded in 1875 by a slave named George Washington, Centralia has grown to become a major food-processing and supply area. Pioneers constructed an unusual blockhouse along the Chehalis River to defend against Indians, and this interesting structure can still be seen in Fort Borst Park.

0:00 (0:50) Depart Centralia past profusion of logging operations, opportunistically located within easy access of Columbia and Willamette rivers.

0:06 (0:45) Traveling "Main Street" route through Chehalis, another fine old depot stands proudly on left.

0:12 (0:39) Cross Newaukum River.

0:25 (0:26) Passing through Winlock, note "World's Largest Egg" enshrined in glass monument on right. "Egg Day" festivities, held here each June, likewise recall community's former prominence in poultry industry.

0:35 (0:16) Cross Cowlitz River, which then follows intermittently on right.

0:47 (0:04) After passing through short tunnel, antiquated wooden trestle spans Cowlitz River, on right, which soon empties into Columbia River a few miles downstream.

0:48 (0:03) Approach Kelso-Longview with comely neighborhoods clustered along hillsides. A short distance downline, dramatic drawbridge spans Cowlitz River on right.

0:50 (0:00) Arriving Kelso-Longview, impressive Cowlitz County Courthouse can be seen across river on right.

 KELSO-LONGVIEW, WA - Lumbering has always been the

economic mainstay of the Kelso-Longview area. From the time the first sawmill was built in 1848 to the early 1920s, development was slow, but in 1922 Robert A. Long purchased 60,000 acres of timberland and then built the world's largest forest mill, starting the two cities toward becoming a major lumber-processing center. Located at the confluence of the Cowlitz and Columbia rivers, deep water port facilities give direct access to the world's markets.

0:00 (0:41) Weather permitting, departure from Kelso-Longview may afford views of truncated Mt. St. Helens (8,365 ft.) and Mt. Adams (12,307 ft.) on left, while further north stands imposing Mt. Rainier at 14,410 feet.

0:03 (0:38) On left, pass Kelso-Longview airport.

0:04 (0:37) Cross Coweeman River which too joins Columbia shortly downstream.

0:09 (0:31) Emerge into clearing, affording first view of Columbia River on right. Large stockpiles of timber are corralled out in water awaiting transport. Across river, familiar silhouette of cooling tower readily identifies 460-million dollar Trojan Nuclear Power Plant.

0:13 (0:28) Cross Kalama River.

0:15 (0:26) While passing through Kalama, note towering totem pole, entrenched along river banks on right.

0:24 (0:17) Cross Lewis River.

0:29 (0:12) Pass through pleasant little community of Ridgefield. Just south of town, old wooden bridge crosses Lewis River on right. Sudden onset of marshy terrain reflects abundant water resources of area.

0:36 (0:05) On right, train borders shoreline of Vancouver Lake.

0:40 (0:01) Great Western Malting Company dominates industrial sprawl on outskirts of Vancouver.

0:41 (0:00) Delightful chalet-style station greets passengers on left as train arrives Vancouver.

VANCOUVER, WA - Strategically placed on the Columbia River, where ocean, air, rail and highway transportation converge, Vancouver has become a major shipping hub of the Northwest. Its lengthy history (it is the oldest non-Indian settlement in Washington) saw the likes of a trading outpost of the Hudson's Bay Company, the construction of Fort Vancouver, and the presence of Ulysses S. Grant when he was but a mere lieutenant in the U.S. Army. Both Fort Vancouver and the U.S. Grant Museum are open to the public.

0:00 (0:19) Depart Vancouver, crossing Columbia River (and Washington/Oregon state line) into Portland. In midst of river, traverse Hayden Island, while vessels and dockside facilities of vast shipping industry abound on both banks.

0:10 (0:10) If both are on time, northbound and southbound Coast Starlights should meet about now.

0:13 (0:06) Cross Willamette River, which then follows on left into Portland station. Willamette is another important shipping channel, as evidenced by heavy concentration of industry along its banks. Dramatic bridges span this waterway, with downtown Portland skyline silhouetted in background.

0:18 (0:01) On left, grand old steamboat now provides nostalgic atmosphere for River Queen Restaurant.

0:19 (0:00) Arrive Portland beneath stately clock tower of Union Station.

PORTLAND, OR - Portland claims to be "a beautiful, clean, green American City," and indeed it is. An attractively restored downtown is the heart of this community set amongst forested hills along the Columbia River. Its mild climate makes it one of the most desirable cities in which to live in the Pacific Northwest.

And there seems to be energy here. Its seaport ships huge amounts of grain, major electronics firms have located here, there is a snappy new light rail system, and the city is still small enough to enjoy.

Union Station, 800 NW 6th Ave., an older section of downtown, but handy to Portland's city center. There are redcaps, luggage carts, a newsstand, vending machines, a snack bar and a very good restaurant. Pay-parking is in front of the station.

For arrival and departure information, call (503) 273-4865. For reservations and other information, call (503) 241-4290.

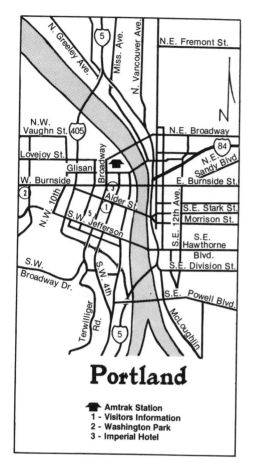

Portland

Amtrak Station
1 - Visitors Information
2 - Washington Park
3 - Imperial Hotel

Ticket window open daily, 7:30 am to 5:30 pm; waiting room, 7 am to 9:45 pm.

Cab stand at the station; Broadway Cab, 227-1234 and Radio Cab, 227-1212. **Local bus** stop is one block south of the station (chart in station). There is a direct Hertz **rental car** phone in the station, 249-5727. MAX (Metro Area Express) is Portland's new trolley (light rail) system that loops through the downtown core, then crosses Steel Bridge to reach the eastern suburbs, running during the day at 15-minute intervals. Buses and MAX are free within the downtown area; call 233-3511 for recorded information. **Greyhound** is only two blocks from the station at 550 NW 6th Ave., (503) 243-2323. **Portland International Airport** is eight miles northeast of the station.

Greater Portland and Visitors Assn., 26 SW Salmon, 97204; (503) 222-2223.

Imperial Hotel, 400 SW Broadway (at Stark), 97205; (503) 228-7221. Nice accommodations at reasonable rates; will pay for cab from the station which is eight blocks. $58.

Washington Park, 4001 SW Canyon Road, is one of the nation's nicest, has thousands of roses, a zoo with a train, Japanese gardens, a science museum, and an outstanding Western Forestry Center with exhibits of paper mills, lumbering and other unique aspects of this industry. **Gray Line,** (503) 226-6755, has some excellent tours of the city, the northern Oregon coast, the Columbia River and Mt. Hood. The **Annual Rose Festival** is held in early June, with a parade, band and symphonic concerts, sporting events and many other activities throughout the week.

0:00 (1:12) Depart Portland and immediately cross Willamette River. Colorful "butterfly" mural can be seen in midst of commercial district on right. After running on Burlington Northern rails since Seattle, we follow main line of Southern Pacific for remainder of trip to Los Angeles.
0:13 (0:59) On left, pass campus of Reed College.

Proceed for next few miles through attractive suburbs of Milwaukie and Gladstone. On clear days, Mt. Hood may be viewed on left, towering 11,235 feet in midst of Cascade Range. Mountains of Coast Range can be seen on right.
0:27 (0:45) Cross Clackamas River.
0:29 (0:43) Slip through historic Oregon City, end of Oregon Trail and one-time territorial capital. Pioneers believed Willamette Valley to be "The Great Heartland."
0:30 (0:42) Large hydroelectric facility harnesses power from Willamette River which rejoins momentarily on right.

For next several miles, enjoy colorful character of small agricultural communities, as train travels directly through town centers enroute to state capital.
0:40 (0:32) Cross Molalla River.
0:45 (0:27) Cross Pudding River.
0:53 (0:19) Passing through Woodburn, old Southern Pacific steam engine is preserved on left.

1:12 (0:00) Arrive Salem, passing directly adjacent to state government offices on right. Most prominent is gold-colored statue of early pioneer, standing atop marble tower of State Capitol Building. Immediately thereafter, pass campus of Willamette University, oldest such institution in the West.

SALEM, OR - There is some dispute over just who named this capital city of Oregon, but it does seem certain that it was named after Salem, Massachusetts. The capitol, one of the nation's newest, is constructed of beautiful white marble with fine murals and sculptures.

0:00 (0:27) Depart Salem.

0:04 (0:23) On left, pass Salem's Municipal Airport.

0:15 (0:12) Oregon's largest llama herd can be seen on right. These sure-footed camel cousins are becoming popular with hikers, both as pack animals and as wilderness companions.

0:19 (0:08) At south end of Jefferson, cross Santiam River.

0:27 (0:00) Arrive Albany through well-kept residential district. Old stone depot is interesting, yet unobtrusive like rest of town.

ALBANY, OR - The first steamboat reached Albany in 1852, the same year its first industry—a grist mill—was put into production. Finally, in 1870, the railroad reached here, but not until the builder of the then O&C Railroad received a $50,000 "incentive" from the residents so they would not be bypassed by the line. Albany is the home of the World Championship Timber Carnival, featuring tree topping, speed climbing, bucking, log rolling and axe throwing. Also, the largest Veterans' Day celebration in the nation is held here.

0:00 (0:37) Depart Albany.

0:08 (0:30) Cross Calapooia River.

0:25 (0:14) After passing through Harrisburg, cross Willamette River, having narrowed considerably since last observation.

0:36 (0:03) Approach Eugene through large Southern Pacific rail yards, while colorful murals adorn building walls on right.

0:40 (0:00) Lane County Jail borders on right as train arrives Eugene, Amtrak's westernmost stop.

EUGENE, OR - Lumbering remains Eugene's economic mainstay, while the University of Oregon lends a college atmosphere to this west-central Oregon community. Outdoor recreational opportunities are plentiful, most notably on the McKenzie River, which provides excellent fishing and boating.

0:00 (2:58) Departing Eugene, another interesting mural can be seen on right as train heads southeasterly toward Willamette National Forest.

0:02 (2:56) Train skirts University of Oregon campus on right before crossing Willamette River into sister-city of Springfield.

0:19 (2:39) Cross Willamette River, and follow to its source atop Cascade Summit. Numerous crossings occur throughout this stretch.

The ensuing 75-mile ascent is one of the most scenic routes in the country, with the jutting peaks of the Cascade Range providing a dramatic backdrop for the dense and colorful vegetation of the Willamette National Forest.

As the train slowly winds through tunnels and snowsheds, quaint little towns, snuggled within the wilderness, offer fascinating glimpses of a robust, pioneer life style. Majestic waterfalls, tumbling down the mountainsides, further embellish this spectacular scenery.

0:34 (2:22) On left, Lookout Point Reservoir dams Willamette River.

0:56 (1:59) Small town of Westfir is highlighted by beautiful covered bridge, spanning Willamette River on right.

1:00 (1:55) Begin climbing "The Hill" at Oakridge, an ambitious ascent of over 3,600 feet in 44 miles, that culminates atop Cascade Summit.

1:04 (1:51) Cross Salmon Creek.

1:45 (1:10) Arrive 4,840-foot Cascade Summit. Southern descent is much more gradual, proceeding well into California before losing appreciable altitude. Snow-depth gauges can be seen on right between summit and Chemult.

1:53 (0:54) Deep blue waters of Lake Odell border on left. Back on right and left, brief clearings in forest permit inspiring vistas of Cascade peaks.

2:22 (0:25) Cross Little Deschutes River.
2:47 (0:00) Arrive Chemult. Depot is conspicuous because of absence. In its place, a mere wooden gangplank escorts passengers onboard.

CHEMULT, OR - Situated between the Deschutes and the Winema national forests, Chemult is in the very heart of Oregon's mountains and lakes recreational lands. Bend, just 57 miles to the northeast, with year-round sunshine and the likes of swimming, golf, tennis, canoeing, hiking and horseback riding is one of the more popular Oregon vacation spots.

0:00 (1:13) Depart Chemult through dense woodlands of Winema National Forest. Milling and logging concerns are a most frequent sight throughout this stretch.
0:20 (0:56) Famed Crater Lake is perched high in the mountains, just 15 miles to the right.
0:37 (0:36) Cross Williamson River, which follows periodically on right. A few miles downstream, river plunges unexpectedly into colorful, rocky gorge.
0:49 (0:24) Pass through Chiloquin. Nearby Collier Memorial State Park features largest museum of logging equipment in U.S. Just outside town, cross Sprague River, which proceeds to join Williamson River, and flow south into Upper Klamath Lake.
0:59 (0:14) On right, begin skirting shoreline of Upper Klamath Lake, with Mt. McLoughlin (9,495 ft.) towering in distance. Between April and September, large white pelicans are a popular attraction of area.
1:13 (0:00) Arrive Klamath Falls.

KLAMATH FALLS, OR - Klamath Indians once cooked with steam from a vast reservoir of geothermal energy which still lies beneath this area. Thought to be one of the world's largest such stores of energy, it is currently used to heat businesses, schools and homes.
0:00 (2:25) Depart Klamath Falls.
2:25 (0:00) Arrive Dunsmuir.

DUNSMUIR, CA - This small recreational community is nestled in the foothills of 14,162-foot Mt. Shasta. Once a major railroad center of the Southern Pacific, it now enjoys an economy dominated by small resorts offering fine fishing in the summer and skiing in the winter.
0:00 (1:49) Depart Dunsmuir.
1:44 (0:00) Arrive Redding.

REDDING, CA - Lumbering and salmon fishing are both important to Redding, but its location at the northern terminus of the Sacramento Valley (the most northern point in California where orange and palm trees grow naturally) provides the weather and geography to attract thousands of vacationers to the area. Beautiful Lake Shasta, with its 370 miles of shoreline, offers boating and fishing, while wild and scenic rivers provide white-water canoeing for the more adventuresome. Additional attractions include tours of Shasta Caverns (reached only by boat) and Shasta Dam, three times as high as Niagara Falls and one of the most impressive structures in America. This is also the gateway to Lassen Volcanic National Park.
0:00 (1:12) Depart Redding.
1:14 (0:00) Arrive Chico.

CHICO, CA - Gold attracted the earliest settlers to this area, but it was rich agricultural lands that enticed many to stay. Chico was founded by one of California's most famous citizens, General John Bidwell, when he formed a 28,000-acre farming enterprise named Rancho Del, and which became the most renowned agricultural establishment in the state. Today, ample harvests of rice, almonds, walnuts, peaches, prunes and olives are produced in the area as well as numerous other crops and cattle. Bidwell's elaborate mansion is now a state park. Chico is not only a modern trade center, but is also home of California State University, Chico, where 12,000 students seek degrees in 20 fields, including business, education and nursing. South of here is Oroville Dam—the highest and largest earth-filled dam in the country.
0:00 (0:41) Depart Chico.

0:40 (0:00) Arrive Marysville.

MARYSVILLE, CA - As in the case of Chico, Marysville got its start when early-day prospectors flocked here to work placer claims in the area's streams. Also, as in Chico's case, the permanence of Marysville has been largely due to agriculture. Fruit and other crops are important to this Sacramento Valley town.

0:00 (0:59) Depart Marysville.

0:59 (0:00) Arriving Sacramento, gracious Spanish architecture highlights many buildings of downtown district on left. Ornamental-domed tower is City Hall, whose weighty bronze doors require at least two strong men to open for business each morning.

SACRAMENTO, CA - To describe Sacramento as a treasure chest of Western historical lore would still be something of an understatement. Consider first that the famous California "Gold Rush" began here when nuggets were discovered at Sutter's Mill in 1848. Only 12 years later, the Pony Express was welcomed into town at the completion of its first historic run. And in 1863, a group of Sacramento visionaries began charting a route across the Sierra Nevadas that would eventually become the most ambitious link in the nation's first transcontinental railroad.

Such monumental distinctions would seemingly be hard to surpass, although Sacramento's current role as one of the world's largest food production centers assures it a status of increasingly vital importance. The city, too, maintains statewide prestige as the capital of California.

As might be expected, historical highlights are the emphasis of Sacramento's major attractions, from the reconstructed facilities of Sutter's Fort, to the splendid array of Victorian homes preserved throughout the city. Of particular interest to train buffs is the California State Railroad Museum, located only one block from the Amtrak station. Here, sound effects and even simulated motion are used to re-create the romantic atmosphere surrounding the glory years of the railroad.

0:00 (0:20) Departing Sacramento, stately Capitol Building can be seen on left.

Built in 1869, gilded globe still remains atop dome, despite protestations of original architect who described it as "simply ridiculous and abominable—a slur on our tastes forever."

During 1906 remodeling, "modern" conveniences replaced 45 fireplaces that once heated building. Iron hitching posts surrounding carriage entrance were also lost at that time.

On immediate left is aforementioned California State Railroad Museum. Sacramento Locomotive Works are on right.

0:02 (0:17) Proceed across Sacramento River, noting on left riverboats along shore and interesting drawbridge a few blocks downstream.

0:10 (0:06) At considerable expense, railroad and highway have been elevated for several miles permitting underlying lands to be flooded for rice farming. On left, over 4,000 columns hold road above muddy croplands.

0:20 (0:00) Arrive Davis. Spanish motif of this handsome station is popular style of depots throughout southern California.

DAVIS, CA - Long known for its prolific production of agricultural crops, Davis is noted more recently for its pioneering attitude in the field of energy conservation. In 1975, the City Council enacted the nation's first energy conservation building code, setting standards for all new houses and apartments. A citywide recycling program is also highly successful. Most impressive, however, is Davis' claim that its many miles of scenic bicycle paths account for as much as 25% of the city's total vehicle traffic.

0:00 (0:44) Departing Davis, border University of California at Davis campus on right. Grapevines are part of school's renowned wine research program.

0:08 (0:18) Elongated antique shed at left sags with age, but still provides shelter for several hundred sheep.

0:24 (0:10) Passing through Suisun-Fairfield, stately, white-pillared Solano County Courthouse stands distinctively on right at terminus of palm-lined Union Avenue. Shortly thereafter, emerge upon waters of Suisun Bay.

0:34 (0:10) On immediate left, hundreds of Merchant Marine vessels are clustered in storage along shoreline, readily conjuring up images of Normandy invasion. Ships are awaiting tow to Sacramento where they will be unceremoniously cut into scrap. Meanwhile, invasion of different sort is evidenced on forward left, where docks are often overflowing with thousands of Japanese auto imports. Last ship before bridge is fabled Glomar Explorer, easily identified by helicopter pad on stern. Although ostensibly a research vessel, it has performed such feats as raising a sunken German submarine during World War II.

0:38 (0:06) Cross drawbridge spanning Suisun Bay. Structure is over one mile long and stands 70 feet above water. Prior to its construction in 1930, train was broken down into sections and ferried across bay. Once on southern shore, entangled maze of refinery apparatus escorts train into Martinez.

0:47 (0:00) Arrive Martinez. While in station, Martinez Museum can be seen in old frame house on left.

 MARTINEZ, CA - This important commercial and military port was also the home of John Muir, one of the nation's earliest and most outspoken conservationists. His house is now preserved as a National Historic Site. Joe Dimaggio Drive is on the right side of the train, honoring the "Yankee Clipper" who was raised here.

0:00 (0:30) Depart Martinez along Carquinez Strait, connecting Suisun and San Pablo bays. Carquinez Bridge looms impressively in foreground right, while on left, famed golden hills are subtly encroaching upon landscape.

0:09 (0:20) With town of Crockett huddled on hillside left, travel directly through midst of C & H sugar refinery. Immediately thereafter, train bears south along shores of San Pablo Bay.

0:29 (0:00) Arrive Richmond.

RICHMOND, CA - Richmond's popularity as a convenient suburban stop is enhanced by its trackside connections with BART, a rapid transit system servicing many outlying regions throughout the Bay Area.

0:00 (0:12) Departure from Richmond affords first view of dramatic San Fran-

cisco skyline across bay. Golden Gate Bridge can be seen north of city, while Bay Bridge connects with Oakland to the south. Alcatraz Island is also visible below Golden Gate Bridge.

0:05 (0:07) On right, pass Golden Gate Race Track.

0:07 (0:05) Intimidating "jumps" provide challenge for water-skiers at Aquatic Park on right.

0:12 (0:00) Arrive Oakland. Amtrak buses are waiting at station for passengers enroute to San Francisco.

 OAKLAND, CA - See page 192.

SAN FRANCISCO, CA - It was in 1848, when the "city" had approximately 800 residents, that Sam Shannon discovered gold and started San Francisco's first boom. It has never been the same since. It soon became a bustling, thriving supply center and international port, as people and goods streamed into the area. The city has had its setbacks—the most notable being the devastating earthquake that rocked the area April 18, 1906. The entire business district (as well as many other parts of the city) was completely destroyed. But rebuilding was rapid, and expansion continued. The 1989 quake that registered a hefty 6.9 on the Richter Scale severely damaged two areas of the metroplex, but the city has rebounded from that disaster with style.

Two bridges have been key to San Francisco's development. The Bay Bridge linked the peninsula to Oakland in 1936, and then the Golden Gate Bridge was completed in 1937, giving the city an important direct highway to the north. World War II saw further growth as the area became an important military region. Today the city has a solid based economy and is the financial hub of the West.

Tourism has also boomed in the City by the Bay—and it's no wonder. Superior restaurants, fashionable stores, a sophisticated blend of cultures, all in a perfect setting. It's America's Paris—but perhaps better.

Transbay Terminal, 425 Mission St., is in the lower downtown, just

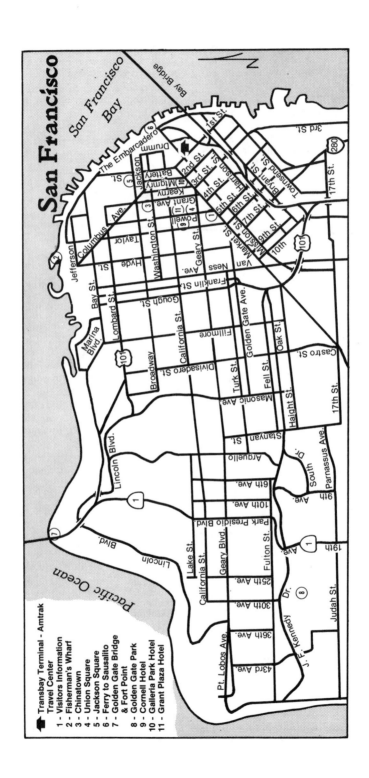

San Francisco

Transbay Terminal - Amtrak
Travel Center
1 - Visitors Information
2 - Fisherman's Wharf
3 - Chinatown
4 - Union Square
5 - Jackson Square
6 - Ferry to Sausalito
7 - Golden Gate Bridge
    & Fort Point
8 - Golden Gate Park
9 - Cornell Hotel
10 - Galleria Park Hotel
11 - Grant Plaza Hotel

off Market Street. Amtrak passengers are bused between here and the Oakland Amtrak station. The terminal has two snack bars, a coffee shop and a mini-mart. There is covered pay-parking and a large transit directory upstairs for city bus and BART users. There are no redcaps, but station personnel will assist with luggage.

For reservations and other information, call (415) 982-8512. The waiting room is open 24 hours.

(CalTrain commuter trains south to San Jose leave from the S.P. 4th Street Station at 4th and Townsend, just over a mile from the Transbay Terminal.)

Cab stand is at the terminal; Yellow Cab, 626-2345; City Cab, 468-7200. BART (subway) is approximately five blocks at Montgomery and Market streets, and also at Drumm and Market streets. Call 788-2278. For **local bus and cable car** information, call 673-6864. Most all major **rental cars** are located nearby. **Greyhound,** 433-1500 and **Trailways,** 982-6400, are at the terminal. The **airport** is 16 miles south of the Transbay Terminal. The **Airport Bus Terminal** is at Ellis and Taylor streets.

Powell and Market streets, lower level of Hallidie Plaza. For current activities recording, call 391-2001. Write or call **San Francisco Convention and Visitors Bureau,** P.O. Box 6977, San Francisco, CA 94101, (415) 391-2000.

Cornell Hotel, 715 Bush St., 94104; (415) 421-3154. European flavored, small and unpretentious. Well managed and comfortable. Fine restaurant in the basement. Breakfast included. Just off Powell, eight blocks from Transbay Terminal. $60.

-**Galleria Park Hotel,** 191 Sutter St., 94104; (415) 781-3060 or 800-792-9639 (outside CA). Luxurious rooms. Close to Union Square shopping, yet only four blocks from Transbay Terminal. $120.

-**Grant Plaza,** 465 Grant Ave. (at Pine), 94108; (415) 434-3883. Modest accommodations at a budget price. Excellently located at the gateway to Chinatown, five blocks from Transbay Terminal. $42.

Sightseeing in San Francisco is relatively easy (except for the hill climbing) due to its unusual compaction and good public transportation.

Fisherman's Wharf, in the area of Jefferson and Taylor streets, is a fine collection of restaurants specializing in seafoods, unusual shops and harbor cruise boats. This is also the location of **Ghiradelli Square** and **The Cannery.**

Golden Gate Bridge and Fort Point, at the north end of the city on U.S. 101, is the world's most famous and attractive suspension bridge in a spectacular setting. **Golden Gate Park,** 1017 acres bounded by Fulton Street, Stanyan St., Lincoln Blvd. and the Pacific Ocean, has many points of interest including: Asian Art Museum, Japanese Tea Garden, Shakespeare's Garden, Golden Gate Golf Course, bridle paths, lakes and beautiful landscaping.

Chinatown, several blocks in the area of Grant and Washington, has many restaurants and shops and the largest Chinese community outside of the Orient.

Union Square, at Geary and Powell streets, is the center of the San Francisco shopping and hotel district. **Jackson Square,** actually a block bounded by Jackson, Montgomery, Gold and Sansom streets, was once the province of design professionals and home furnishing buyers, but has become a popular spot for sightseers. Antique shops, art dealers, and other shops in a 19th-century setting. There are elegant wholesaler window displays. The entrance is on Jackson and Montgomery streets.

Cable Cars provide transportation and great fun. The **ferry to Sausalito** can be taken from the Ferry Terminal at Market St. and The Embarcadero. An excellent, inexpensive way to see the bay and the city skyline.

0:00 (1:13) Depart Oakland. Gleaming BART trains contrast sharply with an otherwise uninspiring industrial "Bowery."

0:02 (1:11) On right, impressive Bay Bridge, spanning San Francisco Bay, links cities of Oakland and San Francisco.

0:08 (1:02) Rail fans will be intrigued by cornucopia of older rail passenger cars, both Amtrak and private varnish, reposing in coach yard on right.

0:09 (1:04) Wharfside shops, restaurants and motels of Jack London Square cluster around colony of sailboats and other pleasure craft on right. This may become Oakland stop for Amtrak.

0:19 (0:54) Scene of prim Oakland Hospital, on right, has been gratuitously "enhanced" by lengthy graffiti-laden wall.

0:23 (0:50) Inverted dish, on right, is Alameda County stadium, home of baseball's Athletics and former turf of erstwhile Oakland Raiders.

0:39 (0:34) Flower farm presents a spectrum spectacular on left.

0:46 (0:27) White mountains of pure salt extracted from Bay by Morton and Leslie salt companies loom on right.

0:55 (0:18) Small cove provides shelter for multitude of small sailing craft. Larger structures across Bay are blimp hangers of Moffet Field Naval Air Station, built during thirties and now on National Historic Register.

0:57 (0:16) Tops of roller coasters and several other thrill rides are lofty protrusions above Mariotts Great America amusement park on right.

1:06 (0:07) Scores of tank-like vehicles beside FMC plant on left are armored personnel carriers, both M113s and more sophisticated Bradley Fighting Vehicles. Many of M113s are destined for Pakistan while Turkey and Saudi Arabia are major customers for controversial Bradleys—a vehicle that performs well in desert heat, but, according to critics, is slow and vulnerable.

1:08 (0:05) View of University of Santa Clara, on right, is dominated by athletic stadium and bubble-enclosed sporting facility.

1:10 (0:03) Ancient brick roundhouse with turntable highlights expansive Southern Pacific rail yards at San Jose.

1:13 (0:00) Arrive San Jose.

SAN JOSE, CA - Spanish conquistadores were the first to set eyes on the lush Santa Clara Valley in 1769. Soon thereafter, in 1777, San Jose was founded, making it the oldest incorporated city in California. Orchards and vineyards abound, and familiar names, such as Paul Masson and Almaden, have wineries here. Education also thrives. Stanford University, Santa Clara and San Jose State College are all situated here, the latter being the state's oldest institutions of higher learning—founded in 1874. Transfer here for peninsula Caltrain service to San Francisco.

0:00 (1:21) Departing San Jose, double-decked Caltrains line tracks on left.

0:16 (1:02) Town of Coyote more or less marks point where industrial and citified environs of Bay area give way to rich agrarian lands of central California.

0:32 (0:48) Even sealed environment of The Coast Starlight does not always prevent one's nose from verifying that Gilroy is known as "The Garlic Capital of the World."

A great festival is held here each year when cooks and connoisseurs from around the world come to prepare and savor garlic delicacies during the first full weekend in August. Up to ten tons of garlic can be depleted during this gala event. Although the town may occasionally reek a bit, it boasts some nice points of interest which can be observed on the right. First is the attractive St. Mary's Church adorned with its shiny gold bell; a bit further downline is the Old City Hall with its highly unusual clock tower; an interesting zodiac-looking mural enhancing the wall of a track-side building; and then the Spanish-styled depot itself.

0:37 (0:42) Extensive garlic fields now border each side of track.

0:41 (0:34) Starlight now moves one valley westward by traversing through Gabilan Range to reach Salinas River Valley. This pleasant stretch features golden-soft, rolling hills and bare-trunked eucalyptus trees that occasionally line each side of track. Trees were originally imported from Australia for use as ties during early railroad construction.

0:52 (0:28) Enormous cavern, on left, was once a dolomite quarry, but after being fairly depleted, aggregate became primary product from this huge hole. Assortment of loading contrivances raise mined material from below and then directly onto rail cars.

0:55 (0:15) Acres and acres of truck farms now spread out across valley.

1:10 (0:12) At Slough, numerous species of waterfowl, including egrets, herons and pelicans, frequent backwater on left.

1:12 (0:10) On right, Moss Landing Power Plant of Pacific Gas and Electric Co. uses natural gas and oil as its power source. Just to south, emitting white clouds of "smoke," is Kaiser Refactories which manufacture firebrick and related products.

1:14 (0:08) Big, bushy "weeds" in field surrounding Castroville are actually tops of artichoke plants. Forget the garlic, we are now in "The Artichoke Capital of the World."

1:19 (0:04) Graves School, a lonely but lovely "one-roomer," makes a nostalgic centerpiece for vegetable field on right.

1:23 (0:00) Arrive Salinas.

SALINAS, CA - Much of the flavor of Salinas' environs has been captured in the writings of Pulitzer Prize winner John Steinbeck, who wrote in glowing prose about his home town's locale. Sometimes referred to as the country's "Salad Bowl," its warm temperatures and abundant sunshine foster an agricultural cornucopia. This is the edge of the Big Sur country, and the Monterey Peninsula is just 12 miles to the west.

0:00 (2:38) Depart Salinas. On right, in downtown Salinas, ancient church-building-turned restaurant features four skinny towers protruding from its top, bedecked with attractive golden mosaic.

0:05 (2:31) Schilling spice operation is on left.

0:08 (2:29) On right, large Firestone facility appears somewhat out of place amidst surrounding croplands.

0:22 (2:16) Sprawling "confines" of Soledad Correctional Facilities are just to left.

0:29 (2:09) On right, Salinas River now accompanies train along its course through Salinas River Valley.

0:39 (1:59) Just before 1,305-foot tunnel, colorful single-engine planes parked on right are used for dusting crops with pesticides. Tunnel (number 5½) was constructed in 1923 for curve-reducing line change.

0:46 (1:51) Crates of local produce, including lettuce, grapes, tomatoes, onions and carrots, await shipment on docks of packing companies in King City.

0:50 (1:49) An early bit of Americana appears on side of weather-beaten barn, on right, encouraging populace to "Chew Mail Pouch Tobacco."

0:55 (1:44) Swooping S curve of U.S. 101 curls across valley floor in distance to right.

0:56 (1:43) At southern end of San Lucas, small Christ-figure hovers protectively above tiny cemetery, nestled below trackside on right.

1:08 (1:29) Many operating wells can be seen while passing through extensive oil fields of San Ardo.

1:13 (1:24) Train rejoins Salinas River on right, and crosses a few miles downline.

1:26 (1:13) On right, pass Camp Roberts facilities of California National Guard.

1:32 (1:10) Unusual "bell wall" highlights grounds of Mission San Miguel on right. Intriguing adobe structure, built in 1797, boasts best-maintained interior of all California missions.

1:36 (1:06) Endless rows of white fences identify most attractive horse farm on left.

1:40 (1:02) Glide through Paso Robles, historic stage stop and approximate halfway point between San Francisco and Los Angeles.

1:49 (0:54) On right, at Templeton, billboard for Pesenti Winery entices passersby with "tours and tasting room." Although recently rediscovered in region, wine-making was introduced by Franciscans 200 years earlier, cultivating vineyards on mission grounds to supply needs of church.

1:56 (0:47) On outskirts of Atascadero, Santa Lucia foothills border attractive golf course on right.

For the next half hour, the ensuing negotiation of Cuesta Grade can be subtly enthralling. Although not what one might describe as spectacular, this small adventure nevertheless seems to capture much of what is romantic and unique to rail travel itself.

The monolithic rock formations, protruding suddenly out of nowhere, seem to typify the many curiosities that are encountered "off the beaten path." The frequent tunnels, engineering marvels unto themselves, at once accentuate the myriad of sounds that are as much a part of the rail experience as the vistas that loom outside.

Winding gracefully around two horse-shoe curves into San Luis Obispo, the entire train comes into view. Marvel at its simplicity and the simple pleasures it can provide.

2:32 (0:08) Reversing ten-degree horse-shoe curves, Goldtree and Servano, are fitting finale to Cuesta journey—and also herald a return to "civilization" with fortress-like California Men's Colony dominating scene on right.

2:33 (0:07) Cross splendid old trestle, seen moments earlier during descent of Cuesta Grade.

2:36 (0:02) On left, note athletic field and campus of California Polytechnic State University.

2:38 (0:00) Arrive at San Luis Obispo's attractive 1934 depot.

SAN LUIS OBISPO, CA - Originally a mission founded in 1772—Mission San Louis Obispo de Tolosa, named for a 13th-century French saint and bishop (because a nearby volcanic peak was thought to resemble a bishop's cap)—this city is now one of the more popular destinations for those wishing to explore the scenic central coast of California. Morro Bay, Pismo Beach, San Simeon and local wineries are some of the area's highlights. California Polytechnic State University, with an outstanding agricultural program, and smaller Cuesta College are both located here.

0:00 (2:06) Departing San Luis Obispo, note turntable on right, used to reverse direction of locomotives. Proceed thereafter on slow, winding route through more hills of Santa Lucia Range.

0:06 (2:00) If both are on schedule, north-bound and southbound Coast Starlights should meet about now.

0:17 (1:49) Passing through Grover City, old Amtrak coaches have been converted into restaurant on right.

0:27 (1:39) Cross Santa Maria River on outskirts of Guadalupe. Once in town, note beautiful old mission on left.

0:39 (1:27) Another working oilfield abuts trackside at Casmalia.

After Casmalia, the Starlight enters Vandenberg Air Force Base, America's western spaceport. Here, the Strategic Air Command conducts missile crew training and tests both Peacekeeper and Minuteman ICBMs as well as numerous varieties of smaller missiles. It is the only military installation of its kind.

The base is huge. With 154 square miles of real estate and a working population of 12,000, it is the Air Force's third largest. More than 1,600 launches have been conducted here. And although space shots are usually associated with Cape Canaveral, Vandenberg has placed half again as many satellites into orbit as the Cape. Vandenberg's location is ideal for putting objects into polar orbit which allows surveillance of the entire globe.

Various launch complexes can be spotted for the next 25 minutes or so.

0:43 (1:23) Vandenberg's Minuteman Area is off to right.

0:51 (1:15) Three-mile-long Vandenberg Airfield is on left. Strip can accommodate space shuttle landings should base become site for future shuttle launches.

0:52 (1:14) Pacific Ocean now comes into full view. For next 113 miles, spectacular vistas abound as train skirts atop seacliffs, overlooking frothy tumult of pounding surf. Because of Vandenberg and two large ranches, public can see much of this country only by train.

0:56 (1:10) Cross Santa Ynez River. Unusually colorful ground cover is most pronounced over next few miles.

1:00 (1:06) Gantries of SLCs (space launch complexes) Four and Five are spread out for next two miles on left.

1:03 (1:03) Pernales (or Honda) Point, on right, has often been confused for Point Arguello a bit further south, causing more than one maritime calamity after ships have mistakenly turned eastward.

1:04 (1:02) SLC Six, nicknamed "Slick Six," lies huddled in hills on left. This 2.5-billion-dollar spacecraft facility is world's most sophisticated. Designed to be first space shuttle launch facility on West Coast, complex was placed on indefinite hold after 1986 "Challenger" disaster.

1:05 (1:01) Lighthouse on right deters ocean-going vessels from jutting cliffs of Pt. Arguello. Stout rock reef protects tower and keeper's residence from inclement seas.

1:14 (0:52) Exit southern boundary of

Coast Starlight, near San Luis Obispo, California

Vandenberg Air Force Base at Jalama Beach.

1:18 (0:48) Another lighthouse sits prominently atop bluff of Pt. Concepcion. Los Angeles is only about 30 miles south of here, but a much greater distance east, since California's coastline curls sharply inward at this point.

1:41 (0:25) Picnic tables and grassy tracts adorn Refugio State Beach on right. On left, Santa Ynez Mountains loom in background, stretching south past Santa Barbara.

1:48 (0:18) On right, pass El Capitan State Beach.

1:50 (0:16) Small lagoon sits picturesquely below trackside on right. Off-shore drilling rigs and associated facilities at beachside are frequent sights throughout duration of Pacific Coast run.

1:51 (0:15) Late one February evening in 1942, only two months after Pearl Harbor, a Japanese submarine surfaced offshore and lobbed several rounds from its deck cannon into Ellwood oil field off to right. Damage was light, but incident heightened pressures to relocate West Coast Japanese Americans.

1:53 (0:13) Before turning inland toward Santa Barbara station, note San Miguel Island out on right. Three more islands extend south, forming chain that delineates Santa Barbara Channel. Explorer Juan Cabrillo, who discovered islands in 1542, is buried on San Miguel.

1:57 (0:09) In distance on right, lofty bell tower is landmark of University of California at Santa Barbara campus.

2:04 (0:02) Historic Santa Barbara Mission can be seen on left. Dubbed "Queen of the Missions," distinctive structure is only one in California to employ twin-tower design. Lovely fountain fronting building is fed by aqueduct, built by Indians in 1808.

2:06 (0:00) Arrive Santa Barbara. Immediately left of station is 100-year-old Moreton Bay fig tree, its lengthy branches spread majestically across four-lane thoroughfare.

SANTA BARBARA, CA - In 1782, the Santa Barbara Presidio Real, which means "Royal Fortress," was constructed, marking the beginning of the city but the end of Spain's fortress construction in the New World. Then in 1786, the Santa Barbara Mission was founded which was just one of 21 built by Spanish Franciscans. Although the flags of Mexico, independent California and the U.S. have also flown over Santa Barbara, its Spanish heritage still pervades. Even after a devastating earthquake in 1925 destroyed most of the city, rebuilding made liberal use of white adobe and red-tile roofs, using distinctive Spanish-Moorish architecture. Situated on a sweeping palm-lined beach with mountains for a backdrop, Santa Barbara is one of America's jewels.

0:00 (0:40) Depart Santa Barbara south-bound through host of well-endowed residential neighborhoods.

0:04 (0:36) Lagoon, on right, is bird refuge and centerpiece of zoological gardens.

0:05 (0:35) Passing through beautiful little community of Miramar, old station house and passenger cars have been cleverly converted to a restaurant on left.

0:07 (0:33) Overexposed sunbathers are often quite "visible" as train passes by Summerland nude beach on right.

0:10 (0:30) Huge snowman and friends are year-round attraction on left.

0:18 (0:22) As seacliffs dissipate at Mussel Shoals, remainder of coastline route travels directly along beach into Ventura. Lengthy causeway, seen here on right, extends out to rocky islands where first completely underwater oil well began production in 1964. Tracks follow old stage road that was only open while tide was out.

0:29 (0:11) Cross Matilija Creek as it spills into ocean.

0:30 (0:09) Now heading inland, Ventura County Fairgrounds are conspicuous on right, while resplendent San Buenaventura Mission stands proudly on left. Since first constructed in 1809, mission has been used continuously, except for four-month period in 1812 when series of violent earthquakes required its temporary closure. San Buenaventura was also only California mission to ever use wooden bells, which have subsequently been removed from belfry and now are preserved in Mission Museum.

0:35 (0:05) Cross Santa Clara River.

0:40 (0:00) Arrive Oxnard.

 OXNARD, CA - A fertile plain makes Oxnard a citrus center and food-processing hub. Sugar was once important, but this has given way to lima beans which make up nearly half of the world's supply.

0:00 (0:20) Depart Oxnard through bountiful farmlands and orchards of Simi Valley.

0:09 (0:11) In Camarillo, quaint mission-style church sits atop hillside on left. On eastern outskirts, imposing plantation-type estate overlooks fields on left.

0:19 (0:01) Scenic Simi Creek crosses beneath tracks several times as it lazily meanders through area of Moorpark.

0:20 (0:00) Arrive Simi Valley.

SIMI VALLEY, CA - This is a northern suburb of Los Angeles.

0:00 (0:40) Depart Simi Valley and continue toward Santa Susana.

0:13 (0:35) At Santa Susana, train suddenly embarks on unlikely adventure across "mini-pass" of Santa Susana hills. Imposing rock formations, cactus fields and frequent tunnels (a popular setting for numerous Hollywood Westerns) highlight this delightful, yet seemingly incongruous intrusion. Once at "summit," descend into sprawling expanse of Los Angeles megalopolis.

0:21 (0:27) Passing through Chatsworth, proceed through residential district with swimming pools, an ever-popular adjunct of many homes.

0:28 (0:20) Approaching Van Nuys, scene becomes largely industrial. Sperry, Anheuser Busch, General Motors and Schlitz are but a few of the more renowned corporations whose facilities dot this stretch.

0:29 (0:19) On right, pass Van Nuys airport.

0:36 (0:12) Good view of Santa Monica Mountains is now afforded on right, while San Gabriels border in background on left.

0:38 (0:10) On left, pass Hollywood-Burbank airport.

0:48 (0:00) Arrive Glendale. This tidy

Spanish-style depot, replete with ornamental scroll-work, has been used as a backdrop for many motion pictures.

GLENDALE, CA - Last stop before Los Angeles, and situated on the edge of Hollywood, Glendale is enhanced by many impressive hillside homes.

0:00 (0:14) Departing Glendale, note lush acreage of Forest Lawn Memorial Park on left. Palatial, castle-like building in foreground is "Great Mausoleum." As well as its conventional use, mausoleum boasts a vaunted collection of memorial art, including replicas of Michelangelo's major works, and a glorious stained-glass recreation of da Vinci's "Last Supper."

Also prominent is "Hall of Crucifixion-Resurrection," seen atop Mt. Forest Lawn. Dedicated in 1951, building houses Jan Styka's magnificent painting, "The Crucifixion," which measures 195 feet long and 45 feet high.

0:05 (0:09) Parallel concrete channel on right that sometimes becomes Los Angeles River.

0:06 (0:08) Perched atop bluff on right is Dodger Stadium, home of Major League Baseball's 1988 champions.

0:09 (0:05) On left, Lawry's California Center is notable manufacturer of spices and food products.

0:10 (0:04) On left, cluster of tall buildings is Los Angeles County Hospital which operates in conjunction with University of Southern California.

0:11 (0:03) Crossing Los Angeles River avails good view of downtown Los Angeles skyline on forward right. Predominant older tower is Los Angeles City Hall, while double-domed building in foreground houses Post Office annex.

0:13 (0:01) On left, pass Los Angeles County Jail.

0:14 (0:00) Arrive Los Angeles.

LOS ANGELES, CA - Los Angeles is big. It has nearly 14 million inhabitants and will someday overtake New York City as the nation's largest metropolitan area. The largest Hispanic population outside of Mexico is here and the largest assemblage of Japanese outside of Japan call this home. The suburb was invented here after World War II, and expansion has never stopped.

Los Angeles' reputation is as mixed as its populace—flakey fads and funky fashions; perpetual sunshine and perpetual smog; freeways free of nothing but tolls; Tinsel Town with a lot of tarnish. But obviously, there is a huge attraction here; it is one of the most visited cities in the world.

The first visitor to arrive was Juan Cabrillo, a Portuguese conquistador who landed here in 1542. This was the discovery of California and it was claimed in the name of Spain. Two hundred years later the area was reached by an overland expedition, and in 1781 Governor Felipe de Neve established by proclamation the "City of our Lady Queen of the Angels." In 1822, Spanish rule ended and the city became part of the California Territory.

All southwestern trains wind up in LA, so it is a city that western rail passengers have come to know, even if for only an "overnight" between trains. Whether you're making connections or have come to see Southern California, it's possible to see some of the sights, contrary to conventional wisdom, without owning or renting a car. Amtrak's service between San Diego and Santa Barbara opens up myriad possibilities.

Union Passenger Terminal, 800 North Alameda St., 90012. One of the nation's most attractive stations, built in California Mission/Moorish style, and located in the heart of Los Angeles, is now being renovated to accommodate shops and a bus terminal. The station has a parcel check for ticketed passengers, luggage carts, redcaps, handicap transfer, a restaurant, food and beverage vending machines, newsstand, gift shop and adjacent pay-parking.

Call (213) 624-0171 or 800-USA-RAIL for arrival and departure information as well as reservations and other information. Ticket window hours are 5:45 am to 11 pm; the waiting room is open 24 hours.

Cab stand at the station; Independent, 385-8294; L.A., 627-7000; United Independent, 653-5050. **Local bus** at the station; 626-4455. Budget, (213) 747-0090, and National, (213) 746-3194, have free pick up at the station. **Grey-**

Los Angeles

Amtrak Station
1 - Visitors Information
2 - Downtown Area (Hotels)
3 - Queen Mary
4 - Disneyland

5 - Six Flags Magic Mountain
6 - Universal Studio Tours
7 - NBC Studio Tours
8 - Knotts Berry Farm

hound, (213) 620-1200. **Los Angeles International Airport** is approximately 18 miles southwest of the station. Amtrak has **connecting bus** service to various Southern California towns, including Bakersfield for San Joaquin trains.

Visitor Information Center, 695 S. Figueroa St., 90071; (213) 689-8822.

Figueroa Hotel, 939 Figueroa St., 90015; (213) 627-8971 or 800-421-9092. Medium size, older hotel, wonderfully maintained with spacious accommodations. Warm, Spanish-style lobby.

National rental cars on the premises. Laundromat. About a $7 cab ride (two miles) from the station. Near shopping, convention center and financial district. $72.

-Best Western Inntowne Hotel, 925 S. Figueroa St., 90015; (213) 628-2222. Free downtown (and Amtrak) shuttle service. Laundromat. Next to Figueroa Hotel listed above. $80.

-Best Western Hotel Tokyo, 328 E. First St., 90012; (213) 617-2000. Japanese speaking staff, next to Japanese Village Plaza. Opened in 1987. Very handy to the

Los Angeles Union Passenger Terminal

station, about four blocks. $82.

There are two older downtown hotels for the economy-minded, also fairly close to the station:

-Stillwell Hotel, 838 S. Grand Ave., 90017; (213) 627-1151 or 800-553-4774. A nicely remodeled, quiet, budget accommodation, with some older clientele. Across from the Chase Plaza. Laundromat. About two miles from the station. $45.

-Clark Hotel, 426 South Hill St., 90013; (213) 624-4121. Currently undergoing a much-needed renovation project, starting with the upper floor. About a mile from the station. Hotel looks closed because of subway construction but offers newly remodeled rooms at $50.

It's possible to breathe in much of the city's beginnings just outside the station. **El Pueblo de Los Angeles State Historic Park,** immediately across from station, is the birthplace of Los Angeles. Many rebuilt structures are around the old plaza. **Avila Adobe** is the oldest existing house in Los Angeles. **Olvera Street** has numerous picturesque Mexican shops and restaurants along one of the first streets in the old city. A great place to spend some time while waiting for a train. The two Mexican restaurants, La Golondrina and El Pasco, are popular lunch spots. La Golondrina (the swallow) is in the first brick edifice in LA, built in 1850.

The Museum of Contemporary Art is about a mile from the station, downtown at 250 S. Grand Ave., and **The Music Center of Los Angeles,** at 135 N. Grand, is home of the Los Angeles Philharmonic Orchestra, Joffrey Ballet and other performing arts.

Grayline has various **city tours,** with hotel pick up and drop off.

Of course, **not** within walking distance are some of LA's most popular destinations: Disneyland, The Lakers, The Queen Mary, Universal Studios, goofy Venice, cruises to Catalina and Knott's Berry Farm, to name but a few.

Los Angeles
San Diego

San Diegans

Although it's not officially called the Southern California Corridor, that's what it is. It takes several trains daily, scurrying both directions between Los Angeles and San Diego, to handle the demands of this densely peopled strip of Southern California coast. Although speeds can reach 90 mph at times, a clutter of stops holds the running time for most of the trains to 2¾ hours—a time freeway drivers can usually better. However, the train ride hardly compares to the freeway hassle.

Stops along the Santa Fe's "Surf Line" include Anaheim (Disneyland) and San Juan Capistrano (fine beaches and its mission of swallow fame). South of Capistrano the views are particuarly good where the tracks hug the shore for several miles, as sunbathers and surfers speckle the beaches on one side and cliffside houses with ocean views are almost as abundant on the other.

The ultimate southbound destination, of course, is San Diego, where the classic mission-style Santa Fe station is located just a stone's throw from the ever-popular harbor area. The "Tijuana Trolley" departs regularly for the Mexican border.

Train service is from early morning to early evening and is handled with Amfleet equipment. Snacks and sandwiches are available on each train while checked baggage is only available on selected trains. Telephones are available in the food service cars and in Custom Class cars. The reserved Custom Class Service, with roomier seating and free coffee, tea, orange juice and newspapers, is for a slightly higher fare.

Besides "Thruway" buses, two San Diegans, one northbound and one southbound, have extended runs to and from Santa Barbara.

Route Log

For route between Santa Barbara and Los Angeles, see page 272.

 LOS ANGELES, CA - See page 273.

0:00 (0:34) Backing out of Los Angeles Union Passenger Terminal, and then curling north at Mission Tower, San Diegan positions itself on main line of Santa Fe for its southward jaunt. (San Diegans have sometimes used "push-pull" equipment. When this occurs, backing maneuver is omitted.)

0:05 (0:29) Excellent view of Los Angeles cityscape on right where distinctive white-towered City Hall has center stage. Take note of old stone bridges that cross over tracks along this section. Their sculpted pilasters are reminiscent of ancient Rome and memorialize an era of Los Angeles long gone. Los Angeles River, encased in concrete on left, parallels our course for several minutes.

0:07 (0:27) Amtrak coach yard is on immediate right where a gaggle of Superliner cars are stored and await service on trains such as Desert Wind, Sunset Ltd., Southwest Chief and Coast Starlight.

0:09 (0:25) Diesel shops, roundhouse and its companion turntable are on right where twenty or so F-40 Amtrak diesels can generally be counted. Upon passing this facility, train curves sharply to left and crosses Los Angeles River.

0:12 (0:22) Acres of truck trailers used on piggyback freight trains are assembled on left at north end of Santa Fe rail yards.

0:14 (0:20) Office building of Santa Fe Railroad on left marks southern end of yards.

0:24 (0:10) Pass through refinery operations and active oil wells of Santa Fe Springs. One of area's larger tank farms will soon be seen on left.

0:31 (0:03) Perhaps more than one hundred assorted light aircraft at airport serving Fullerton area are in very midst of dense residential area on right.

0:34 (0:00) Arrive Fullerton. Note home of well-known Donald Duck citrus juice on left just before reaching station. The Santa Fe station, on left, is a delight. Its pink-stucco facade topped with a dark, red-tile roof is further enhanced by unusually large arch-shaped windows and accents of fine grill work. Landscaping with palms furnishes a near-perfect setting for this lovely station.

 FULLERTON, CA - As you may have guessed from the citrus juice operation just mentioned, Fullerton has had its roots in the citrus industry. Los Angeles' growth to the south has now made Fullerton virtually indistinguishable from its much larger northern neighbor.

0:00 (0:07) Depart Fullerton.

0:03 (0:04) Old Victorian house on immediate left appears to feel a bit uncomfortable surrounded by far less distinctive but newer homes.

0:06 (0:01) Nearing Anaheim, the obvious question is: "Where's Disneyland?" Look off to the right—a sharp eye can spot The Matterhorn, its white top jutting into the California haze.

0:07 (0:00) Arrive Anaheim's $853,000 modernistic station immediately below on right. Looming immediately behind is Anaheim Stadium, home of California Angels and Los Angeles Rams.

ANAHEIM, CA - Although best-known for Disneyland, that granddaddy of all theme parks, it should also be thought of as the Valencia orange heartland of California. Even the county's name

is Orange. Its agricultural heritage is more than one hundred years old, having received its start when ex-Fortyniners-turned-farmers moved here from San Francisco and German colonists came here to raise grapes. The name is derived from the nearby Santa Ana River and "heim," the German word for home.

0:00 (0:09) Depart Anaheim.

0:04 (0:05) Old Orange Station is on left, while downtown high rises of Orange are just off to right.

0:09 (0:00) Arrive Santa Ana.

SANTA ANA, CA - We are still in Orange County—as a matter of fact this is the county seat.

0:00 (0:18) Depart Santa Ana.

0:04 (0:14) On right, two enormous hangars which housed World War II blimps are now part of U.S. Marine helicopter operations at El Toro. These two monstrous blisters are actually constructed of wood. Range of Santa Ana Mountains forms a high horizon on left.

0:07 (0:11) Jets of Marine Corps Air Station at El Toro can be seen parked on runways at left.

0:15 (0:03) Cruise through orange orchards which line either side of tracks.

0:18 (0:00) On arrival at San Juan Capistrano, famous mission with its attendant bell tower can be seen on left adjacent to tracks. Also, note attractively landscaped walkways and bike paths on left just before arriving. Depot itself is also on left, complete with a good restaurant. Northbound passengers might note a Border Patrol bus parked near station which is awaiting illegal aliens frequently ousted from northbound trains by U.S. customs officials who quietly "sweep" coaches.

SAN JUAN CAPISTRANO, CA - The community grew up around the mission which was established in 1776, making the building the oldest in the state. Although this was one of the most beautiful missions built in California, some of its most attractive features were destroyed by an earthquake in 1812. It is world-renowned for its large swallow population that departs about October 23 and returns about March 19 of each year.

0:00 (0:28) Depart San Juan Capistrano.

0:04 (0:24) Suddenly, after having trav-

San Diegan – Southern California Coast

eled without a hint of ocean, The San Diegan spurts out onto beaches of Capistrano, with Pacific Ocean spreading out before us.

For the next 45 minutes, passengers on the right will be treated with seaside vistas. Those on the left will be able to look up to catch sights of homes perched precipitously on clifftops with stunning ocean views.

0:09 (0:19) This is San Clemente, identified by a lovely little park rising above the tracks on left and a popular wharf restaurant on pier jutting out over ocean on right. President Nixon's California home was here during his presidency. This is a stop for some San Diegan trains.

0:16 (0:12) Two gigantic concrete beehives contain reactors of San Onofre Nuclear Generating Station sandwiched between tracks and beach on right.

0:17 (0:11) Northbound vehicular traffic on highway at left is frequently backed up while U.S. immigration officers make a check for illegal aliens. Approximately 2,000 Mexicans and Central Americans are returned each day by officers working this area of California.

0:23 (0:05) San Diegan now slips through confines of Camp Pendleton Marine base.

0:26 (0:02) Dozens of small sailing vessels clustered in yacht basin on right create a highly appealing maritime scene. Over 800 pleasure craft can be berthed here at any given time.

0:28 (0:00) Arrive at Oceanside where at left ultra-modern, both in design and function, transit center progresses up hillside with structures housing Amtrak and Greyhound terminals, while local transit buses are just to its left. Santa Fe rail yards are on right.

 OCEANSIDE, CA - This community, which has a reputation

for being "lean and mean," is closely tied to Camp Pendleton U.S. Marine Base that stretches for more than 20 miles northward from the city.

0:00 (0:16) Depart Oceanside.

0:03 (0:13) Carlsbad, which has outstanding three-storied Victorian structure adorning hillside on right, is also home for military boys' school whose students occasionally find excitement by rattling San Diegan's sides with stones.

0:05 (0:11) Monolithic concrete structure on beach at right is San Diego Gas and Electric's first power plant.

0:14 (0:02) Del Mar's horse racing track, one of the finest in Southern California, is just to left.

0:16 (0:00) Arrive Del Mar where one more attractive beach awaits, and luxury apartments are above station on left.

 DEL MAR, CA - This pleasant oceanside village has 5,000 mostly upscale residents.

0:00 (0:30) Depart Del Mar.

0:01 (0:28) San Diegan makes a swing inland while last view of ocean is afforded back to right.

0:07 (0:23) While snaking through very rugged terrain, note novel red sculpture in front of nine-story glass building on left—rather like a rocket coming out of an egg beater.

0:21 (0:09) Tropical palm setting of Hilton resort is on right.

0:22 (0:08) Mission-style tower of University of San Diego can be seen atop bluffs on left.

0:24 (0:06) Convair Division of General Dynamics Corp. is just to right of tracks.

0:25 (0:05) San Diego's Lindbergh Field, unique because of its location being near very heart of city it serves, is off to right.

0:30 (0:00) Arrive at San Diego's eye-catching mission-style Santa Fe station. Downtown skyline is just beyond on left and maritime scenes of San Diego Harbor are just a block away on right.

SAN DIEGO, CA - It was in 1769 that Gaspar de Portola, Junipero Serra (a Franciscan priest) and several Spanish soldiers ventured north from Mexico to establish a mission here on Presidio Hill. This first European settlement gave birth to what is now California. However, this was not the first discovery of the area. More than 200 years earlier, Juan Cabrillo sailed into a splendid natural harbor that now serves as home to one of the nation's largest naval bases.

A mild Mediterranean-like climate, together with the Pacific Ocean and the town's proximity to the Mexican border, have combined to make San Diego one of the country's favorite vacation spots. There are 70 miles of beaches and easily as many miles of golf courses. Electronics, aerospace, medical research and tourism fuel its growth—a growth San Diego, so far, has handled quite well.

San Diego Station, 1050 Kettner Blvd., built by the Santa Fe and located on the west edge of the older downtown area, is one of the most attractive depots in use today. Its scale, its Spanish motif, the palm-lined landscape, all blend perfectly in this Southern California setting. There are luggage carts, redcaps, three nearby restaurants, a snack bar, food and beverage vending machines and a newsstand. Pay-parking is adjacent to the station.

Ticket window hours are 5:15 am to 9 pm; the waiting room is open 5:15 am to 11:30 pm. For reservations and other information, call 800-USA-RAIL.

Cab stand is at the station; Yellow Cab, 234-6161. **Local buses** stop one block away at Kettner and Broadway, 233-3004. Avis and Budget **rental cars** are located at the station. The **"Tijuana Trolley,"** the first trolley line built in the United States in 20 years, was completed in 1981 and connects downtown San Diego with San Ysidro, CA adjacent to Tijuana, Mexico 16 miles to the south. These trolleys can be boarded across the street from the station; 231-8549 (recorded). **Greyhound/Trailways,** (619) 239-9171. **Mexicoach** has departures from the station. **International Lindbergh Field** is four miles north of the station.

Visitor Information Center, 11 Horton Plaza, 1st Ave. and F, (619) 236-1212. Recorded visitor information, (619) 239-9696. Write San Diego Convention & Visitors Bureau, 1200 Third Ave., Suite 824, 92101.

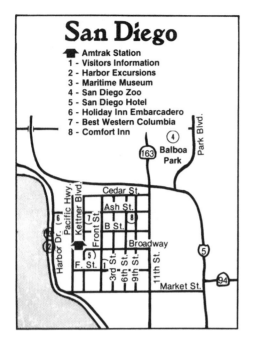

San Diego

🔺 Amtrak Station
1 - Visitors Information
2 - Harbor Excursions
3 - Maritime Museum
4 - San Diego Zoo
5 - San Diego Hotel
6 - Holiday Inn Embarcadero
7 - Best Western Columbia
8 - Comfort Inn

16 miles south, can be reached by the "Tijuana Trolley" which starts at the station and runs east along "C" Street.

The **San Diego Zoo,** considered by many as the nation's finest, is in **Balboa Park** where there are also numerous museums and lush tropical gardens. **Sea World of San Diego,** at 1720 South Shores Rd., is one of the world's largest marine life parks.

Hotel San Diego, 339 W. Broadway, 92101; (619) 234-0221; toll free, 800-621-5380. A refurbished older hotel. Four blocks from the station; courtesy shuttle. $60.

-Best Western Columbia, 555 West Ash St., 92101: (619) 233-7500. Five blocks from the station. $75.

-Comfort Inn, 719 Ash, 92101; (619) 232-2525. About 15 blocks from the station. $57.

-Holiday Inn Embarcadero, 1355 North Harbor Dr., 92101; (619) 232-3861. High rise with balconies, on the bay. Five blocks from the station; courtesy shuttle. $74.

Horton Plaza, bounded by Broadway, G St., 1st and 4th avenues, one of the most architecturally bizarre shopping malls anywhere, is located in the heart of downtown. It's a delight just to walk through this post-modernism maze of levels and balconies.

Also, next to downtown is the harbor and its **Maritime Museum,** 1306 Harbor Dr., with three ships including the 100-year-old merchant sailing ship, the Star of India. **Cruises of San Diego Harbor** are available at the foot of Broadway. **Tijuana,**

San Joaquins

These trains, combined with connecting bus service at each end, join San Francisco and Los Angeles through California's San Joaquin Valley. With major stops consisting of Oakland, Martinez, Fresno and Bakersfield, it would be easy to assume The San Joaquins might someday be renamed The San Ho Hums. Don't sell them short! The traveler who makes the entire run encounters a wide range of both pleasing and interesting scenes. And ridership is high, due in part to the large number of dedicated connecting buses serving other population centers.

In petroleum-rich Kern County the tracks pass through an oil field with more working wells per square mile than will be seen on any other passenger train route in North America. Then the heart of the Valley—one of America's most fertile and productive—has a seemingly unending procession of almond, plum, pistachio and fig groves as well as wine and raisin-grape vineyards, and even occasional cotton fields. These checker the flattened landscape for miles on end but never become monotonous. At the north end of the Valley, there is a dramatic change when the terrain becomes rolling and the Bay Area's maritime scenes suddenly grab one's attention.

San Francisco itself becomes the perfect starting or ending point for this journey. It is only a short connecting bus ride from Oakland's station to the Transbay Terminal nicely situated in downtown San Francisco within easy walking distance of cable cars, The Embarcadero and the ferry to Sausalito.

There are two departures daily from both Oakland and Bakersfield, with trains leaving each city early in the morning and late in the afternoon. A third train is also planned. The 312-mile trip takes six hours, with connecting bus service between Bakersfield and Los Angeles adding three more hours and the bus between Oakland and San Francisco another 20 minutes—all told, 9½ hours. This is somewhat faster than The Coast Starlight following the coast route. There is also direct bus service connecting The San Joaquins with The San Diegan trains and The Desert Wind. Several other bus connections to numerous central California towns are offered along the route.

There is no checked baggage, so bags must be carried on board. The morning train out of Oakland and the evening train out of Bakersfield offer complete meal service while the other trains have sandwiches and beverages. Superliner coaches have been in use, although Amtrak's new horizon equipment may be placed into service on this run.

Route Log

BAKERSFIELD, CA - Although agriculture is important (as it has been since the town's humble birth in 1869), oil is king in this community of 100,000. Except for a short bit of excitement in 1885 with the discovery of gold in the area, Bakersfield's real blossoming occurred when oil was discovered at the close of the last century.

Connecting motor coach service serves Los Angeles and its various suburbs and Barstow.

0:00 (0:24) Depart Bakersfield's small trailer-station, and slip through Santa Fe rail yards. Rail fans will want to watch for roundhouse which will be on left shortly after departure.

0:05 (0:19) At end of yards, cross large irrigation canal and swing northward which will be our course until we depart Stockton four hours from now. Here San Joaquins pass through that massive oil field mentioned above, with seemingly hundreds of pumps crowded together making a truly impressive industrial scene. A large refinery is just to right.

0:19 (0:05) Through Shafter, then almond groves line both sides of tracks. In late winter, these trees will be covered with millions of pinkish-white blossoms. Groves will appear off and on until we reach Stockton.

0:21 (0:03) Note staked grapevines, which will also be evident for miles to come. Grapes grown in this region are mostly dried into those "California Raisins," while those north of Fresno will become fine California wine.

0:24 (0:00) Arrive Wasco.

WASCO, CA - This is one of several farming communities that dot the valley.

0:00 (0:44) Depart Wasco and resume ramblings through formal orchards and vineyards.

0:14 (0:30) Sign on left identifies Colonel Allensworth Park named in honor of U.S. Army's first black colonel.

0:22 (0:22) Continue through flat, flat country which almost eliminates the necessity for field-leveling usually essential for ditch irrigation.

0:27 (0:17) On entering Corcoran, note huge cotton gin operation and then attractive, unused Santa Fe station, both on left.

0:44 (0:00) Arrive Hanford.

HANFORD, CA - Oddly enough, Hanford boasts one of the best Chinese restaurants in the United States— the Imperial Dynasty. Customers have included presidents, foreign dignitaries and other notables. Motor coach service connects to Visalia—gateway to Kings Canyon and Sequoia national parks.

0:00 (0:32) Depart Hanford.

0:03 (0:29) Dozens and dozens of homeowners on left have obviously been receptive to sales pitch of aggressive redwood fence salesman.

0:10 (0:22) Cross Kings River.

0:18 (0:14) Impressive expanse of grape vineyards spills across thousands of acres, stretching for miles along both sides of tracks.

0:27 (0:05) Cribari Winery is just to right as train slows for Fresno.

0:29 (0:03) Prior to arrival at Fresno, raisin plant is just to left of tracks, with interesting old water tower and faded sign proclaiming "Sunmaid Raisins." Although upper floors are not used, lower portion still is in operation during raisin season. Modest skyline of downtown Fresno is on left.

(Amtrak had plans to shift from Santa Fe and use Southern Pacific tracks between Calwa, four miles south of Fresno, and Stockton. Segment below, however, is log for Santa Fe route still in use at press time.)

0:32 (0:00) Arrive Fresno.

FRESNO, CA - This is the heart of the San Joaquin Valley and the raisin center of the world. Sunmaid has the world's largest dried fruit packing plant here, and the largest fig orchards are in the immediate area. The county claims to be the most farm-productive in the country. Wineries and winery equipment production are also important.

0:00 (0:29) Depart Fresno's rather bedraggled depot and immediately pass by attractive Santa Fe offices on left. Crossing Fresno Street, note historic water tower in downtown a block to left, looking like an extremely squat rocket. Then on immediate right, wildly painted mural adorns wall in small park next to tracks.

0:08 (0:21) Still in suburbs, campus of Fresno State College is on left.

0:19 (0:10) After appealing golf course on left, cross high over waters of San Joaquin River.

0:28 (0:00) Arrive Madera.

MADERA, CA - This is one of the large agricultural communities in the area.

0:00 (0:30) Depart Madera and cross Fresno River.

0:06 (0:24) To right and forward of train, Cathedral Range of Sierra Nevada Mountains, rising to over 13,000 feet above sea level, contains spectacularly beautiful Yosemite National Park which Horace Greeley once called "the greatest marvel of the continent."

0:09 (0:21) Grove of pistachio trees stands just to left of tracks.

0:11 (0:19) Visions of Thanksgiving are aroused as we pass by turkey farm on right.

0:24 (0:07) As we slowly swing to left at Planada, large grove of scraggly trees on right, short and stubby, are kadota figs.

0:26 (0:05) Goodyear plant on left turns out large quantities of plastic bags.

0:31 (0:00) Arrive Merced.

MERCED, CA - Here connecting motor coach service carries rail travelers directly to and from lovely Yosemite National Park, some 75 miles to the east.

0:00 (0:21) Depart Merced and note picturesque courthouse two blocks away on left and facing tracks.

0:07 (0:14) Castle Air Force Base is on right at Atwater, where assorted World War II aircraft, tethered next to tracks, are on public display, and include B-29 flown in by General Jimmy Doolittle—his last military flight.

0:11 (0:10) Magnificent stands of almond trees spread out on each side of right-of-way.

0:12 (0:09) Over Merced River, most impressive stream seen on trip so far, which joins San Joaquin River west (left) of here.

0:18 (0:03) Low-lying mountains on distant horizon to left comprise Diablo Range.

0:21 (0:00) Arrive Turlock.

TURLOCK, CA - This is actually Denair, just east of the much larger town of Turlock where locals find diversion by holding a harnessed turkey race each October.

0:00 (0:14) Depart Turlock.

0:03 (0:10) Aircraft hangar in midst of almond grove on left generally has crop-dusting biplanes parked in front, but where is runway? Frequent grade crossings in this area give train's air horn a constant workout.

0:07 (0:06) Cross Tuolumne River.

0:11 (0:02) Pass over concrete-lined Hetch Hetchy Aqueduct cutting cleanly across valley and built to transport water from Sierra Nevadas to Bay Area. A Reagan Administration official once proposed that the Hetch Hetchy Reservoir be permanently drained and its valley turned into another Yosemite. San Franciscans, however, voiced some objections to idea.

0:13 (0:00) Arrive Riverbank where its green-trimmed, white-frame station offers pleasant change for depot-watchers.

RIVERBANK, CA - Riverbank began as a ferrying point on the Stanislaus River during the gold rush of the 1880s. Later the Santa Fe Railroad came through the valley and the settlement soon sprouted into a railroad town. This is Amtrak's stop for nearby Modesto, where Gallo operates the world's largest winery. If Amtrak moves to the Southern Pacific tracks as planned, Modesto itself would become a stop.

0:00 (0:25) Depart Riverbank.

0:01 (0:24) Cross Stanislaus River.

0:12 (0:13) Grape vineyards are virtually everywhere along this portion of route. Franzia Wineries have contracted to buy most of crop grown throughout immediate area.

0:25 (0:00) Arrive Stockton.

STOCKTON, CA - This is California's only inland seaport, with a deep-water channel connecting the city to the Bay Area some 78 miles to the west.

0:00 (0:36) Depart Stockton.

0:26 (0:10) Pacific Gas and Electric power plant is on right.

0:28 (0:08) Enter Antioch, then first evidence of Bay Area's presence will be seen on right where shipping channel of San Joaquin River is just visible. Seagoing vessels are able to navigate into this area via San Francisco Bay. Although hard to spot, San Joaquin and Sacramento rivers join on right as they continue toward San Francisco Bay and Pacific Ocean. Soon, Dow Chemical plant will be on immediate right, where a plethora of blaze-orange windsocks flutter from various positions throughout facility to identify wind direction in case of escaping chlorine gas.

0:36 (0:00) Arrive Antioch-Pittsburg.

ANTIOCH-PITTSBURG, CA - This is one of the Bay Area's most industrialized areas.

0:00 (0:23) Depart Antioch-Pittsburg.

0:07 (0:16) At one time, trains would grind to a halt here, then creep forward, only to repeat process while switching from Santa Fe to Southern Pacific tracks at Port Chicago. This 15-minute line change has been eliminated by new transfer track exchange trackage allowing trains to breeze through at 50 miles per hour.

Port Chicago was once a small lumber town called Bay Point. It had a city-owned saloon that was profitable enough to finance the community's water, street lights, sewer and other public services.

0:10 (0:13) Numerous ships across waterway, on right, and anchored side by side have been "mothballed" by U.S. Navy and await salvage operations at Sacramento. Concord Naval Weapons facility is here, with acres and acres of ammunition storage. U.S. Government relocated it a few years back to prevent recurrence of a catastrophe that leveled Port Chicago's buildings when two munitions ships blew up during World War II.

0:11 (0:12) Lift-span rail bridge of Southern Pacific, directly ahead and to right, carries California Zephyr and Coast Starlight across narrows of Carquinez Strait. Second bridge carries Interstate 680 auto traffic, which is major north-south bypass of Bay Area.

0:14 (0:09) Just before reaching bridge, look directly across strait where grey, unmarked Glomar Explorer, sporting a white heliport platform on its stern, is anchored. It's normally the last ship just before rail bridge. This deep-sea research vessel made headlines some years back when it attempted to retrieve a sunken Russian sub from ocean's floor.

0:16 (0:07) At left, expansive Shell refinery and tank farm snuggle against hillside.

0:19 (0:04) Approaching the station at Martinez, note Southern Pacific trackage that crosses bridge on right, making a steep descent alongside us. This is where we join routes of The California Zephyr and The Coast Starlight.

0:23 (0:00) On arrival at Martinez note semaphore that landscapes station on left.

MARTINEZ, CA - This important commercial and military port was also the home of John Muir, one of the nation's earliest and most outspoken conservationists. His house is now preserved as a National Historic Site. Joe Dimaggio Drive is on the right side of the train, honoring the renowned "Yankee Clipper" who was raised here.

0:00 (0:29) Depart Martinez along Carquinez Strait, connecting Suisun and San Pablo bays. Carquinez Bridge looms impressively in foreground right, while on left, famed golden hills are subtly encroaching upon landscape.

0:09 (0:20) With town of Crockett huddled on hillside left, travel directly through midst of C&H sugar refinery. Immediately thereafter, train bears south along shores of San Pablo Bay and passes beneath Carquinez Bridge.

0:12 (0:17) Dart into momentary darkness while passing through trip's first (and last) tunnel.

0:13 (0:16) Union Oil refinery, on left, truly "graces" hillside with its pastel storage tanks set off by ecologically inspired landscaping.

0:27 (0:02) Huge Standard Oil of California refinery stretches across face of slopes across Bay just before Richmond.

0:29 (0:00) Arrive Richmond.

RICHMOND, CA - Richmond's popularity as a convenient suburban stop is enhanced by its trackside connections with BART, a rapid transit system servicing many outlying regions throughout the Bay Area.

0:00 (0:07) Departure from Richmond affords first view of dramatic San Francisco skyline across bay. Golden Gate Bridge can be seen north of city, while Bay Bridge connects with Oakland to the south.

0:05 (0:02) On right, pass Golden Gate Field Race Track.

0:07 (0:00) Arrive Berkeley.

BERKELEY, CA - This stop provides service for the main campus (there are nine of them) of the University of California. Thirty thousand students study in buildings of striking beauty; most notable architecture is the acclaimed University Art Museum.

0:00 (0:06) Depart Berkeley.

0:02 (0:04) Last, grand view of San Francisco can be captured, again off to right, where Alcatraz Island can now be seen directly below Golden Gate Bridge.

0:06 (0:00) Arrive Oakland, train's final destination. Bus connections are available at station for passengers enroute to San Francisco.

 OAKLAND and SAN FRANCISCO, CA - See pages 192 and 265.

Other West Coast Service

The **Mount Rainier** is an unreserved train that travels from Seattle to Portland in the evening, and from Portland to Seattle in the morning. Food service consists of sandwiches, snacks and beverages. Checked baggage is not handled, but hand baggage may be carried on board.

Caltrain/SP provides train service between the Southern Pacific station in San Francisco (4th & Townsend) and Amtrak's station in San Jose.

Alaska Railroad

They say Alaska is different. But, just how different is—well—what really makes the difference. Winters can get so cold that locals sometimes leave their cars running all night; then summers can be so warm that weekends are spent waterskiing. Alaska stretches farther west than Hawaii—and farther east than Maine (since the Aleutians actually cross the International Date Line). Vertically, the state juts from sea level to over 20,000 feet—the highest point in North America. And there is no state income tax; it works the other way around in that Alaska pays its residents an annual allotment out of a fund created from pipeline revenues. Alaskans can continue to tick off such contrasts almost indefinitely.

The principal railroad in Alaska is owned by the state, and one may rightfully conclude that it, too, is a different breed. Passenger trains are immaculately maintained, inside and out. Windows throughout are clear and clean, even in the dome cars, while white linen tablecloths and real china grace the diner, where the bill of fare runs from simple sandwiches to Alaskan Seafood Saute. Almost an overabundance of leg room exists in the coaches. Attractive and enthusiastic tour guides are in each coach to keep passengers informed about interesting points along the route and to answer any questions passengers may have. It is the only U.S. railroad that makes unlimited flag stops; and it's the railroad that was originally constructed to haul gold from the gold fields around Fairbanks, and is now one of the state's top tourist attractions.

For those wanting to go really deluxe, both Gray Line of Alaska and Princess Tours are operating their own full-length dome cars between Anchorage and Fairbanks. These cars are attached to the rear of the regularly scheduled trains and provide upper-level viewing for every passenger. Private dining facilities are on the lower level. Gray Line has four cars, each with surprisingly minimal upper-level sway. Princess runs two cars of equal elegance and offers a large viewing platform on the end-car. See a travel agent to book either tour.

Most all passengers on the Anchorage-Fairbanks run stop over at Denali National Park to at least take the wildlife tour (and try, weather permitting, to get some more views of Mt. McKinley). If you plan to spend only one night in the park and travel the entire rail route, consider an Anchorage departure. This allows time to complete the wildlife tour that starts early morning the second day. If you're spending two nights at the Park, you can just as easily depart from Fairbanks. A Fairbanks-to-Denali-to-Fairbanks round trip also works well with a one-night Denali layover.

More and more travelers are discovering the route between Anchorage and Seward. Although the Denali experience on the Anchorage-Fairbanks trip is incomparable, the run down to Seward is one of the most spectacular in the world. Not only are the mountains more Swiss-like, the train passes within one-half mile of three magnificent glaciers.

A one-day, round-trip excursion leaves

plenty of time to explore Seward (a delight) or take a half-day cruise of Resurrection Bay.

Scheduling for Anchorage-Fairbanks: During the summer season, which is normally from mid-May to mid-September, trains run daily. An "Express" run, from late May through mid-September, making intermediate stops only at Wasilla, Talkeetna, Denali National Park and Nenana, is made seven days per week in each direction. Departure time from both Anchorage and Fairbanks is 8:30 am. A "Local" train, making numerous stops, operates during the summer on a thrice-weekly schedule.

The Express takes approximately twelve hours between the two cities. The Local operates only between Anchorage and Hurricane Gulch, making a round trip each of the three days it operates. During the winter months there is only one train per week, departing Anchorage at 8:30 am on Saturdays and leaving Fairbanks at 8:30 am on Sundays. Viewing in the winter, of course, is minimal due to the limited amount of daylight. The Express trains carry standard coaches and dome cars, and offer complete meal and beverage service. Other trains use rail diesel car equipment and have vending-machine snacks only.

Scheduling for Anchorage-Seward: Two attached rail diesel cars make the round trip daily, departing Anchorage at 7 am and arriving back in Anchorage at 10 pm. The trip takes four hours each way, and trains operate from Memorial Day weekend through Labor Day. Sandwiches and beverages are available on the train, both directions.

Scheduling for Whittier Shuttle: From late May to mid-September the railroad provides a shuttle service between Portage (a stop on the Anchorage-Seward line) and Whittier, where there is ferry service to and from Valdez. This unique transport, offering not only coaches but flat cars carrying motor vehicles with their passengers, is Whittier's only land connection to the rest of Alaska. There are numerous departures throughout the day and evening Thursday through Monday. There are several departures during the afternoon and evening Tuesday and Wednesday. The 1:30 pm shuttle from Portage connects with the 3 pm ferry departure at Whittier, while the 2:30 pm ferry arrival connects with the 3:30 pm shuttle to Portage. Those wanting to spend additional time in Whittier may do so by taking a train that allows for that.

Service is also provided daily between Anchorage and Whittier, with motor coach providing transportation between Portage and Anchorage. Departures are from Anchorage at 11:45 am and from Whittier at 3:30 pm.

Reservations and Fares: Reservations are required on all trains operated by the Alaska Railroad. Some sample fares: Anchorage to Denali Park, $62 one way; Anchorage to Fairbanks, $88 one way. For more information, write or call: Passenger Services Department, The Alaska Railroad, P.O. Box 107500, Anchorage, AK 99510; (907) 265-2494, or 800-544-0552 for reservations.

The Railroad also offers several tour packages that offer worthwhile savings.

Route Log

Anchorage-Fairbanks

ANCHORAGE, AK - Anchorage is the largest city (geographically) in the U.S., having incorporated huge amounts of real estate within its boundaries. In spite of this, the downtown is fairly easily managed on foot. About a day or two will allow you to take in most things Alaska's largest city has to offer; the town is really more of a base for seeing the southcentral part of the state. (Non-Anchorage residents like to say: When you're in Anchorage, you're only 30 minutes from Alaska.) Most flights from the Lower 48 come into Anchorage, and air fare is usually considerably less than flying to Alaska's second largest city, Fairbanks.

This is the ideal base for riding the Alaska Railroad, being the focal point of the system. The four popular rail destinations are easily reached from here: Fairbanks, that still-frontier city to the north; Denali National Park, with its wildlife tours and Mount McKinley; Seward, a delightful seaport on Resurrection Bay, and reached by one of the most dramatic train rides in North America; and Whittier, the unique marine (ferry boat) access to Valdez through oil-free portions of Prince William Sound.

Anchorage is located on Knik Arm of Cook Inlet and shielded from heavy rainfall by the Kenai Mountains to the south. Having a moderate climate, its mild summers are comparable to those of Seattle. Very little evidence is left of the earthquake that registered 8.6 on the Richter Scale and devastated the city in 1964, nor were Anchorage's shores fouled by the 1989 oil spill.

Alaska Railroad Station, 421 W. First Ave., Pouch 107500, 99501, is on the edge of the downtown area. There is a covered walkway leading up the hill to town, and parking is available in front of the station. Long-term parking needs a permit, available at the ticket window.

If you wish to sit with someone, keep in mind that people line up early for boarding. One day there may be plenty of seating, but the next may be full. Reservations are important. Ticket window hours are 6 am to 11 pm. Call (800) 544-0552, or (907) 265-2494.

Cabs: Yellow Cab, 272-2422; Checker, 276-1234. Two blocks to **local buses,** with main transit center at 6th Ave. and G St.; call 343-6534. National, 274-3695; Budget, 243-0150; and Avis, 277-4567 have **rental cars** near the station. Alaskan Express, 279-0761, has **bus service** to Fairbanks, Haines, Whitehorse and Skagway. **Anchorage International Airport** is about four miles southwest of downtown.

Log Cabin Visitor Information Center, W. 4th Ave. and F Street. Call (907) 274-3531, or write Anchorage Convention & Visitors Bureau, Plaza 201 E. 3rd Ave., 99501. Information on special

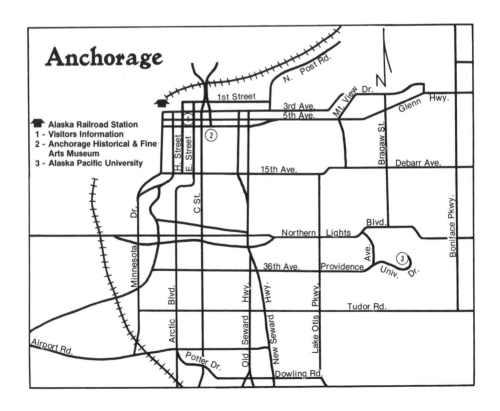

Anchorage

■ Alaska Railroad Station
1 - Visitors Information
2 - Anchorage Historical & Fine Arts Museum
3 - Alaska Pacific University

events, call 276-3200.

Accommodations in Anchorage are expensive, particularly in the downtown area. There are a few Bed and Breakfasts in the downtown area which are somewhat more economical. Anchorage reservations in the summer should be made well in advance.

-**Voyager Hotel,** 501 K Street, 99501; (907) 277-9501 or 800-247-9070. A small, tastefully decorated hotel in a good location; well managed and one of the most reasonably priced of Anchorage's best hotels. Ten blocks from the station. $89.

-**8th Ave. Hotel,** 630 W. 8th Ave., 99501; (907) 274-6231, 800-478-4837 (AK only). A recently converted small apartment building, in a good location, with spacious (suite) accommodations. Nine blocks from the station. One of Anchorage's best values. $80.

-**Holiday Inn,** 239 W. 4th Ave., 99501; (907) 279-8671. Popular with tour groups. Downtown, four blocks from the station. $84 to $120.

-**Anchorage Hotel,** 330 E. St., 99501; (907) 272-4553 or 800-544-0988. A beautifully restored small, historic hotel in the heart of downtown. Four blocks from the station. $109 to $119.

-**Bed and Breakfast-Alaska Private Lodgings,** P.O. Box 200047, Anchorage, AK 99520; (907) 258-1717. A bed and breakfast information and reservation service, including downtown B & Bs.

Be sure to get an **Anchorage Visitors Guide** by writing or stopping at the Visitors Center. It has an elaborate walking tour of downtown, as well as other area attractions. Some highlights of the walking tour include: The **Log Cabin Visitors Center** itself; a walk down 4th Ave., Anchorage's **"Main Street;"** the **Anchorage Historical and Fine Arts Museum,** 121 West 7th Ave., depicting Anchorage and Alaska native cultures; **Resolution Park** at the west end of 3rd Ave., with a view of Knik Arm and Mt. McKinley (on a clear day); and **free films** about the area shown in the Arco Building at 7th and G streets.

If you have a car, or want to take the bus, **The Alaska Zoo** at Mile 7 on O'Malley Road has various species of Alaskan wildlife, including polar bears.

0:00 (1:23) Depart Anchorage with front range of Alaska Mountains looming in distance. A grand spectacle unto themselves, natives regard these mountains as mere "foothills" in respect to monumental peaks that will soon border route a few miles north.

0:04 (1:19) Cross Ship Creek. A mile west, waters widen before flowing into sea, availing several inland docks to ocean-going vessels.

0:08 (1:15) Train skirts fringe of Elmendorf Air Force Base on left, and Fort Richardson Army Installation on right. Elmendorf is Alaska's largest air base.

0:13 (1:10) On left, myriad of military aircraft are poised alongside Elmendorf runways.

0:14 (1:09) Proceed through birch-lined gullies, keeping eyes peeled for great Alaskan moose; 125-mile stretch between here and Curry is favorite haunt of this curious beast.

0:20 (1:03) Brief clearing on forward left provides first breathtaking glimpse of Mt. McKinley. Jutting 20,320 feet skyward, peak is tallest in North America, and actually highest in world if measured from base to crest.

Along the route, "mileposts" are conspicuously tacked on trees and telephone poles, and represent the distance from the line's southern terminus at Seward. Many subsequent entries will be prefaced by milepost designations (MP) as a further aid in identification.

0:29 (0:54) Cross Eagle River, its waters moving swiftly through small canyon.

0:45 (0:38) MP 136. At Birchwood, small airport seen through trees on left is but one of countless such facilities throughout Alaska. Vast distances of forbidding wilderness make airplane most popular and practical means of transportation.

0:48 (0:35) MP 138. On left, begin bordering Knik Arm, an inlet of Pacific Ocean. Tides here can reach 40 feet—third highest in world. In distance, Mt. Foraker (17,400 ft.), Mt. Hunter (14,573 ft.), Mt. Russell (11,670 ft.) and Mt. Dall (8,756 ft.) are a formidable supporting cast surrounding mighty Mt. McKinley.

0:54 (0:29) MP 141. Eklutna Village is home of Russian Orthodox Church established in 1835. Its adjacent cemetery is most unusual, with colorful "spirit houses" built atop gravesites to preserve souls of those buried here.

1:01 (0:22) MP 146. Traverse series of bridges across Knik River. Prior to 1964 earthquake, river was outlet for ice-flows and floodwaters descending from Lake George. Barren trees dot sunken landscape that became tidal flats after quake.

1:08 (0:15) MP 151. At Matanuska, begin travel through scenic agricultural valley, with surrounding peaks an added embellishment. In 1930s, poverty-stricken farmers from Minnesota, Wisconsin and Michigan were allowed to homestead here in a federally sponsored socialistic experiment. Although the effort failed, many stayed, and numerous attractive spreads can still be seen scattered throughout the region.

Despite a brief growing season (100-120 days), long hours of daylight compensate for this shortcoming. A record-size 76-pound cabbage grown in this region evidences potential of these northern farmlands.

1:12 (0:11) Nearby Pioneer Peak of Alaska Range dominates skyline. To immediate right of Pioneer are East Peak, Middle Peak (with two points) and Goat Mountain (looking somewhat truncated).

1:23 (0:00) MP 159. Recreational lakes border town on arrival Wasilla.

WASILLA, AK — This is a service hub of the Matanuska Valley. On the right, perched on "temporary" cribbing, Teeland's Country Store is the oldest business in Matanuska and Anchorage area. As well as retail merchant, Teeland's was once a veritable museum with old photos, antiques and native artifacts on display. Off to right is a McDonalds with its own caboose. Establishment reportedly had longest line of any McDonalds on opening day.

0:00 (1:29) Departing Wasilla, note towering totem pole fronting property of Kashim Inn.

0:21 (1:08) MP 174. Cross Little Susitna River.

0:30 (0:59) MP 181. On left, clusters of cozy cabins encircle shoreline of Nancy Lake, a popular recreational resort.

0:39 (0:50) MP 185. Pass through Willow,

once deemed by voters as future site of state capital. Electorate later nixed move by failing to approve necessary funding. Town's centrality was prime consideration for proposed move from Juneau.

0:55 (0:34) Cross Kashwitna River. For next 45 miles, enjoy spectacular views of Mt. McKinley on left if skies cooperate. (There's a seven-in-ten chance they won't.) Service personnel will generally open vestibule doors to accommodate photographers, while engineer purposefully slows train where vistas are most dynamic. Enthusiasm that pervades crew adds immensely to this delightful adventure.

1:16 (0:13) MP 224. Susitna River joins and follows on left. It will accompany train for next 40 miles.

1:29 (0:00) MP 226. Arrive Talkeetna.

TALKEETNA, AK - A robust frontier atmosphere is well preserved at Talkeetna, a popular staging ground for Mt. McKinley expeditions. The town's name is derived from an Indian word meaning "place where rivers meet"— a reference to the nearby confluence of the Talkeetna, Chulitna and Susitna rivers.

The white building over to the left is Fairview Inn which housed and fed President and Mrs. Warren G. Harding in 1923 when the president was in Alaska to drive the golden spike at Nenana. Harding died about two weeks later in San Francisco, supposedly from food poisoning.

The town has both spirit and a sense of humor. One of its annual celebrations includes a "moose-nugget-throwing" contest.

0:00 (4:25) Depart Talkeetna and cross Talkeetna River.

Over the next immediate stretch, the train begins a gradual ascent of the Continental Divide that culminates 85 miles north at the summit of Broad Pass. Subtle geographic changes can be detected enroute, with the terrain and vegetation reflecting more alpine-like environs. Brilliant pink flowers, growing profusely along right-of-way in July, are fireweed. The large, white flowery plants in moist areas are cow parsnips—sometimes called wild celery.

0:34 (3:51) MP 248. Pass through Curry, halfway between Seward and Fairbanks.

Because of this strategic position, a resort hotel was built here in 1923, off to right. Hostelry sported tennis courts and even an undersized golf course. Years took their toll until, finally, a fire in 1957 ended its colorful career.

0:50 (3:35) MP 258. Sole resident of Sherman has proudly pronounced his home "City Hall," on right.

0:58 (3:27) MP 264. Cross Susitna River as it departs to east.

1:01 (3:24) MP 266. Cross Indian River first of several times as train traces its course through colorful canyon. When train makes its third crossing (in a few minutes) watch for salmon in pool below on left. Just before that, also on left, will be a small cross above river, erected by two mountaineers in remembrance of a friend killed in a climbing accident.

1:19 (3:06) Emergence from canyon affords another fabulous panorama of Mt. McKinley grouping on left. Range is now only 46 miles away—its closest proximity to rail line.

1:42 (2:43) MP 284. A few anxious moments are in store as train crosses Hurricane Gulch from dizzying height of near 300 feet. Chulitna River joins on left and follows route intermittently to its source atop Broad Pass. This 918-foot trestle was most expensive and difficult to build on entire line. View to left is particularly stunning.

1:47 (2:38) MP 287. Footbridge, relic of prospecting times, stretches ladder-like across river on left.

1:51 (2:34) MP 289. Honolulu (without palm trees) is situated halfway between Anchorage and Fairbanks.

1:56 (2:29) MP 292. Cross east fork of Chulitna River.

2:01 (2:24) MP 295. Approaching summit of Broad Pass, journey through midst of wide alpine valley, with jagged peaks flanking this treeless expanse.

2:05 (1:36) MP 297. Frequently, siding called Colorado is where northbound and southbound express trains meet. Tour guides swap trains here, enabling them to return home (Anchorage or Fairbanks) on same day as departure. (Train may wait here for some time. Log times are adjusted for an approximate 40-minute delay each direction.)

3:00 (1:25) MP 304. On right, imaginative design highlights log house at town of Broad Pass. Adjacent "storage cache," perched atop tower, keeps provisions beyond reach of uninvited guests.

3:09 (1:16) MP 309. Summit Lake borders on right, while imposing peaks of Mt. Deborah (12,399 ft.) and Mt. Hayes (13,832 ft.) hover in background.

3:10 (1:15) MP 310. Marker on right designates summit of Broad Pass. Elevation of 2,363 feet is highest point along Alaska Railroad, yet pass is still lowest crossing of Continental Divide in entire Rocky Mountain chain.

3:25 (1:00) MP 319. Return to hillier terrain as train passes through Cantwell, marked by airstrip on left. On outskirts of town, note overgrown cemetery along hillside on left. Several gravesites are adorned with spirit houses similar to those found in Eklutna.

3:31 (0:54) MP 323. Cross Windy Creek into southeastern region of Denali National Park. Train then climbs atop bluffs overlooking Nenana River Valley on right. River generally parallels route for next 90 miles.

3:57 (0:28) MP 334. At Carlo, handsome log home and another storage cache can be seen on right.

4:18 (0:07) MP 345. Approaching park station, Nenana River Valley is now totally encircled by towering peaks of Alaska Range. Setting is one of most inspiring along entire run.

4:25 (0:00) MP 347. Traverse lofty bridge across Riley Creek as train arrives Denali. Denali is Indian word for "the great one," with obvious reference to nearby Mt. McKinley. Note airpark beside tracks on right.

DENALI NATIONAL PARK, AK - Mt. McKinley is the central fixture of this alpine wonderland, presiding majestically over 3,000 square miles of pristine wilderness. Although a worthy draw in its own right, many other attractions add to the magic of this enchanting tourist haven.

Abundant wildlife roam freely throughout the park, with caribou, fox, grizzly bear and Dall mountain sheep only a few of the many species to behold. Over 100 varieties of birds have been identified and represent migrations from six different continents. Free shuttle buses take visitors deep into the park, with early-morning departures generally offering the best viewing. Wildlife tours (also by bus) offer guided sojourns along the park's one road. Rangers offer dog sled demonstrations daily, just a short bus ride from the Riley Creek Information Center.

From spring until midsummer, colorful wildflowers spread a regal blanket across the high mountain tundra. Ranger-led nature hikes and campfire chats help visitors further appreciate such spectacles, as well as other aspects of the area's complex ecosystem.

Private operators offer exciting alternatives for backcountry exploration, with flightseeing, rafting and horseback treks quite popular. In wintertime, cross-country ski tours and dog-sled excursions are available for the more adventuresome.

Accommodations at Denali are rather expensive, and tour packages generally offer savings.

The spacious Denali National Park Hotel (907-683-2215) is the "base camp" for many of the park's activities and the only easy walk from the station. Shuttle buses serve most other nearby hostelries. Nearby McKinley Chalets (907-683-2407) is another logical choice for staying overnight. Denali Crows Nest Log Cabins (907-683-2723) are somewhat less expensive. Perhaps the most economical are McKinley/Denali Bed and Breakfast cabins (907-683-2733) that start around $55. For central reservations information, call (907) 274-5366.

0:00 (1:44) Departing Denali, note cluster of old Pullman cars on left that once provided lodging following fire at McKinley Hotel, and remain as hotel's calling card.

0:10 (1:34) MP 351. Dall sheep are frequently seen between here and milepost 354. On forward right, impressive highway bridge spans Nenana River.

0:17 (1:27) MP 353. Cross northeastern boundary of Denali National Park, passing under previously cited bridge before entering short tunnel. Emerge amidst beautiful Nenana River canyon, winding precarious-ly atop colorful rock ledges while river rages through gorge below.

0:30 (1:14) MP 357. Approaching Healy, note coal seams exposed in rock strata on right. Branch line of railroad extends up valley to east, servicing extensive coal-mining operations.

0:42 (1:02) MP 362. North of Healy, coal crushing and loading occurs here at "Usibelli Tipple," Alaska's only coal mine camp. Coal itself is mined at nearby Suntrana. Watch for coal seams along right-of-way.

0:44 (1:00) MP 363. Beyond Healy, rugged terrain is gradually displaced by more gentle, rolling landscape with birch and aspen groves and scrub brush reminiscent of earlier stretches. On right, old railroad cars are positioned in midst of Nenana River as flood control measure. Such sightings are common over next several miles.

0:53 (0:51) MP 370. Cross Nenana River which then follows on left.

1:20 (0:24) MP 391. Train borders grounds of Clear Military Installation. On left, massive radar apparatus is part of "early warning" defense monitor.

1:43 (0:01) MP 411. Nenana River flows into Tanana River on left approaching community of Nenana. Here, railroad operates barge system that services rural outposts nearly 800 miles to west and over 500 miles to east. On forward right, Mears Memorial Bridge stretches dramatically across Tanana River. Structure is one of longest single-span bridges in world. Turning east into town, note visitors center on right, housed in quaint log cabin with sod roof.

1:44 (0:00) Arrive Nenana's restored station, which now houses Alaska State Railroad Museum.

NENANA, AK - Originally one of Alaska's historic roadhouses was located here; then when the railroad arrived, the town flourished as a construction base. President Warren G. Harding drove a golden spike here in 1923, which concluded the Alaska Railroad's construction. But Nenana has a greater claim to fame—the annual "Ice Classic" lottery. Annually, entrants try to guess the time of the spring ice breakup in the Tanana

River, and those with the right time share over $100,000 in prize money.

0:00 (1:50) Depart Nanana, and immediately pass wooden tower on left which is placed on ice to act as a giant trigger to stop official time clock for aforementioned lottery.

On outskirts of town, train heads south into U-turn prior to traversing Mears Bridge. While crossing river, note "Indian fish wheels" positioned along banks. Paddles are propelled by river current and capture salmon swimming upstream to spawn; catch is then deposited into containers on shore. Once across river, monument on left commemorates site where golden spike was driven.

1:27 (0:33) MP 460. Forested hills surrounding Fairbanks provide scenic setting for many outstanding homes secluded in their midst.

1:39 (0:11) MP 465. Picturesque farmstead on left operates in conjunction with University of Alaska, supplying school with fresh produce and meat. Other campus facilities stand immediately to east.

1:43 (0:08) Phillips Field stretches across pasture on right, colorfully bedecked with multitude of small aircraft.

1:46 (0:04) Proceed through industrial district as Chena River joins on right.

1:50 (0:00) Arriving Fairbanks, elegant steeple of Immaculate Conception Catholic Church protrudes above treetops on forward right. Formerly ensconced across river, hierarchy subsequently wanted it moved closer to Catholic hospital. Thus, in 1911, church was jacked up and dragged across ice to its present site.

FAIRBANKS, AK - They count the winters here—not the years. This is the northernmost city in the U.S., only 130 miles south of the Arctic Circle. Temperatures can easily drop to 65 below. It's a hearty lot that live here, but even

Alaska Railroad - Dining Car

293

then, there are limits. It's now policy to close the schools when the thermometer dips to a frigid minus 50.

In spite of its ice-box image, summers can be spectacularly beautiful, with shorts almost as common as in Los Angeles. Annual average precipitation in Fairbanks is a mere 11 inches, but the area's brief growing season somehow produces unusually lush foliage on the hills that surround the town.

A mixture of old and new, rugged and civilized, Fairbanks got its start in 1902 as a gold-mining settlement when Felix Pedro (pronounced Pee-dro) discovered gold sixteen miles north of here. Fairbanks still maintains a frontier atmosphere, most evident when you walk through downtown. It is Alaska's second largest town (population 23,000), and is supported by pipeline-related industries, mining, aviation, government and tourism.

Alaska Railroad Passenger Depot, 280 N. Cushman, Fairbanks, AK 99701. Located on the edge of downtown, just across the Chena River. The station has food and beverage machines and adjacent free parking.

For reservations and other information, call (907) 456-4155.

Cabs are at the station at train times; Northern Lights, 456-2557 and North Pole Taxi, 488-7900. Hertz has **rental cars** in the downtown area; 452-4444 or 800-654-3131. **Local Borough Bus** is four blocks from the station, 456-3279. **Fairbanks International Airport** is approximately five miles southwest of downtown.

Fairbanks Convention and Visitors Bureau, 550 First Ave., 99701; (907) 456-5774.

During the middle of the summer, Fairbanks' accommodations are under siege and rather expensive. Reservations should be made several months in advance, particularly if you plan to be here during "Golden Days" in the latter part of July. Since many of Fairbanks' attractions are west of downtown, many visitors prefer to stay out along Airport Way, a newer part of town, albeit striplike.

-**Super 8,** 1909 Airport Way, 99701; (907) 451-8888 or 800-843-1991. Nicely main-

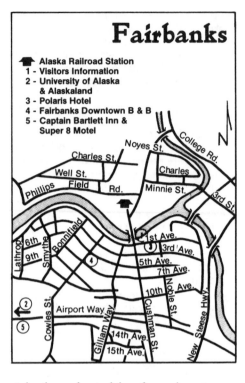

Fairbanks

Alaska Railroad Station
1 - Visitors Information
2 - University of Alaska & Alaskaland
3 - Polaris Hotel
4 - Fairbanks Downtown B & B
5 - Captain Bartlett Inn & Super 8 Motel

tained, a short drive from downtown. They will pick up and deliver train passengers. $82.

-**Captain Bartlett Inn,** 1411 Airport Way, 99701; (907) 452-1888 or 800-544-7528. A long-time popular motel, a short drive from downtown. They offer train station pick up and drop off. $96.

-**Polaris Hotel,** 407 First Ave., 99701; (907) 452-5574. This downtown landmark has been reasonably well maintained and is but a few blocks from the station. $89.

-**Fairbanks Downtown Bed & Breakfast,** 851 6th Ave., 99701; (907) 452-7700. A nicely run B&B in an older home on the fringe of downtown. Quiet neighborhood. $55.

Downtown Fairbanks is interesting to poke around. Unusual shops without a lot of glitz are in the heart of downtown. Be sure to pick up a walking tour brochure at the visitors center.

-**Workshop on Alaska** is a great way to start or end your Alaska vacation, if you have the time. This five-day course in July, presented by the University of Alaska, offers a look at everything that is unique about this great state: Northern Lights, permafrost, the oil pipeline, musk oxen, gold dredging, history—complete with field trips and salmon bakes. Tuition is $225 and rooms are provided on-campus for $8 per person (double). Write Conference on Institutes, University of Alaska Fairbanks, 117 Eielson Bldg., Fairbanks, AK 99775; or call (907) 474-7800.

-**University of Alaska Museum,** on University of Alaska-Fairbanks campus, has 10,000 feet of display space divided into six sections. Five are devoted to geographic features of the state while the sixth is devoted to traveling shows. A good place to begin a tour of Fairbanks and the surrounding area.

-**Alaskaland** is a 44-acre city "theme park" which is the site of many attractions providing visitors with a good look at Fairbanks' past and present. Located between downtown and the airport along Airport Way at Peger Rd.

-**Riverboat "Discovery"** provides rides on Alaska's only remaining sternwheeler riverboats and makes a 20-mile trip on the Chena and Tanana rivers each day in the summer. Highlight is a stop at a reconstructed Indian Village, with demonstrations of native lifestyle. (Very popular with large tour groups.)

Anchorage-Seward Route Log

 ANCHORAGE, AK - See page 287.

0:00 (3:57) Depart Anchorage, briefly following Knik Arm on right.

0:05 (3:52) If residents of suburbs near tracks are not yet awake, they soon will be, as engineer sounds air horn at several crossings. Jogging trail beside tracks will be quite busy during evening on return.

0:19 (3:34) Alaska's largest shopping mall, Diamond Center, is on left. Suburban mall had typical negative impact on downtown area when it opened a few years ago.

0:21 (3:32) Huge car-squashing operation on right is rather fascinating eyesore.

0:26 (3:26) Airstrip creates common backyard for long row of fine homes and parked aircraft bordering track on right. Some homes have been designed to also act as hangars.

0:29 (3:21) Marsh with viewing boardwalks is Potter State Game Refuge where numerous waterfowl find sanctuary. Water on right is Turnagain Arm—supposedly receiving its name when Captain James Cook explored region, having to continually adjust his vessel's course.

0:38 (3:14) Scenery becomes more dramatic as Hawaii-like mountains with thick vegetation rise steeply from water's edge across bay. Cascading waterfalls enhance this Alaskan setting. Watch for Dall sheep above tracks. Two 1896 gold-mining districts, Sunrise and Hope, lie along far shore, but are no longer active.

0:48 (3:03) Colorful moose mural adorns utility trailer behind mailboxes on left.

1:16 (2:35) At Girdwood, one of five chairlifts of Alyeska Ski Resort is visible on ridge to left. Alyeska is state's largest ski area.

1:31 (2:20) Broken trees, above on left, identify active snowslide area.

1:32 (2:19) Very attractive waterfall displays its plumage to left of tracks.

1:36 (2:15) Twentymile Glacier rests at top of valley to left.

1:39 (2:06) Train pauses for a few moments at Portage. Road to left leads to Portage Glacier viewing. Tracks curling off to left are Whittier Cutoff—Alaska Railroad's connection to Whittier-Valdez ferry service. Motor vehicles can board flatcars to be transported to Whittier and ferry connection. (Whittier has no road link to rest of state.) Note vehicle loading lanes on immediate right. This area was hard hit by 1964 earthquake, sinking nearly 12 feet. High tides covered tracks, and trains could only pass while tides were out. Soon, rails and highway separate and won't meet again until Moose Pass.

1:58 (1:55) Spencer Glacier looms, almost menacingly, on left. Engineer usually stops train here to accommodate photographers.

2:05 (1:50) Enter a tunnel and 30 seconds later emerge, clinging to Placer River Gorge, where river, full of glacial silt, has carved deeply into earth. Segments of movie *Runaway Train* were filmed along this stretch of track.

2:11 (1:45) Superb waterfall gushes down mountainside across valley to right.

2:16 (1:40) Dirty-faced Bartlett Glacier dominates scene on left. Famous "Loop,"

Alaska Railroad – Princess Tour Observation Car

a trestle that crossed over itself, once allowed tracks to negotiate rugged terrain. Loop has been replaced by some exceptional hairpin curves—and more powerful locomotion.

2:25 (1:32) Up to left is one more snowy monolith—spectacular Trail Glacier. Over one-half of world's glaciers are in Alaska.

2:52 (1:02) Waters of Upper Trail Lake spread along tracks on right.

2:56 (0:58) Village of Moose Pass is on right, where Seward Highway connects with road to fishing port of Homer. Town was originally construction camp for Alaska Railroad. Middle Trail Lake can be spotted through trees to left.

3:01 (0:53) Lower Trail Lake now accompanies tracks on right.

3:08 (0:51) On right, 24-mile-long Kenai Lake is fed by Snow River to east and is drained by Kenai River at west end.

3:42 (0:12) Nearing Seward, cross Salmon Creek, where fishing for sea-run Dolly Varden is popular.

3:48 (0:06) Seward's airport now appears on left where assorted helicopter and fixed-wing craft can be seen. Resurrection Bay is just beyond. Bay was named by explorer Alexander Baranoff when, in 1791 on Resurrection Sunday, he found shelter from a ferocious storm.

3:49 (0:05) Railroad's Seward yards swing off to left. On return run, train will back into these yards before heading north toward Anchorage.

3:50 (0:04) Huge piles of coal have been brought here from Interior Alaska coal mines, and will soon be loaded by elaborate equipment onto freighters, mostly bound for Korea.

3:51 (0:03) Cruise ships and freighters can often be spotted in harbor on left.

3:54 (0:00) Arrive Seward adjacent to town's colorful Small Boat Harbor at town's northern edge.

SEWARD, AK - Situated on beautiful Resurrection Bay and ringed by snow-capped mountains, Seward is one of Alaska's more appealing locales. It was further blessed when the 1989 oil spill avoided its shores. Although it rains a lot in Seward, its temperate climate makes it a popular visitor destination.

Named for Lincoln's Secretary of State, William H. Seward, who negotiated Alaska's acquisition from Russia in 1867, the town was established in 1903 by railroad surveyors as an ocean terminal. Tourism and fishing industries are now as important as its shipping activity.

March 27, 1964, Alaska's Good Friday earthquake hit Seward with a vengeance. All of the docks that ring the city were destroyed, and nearly all of the Alaska Railroad yards were lost when a huge wedge of waterfront disappeared into the bay. Tank farms at each end of town burst into flames and created an image of total devastation. But Seward recovered.

Daily **bus** service to Anchorage. **Ferry** service to Valdez and Kodiak. **National Car Rental** downtown at 3rd & "E" streets; (907) 274-3695.

The **Visitor Information Center** is located in the center of town at 3rd and Jefferson streets, in a vintage rail car. Write Box 749, Seward, AK 99664; or phone (907) 224-3094.

-The **Breeze Inn,** at the Small Boat Harbor and near the station, Box 2147, 99664-2147; phone (907) 224-5237; overlooking the bay.

-The **New Seward Hotel** & Saloon, located downtown, Box 670, 99664; phone (907) 224-8001; well-maintained older hotel.

-**Marina Motel,** near Small Boat Harbor, Box 1134, 99664; phone (907) 224-5518.

The entire town of Seward is within walking distance of the train. Head south and you'll see it all. The **Kenai Fiords Visitor Center** in the Small Boat Harbor has several short films about the Seward area and is worth a stop. Seward has a very fine **museum** located downtown at 3rd and Jefferson, across from the Visitor Center, with earthquake displays, railroad memorabilia and other well-presented historic displays. The **University of Alaska's Marine Education Center,** at the south end of Third Street, has some modest but interesting exhibits on local sea life. In 1989, an **Otter Research Center** was established just across the street, to scrub oil-covered sea otters. It is not open to the public, but seeing it from the outside gives an idea of the magnitude of the otter rescue effort.

Canadian Rail Service

Whether a traveler is in search of breathtaking mountain scenery, spectacular and rugged coastlines, North America's only walled city, or simply a remote Indian village—it can be found using Canada's rail system. The Canadian, the country's transcontinental train, traces a twisting route of trestles and tunnels through the majestic Rockies, including Jasper National Park, while the Skeena traverses the beautiful wilderness of central British Columbia. The British Columbia Railway snakes along fiord-like Howe Sound, then takes on the direct challenge of the Coastal Range. A northland adventure is offered by the Hudson Bay which makes an excursion to that immense body of water, where Churchill hunkers down on its desolate and polar-bear-populated shoreline. And in the East, the Ocean, after departing Montreal, makes a swing through the Maritime Provinces of New Brunswick and Nova Scotia, before making a triumphant entrance into Halifax along one of the world's most attractive inner harbors—Bedford Basin.

Although, as a general rule, the rolling stock is older than that found in the U.S. (it's the equivalent of Amtrak's Heritage Fleet), this equipment is well-maintained and very comfortable. Also, modern LRC equipment (Light, Rapid, Comfortable) has gone into service in the heavily populated areas in and around Toronto and Montreal, allowing higher speed with unique automatic tilting capability on curves. Domes are included on transcontinental trains affording great roof-top views of the passing scenes.

As in the U.S., Canada has relegated the operation of most of its passenger train service to a government-owned corporation—VIA Rail Canada. Unfortunately, effective January 15, 1990, the Canadian government severely curtailed VIA's operations. The legendary Canadian no longer runs on CP rail tracks, leaving transcontinental passengers with only one choice of routes, through Edmonton rather than Calgary. Long-distance trains have been relegated to only triweekly service. On the brighter side, most of the former system's routes still see service, albeit less frequently.

In the East, logical access between VIA and Amtrak occurs with direct trains from New York to either Montreal or Toronto. VIA can also be found at the border towns of Windsor and Sarnia, Ontario across from the Amtrak-served cities of Detroit and Port Huron, Michigan. A train also connects Chicago and Toronto, crossing the border at Sarnia. Also, connecting bus service is available between VIA in Vancouver and Amtrak in Seattle and between VIA in Winnipeg and Amtrak in Grand Forks, North Dakota.

Reservations - It is a good idea to make reservations as early as possible for those trains requiring them. Reservations can be made by calling any of the toll-free numbers in the Appendix. Of course, travel agents are always available to make reservations. Timetables can also be acquired at VIA stations or by calling their toll-free numbers.

Tickets - Although tickets would generally be purchased through a sales office or a travel agent, it is possible to buy them after boarding the train, but only to the nearest major city. As in the U.S., major credit cards are accepted.

Fares - Fares are generally comparable to those in the U.S. However, several special discounts are available, and it is important to give each consideration in trying to arrive at the lowest fare. These specials can make Canadian rail travel very economical—particularly long-distance travel in the off season. A travel agent or VIA sales office will be able to help in making these determinations. Children, persons 60 or older, those traveling round trip and groups are all entitled to discounts.

And perhaps the greatest bargain, if one plans to travel extensively, is the CANRAILPASS. Here, a travel card is purchased allowing unlimited travel for one fixed price. The price varies, depending on the territory in which travel is permitted, the length of time the pass can be used, and the time of year that travel will take place.

Flag Stops - Myriad flag stops exist on Canadian routes—so numerous, no effort has been made to include all of them in *Rail Ventures* logs.

Customs - For citizens of the U.S., entry into Canada is relatively simple, with no passports or visas required. Some evidence of citizenship should be carried by native-born U.S. citizens such as birth, baptismal or voter's certificate. A drivers license or social security card is not necessarily considered evidence of citizenship. Naturalized citizens should carry a naturalization certificate or some other evidence of citizenship. Persons under 18, not accompanied by an adult, should have a letter from a parent or guardian giving them permission to travel in Canada.

Persons not citizens or legal residents of the U.S. generally will need a passport or some other acceptable travel document. These persons who wish to return to the U.S. should check with a U.S. Immigration Office to make sure they have the necessary papers.

Timetables - To order a VIA timetable, call one of the VIA phone numbers listed in the Appendix.

Montreal
Halifax

Atlantic

Linking the Nova Scotian coastal city of Halifax with Montreal, the Atlantic affords its passengers lovely countryside scenes in southern New Brunswick, and, best of all, an outstanding trip around Bedford Basin—that truly spectacular inner harbor at Halifax. Because the Canadian Pacific Railway, some 100 years ago, needed access to an eastern port that was ice free, there is a unique aspect of this trip. Although the Atlantic is a Canadian train running on Canadian-owned tracks, its route short-cuts across United States soil. Stops are made at several towns in northern Maine, ironically providing the only rail passenger service in the state.

Since the US-Canadian border is crossed twice, customs inspections are inevitable. Fortunately, this procedure no longer involves passengers who are neither getting on nor off in Maine.

Westbound Schedule (Condensed)
Halifax, N.S. - Early Afternoon Departure
Moncton, N.B. - Late Afternoon
Saint John, N.B. - Early Evening
Jackman, ME - Middle of the Night
Montreal, Que. - Early Morning

Eastbound Schedule (Condensed)
Montreal, Que. - Early Evening Departure
Jackman, ME - Middle of the Night
Saint John, N.B. - Early Morning
Moncton, N.B. - Late Morning
Halifax, N.S. - Late Afternoon Arrival

Frequency - Three times a week, departing both Halifax and Montreal—Monday, Thursday and Saturday.

Seating - Standard coaches and Day-nighters.
Dining - Complete meal and beverage service as well as lighter fare.
Sleeping - Dayniter coach, berths, roomettes, and bedrooms.
Baggage - Checked baggage at larger towns.
Reservations - All-reserved train.
Length of Trip - 752 miles in 20½ hours.

Route Log

HALIFAX, N.S. - Halifax was founded by Edward Cornwallis in 1749 as an army and naval base for the English after the French established an imposing fortress at nearby Louisbourg. The deep harbour, protected by both islands and bluffs, made it an ideal naval base, particularly after the Citadel Hill Fortress was constructed as protection. Halifax has remained a military center to this date.

Because of its excellent harbor, Halifax has always been oriented toward ocean industries with ship-repair facilities, containerization docks and various other ship-yards still dominating its waterfront. It's a remarkably clean city and attracts thousands of visitors every year, many using this provincial capital as a base for touring the rest of the province. The shores, particularly to the south, are noted for their ruggedness.

In 1917 the largest man-made explosion (prior to the atom bomb) occurred in Halifax Harbor when, on December 6th of that year, The Mont Blanc, a freighter loaded with ammunition, collided with the Imo. The Mont Blanc caught fire and 26 minutes later she blew up, devastating large portions of Halifax and Dartmouth and killing 1,900 persons.

VIA Station, 1161 Hollis St., is a nicely remodeled station on the edge of downtown. There is a snack bar, a newsstand and redcaps. Thirty-minute free parking is in front of the station. Pay-parking is at the rear of the station.

Ticket windows and waiting room are open 8 am to 6:30 pm. Call 429-8421 for reservations and other information.

Cab stand and **local buses** at the station; Yellow Cab, 422-1551 and Casino Taxi, 429-6666. Metro Transit, 421-6600. **Bus terminal** for Acadian Lines, 454-9321. Tilden **rental cars** are nearby and there is a direct phone line from the station. The **airport** is located across the bay and southeast of Dartmouth.

Tourism Halifax, Old City Hall, Duke and Barrington streets; (902) 421-8736. A provincial information office is in The Old Red Store on the wharf at Historic Properties; (902) 424-4247. Write: Box 1749, B3J 3A5.

Hotel Nova Scotian, 1181 Hollis St., B3H 2P6; (902) 423-7231. Comfortable, well-maintained hotel, adjoins the station. $104.

-Halliburton House Inn, 5184 Morris Street, B3J 1B3; (902) 420-0658. A smaller hotel occupying a Registered Heritage Property. Breakfast and afternoon tea are included. Only two blocks from the station. $95.

Many attractions are within walking distance. A map of Halifax describing a **walking tour** may be obtained from the Visitors Bureau which is about a 15-minute walk north of the VIA station. Points of interest include: the old waterfront where the **"Bluenose II,"** a replica of the famous racing schooner and used for pleasure cruises, is often berthed (the original Bluenose, built in 1921, kept the International Fisherman's Trophy in Canada for 20 years); **Historic Properties** which is made of nicely restored buildings along the waterfront; and the **Maritime Museum of the Atlantic,** which includes exhibits of such nautical

subjects as a "skinned" torpedo and flotsam from the Titanic.

The Citadel, located on a hill overlooking the harbor with a large star-shaped fortress, replacing the earlier wooden one built by Cornwallis, also has Maritime and Historic Museums.

Musquodoboit Railway Museum, the largest in eastern Canada, is located at Musquodoboit Harbor north of Halifax.

0:00 (1:27) Depart Halifax.
0:12 (1:10) Tracks now make an encompassing arc along westerly shore of beautiful Bedford Basin, on right. Everything

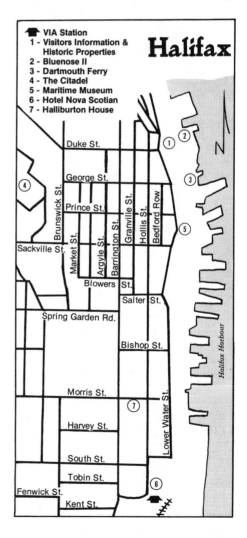

VIA Station
1 - Visitors Information & Historic Properties
2 - Bluenose II
3 - Dartmouth Ferry
4 - The Citadel
5 - Maritime Museum
6 - Hotel Nova Scotian
7 - Halliburton House

Halifax

Halifax Station

from giant oceangoing freighters to smallest pleasure craft speckle harbor, creating a scene that captures very essence of Canada's Maritime Provinces. Two suspension bridges in distance span harbor entrance and connect twin cities of Dartmouth (on left) and Halifax. It was in that general area that munitions ship, Mont Blanc, exploded in 1917.

0:19 (1:08) Eastbound Atlantic pauses briefly at Windsor Junction, where line branches off to left toward Yarmouth.

0:46 (0:40) Elongated waters of Shubenacadie Grand Lake form inviting scene on left as train cuts through rolling Nova Scotian countryside. Many other small lakes can be observed through here.

1:02 (0:25) Cross Shubenacadie River and slip through nice-appearing town with same unusual name (an Indian word meaning "where the potato grows").

1:27 (0:00) Arrive Truro.

TRURO, N.S. - Located at the tip of Cobequid Bay, actually an extension of the high-tidal-action Bay of Fundy, Truro is one of the largest of the early-Acadian settlements. Here, railroad-

ing and manufacturing play important economic roles, while higher education is also prominent. It is the home for Nova Scotia Agricultural College and Nova Scotia Teachers College.

0:00 (1:20) Depart Truro and start a twisting trek across upper thumb of Nova Scotia.

0:18 (1:02) Cross Canada Highway 104 and then travel 87 feet above small, but lovely, Folly River.

0:30 (0:50) Train grinds over summit where Folly Lake lies nestled just to right of tracks.

1:00 (0:20) Cross River Phillip coursing through pine-laden forests.

1:20 (0:00) Arrive Springhill Jct.

SPRINGHILL JUNCTION, N.S. - This very small town (population 203) was named for springs found in nearby hills.

0:00 (0:22) Depart Springhill Jct.

0:22 (0:00) Arrive Amherst.

AMHERST, N.S. - Geography buffs will be happy to learn that this is the geographical center of the

Maritime Provinces. It is also a manufacturing center, producing such varied products as clothing, structural steel, dairy goods and tanning oils.

0:00 (0:17) Depart Amherst.

0:07 (0:10) Enter New Brunswick and leave Nova Scotia.

0:11 (0:06) Historic Fort Beausejour, perched atop knoll on right, stands silent guard over Tantramar Marshes which stretch across 84 square miles on left. These marshes were once tidal flats until French Acadians, more than 200 years ago, resourcefully constructed elaborate dike systems, turning what was once muddy bogs into fertile farmlands. Dikes are still visible today.

0:17 (0:00) Arrive Sackville.

SACKVILLE, N.B. - This city of 5,800 persons rejoices in the distinction of possessing the only harness shop in North America still producing horse collars. It is also the location of Mount Allison University, which, in 1875, awarded the first degree given to a woman in the British Empire. Sackville was a seaport until a landslide changed the course of the Tantramar River in 1920.

0:00 (0:51) Depart Sackville.

0:51 (0:00) Arrive Moncton.

MONCTON, N.B. - The present location of the city was first occupied for a short while in the mid-1700s by French Acadians who reclaimed the surrounding marshes by constructing dykes along the river. However, the site was ultimately abandoned when the British forced the Acadians to leave and totally destroyed the settlement. Later, in 1766, several German families from Pennsylvania moved to what is now Moncton, a simplification of the name of Lieutenant General Robert Monckton, who served under Wolfe's command, and captured nearby Fort Beausejour in 1755.

Although shipbuilding was once an important industry in Moncton, it gradually declined and the town with it. Finally, new life came with the railroad, and Moncton became a major rail and trade center for eastern Canada. Several of New Brunswick's attractions are nearby.

VIA Station, 1240 Main St., has storage lockers, redcaps, a snack

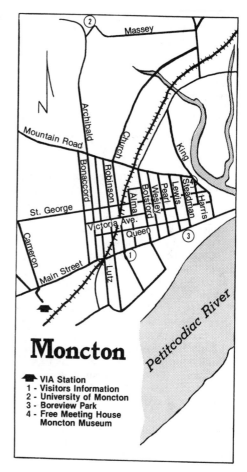

Moncton

- VIA Station
- 1 - Visitors Information
- 2 - University of Moncton
- 3 - Boreview Park
- 4 - Free Meeting House
   Moncton Museum

bar and a newsstand. Pay-parking is adjacent to the station. A shopping mall is within easy walking distance.

For reservations and information, call (506) 853-8012; for arrival and departure information, 857-0372. Ticket window and waiting room are open 9:30 am to 10 pm.

Cab stand at the station; Air Cab, 857-2000. Nearest **local bus** stop, one block from the station, Main at Highfield Square. **SMT bus** terminal, 859-5060. Tilden will pick up and deliver **rental car** customers, 857-0644. **Moncton Municipal Airport** is approximately five miles east of the station.

Moncton Marketing and Promotion, 774 Main St., E1C 1E8; (506) 853-3333.

Keddy's Brunswick Hotel, Highfield and Main St., E1C 8N6; (506) 854-6340 or 800-561-7666. One block from the station. $75.

-Colonial Inn, 42 Highfield St., E1C 8T6; (506) 382-3395. Two blocks from the station. $67.

In town, the **Acadian Museum** at the University of Moncton, the only French university in the Atlantic provinces, has displays featuring the Acadian culture of the Moncton area. The **Tidal Bore** can be viewed from Bore Park where the tide comes in. As the tide moves across the vast mud flats, they become a mile-wide river, often 30 feet deep. Timetables for witnessing this event are available at the information center.

Centennial Park has displays including "Old 5270," a Pacific class steam locomotive, a CF-100 jet fighter and a World War II Sherman tank.

Not far from Moncton, **Hopewell Cape** has unusual "flower pot" rocks formed by the enormous tides of the Bay of Fundy.

Fort Beausejour National Historic Park is located just off the Trans-Canada Highway, 35 minutes southeast from Moncton. The fort was built by the French between 1751 and 1755, but was captured by the English before completion. The fort has a commanding view across the expanses of the Tantramar Marsh where the Acadians reclaimed most of the land from the Fundy tides by using extensive systems of dykes.

0:00 (0:57) Depart Moncton.
0:07 (0:50) Last look at Shepody Bay is afforded just off to left.
0:30 (0:27) Cross Petitcodiac River.
0:57 (0:00) Arrive Sussex.

SUSSEX, N.B. - Recent potash discoveries here have enlivened the town's economy. The only other Canadian potash deposits are in western Saskatchewan. The town has long been an important dairy and craft center.
0:00 (0:52) Depart Sussex.
0:12 (0:40) Through Norton, note many homes with rather interestingly similar architecture—large white structures with black, hippish roofs.
0:15 (0:37) Eye-catching (and tongue-twisting) Kennebecasis River flows along

with train, on right.
0:18 (0:34) One of few remaining covered bridges in this region is on right, charm being further enhanced by two churches that form backdrop.
0:34 (0:22) Kennebecasis Bay can now be seen on right with its residential studded shore line. Note fine-looking mansion on hill on far side of water.
0:44 (0:12) Through Rothebay with its numerous summer homes and scattered pleasure craft floating at their docks.
0:52 (0:00) Arrive St. John. VIA station stands near site of former Union Station demolished in 1971.

ST. JOHN, N.B. - This is Canada's oldest incorporated city (1785), founded by thousands of Loyalists who landed here in 1783. Benedict Arnold came here to live after having to leave the United States. The city claims some firsts: the first newspaper and the first bank in Canada, and the first police force in North America.
0:00 (0:55) Depart St. John.
0:08 (0:47) Train crosses high above St. John River. If tide is out, famous Reversing Falls Rapids can be seen below on right. Twice each day, high Fundy tides cause reversal in water's flow.
0:09 (0:46) Impressive Kimberly Clarke paper mill is on immediate right with its intimidating structures and huge piles of wood chips.
0:16 (0:39) Stunning view of St. John River's Grand Bay on right. Numerous cottages can be seen snuggled along shoreline.
0:20 (0:35) Train now bids farewell to river as tracks climb northwesterly toward Fredericton.
0:30 (0:25) New Brunswick's rural charm continues with another covered-bridge scene on left.
0:52 (0:04) Pass by expansive facilities of Gagetown Armed Forces Base, one of largest (geographically) in Commonwealth.
0:57 (0:00) Arrive Fredericton Junction.

FREDERICTON JCT., N.B. - This is the closest the main line comes to Fredericton. Not much here, but it is a stop for connecting buses to the city itself. Fredericton is the cultural center of New Brunswick, as well as the provincial capital.

0:00 (0:50) Depart Fredericton Jct.

0:05 (0:45) Forest lands continue, with birch stands offering their white-barked trunks to lighten this heavily wooded region. Lakes and dairy farms are abundant as we approach the state of Maine.

0:50 (0:00) Arrive McAdam, where gargantuan station, constructed in 1901 from locally quarried granite, is now a national historic site. This three-story dinosaur was originally a combination station and hotel, but hostelry closed in 1959.

MCADAM, N.B. - This was once a major passenger train hub, with branch lines serving various New Brunswick destinations, including St. Andrews, where CP once ran and operated the still-famous Algonquin Hotel.

0:00 (0:10) Depart McAdam, and in a few moments enter the state of Maine upon crossing St. Croix River.

Enter Eastern time zone. Westbound passengers move clocks forward one hour. Eastbound, back one hour.

0:10 (0:00) Arrive Vanceboro.

VANCEBORO, ME - This is a customs stop for westbound trains. Inspections usually go rather swiftly, but there can be occasional delays.

0:00 (4:37) Depart Vanceboro.

The train now traverses the southern edge of the upper wilderness of Maine, still following the Canadian Pacific's track during the dead of night. Occasional stops are made when civilization is contacted at **DANFORTH, MATTAWAMKEAG, BROWNVILLE JUNCTION,** and **GREENVILLE.**

4:37 (0:00) Arrive Jackman.

JACKMAN, ME - This border station is a customs stop for eastbound passenger trains.

0:00 (1:10) Depart Jackman.

0:40 (0:30) Leave United States and cross into Quebec.

1:10 (0:00) Arrive Megantic.

MEGANTIC, QUE. - Another Canadian town that has largely descended from Loyalist settlers, this community is at the tip of ten-mile-long Lake Megantic—a fisherman's pristine haven.

0:00 (2:08) Depart Megantic.

2:08 (0:00) Arrive Sherbrooke.

SHERBROOKE, QUE. - As one might suspect from observing the surrounding forests, the city's economy is heavily dependent on wood products, including lumber, pulp and paper. Winter recreation is also becoming important.

Located at the confluence of the Magog River and the Saint Francois, the city has an attractive setting, spread out across numerous hills with the Magog cutting an impressive chasm through the heart of town. The University of Sherbrooke is here, and boasts a fine art gallery and rather handsome campus.

0:00 (0:43) Depart Sherbrooke, following along banks of impressive Saint Francois River.

0:43 (0:00) Arrive Richmond.

RICHMOND, QUE. - This is a small agrarian-oriented community, and the point where the tracks now diverge from the attractive Saint Francois River Valley. Richmond began with the arrival of the Grand Trunk Railroad in 1853.

0:00 (0:55) Depart Richmond.

0:53 (0:02) Cross Yamaska River.

0:55 (0:00) Arrive St. Hyacinthe.

ST. HYACINTHE, QUE. - This town of 40,000 serves as a trade center for local farming activities, and also is home for those who don't mind commuting to Montreal, some 33 miles to the west. The town was not named for lily-like flower but a local landowner.

0:00 (0:33) Depart St. Hyacinthe, then pass town's golf course on outskirts at left.

0:10 (0:23) Royal Hills, those unusual mountains on left, are of volcanic origin dating back millions of years. A quarry can be seen on the slopes of St. Hilaire, two miles away, which is a source of rare minerals, many being found only in this locale. Rougemont Mountain is eight miles distant, while 1,350-foot Yamaska Mountain is 12 miles from here.

0:15 (0:18) Trundle over impressive Richelieu River which drains Lake Champlain, directly south of us in New York State, into the St. Lawrence.

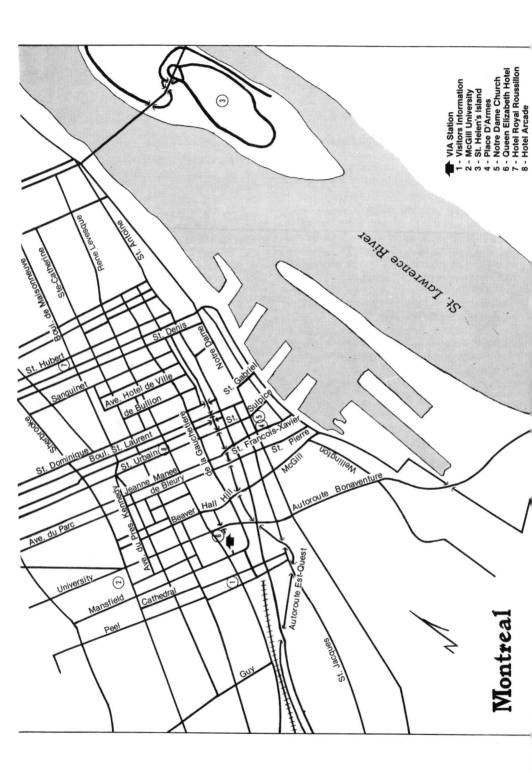

Montreal

VIA Station
1 - Visitors Information
2 - McGill University
3 - St. Helen's Island
4 - Place D'Armes
5 - Notre Dame Church
6 - Queen Elizabeth Hotel
7 - Hotel Royal Roussillon
8 - Hotel Arcade

St. Lawrence River

306

0:33 (0:00) Arrive St. Lambert.

ST. LAMBERT, QUE. - We are now immediately across the St. Lawrence from our destination, Montreal. St. Lambert Lock, a lift station for the St. Lawrence Seaway traffic, is here.

0:00 (0:12) Depart St. Lambert and start ascent necessary for crossing St. Lawrence River on Victoria Bridge.

This structure was once known as the Jubilee Bridge when it was opened in 1898. It handled two sets of rails, an electric interurban line and auto traffic, and was one of the world's longest bridges at 1¼ miles. Those two concrete-lined channels below us are the St. Lawrence Seaway and the St. Lambert Lock which is just one of many locks needed to raise or lower shipping using this waterway. The Seaway is narrow and unfortunately cannot handle larger ships of today's maritime fleet. The islands to the right were home to Canada's very successful 1967 world's fair—Expo 67. The geodesic dome was the U.S. Pavilion. The skyline of Montreal is a dramatic scene on the right.

0:06 (0:06) Leaving Victoria Bridge, we enter Montreal through Canadian National rail yards.

0:08 (0:04) Slip over nicely landscaped Canal Lachine (pronounced luh-sheen), built years ago to circumvent Lachine Rapids, but discontinued operations when Seaway was opened.

0:10 (0:02) Sink underground as we near end of line.

0:12 (0:00) Arrive Montreal's Central Station.

MONTREAL, QUE. - Montreal is one of North America's oldest cities. In 1535 Jacques Cartier discovered this location which was already inhabited by 4,000 Iroquois Amerindians. However, it wasn't until 1642 that a permanent settlement was established by French Jesuit missionaries.

Although the British captured the town in 1760 during the Battle of the Plains of Abraham (which ultimately led to all of Canada becoming British), Montreal, to this day, remains a city of charming French character. Three-fourths of its populace still speak that language, and the city has a distinct European look and feel.

Located on a collection of islands in the St. Lawrence River, and only 117 feet above sea level, it is dominated by 765-foot Mount Royal from which the city derives its name. Winters here can be hard, but miles of underground shopping and a good subway system make it a town to be visited during any season.

Central Station, 895 la Gauchetiere W. (at University), is located in the very heart of downtown. This is one of VIA's busiest and best stations. Escalators leading down to train platforms stretch across its central plaza while stores and services are ensconced along the perimeter. There are numerous snack bars, restaurants and shops that line the underground arcades leading to other buildings in downtown Montreal. There are redcaps, and pay-parking is adjacent to the station.

Ticket windows are open 6:30 am to 11:35 pm; the waiting room is open 5 am to 12:15 am. For reservations and other information, call (514) 871-1331.

Cab stand at the station; Diamond, 273-6331, and LaSalle, 277-2552. Tilden and Budget **rental cars** are at the station. Local buses stop at the station, 288-6287. **Intercity bus** terminal, Voyageur, (514) 842-2281. **Montreal International Airport** is about 15 miles west of downtown.

Visitor Information Center, 1001 Square Dorchester (at Peel); (514) 871-1595. Write Greater Montreal Convention & Tourism Bureau, 1010 Sainte-Catherine Street West, Suite 410, H3B 1G2.

The Queene Elizabeth Hotel, 900 Dorchester Blvd. W. (at Mansfield), H3B 4A5; (514) 861-3511 or 800-828-7447. One of Montreal's best. Located above Central Station. $150.

-Hotel Royal Roussillon, 1610 rue St-Hubert, H2L 3Z3; (514) 849-3214. Attractive accommodations, one of downtown Montreal's best values. Easily reached by subway; get off at Berri-de-Montigny Station (Boul. de Maisonneure). About a mile north of VIA's Central Station, in a quiet neighborhood. $60.

-Hotel Arcade, 50 Rene-Levesque Blvd. West (formerly Dorchester Blvd.), H27 1A2; (514) 874-0906. New hotel with small rooms. Five blocks from the station. $70.

Two Bed and Breakfast reservation services include:

-A Downtown Bed & Breakfast Network, 3458 Laval Ave. (at Sherbrooke St.), H2X 3C8; (514) 289-9749. A reservation service for 85 B&Bs in the downtown area, including this location.

-Montreal Bed & Breakfast, 4912 Victoria Ave., H3W 2N1; (514) 738-9410.

Much of Montreal is underground, with shops, restaurants and services lining miles of walkways underneath portions of the city. A **walking tour** of the old city, roughly defined by McGill, Notre-Dame, Berri streets and the St. Lawrence River, can be taken starting at Place D'Armes (at St. Sulpice and Notre Dame St.). Here one can see Notre Dame Church, Saint-Sulpice Seminary and the Bank of Montreal Museum. From this point, walk east along cobblestone streets to see Place de la Justice and artists exhibiting works. Upon reaching the church and Bonsecours Market, head west and pass by Place Royale, the d'Youville Stables and the Old General Hospital. The old city also has many galleries, charming shops and cafes.

St. Helen's Island has several attractions including: **The Montreal Aquarium** with fine displays of marine life; **St. Helen's Island Museum** at the Old Ford, Montreal's Military and Maritime Museum, with various military and naval artifacts dating from the 15th century; and **LaRonde,** a spectacular amusement park, resulting from the world's fair (Expo '67) held here in 1967.

The **Montreal Museum of Fine Arts,** 1379 rue Sherbrooke W., with excellent permanent art collections as well as traveling exhibits.

Mount Royal Overlook has a great view and a steep climb—206 steps up a stairway with only two landings. Go up Peel Street, through McGill University to Mount Royal Park to the base of the stairs, then climb!

Some distance northeast of downtown, but reached by subway, is the **Botanical Gardens,** 4101 rue Sherbrooke E. Get off the subway at Pie IX Station (the stop for the **Montreal Expos** stadium). There are over 25,000 species and plant varieties, 30 outdoor gardens and nine greenhouses. This is one of the most outstanding botanical gardens in the world.

Montreal   Halifax

Ocean

The Ocean is VIA's connection to the Atlantic provinces avoiding those customs stops made by the Atlantic. As a result, many travelers prefer this route over the Atlantic's trip through Maine.

This is an overnight trip to (and from) Montreal, skirting around the topside of Maine. The result is a trip along the St. Lawrence River during the western leg of the journey, with the segment between Levis, Que. and Campbellton, N.B. normally traveled in darkness.

Westbound Schedule (Condensed)
Halifax, N.S. - Early Afternoon Departure
Moncton, N.B. - Late Afternoon Departure
Campbellton, N.B. - Late Evening
Levis, Que. - Early Morning (Ferry Service
    to Quebec City)
Montreal, Que. - Early Morning Arrival

Eastbound Schedule (Condensed)
Montreal, Que. - Early Evening Departure
Levis, Que. - Late Evening (Ferry Service
    to Quebec City)
Campbellton, N.B. - Early Morning
Moncton, N.B. - Late Morning
Halifax, N.S. - Late Afternoon Arrival

Frequency - Three times a week, departing both Halifax and Montreal Sunday, Wednesday and Friday.

Seating - Standard coaches and Dayniters.

Dining - Complete meal and beverage service as well as lighter fare.

Sleeping - Dayniter coach, berths, roomettes, and bedrooms.

Baggage - Checked baggage at larger towns.

Reservations - All-reserved train.
Length of Trip - 840 miles in 20½ hours.

Route Log

For route between Halifax and Moncton, see that portion of the Atlantic route log, page 301.

 MONCTON, N.B. - See page 303.

0:00 (1:00) Depart Moncton.

From Moncton to Rogersville, the Ocean follows eastern margin of interior New Brunswick wilderness, occasionally touching small villages, many of which sprung up when the railroad was completed.
0:26 (0:34) Cross Richibucto River.
0:54 (0:06) Cross Kouchibouguacis River.
1:00 (0:00) Arrive Rogersville.

ROGERSVILLE, N.B. - This small trading center of 1,061 persons is named in honor of James Rogers, former Bishop of Chaltham.
0:00 (0:31) Depart Rogersville.
0:21 (0:10) Cross impressive Miramichi River, burgeoning with waters originating from much of central New Brunswick, and which finally empties into Miramichi Bay in Gulf of St. Lawrence on right (too far to be visible).
0:31 (0:00) Arrive Newcastle.

NEWCASTLE, N.B. - Situated on the tip of Miramichi Bay, shipping through its fine port facilities generates much of this city's business. Pulp production is also an important economic mainstay. Of interest is McDonald Farm, northeast of here, which is a working farm carefully restored to depict rural life in the early 1800s. Miramichi Folksong Festival is celebrated here each summer.

0:00 (0:50) Depart Newcastle and continue through forested lands of eastern New Brunswick.

0:11 (0:39) Conclusions are easily drawn about local pastimes (and winter weather) when observing homemade hockey rink on left.

0:44 (0:06) Cross large Nepisiguit River just before it flows into Nepisiguit Bay.

0:50 (0:00) Arrive Bathurst (pronounced bat-hurst).

BATHURST, N.B. - This city of 16,300 is the urban focal point for mining and other industry in northeastern New Brunswick. Tourists have also found this area with its many scenic waterfalls and beaches. A pretty drive leads to nearby Caraquet where Acadian Historical Village is located—a re-created settlement depicting Acadian lifestyle of the early 1800s.

0:00 (1:20) Depart Bathurst and trace course along Chaleur Bay, on right, until Campbellton.

0:04 (1:16) Cross Tetagouche River.

0:34 (0:46) Pass through small coastal community of Jacquet River (flag stop) where good crab and lobster fishing is afforded along shoreline, and then cross Jacquet River.

0:49 (0:31) Apparent narrowness of bay is caused by Heron Island about five miles off shore to right.

1:07 (0:13) This is Dalhousie Jct., with newsprint mills and popular public beaches nearby.

1:20 (0:00) Arrival at Campbellton is marked by lovely view of bay.

CAMPBELLTON, N.B. - In 1760, the bay serving this port city provided the setting for the last naval engagement of The Seven Years War. Superb fishing is found throughout this region of New Brunswick, and a well-attended Salmon Festival is held here each July. Nearby Sugarloaf Provincial Park provides not only fishing, but camping and winter sports as well.

0:00 (0:24) When departing Campbellton, impressive bridge can be seen on right, spanning tip of Chaleur Bay, fed at this

point by fish-filled Restigouche River.

0:23 (0:01) Cross Restigouche River and, at midpoint, enter Quebec and leave New Brunswick.

Gain one hour as train passes from Atlantic to Eastern Time. Set your watch back (forward if eastbound) one hour.

0:24 (0:00) Arrive Matapedia.

MATAPEDIA, N.B. - The name Matapedia stems from a similar Indian word meaning "river breaks into branches." Technically speaking, rather than separating, Matapedia and Restigouche rivers join here, just before rushing into bay. This is also where the rail line to Gaspe departs our route.

0:00 (6:30) Depart Matapedia.

From here to just beyond Amqui, the Ocean stays in the exciting Matapedia River Valley where the swift, sometimes torrential waters of the Matapedia are always a stone's throw from the tracks. Since the Ocean runs along this stretch in darkness, forested hills, spotted with intermittent lakes and harboring considerable wildlife, as well as an occasional picturesque farmstead, are scenes afforded passengers only if the train is considerably off schedule.

Several communities are nighttime stops between here and Levis, including: **CAUSAPSCAL, AMQUI, SAYABEC, MONT-JOLI, RIMOUSKI, TROIS-PISTOLES, RIVER-DU-LOUP** and **MONTGAMY.**

7:15 (0:00) Arrive Levis, where ferry service to Quebec City is available. Quebec City is immediately across St. Lawrence River on right.

QUEBEC CITY, QUE. - Champlain founded Quebec City in 1608 as a fur-trading post, and in 1620 he established a fort on the higher plateau portion of the city. The city soon developed as a city on two levels with the upper portion, 305 feet above sea level, being a natural defensive fortification, and becoming a military and administrative area. A stone wall was constructed surrounding a portion of this upper city with an entrance through three large gates. The lower city was primarily trade-oriented.

Today, an unusual tubular elevator, "Funiculaire," connects these two levels.

Quebec City's strategic location made it the focal point of two major battles. In 1759 an attack across the Plains of Abraham occurred when the British, led by Wolfe, scaled the cliffs of the city and defeated the French commanded by Montcalm. Then in 1775, American Patriots made an effort to siege Quebec City, and a force led by Benedict Arnold mounted an unsuccessful attempt to capture it. Additional fortifications were built, but were never used as this was the last effort made to take the city by force.

Today, Quebec City is the provincial capital of Quebec. Its strong French-European flavor (over 90% of the population speaks French) and uniquely quaint appearance (it is the only walled city north of Mexico) have made this a popular tourist destination point.

VIA Station, Gare du Palais, 450 rue de la gare du Palais. This grand old station was built by the Canadian Pacific Railway in 1916 and served Quebec City as a rail station until its closure in 1976, forcing downtown passengers to use the suburban Sainte-Foy station. The early 1980s saw a remarkable renovation ($28 million) and service once again restored to the heart of the city starting in late 1985. (The suburban VIA station in Ste-Foy is still operational.)

There are storage lockers, luggage carts, a restaurant, a snack bar, a newsstand and underground pay-parking.

For reservations, call (418) 692-3940; for arrivals and departures, (418) 524-6452. Ticket windows are open very early mornings, late mornings and afternoons. The waiting room is open from about 5:30 am to 11 pm.

Cab stand is at the station and there is a direct phone line. **Bus** terminal on Boulevard Charest, between Dorchester and Caron. Tilden and Budget **rental cars** are within walking distance. There is **ferry** service from Quebec City to and from Levis across the St. Lawrence River for VIA train service to the Atlantic provinces. This ferry service is operated on a 24-hour basis, departing every half hour from 6 am to midnight—less frequently from midnight to 6 am. **Quebec Municipal Airport** is northwest of the

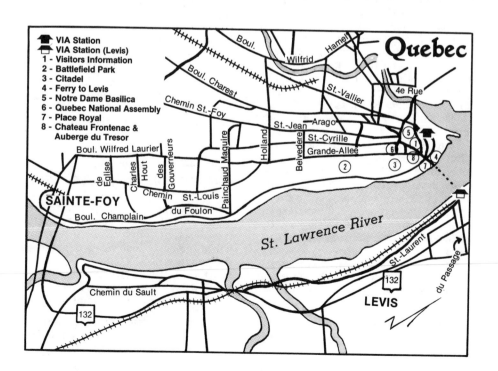

311

city.

? Tourisme Quebec, 12 rue Sainte-Anne; (418) 643-2280, or 800-443-7000 (Eastern U.S.), or 800-363-7777 (Western U.S.). Write Tourisme Quebec, C.P. 20000, G1K 7X2.

Quebec has a central room-reservation service, 800-463-1568 (for the U.S. and Canada). There are also Bed and Breakfast possibilities; call (418) 527-1465 for B&B reservation service.

-**LeChateau Frontenac,** 1 rue des Carrieres, G1R 4P5; (418) 692-3861 or 800-828-7447. Quebec's most famous landmark. A mile from the station. $150.

-**Auberge du Tresor,** 20 rue Ste-Anne (at du Fort), G1R 3X2; (418) 694-1876. Small, moderately priced hotel, excellently located across from LeChateau Frontenac, next to the tourism office. One mile from the station. $75.

A few In-Town Attractions: The Citadel, with its enormous walls overlooking the entire city, is the largest fortification in North America still garrisoned by regular troops. This British-built fortress can best be seen by guided tours.

If you do nothing else, be sure to stroll along **Dufferin Terrace,** a boardwalk in front of the Chateau Frontenac Hotel that connects to the **Promenade des Gouverneurs** following the cliffside with sweeping views of the St. Lawrence River and its maritime activity.

Place Royale, in the lower town along the St. Lawrence River, is the birthplace of Quebec City, and several of the 18th-century houses are open to the public.

The Notre-Dame-des-Victoires Church is one of the oldest in North America. Also, the **Quebec Fortifications,** 2 rue d'Auteuil, C.P. 2474, built due to the city's strategic location, were designed by the French engineer Gaspard Chaussegros de Levy. Covering a large portion of the city, pathways allow easy viewing.

The Cite Parlementaire, which houses Quebec's National Assembly, is located just outside of the walls of the city.

0:00 (0:22) Depart Levis, and soon begin climb from water level to slightly higher plain for remainder of run into Montreal.

Some marvelous views of Quebec City and St. Lawrence River with its ocean-going traffic will be afforded on the right as we make this climb.

0:22 (0:00) Arrive Charney.

CHARNEY, QUE. - At this juncture, trains on the south side of the St. Lawrence traveling from Montreal and Quebec City depart from this line and curl northward to make a spectacular crossing of the river before entering Ste-Foy.

0:00 (1:46) Depart Charney.

0:03 (1:43) Cross a river named Chaudiere, a French translation of an Indian word meaning "boiling kettle."

0:23 (1:23) Through Laurier, a small town of 1,000 named after Wilfred Laurier, an early Prime Minister of Canada.

0:31 (1:15) Cross swift-moving Henri River.

1:02 (0:44) Note rows of rocks in field on right, waste product of a farmer's effort to make his field more productive.

1:07 (0:39) Cross Becancour River at milepost 66.8.

1:21 (0:25) At St. Leonard, cruise high above Nicolet River.

1:32 (0:14) Under Trans-Canada and Quebec Autoroute 20, stretching from Victoria, British Columbia to Saint John's, Newfoundland.

1:38 (0:08) Passing through St. Cyrille where St. Cyrille's Church, with a large silver dome and two lesser domes gracing its grey-stone walls, is centerpiece of town on right.

1:44 (0:02) Note attractive rapids below as Ocean spans St. Francois River.

1:46 (0:00) Arrive at Drummondville's rather tired-looking depot.

DRUMMONDVILLE, QUE. - Le Village Quebecois d'Antan is located here, a fine collection of restored buildings with a costumed staff depicting typical activities in 19th-century Quebec, one of the major historical attractions of the province.

0:00 (0:40) Depart Drummondville.

0:38 (0:02) Cross Yamaska River.

0:40 (0:00) Arrive St. Hyacinthe.

For route between St. Hyacinthe and Montreal, see that portion of the Atlantic route log, page 305.

Ocean – Richelieu River Bridge

Other Atlantic Service

The **Chaleur** makes overnight runs between Montreal and Gaspe three times a week, departing both Montreal and Gaspe on Monday, Thursday and Saturday. Montreal departures are early evening and Gaspe arrivals are late morning the next day. Gaspe departures are midafternoon and Montreal arrivals are early morning the next day. The route from Montreal follows the route of the Ocean to Matapedia, at which point the train heads east along the spectacular south shore line of the Gaspe Peninsula. This reserved train is equipped with coaches, Dayniters, sleeping cars and complete meal service.

Labrador, the mainland portion of Newfoundland, can be experienced by train if one travels to Sept-Iles, Que. on the north shore of the St. Lawrence River. There, early evening each Monday (or early morning on Tuesday) and early morning each Thursday, a train with coaches and a snack bar makes a journey northward across western Labrador to Labrador City, with the Thursday train

splitting at Ross Junction so that half goes on northward to Schefferville, Quebec. A dome car is put into use during the summer for better scenery viewing. The return trips are Wednesday and Friday. Trains are unreserved.

Because the schedules are subject to change, the railroad suggests calling a week in advance to verify specific dates and times. Call the station in Sept-Iles, (418) 968-7805.

Montreal • Quebec
Toronto
Windsor

Corridor Service

The very heart of VIA's network is the so-called "Corridor," stretching from Quebec City to Windsor, Ontario, with branches to Sarnia, Niagara Falls, Ottawa and Kitchener. And the heaviest used portion is that high-speed track connecting Canada's two largest cities, Montreal and Toronto. LRC trains (light, rapid, comfortable) operate throughout the Corridor.

A multitude of Rapidos, VIA's express trains with VIA 1 service (early boarding privileges, meals served at your seat, complimentary newspapers and magazines), make the trip between Montreal and Toronto any given weekday. Several more Rapidos connect Ottawa with Toronto, by way of Kingston. Additional trains make runs between Toronto and the border cities of Sarnia, Windsor and Niagara Falls.

Route Log

This route log covers Montreal-Toronto-Windsor and Montreal-Ottawa. The Toronto-Sarnia route is included in the log of the International, page 133, Toronto-Niagara Falls in the log of the Maple Leaf, page 59, and Montreal-Quebec City in the log of the Ocean, page 312.

MONTREAL-TORONTO

 MONTREAL, QUE. - See page 307.

0:00 (0:18) Depart Montreal's Central Station on CN tracks. In about 60 seconds emerge from underground, heading southeast, and soon parallel St. Lawrence River.

0:04 (0:14) Cross Lachine (pronounced "luh-sheen") Canal, with its very attractive landscaping. Canal was constructed prior to St. Lawrence Seaway providing bypass around treacherous Lachine Rapids of St. Lawrence River. Nine miles in length, it ceased operations in 1965.

Unfortunately, the Seaway no longer serves as it was originally intended. Many of today's freighters cannot be accommodated by the waterway's rather narrow channel, and the ice blocks traffic west of Montreal three months or more each winter. From time to time, proposals are put forth to modernize the system, but the costs would be enormous.

0:05 (0:13) Several tracks now depart to left to cross Victoria Bridge over St. Lawrence and then on to either Maritime Provinces or New York City.

0:09 (0:09) Re-cross Lachine Canal.

0:12 (0:06) Now slip beneath enormous pile of spaghetti called an interchange, which scrambles and then unscrambles traffic carried by Trans-Canada 20 and Autoroute 15.

0:15 (0:03) Sets of CN and CP tracks branch to right toward huge marshalling yards for both lines.

0:18 (0:00) Arrive Dorval.

 DORVAL, QUE. - This is a western suburb of Montreal, home to Montreal International Airport just off to the right.

0:00 (0:29) Depart Dorval.

0:04 (0:25) Note two attractive golf

courses lining tracks on right.

0:08 (0:21) Stone buildings and round barn on right are part of McDonald College's experimental farm.

0:09 (0:20) Cross smaller of two tongues of Ottawa River to reach Isle de Perrot. River is principal branch of St. Lawrence. Its origin is in central Quebec, some 160 miles above Ottawa, and forms partial boundary between Quebec and Ontario. Rapids and falls make most of it unnavigable, but significant elevation change makes stream ideal for hydroelectric power.

0:12 (0:17) Now cross larger segment of river and upon reaching Quebec's mainland, enter Vandreuil, named for early-day governor of Canada.

0:22 (0:07) A final glimpse can be caught of St. Lawrence off to left.

0:29 (0:00) Arrive Coteau.

COTEAU, QUE. - This is the final stop in the province of Quebec and the outer fringe of Montreal's populous suburbs.

0:00 (0:30) Depart Coteau, where rural countryside and occasional forests begin to prevail over cosmopolitan scenes just reviewed.

0:07 (0:23) Enter Ontario and leave Quebec.

0:30 (0:00) Arrive Cornwall.

CORNWALL, ONT. - Cotton, oddly enough, was once an important product of this most easterly Ontario city, and it was in one of Cornwall's cotton mills that Thomas Edison installed equipment to achieve the first electric illumination of a factory. Today, the city is headquarters for the St. Lawrence Seaway Authority.

0:00 (0:36) Depart Cornwall.

0:34 (0:02) Spanning St. Lawrence, on left, is International Bridge reaching across to Ogdensburg, New York.

0:36 (0:00) Arrive Prescott.

PRESCOTT, ONT. - As the only deep-water port between Montreal and Toronto, shipping has become an important aspect of the city's economy. Of particular interest is Fort Wellington; it occupied a strategic point on the St. Lawrence and saw action during the War of 1812.

0:00 (0:13) Depart Prescott.

0:07 (0:06) Final glimpse of St. Lawrence is afforded on left. Large facility on left is plant of chemicals-producing giant—duPont.

0:13 (0:00) Arriving in Brockville, somber brick structure of Brockville Psychiatric Hospital dominates scene off to left. Also, to left, can be glimpsed a portal of an abandoned rail tunnel that burrowed beneath the town and had doors on each end (a rarity) to prevent ice from forming on its roof.

BROCKVILLE, ONT. - Named after a War of 1812 hero, General Sir Isaac Brock, the city is situated at the eastern end of the popular Thousand Islands resort and vacation area. Oscar of the Waldorf once served as a personal chef for George C. Boldt (who lived in this area) and concocted a salad dressing in honor of these St. Lawrence River jewels.

0:00 (0:23) Depart Brockville.

0:23 (0:00) Arrive Ganonoque.

GANONOQUE, ONT. - A popular embarkation point for touring the Thousand Islands area by boat as well as plane. Boat cruises take from one-and-a-half to three hours, some including stopovers at the unfinished castle built by George Boldt.

0:00 (0:18) Depart Ganonoque.

0:12 (0:06) Cross Cataraqui River and historic Rideau Canal, with Kingston Mill lock off to right.

0:18 (0:00) Arrive Kingston.

KINGSTON, ONT. - At one point, during its evolution from a fur-trading post to a vibrant industrial center, Kingston was actually the nation's capital. With its location at the point where Lake Ontario empties into the St. Lawrence, this was a logical choice. It is also at the southern terminus of the Rideau Canal which connects the St. Lawrence with Ottawa to the north.

Bellevue House, once the home of Canada's first prime minister, Sir John A. Macdonald, has been restored and furnished for public viewing. Also of interest is Old Fort Henry, now a living museum of military artifacts, with uniformed "soldiers" and booming cannons.

0:00 (0:22) Depart Kingston, as scenery remains that of rolling to flat grasslands punctuated only with occasional groves of trees.

0:03 (0:16) Beautiful Collins Bay can be seen glimmering off to left.

0:22 (0:00) Arrive Napanee.

NAPANEE, ONT. - During its waterpower heyday, Napanee, now a town of about 5,000, boasted tanneries and mills that produced flour, oatmeal, paper, woolen and leather goods, tools and furniture.

0:00 (0:20) Depart Napanee and span Napanee River on 222-foot viaduct, while falls can be seen to left.

0:20 (0:00) Arrive Belleville.

BELLEVILLE, ONT. - This is the gateway to Quinte's Island in the St. Lawrence, where vacationers find long, sandy beaches to be most alluring. The city also offers splendid recreational pursuits with golf, swimming and an excellent yacht harbor.

0:00 (0:13) Depart Belleville.

0:12 (0:00) Arrive Trenton Jct.

TRENTON JCT., ONT. - This stop serves the attractive community of Trenton which has much the same recreational opportunities as does Belleville. Trenton is also the entrance to the elaborate Trent-Severn Canal which provides a 240-mile waterway through some 44 locks, and leads to Georgian Bay on Lake Huron.

0:00 (0:26) Depart Trenton Jct.

0:26 (0:00) Arrive Cobourg.

COBOURG, ONT. - In earlier times, this quaint community of 11,000 persons served as a lake port for steamers and a staging point on the road connecting Toronto, Kingston and Montreal.

0:00 (0:33) Depart Cobourg.

0:05 (0:28) Lake Ontario finally comes into view, about a mile south (left) of us.

0:33 (0:00) Arrive Oshawa.

OSHAWA, ONT. - Originally a lake port, this city has become a major auto-manufacturing center for Canada. Of special interest is the Canadian Automotive Museum with a splendid col-

lection of early automobiles. Parkwood, former home of Canadian auto magnate R. S. McLaughlin, features antiques and gardens.

0:00 (0:17) Depart Oshawa.

0:14 (0:03) Frenchman Bay and Pickering Nuclear Generating Plant are on left.

0:17 (0:00) Arrive Guildwood.

GUILDWOOD, ONT. - This is the eastern edge of Metropolitan Toronto, just 13 miles from the heart of the city.

0:00 (0:16) Depart Guildwood.

0:12 (0:04) Toronto's modernistic skyline now appears ahead of us with tall, spectacular spindle of CN Tower rising 1,821 feet, world's tallest free-standing structure.

0:16 (0:00) Arrive Toronto's Union Station.

TORONTO, ONT. - In the 1600s, the Iroquois Indians had a small village on what is now the site of Toronto. However by the 1700s, the village was gone, and the French had established a mission and fort at this spot. This outpost was short-lived, for in 1759 the occupants burned it to the ground to prevent the British from capturing it. Then in 1793, 30 years after the Treaty of Paris gave Canada to Britain, the town of York was established on this site by John Graves Simcoe, the first governor of Ontario (then known as "Upper Canada"). This modest settlement was the present-day city's forebear.

Situated on the shores of Lake Ontario, Toronto is a commercial and cultural metropolis comprised of 3.6 million people. It lays claim to being Canada's biggest city and the capital of Canada's most populous province, Ontario.

Downtown is robust and sparkling, busy with theaters, fine restaurants, major sporting events and cosmopolitan shopping. People are attracted here, both day and night, in a way that would make any city planner envious. Actor and noted traveler Peter Ustinov once referred to the town as "New York run by the Swiss." That summed it up well.

Getting around Toronto is both relatively easy and inexpensive, making the city all the more appealing. There are trolleys,

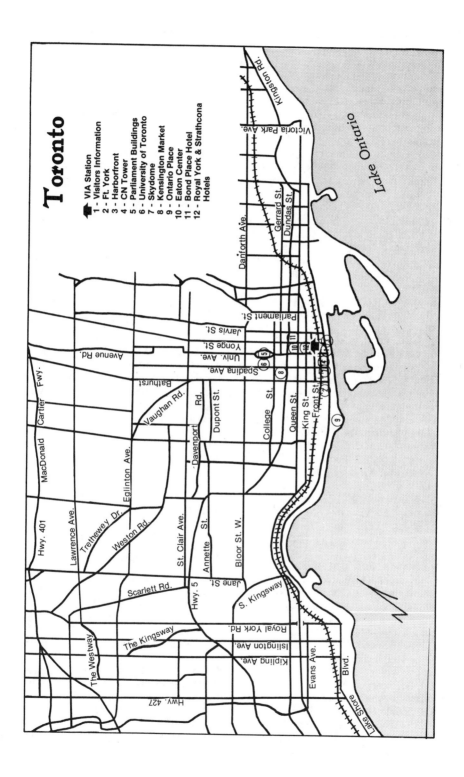

Toronto

- VIA Station
- 1 - Visitors Information
- 2 - Ft. York
- 3 - Harborfront
- 4 - CN Tower
- 5 - Parliament Buildings
- 6 - University of Toronto
- 7 - Skydome
- 8 - Kensington Market
- 9 - Ontario Place
- 10 - Eaton Center
- 11 - Bond Place Hotel
- 12 - Royal York & Strathcona Hotels

Lake Ontario

buses, GO Trains (commuter rail) and perhaps the world's cleanest and safest subway (a reflection of the city itself) that provide Toronto with one of the best urban transit systems found anywhere.

🚇 **Union Station,** Front Street West, between Bay and York streets, is a bustling, attractive station nicely located in the downtown area. Its grand facade is adorned with 22 pillars of Bedford limestone. There are storage lockers, restaurants, snack bars, newsstand and redcaps.

The station was opened by the Prince of Wales in 1927 and has been changed little throughout the years. Some modern appurtenances include an electronic arrival and departure board and a first class lounge for VIA-1 ticket holders. Pay-parking is adjacent to the station. An underground arcade leads to many shops and stores beneath downtown Toronto.

Call 366-8411 for reservations and information.

🚌 **Cab** stand is at the station, but cabs can be scarce during rush hours; call 366-6868 or 363-5757. Nearest **local bus** stop is in front of station; call 393-INFO. Tilden and Budget **rental cars** are available at the station. Both **GO-Trains** and the **subway** serve this station. **Greyhound** and **Voyageur** buses (and others) are at 610 Bay St. at Dundas, about a mile from the station. **Pearson International Airport** is 12 miles northwest of downtown.

❓ **Metropolitan Toronto Convention & Visitors Association,** Queen's Quay Terminal at Harbourfront, P.O. Box 126, 207 Queen's Quay West, M5J 1A7; (416) 368-9821.

🛏 **Strathcona Hotel,** 60 York St., M5J 1S8; (416) 363-3321. Recently remodeled, providing nice accommodations at reasonable rates. Only a block from the station. $75.

-**Bond Place Hotel,** 65 Dundas St., M5J 1E3; (416) 362-6061. Well managed, comfortable hotel; near good shopping (Eaton Center). About a mile and a half from the station, but reached by subway (Dundas station is within three blocks). $85.

-**Royal York Hotel,** 100 Front St. W, M5J 1E3; (416) 368-2511. Elderly, dignified Toronto landmark, directly across from the station and can be reached by an underground arcade. $134.

⭐ Downtown Toronto is an attraction in and of itself. For shopping there is the stunning **Eaton Centre,** which houses 300 shops and restaurants and 18 movie theaters under a cavernous arched glass arcade, anchored by two of Toronto's department stores. Close to the station, and visible for miles, is the **CN Tower,** the world's tallest (1,821 feet) freestanding structure. On top, of course, is a revolving restaurant and an observation gallery. And, vying for "8th Wonder" status is Toronto's new **SkyDome** sports complex, with its retractable roof, North America's largest McDonald's and a 350-room hotel. It's the house of the Blue Jays. The venerable **Kensington Market,** at Dundas and Spadina, is an old Jewish market occupying several blocks, and appearing very much like a European bazaar with produce, live chickens, bagels and custard tarts. Chinatown is adjacent to the market.

A trip west on **Bloor Street,** easily toured by subway, savors the diversity of Toronto. Downtown Bloor has an assemblage of high fashion stores that fan out to the north. Farther west is the University of Toronto, followed by the Annex, a Ukrainian neighborhood with its European atmosphere. And on the lake is **Harbourfront,** with its marina, shops and ferryboats to the Toronto Islands.

TORONTO-WINDSOR

For route between Toronto and London, Ontario, see that portion of International Log, page 133.

0:00 (0:30) Departing London, many of town's earliest three- and four-story buildings, one block to right, are in vivid contrast with London's newer downtown.
0:02 (0:28) Cross Thames River.
0:03 (0:27) Cross Thames River one more time.
0:05 (0:25) Although hockey is Canada's national sport, soccer is also popular during warmer months. Fields for that latter sport are in park at left.
0:13 (0:17) Tobacco kilns, those skinny barns with multiple doors, dot field on left.

0:30 (0:00) Arrive Glencoe's 1890s station.

GLENCOE, ONT. - This town of 1,700 is VIA's stop for the agricultural area to the west of London. Glencoe was once the end of the line for the Canada Air Line Railway.

0:00 (0:31) Depart Glencoe.

0:14 (0:17) Seven more tobacco farms appear in fields at left, attesting to hot and lengthy growing season and soil well-suited to that crop.

0:25 (0:06) Asparagus can frequently be seen growing in field on left. Cabbages, tomatoes and soybeans are also grown by area farms.

0:31 (0:00) Arrive Chatham, where older red-brick station greets arriving passengers.

CHATHAM, ONT. - Just as its namesake in England, Chatham (pronounce it without the h) rests near the mouth of the Thames River. The city has played an important role in shaping American history, acting as a northern terminus for the American Civil War's underground railway (a clandestine routing of slaves to the North and freedom), scene of a major battle during the War of 1812, and where John Brown hatched his plot to attack the federal armory at Harper's Ferry.

0:00 (0:44) Depart Chatham.

0:15 (0:39) Canals with myriad pleasure craft create surprising contrast to agricultural scenes which have dominated trip.

0:16 (0:38) Lake St. Clair now appears on right. Marinescapes continue; boats, lakefront homes, ducks and geese line waters edge for several miles.

0:28 (0:16) Train now cuts directly through very attractive marina.

0:44 (0:00) Arrive Windsor.

WINDSOR, ONT. - Windsor lies just across the Detroit River (one of the busiest shipping channels in the world) from the city of Detroit, making it a major port of entry to Canada. Because of the bend in the Detroit River (and hence in the U.S.-Canada border), Windsor is actually south of its American cousin.

The French first settled the area in the early 1700s with British locating nearby in the late 1700s. Agriculture and distilling were important aspects of Windsor's economy in the late 1800s, which saw the founding of the Hiram Walker distillery in 1858. Today, Windsor is a busy manufacturing city of 250,000 people, with General Motors, Ford and Chrysler having plants and supply industries here.

VIA Station, 298 Walker Rd., just south of Riverside Drive E., is about 1½ miles from downtown. There are storage lockers, food and beverage vending machines, a snack bar and pay-parking a block away.

For information and reservations, call 256-5511; for arrival and departure information, call 254-5252. Ticket windows and the waiting room are open from early morning on into the evening.

Cab stand is at the station; Capital Cab, 255-9444. **Local bus** service is one block from the station; Transit Windsor, 944-4411. **Tunnel bus** between Windsor and Detroit stops just east of 500 Ouellette in downtown Windsor and at the Renaissance Center in Detroit. **Greyhound,** (519) 254-7575. **Windsor Airport** is about 4½ miles south of the station.

Convention and Visitors Bureau, 80 Chatham St. E., N9A 2W1; (519) 255-6530.

Relax Plaza, 33 Riverside Dr. E., N9A 2S4; (519) 258-7774 or 800-661-9563. By the river, two miles from the station. $68.

-Inn General, 430 Ouellette Ave., N9A 1B2; (519) 253-7281. Near the tunnel to Detroit, two miles from the station. $65.

-Holiday Inn, 480 Riverside Dr., N9A 5K6; (519) 253-4411. By the river, 2½ miles from the station. $114.

Hiram Walker and Sons, Ltd., 2072 Riverside Dr. E., one of the world's leading distilleries, has tours of this Canadian Club producer, adjacent to the VIA station.

Windsor has an outstanding collection of parks and gardens. Some of the best floral displays will be found at **Jackson Park Sunken Garden,** Tecumseh Rd. at Ouellette Ave. There are fountains as well as a World War II Lancaster bomber display. The **Dieppe Gardens,** located on Riverside Drive at the foot of Ouellette

Ottawa Station

Ave., have an excellent view overlooking the Detroit River and the Detroit skyline. There is also a 1911 steam locomotive on display. **Coventry Gardens and Peace Fountain,** Riverside Dr. E. at Pillette Rd., are a six-acre riverfront park with a 75-foot floating fountain in the Detroit River.

Hiram Walker Historical Museum, located downtown at 254 Pitt St. W., has various artifacts from southern Ontario history and a War of 1812 exhibit.

MONTREAL-OTTAWA

 MONTREAL, QUE. - See page 307.

0:00 (0:18) Depart Montreal's Central Station on CN tracks. In about 60 seconds emerge from underground, heading southeast, and soon parallel St. Lawrence River.

0:04 (0:14) Cross Lachine (pronounced "luh-sheen") Canal, with its very attractive landscaping. Canal was constructed prior to St. Lawrence Seaway providing by-pass around treacherous Lachine Rapids of St. Lawrence River. Nine miles in length, it ceased operations in 1965.

0:05 (0:13) Several tracks now depart to left to cross Victoria Bridge over St. Lawrence and then on to either Maritime Provinces or New York City.

0:09 (0:09) Re-cross Lachine Canal.

0:12 (0:06) Now slip beneath enormous pile of spaghetti called an interchange, which scrambles and then unscrambles traffic carried by Trans-Canada 20 and Autoroute 15.

0:15 (0:03) Sets of CN and CP tracks branch to right toward huge marshalling yards for both lines.

0:18 (0:00) Arrive Dorval.

DORVAL, QUE. - This is a western suburb of Montreal, home to Montreal International Airport just off to the right.

0:00 (1:45) Depart Dorval.

0:04 (1:41) Note two attractive golf courses lining tracks on right.

0:08 (1:37) Stone buildings and round barn on right are part of McDonald College's experimental farm.

0:09 (1:36) Cross smaller of two tongues of Ottawa River to reach Isle de Perrot. River is principal branch of St. Lawrence. Its origin is in central Quebec, some 160 miles above Ottawa, and forms partial boundary between Quebec and Ontario. Rapids and falls make most of it unnavigable, but significant elevation change makes stream ideal for hydroelectric power.

0:12 (1:33) Now cross larger segment of river and upon reaching Quebec's mainland, enter Vandreuil, named for early-day governor of Canada.

0:22 (1:23) A final glimpse can be caught of St. Lawrence off to left.

0:29 (1:16) Through Coteau, then cross not-too-impressive Delise River.

0:33 (1:12) Note quaint, silver church in St. Polycarpe, to left.

0:43 (1:02) Leave province of Quebec and enter Ontario.

0:47 (0:58) Interesting remains of several stone fences are on right.

0:50 (0:55) Delightful appearing golf course is on right, accented with ponds and pedestrian bridges.

0:52 (0:53) Through Alexandria, one of many small agrarian trading centers in eastern Ontario.

1:04 (0:41) Maxville is "Home of the Glengary Highland Games," as proclaimed on building to right. Most important Highland gatherings in North America take place here in August (Saturday before first Monday) when pipe bands and dancers show their talents.

1:08 (0:37) Very attractive silver-spired church punctuates Moose Creek's modest skyline on right.

1:18 (0:27) At Casselman, just 29 miles east of Ottawa, note very unusual architecture of church one block to right.

1:19 (0:26) Cross South Nation River.

1:32 (0:13) Carlsbad Springs and Caldonia Springs, both north (right) of here, were once frequented for their supposedly therapeutic waters.

1:44 (0:01) Ottawa's skyline now dominates right forward.

1:45 (0:00) Arrive at Ottawa's very slick and airy station.

OTTAWA, ONT. - As the capital of Canada, Ottawa is a governmental oriented city with very little industry. It is handsomely situated on rounded promontories that are set amongst three rivers and a canal.

Although Champlain used this spot as a base for exploring along the Ottawa River, there was no settlement here until the early 1800s. It was first called Bytown (after Colonel By who constructed the Rideau Canal as a waterway for British gunboats) and was only a small lumbering community when it was designated the capital of Canada by Queen Elizabeth in 1857. Shortly thereafter, it was renamed Ottawa and subsequently developed into a very carefully planned community.

Today, it is marked by very "British"-looking buildings, six national museums, beautiful parks and abundant flower gardens with showy displays of brilliant colors—particularly the thousands of tulips that bloom in late May.

Ottawa Station, 200 Tremblay Road, is a modernistic steel and glass structure completed in 1966, located about two miles from the downtown area. There are storage lockers, handcarts, a newsstand, gifts, a restaurant and a coffee shop, and a barbershop. Free parking is adjacent to the station.

For reservations and information, call (613) 238-8289. For arrivals and departures, call 238-4706. Ticket windows are open from early morning to early evening.

Cab stand at the station; 238-1111. A new **Transitway** system to downtown stops at the station. Budget and Hertz have direct phone lines for **rental cars. Voyager bus** terminal, 265 Catherine, (613) 238-5900. **Ottawa International Airport** is approximately 13 miles southwest of the station.

Visitor Information, National Arts Center (Elgin Street entrance); (613) 237-5158. Write Visitors & Convention Bureau, 222 Queen St., K1P 5V9.

Lord Elgin Hotel, 100 Elgin St. at Larier, K1P 5K8; (613) 235-3333. Small but very attractive rooms. One of Ottawa's better downtown values. Excellent location. Two miles from the station. $74.

In the downtown area, the **Canadian Parliament Buildings** are set on Parliament Hill overlooking the Ottawa River. Changing of the Guard takes place at 10 am in the summer. Some of the best shopping is at **Rideau Center,** across the canal on Rideau Street and Sparks Street Mall. Various stage productions appear regularly at the **National Arts Center.**

Two of the more outstanding museums are the new **Canadian Museum of Civilization,** in Hull directly across from Parliament Hill, which has 750,000 artifacts on display, History Hall with life-size historic structures, including a prairie depot, an IMAX/OMNIMAX theatre, and much more, and **National Museum of Science and Technology,** at 1867 St. Laurent Blvd., about a mile or so southeast of the station, is great for the entire family. Exhibits include such things as autos, buggies and trains. The **National Aviation Museum** is at Rockcliffe Airport.

Toronto-Kitchener-London

 TORONTO, ONT. - See page 316.

0:00 (0:33) Depart Toronto's Union Station. In a moment, CN Tower will soar skyward on left, then $400 million SkyDome, home to Toronto Blue Jays, will dominate all else on left.

0:20 (0:13) On outskirts of Toronto, train angles through Weston Golf Course.

0:33 (0:00) Arrive Brampton.

 BRAMPTON, ONT. - A plethora of nurseries and greenhouses give Brampton the nickname "Flower City." Nearby, the Great War Flying Museum has a fine collection of World War I memorabilia.

0:00 (0:37) Depart Brampton.

0:37 (0:00) Arrive Guelph where armory-looking city hall sits behind 1911 station on left.

 GUELPH, ONT. - This community has a fine assemblage of architectural styles utilizing locally quarried limestone.

0:00 (0:18) Depart Guelph.

0:18 (0:00) Arrive Kitchener's attractive brick station.

 KITCHENER, ONT. - Kitchener and its twin, Waterloo, were originally founded by Pennsylvania Mennonites. Later an influx of German immigrants gave the area an Old Country flavor that persists today.

0:00 (0:35) Depart Kitchener and soon enter some of the most productive dairy country in the world.

0:35 (0:00) Arrive Stratford where sign on station proclaims "The Festival City."

 STRATFORD, ONT. - The Stratford Festival was born here in 1953. From a humble beginning of Shakespearean plays, the event has become world renowned and has expanded to three theaters. The annual celebration now runs from May through October.

0:00 (0:38) Depart Stratford.

0:38 (0:00) Arrive London.

 LONDON, ONT. - See page 135.

Jonquiere

Montreal

Train to Jonquiere

The train is the way to go to Jonquiere. The tracks slice through undulating, forested Laurentians laced with meandering rivers and liberally sprinkled with glossy-surfaced lakes, some of Canada's most attractive wilderness. Sparkling waterfalls, spectacular rock cuts and airy trestles add to the excitement. During the fall, the foliage is exquisite and there is always a chance of spotting some caribou, moose or bear. Numerous hunting and fishing clubs, with names such as Jacques Cartier, Iroquois and Orleans, are strung along the route causing the train to make frequent but interesting unscheduled stops.

The service is only thrice-weekly, the pace unhurried, and the atmosphere on board is relaxed and friendly. You might wish to pack a lunch, however, as the snack bar food leaves quite a bit to be desired. If you can only take the train one way, the return run from Jonquiere would be recommended since the more scenic portions will be traversed during full daylight.

The tracks were actually built by four different railroads, the earliest construction occurring a century ago. That first section was only a three-mile stretch between L'Assumption and L'Epiphanie, built in 1885-86 by the rather obscure L'Assumption Railway.

Northbound Schedule (Condensed)
Montreal, Que. - Early Afternoon Departure (Monday, Wednesday and Friday)
Hervey, Que. - Late Afternoon
Jonquiere, Que. - Late Evening Arrival

Southbound Schedule (Condensed)
Jonquiere, Que. - Late Morning Departure, Tuesday and Thursday; Early Afternoon Departure, Sunday
Hervey, Que. - Late Afternoon (Early Evening, Sunday)
Montreal, Que. - Midevening (Late Evening, Sunday)

Frequency - Tri-weekly (see above).
Seating - Coaches.
Dining - Food and beverage service.
Reservations - Unreserved train.
Length of Trip - 308 miles in 9 hours.

Route Log

 MONTREAL, QUE. - See page 307.

0:00 (0:10) Depart Montreal's Central Station in complete darkness for eight minutes while encased by Mount Royal Tunnel. This shaft burrows through Mt. Royal, then emerges three miles northwest of its downtown starting point.
0:09 (0:00) Arrive Mount Royal.

MOUNT ROYAL, QUE. - Although you can't tell by looking (the train is below grade here), we have stopped in a citified portion of Montreal called Mount Royal.

0:00 (0:10) Depart Mount Royal.
0:05 (0:05) After curving to right for a northeasterly course out of Montreal, look back to right where beehive-domed Saint Joseph Oratory Museum, known for its beautiful stained glass windows and mosaics, is at Mount Royal's base; one of

the world's most unusual Catholic shrines.

0:13 (0:00) Arrive Ahuntsic.

AHUNTSIC, QUE. - This stop is in a section of Montreal with intermixed modest income housing, newer apartments and industrial operations.

0:00 (0:15) Depart Ahuntsic.

0:05 (0:11) Enormous expanse of stone quarry is just to right of tracks.

0:14 (0:02) Cross multi-laned Route 40, which is major artery between Montreal and Quebec City.

0:16 (0:00) Arrive Pointe-aux-Trembles where waters of St. Lawrence River are visible about three blocks distant on right.

POINTE-AUX-TREMBLES, QUE. - This is the easternmost suburban stop before escaping the metropolitan confines of Montreal and shifting to the pastoral scenes of rural Quebec. From here, the landscape becomes dotted with farmsteads and dairy silos, mild-eyed cattle graze contentedly everywhere and small communities make intermittent appearances, each seeming to have a greystone church topped with a silver-spired steeple. In spite of its northern location, the area is ideal for tobacco, and fields of this crop, as well as curing barns, can soon be spotted along the route.

0:00 (0:26) Depart Pointe-aux-Trembles.

0:05 (0:21) Cross River des Prairies, actually an offshoot of Ottawa River, just west of its joinder with St. Lawrence. It takes two tries for us to get across. This river and St. Lawrence encircle Montreal, giving it an island status.

0:12 (0:14) Oldest portion of rail line to Jonquiere is along this stretch between milepost 117 and 114, originally built by the L'Assumption Railway in 1885-86.

0:18 (0:08) Cross LacOuareau River.

0:26 (0:00) Arrive Joliette.

JOLIETTE, QUE. - This city of 18,000 has long been an important rail head and trade center serving the De Laundrie region of Quebec, the only Quebec region named after a woman. The town was founded in 1832 by her husband, Barthelemy Joliette, a local deputy, notary and businessman. This is tobacco country, with picking occurring in August. Archery range used during 1976 Olympic Games is still located here.

0:00 (1:04) Depart Joliette and cross L'Assumption River.

0:05 (0:59) Typical tobacco curing barns stand in field on right.

0:07 (0:57) At milepost 97, thick stand of dairy silos in distance gives appearance of small town on horizon. Train is now traveling at a comfortable 60 mph.

0:27 (0:37) Small village of St. Justin, at milepost 78, is demarcation point between plains just visited and wooded, rolling terrain yet to come. Route becomes more and more scenic.

0:29 (0:35) Suddenly, at milepost 76.3, we seem to soar through space as train crosses 175 feet above Maskinonge River, breathtaking because of its abruptness. Don't miss views of surrounding countryside, particularly to right.

0:43 (0:21) Another airy crossing occurs at milepost 65.1 where train traverses 1,071-foot-long bridge over Riviere-du-Loup; again, nice views are afforded.

0:49 (0:15) At milepost 61, cross 165 feet above West Yamachiche River.

0:53 (0:11) Cross East Yamachiche River at milepost 58.

1:00 (0:04) Cross small stream at bottom of Lavern Gully at milepost 52.

1:02 (0:02) Momentary darkness prevails as train chugs through 610-foot tunnel— second of only two tunnels on route, first being Mount Royal Tunnel at beginning of our trip. Upon exiting, cross Shawinigan River at milepost 50.

1:04 (0:00) Arrive Shawinigan.

SHAWINIGAN, QUE. - Located on the St. Maurice River, Shawinigan is the birthplace of Quebec's chemical industry. Cheap hydroelectric power (totalling a whopping 400,000 horsepower) produced at the falls on the river has accounted for aluminum, paper and chemical industries locating here. The town's Indian name means "angular portage."

0:00 (0:32) Depart Shawinigan.

0:06 (0:26) Fine view of Saint Maurice River is afforded on right.

0:11 (0:21) Now, cross high above Saint Maurice River on a 722-foot-long trestle at milepost 43.5.

0:12 (0:20) One of Shawinigan's major industries is on left. Logs are floated down St. Maurice River to damsite where Canadian International Paper's operation turns them into pulp for paper products. Much of pulp is exported south to U.S.

0:17 (0:15) Stop at CN rail yards of Garneau at milepost zero. Milepost numbers, which have been growing smaller, now get progressively larger as we move farther toward Jonquiere.

0:21 (0:11) Depart Garneau.

0:26 (0:06) Three-spired church, about one block from tracks on right, identifies village of Herouxville at milepost 3.

0:30 (0:02) Cross small Riviere des Envie at milepost 6.5.

0:32 (0:00) Arriving St. Tite, take note of neat red and white house with matching windmill in front, just to right of tracks.

ST. TITE, QUE. - This small town of 3,000 calls itself "The City of Leather" for the gloves and boots manufactured here.

0:00 (0:17) Depart St. Tite.

0:05 (0:12) Sylvan setting on right features small lake with cottages nestled along its idyllic shoreline.

0:11 (0:06) Twin spires grace unusually attractive church of Ste-Thecle on left.

0:17 (0:00) Arrive Hervey Jct. at milepost 18.7.

HERVEY JCT., QUE. - This rather unimpressive-looking small town is a division point for the railroad. Tracks seen taking off to the left at this junction lead north and then west across a vast lakeland wilderness. The cities of Senneterre and Cochrane, the latter being some 495 rail miles from here, are both reached by this line.

0:00 (0:44) Depart Hervey Jct.

0:09 (0:35) At milepost 23, narrow landing strip on right leads directly into pretty little town of Lac-aux-Sables, testing pilot's skill and townsfolk's nerves.

0:10 (0:34) Expansive waters of very scenic Lac-aux-Sables are on left. Forest now becomes almost continuous while small lakes become more abundant.

0:23 (0:21) Just beyond milepost 30, bridge 323 feet in length carries us over Batiscan River which then follows along left side of train. During autumn, foliage is quite spectacular from here on to Jonquiere.

0:43 (0:01) On outskirts of Riviere-a-Pierre, note small hockey rink on right, not only attesting to widespread popularity

of Canada's national pastime, but evidence that winters are definitely on the chilly side.

0:44 (0:00) Arrive Riviere-a-Pierre at milepost 40.

RIVIERE-A-PIERRE, QUE. - Numerous two-story buildings with a variety of architectural styles pervade Riviere-a-Pierre. From this quaint village, the tracks now turn left 45 degrees and head due north (we've been going northeast) until reaching Chambord, some 120 miles away.

0:00 (1:43) Depart Riviere. For those traveling during the fall, darkness sets in about now. The return trip, however, offers daylight along the scenic stretches north of here.

From here to Chambord, the undulating, forested countryside is liberally sprinkled with lakes and hunting camps, each with its own particular character.

0:18 (1:25) Lovely Batiscan River, which is flowing south to the St. Lawrence, joins our route again and becomes a familiar scene during the next 50 miles.

0:27 (1:16) White, frothy rapids of Batiscan are particularly appealing for short stretches in either direction from milepost 57.

0:34 (1:09) On left, impressive rocky cliffs of Linton add special flavor to route at milepost 62.

0:41 (1:02) Near milepost 64, on left, three collections of stone piers poking out of river are remains of bridge that carried tracks some fifty years ago.

0:53 (0:50) Note fire lookout tower at tip of mountain on left.

1:07 (0:36) Stadacona, typical of small settlements throughout this region, is at milepost 76.4.

1:38 (0:05) Cross over rapids and bid farewell to Batiscan River which has been our companion since leaving Riviere-a-Pierre.

1:42 (0:00) Arrive Lac Edouard at milepost 95.

LAC EDOUARD, QUE. - This remote village is situated on a lake by the same name, one of the region's larger bodies of water. Cottages mark the shoreline and also huddle here and there throughout the nearby woods. Note the old rail station to the left of the tracks.

0:00 (1:48) Depart Lac Edouard. While following lake's edge for a few moments, it is understandable, upon seeing such pristine beauty, why the area has become inhabited.

0:18 (1:31) On right, near milepost 105 and just before reaching Summit Club, watch for pretty Summit Lake with inviting cabins along its shoreline.

0:48 (1:02) From mileposts 115 to 117 excellent views of northern tip of Kiskissink Lake are afforded. Small boats are evidence that lake is popular with fishermen.

0:52 (0:59) Near milepost 119 note cabin on hill to right, elaborately decorated in Western style with wagon wheels, while rock bridge leads to another small cottage.

1:13 (0:38) One of area's larger lakes, Mirage, is just to left, between mileposts 128 and 130. Pontoon planes can often be spotted here.

1:14 (0:37) Cross Wip River at milepost 129.

1:29 (0:23) Cross Noisy River as it tumbles toward Lake Bouchette to left.

Civilization is found once again upon arrival at Lac Bouchette, one of the larger settlements in the surrounding region, and located on paved Highway 155 leading to Chambord. As a matter of fact, the train straddles the highway as it stops here at milepost 143.

1:30 (0:22) On left is Lake Ouiatchouan at milepost 144, situated at northern tip of Lake Bouchette.

1:53 (0:00) At milepost 159.5, arrive Chambord (Jct.) where most of remaining passengers usually detrain. Town of Chambord is off to left.

CHAMBORD, QUE. - This charming town (call it shomball) on a cove of Lac St. Jean is a popular resort for those seeking recreational opportunities afforded by the lake. Here, fishing for the ouananiche, an aggressive freshwater salmon, is a major attraction, while rivers of the region offer walleye, pike and speckled trout. The lake itself is huge, sometimes being referred to as an inland sea, having a circumference of 140 miles. Note crucifixion scene on the left.

0:00 (1:02) Depart Chambord.

0:03 (0:59) Lac Saint Jean now comes into view to left.

0:15 (0:47) At milepost 169, train slips through town of Metabetchouan, where well-known musicians' camp is located. Note outstanding Gothic-style church on right which is constructed of pink granite quarried nearby.

0:20 (0:42) Last view of Lac Saint Jean on left before train twists to east on its final leg.

0:42 (0:20) Church on left, with its modern sweeping lines, is centerpiece of town of Larouche.

1:00 (0:02) Cross Sables River on 231-foot bridge.

1:02 (0:00) Arrive Jonquiere.

JONQUIERE, QUE. - This city exemplifies what all industrial cities should be. Owing its robustness to the free world's largest aluminum manufacturing complex, Jonquiere is modern, clean and attractive. A super-abundance of hydroelectric power has caused Alcan to locate its largest aluminum plant here, even though bauxite (aluminum ore) must be brought in by ship from such faraway places as South America and Africa. One can easily feel the vibrant spirit that has made this city a truly progressive metropolis.

The area was first settled in the early 1800s when Peter McLeod and 21 other men (a collection of Indians and Scotsmen) arrived here to construct and operate a sawmill, its lumber to be sold to Great Britain for her Merchant Marine. Soon, however, interests turned to farming the land that had been cleared, and, in spite of the sometimes bitter winters, the 120-day growing season fostered both vegetable and dairy farming.

Today, paper and aluminum dominate the region's economy, with 75% of the population afforded employment by these two industries. Oceangoing vessels find their way along the St. Lawrence and then up the Saguenay River (meaning "where we set sail") to the port at nearby La Baie. Here, bauxite from South America is offloaded and shipped by rail to aluminum plants in Chicoutimi, Jonquiere and Alma. Inexpensive hydroelectric power, critical in aluminum production, is the reason the plants are in this remote locale.

? Visitor Information, Bureau de tourisme et des congres de Jonquiere, 2665, boul. du Royaume and 3968, boul. Harvey; (418) 548-4004. Write Association touristque du Saguenay—Lac-Saint-Jean—Chibougaman, 198, rue Racine Est, bureau 200, Chicoutimi, Quebec, G7H 1R9; or call year round (418) 543-9778.

-Hotel Roussillon Saguenay, 2675, boul. du Royaume, G7S 5B8; (418) 548-3124. Large, attractive hotel, about five miles from the station. $63.

-Hotel Jean Dequen, 2841 boul. du Royaume, G7S 4K6; (418) 548-7173. Small 12-room hotel, about two miles from the station. $35.

There is much to do in this remote but fascinating area, although you might consider brushing up on your French. Ninety-eight percent of the populace speak that language, and bilingualism is even less of a trait here than in Quebec City and Montreal (although English is spoken at the hotels listed above). This is part of the region's appeal and adds to the adventure. Highlights include: breathtaking **scenic cruises** on North America's longest fiord; tours of the **Alcan aluminum plant,** the Free World's largest; tours of **Shipshaw,** an Alcan dam and enormous power plant; and, in nearby Chicoutimi, the excellent **Saguenay-Lac St. John Museum** with regional artifacts.

Other Quebec Service

There is triweekly service from **Montreal to Senneterre and Cochrane,** with sleeping cars and snack and beverage service to Senneterre. Coach seats are unreserved.

Cochrane
North Bay
Toronto

Northlander

The Northlander is unique among North American trains. It's not the scenery or even the places visited that are so different, it's the train itself that makes this trip special.

The feeling is one of solid, art-deco luxury. This articulated (the cars are permanently joined, avoiding noisy vestibules) streamliner is owned and operated by the Ontario Northern Railway, chartered by the province of Ontario. The trains have three cars: the "A" car is European-compartment-style with three-facing-three seating; the non-smoking "C" car has spacious two-and-one seating, utilizing what may be the most comfortable seats in railroading; and the dining "B" car is bright and airy with attractive, friendly waitresses—somewhat reminiscent of what airline stewardesses were once always like. Windows have venetian blinds encased between the double panes of glass, and announcements come over the train's PA system crisp and ungarbled.

The ONR operates two identical sets that were once luxury Trans European Express trains, built by the Swiss, and operated between Paris and Zurich. They were put up for sale by the Swiss government in 1977 and Ontario quickly snapped them up (which created an uproar for not buying Canadian).

These Northlanders make a mostly daylight run between Toronto and Cochrane (although a bus is utilized for the last few miles between Porquis and Cochrane). Cochrane is the southern terminus of the famed Polar Bear Express to Moosonee.

Northbound Schedule (Condensed)
Toronto, Ont. - Early Afternoon Departure
North Bay, Ont. - Late Afternoon
Cochrane, Ont.* - Late Evening Arrival

Southbound Schedule (Condensed)
Cochrane, Ont.* - Early Morning Departure
North Bay, Ont. - Early Afternoon
Toronto, Ont. - Early Evening Arrival

*Connecting motor coach carries passengers 28 miles between Porquis and Cochrane. (Rail service may be extended to Cochrane.)

Frequency - Daily, except Saturday.
Seating - See above.
Dining - Full meal service.
Baggage - Carry-on only.
Reservations - All-reserved train. Seats are assigned prior to boarding.
Length of Trip - 482 miles in 10½ hours.

Route Log

For route description between Toronto and Washago, see that portion of Canadian log, page 344.

0:00 (0:19) Depart Washago, and terrain immediately begins to shift from rich farming countryside to rugged, forested lakelands called Muskoka. Last ice age carved granite base rock into dramatic shapes making numerous rock cuts necessary along route.

0:04 (0:15) Cross one of region's numerous canals where pleasure craft create

colorful scene, on right.
0:19 (0:00) Arrive Gravenhurst.

GRAVENHURST, ONT. - Long popular with the rich and famous, this serene Victorian town is still a tourist center for those wanting to visit the Muskoka Lakes region. The town holds popular summer stock comedies and musicals in the elegantly refurbished Gravenhurst Opera House. And every summer, free Sunday band concerts are performed from a floating stage on Gull Lake.

0:00 (0:33) Depart Gravenhurst.
0:01 (0:32) Aforementioned Gull Lake is just through trees on right.
0:12 (0:21) Pass high over south branch of Muskoka River where falls can be seen at right and boats can occasionally be spotted on left, as train enters Bracebridge. Community of 9,000 is geared to tourism, draw being beautiful Lake Muskoka, just to west of town.
0:29 (0:04) Siding Lake appears at left.
0:33 (0:00) Arrive Huntsville.

HUNTSVILLE, ONT. - This is another lake-country resort town and offers boat cruises along the Muskoka River to Peninsula Lake. Also, Algonquin Provincial Park, a popular canoeing and fishing area, is just east of here.

0:00 (1:01) Departing Huntsville, Lake Vernon is off to left.
0:01 (1:00) Cross very scenic Hunters Bay.
0:04 (0:57) Lumber mill, a frequent sight throughout Canada's forest lands, is on right.
0:24 (0:37) Golf course, on left, is very inviting scene. North branch of Magnetawan flows nearby, a stream we must cross several times.
0:33 (0:28) Through Burk's Falls where old station once served those boarding popular Magnetawan River steamer.
0:54 (0:07) Through attractive Sundridge, which caters to fishermen hoping to land deep-water trout found in waters of Lake Bernard, on right.
1:01 (0:00) Arrive South River.

SOUTH RIVER, ONT. - Here, canoeists find ready access to Algonquin Provincial Park.

0:00 (0:56) Depart South River.
0:01 (0:55) Cross South River where waterfalls can be seen off to left.
0:07 (0:49) High trestle carries tracks over small Viaduct Creek.
0:15 (0:41) Through town of Trout Creek, where small white church on right seems to wear an ice cream cone for a steeple top.
0:21 (0:35) Outstanding view of charming valley farmlands now presents itself, off to left.
0:51 (0:05) Entering outskirts of North Bay, our CN tracks intersect those of CP Rail.
0:56 (0:00) Arrive North Bay's ONR Station.

NORTH BAY, ONT. - Rail buffs will recognize North Bay as home base for the Ontario Northland Railway. Chartered in 1902 as the Timiskaming and Northern Ontario Railway, it started out to serve the farming country north of here, but ultimately found its way to Moosonee, its northern terminus on James Bay, in 1932.

North Bay is a popular destination for fishermen, particularly those wanting to try their luck on adjacent Lake Nipissing. Hunting is also an important North Bay recreational activity.

Boat cruises, leaving from Government Dock near downtown, are quite popular.

ONR Station is located at Fraser and Chippewa streets on the north edge of downtown. If your trip originates here, be sure to check with an ONR attendant in the station's rather pleasant lobby for a seat assignment before boarding the Northlander.

For **Deluxe Cabs,** call 472-4100. For **Tilden rental cars,** call 474-3030.

Write **Chamber of Commerce,** 509 Main E., North Bay, Ont., P1B 1B7; phone (705) 472-8480.

-The **Empire Hotel,** 425 Fraser St., P1B 8K6, (705) 472-8200, is located in the heart of downtown and has quite comfortable rooms. $54.50.

0:00 (1:33) Depart North Bay, backing first to east and then to south.
0:04 (1:29) Having positioned itself on ONR's main line, Northlander again heads

northward.

0:09 (1:24) Numerous small boats are docked at Trout Lake Marina on immediate right.

1:31 (0:02) Arm of Temagami Lake, at left, reaches to edge of town. Note nicely manicured park, boat docks and walkways along shore, a project of Ontario's Development Program.

1:33 (0:00) Arrive Temagami, a Cree Indian word for "deep water."

TEMAGAMI, ONT. - This logging community (mostly harvesting white pine) is also a hunting and fishing center.

0:00 (0:41) Depart Temagami.

0:06 (0:35) Lakes are everywhere; one of area's large bodies of water now appears at right.

0:20 (0:21) Note unusual approach to supporting telephone poles which are propped upright with an abundance of rocks.

0:30 (0:11) Dam on left holds back Montreal River.

0:41 (0:00) Arrive Cobalt.

COBALT, ONT. - Mining was Cobalt's reason for being. It started in 1903 when, legend has it, a blacksmith heaved his hammer at a fox and missed. The heavy tool chipped into a rock and disclosed what turned out to be the world's richest silver vein. The community still bears the imprint of its early helter-skelter construction. Today, Cobalt's Northern Ontario Mining Museum has perhaps the best display anywhere of native silver.

0:00 (0:14) Depart Cobalt.

0:06 (0:08) Looking right, Lake Timiskaming is beautiful setting for Haileybury. Land on far side of lake is province of Quebec.

0:10 (0:04) Plant at right processes some of Ontario's trees into particle board.

0:14 (0:00) Arrive New Liskeard.

NEW LISKEARD, ONT. - This is a farming and dairying center. Northbound passengers may question this, but once the Northlander departs, there can be no doubt. The Little Clay Belt, as it is called, starts just north of town. This fertile farming area can produce many crops grown in more southern climes in spite of a shorter growing season.

0:00 (0:24) Departing New Liskeard, note hundreds of canoes stacked on end in lot of manufacturer on left.

0:02 (0:22) Now, enter upon fertile farmlands of Little Clay Belt, just described. If Iowa were flat, it would look like this.

0:23 (0:01) Cross high over Englehart River.

0:24 (0:00) Arriving Englehart, note 1921 steam locomotive (a 4-6-2, #701), built for the Timiskaming and Northern Ontario Railway and nicely maintained in its green and gold colors, on left.

ENGLEHART, ONT. - This town has its roots in both lumbering and railroading.

0:00 (0:30) Depart Englehart's nicely renovated station. Large pulp mill can be seen off to left.

0:08 (0:22) High trestle carries Northlander above Blanche River.

0:30 (0:00) Arrive Swastika.

SWASTIKA, ONT. - Gold was discovered just south of here after the turn of the century. Swastika was born and soon found itself at the center of one of Canada's richest mineral finds.

0:00 (0:45) Depart Swastika.

0:05 (0:40) Cross arctic divide, beyond which all streams flow north to James Bay. Numerous rivers and creeks are crossed before reaching Matheson.

0:45 (0:00) Arrive Matheson.

MATHESON, ONT. - Matheson, entrenched in Ontario's northern mining region, still maintains itself as an agricultural trade center.

0:00 (0:20) Depart Matheson.

0:12 (0:08) Crossing Driftwood River, look to left to see Monteith Correctional Centre. Just west of here, two famous gold mines, the Dome and the Hollinger, were discovered in the early 1900s.

0:20 (0:00) Arrive Porquis.

PORQUIS, ONT. - Those continuing on to Cochrane transfer to an awaiting coach. The drive takes about 40 minutes, and passengers are delivered to Cochrane's ONR station. (There are plans, however, to extend the Northlander into Cochrane.)

COCHRANE, ONT. - Cochrane has all the appearances of a modern-day frontier town, a bustling little city thriving on a blend of tourism, hunting, fishing, mining, lumbering and railroading. This is the southern terminus of the Polar Bear Express, Ontario Northland's popular train to Moosonee on James Bay.

ONR Station is situated on the edge of Cochrane's small downtown area. This nicely maintained depot has storage lockers, cab stand, a restaurant and an adjacent railway museum housed in four historic rail cars.

Write **Cochrane Visitors Center** (June through Labor Day), Cochrane, Ont., P0L 1C0.

Tilden rental cars are one mile from the station, next to the Northern Lites Motel. The inter-city **bus terminal** is the train station.

Reservations should be made well in advance, particularly during Cochrane's busy summer season.

-The **Northern Lites Motel,** Highway 11, Box 1720, P0L 1C0, (705) 272-4281, is a short cab ride, or a healthy mile walk, from the station and downtown. Rooms are nice and large, and a good restaurant is open throughout the day. $54.

-(The **ONR** has plans to expand the rail station, which would include 32 motel units. Completion could occur as early as the summer of 1990. For information, call (416) 965-4268, or (705) 472-4500.)

Polar Bear Express

The Polar Bear Express heads north from Cochrane, Ontario into a land of muskegs, wilderness rivers, moose and bears—but, sorry, no polar bears. The end of the line is James Bay, the southernmost extension of Hudson Bay where Moosonee and its sister outpost, island-ensconsed Moose Factory, live an isolated existence. (Sorry again, there is no moose factory at Moose Factory.)

The draw is the uniqueness of the region and the opportunity to visit Ontario's oldest permanent English-speaking settlement—curiously named Moose Factory. That settlement of 1,600 Cree Indians and whites is reached from Moosonee by boat in the summer, by road across the frozen Moosonee River in the winter, and by helicopter during the ice breakup season. Much of its pioneer past has been maintained, and touring historic buildings and other artifacts gives visitors a strong sense of "the way it was."

A Hudson's Bay Company fort was established on what was then called Hayes Island in 1673, but within 13 years the French captured the installation that had been defended by only 16 men. The English regained it by treaty in 1732. This remote trading post remained virtually unreachable by land until 1923, when the Temiskaming Northern Ontario Railway, now the Ontario Northland, reached Moosonee. These two largest isolated communities in Ontario still remain relatively unknown.

Schedules and Equipment - The Ontario Northland Railway, owned and operated by the Province of Ontario, runs round-trip excursion trains (The **Polar Bear Express**) daily, except Friday, from late June through early September. Passengers are transported in luxuriously refurbished rail cars that contrast sharply with the surrounding countryside. Departures from Cochrane are early morning and from Moosonee early afternoon. The trip takes just over four hours in each direction.

In addition to these summertime excursions, there is a **local** that runs twice a week in the summer and three times a week the remainder of the year. The local is another experience, carrying Indians and hunters from flag stop to flag stop as well as tourists to Moosonee. In the off-season it uses the same equipment as the Polar Bear Express, but is a mixed train and takes longer to get there. Its off-season departures from Cochrane are midmorning on Monday, Wednesday and Friday and returns leave early morning on Tuesday, Wednesday and Friday.

Food service is available on both trains.

Reservations are required for the Polar Bear Express excursion trains. For reservations and information, including tour packages, write Ontario Northland Transportation Commission, 65 Front St. W., Toronto, Ont., M5J 1E6; or phone (416) 965-4268 (Toronto), or (705) 472-4500 (North Bay).

Route Log

 COCHRANE, ONT. - See page 330.

0:00 (4:20) Depart Cochrane as polar bear on town's water tower, on right, watches over all from above.

(Note: Mileposts are quite visible on this line and are included as additional reference points.)

0:10 (4:10) MP 5. Cochrane's airport handles normal variety of wheeled aircraft on runways as well as seaplanes on waters of Lillabelle Lake, on right.

0:13 (4:07) MP 7. Farms interspersed with wooded hills will prevail for several miles as train crosses northern rim of Ontario's Clay Belt.

0:19 (4:01) MP 11. Abitibi River is on right. Stream will be followed off and on as it drifts toward James Bay.

0:28 (3:52) MP 18. Large sawmill of Ontario Paper Company is on right at Gardiner.

1:01 (3:19) MP 43. At Island Falls, cabin on right has own little rail conveyance parked on walkway of cross ties on right.

1:02 (3:18) MP 44. One of numerous Ontario Northland communication towers is on right. Company has $20 million invested in system that handles radio, telephone and television transmissions to and from remote Northlands.

1:04 (3:16) MP 45. Cross broad waters of Abitibi River where Abitibi River Island Falls Power Plant and Dam can be glimpsed upriver on right.

1:05 (3:15) MP 46. Under powerline leading from power station, then pass another lumber operation of Ontario Paper Company.

1:09 (3:11) MP 49. Expanse of dead trees was caused by June 1976 forest fire.

1:16 (3:04) MP 55. Green wooden boxes at trackside hold shims of wood used for leveling tracks affected by springtime frost heaves. This phenomenon is typical wherever muskeg or permafrost is prevalent.

1:33 (2:47) MP 69. Fraserdale is the northernmost point for road service in this region.

1:39 (2:41) MP 74. Terrain grows more rugged with aspen and black spruce everywhere.

1:48 (2:32) MP 80. Cross 50th Parallel.

2:06 (2:14) MP 93. Huge Otter Rapids generating facility is on right, one of four highly automated hydroelectric stations in region operated by microwave signals from central location.

2:10 (2:10) MP 96. Note "stuffed folks" standing in yard of Miller's cabin, on right, at Coral Rapids. Diamonds have actually been found in this vicinity. We are now halfway to our destination.

2:47 (1:33) MP 126. Lignite, a very low grade of coal, lies just beneath the surface. Mining these deposits has been considered, but development has yet to occur due to low quality and cost of removal.

3:01 (1:19) MP 131. Cross Onakawana River.

3:09 (1:11) MP 138. Cross first of several "upside-down bridges" on route, designed to permit ice flows and other floating objects to clear structure. Supporting girders are above instead of below bridge, although difficult to see as train passes above.

3:15 (1:05) MP 142. Cross Moose River on 1,800-foot-long trestle, longest on route. Crossing here during ice breakup in spring can be spectacular as tons of ice drift downstream toward James Bay.

3:37 (0:43) MP 158. Cross Otakwahegan River.

3:39 (0:41) MP 159. Cross 51st Parallel.

3:40 (0:40) MP 160. Occasional temporary goose-hunting camps may be spotted through trees. Indians are permitted to hunt year round by aboriginal right.

3:44 (0:36) MP 162. Cross Cheepash River. Extensive gypsum deposits are nearby.

4:02 (0:18) MP 174. Cross Kwataboahegan River on second upside-down bridge. Others will be at mileposts 176 and 180.

4:20 (0:00) MP 186. Arrive Moosonee, where "Sons of Martha" monument on right commemorates workers who built the Abitibi generating station and extension of railroad to Moosonee. Handsome church, farther to right, is Cathedral of the Oblates Mission.

 MOOSONEE, ONT. - This is the northern terminus of the ONR. First impressions are not great, as the town has never fully entered the 20th century. Streets are either muddy, dusty or frozen, depending on the season. But the town has spirit and has been doing a lot to make things more attractive—new sidewalks, boardwalk at the docks, etc.

All-terrain vehicles (ATVs) have been banned from the main streets to give tourists better use of the town. (Here, nearly everyone has at least one ATV.) Buildings range from neo-government to early ramshackle, but there is a certain fascination here. Perhaps it's the frontier.

Cree Indians are the major inhabitants, whose lifestyle reflects their long adaptation to living in this remote region. Government and tourism are the major economic mainstays, with the latter holding forth during a very limited season. It is a jumping-off point for hunters and others needing to head farther north toward the arctic.

In the fall, the town bustles with goose hunters heading to various hunting camps, many such outposts being surprisingly posh and expensive. But Moose Factory Island is where most "tourists" go.

During the winter, the scene changes. This is when the ground (and the river) is frozen, making it possible to travel virtually anywhere by snowmobile. Indian villages north of here, inaccessible by land during the summer months, are reached by "The Winter Road" that consists of packed snow from hundreds of snowmobiles and ATVs. Instead of a time of confinement, it's a time of release.

If you plan to stay overnight, choices are quite limited. Be sure to make reservations well in advance if you plan to be here during the summer.

-Polar Bear Lodge, Box 305, (P0L 1Y0); (705) 336-2345. Surprisingly comfortable accommodations, with a good restaurant, looks out on the Moosonee River and boat docks, and is about ¾ mile from the station. Open all year. $69.30, including tax.

-Moosonee Lodge, Box 124, (P0L 1Y0); (705) 336-2351. Open May to October. Also on the river and about ¾ mile from the station. $69.30, including tax.

Ontario Northland – Moosonee, Ontario

(Before starting out to explore the area, be sure to obtain an ONR guide booklet that describes the area and has a fold-out map.) In Moosonee a visit to the **Museum Car,** which stands across from the station, is easy to work into one's schedule. From there, it's about a half mile straight down First Street (which curves to the left) where the **boats dock.** Just beyond the docks, on the town side of the road, is **Revillon Freres Museum** with artifacts and photos of early Moosonee days.

At the docks, large Rupert House canoes offer an interesting adventure in reaching **Moose Factory,** situated in the Moosonee River. (ONR suggests buying a one-way fare, since there are many boats, and your return, therefore, can be at any time. They also suggest being at the dock for the return at least an hour before train time.) Guided tour boats are also available.

Once on the Moose Factory Island, there are numerous sights to explore. Highlights include: the **Centennial Park Museum,** operated by Ontario Northland Transportation Commission, which has displays explaining how the area was developed from the formation of the Hudson's Bay Company; **St. Thomas Church,** with its unique floor holes to allow floodwaters to enter, thus avoiding a recurrence of an episode when the church floated away; **Anglican Church Parish Hall** where local crafts can be purchased as well as light lunches and refreshments; and the **cemetery** with tombstones dating back to early traders and missionaries.

Hearst

Sault Ste. Marie

Algoma Central

To "ride in the tracks of the black bear," you have to get up early. At the Algoma Central Railway's Sault Ste. Marie ("The Soo") depot, boarding begins at 7:00 am, and it's wise, when you're one of a possible 1,200 planning to ride, to get aboard as soon as possible, especially if you have a family or group that wants to sit together. Usually, by 7:45 only scattered seats remain available.

The ACR's Agawa Canyon Tour train is very popular; some summers have seen more than 100,000 passengers boarding the silver coaches with maroon letterboards and a black bear and his tracks on their flanks. ACR trains are clean, well-managed, and attractive. The mostly gray locomotives are splashed with a wide, deep-red stripe with yellow trim that is extremely eye-catching.

Incorporated in 1899, the ACR's route wound through dense forests and rugged hills and crossed many rivers and deep ravines. The first 56 miles of rail north of The Soo reached only 42 miles away! Its name at that time, the Algoma Central Hudson Bay Railway, or AC & HB, led some wags to call it the "All Curves and High Bridges."

Besides its most popular Agawa Canyon Tour Train, the ACR operates a Snow Train and its regular Soo-Hearst passenger trains.

Agawa Canyon Tour trains usually arrive back at The Soo on time at 5:00 pm with passengers so enthused about their "ride in the tracks of the black bear" that they crowd shoulder-to-shoulder into the depot's interesting gift shop. Veterans of the trip advise shopping the day before when picking up tickets, preferably before that day's train arrives back at The Soo.

Frequency - Varies by train. Canyon Tours run from early June through mid-October. The Snow Train runs Saturdays and Sundays only from January through March. The Regular Passenger Trains #1 and #2 operate six days a week from mid-May to mid-October, and weekends only the rest of the year (northbound Fri., Sat., Sun.; southbound Sat., Sun., Mon.).

Seating - Coaches only. ACR recommends picking up tickets a day in advance for all trains, even though reservations are available and required only for the Snow Train.

Dining - Varies by train. Dining cars, operated by E. J. Merini Catering, stay with the Canyon Tour and Snow Trains the entire trip, and provide hot breakfasts and lunches, as well as snacks and box lunches. Lunch can be ordered on board Trains #1 and #2 before arrival at Hawk Junction, where passengers can pick up their orders on arrival.

Baggage - No service on Canyon Tour trains. But the regular trains, to which the Snow Train is attached between The Soo and Eton, provide baggage cars that carry an unbelievable variety of articles from fishing poles to snowmobiles.

Reservations - Write to: Algoma Central Railway, Passenger Sales, 129 Bay Street, Sault Ste. Marie, Ontario, Canada P6A 1W7. Or phone (705) 254-4331.

Length of Trip - 296 miles in 10 hours.

Route Log

(A more detailed log of the route between Sault Ste. Marie and Canyon is furnished by ACR in its "Guide to Agawa Canyon Tour." Since mileposts are quite visible on this route, they are shown below after the passing times. Since Trains #1 and #2 stop almost anywhere and everywhere, no attempt has been made to list all stops and times are approximate.)

SAULT STE. MARIE, ONT. - The ACR is heavily involved in the development of The Soo waterfront. It owns the Station Mall shopping center and the Holiday Inn overlooking the river, both near the depot. Tours of the Soo Locks are available nearby.

Get Soo area information from Algoma Kinniwabi Travel Association, 616 Queen St. E., Sault Ste. Marie, Ontario, Canada P6A 2A4, Phone (705) 254-4293.

Two good hotels are close to the station: the **Stel Empire Inn,** (705) 759-8200, $90, is two blocks; and the **Holiday Inn,** (705) 949-0611, $94, is about four blocks away. Both are near the Station Mall with shopping, restaurants and theaters. Somewhat farther from the station (seven blocks) and with lower rates are the **Downtown Motel,** (705) 253-5639, $49, and the **Northwest Inn,** (705) 942-1970, $49.

0:00 (3:30) Milepost 0. Depart The Soo from ACR's 1973 depot. Some of The Soo's more interesting sights appear in rapid succession on left: Canadian Lock, St. Mary Paper Mill with its Gothic-like structures, mile-long International Bridge and Algoma Steel Corporation.
0:39 (2:51) MP 19. Cross 810-foot-long, 100-foot-high trestle with a sweeping view of Bellevue Valley to left. Lake Superior can be glimpsed in far distance.
1:30 (2:00) MP 57. Idyllic Trout Lake is at right, with cabins and canoes adding woodland charm.
1:38 (1:52) MP 62. On right, boulder-strewn Pine Lake is one of trip's prettiest scenes.
2:20 (1:20) MP 81. Cross Batchewana River.

2:44 (0:46) MP 92. Curve right across Montreal River on ACR's most famous trestle, 130 feet high and 1,550 feet long. Below us to left, ground level drops another 100 feet below base of trestle where one of three dams generating electricity for The Soo is located.
2:52 (0:38) MP 97. Crest highest point on ACR, 1,589 feet above sea level.
3:06 (0:24) MP 102. Begin our descent to canyon floor: 500 feet in 12 miles. Terrific view to left, all the way to Lake Superior. Deep within canyon, Agawa River meanders prettily.
3:20 (0:10) MP 112. At canyon level, cross Agawa. Bridal Veil Falls appears to right, Black Beaver Falls to left.
3:30 (0:00) MP 114. Arrive at Canyon.

CANYON - This is the destination of the Agawa Canyon Tour Train. Here the crew switches the locomotives to the opposite end of that train in preparation for the return trip. The ACR's Guide provides detailed information about, and a map of, the canyon. It suggests planning activities for the two-hour layover before arrival—there's too much to see and do here in just one trip. (Trains #1 and #2 pause here, but not long enough for through passengers to detrain and see any of the sights.)

Things to do here include:
1. Picnic in the developed park near the train or farther away in a more rustic area. Several locations have water pumps.
2. Watch (or join) kids in the play area in the horseshoe pits or on swings, slides or an operating handcar on a set of tracks.
3. If you have the required license, fish the river for speckled trout.
4. View one or both waterfalls.
5. Walk up to the lookout points—the intermediate one is fairly easy to reach; the upper point requires a long climb up wooden stairs. But the view is spectacular, looking over the canyon, the river and the train. The Guide wisely recommends allowing at least 40 minutes for the round trip.
0:00 (1:24) MP 114. Depart Canyon.
0:06 (1:18) MP 117. River's descent is punctuated by series of lovely cascades and waterfalls, on right.
0:11 (1:13) MP 120. Cross notorious "Chi-

Algoma Central – Hawk Junction, Ontario

nese Bridge," built by a Canadian manufacturer for Nationalist China. Firm had contract nullified by Chairman Mao when he came into power, so bridge was sold at a reduced price to an opportunistic Algoma Central.

0:16 (1:08) MP 123. Sign for Windy Lake Lodge identifies flag stop for fishermen in summertime and skiers in winter. Many backcountry hostelries are sprinkled along this stretch of ACR tracks to accommodate sportsmen who prefer their wilderness liberally laced with comfort.

0:31 (0:53) MP 132. At Millwood, large lumbering operation is on left.

1:00 (0:24) MP 149. Woods present nice stand of birch trees, at right. Similar in appearance to aspens, which are also found along route, birches are distinguished by their whiter-than-snow trunks. Spruce is a prevalent evergreen, while maple is a common hardwood.

1:10 (0:14) MP 157. Train experiences brief encounter with "outside" world as tracks cross Canada's Highway 101.

1:24 (0:00) MP 165. Arrive Hawk Junction.

HAWK JUNCTION, ONT. - There should be enough time to stretch for a few minutes at this Algoma Central division point. The ACR rail yards provide an interesting array of equipment —snowplows, cabooses, diesel locomotives —and long strings of red-painted baggage carts at trackside. If you ordered a hamburger, it will be waiting for you, probably warming on the hood of the cook's car by the station. (These burgers are really better than they sound.)

This is a jumping-off point for the old trappers' canoe route.

0:00 (3:24) MP 165. Depart Hawk Junction and head deeper into wilderness of Canadian Shield. Watch for moose, bear and white-tailed deer.

0:28 (2:56) MP 184. Dubreuilville is scene of bustling lumber operation, with conveyors, cranes, tracks and a wood burner all laboring at left.

0:45 (2:39) MP 195. At Franz, cross main line of CP rail, route of VIA's Sudbury-White River triweekly rail diesel car service.

0:59 (2:25) MP 206. At Wabatong, note

"Petticoat Junction" cottage by Lake Wabatongushi, on right.

1:05 (2:19) MP 210. Finger-like Oba Lake extends along tracks at left. Until now, waters have flowed to south. North of here, streams drain across Arctic Watershed north to Hudson Bay.

1:09 (2:15) MP 212. Cross portion of Lake Oba on quarter-mile-long bridge constructed not on a firm foundation, but on buoyant footings that literally float tracks on lake's surface.

1:14 (2:10) MP 215. Expansive body of water on left is Lake Tatnall.

1:49 (1:35) MP 245. Briefly merge with CN main line and yards at Oba. "The Last Resort" stands at right, presumably final home of retired wag. CN tracks carry VIA's transcontinental trains.

2:10 (1:14) MP 254. Moose rack over door of hunter's cabin, on left, is most appropriate decoration.

2:40 (0:44) MP 275. Mead is first town since Hawk Junction that has luxury of paved highway access.

3:11 (0:13) MP 296. After traveling north all day, train curls east and slows as it enters outskirts of Hearst.

3:23 (0:01) MP 295. Pass one of Hearst's numerous lumber mills, on left. Plywood industry has long been a Hearst mainstay.

3:24 (0:00) MP 296. Arrive Hearst.

HEARST, ONT. - If you visit Hearst in the summer or fall, it's a good idea to have reservations. This is a sportsman's haven with thousands of nearby lakes supplying outstanding fishing as well as excellent goose hunting. Just as important is big game hunting, particularly for moose that abound in this region. Snowmobiling on 130 miles of trails is also popular in the winter months.

Lumbering is the principal industry in this largely French-speaking community. Several large sawmills operate here, some offering tours.

The **station** is a small, efficient facility with CN markings but used by the Algoma Central. It is centrally located, directly behind two of the town's nicer motels and two blocks from George (Main) Street.

The Hearst trains are unreserved, and tickets are not sold until 7:45 am the day of departure. Credit cards are not accepted. (Although MasterCard and VISA are accepted by ACR at Sault Ste. Marie, they cannot be used at the Hearst station.)

Bus service is available to and from Kapuskasing, connecting to VIA's Northland.

The Queen's Motel, (705) 362-4361, is directly in front of the station and has large, comfortable rooms, a sauna and whirlpool, and an indoor pool. $42. The adjacent **Companion Motel,** (705) 362-4304, also has nice accommodations. It has an excellent restaurant and an interesting lounge filled with local color. $45.

White River   Sudbury

Sudbury to
White River

White River is still served by VIA, but just barely. The Canadian was removed from the CPR line through White River in January of 1990, but VIA received a mandate to continue service to that town. As a result, rail diesel cars still make triweekly runs between Sudbury and White River. Trains depart Sudbury midmorning, Tuesday, Thursday and Saturday, and depart White River midmorning, Wednesday, Friday and Sunday. The trip takes approximately nine hours.

Route Log

SUDBURY, ONT. · The town was founded in 1823 during the construction of the Canadian Pacific Railway, and it was during this activity that sufficient ore discoveries were made in order to induce serious mining. Today, Sudbury is the largest nickel-producing area in the world. The "Sudbury Basin" is a depression in the earth approximately 17 miles wide and 35 miles in length around which most of the mining activity is carried on by Inco Metals and Falconbridge.

Although geologists are unsure, many believe this basin was formed nearly two billion years ago when an enormous meteorite, several miles across, had a spectacular collision with the earth. The "irruptive" nickel which appears on the edges of the basin gives much of the countryside a lunar-surface appearance. Geologic formations, including "shatter cones," are so unusually similar to features thought to exist on the moon that

U.S. astronauts studied the area prior to their moon landings.

There are two **VIA Stations** in the Sudbury area. The CP station at 233 Elgin Street is a well-maintained facility on the edge of downtown, and now only serves the RDC service to White River. VIA's transcontinental train uses the CN station in nearby Capreol.

For reservations and other information, call 800-268-9520.

Cab stand at the CP station; metro 673-6000. **Greyhound,** on Falconbridge Highway, is about three miles from downtown. (Greyhound will discharge passengers downtown, about ¾ mile from the CP station.) Call 560-1444. **Local bus,** 560-1111. The **airport** is several miles northeast of town.

The Sudbury Regional Development Corporation, 200 Brady St., P3E 5K3; (705) 673-4161 or (705) 674-3141.

Senator Hotel, 390 Elgin St., P3B 1B1; (705) 675-1273. Well-managed hotel with nice rooms and a very good restaurant. Some rooms overlook rail yards and station. Two blocks from the CP station. $60.

-**President Hotel,** 117 Elm, P3C 1T3; (705) 674-7517. In downtown area, about ¾ mile from the CP station. $62.

One of Sudbury's principal attractions is the **Big Nickel Mine** with half-hour tours. Also, smelter slag pourings each night are both erie and beautiful; call 682-2087 for times. **Science North** is the region's most popular place to visit, containing hands-on science exhibits.

0:00 (0:53) Departing Sudbury, Community Arena stands in forefront of downtown hub on right, while attractive residential district overlooks activity from atop bluffs on left.

0:02 (0:51) On right, many businesses use murals as clever means for advertising goods and services.

0:04 (0:50) Multi-domed St. Volodymyr Ukrainian Greek Orthodox Church on right is a most impressive example of Ukrainian Baroque architecture.

0:06 (0:48) On outskirts of town, train winds through small mini-canyons carved within rocky terrain. Nickel open-pit mines are a frequent observation throughout this stretch. Watch for molten slag being dumped.

0:10 (0:43) Pass through Azilda, named for first white woman settler in this region. Like many other small towns along route, Azilda is a flag stop where passengers may entrain or detrain when prior notice is given.

0:17 (0:35) Typical of most small Ontario communities, elegant church on left at Chelmsford is prominent centerpiece of town.

0:27 (0:27) Cross aptly named Vermilion River.

0:32 (0:23) Beautiful Onaping Falls tumble down by trackside on right.

0:35 (0:20) West of Levack, and continuing nearly to Winnipeg, route wends its way past myriad lakes, so numerous that individual identification would be impractical. At once a scenic wonderland of shimmering beauty, wetlands of Ontario are as well a recreation haven, with hunting and fishing camps nestled picturesquely along many shorelines. Famous Canadian moose is also a frequent visitor to these parts, often seen lumbering through neighboring marshes.

0:39 (0:16) More waterfalls embellish scenery on right.

0:47 (0:09) Beaver colonies, like those entrenched on right, are perhaps most intriguing architectural structures seen throughout lakelands.

0:55 (0:00) Arrive Cartier.

 CARTIER, ONT. - A small settlement of about 1,500, named for Sir Etienne Cartier.

0:00 (3:16) Depart Cartier.

0:16 (3:00) Unusually large red weather vane atop shed makes wind-watching a breeze for residents of adjacent home, on left.

0:36 (2:37) Just past Sheahan, cross Spanish River which then follows on right.

0:55 (2:21) Names of many towns along route are derived from Indian geographic descriptions. One such example is found here at Metagama, which, when translated, means "river flows out of lake." Name refers to Spanish River which finds its source a few miles north in Biscotasi Lake.

1:20 (1:56) Ducks and geese are sometimes amusing attraction at Biscotasing, waddling about well-kept grounds of station house on right. Resort community is set atop hillside on left, overlooking arm of Biscotasi Lake. Weathered church is particularly picturesque.

1:44 (1:33) Large timber mill operation, on right at Ramsey, is one of first to be observed in countless succession of such facilities seen throughout Canada. While some enterprises harvest woodlands for lumber, pulping operations are much more prevalent, and represent one of country's most prodigious industries.

2:25 (0:56) On left, follow then cross Wakamagasing River, approaching quaint little town of Sultan.

3:00 (0:21) Cross Nemegosenda River just before passing through Nemegos.

3:14 (0:11) Apparently not designed for sleepwalkers, note island cabin, curiously isolated in midst of Lake Poulin on right.

3:15 (0:10) At Devon, freight chutes on right facilitate loading of wood chips—an important by-product of milling process, used in manufacture of particle board and paper pulp.

3:25 (0:00) Arriving Chapleau, finely preserved CPR steam locomotive, number 5453, is proud fixture of park on left.

CHAPLEAU, ONT. - Although logging is now Chapleau's main thrust, at one time this was the most important railroad town between Sudbury and Lake Superior. Solid bedrock of the Canadian Shield, when not protruding, is frequently only a foot or so below the surface, and construction of the Canadian Pacific through this area was extremely difficult. Cuts were stubborn and lack of soil for fills was just as troublesome, with soil being shipped in for embankments. Furthermore, there were treacherous sink holes which would sometimes not make themselves known until after several trains had rumbled over them.

Besides logging, Chapleau is a hub of great fishing and hunting with good fly-in services available. Three provincial parks are within 50 miles of this attractive forest community. Next to the steam locomotive is Centennial Museum with natural history and pioneer exhibits, as well as the Rotary International Friendship Table which has wood inlays from around the world. On the station lawn is a monument to Louis Hemon, well known Canadian author, who died near here when struck by a train.

0:00 (3:07) Departing Chapleau, beautiful homes border edge of Kebsquasheshing Lake, both right and left.

0:14 (2:53) Sign at right indicates location of Chapleau Crown Game Preserve. Tracks form southern boundary of this park for several miles.

0:39 (2:28) "Encompassing waterfront vistas" would be appropriate advertisement for structure, half-submerged in Lake Windermere on left.

0:50 (2:17) Small red shack at right was once depot for Bolkow.

1:27 (1:40) Approaching Missanabie, cross arm of Dog Lake, one of region's largest. Once in town, note general store and old hotel huddled scenically along lake shore on left.

2:00 (1:10) Pass through picturesque community of Franz, tucked neatly in cove alongside Hobon Lake. Here, tracks of CP Rail cross those of legendary Algoma Central. Latter is known for spectacular autumn leaf excursions.

2:15 (0:57) Note dam on left as train crosses Magpie River. Structure was one of earlier hydro-power facilities in region.

3:09 (0:06) Join White River on left, then cross several times subsequently. As name might imply, surging falls and foamy rapids are common throughout its course.

3:15 (0:00) Arrive White River.

 WHITE RIVER, ONT. - This small village of 850 is situated at one of the few highway intersections in this region, making it a popular base for hunters and fishermen. Its weather station records some of the coldest temperatures in North America. The mercury once dipped to minus 72 degrees Fahrenheit —just 6 degrees above the Canadian record.

Canadian

You might suspect a trip spanning the dominion of Canada on board the only transcontinental train in the Western Hemisphere would be a scenic delight. Good suspicion! Nearly every shape and form of Canada's interior beauty sweeps by on this second-longest train ride anywhere. (The longest ride of all shows you a lot of Siberia.) It's almost as though mountains, plains, lakes, rivers and forests were carefully positioned in dramatic sequence just to titillate those cruising on the Canadian.

But it's more than just scenery. From start to finish, the Canadian rolls across 3,000 miles of history. A transcontinental railroad was talked about in Canada as early as 1871, when suggestions of such a project were used to prop up negotiations to bring British Columbia into Confederation. And there was another incentive: Canada could ill-afford to ignore the 1869 golden-spike accomplishment of its neighbor to the south. Not without its detractors, the monumental effort finally began, almost casually at first, but with the appointment of William Cornelius Van Horne in 1881, construction pushed forward with resolve. The tortuous Rockies, the bitter Canadian winters, the locomotive-swallowing muskegs of Ontario, all were formidable adversaries. But on November 7, 1885 the last spike in the last section of track was ceremoniously tapped in at Craigellachie, British Columbia. The following year the railroad was ready, and the first trans-Canadian passenger train puffed out of Montreal on June 28, arriving at its western terminus of Port Moody on July 4. The line was the Canadian Pacific Railway Company, later abbreviated to CP Rail when it reorganized in 1971.

The first train was not called the Canadian, however. Early designations included Trans-Canada Ltd. and Dominion. The name Canadian wasn't bestowed until 1955 when what was then the world's longest dome train pulled out of Montreal, composed of streamlined, stainless steel cars built at Budd Company's Red Lion plant. (By the late 1960's, the train had reached its greatest length— 22 cars, including ten sleepers and two diners.)

But another transcontinental line was soon added to compete with the CP. This new route was built by a collection of public and private railroading efforts in the early 1900s, taken over by the Canadian government and operated as the Canadian National Railway, now known as the CN. This more northern and more remote route avoided the muskegs along the top of Lake Superior and the arduous Kicking Horse Pass. The line went through Edmonton and Jasper before crossing Yellowhead Pass and curling southwest to Vancouver. It is this "second" transcontinental route that is now followed by the Canadian. The shift from the CP occurred January 15, 1990 when VIA's operations were severely curtailed.

Heading westward from Toronto, the Canadian encounters the lake-studded forests of Ontario's Canadian Shield country before a brief pause at Winnipeg. The route then angles across the ultra-flat expanses of Canada's wheatlands before reaching Edmonton, where soon thereafter, passengers get their first look at the Canadian Rockies—dead ahead. The ensuing trip through these giant bastions of western Canada is the crowning touch to a journey ranked as one of the best of all travel experiences.

Westbound Schedule (Condensed)
Toronto, Ont. - Late Night Departure
Capreol (Sudbury), Ont. - Early Morning (2nd Day)
Winnipeg, Man. - Midmorning (3rd Day)
Edmonton, Alta. - Early Morning (4th Day)
Jasper, Alta. - Early Afternoon (4th Day)
Kamloops, B.C. - Late Night (4th Day)
Vancouver, B.C. - Early Morning (5th Day)

Eastbound Schedule (Condensed)
Vancouver, B.C. - Late Night Departure
Kamloops, B.C. - Early Morning (2nd Day)
Jasper, Alta. - Midafternoon (2nd Day)
Edmonton, Alta. - Late Night (2nd Day)
Winnipeg, Man. - Early Evening (3rd Day)
Capreol (Sudbury), Ont. - Late Night (4th Day)
Toronto, Ont. - Early Morning (5th Day)

Frequency - Three times each week. Toronto departures are Tuesday, Thursday and Saturday. Vancouver departures are Monday, Thursday and Saturday.
Seating - Standard coaches, Dayniters and dome cars.
Dining - Dining car with complete meal and beverage service.
Sleeping - Sleeping cars with berths (sections), roomettes and bedrooms; Dayniter coaches.
Baggage - Checked baggage handled at most stops.
Reservations - All-reserved train.
Length of Trip - 2,765 miles, departing late night on the first day and arriving early morning on the fifth day (approximately 84 hours).

Route Log

 TORONTO, ONT. - See page 316.

0:00 (0:46) Depart Toronto.

A departure note. The train must leave heading east before curling north and then west into MacMillan Yard. From here, it must back into the Newmarket subdivision at Snyder where it is finally in position to proceed northward to Newmarket, Barrie and Orillia. This process takes about one hour. Arrivals by the Canadian at Toronto are a simple direct approach from the north and west without all the time-consuming maneuvering.

Times shown between here and Newmarket are for eastbound (Toronto-bound) trains only.

--- (0:45) CN Tower, world's tallest free-standing structure at 1,821 feet, soars skyward on right.

--- (0:44) $400-million SkyDome, on right, overshadows lower downtown Toronto. This bulbous edifice, completed in 1989, was built to house baseball's Blue Jays, shops, restaurants and a 350-room hotel. On nicer days, roof can be retracted to an open position in 30 minutes to put 90% of its spectators in sunshine. While passing this stupendous coliseum, be sure to look up to see whimsical groupings of "spectators" protruding from building like modern-day gargoyles.

--- (0:42) Tops of brick buildings and sign on grassy knoll are all that can be seen of Historic Fort York Park, on right. Park features restored British garrison from War of 1812.

--- (0:36) General Electric's Chemical Materials Division Plant #3 is on right.

--- (0:17) Final look at Toronto's skyline is afforded back on right.

1:12 (0:00) Arrive Newmarket.

NEWMARKET, ONT. - Its proximity to Toronto and the rich agricultural lands that surround it make Newmarket an important regional trading center. Of particular interest is the town's historic Quaker Meeting House.

0:00 (0:31) Departing Newmarket, former leather works has been elegantly transformed into The Old Davis Tannery Centre shopping mall, adorned with purple awnings and a wonderful four-faced clock tower, on right.

0:01 (0:30) In early 1900s Canadian Government planned to make Newmarket a

Great Lakes port by converting Little Holland River into a canal connecting with Lake Simcoe. Although plan was ultimately aborted, locks on right still survive.

0:31 (0:00) Arrive Barrie with Kempenfelt Bay, an arm of Lake Simcoe, at right.

BARRIE, ONT. - This commercial center of 35,000 is situated on the shores of Kempenfelt Bay, the western arm of giant Lake Simcoe. Barrie is home to the Base Borden Military Museum with its unusually large collection of military memorabilia, and the Simcoe County Museum and Archives devoted to tracing the history of man in this area.

0:00 (0:25) Depart Barrie.

0:01 (0:24) In small park at right, 4-6-0 CN steam locomotive 1531 has been lovingly preserved.

0:02 (0:23) Modernistic work of metal art, on right, appears to be contemplating flight.

0:03 (0:22) Unusual archway spans city street in downtown Barrie, on left.

0:06 (0:19) Numerous small watercraft are docked at marina, on right, creating pleasant maritime scene.

0:22 (0:03) Large complex of brick buildings, attractively ensconced on hillside left, is Huronia Regional Centre, an institution that houses and works with the handicapped.

0:25 (0:00) Arrive Orillia.

ORILLIA, ONT. - This town of 24,000 is situated on the Trent-Severn Canal System, and has an economy maintained by light industrial activities. Stephen Leacock, Canada's foremost humorist, wrote many of his works while living here, and his home, a 19-room lakeshore mansion, can be toured by the public.

0:00 (0:16) Depart Orillia.

0:04 (0:12) Train creeps across swing bridge spanning Trent-Severn Waterway. This 1,006-mile marine system, comprised of rivers, canals and lakes, snakes across Ontario countryside linking Lake Ontario with Georgian Bay. Like Erie Canal, commercial traffic has all but disappeared from its waters while recreational use has blossomed and now dominates.

0:16 (0:00) Slip past old concrete water

tower, at right, on arrival Washago.

WASHAGO, ONT. - Nicely situated at the very northern tip of Lake Couchiching, an adjunct to larger Lake Simcoe, Washago comes from a similar Indian word meaning "sparkling waters."

0:00 (1:42) Depart Washago.

0:14 (1:28) Lakeside resort on right often has seaplanes parked in easy view of tracks.

1:00 (0:42) Expansive waters of Lake Joseph are now on right.

1:32 (0:08) Stop momentarily while train switches from CP line to tracks of CN.

1:41 (0:01) Canadian rumbles high above Seguin River on lengthy trestle (1,695 feet). Parry Sound is off to left while town of same name comes into view on right.

1:42 (0:00) Arrive Parry Sound.

PARRY SOUND, ONT. - Excellent fishing, swimming, hunting and boating have made this Georgian Bay community of 5,000 a very popular destination resort area. This is the main access to that area known as 30,000 Islands, the world's largest concentration of islands, which are situated along the shore of the Bay—an eastern satellite of Lake Huron.

0:00 (3:10) Depart Parry Sound on CN tracks.

0:40 (2:30) Cross Shawanaga River.

1:00 (2:10) Cross Magnetawan River.

2:00 (1:10) Cross French River, once a major canoe route between Lake Superior and Montreal.

3:00 (0:10) Black rock outcroppings and white-barked birch trees create bizarre landscape on approach to Sudbury Junction.

Millions of years ago, an enormous meteorite slammed into the earth's crust, forming a gouge some 35 miles in length and exposing rich deposits of nickel and other ores. During the construction of the railroads in the 1800s, these deposits were finally discovered in what is now known as the Sudbury Basin. Sudbury is now the world's largest producer of nickel; the large stack visible in the distance to the left belongs to Inco's smelter and is the world's tallest at 1,250 feet.

Over the years, acid rain from the

smoke of Sudbury's mining operations has largely denuded the immediate landscape, but more recent environmental technologies have improved the local scene. As a matter of fact, Sudbury boasts some of the region's finest flower gardens. **3:10** (0:00) Arrive Sudbury Junction.

SUDBURY JCT., ONT. - This is a brief stop in Sudbury's outskirts. For a description of Sudbury, see page 340.

0:00 (0:32) Depart Sudbury Junction, and skim past eastern edge of greater Sudbury.

0:30 (0:00) Arrive Capreol.

CAPREOL, ONT. - This is another station used for Sudbury area passengers. Capreol is just a few miles north of downtown Sudbury.

0:00 (0:54) Depart Capreol.

Over the next several miles, the geography becomes increasingly alpine in nature. Rolling hills assume more rugged, angular features, while clusters of evergreens stand tall amidst a thicketed ground cover. Various species of pine, oak and ash, as well as tamarack, balsam, fir, white spruce, birch and hemlock are found in the Great Lakes Forest Region.

Geographic features encountered are characteristic of the Canadian Shield, with extensive lake systems and dense forests nurtured by soil that thinly covers bedrock. This bedrock is 500 million to 5 billion years old and covers one half of Canada as well as portions of the northern U.S. Muskegs (peat bogs) are abundant. Minerals are found throughout the region and mining is still prominent. Many ancient glacial lakes have gradually filled in with clay, creating rich agricultural areas. Approximately one sixth of Ontario (an Iroquois word which could mean "beautiful lake") is covered by fresh water lakes—nearly a half million of them.

0:01 (0:53) Cross very pretty Vermilion River which will accompany route beyond Laforest.

0:54 (0:00) Arrive Laforest.

LAFOREST, ONT. - This settlement is typical of many found along the railroads through this section of Ontario—small, isolated (no road access) and devoted to a frontier existence. At one time, schooling for children living in these remote reaches was provided by portable "schoolhouses" that consisted of a specially equipped and staffed rail car that would be towed into town by train, left on a siding for a few days, then moved on to the next village.

0:00 (0:55) Depart Laforest.

0:12 (0:43) On right, Key's Camp is just one of many hunting and fishing camps that dot CN's route through this lake country. Colorful canoes add charm to this woodland setting.

0:27 (0:28) Ruel Shoo-Fly Camp is another sportsman's retreat.

0:55 (0:00) Arrive Westree.

WESTREE, ONT. - This is one of the smaller stops, population 10 (more or less).

0:00 (0:30) Depart Westree.

0:18 (0:12) Cross Muskegoma River on 850-foot trestle.

0:19 (0:11) While birch and aspen forests give way to their coniferous relatives, pine and fir, the terrain continues rocky and marshy.

0:29 (0:01) Minisinakwa Lake is on left.

0:30 (0:00) Cross Minisinakwa River and arrive Gogama.

GOGAMA, ONT. - This good-sized town (over 600 population) has avoided isolation by situating just off the main highway between Timmins and Sudbury.

0:00 (1:26) Depart Gogama.

0:04 (1:22) Cross Timmins-Sudbury highway.

0:06 (1:20) Cross broad waters of Macaming River.

1:26 (0:00) Arrive Foleyet.

FOLEYET, ONT. - A lumbering community, located on the Timmins-White River highway and the Ivanhoe River, Foleyet is host to numerous moose hunters during the fall. Bear and other game are also found in the region.

0:00 (0:48) Depart Foleyet.

0:48 (0:00) Arrive Elsas.

ELSAS, ONT. - Elsas is a tiny, remote forest outpost, nicely ensconced on Kapuskasing (accent the first and third syllables) Lake. It seems half the town meets the baggage car to receive or send some sort of freight—boxes of french fries, furniture, a dog or two, the mail pouch.

0:00 (1:28) Depart Elsas along northern edge of immense Chapleau Game Preserve—one of world's largest.

0:02 (1:26) Nice view of Lake Kapuskasing is afforded on left.

0:50 (0:38) Cross Fire River.

1:00 (0:28) Cross Lower Minnipuka Lake.

1:28 (0:00) Merge with tracks of Algoma Central upon arrival Oba.

OBA, ONT. — Oba's claim to fame is its location on the intersection of the Algoma Central Railway with the CN tracks. The Algoma Central connects Sault Ste. Marie, 245 miles to the south, with Hearst just 51 miles to the north. The line penetrates the spectacular Algoma Canyon, and excursion trains out of Sault Ste. Marie are extremely popular during the height of fall color.

0:00 (0:41) Depart Oba.

0:12 (0:29) Cross Kabinakagami River, another stream whose waters ultimately reach Hudson Bay.

0:27 (0:14) Cross Shekak River.

0:32 (0:09) Sawmill, at left, is one of but many along this stretch of right-of-way.

0:41 (0:00) Arrive Hornepayne.

HORNEPAYNE, ONT. - This is the first town since Capreol that resembles a 20th-century community. Nearly 2,000 people live here, and the city has a city-center building, visible from the train, that houses schools, stores, athletic facilities and various city services.

0:00 (1:00) Depart Hornepayne.

1:00 (0:00) Arrive Hillsport.

HILLSPORT, ONT. - This community of 80 is another town devoted to lumbering.

0:00 (0:45) Depart Hillsport.

0:45 (0:00) Arrive Caramat.

CARAMAT, ONT. - Caramat is nicely situated on a small lake by the same name.

0:00 (0:25) Depart Caramat.

0:24 (0:01) Large pole-producing mill is on immediate left.

0:25 (0:00) Arrive Longlac.

LONGLAC, ONT. - This forest products oriented town anchors the northern tip of 44-mile-long Long Lake, once an important canoe route that was part of a thriving fur trade. Plywood plants now are the community's principal employers.

0:00 (0:39) Depart Longlac.

0:39 (0:00) Arrive Nakina.

NAKINA, ONT. - This is a major outfitting center for sportsmen who hunt and fish the region. Like the other communities along the route, Nakina was nurtured by the building of the railroad. The line from here to Armstrong was constructed by the National Transcontinental Railway and was opened on June 1, 1915. That same enterprise built the line from here to Longlac in 1923.

0:00 (1:34) Depart Nakina, as lakes grow more sparse.

1:15 (0:19) Note fire lookout tower off to left.

1:28 (0:06) Crossing Jackfish Creek on 798-foot-long, 74-foot-high trestle, look to left for view of northernmost waters of Lake Nipigon.

1:34 (0:00) Arrive Ferland.

FERLAND, ONT. - Just to the south of this lumbering hamlet is aforementioned Lake Nipigon, Ontario's largest body of water. It stretches 60 miles from north to south and bulges to 40 miles across at its widest point.

0:00 (0:46) Arrive Ferland.

0:07 (0:39) Cross Mud River on 60-foot-high trestle.

0:46 (0:00) Arrive Armstrong.

ARMSTRONG, ONT. - This forest outpost of 600 is yet another community closely tied to both the railroad and the timber industry. However, unlike so many towns along the CN route, it is not reached solely by rail. It's possible to drive 150 miles straight south and reach the Great Lakes port city of Thunder Bay.

0:00 (10:00) Depart Armstrong.

Both westbound and eastbound trains are scheduled to cross the stretch of tracks between here and Minaki, Ontario during darkness. Stops are made at **SAVANT LAKE, SIOUX LOOKOUT, RED LAKE ROAD** and **REDDITT** as well as numerous flag stops.

Gain one hour as train passes from Eastern to Central Time. Set your watch back (forward if eastbound) one hour.

10:00 (0:00) Cross Winnipeg River and note fine old lodge in distance. Arrive Minaki.

 MINAKI, ONT. - Scenic Gun Lake is just to the south of Minaki, where the Minaki Lodge, the structure visible off to the left when entering town from the east, once hosted weekenders that arrived here from Winnipeg by special excursion trains. Originally a CN hostelry, the lodge still operates, having been remodeled by the province of Ontario.

0:00 (2:15) Depart Minaki.

0:05 (2:10) Lakes abound and scenery becomes more attractive than ever.

0:21 (1:54) Through hamlet of Malachi as Lake Malachi, on left, routinely treats villagers to a stunning view.

0:30 (1:45) Note waterfall to right.

0:33 (1:42) Cross into Manitoba, boundary being readily identified by marker on right. We have just entered Whiteshell Provincial Park, a dreamland for canoe paddlers.

1:10 (1:05) Cross main line of CP Rail and former route of the Canadian. Route now runs straight as an arrow directly west toward Winnipeg.

1:25 (0:50) Through Elma, as countryside turns more pastoral. Farms through here were originally 160-acre homesteads granted by government.

2:00 (0:15) Country is now all farming and flat as a pancake, as prairies take over.

2:15 (0:00) Cross Red River Floodway on 903-foot viaduct as train arrives at Transcona.

 TRANSCONA, MAN. - This is an eastern Winnipeg suburban stop.

0:00 (0:17) Depart Transcona; Winnipeg's downtown skyline is directly ahead.

0:13 (0:04) Cross 55 feet above Seine River.

0:15 (0:02) Cross Red River.

0:17 (0:00) Arrive Winnipeg's CN Station.

 WINNIPEG, MAN. - In 1738 the French explorer Gaultier built Fort Route on the present site of Winnipeg. It wasn't until 1812, however, that a permanent settlement was established when Selkirk Settlors (led by Lord Selkirk) arrived and settled along the banks of the Red River, land which was granted to them by the Hudson's Bay Company.

In 1835, the Hudson's Bay Company, whose home offices are now in Winnipeg, built Fort Garry to further protect its fur-trading activities. Then in 1881, with the arrival of the Canadian Pacific Railway, Winnipeg became a major center of railroad activity.

Agricultural lands attracted various immigrant nationalities in the early 1900s, which gave the town its first real growth and assured its permanence. Today, it is not only the oldest city in the prairie provinces of Manitoba and Saskatchewan, it is also the largest with 600,000 residents. It is the capital of Manitoba.

VIA Station, 123 Main Street, on the edge of downtown, is a handsome structure designed by Warren and Wetmore, architects of New York's Grand Central Terminal. It has a sizeable waiting room, snack bar, restaurant, gift shop, barbershop and storage lockers. There are luggage carts, but they can't be used on the escalators to the train platforms. A new, attractive ticketing area has been installed and an interesting model railroad display by the Winnipeg Model Railway Club is just off the main lobby. There is pay-parking and limited free parking.

Station hours are 7:30 am to 10:30 pm. Call 949-1830 for reservations and information; 949-8780 for arrivals and departures.

Both **cabs** and **local buses** are at the front of the station. There is a **cab phone** just inside the station entrance. **Amtrak Thruway Bus** between Winnipeg VIA station and Grand Forks, North Dakota arrives here late morning and departs midmorning. **Greyhound,** 478 Portage, 775-8301; **Grey Goose,** 301 Burnell, 786-8891. **Winnipeg International Airport** is approximately four miles west of downtown.

Tourism Winnipeg, 232-375 York Ave., R3C 3J3; (204) 943-1970.

Gordon Downtowner Motor Hotel, 330 Kennedy St., R3B 2M6; (204) 943-5581. Extra large, bright and attractive rooms on the northwest edge of downtown. Thirteen blocks from the station. $49.

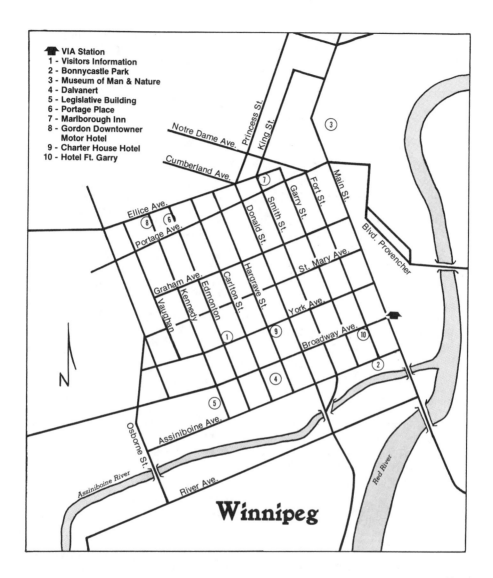

VIA Station
1 - Visitors Information
2 - Bonnycastle Park
3 - Museum of Man & Nature
4 - Dalvanert
5 - Legislative Building
6 - Portage Place
7 - Marlborough Inn
8 - Gordon Downtowner
    Motor Hotel
9 - Charter House Hotel
10 - Hotel Ft. Garry

Winnipeg

-**Marlborough Inn,** 331 Smith Rd., R3B 2G9; (204) 942-6411. Recently remodeled historic hotel. Eight blocks from the station. $65.
-**Charter House Hotel,** 330 York Ave., R3C 0N9; (204) 942-0101 or 800-782-0175. Handsome rooms in a central location. Six blocks from the station. $65.
-**Hotel Fort Garry,** 222 Broadway, R3C 0R3; 942-8251 or 800-665-8088. Historic hostelry, recently restored to its original luxurious state. One block from the station. $99.

Some of Winnipeg's downtown points of interest, all walkable by the energetic, include: **Dalnavert,** 61 Carlton St., a restored Victorian home of the son of Canada's first prime minister; **Bonnycastle Park,** a lovely setting on the Assiniboine River, only two blocks from the station; the **Legislative Building,** Broadway and Kennedy, one of North America's more beautiful public buildings with colorful flower gardens; the **Manitoba Museum of Man and Nature (and Planetarium),** 190 Rupert Ave., has exhibits depicting history of Manitoba, and is one of Canada's finest museums. The **planetarium** has programs year-round, and **Portage Place,** on N. Portage Ave., spans three blocks and contains 150 shops, restaurants, offices and movie theaters, including an IMAX large-screen movie system. Its centerpiece is a restored clock from the Old City Hall, and contains a 20-bell carillon.

Railfans (and others as well) will enjoy the **Prairie Dog Central** steam train that offers a 36-mile (two-hour) trip to Grosse-Isle from the CNR St. James Station, 1661 Portage Ave., just west of St. James St., Sundays, June through September. **Assiniboine Park and Zoo** has more than 1,200 animals at Corydon Ave., west of Shaftsbury. There is also a miniature railway in the park.

0:00 (0:57) Depart Winnipeg.
0:01 (0:56) Cross Assiniboine River near its juncture with Red River. Waters will ultimately flow north into Lake Winnipeg.
0:03 (0:54) On right, ornate dome is distinctive feature of Winnipeg's Legislative Building. Red River now follows momentarily on left.
0:32 (0:25) An interesting two-story depot on right and an old church on left are highlights through Elie. On western edge of town, cross Milk River, with neighborhoods of gracious homes lining its banks.
0:50 (0:07) At Nattress, cross Assiniboine River.
0:54 (0:03) Horse farm appears on right where newborn colts can often be seen cavorting with their proud mothers.
0:57 (0:00) Arrive Portage la Prairie.

 PORTAGE LA PRAIRIE, MAN. - Literally translated as "prairie portage," the city is situated at the narrowest point between the Assiniboine River and Lake Manitoba. This spot once served as a resting point for both Indians and early settlers transporting their canoes between these two important waterways.

A fort was established at this strategic site in 1738, and from 1867 to 1868 the town held the distinction of being capital of the "Republic of Manitobah." Today, it remains a transportation hub of the prairies, with the CN and CP rail lines

making a unique prairie intersection, while the Trans-Canada and Yellowhead highways join here.
0:00 (1:01) Depart Portage la Prairie where our CN tracks gradually swing to right away from CP main line that continues on to Calgary.
0:07 (0:54) Glide across large depression which carries excess waters of Assiniboine River during those unusual moments when it is in flood stage.
1:01 (0:00) Arrive Brandon North, where what has to be world's smallest station awaits on left. Not much larger than a playhouse, depot is actually complete with desk and benches.

 BRANDON NORTH, MAN. — This northern "suburb" stop serves the town of Brandon, a few miles off to left.
0:00 (0:14) Depart Brandon North.
0:14 (0:00) Arrive Rivers.

 RIVERS, MAN. - Named for the president of the Grand Trunk Railway, this town is but one of many wheat-oriented communities of Manitoba.
0:00 (2:12) Departing Rivers, note one of few baseball diamonds which can be observed while traveling Canada by rail—hockey is a more important sport in this part of world. Watch for hangar-like buildings in several communities along this route which house both hockey and curling rinks.
0:35 (1:37) Train is now cruising along a mesa top, with nice view of Assiniboine River twisting and turning through valley below.
0:37 (1:35) Cross Minnewashtack Creek on trestle over 1,500 feet in length.
0:41 (1:31) Trestle carries us high over Birdtail Creek.
1:03 (1:09) After milepost 213, watch for sign on right which pinpoints Manitoba-Saskatchewan border. From here on, landscape will begin to flatten more and more as we move westward.
1:07 (1:05) Strings of rail tank cars frequently line siding awaiting cargo from potash mine on left. Mineral is used in manufacture of fertilizer.
1:22 (0:42) Another potash plant can be seen to left across valley. Another similar plant can be seen to left in about eight

more minutes.

2:11 (0:01) Passing through extensive rail yards of Melville, note quaint onion-domed church to right.

2:12 (0:00) Arrive Melville.

 MELVILLE, SASK. - One of the larger towns along the route, this is a rail division point. Notice enclosed hockey rink just behind Melville's rather attractive, chalet-style depot.

0:00 (2:19) Depart Melville.

0:23 (1:56) Two churches in Goodeve are particularly eye-catching, one single-steepled and one three-spired.

0:31 (1:48) Russian influence is apparent in this part of Saskatchewan. Note Mosque-appearing church in Hubbard.

0:47 (1:32) Here is another church with Russian flavor as we pass through town of Jasmine.

1:04 (1:15) Seemingly in middle of no-where, a horse track and arena suddenly appear.

1:17 (1:02) Hills on either side of us are Touchwood Hills, named after dead poplar trees which make excellent firewood.

1:21 (0:58) Soon after milepost 77, some Indian influence is noticed from both fence and facing of house in Quinton—the one-and-only house in Quinton.

1:59 (0:20) Cross over Peter Lake at milepost 101.

2:10 (0:09) Now pass over much larger Boulder Lake.

2:19 (0:00) Arrive Watrous.

 WATROUS, SASK. - This town actually has motels, the first we've seen for some time. This is a resort community with hot mineral springs four miles north of here which the Indians believed had unusual curing properties.

0:00 (1:05) Depart Watrous. (Travel between Watrous and Saskatoon is during the middle of the night.)

1:05 (0:00) Just before arriving Saskatoon, cross the South Saskatchewan River.

SASKATOON, SASK. - Located on the prairies of Saskatchewan,

it is the second largest city in the province with a metropolitan population of 150,000. Founded in 1882 as a temperance colony, it has grown to prominence as a center of one of the richest agricultural regions of Canada. It is sometimes referred to as the "City of Bridges" due to the large number that cross the South Saskatchewan River here.

VIA Station, Chappell Dr., is located four miles from downtown, reached by traveling west on 11th St. to Chappell. The station has storage lockers and vending machines. Free parking is adjacent to the station.

For arrival and departure information, call (306) 384-5665. For reservations and other information, call 800-665-8630.

Cab stand is at the station; United Cabs, 242-1206. United Cabs also has **limo service** to and from downtown. Nearest **local bus** stop is at the corner of Dieppe St. and Elevator Rd., four blocks from the station; 242-1206. **Saskatoon Airport** is approximately eight miles north of the station.

Saskatoon Visitor and Convention Bureau, 102 310 Idylwyld Dr. N., Box 369, S7K 3L3, (306) 242-1206.

Sheraton Cavalier, 612 Spandia Cres. E., S7K 3G9; (306) 652-6770. Downtown location, two blocks from shopping. Five miles from the station. $78.

The Mendel Art Gallery and Civic Conservatory is located at 950 Spandia Crescent East, on the west bank of the South Saskatchewan River, just a short walk from the business district. The gallery has permanent Canadian paintings and sculpture, as well as local, national and international shows.

The **Saskatchewan Western Development Museums,** Saskatoon Branch at 2610 Lorne Ave. (two blocks off Ruth St. exit) has exhibits of the development of western Canada. The **Ukrainian Museum of Canada,** 910 Spandia Cres. E., has exhibits of Ukrainian culture in Canada.

0:00 (1:10) Depart Saskatoon.
0:13 (0:57) On right, former station at Gandora now serves as a private home.
1:10 (0:00) Arrive Biggar.

BIGGAR, SASK. - Biggar is smaller than most towns with three museums. Biggar Museum and Gallery tells the story of the area's settlement. The Homestead Museum features a pioneer home, rural schoolhouse, general store and sod home, while five miles east, Kisser's Western Relics Museum indeed displays Western relics.

0:00 (1:03) Depart Biggar.
1:03 (0:00) Arrive Unity.

UNITY, SASK. - This small prairie community has its own salt plant that offers tours that allow visitors to see how a variety of salt products are manufactured.

0:00 (1:22) Depart Unity.
0:32 (0:50) Large Manitou Lake off to right is notable for its good-sized island in its middle.
0:43 (0:39) Leave Alberta and enter Saskatchewan. Provincial boundary is marked by sign at right.

Leave Central Time and enter Mountain Time. Set your watch back an hour (forward if eastbound).
0:54 (0:09) Cross Ribstone Creek (three times).
1:22 (0:00) Arrive Wainwright.

WAINWRIGHT, ALTA. - Wainwright Canadian Forces base is just southwest of this Alberta community. Petroleum production has also been an economic mainstay.

0:00 (0:50) Depart Wainwright.
0:10 (0:40) Train now makes an airy crossing of impressive Battle River which lies some 200 feet below. Steel trestle is nearly 3,000 feet in length.
0:40 (0:10) Numerous sink holes throughout this area provide good habitat for migrating waterfowl, including Canadian geese. These small ponds now dot landscape on both sides of tracks.
0:50 (0:00) Arrive Viking.

VIKING, ALTA. - The name of this Alberta farming community reflects its Scandanavian heritage. Nearby quartzite rocks, carved by Cree Indians, are thought to relate to buffalo fertility rights.

0:00 (1:20) Depart Viking.

Edmonton, Alberta

0:13 (1:07) Russian Orthodox Church, with its silver and white onion-shaped dome, is architectural jewel of Holden, across small lake on right.

0:25 (0:55) Small red grain elevator on left serves as statement of sorts. Instead of "Alberta Pool," west side has been enscribed "Dirty Shorts."

0:32 (0:48) Huge Beaver Lake can be spotted in distance to right.

0:43 (0:37) Now, large Cooking Lake is on left.

1:06 (0:14) After passing through yards at Clover Bar, cross Saskatchewan River where refineries are most evident on fringe of Edmonton.

1:14 (0:06) Sizeable coliseum on left is home to National Hockey League's Edmonton Oilers.

1:16 (0:04) Edmonton's professional football team uses stadium on immediate right.

1:20 (0:00) Arrive Edmonton.

EDMONTON, ALTA. - Edmonton has a shopping mall like Crocodile Dundee has a knife. Totally intimidating any would-be competitors, it's the largest in the world. A super-extravaganza that has to be seen to be believed, with stores and more stores (there are over 40 shoe stores alone), it has its own amusement-park attractions that include three roller coasters, a floating replica of the Mayflower (complete with submarine rides around its perimeter), a nifty theme hotel and a beach with surf— all under one immense roof. And some people even go to the Mall just to shop.

With such a dynamo on the west edge of town, it would seem Edmonton's downtown area might wither, even though the town is the provincial capital. This has not happened. The downtown has its own delightful shopping malls, a modern subway and enclosed pedestrian walkways that keep the city vibrant—both day and night, summer and winter.

VIA Station, 1004-104 Ave. in the CN Tower at 100 Street, constructed in the 1960s as part of an urban development project, has an unusual circular interior design with a gift shop, snack stand, storage lockers and pay-parking. (There are free luggage carts, but they have limited usefulness since they

353

can't be taken up the escalators to the train platforms.) Hours are 9:30 am to 6 pm, Mon.-Fri.; 10 am to 6 pm, Sat. and Sun.

For arrivals and departures, call (403) 422-6032; for reservations, 800-665-8630.

Cab stand and **local buses** are at the station. Yellow Cab, 462-3456; Checker Cabs, 455-2211. For **LRT (Subway)** and other transit information, call 421-4636. **Subway** is free within the downtown area and runs along Jasper Avenue and 99 Street. Nearest subway stop is Churchill Station, two blocks away on 99 Street. **Greyhound,** 10324-103 St., is four blocks from the station; 421-4211. Tilden offers **rental car** delivery at sta-

tion, 422-6097. The **airport** is 17 miles southwest of the city.

Visitor Information Center, Edmonton Convention & Tourism Authority, 9797 Jasper Ave., No. 104, T5J 1N9; (403) 422-5505.

Best Western Ambassador Motor Inn, 10041-106 St., T5J 1G3; (403) 423-1925. On west edge of downtown, near subway, nine blocks from the station. $45.

-**Edmonton House,** 10205-100 Ave., T5J 4B5; (403) 424-5555. An all-suite hotel with spacious rooms and lots of extras: pool, exercise room, ping pong, sauna and covered parking. An excellent value. Six blocks from the station. $72.

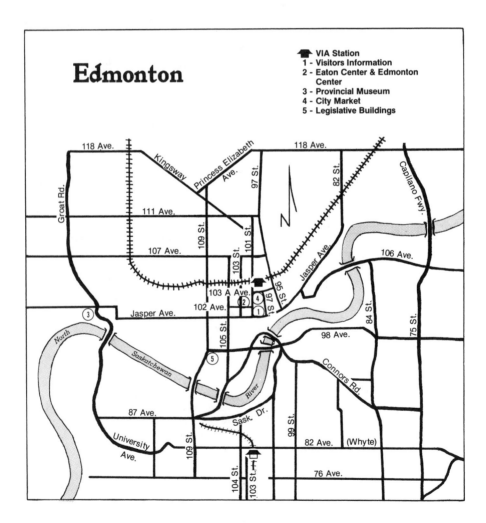

Edmonton

- VIA Station
1 - Visitors Information
2 - Eaton Center & Edmonton Center
3 - Provincial Museum
4 - City Market
5 - Legislative Buildings

-**Fantasyland Hotel & Resort,** at West Edmonton Mall, 17700-87 Ave., T5T 4V4; (403) 444-3000—From Canada, 800-661-6454, or from USA, call collect and give operator name of your state. For a real splurge, ask for the Canadian Rail Room (there are five) complete with railroad berths, jacuzzi, operational signal crossing, domed ceiling, clocks displaying time zones, and more—all in utter elegance. Or ask about other theme rooms. $180 for Canadian Rail Room. $120 for standard rooms.

Within walking distance, shopping is available at the **Eaton Center,** including miniature golf and movies, just three blocks from the station, at 101 St. and 102 Ave. Across 101 St. is the **Edmonton Center** with still more shops and restaurants. The **Provincial Museum of Alberta,** 12845-102 Ave., has worthwhile nature and cultural exhibits. If you should be in Edmonton on a Saturday during the warmer months, a real treat is the city **market** at 102 Ave. and 97 St., with farmers' produce, flowers, fish and crafts.

And, of course, for more shopping and sheer fun, there's the **West Edmonton Mall** described in the introduction above. Take a Number 10 bus westbound on Jasper Ave. from downtown.

0:00 (1:25) Depart Edmonton westbound in shadows of contemporary skyscrapers.
0:06 (1:20) Grassy parkway separates tracks from attractive residential district on left.
0:08 (1:18) On right, pass Edmonton Municipal Airport (International Airport is much farther south) with multitude of aircraft parked nearby. Immediately thereafter, proceed through industrial sector, with large logging concerns predominating. Such operations are common throughout Canada, and represent one of country's most important industries.
0:52 (0:34) "Onion-domed" church on right at Carvel is fine example of Byzantine architecture. This most distinctive design commonly characterizes churches of Russian, Greek and Ukrainian denominations.
0:53 (0:33) Series of small lakes provide convenient weekend retreats for work-weary urbanites. Mink Lake on left, and

Johnny's Lake, just downline on right, are two of these.
1:01 (0:25) Cross into Wabamun via bridge spanning arm of Wabamun Lake. Town's name is derived from Indian word for "mirror," a reference to adjacent lake.
1:13 (0:12) Golf course on left is additional draw for Gainford area.
1:23 (0:02) With highway bridge paralleling on left, cross beautiful Pembina River approaching Evansburg.
1:25 (0:00) Arrive Evansburg.

EVANSBURG, ALTA. - This stop serves the western fringe of Edmonton's widespread area. The town derives its name from a former mayor of this city.

0:00 (1:10) Depart Evansburg admist rolling farmlands of western Alberta.
0:10 (0:59) Another onion-domed church is prominent fixture on left at Wildwood. West of town, proceed along fringe of Chip Lake on left.
0:40 (0:30) Old tractor tires make unusual fence, encircling house on right at Peers.
0:54 (0:16) High trestles across Wolf Creek and McLeod River provide sudden drama to this stretch.
1:10 (0:00) Arrive Edson.

EDSON, ALTA. - Located approximately halfway between Edmonton and Jasper, Edson serves as a trading hub for its immediate area. It was named in honor of a vice-president of the Grand Trunk Pacific Railway, Edson Chamberlain.

0:00 (1:05) Depart Edson, passing large cemetery on right.
0:18 (0:48) Cross Sundance Creek atop another lofty bridge.
0:21 (0:45) At Bickerdike, charming chalet-style depot sits on right, with lush farmlands a picturesque backdrop. Ominously named Octopus Lake can be seen on left.
0:32 (0:33) With McLeod River bordering on left, peaks of Rocky Mountains can now be discerned, jutting above horizon in distance.
0:35 (0:31) On right, grounds of Medicine Lodge Detention Center are adorned by colorful array of miniature totem poles.
0:42 (0:24) Train skirts shoreline of Obed

Lake on right. Hills now encroaching on landscape preview arrival into Rocky Mountains.

1:01 (0:05) Approaching Hinton, huge St. Regis pulp plant on right is one of Canada's largest.

1:05 (0:00) Arrive Hinton. Depot's A-frame design lends appropriate atmosphere to this recreation gateway.

HINTON, ALTA. - This is the eastern gateway city to Jasper National Park. One of Alberta's two major pulp-processing plants, a St. Regis Pulp and Paper Mill, is located here with tours offered to the public. Also, the Alberta Forestry Museum has interesting exhibits of work of Canada's early forest rangers.

0:00 (1:08) Depart Hinton.

0:02 (1:06) Incongruously stowed amidst trees on left, once-proud riverboat steamer now languishes in weather-beaten neglect.

0:05 (1:03) Climb atop bluffs overlooking Athabasca River Valley on right. Within several miles, train emerges in heart of Jasper National Park, with towering peaks and shimmering lakes an encompassing spectacle to behold.

1:08 (0:00) Arrive Jasper where a steam locomotive, a totem pole and a "bear" all greet passengers.

JASPER, ALTA. - Jasper National Park, named after Jasper Hawes, a fur trapper in this area in the early 1800s, is located in the midst of majestic mountain scenery. Like Banff, it is understandably one of the more popular vacation areas in the Canadian Rockies.

VIA Station, 607 Connaught Drive, has a snack bar, a gift shop, storage lockers, luggage carts, a newsstand and redcaps. Free parking is adjacent to the station.

For reservations and information, call 800-665-8630; for arrivals and departures, 852-3168. Ticket window and waiting room hours are 8 am to 10:30 pm.

Cab stand is at the station; Jasper Taxi, 852-3146. **Greyhound** bus terminal and **tour buses,** including icefield tours, are adjacent to the station.

Information Center, 632 Connaught Drive (at Hazel). Write **Jasper Park Chamber of Commerce,** P.O. Box 98, Jasper, Alberta T0E 1E0. Call

(403) 852-3858.

Whistler's Motor Hotel, Box 250, T0E 1E0; (403) 852-3361. Across the street from the station. $69.

-Jasper Inn Motor Lodge, P.O. Box 879, T0E 1E0; (403) 852-4461. Limo service to and from the station. Four blocks from the station. $105.

Pyramid and Patricia lakes, located about five miles from town on Pyramid Lake Road, are fine examples of glacial lakes in an alpine setting. **Maligne Canyon, Medicine Lake and Maligne Lake** are located east of Jasper in the Maligne Valley. A spectacular gorge leads to the two lakes; Maligne Lake is in a breathtaking mountain setting. **Punchbowl Falls and Miette Hot Springs** are both east of Jasper, the furthest being Miette Hot Springs about 38 miles from town. The falls can be seen about 8 miles before reaching the hot springs, the latter being the hottest spring in the Canadian Rockies.

Mount Edith Cavell, 19 miles south of town off 93A access road, with its Angel Glacier is one of the more spectacular peaks in the Jasper area. **Athabasca Falls** are 20 miles south of Jasper, with various viewpoints offering excellent views of these magnificent cascades.

0:00 (1:53) Depart Jasper and head toward Yellowhead Pass and some of North America's most magnificent scenery! Trident Range will be on our left and Victoria Cross Range on our right as we make this ascent. Waterfalls, streams, snowfields and tunnels make this a railroading spectacular.

0:24 (1:29) Those small wire fences that occasionally appear on uphill side of right-of-way are slide detectors which activate a red signal should there be a rockslide or snowslide blocking tracks.

Gain one hour as train passes from Mountain to Pacific Time. Set your watch back (forward if eastbound) one hour.

0:37 (1:16) Crest Yellowhead Pass at milepost 17.5. This is border between Alberta, just behind, and British Columbia, just entered. Tracks are only 3,718 feet above sea level; however, many of surrounding peaks soar to more than 11,000 feet. Yellow-

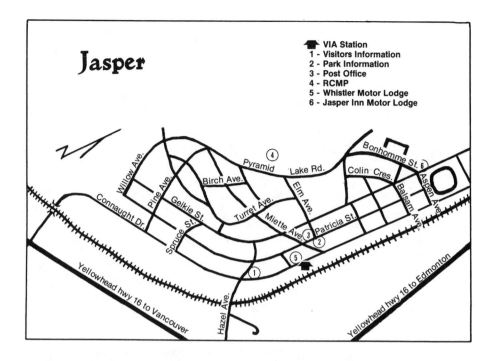

Jasper

- VIA Station
- 1 - Visitors Information
- 2 - Park Information
- 3 - Post Office
- 4 - RCMP
- 5 - Whistler Motor Lodge
- 6 - Jasper Inn Motor Lodge

head is one of lowest passes along entire North American Continental Divide. At this northerly point, waters flowing to east actually, sooner or later, find their way into Arctic Ocean.

0:42 (1:11) Beautiful Yellowhead Lake stretches serenely beside tracks on left. Yellowhead Mountain is highest peak directly across lake.

1:03 (0:50) And now, Moose Lake is alongside of us at left, even larger than Yellowhead.

1:14 (0:39) Red Pass Junction, at milepost 43.9, is a flag stop.

This is where the rail lines divide, with our CN line heading to the left (south) toward Kamloops and Vancouver, while the other (route of the Skeena) continues west to the end of the line at Prince Rupert.

1:19 (0:34) Through short tunnel.

1:30 (0:24) This is avalanche country, apparent as train drifts through another snowshed.

1:35 (0:20) Looking back, view is superb. One of dominant peaks is Mt. Robson at 3,954 meters—that's 12,972 feet—Canada's highest.

1:44 (0:09) Rugged peaks to left comprise Selwyn Range.

1:53 (0:00) Arrive Valemount.

VALEMOUNT, B.C. - This is a popular recreation area, particularly for fishermen. The town is situated at the very northern end of the Canoe Reach of skinny Kinbasket Lake.

0:00 (1:40) Depart Valemount.

0:05 (1:35) Excellent views are afforded in all directions; Premier Range is forward to right.

0:12 (1:24) To right, spectacular snowfields of Albreda Glacier create a perpetual blanket of white. Train is now paralleling course of Thompson River which will be followed into Kamloops.

1:15 (0:25) Note spectacular falls off to left.

1:40 (0:00) Arrive Blue River.

BLUE RIVER, B.C. - This small way-stop is in a truly idyllic setting, also popular with fishermen, as was Valemount.

0:00 (1:50) Depart Blue River.

0:24 (1:26) Enormous rapids below, on left, make it clear we are headed downhill.

Canadian – Canadian Rockies

Tunnel creates momentary darkness.

0:25 (1:25) River now squeezes through Little Hells Gate Gorge.

1:37 (0:13) Two large sawmills, on left, consume huge amount of local timber stands.

1:50 (0:00) Arrive Clearwater.

CLEARWATER, B.C. - This is a lumbering and farming community. Countryside will evidence more agricultural qualities as we approach Kamloops.

0:00 (1:45) Depart Clearwater, where Clearwater River, on right, adds to already burgeoning North Thompson River.

0:24 (1:21) Note small aerial tram, to left, that offers forest rangers unique ride to fire lookout on Baldy Mountain.

1:10 (0:35) "Current Ferry," on right, uses force of stream to propel it across North Thompson.

1:45 (0:00) Arrive Kamloops CN station, situated on northern edge of city.

KAMLOOPS, B.C. - The city is located at the confluence of the North and South Thompson rivers. The first white men to reach the area were fur traders representing the Pacific Fur Trade Company. They arrived here in 1811 and found the Kamloops Indians (of the Shuswap Tribe) eager to trade. This led to the construction of outposts which were eventually taken over by the Hudson's Bay Company in 1821.

Gold was discovered near here in the early 1850s spurring further development. British Columbia became a province of Canada in 1871, permitting the Canadian Pacific Railway to be extended to Kamloops three years later.

Even though this is Canada, Kamloops has a semi-arid climate with temperatures frequently soaring into the 90s during the summer months. Locals take to the beaches of the Thompson River in droves on warmer weekends, a favorite spot being just to the right of the tracks upon departure westbound from VIA's downtown station. It is so warm that Kamloops has a surprising five-month, frost-free growing season.

There are two VIA stations in Kamloops:

-**CN Station,** north of town and just off to the west of Hwy. 5, is open one hour before train time and closes on departure. There are soft drink and snack vending machines. This is the station used by the Canadian.

-**CP Station,** 3rd and Lansdowne, with a small waiting room, has direct phones to taxis, a few gift items for sale, but no lockers. Free parking is adjacent to the station.

For reservations and other information, call 800-665-8630.

 Cabs include Yellow Cab, 374-3333 and Kami, 374-5151. **Greyhound** is at 725 Notre Dame, 374-1212. **Rental cars** include Budget, 374-1456, with local delivery, and Tilden, 376-4911. For **local bus** information, call 376-1216.

Kamloops Travel InfoCentre, 10-10th Ave., V2C 6J7, located off 10th Avenue on the south bank of the South Thompson River, about a mile from the CP Station; (604) 374-3377.

Stockmen's Inn, 540 Victoria St., V2C 2B2; (604) 372-2281. Attractive four-story motel in the heart of downtown. Three blocks from the CP Station. $83.

-**Whistler Inn,** 375-5th Ave., V2G 6J5; (604) 828-1322. Five blocks from the CP Station. $60.

-**Scotts Motor Inn,** 551-11th Ave., V2C 3Y1; (604) 372-8221. About a mile from the CP Station but a good value. Also, convenient drive to the CN Station. $48.

Kamloops Museum and Art Gallery is located downtown at 207 Seymore Street, about three blocks from the CP Station. Exhibits depict life going back to the fur trade era. Kids should enjoy the **Kamloops Wildlife Park** and the **Waterslides** located 10 miles east of Kamloops on the East Trans-Canada Highway. There's even a miniature railway.

0:00 (4:00) Depart Kamloops.

0:01 (3:59) Make first of many river crossings between here and Vancouver, as North Thompson is crossed with view of Kamloops to left. Soon cruise beside Kamloops Lake on left. After lake, route will first follow Thompson River and then Fraser River into Vancouver—no more passes to surmount.

CN and CP tracks parallel each other on opposite riverbanks, frequently exchanging sides.

0:50 (3:10) Cross to southern shore of Thompson.

0:55 (3:05) To right is Walhachin, now a mere grove of cottonwoods. In early 1900s, prior to WWI, settlers irrigated this arid land, hoping to create their own "Garden of Eden." However, men were called to arms leaving their beloved land to the elements. A devastating flood washed out their aqueduct, and Walhachin ultimately met its demise.

1:00 (3:00) Cross to Thompson right-hand shore.

1:33 (2:27) Through arid flag stop of Ashcroft, and now swing southward, still following river.

1:51 (2:09) Rapids of Black Canyon churn Thompson into frantic froth.

2:43 (1:17) Above to right, waterfall from Murray Creek literally shoots out from mountainside during springtime.

2:45 (1:15) It is still apparent, on slope to right, where landslide occurred August 13, 1905, when lower portion of mountain came rumbling across valley in matter of seconds, damming waters of Thompson River. Five Indians were buried alive and thirteen more were drowned when waters backed over nearby village.

3:00 (0:53) Train enters "Jaws of Death," a particularly treacherous section of river, as canyon becomes narrow gorge.

3:16 (0:44) Cross Fraser River, just across from Lytton, where muddy waters of Thompson merge into much clearer Fraser on left. Simon Fraser, fur trader and explorer of British Columbia, put ashore at this point on June 18, 1808. Lytton, with its significant Indian population, lays claim to being longest continually occupied spot in North America.

3:20 (0:40) At Cisco Flats, both railroads now decide to exchange river banks in dramatic style. Original Canadian Pacific bridge was fabricated in Britain more than 100 years ago, arriving at Port Moody by ship, moved in sections by rail (of course) to present-day site, then erected by San Francisco Bridge Company. Bridge was eventually replaced.

4:00 (0:00) Arrive Boston Bar.

BOSTON BAR, B.C. - This village was originally a gold-mining center. A unique cable tram, only large enough to hold one automobile, serves as an aerial ferry between North Bend, immediately across the Fraser, and the Trans-Canada Highway here at Boston Bar.

0:00 (2:05) Depart Boston Bar.

0:17 (1:48) Canyon narrows to mere 110 feet forming "Hells Gate," where 200 million gallons of water per minute drain from 84,000 square miles of British Columbia. Each year, 2 million sockeye salmon swim upstream against this torrent to reach their spawning grounds. Simon Fraser reported it as "an awesome gorge."

The Pacific salmon industry was nearly ruined when rockslides in 1914, triggered by construction in the canyon, made passage so narrow that salmon spawning was cut by 90 percent. Subsequently, Canadian/U.S.-built fishways slowed the stream flow enough to bring the salmon population back to normalcy. Now, a tramway swoops bright red gondolas to the bottom carrying 28 passengers per load for impressive view of the canyon. Whitewater rafters can often be seen challenging the rapids and a treacherous whirlpool called "Devil's Wash Basin."

0:34 (1:31) Graceful structure of Alexandra Bridge spans Fraser on right.

The original Alexandra Bridge was built by Joseph Trutch in 1863 as part of the famed Cariboo Road. It was the first suspension bridge in British Columbia, and actually looked quite similar to its replacement (except the original sported wooden towers). It was destroyed by a flood in 1894, twenty years after its construction.

0:43 (1:22) Waterfall cascades directly overhead while train passes through tunnel.

0:55 (1:10) Obstruction at mouth of Fraser River Canyon is monolithic Lady Franklin Rock, named for widow of Sir John Franklin, Arctic explorer who died in 1847 searching for Northwest Passage. Lady Franklin's efforts to find her husband led her here but she could not probe farther upriver because of this formidable barrier. Her courage, however, inspired numerous expeditions to search for Sir John, ultimately producing thorough exploration of Canadian Arctic region.

0:56 (1:09) Town of Yale is immediately across river.

In its day, Yale was one of the most important and exciting towns in the West. Founded in 1848 as a fur collection point for the Hudson's Bay Company, Yale's place in history was furthered when local gold discoveries occurred in 1858. Then with greater finds 400 miles farther north at Cariboo and Barkersville, construction of the legendary Cariboo Wagon Road started here in 1862.

In 1880, railroad construction was commenced with the blasting of the oldest train tunnel in western Canada, on the CP line just north of here. Andrew Onderdonk was the man chosen to construct various segments of western track, extending from Port Moody to Kamloops Lake. Like his American counterparts farther south, Onderdonk employed thousands of Chinese willing to work hard and often for only about half of that received by white men. The Chinese may have been the real heroes of the Canadian Pacific. Omer Lavellee, in his classic book, *Van Horne's Road,* points out that when construction was completed and all the workers were summarily discharged, a local newspaper observed that a thousand white men rushed into the saloons and soon began to wreak havoc on the town. The Chinese merely went into the woods and ate their rice. The paper then chuckled over this difference between "pagans and Christians."

Yale claims the first railway station west of the Rockies, the first town council in British Columbia and the first girls' finishing school on the B.C. mainland (once visited by the Duke and Duchess of York).

0:58 (1:07) Just after crossing Emory Creek, pass location where Onderdonk's first Yale construction locomotive was unloaded from ship to shore in 1880.

1:18 (0:47) Through flag stop of Hope.

1:50 (0:15) Up valley, to right across river, is Harrison Hot Springs, a fine resort in the mountains. As you might suspect, resort's hot springs are a major attraction. Beautiful Harrison Lake, as well as historic Harrison Hotel, add to area's appeal.

2:05 (0:00) Arrive Chilliwack.

CHILLIWACK, B.C. - This agricultural center is located in a broad, fertile valley, actually the delta of the Fraser River. The delta has taken several million years to form, and now covers bedrock with soil one mile deep.

0:00 (0:28) Depart Chilliwack.

0:28 (0:00) Arrive Matsqui.

MATSQUI, B.C. - This is one more agrarian community and the last stop before reaching Vancouver's densely populated suburbs.

0:00 (1:02) Depart Matsqui.

0:02 (1:00) Now, cross to north banks of Fraser at Page.

0:22 (0:40) Through Mission, a small community named for an Indian school established here in the 19th century.

0:32 (0:30) Cross Stave River. It was near here that Billy Miner pulled off Canada's first train robbery in September, 1904—two years before his $15 holdup east of Kamloops.

0:33 (0:27) Literally pass through large lumber mill and yards.

0:39 (0:21) Fort Langley National Historic Park is immediately across river from ferry dock. Built in 1827 by Hudson's Bay Company, fort functioned as provisioning and administrative center for company and was to end American competition in Northwest. It was here that James Douglas declared British Columbia a crown colony in 1858 and fort became first capital.

0:57 (0:03) Cross Pitt River on 1,749-foot bridge with another center-pivot span.

1:00 (0:00) CP Rail repair shops and yards herald arrival at Port Coquitlam.

PORT COQUITLAM, B.C. - Development of this area, including nearby Port Moody, began with the 1858 gold rush. But the first major boom occurred 27 years later when the western terminus of the Canadian Pacific was planned for nearby Port Moody. Real estate skyrocketed in value, with some lots jumping from $15 to $1,000 each. The first shipment of rails arrived from England at Port Moody in May of 1883, and by August, 1885, the Marquis of Langsdowne, Governor General of Canada, was able to cross Canada for the first time without entering the United States (although not entirely by train since the track was not yet finished above Yale). In November, 1885, the trans-Canada route was complete, and the first transcontinental passenger train ceremoniously pulled into Port Moody at noon on July 4, 1886. The boom soon turned to bust, however, when the railroad was extended to a new Pacific terminal at Vancouver the very next year.

0:00 (0:50) Departing Port Coquitlam, cross river by same name before heading first south then west into megalopolis of Vancouver.

0:50 (0:00) Arrive at Vancouver's stately CN station.

VANCOUVER, B.C. - British explorer Captain George Vancouver discovered this area in 1792. It was a natural for becoming a seaport with its sheltered harbor and nearby forests as an important source of lumber. The arrival of the Canadian Pacific Railroad in 1884 and the development of the fishing industry spurred Vancouver to becoming one of Canada's great cities.

In a sparkling bay and mountain setting, offering relatively temperate weather year-round, the city has become a favorite western vacation spot.

There are two stations in Vancouver. The CN Station in downtown Vancouver on Station Street serves VIA's trains to and from the east. The British Columbia Railway Station, actually in North Vancouver, serves BCR rail diesel cars which travel north to Lillooet and Prince George, as well as the popular Royal Hudson summer-excursion trains to Squamish.

-VIA Station, 1150 Station St., is a handsome facility built along classic lines.

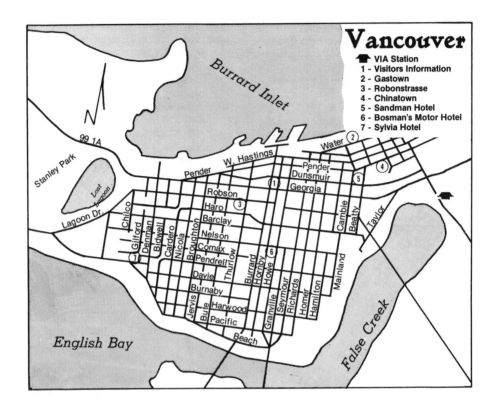

Vancouver

🚍 VIA Station
1 - Visitors Information
2 - Gastown
3 - Robonstrasse
4 - Chinatown
5 - Sandman Hotel
6 - Bosman's Motor Hotel
7 - Sylvia Hotel

It is about a mile from the central downtown area. The station has storage lockers, luggage carts, redcaps, a newsstand, vending machines, a snack bar and a restaurant. There is ten-minute free parking with long-term pay-parking two blocks away.

Ticket window hours are 9 am to 6 pm, and the waiting room is open 7 am to 6 pm. For arrival and departure information, call 669-3050. For reservations and other information, call 800-665-8630.

-BCR Station, 1311 W. 1st Ave., is located across Burrard Inlet in North Vancouver. The station has food and beverage vending machines and storage lockers.

Ticket and waiting-room hours are 6:30 am to 9 pm. Call (604) 984-5246 for reservations and information and 984-5264 for recorded information. Write BC Rail, Passenger Sales Service, Box 8770, V6B 4X6.

Note that although **Royal Hudson** steam trains to Squamish leave from this station, they are not operated by BC Rail.

Call Harbour Ferries, (604) 687-9558, for Royal Hudson ticketing and reservations.

Both stations have **cab** stands; Yellow Cab, 681-3311 and Black Top, 683-4567. **Local buses** stop in front of the VIA Station; call 324-3211.

Early morning **bus service** is furnished to the BCR Station from the Vancouver bus terminal, 150 Dunsmuir Street (across from the Vancouver Sandman Hotel) with pick ups from there to Stanley Park entrance, and in the evening, buses meet trains to return passengers by the same route. A fare is charged.

Skytrain, Vancouver's new rapid transit system, running through downtown from the waterfront to New Westminster, stops one block from the station; 261-5100. Tilden and Budget **rental cars** are available at the VIA Station. Bus service to and from The Coast Starlight in Seattle is available at the Vancouver Sandman Hotel, across from the Greyhound terminal; **Greyhound** terminal, 150 Dunsmuir; 662-3222. **Vancouver**

International Airport is a few miles south of the downtown area.

? **Greater Vancouver Convention & Visitors Bureau,** 1055 Dunsmuir St., V7X 1L3; (604) 683-2000 or 800-663-8555 (across from the Burrard Skytrain station).

Vancouver Sandman Hotel, 180 West Georgia St., V6B 4P4; (604) 681-2211. Opposite the bus terminal; buses to The Coast Starlight in Seattle leave from this hotel. Located downtown and about a mile from the VIA Station. $92.

-**Bosman's Motor Hotel,** 1060 Howe St., V6Z 1P5; (604) 682-3171 or 800-663-7840. In the heart of downtown, about two miles from the VIA Station. $89.

-**Sylvia Hotel,** 1154 Gilford St., V6G 2P6; (604) 681-9321. Overlooks beach on English Bay, next to Stanley Park. Popular small, old (1912) hotel. About three miles from the VIA Station. $47.

Stanley Park, at the foot of Georgia St., is considered to be one of the finest parks in the world. On a beautiful peninsula, forming a bridged link to North Vancouver, the park contains a zoo featuring polar bears, penguins, gardens, trails, picnic sites, tennis courts and an aquarium with 9,000 specimens of sealife.

Gastown, Water and Carroll streets, is where Vancouver began. Now an historic site which permits shops to remain open on Sunday (a rarity in Canada), this restored area has fine restaurants, shops and nightclubs. Its zany, steam-spurting clock has become Gastown's trademark. **Chinatown,** extending along Pender St., between Gore and Carroll, is a delight with its color, sounds and smells. This is the second largest Chinese settlement in North America. It's less than a mile from the station. Another downtown lure is **Robonstrasse,** located along a section of Robson Street between Hornby and Bute. It's a shopping area with a charming European atmosphere.

There are two unique attractions in the North Vancouver area. The **Capilano Suspension Bridge** is the world's longest suspension footbridge. It is 70 meters above the Capilano River and is 137 meters from shore to shore. (Not for those who are bothered by heights.) **Grouse Moun-**

tain has shops and a restaurant on the summit, and is reached by Canada's largest aerial tramway. This not only serves skiers, but those wishing to obtain a spectacular panorama of Vancouver.

And rail buffs will want to ride one of the area's biggest attractions, the **Royal Hudson Steam Train.** As its name implies, this is an excursion train pulled by one of the famous Royal Hudson engines, number 2860. The route begins at the British Columbia Railway Station in North Vancouver and makes a six-hour round-trip to Squamish in the summer. The scenery is spectacular. See the BCR Station information above for further details.

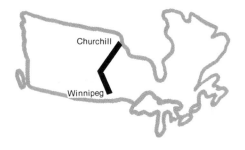

Hudson Bay

Two strands of silvery steel seem to stretch endlessly toward the horizons both fore and aft of the Hudson Bay. Countless Indian village whistle stops help break the tedium, until even these become heavily redundant. While sometimes monotonous (and certainly never hurried), this 1,055-mile trek from Winnipeg to Churchill is always an adventure and truly one of today's unique travel experiences.

Conceived in the 1870s, the line had a checkered history of starts and stops until finally, beginning in the mid-1920s, 3,000 hard-working emigrants, struggling against frost, blizzards and insects, constructed the final 300 miles of iron, reaching Churchill on Hudson Bay in March 1929.

Its purpose was to provide a shorter route to the world's grain markets, as well as direct access to Canada's interior for inbound goods and new emigrants. Although it has never become the epic transport that was once envisioned, it has indeed provided a means of exporting much of Canada's wealth of wheat and has had a profound influence on the development of the North's enormous resources.

After leaving Winnipeg in the late afternoon, the Hudson Bay reaches its northern goal of Churchill in the early morning of the third day. Two nights are spent on the train while making numerous stops to board and detrain local residents traveling from one flag stop to another. Sleeping car accommodations are definitely recommended.

Once there, the day can be spent seeing the sights and still start the return trip that evening. Of course, it's possible to stay longer, but the next return train will not depart for two or three days, depending on the day of the week. The major attraction is polar bear viewing which is best in the fall. It is worth noting that during the summer and fall, reservations should be made well in advance. Package tours are also offered by VIA Rail.

Northbound Schedule (Condensed)
Winnipeg, Man. - Late Evening Departure
The Pas, Man. - Midmorning (2nd Day)
Thompson, Man. - Early Evening (2nd Day)
Gillam, Man. - Middle of the Night (3rd Day)
Churchill, Man. - Early Morning Arrival (3rd Day)

Southbound Schedule (Condensed)
Churchill, Man. - Midevening Departure
Gillam, Man. - Middle of the Night (2nd Day)
Thompson, Man. - Late Morning (2nd Day)
The Pas, Man. - Early Evening (2nd Day)
Winnipeg, Man. - Early Morning Arrival (3rd Day)

Frequency - Departs Winnipeg Sunday, Tuesday and Thursday. Arrives in Churchill Tuesday, Thursday and Saturday. Departs Churchill same day of its arrival and arrives in Winnipeg Thursday, Saturday and Monday.
Seating - Standard coaches.
Dining - Complete meal and beverage

service.

Sleeping - Roomettes and bedrooms.

Baggage - Checked baggage handled between major stops.

Reservations - All coach seats must be reserved for distances over 50 miles.

Length of Trip - 1,055 miles in 34 hours.

Route Log

 WINNIPEG, MAN. - See page 348.

0:00 (0:57) Depart Winnipeg.

0:01 (0:56) Cross Assiniboine River near its juncture with Red River. Waters will ultimately flow north into Lake Winnipeg.

0:03 (0:54) On right, ornate dome is distinctive feature of Winnipeg's Legislative Building. Red River now follows momentarily on left.

0:32 (0:25) An interesting two-story depot on right and an old church on left are highlights through Elie. On western edge of town, cross Milk River, with neighborhoods of gracious homes lining its banks.

0:50 (0:07) At Nattress, cross Assiniboine River.

0:54 (0:03) Horse farm appears on right where newborn colts can often be seen cavorting with their proud mothers.

0:57 (0:00) Arrive Portage la Prairie.

PORTAGE LA PRAIRIE, MAN. - Literally translated as "prairie portage," the city is situated at the narrowest point between the Assiniboine River and Lake Manitoba. This spot served as a resting point for both Indians and early settlers transporting their canoes between these two important waterways.

A fort was established at this strategic site in 1738, and from 1867 to 1868 the town held the distinction of being capital of the "Republic of Manitobah." Today, it remains a transportation hub of the prairies, with the CN and CP rail lines making a unique prairie crossing, while the Trans-Canada and Yellowhead highways join here.

0:00 (2:40) Depart Portage la Prairie.

For the remainder of the evening, the Hudson Bay travels through southern Manitoba farming country that could easily pass for central Nebraska, flat and fertile lands interspersed only with patches of trees.

1:36 (1:04) One should not laugh at bumper stickers proclaiming "Ski Manitoba." A few miles west (left) is Mt. Agassiz Ski Resort in Riding Mountain National Park.

2:40 (0:00) Arrive Dauphin.

DAUPHIN, MAN. - A fort was constructed here as early as 1742 to help establish fur trading in the region, but it wasn't until the railroad arrived in 1896 that European settlers arrived, creating the community that now is a regional trade center. Fort Dauphin Museum has a wide variety of exhibits on display. Canada's National Ukrainian Festival is held here the end of July and the beginning of August.

0:00 (1:36) Depart Dauphin.

1:36 (0:00) Arrive Roblin.

ROBLIN, MAN. - Another farming center. Keystone Pioneer Museum offers displays of agricultural machinery and other rural artifacts.

0:00 (3:55) Depart Roblin.

0:22 (3:33) Enter Saskatchewan and leave Manitoba.

Between here and the town of Hudson Bay, Sask., the train stops at four small communities of east-central Saskatchewan: **KAMSAK, CANORA, STURGIS** and **ENDEAVOUR.**

4:04 (0:00) Arrive Hudson Bay.

HUDSON BAY, SASK. - This eastern Saskatchewan trading center is the last stop on the Hudson Bay's brief westward arc through this province.

0:00 (1:55) Depart Hudson Bay.

1:05 (0:50) Re-enter Manitoba and leave Saskatchewan.

1:55 (0:00) Arrive The Pas.

THE PAS, MAN. - Gateway to the North, it has become a center for lumbering, pulp, fishing and furs, and all traffic to and from the north country passes through this rugged community. Moose, deer and caribou along with walleye, trout, pickerel and pike make this a sportsman's paradise. It is also headquarters for various branches of the provincial government in northern Manitoba. Of interest: Little Northern Museum has Indian and pioneer exhibits; and in February a renowned Trappers Festival is held for three days, when trappers, miners, lumbermen and Indian chiefs indulge in such competitive frolics as woodchopping, dog sledding, singing and dancing.

0:00 (1:12) Depart The Pas and immediately cross icy flow of Saskatchewan River which empties into nearby Cedar Lake—one of Lake Winnipeg's many adjuncts.

0:06 (1:06) Flin Flon Jct. is where line divides, with a branch on left driving straight north to Lynn Lake.

0:32 (0:40) Clearwater Provincial Park, on left, is summer recreational area for residents of The Pas. Clearwater Lake is centerpiece of Park.

0:48 (0:23) Cormorant Lake sprawls in distance to left where myriad species of waterfowl take refuge.

1:09 (0:03) Little Cormorant Lake is on right. Note quarry which has provided pink marble for many of Canada's newer buildings.

1:12 (0:00) Arrive Cormorant at milepost 41.

CORMORANT, MAN. - This little community gets its appellation from the bird with the same name—an aquatic raven. Located on a narrow neck of land between portions of Cormorant Lake, it was the first large village on the Hudson Bay Railway. The early population was largely French and Scottish, many of whom intermarried with area natives.

0:00 (2:30) Depart Cormorant.

1:03 (1:27) Flag stop of Wekusko (Cree for Herb Lake) where an all-weather road leads to gold-mining activities at Snow Lake.

1:12 (1:18) Hargrave Lake is on right.

1:20 (1:10) Dense forests of spruce, tamarack and jack pine continue to border tracks, while tripod-shaped phone poles solve problem of unstable muskeg.

1:47 (0:43) At milepost 109, make only highway crossing between The Pas and Churchill. This road leads from Winnipeg to Thompson.

2:30 (0:00) Arrive Wabowden at milepost 136.

WABOWDEN, MAN. - Perhaps the prettiest community along today's route, Wabowden acts as a transfer point for goods destined for more remote regions. The Brandon Experimental Farm is here and has had successful results with vegetables and small grains. Some small farms are operating nearby.

0:00 (1:12) Depart Wabowden and immediately Bowden Lake appears on left. About two miles beyond (and out of view) is Setting Lake—an elongated body of water which serves as part of extensive Grass River canoe route, connecting Flin Flon with Nelson River.

0:07 (1:05) If both are punctual, northbound and southbound Hudson Bay trains should meet about now. Unless it's summertime, don't be surprised to see snow plastered to front of southbound.

1:12 (0:00) Native dogs anxiously await train at Thicket Portage (milepost 184) where train's cook usually drops off food scraps which are instantly snapped up by these voracious canines.

THICKET PORTAGE, MAN. - This is one of the oldest inhabited villages in the area. Besides its native Indian population, a number of Scandinavian and Icelandic settlers have migrated here because of fishing opportunities. Sturgeon, as well as other commercial fish, are shipped from here to the U.S. A veritable maze of regional waterways focuses on Thicket Portage.

0:00 (1:40) Depart Thicket Portage.

0:30 (1:10) At milepost 199.5, Hudson Bay begins a slow-grinding curl to left and away from main line starting a 30-mile side trip to mining city of Thompson. Terrain becomes increasingly rolling with numerous rock outcroppings and small lakes.

1:28 (---) Hudson Bay slowly backs into wye, pulls out toward main line, and then slowly backs four miles into dead end at Thompson.

1:45 (0:00) Arrive Thompson's VIA station which is about a mile from downtown. A large Inco smelter, visible in distance, is working evidence of city's mining economy.

THOMPSON, MAN. - Like Sudbury, Thompson's reason for existing is nickel. Huge ore deposits are mined and processed by Inco Metals Company, which has created a surprisingly large and modern city in Manitoba's Northland

Route of the Hudson Bay – Northern Manitoba

(714 rail miles from Winnipeg). Tours of Inco's operations are available in the summer but unfortunately require more time than the Hudson Bay permits. Train is normally here long enough to permit a quick trip into town, but first, be sure to verify train's departure time.

0:00 (1:33) Depart Thompson, retracing 30-mile route back to main line.

1:23 (0:00) Arrive Pikwitonei at milepost 213.

PIKWITONEI, MAN. - A Cree word meaning "broken mouth," Pikwitonei was once a major construction terminal for the railroad, with a roundhouse and other shop facilities. Certainly one of the more attractive and substantial-appearing villages along the route, it now survives largely on trapping activities. Canoe access to the region's waterways is also found here.

0:00 (3:10) Depart Pikwitonei, and work still deeper into very heart of Indian country where lifestyles have shown little change across time. Watch for mothers carrying papooses in moss bags and occasional Indian camps along right-of-way.

0:21 (2:49) Train crosses one of region's multitudinous lakes at milepost 225.

0:45 (2:25) At milepost 241, powerful Nelson River is crossed at Manitou Rapids. This 612-foot cantilevered span stretches a lofty 110 feet above river below. Waters of Assiniboine, Winnipeg, Red, English and Saskatchewan rivers, after passing through Lake Winnipeg, all course through this impressive gorge, headed toward Hudson Bay. Whirlpools make these narrows particularly dangerous for canoers. Only significant rock cuts on rail line appear here on each side of chasm.

1:56 (1:14) Train usually stops at Ilford (milepost 285). As populous gathers to pick up mail it is obvious that train's arrival is a daily social event.

2:18 (0:52) Cross under one of world's longest transmission lines carrying power to southern Manitoba from giant hydroelectric plants near Gillam.

2:58 (0:12) Pass through Luke, a flag stop named for mail carrier and trapper Luke Clemens. Some accounts relate that he was a brother of American author Mark Twain (Samuel Clemens), while others indicate he was a nephew.

3:10 (0:00) Arrive Gillam at milepost 326.

GILLAM, MAN. - Before construction was started on the nearby Kettle Generating Station in February 1966, Gillam was a village of only 356 people. With the construction and completion of this great hydroelectric facility (1,272,000-kilowatt capacity), Gillam became a thriving community with a population of more than 3,000. The power plant is situated about five miles from here on the Nelson River. Other hydro-

367

electric projects are also located on the Nelson, just downstream from the Kettle plant. Heavily dependent on the railroad, Gillam has no highway link to the rest of Canada.

0:00 (6:55) Depart Gillam.

0:07 (6:48) At milepost 331, cross Nelson River at Kettle Rapids where lights of massive Kettle Generating Station can be seen two miles upstream, to left, while Long Spruce Generating Station is downstream.

Before long, the Hudson Bay begins to traverse lowland coastal plains which are covered with frozen muskeg. Spruce and tamarack become sparse and stunted. This will be most apparent when dawn breaks, sometime before our arrival at Churchill in its bleak and barren setting. Additional nighttime stops are scheduled for villages of **WEIR RIVER** and **HERCHMER** at mileposts 373 and 412.

5:27 (1:28) At milepost 445, landscape becomes barren for some miles until "one-sided" trees reappear near Churchill River.

6:43 (0:12) At milepost 503, first sight of Churchill is afforded on right where enormous grain elevator protrudes above horizon.

6:55 (0:00) Arrive Churchill at milepost 509.

CHURCHILL, MAN. - Churchill is situated almost 600 miles (approximately 1,100 rail miles) north of Winnipeg on the shores of Hudson Bay, an outpost where the modern world meets the Eskimo frontier. It is an unusually barren but fascinating country where one gets a real taste of life in the North.

The area was first visited as early as 1612 by Europeans looking for a Northwest Passage to the Orient. Then the Hudson's Bay Company, in 1688, established a trading post near the current townsite, commencing trade with shipment of eight casks of whale oil to England.

In 1732, construction of Fort Prince of Wales was commenced by the British across Churchill Harbor from the present townsite, and finally completed several years later. It was one of the most imposing fortresses in North America. Not only was the fort protected by its own forty cannon, there were other guns outside the fort, the

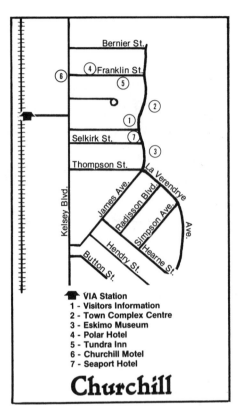

VIA Station
1 - Visitors Information
2 - Town Complex Centre
3 - Eskimo Museum
4 - Polar Hotel
5 - Tundra Inn
6 - Churchill Motel
7 - Seaport Hotel

Churchill

largest being at Cape Merry battery on the shore of the harbor entrance. In 1782 a French naval force sailed into the harbor and the fort, manned by less than 40 troops, surrendered without firing a shot. Today it is a National Historic Park which can be reached by boat in the summer when the park is open to visitors.

As western Canada developed its agricultural lands, demand increased for means of exporting grain, bringing about the eventual construction of the Hudson Bay Railroad (now part of the Canadian National system) in 1929, and the Port of Churchill in 1931 whose five-million-bushel grain elevators dominate the Churchill scene.

During World War II, the United States established Fort Churchill just east of town when the population was about 500. Later, the population grew to almost 10,000 when a Canadian Forces Base was established here, but eventually shrunk to its present-day size of 1,500 after the closing of the base.

Perhaps the most unique feature of Churchill is the annual migration of polar bears through the town in the fall, a bizarre event that has been featured in a National Geographic TV documentary. VIA offers very popular package tours in the fall for those wanting to witness this show.

VIA Station, 74092 Churchill, is on the western edge of this compact community. There are no storage lockers, but the baggage room will hold your luggage if you wish.

Ticket window opens for one hour upon arrival of the train, and one hour before departure. Call 800-282-8070 for reservations and information.

Churchill can be reached only by train or air (and oceangoing freighters in the summer). **Churchill Taxi,** 675-2200. **Rental cars** available at hotels; Tundra rental cars, 675-8831. The **Airport** is near town. Calm Air, 675-8858, has scheduled and charter flights. Pacific Western Transair, 675-8851, has scheduled flights.

Parks Canada has an information center at Bayport Plaza; (204) 675-8863. Write Parks Canada, P.O. Box 127, R0B 0E0.

Polar Motel, Box 124, R0B 0E0; (204) 675-8878. Free shuttle service, about five blocks from the station. $63.

-**Tundra Inn,** 34 Franklin, P.O. Box 999, R0B 0E0; (204) 675-8831. Three blocks from the station. $78.

-**Churchill Motel,** Box 218, R0B 0E0; (204) 675-8853. Free shuttle services four blocks from the station. $65.

-**Seaport Hotel,** Box 339, R0B 0E0; (204) 675-8807. About six blocks from the station. $70.

All of the town is within easy walking distance of the station. The **Town Centre Complex** houses numerous facilities used by the residents and visitors alike. Under one gigantic roof are a health center, library, school, swimming pool, curling rink, cafeteria, theater, gymnasium, and other game rooms. Inuit and Indian art work are displayed throughout the complex. The **Eskimo Museum** has one of the finest exhibits of Eskimo art found anywhere. **Parks Canada Interpretive Center,** located at Bayport Plaza,

has regular slide shows in the months of July and August, on request at other times.

Other points of interest in the Churchill area include **Fort Prince of Wales** (see text above) and **Cape Tatnam Wildlife Management Areas,** with 160 species of waterfowl and other birds. In the fall, polar bear viewing expeditions are available. VIA has package tours that are quite popular.

(Tundra Buggy Tours, 675-2121, has guided polar bear expeditions. Sea North Tours, 675-2195, has tours to Ft. Prince of Wales and Beluga whale watching in the summer.)

Other Manitoba Service

The Pas-Lynn Lake train makes a ten-hour trip from The Pas, departing late morning on Monday, Wednesday and Friday. The return departs Lynn Lake early morning on Tuesday, Thursday and Saturday. The train is unreserved and there is no food service.

Wabowden-Churchill has a Sunday train departing Wabowden early morning and departing Churchill on Saturday, taking nine hours between these destinations. The train is unreserved and there is no food service.

Rocky Mountaineer

Although the 1990 VIA cutbacks substantially reduced the opportunities to view Canada's Rockies by train, VIA still runs its very popular "Rockies by Daylight" train, the weekly Rocky Mountaineer. The trip is designed as a sightseeing excursion and is scheduled so that travel occurs during daylight hours. At night, passengers enroute stay in hotels at Kamloops.

The routes cover Fraser and Thompson canyons between Vancouver and Kamloops. At Kamloops, the train divides into separate sections. One section goes over Yellowhead Pass and past Mt. Robson, Canada's tallest peak, to Jasper, while the other takes a route to Banff/Calgary over Kicking Horse Pass and through the Spiral Tunnels.

Passengers can elect to take one-way trips to either Jasper or Banff/Calgary, or make a round trip. Accommodations at those destinations are not included in the fare, although Kamloops accommodations are included. Light lunches are served on board and are also included in the fare.

VIA also offers a "Majestic Circle Tour" which covers six days. This allows passengers to visit both Banff and Jasper on the same trip, with transportation by motor coach between these two resorts.

Departures are from Vancouver on Sunday mornings and from Jasper or Banff/Calgary Thursday mornings. The excursions are seasonal only and run from late May through early October. Reservations should be made early.

Route Log

For route from Vancouver to Kamloops and from Kamloops to Jasper, see log of the Canadian, page 356.

Banff/Calgary to Kamloops is shown below. (The log runs from east to west in keeping with the format used throughout this book. Although the train runs non-stop between Banff and Kamloops, certain cities are shown as stops to give an easy reference point for the times shown in the log.

CALGARY, ALTA. - Calgary is both the oil and cattle capitals of Canada. Even with its half-million-plus population, there is a cowtown image that Calgary has never really shaken off, an image that lends more than it detracts. This is Canada's Fort Worth.

Fort Calgary was originally established in 1875. Built between the Bow and Elbow rivers by the Northwest Mounted Police, the fort was to assist in fur trading and prevent "whiskey travelers" from adversely influencing local Indians. The Canadian Pacific Railway arrived in 1883 at what is now Palliser Square, putting down sidings and, of course, a station. Initially, the town did not even merit division-point status.

The magnificent Canadian Rockies are but a stone's throw west of here, where Banff and Lake Louise attract summer throngs and winter skiers. This proximity resulted in Calgary's selection as host city

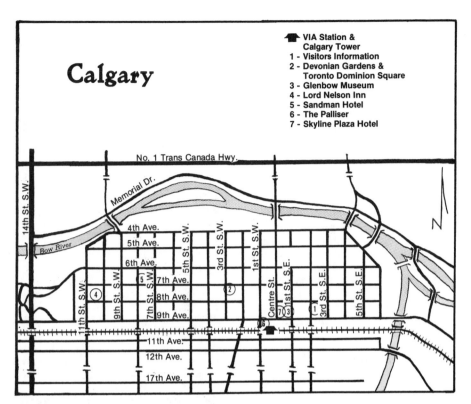

Calgary

for the 1988 Winter Olympics. But Calgary has its own annual summer event that draws thousands each July—the famed Calgary Stampede. This world-famous rodeo is the biggest production of its kind.

VIA Station, 9th Ave. at Centre Street, is beneath the Calgary Tower in the heart of downtown. Attractive pavers for flooring and a stockade false front at the ticket windows create an atmosphere that belies its train-station role. There are storage lockers, redcaps and an elevator to the Palliser Mall where there are restaurants, newsstands and the Palliser Hotel. Ticket window hours are 9 am to 5 pm, and the station is open 24 hours. Pay parking is available.

For arrival and departure information, call (403) 265-8033; for reservations and information, call 800-665-8630.

Both a **cab** stand and **local bus** stop are at the station. Yellow Cab, 250-8311, and Checker Cabs, 272-1111. Tilden has **rental car** pick up and drop off at the station; 237-5063. **C-Train,** Calgary's streetcar LRT system which runs through downtown (free along 7th Avenue), is two blocks north; 276-7801. **Greyhound,** 850-16th St. NW; 265-9111. **Calgary International Airport** is a 25-minute ride from downtown.

Visitor Information Center, 237-8th Ave., T2G 0K8, is three blocks from the station; (403) 262-2766 for information; event line, 262-3866.

Accommodations in downtown Calgary can be expensive, particularly those near the station. At least two good hostelries shown below have relatively economical weekday rates.

-Lord Nelson Inn, 1020-8th Ave. SW, T2P 1J3; (403) 269-8262. About a mile from the station on the west edge of town, has large, attractive rooms with refrigerators, non-smoking floors, free underground parking, and, for rail fans, a view of the CP main line. Three blocks to C-Train. $58, including tax.

-Sandman Hotel, 888-7th Ave. SW; (403) 237-8626. Nicely appointed rooms. Located toward west edge of downtown, nine blocks from the station. $73.

-The Palliser, 133-9th Ave. SW, T2P 2M3; (403) 262-1234 or 800-828-7447.

Elegant downtown landmark, next to the station. A Canadian Pacific hotel. $135.
-**Skyline Plaza Hotel,** 110-9th Ave. SE, T2G 5A6; (403) 266-7331 or 800-648-7200. Very nice downtown hotel, connected by walkway to the station. Hotel is across the street. $145.

Several worthwhile attractions are within walking distance: the indoor **Devonian Gardens** and **Toronto Dominion Square,** 7th Ave. and 2nd St., with three levels of shopping; the **Glenbow Museum,** 1st St. and 9th Ave., housing beautifully exhibited displays of Western Canadian history and culture, one block from the station; the **Calgary Tower,** directly above the station, offering a spectacular view of the city and a revolving restaurant; and **Energeum,** 640-5th Ave. SW, a huge science hall devoted to energy resources displays.

The **Calgary Expedition and Stampede** is a rodeo spectacular held each July at Stampede Park, and can be easily reached from downtown by the C-Train.

0:00 (2:10) Depart Calgary.
0:34 (1:36) Bow River joins us on right, and will now escort Canadian to Lake Louise.
0:45 (1:25) Bearspaw Lake, on right, results from damming of Bow.
1:08 (1:02) View up river, on right, affords stunning panorama of Rockies.
1:10 (1:00) On right, stacks of yellow are product of sulphur plant across river.
1:13 (0:57) Ghost Lake, denying its appellation, is quite visible on right.
1:31 (0:39) Surprisingly glacial-green waters of Kananaskis River flow beneath us and into Bow. Some of Rockies' most awesome monarchs create formidable-looking barrier on left—but in moments, train will meet their challenge, starting a journey marked by spectacular scenery and some incredible feats of railroad engineering.
1:56 (0:14) Enter Banff National Park, one of most popular recreational areas in Canadian Rockies. Awesome Goat Range dominates scene on left. Keep sharp lookout for mountain goats and sheep, as well as elk, deer and other wildlife.
2:10 (0:00) Arrive Banff.

BANFF, ALTA. - Banff National Park, named after Banff, Scotland, has long been one of the most popular resort areas in North America. Truly spectacular mountain scenery and heavy winter snows combine to attract thousands year-round to enjoy hiking, camping, auto touring, skiing and just plain relaxing. The townsite has a permanent population of about 4,000, but in the summer it burgeons, making it advisable to have hotel reservations well in advance.

VIA Station, corner of Elk and Lynx streets, is on the edge of Banff townsite. There are storage lockers, a restaurant, a snack bar, soft drink vending machines, a newsstand, a gift shop and free parking.

For reservations and information, call 800-665-8630. For arrivals and departures, 762-3255.

Cabs and **local buses** are at the station. Banff Taxi, 762-4444. **Avis, Tilden,** and **Hertz** have direct phone lines with pick up and delivery at the station. The **Greyhound** bus terminal is adjacent to the station.

Parks Information Center is at Wolf and Banff Ave.; **Banff Information Center** is at Buffalo and Banff Ave. Write **Banff/Lake Louise Chamber of Commerce,** Box 1298, Banff, Alberta, T0L 0C0. Call (403) 762-3777.

Bow View Motor Lodge, 228 Bow Ave., Box 339, T0L, 0C0; (403) 762-2261. Very spacious, bright rooms. Three short blocks from the station. $70.
-**The Inns of Banff Park,** P.O. Box 1077, 600 Banff Ave., T0L 0C0; (403) 762-4581 or 800-661-1272. Deluxe, with private balconies. Six blocks from the station. $115.

Outdoor activities are Banff's major attractions. These include hiking, camping, fishing, boating and mountain climbing. Horseback riding, bicycling, golfing and tennis are other activities readily available. Year-round swimming in the **Upper Hot Springs Pool** on Mountain Ave., filled with water from natural sulphur hot springs, is a favorite of many visitors. **Bow Falls,** in the Bow River along River Ave., though not spectacular, add considerable charm to the townsite. **Banff Centre,** on St.

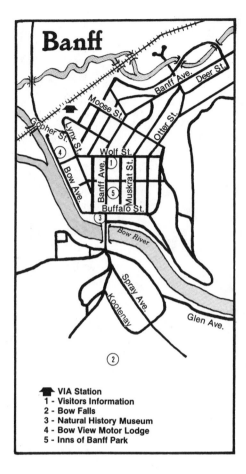

Banff

VIA Station
1 - Visitors Information
2 - Bow Falls
3 - Natural History Museum
4 - Bow View Motor Lodge
5 - Inns of Banff Park

0:00 (0:45) Depart Banff.

0:20 (0:21) Massive shape of 9,393-foot Mt. Eisenhower slips by on right.

0:39 (0:06) At milepost 112, one of highest peaks to be seen on VIA's system is on horizon to left—11,640-foot Mount Temple (3,548 meters).

0:45 (0:00) Arrive Lake Louise.

LAKE LOUISE, ALTA. - This stop provides access to that gem of the Rockies, Lake Louise. The lake, together with its majestic Victoria Glacier, are overlooked by famous Chateau Lake Louise, but cannot be seen from the station.

0:00 (0:55) Depart Lake Louise and commence climb toward Kicking Horse Pass, first of four mountain passes that line route through Rockies. (Rogers Pass, Eagle Pass and Notch Hill will follow in succession.)

0:16 (0:39) Mountaineer conquers summit of 5,403-foot Kicking Horse Pass, crest of Continental Divide, as we enter British Columbia and leave Alberta. Also, enter Yoho National Park and exit Banff National Park. Cairn honors Sir James Hector, discoverer of pass.

0:21 (0:34) Beautiful Wapta Lake lies nestled on right. Patrons of lodge across lake have fine view of passing train as it glides along lake shore.

0:26 (0:29) Breathtaking view is afforded down valley of Kicking Horse River. Lower Spiral Tunnel can be seen down to right as we descend "The Big Hill."

0:31 (0:22) Enter Upper Spiral Tunnel which makes 188-degree curl to left under Cathedral Mountain. After traveling 3,255 feet in darkness, train will exit and be headed in opposite direction!

This tunnel, along with its near-twin, Lower Spiral Tunnel, were constructed in 1908 and reduced the grade of the track bed from a beleaguering 4.4% to an acceptable 2.2%. The Trans-Canada Highway now claims the former right-of-way. Before the tunnels were constructed, trains had to come to a complete stop at three "safety switches" that directed runaways to turnouts—like modern-day escape ramps for "eighteen wheelers."

0:35 (0:20) Make one of several crossings of tumultuous Kicking Horse River.

Julein Road, has theatrical and musical events throughout the summer and winter seasons. **Natural History Museum,** 112 Banff Ave., and **Parks Canada Natural History Museum,** 93 Banff Ave., have numerous interesting displays.

Lake Louise, a few miles from town, is without a doubt one of the prettiest spots in North America. The Chateau Lake Louise overlooks this lovely lake with the magnificent Victoria Glacier as a backdrop.

Moraine Lake and Valley of the Ten Peaks is a few miles east of the Lake Louise access road. A beautiful lake surrounded by ten glaciated mountain peaks.

Route of the Rocky Mountaineer – Kicking Horse Pass

0:36 (0:17) Enter 2,922-foot-long Lower Spiral Tunnel beneath Mount Ogden, while making astonishing 226-degree curve to right—coming almost two thirds of full circle.

0:49 (0:05) Pass through mixture of five tunnels and snowsheds.

0:55 (0:00) Arrive Field.

FIELD, B.C. - Railroading is the reason for Field's mountainside existence. Although the original survey would have placed the railroad above Field, this route was the final outcome. The Roundhouse for helper engines no longer stands, but the turntable can still be seen off to the left. Field was named after Cyrus W. Field who promoted the first trans-Atlantic telegraph cable.

0:00 (1:10) Depart Field and continue gradual descent into valley of Kicking Horse River.

0:28 (0:42) Mount Vaux, 10,892 feet, rules over valley on left.

0:32 (0:38) Jagged peak of Mt. Chancellor can be seen to rear.

0:35 (0:35) Although train now exits Yoho National Park, glorious mountain vistas continue.

0:41 (0:29) Momentary darkness prevails as Canadian pierces first of several tunnels before arriving at Golden.

0:45 (0:25) Curl through former Corey Brothers Tunnel, which once had to be abandoned due to continual cave-ins. Although tunnel was eventually lined with concrete and put back into service, mountain above it had to be removed in 1950's as final solution.

1:08 (0:02) Narrow path of Kicking Horse merges into broad Columbia River Valley, nicely backdropped by Dogtooth Mountain Range on left.

1:10 (0:00) Arrive Golden.

GOLDEN, B.C. - Although the forest industry provides Golden its primary source of income, tourism, for obvious reasons, is also a mainstay. Its central location between the peaks of Yoho and of the Selkirks affords easy access to innumerable hiking trails, fishing streams and lakes. River rafting and mountaineering are also popular.

0:00 (3:00) Depart Golden and trace a course northward through gentle Columbia River Valley.

0:52 (2:08) Columbia River parts company as train swings southward along pretty Beaver River.

Gain one hour as train passes from Mountain to Pacific Time. Set your watch back (forward if eastbound) one hour.

1:04 (1:56) Enter Canada's Glacier National Park—one of western Canada's more rugged regions, dominated by Selkirk Range and perpetual ice.

1:16 (1:44) Our train performs a "death-defying" crossing, 325 feet above Stoney Creek—Canadian Pacific's highest bridge! When completed in 1885, it was highest such structure in the world.

1:23 (1:37) Rather than struggle over Rogers Pass, trains go underground, traversing one of two tunnels.

Eastbound trains use the five-mile-long Connaught Tunnel through Sir Donald Range of Selkirks—second longest rail tunnel in Canada. Construction of Connaught was started in 1913 after more than 200 persons met death in avalanche tragedies on the route over the top between 1885 and 1911. The tunnel was completed in 1916.

Westbound trains use the recently constructed Mount Macdonald Tunnel, which is nine miles long and surpasses the Burlington Northern's Cascade Tunnel (see route of The Empire Builder through Washington state) as the longest in North America. This new tunnel reduces the 2.4% westbound grade to less than 1%, allowing CP Rail to avoid using some 24 helper engines on their westbound freights.

1:31 (1:29) At west portal of Connaught Tunnel, note Illecillewaet Glacier clinging to mountainside, high above to left.

1:33 (1:27) Illecillewaet River escorts train in a steady descent from Rogers Pass.

1:56 (1:04) Three massive snowsheds protect tracks from devastating winter avalanches. At one time there were 31 such sheds protecting descent through Selkirks, totaling five miles in length. Since mountain scenery was important in wooing passenger traffic, original builders installed "summer tracks" outside confining sheds.

2:06 (0:54) Exit Connaught Tunnel at Glacier. High above to left, Illecillewaet Glacier clings to mountainside.

2:29 (0:31) Exit Glacier National Park.

2:40 (0:20) Revelstoke National Park borders train on right.

2:50 (0:10) Cross impressive Illecillewaet River.

3:00 (0:00) Arrive Revelstoke.

REVELSTOKE, B.C. - In a postcard setting of lush forests, streams teeming with fish, towering mountain peaks on all sides, a ski hill and geothermal swimming, Revelstoke offers something for virtually every taste. The Revelstoke Hydroelectric Project, with its immense dam and power plant just north of here, has been a prime source of revenue for the city. Also, typical of so many mountain towns, mining and forest products are economic mainstays.

0:00 (1:49) Depart Revelstoke, with fine view of Mount Begbie and Mt. Macpherson on left. Columbia River, which takes a northerly course around Selkirks rather than through them, is crossed one final time. Route now follows along Tonkawatla River toward Eagle Pass.

0:12 (1:37) Idyllic Wetask Lake on Eagle Pass rests beside tracks on left. CP line now accompanies Eagle River until Sicamous. Supposedly, in 1865, surveyor Walter Moberly discovered pass after sighting eagles flying through this small opening in Monashee Mountains.

0:14 (1:35) View of inviting Clanwilliam Lake is periodically interrupted as three short tunnels are encountered.

0:22 (1:27) Two sturdy snowsheds protect tracks from avalanches as Canadian slips past beautiful Three Valley Lake cradled in Three Valley Gap.

0:25 (1:24) Cross Eagle River.

0:27 (1:22) Griffin (or Green) Lake is just to right of tracks.

0:35 (1:14) Very pretty Kay Falls can be seen cascading down valley side on left.

0:47 (1:02) Here, at Craigellachie, named after a valley in Scotland, final spike was driven into place for last section of trans-Canada railroad. Railroad financier, Donald Smith, performed honors at modest ceremony (last spike was iron, not gold) on November 7, 1885. Line had taken four and a half years to complete. Monument off to right commemorates event at milepost 28.3.

1:05 (0:44) Valley widens in preparation of entering land of Shuswap Lake.

1:10 (0:39) Enter Sicamous where splendid views of Shuswap Lake are first afforded. Here, a swinging span bridge permits boat passage through Sicamous Narrows connecting Shuswap and Mara lakes. Shuswap has 750 miles of shoreline and is home to both Dolley Varden and Kamloops trout, attracting largest aggregation of houseboats anywhere in Canada.

1:12 (0:37) Tracks continue to border serene Salmon Arm of Shuswap Lake.

1:49 (0:00) Arrive town of Salmon Arm.

 SALMON ARM, B.C. - This is the commercial hub of the Shuswap areas, as well as being an agricultural center featuring dairy cows, fruit (apples, strawberries and cherries), vegetables, sheep and poultry. An abundance of tourists in pursuit of water-oriented pastimes will be found during the summer months.

0:00 (2:00) Depart Salmon Arm.

0:02 (1:58) Cross 100 feet above Salmon River, as it nears journey's end at Shuswap Lake.

0:38 (1:22) Lake briefly narrows into South Thompson River before opening into Little Shuswap Lake, on right.

0:59 (1:01) South Thompson River takes on definite form as final view of Shuswap Lake is offered.

1:15 (0:45) Valley continues to widen as farm and ranch lands now blanket valley floor. Watch for occasional canoes plying through broad, still waters of South Thompson on right.

1:32 (0:28) At milepost 113, notorious American robber, Billy Miner, held up Canadian Pacific in 1906 and galloped off with only $15 of loot.

1:56 (0:04) Entering outskirts of Kamloops, site of prehistoric Indian dwellings is off to right.

2:00 (0:00) Arrive Kamloops' CP Rail station, situated on lower edge of downtown.

KAMLOOPS, B.C. - See page 358.

Skeena

The superlative lakes and mountains of Jasper National Park (during the longer days) and the pristine Coastal Range of British Columbia bedazzle Skeena travelers on a wilderness trip between Jasper and Prince Rupert. The ramble along the Skeena River Gorge into Prince Rupert is one of the best excursions on the continent.

At Prince Rupert, still further adventure awaits, where ferry service is available north to Alaska through the spectacular "Inside Passage," or south to Seattle along British Columbia's scenic and rugged Pacific coastline.

Connections are made in Jasper with the Canadian, to and from points east.

Westbound Schedule (Condensed)
Jasper, Alta. - Late Afternoon Departure (Tuesday, Friday, Sunday)
Prince George, B.C. - Late Evening
Smithers, B.C. - Early Morning
Prince Rupert, B.C. - Early Afternoon Arrival (Monday, Wednesday, Saturday)

Eastbound Schedule (Condensed)
Prince Rupert, B.C. - Midmorning Departure (Monday, Thursday, Saturday)
Smithers, B.C. - Late Afternoon
Prince George, B.C. - Late Evening
Jasper, Alta. - Early Morning Arrival (Sunday, Tuesday, Friday)

Frequency - Thrice-weekly, as shown above.
Seating - Standard coach.
Dining - Complete meal and beverage service as well as lighter fare.

Sleeping - Berths, roomettes and bedrooms.
Baggage - Checked baggage handled at Jasper, Prince George and Prince Rupert. At other stations, checked baggage will be handled only when passengers and baggage travel together on the same train, and passengers should advise train conductor of their checked baggage prior to arrival at destination.
Reservations - Reserved coach seats upon purchase of tickets.
Length of Trip - 721 miles in 22 hours.

Route Log

0:00 (3:40) Depart Jasper and head toward Yellowhead Pass.

Some of North America's most magnificent scenery will soon appear! The Trident Range will be on our left and the Victoria Cross Range on our right as we make this ascent. Waterfalls, streams, snowfields and tunnels make this a railroading spectacular.

0:27 (3:13) Those small wire fences, seen here on uphill side of right-of-way, are slide detectors which activate a red signal should there be a rockslide or snowslide.

Gain one hour as train passes from Mountain to Pacific Time. Set your watch back (forward if eastbound) one hour.

0:42 (2:59) Crest of Yellowhead Pass is reached at milepost 17.5. Enter province of British Columbia and leave Alberta. We are only 3,718 feet above sea level, however, many of surrounding peaks soar to more than 11,000 feet. Yellowhead is one of lowest passes along entire North American Continental Divide. Waters flowing to east ultimately find their way to Arctic Ocean.

0:47 (2:53) Yellowhead Lake stretches serenely beside tracks on left. Yellowhead Mountain is highest peak directly across lake.

1:11 (2:29) Moose Lake now appears alongside at left, even larger than Yellowhead.

1:24 (2:16) Red Pass Junction at milepost 43.9 is flag stop where two rail lines divide. One CN line heads to left (south) down Blue River toward Kamloops and Vancouver, while Skeena will continue on due west, following route of Fraser River as far as Prince George. After that, Skeena River will be traced to train's final destination, Prince Rupert.

1:42 (1:58) Along this stretch, if sky is clear, passengers are treated to a fine view of Mt. Robson which bolts up at end of a valley on right. A dramatic scene indeed, with snowfields clinging to its red, stratified face. It's unmistakably Canadian Rockies' highest at 12,972 feet. Have your camera ready.

2:02 (1:38) Rearguard Falls in Fraser River are formidable obstacle for salmon that come all this way from Pacific Ocean. Falls, however, present a final and insurmountable barrier to salmons' journey. Mountains now start to become less rugged and somewhat softer as train continues westward.

3:21 (0:19) Pass high above Shuswap River.

3:34 (0:06) Dairy cattle grazing in pastures tucked away amongst rolling forests create delicate pastoral scenes.

3:40 (0:00) Arrive McBride.

MCBRIDE, B.C. - This is the first "city" (pop. 800) west of Jasper, having been established during the construction of the Grand Trunk Pacific in 1912. A sportsman's delight, the area offers about any kind of quarry, from Dolly Varden trout to grizzly bear.

0:00 (4:45) Depart McBride.

0:05 (4:40) Below, on right, Oscar's Wildlife Museum makes a bizarre sight with various colored tractor tires for a fence, and a bear and a moose painted on building's side.

0:29 (4:16) Into a tunnel.

Darkness usually prevails (except longest of days when westbound) between here and Prince George.

4:45 (0:00) Arrive Prince George.

PRINCE GEORGE, B.C. - Although many rail travelers stop here only to change trains (VIA to British Columbia Railway or vice versa), there is reason to spend a little extra time in Prince George—especially for railfans. A growing rail museum, nurtured by an energetic group of local rail enthusiasts, has an excellent collection of rail cars and equipment; and there's even a small passenger train operation in the city's Fort George Park.

Prince George was little more than a spot on the map until the Grand Trunk Pacific reached this site in 1910. Lumbering and mining contributed to steady growth, and today, Prince George is a city of 70,000, still largely dependent on those two industries.

There are two stations in Prince George: The VIA Station, which is on the edge of downtown; and the British Columbia Railway (BCR) Station located on the outskirts of the city, about four miles south of the VIA Station. Pay shuttle service is available between these two stations, also serving downtown hotels.

-VIA Station, First Ave. and Quebec, serves VIA's east-west route through central British Columbia. There are storage lockers, handcarts and beverage vending machines.

For reservations, call 800-665-8630; for arrival and departure information, call 564-5233. The station is open at train times and during other parts of the day, and is closed Sundays.

-BCR Station, 1108 Industrial Way. This is a small but very neat station in an industrial area of the city. For information, call 561-4033. Waiting room and ticket office are open at train times, 6 am to 2:30 pm during the summer, reduced hours the rest of the year. There is very limited long-term free parking. The station also has a small gift counter. Write BC Rail Ltd., Passenger Sales & Service, Box 8770, Vancouver, B.C. V6B 4X6.

Cabs have a direct line at the VIA Station. Prince George Taxi, 564-4444. **Limo** service between stations (which will also deliver to most hotels) for a $3 charge, 562-6990. Budget, 564-8395 and Tilden, 564-4847 are two blocks from the VIA Station; Hertz is at Simon Fraser Inn, 561-4847. **Local bus** information, 563-0011. **Greyhound Bus** terminal, 1566 12th, 564-5454.

Prince George Visitors and Convention Bureau, 1198 Victoria St., V2L 2L2; (604) 562-3700.

The Coast Inn of the North, 770 Brunswick Street, V2L 2C2; (604) 563-0121. Very nice high-rise hotel. Eight blocks from the VIA Station. $84.

-Simon Fraser Inn, 600 Quebec St., V2L 1W7; (604) 562-3181. Very attractive rooms. Six blocks from the VIA Station. $54.

-Goldcap Motor Inn, 1458-7th Ave., V2N 3P3; (604) 563-0866. Good value. Seven blocks from the VIA Station. $54.

-Park Place Bed & Breakfast, 1689 Birch St., V2L 1B3; (604) 563-6326. Quiet neighborhood, across from Fort George Park. $35.

-The Prince George Railway Museum, off of River Road and close to downtown, has a very fine assortment of rail cars, artifacts and other equipment, as well as a gift shop. The jewel is the Nechaco, a 1913 Pullman that was beautifully restored for EXPO 86. The **Fraser-Fort George Regional Museum,** located in Fort George Park, has a good number of well-displayed artifacts from the region's past. Also in Ft. George Park is the **Ft. George Railway,** offering rides in coaches pulled along a half-mile of track by a Grand Trunk Pacific six-ton work "dinkey," which has unusually small drive wheels that allowed it to operate on very steep grades.

0:00 (1:55) Departing Prince George, follow Nechaco River as it journeys westward toward Vanderhoof and British Columbia lakelands. Country is known for its timber and minerals.
0:55 (1:00) At Isle Pierre, "current ferry" (using stream's force as only source of power) transports vehicles across river.
1:55 (0:00) Arrive Vanderhoof.

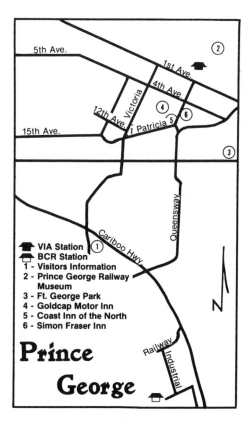

VIA Station ①
BCR Station
1 - Visitors Information
2 - Prince George Railway Museum
3 - Ft. George Park
4 - Goldcap Motor Inn
5 - Coast Inn of the North
6 - Simon Fraser Inn

Prince George

VANDERHOOF, B.C. - This is the geographical center of British Columbia. It is also home to 50,000 Canadian geese that find refuge in the adjacent Nechaco Bird Sanctuary.

But each year, the third weekend in July, birds of an entirely different kind gather here when Vanderhoof holds Canada's largest "camp-in" air show. Canadian and U.S. military jets, aerobatics teams, antique fighters and numerous WWII aircraft entertain 20,000 spectators for two exciting days. If you're an airplane fanatic, you'll want to contact: Vanderhoof International Airshow, Box 1248, Vanderhoof, B.C., V0J 3A0, or phone 604-567-3144.
0:00 (1:11) Depart Vanderhoof.
0:02 (1:09) Lumbering operations become more evident; Nechaco sawmills are on left.
0:05 (1:06) Huge Westar Timber Plateau operations sawmill is on left.
0:36 (0:35) Just north of Fort Fraser, "last spike" was driven on April 7, 1914 to

complete Grand Trunk Pacific line. After financial problems, railroad was absorbed into Canadian Pacific.

0:37 (0:34) Passing through Fort Fraser, note large depot-like building on right, recently built to house "Last Spike Pub."

0:38 (0:33) Cross broad waters of Nechaco River.

0:45 (0:26) Skeena now skirts border of Fraser Lake on right. In July, fireweed along right-of-way and in nearby fields produces brilliant splashes of reddish purple.

0:53 (0:18) Lumbering industry remains quite evident as Skeena passes Fraser Lake Sawmills.

1:01 (0:10) Cross Stellako River. Its five-mile length reputedly makes it shortest river in province.

1:09 (0:02) Just before Endako, road to left leads to Endako Mine, world's largest open-pit molybdenum mine.

1:11 (0:00) Arrive Endako.

ENDAKO, B.C. - This is a service center, largely dependent on railroading (it's a division point) and, of course, the aforementioned Endako Mine.

0:00 (0:49) Depart Endako and follow Endako River.

0:31 (0:18) Yet another sawmill, this time Babine Forest Products sawmill on right.

0:37 (0:12) Tintagel Cairn, visible on right (through bushes), contains stone core which was once part of Tintagel Castle in Cornwall, England. Castle was reputed birthplace of King Arthur (of Round Table fame), and stone was brought here during Canada's centennial in 1967 to help preserve community's heritage. Cairn also contains time capsule to be opened in 2067.

0:42 (0:07) Body of water, on left, is Burns Lake.

0:49 (0:00) Arrive Burns Lake.

BURNS LAKE, B.C. - Originally, Burns Lake was a mere telegraph relay cabin along the Collins Overland Telegraph Line. But when the railroad arrived in 1908, it gained civilized substance.

One of the town's earliest pioneers was quite successful in the hotel business. No longer needing his small cabin, he converted it into a gambling hall. This venerable establishment, known as "The Bucket of Blood," has been restored and now reposes next to the local museum.

The main street has a distinct curve, created when the town's surveyor ran the road around a settler's barn and corral. The landowner, however, claimed the surveyor was drunk and had merely followed a cow path through town.

British Columbia's largest provincial park, Tweedsmuir (and B.C.'s smallest, Deadman's Island) is near here, and today Burns Lake is an important recreational outpost. Rockhounding is also popular, with large opal and agate deposits located nearby.

0:00 (1:07) Depart Burns Lake.

0:11 (0:56) Decker Lake now extends along tracks on left. Babine Lake, longest natural body of water in province, is just north of here, but too distant to see from train. Naturally, with such a proliferation of lakes, moose are common to the area and can often be spotted along right-of-way.

0:17 (0:50) Skeena slips past one more large sawmill, an operation of Decker Lake Forest Products.

1:07 (0:00) Arriving Houston, "World's Largest Flyrod," on left, just east of visitors center, is an obvious statement about region's most popular sport. Also, note sawmill display on west side of visitors center.

HOUSTON, B.C. - This community of 3,000 persons is the home of two giant lumbering companies, one of which, Northwood Pulp and Timber, has the largest enclosed sawmill in the world. Tours are available. Mining and tourism round out Houston's economy, with rockhounding, snowmobiling and cross-country skiing being popular outdoor activities.

0:00 (1:02) Depart Houston through farm- and ranchlands, set scenically amidst Bulkley River Valley. Peaks of Coastal Range loom in distance, soon to escort Skeena on final leg into Prince Rupert.

0:01 (1:01) Stark, white-frame Christian Reformed Church faces tracks on left.

0:03 (0:59) Just west of Houston, tracks that veer off to left serve those two huge sawmills, mentioned just above. Steam from those operations is visible above trees. Here, Morice River flows into

Bulkley.

0:45 (0:17) Pastoral splendor of Bulkley River Valley is epitomized by area surrounding Telkwa where dairy cows, green pastures and hay meadows are backdropped by towering Hazelton Mountains.

0:48 (0:14) Through Telkwa, one of oldest communities in valley, where Telkwa and Bulkley rivers meet. Salmon and steelhead fishing and canoeing are favored activities. Novice and intermediate paddlers are particularly attracted to waters.

1:02 (0:00) Arriving Smithers, Hudson's Bay Mountain on left is regally graced with Kathlyn Glacier.

SMITHERS, B.C. - Established in 1913 as a division point on the Grand Trunk Pacific, Smithers was the first village to be incorporated in British Columbia. It now has a population of 4,500, making it the Valley's trading center. In 1979, most Main Street businesses were given a facelift, and now bear a resemblance to a Bavarian village—blending nicely with the town's alpine setting.

Smithers' visitor center occupies what was once a buffet club car on the CN line between Toronto and Montreal.

0:00 (1:14) Departing Smithers, challenging golf course on right annually hosts prestigious Labor Day tournament.

0:08 (1:06) Handsome homes dot shoreline of Lake Kathlyn on right, with reflection of Skeena Mountains cast majestically across water. Skeenas are subclassification of Coastal Range. To left is impressive Kathlyn Glacier, cradled in Hudson Bay Mountains.

0:20 (0:54) High Bridge across frothy Trout Creek is first of several dramatic spans soon traversed.

0:30 (0:43) Pass through Moricetown, largest Indian village in Valley. East of here, although not visible from train, Bulkley River squeezes through narrow gorge called Moricetown Canyon, where Carrier Indians still "subsistence fish" for salmon traveling to spawn in Babine Lake. Carriers once used fish traps (no longer legal); now, they fish with long gaffing poles, spearing these large fish with utmost skill.

0:40 (0:33) On right, Bulkley River descends into gorge—a preview of exciting canyons awaiting downstream.

0:42 (0:31) Rail buffs should seize opportunity to photograph train as it winds gracefully (to right) across towering Boulder Creek trestle. A short distance downline, bridge across Porphyry Creek

Skeena – Kitwanga, British Columbia

affords similar possibilities.

0:59 (0:15) From high atop rocky ledges, train now embarks on inspiring four-mile adventure through cuts and tunnels of magnificent Bulkley Canyon. Below, cliffs compress Bulkley River into a surging torrent of white water. On opposite bank, waterfalls tumble down into river, further enhancing this spectacular stretch.

1:14 (0:00) Arrive New Hazelton.

NEW HAZELTON, B.C. - Three towns are clustered together here (New Town, Old Town and South Town) as well as myriad nearby Indian villages— all of which make up the area called "The Hazeltons." Indian lore pervades the region, and a reconstructed Indian village from the early 1900s can be explored. Numerous totem poles—one said to be the world's oldest—are found throughout the area. Also, one of the largest collections of Indian carvings outside of a museum is located here. The area is famous for its stylized West Coast Indian art, sought after by international collectors.

0:00 (2:16) Depart New Hazelton. On left, imposing peaks are some of region's tallest, extending 8,000 feet above sea level. Mount Roche deBoule, with its 3,000-foot cliffs, dominates.

0:08 (2:08) Trestle across Sealy Gulch is not for faint-of-heart, perched nearly 200 feet above deep gorge.

0:10 (2:06) On right, Bulkley River has emerged from canyon, and now carves swath through verdant pasturelands. In distance, Hazelton Mountains frame this most picturesque setting.

Shortly downstream, Bulkley River flows into Skeena River, descending from north.

0:35 (1:41) Cross Skeena River which then borders route on left into Prince Rupert. On opposite bank, quaint little town of Nash makes enchanting centerpiece of scene seemingly plucked from travel poster.

0:48 (1:28) Kitwanga, a Skeena flag stop, is starting point for Stewart-Cassiar Highway 37 which winds through wilderness north of here and traverses some of most spectacular scenery in British Columbia. Kitwanga is Indian for "people of the place where there are rabbits." One of

region's many totem poles is on left, immediately after passing burned-out rail station. In winter (when trees are defoliated), St. Pauls Anglican Episcopal Church can sometimes be glimpsed off to left, together with free-standing ornate bell tower. Also, street lined with totem poles (called "Tour of Totems") might be glimpsed to left. Then Skeena passes through Indian cemetery with many graves individually fenced in a profusion of styles.

0:58 (1:18) Beautiful farmhouse adorns landscape on right at Woodcock. Jagged, dramatic Seven Sisters Range is at left, with seven very pronounced peaks.

1:06 (1:10) Old post office and general store are venerable structures seen on left at Cedarvale. An independent mission was established here in 1888. Its effectiveness earned town nickname "The Holy City," and for many years absolutely no work was performed on the Sabbath.

Descending gradually toward sea level, proceed along the scenic Skeena River Valley, with awesome glaciers stretched atop nearby peaks. At trackside, colorful mosses and ferns soften the terrain—a remarkable contrast to the rugged alpine climes looming just above.

1:41 (0:34) Old hotel is nostalgic relic on right at Pacific, now struggling to support its own weight.

1:59 (0:17) At Usk, note another "current ferry" that shuttles between homes on riverbanks. Flow of stream forces cable-guided craft from one side to other, while sign on far side instructs motorists to call for service by either ringing gong on pole or honking horn.

2:16 (0:00) Arrive Terrace.

TERRACE, B.C. - The largest community between Prince George and Prince Rupert, with a metropolitan population of 18,000, is the center of large lumbering operations as well as government, transportation and service industries. Visitors will find much of interest in the region, including lava beds, fossils, hot springs—and as always throughout the province—fishing. A 92½-pound salmon was taken by a rod and reel from the Skeena near here, a world's record.

Kitimat, a planned community built in

Current Ferry – Skeena River

the 1950s, just 50 miles south, has several industries that can be toured. Most renowned is Alcan's aluminum smelter, one of the world's largest. (Call first for Alcan reservations, 604-639-8259).

0:00 (2:10) Depart Terrace through industrial district, with logging operations again most abundant. Two more totem poles will appear at right.

0:04 (2:06) Cross Kitsumkaylus River, first of countless tributaries swelling Skeena River enroute to Pacific Ocean. Mountains of Kitimat Range now border route on both sides.

0:48 (1:22) Stretch between mileposts 39 and 50 features several sets of spectacular waterfalls cascading down near trackside. (Mileposts are conspicuously tacked on adjacent poles.)

1:01 (1:09) All that remains of Kwinitsa are two small sheds. Lovely little station that once stood at trackside was moved to Prince Rupert where it now serves as railroad museum near Prince Rupert's VIA station.

1:16 (0:54) Highway and tracks once shared narrow shelf along river, making vehicular traffic uncomfortable partner of trains through here. At one point, highway actually went beneath power-line tower. Thousands of tons of rock have recently widened base for more roomy arrangement.

1:27 (0:43) Rustic fishing piers on left are entrenched in general area where freshwater and saltwater begin to mix. At this point, river has widened to near half-mile breadth. Watch for harbor seals that sometimes frequent this segment of river.

1:37 (0:33) Fishing industry quickly takes center stage approaching Prince Rupert. Villages at Cassiar, Sunnyside and North Pacific are surrounded by colorful assemblage of boats, with daily harvests proudly displayed across docks.

Waters now broaden into Chatham Sound, encircling Smith, Lelu and Ridley islands. Ridley is an aspiring seaport, with coal and grain facilities recently built to cultivate Asian markets.

1:47 (0:23) Cross bridge onto Kaien Island, home of Prince Rupert. Continue along docks, past terminals for Alaska and British Columbia ferries.

2:10 (0:00) Arrive Prince Rupert, its depot tucked neatly within rocky cove.

PRINCE RUPERT, B.C. - When you come to Prince Rupert, bring your raincoat. Its location on Kaien Island, where the Skeena River dumps into the Pacific, accounts for many misty days—some more misty than others. Even the Chamber of Commerce does not deny that the city gets more than its share of rainfall; they simply call it the "City of Rainbows."

But it's part of the atmosphere that makes Prince Rupert a bit like a miniature San Francisco. Dazzling floral displays in the town parks, neat clapboard homes shelved on the hillsides, an interesting waterfront, complete with fishing fleets and seafood eateries, and some gorgeous harbor sunsets. Yet most people are here to catch ferryboats—ferries to Vancouver and Vancouver Island to the south; ferries up Alaska's Inside Passage to the north; ferries to the Queen Charlotte Islands to the west.

And, of course, more than a few travelers arrive or leave by train. Prince Rupert's history began with the arrival of the Grand Trunk Pacific (now the CN) in 1914, built to compete with the Canadian Pacific's transcontinental route. Soon, fishing and fish processing rose to prominence, then the timber industry. Today, tourism has been added as an economic bulwark.

VIA Station is situated on the harbor, directly below downtown. The station is open several hours each day except Sunday. The station has storage lockers, a literature rack, including city maps, and complimentary coffee. There is limited short-term parking; long-term parking is two blocks from the station.

For arrival and departure information, call (604) 627-7304. For reservations and other information, 800-665-8630. Ticket window and waiting room hours vary, depending on train schedules.

Skeena **Taxi,** 624-2185. **Local buses** are four blocks from station; 624-3343. Tilden **rental cars** are available

by calling 624-5318, or Budget by calling 627-7400. Greyhound **Bus** depot is at 6th St. and 1st Ave., 624-5090. **Alaska State Ferries** sail northward up the scenic Inside Passage to Ketchikan, Wrangell, Petersburg, Juneau, Haines, Sitka and Skagway. **British Columbia Ferries** offer service to Vancouver and Vancouver Island, as well as the Queen Charlotte Islands.

Prince Rupert Visitors Bureau is located at 1st Avenue and McBride St. in the Museum Building, P.O. Box 669, V8J 3S1. Call (604) 624-5637.

Prince Rupert has numerous good accommodations, and pricing seems to fairly reflect the degree of quality and location. Those shown below are in the downtown area, except for the bed and breakfast which is within easy walking distance of downtown. If you plan to walk to any of these accommodations from the station, be prepared to climb. A cab is recommended.

-Crest Motor Hotel, 222 West 1st Ave., Box 277, V8J 3P6; (604) 624-6771. An outstanding hostelry, complete with an elegant dining room, on a bluff overlooking the harbor. $85 to $90 (seaside).

-Prince Rupert Motor Inn, 1st Ave. and 6th St., Box 700, V8J 3P9; (604) 624-9107. Excellent downtown location, overlooking the harbor with a nice restaurant. $56.

-Aleeda Motel, 900 3rd Ave. West, V8J 1M8. Small, quiet, nicely maintained motel with large rooms, all with balconies. $50.

-Raffles Inn, 1080 3rd Ave. West, V8J 1N1; (604) 624-9161. On the edge of downtown. $42.

-Allen's Bed and Breakfast, 401 4th Ave., V8J 1P7; (604) 624-6100. Located in a residential area immediately above downtown. Hosted by a former halibut fisherman who serves large breakfasts to order. All rooms share bath. $44.

The following are in the downtown area. Be sure to visit the city's **Sunken Gardens,** small but immaculate, and **Service Park,** again small but colorful. **Sunsets** on the harbor, weather permitting, can be spectacular. Have a good seafood dinner at **Smiles** on the waterfront; be sure to ask for a table with a view

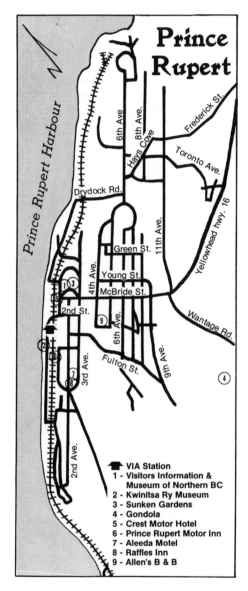

Prince Rupert

Prince Rupert Harbour

6th Ave.
8th Ave.
Hays Cove
Frederick St.
Toronto Ave.
Drydock Rd.
11th Ave.
Yellowhead hwy. 16
Green St.
4th Ave.
Young St.
McBride St.
2nd St.
6th Ave.
Wantage Rd.
3rd Ave.
Fulton St.
9th Ave.
2nd Ave.

◆ VIA Station
1 - Visitors Information &
    Museum of Northern BC
2 - Kwinitsa Ry Museum
3 - Sunken Gardens
4 - Gondola
5 - Crest Motor Hotel
6 - Prince Rupert Motor Inn
7 - Aleeda Motel
8 - Raffles Inn
9 - Allen's B & B

It contains an excellent telegraph exhibit.

For a commanding view of the town and the harbor, ride the **gondola** to the top of Mt. Hays, a few minutes by car from downtown. A bit farther is Port Edward, where the century-old **North Pacific Cannery** has been restored as a museum for the fishing industry.

of the marina. **Shopping,** of course, is in the downtown area, including two malls. The very fine **Museum of Northern British Columbia,** with exhibits of Indian and regional culture, is at the visitors center. And next to the VIA station is a small but wonderful **Railroad Museum** in the former Kwinitsa depot, depicting how life used to be for those who worked and lived in those remote outposts.

British Columbia Railway

Somehow, Norway's rugged and spectacular fiords have been magically transported to Canada. Self-propelled Dayliners (rail diesel cars) of the incredible British Columbia Railway brush along the water's edge as lofty peaks soar dramatically overhead. Traveling 461 miles from North Vancouver to Prince George, the railroad wends through ever-changing but always marvelous scenery, ranging from that just described to the more arid interior mountains of British Columbia.

"Cariboo Class" accommodations are available on through trains, with more roomy seating, complimentary meals, and bar service.

Note that this train uses the BCR stations in North Vancouver and Prince George—not the VIA stations. See North Vancouver (below) for ticket information.

Northbound Schedule (Condensed)
North Vancouver, B.C. - Early Morning Departure
Squamish, B.C. - Early Morning
Pemberton, B.C. - Late Morning
Lillooet, B.C. - Early Afternoon
Exeter, B.C. - Midafternoon
Williams Lake, B.C. - Late Afternoon
Prince George, B.C. - Late Evening Arrival

Southbound Schedule (Condensed)
Prince George, B.C. - Early Morning Departure
Williams Lake, B.C. - Late Morning
Exeter, B.C. - Early Afternoon
Lillooet, B.C. - Midafternoon
Pemberton, B.C. - Late Afternoon
Squamish, B.C. - Early Evening

North Vancouver, B.C. - Late Evening Arrival

Frequency - Summer: Daily each direction between North Vancouver and Prince George. Remainder of year: Daily, each direction between Vancouver and Lillooet; Sunday, Wednesday and Friday, northbound continues on from Lillooet to Prince George; Monday, Thursday and Saturday, southbound from Prince George to Vancouver.

Seating - Dayliner coaches. Cariboo Class has more luxurious seating, but is often more heavily used.

Dining - Food service available on through trains. Cariboo Class includes meals at no extra charge. Coach passengers can purchase light snacks.

Baggage - Checked baggage handled only on through trains to and from Prince George. Baggage for flag stops where agents are not on duty must be claimed from train baggageman before arrival.

Reservations - Reserved seats are required on all trains operating north of Lillooet.

Length of Trip - 461 miles in 13 hours.

Route Log

NORTH VANCOUVER, B.C. - North Vancouver, just across Burrard Inlet from Vancouver, is the southern terminus of the BCR. The station is located at 1311 W. 1st Ave., North Vancouver. Call (604) 631-3500 for BCR trains to Lillooet and Prince George and 984-5264 for recorded information. Ticket window and waiting room hours are 6:30 am to 9 pm. There is free parking adjacent to the station. Write BC Rail, Passenger Sales Service, P.O. Box 8770, V6B 4X6.

Note that although **Royal Hudson** steam trains to Squamish leave from this station, they are not operated by BC Rail. Call Harbour Ferries (604) 687-9558 for Royal Hudson ticketing and reservations.

Early morning bus service is furnished to the BCR Station from the Vancouver bus terminal, 150 Dunsmuir Street (across from the Sandman Inn), with pick ups from there to Stanley Park entrance. In the evening, buses meet the trains to return passengers by the same route. A small fare is charged.

0:00 (1:19) Depart North Vancouver.

0:01 (1:17) On left is graceful Lions Gate Bridge.

0:03 (1:16) Cross Capilano River at confluence with English Bay on left.

0:12 (1:07) Dense, lush foliage contrasts nicely with modernistic high rises and beautiful homes of affluent West Vancouver.

0:20 (0:56) A long tunnel (1,700 feet) precedes first view of magnificent Howe Sound on left. Immediate waters are Horseshoe Bay. Area is renowned for its salmon fishing.

0:40 (0:31) Dome of 5,330-foot Mt. Wrottesley dominates opposite shore.

0:57 (0:15) Britannia Beach, at milepost 30, is where mining and smelting operations once stood at base of 6,645-foot Mt. Sheen. Barren top of 6,815-foot Mt. Sedgewick is forward on left, across bay.

1:03 (0:11) Forward on left is sharply defined Mt. Garibaldi, looming 8,787 feet above Squamish.

1:12 (0:02) On right, at milepost 39, is Stawamus Chief—reputed to be second largest rock in world. Monolith is a favorite with rock climbers who pit their skills (and luck) against its massive granite face which rises 2,138 feet above the bay.

1:14 (0:00) Arrive Squamish at milepost 40.

SQUAMISH, B.C. - Situated at the northern tip of Howe Sound, near Garibaldi Provincial Park and the northern terminus of the Royal Hudson

steam train, it is understandable why tourism is big business in Squamish. BCR locomotive shops are located here.

0:00 (1:41) Depart Squamish where rails follow route of Squamish River.

0:09 (1:31) Commence through beautiful Cheakamus Canyon at milepost 47.

0:32 (1:06) Blue-green color of Cheakamus River on right is typical of mountain glacial streams.

0:58 (0:40) Quaint chalet architecture pervades year-round resort of Whistler (named after marmots which make a loud whistling sound) where skiing is a major attraction.

1:00 (0:38) At Alta Lake, train crests summit of Coastal Range at 2,199-foot elevation (milepost 74). From here a gradual descent leads to fertile Pemberton Valley where root crops, such as potatoes and turnips, thrive.

1:09 (0:31) At milepost 79, long and narrow Green Lake on left has 7,000-foot Rainbow Mountain for fine backdrop.

1:38 (0:05) Cascades of Green River rapids and then Nairn Falls add to charm of grand entrance to Pemberton.

1:43 (0:00) Arrive Pemberton at milepost 95.

PEMBERTON, B.C. - This is the major trading center for the lush Pemberton Valley. It was near here, along the Lillooet River, that early-day prospectors streamed by, seeking their fortunes during the gold-rush days. Massive Mount Currie towers above valley on right, at 8,364 feet.

0:00 (2:05) Depart Pemberton and cross Lillooet River.

0:05 (1:55) At milepost 99, pass through flag stop of Mt. Currie, serving one of British Columbia's largest Indian reservations.

0:07 (1:53) Train is now escorted by Birkenhead River until its arrival at Birken at top of Cascade Range.

0:30 (1:33) At Birken, milepost 114, surroundings begin to appear more arid than Coastal Range. Note that mountains are less glaciated and have a softer look. Birkenhead Provincial Park is in mountains just to left.

0:51 (1:10) At milepost 123, train begins journey along 15 miles of Anderson Lake

BCR Dayliner – Fraser River, near Lillooet

shoreline, on right.

0:53 (1:08) Views are momentarily taken away as Dayliner cuts through a short tunnel.

0:56 (1:05) Boxcar lies unretrieved in lake on right, an unfortunate victim of some former misadventure.

1:06 (0:58) At milepost 129, McGillivray Falls are on left.

1:24 (0:40) Seton Portage, at milepost 139, lies between Anderson and Seton lakes, and was site of first railway in province. Wooden rails were used to portage boats between lakes!

1:26 (0:38) Into darkness again, this time for 30 seconds, and emerge along banks of lovely Seton Lake, nestled between Mt. McLean on left and Cayoosh Range across lake. Penstocks, those giant tubes on left, bring water from higher environs to power hydroelectric plant of B.C. Hydro and Power Authority. BCR is constructing a 2,940-foot tunnel along lake to avoid troublesome landslides.

1:35 (0:29) At milepost 142, Shalalth was gateway to placer gold mining of Bridge River more than 100 years ago. (This type of mining obtained gold from gravel deposits and is pronounced "plass-er.")

2:03 (0:05) At north end of Seton Lake, 9,200-foot Mt. Brew towers above valley on right.

2:08 (0:00) Arrive Lillooet.

LILLOOET, B.C. - Located at the confluence of the Fraser River and Cayoosh Creek, placer mining during the last century made Lillooet, pronounced "Lil-loo-ett," a boom town of the gold-rush era. It was also an important provisioning point on the Cariboo Highway that led to the north. In spite of its mountain setting, temperatures frequently soar above 100 degrees during the summer, which partially accounts for the fine crops of watermelon, vegetables and fruit that are grown here.

0:00 (2:32) Depart Lillooet.

0:06 (2:26) Cross Fraser River, spanned by attractive silvery-steel bridge, and commence steep climb out of canyon for next 30 miles, gaining 3,000 feet in elevation before emerging on Cariboo Plateau at Kelly Lake.

0:48 (1:42) At milepost 183, after passing through Moran, Fraser River snakes through canyon, a dizzying 2,678 feet below.

1:05 (1:25) Kelly Lake, at milepost 193, rests in a glorious setting, with Marble Range forming a most scenic backdrop on left. This is edge of great cattle country of the Cariboo.

1:19 (1:09) Through flag stop of Clinton, center of ranching, where renowned Clinton Ball is held each May during town's annual rodeo.

1:34 (0:54) At milepost 215, flag stop of Chasm is aptly named for a deep canyon on right, formed at close of ice age when a stream from melting ice cut through lava-formed Fraser Plateau.

2:08 (0:19) At milepost 243, Horse Lake is heart of guest ranch country and is highest point on British Columbia Railway, 3,864 feet above sea level. From here, Dayliner begins a gradual descent into cattle country of Williams Lake through forested, rolling countryside interspersed with open fields and meadows.

2:35 (0:00) Arrive Exeter.

EXETER (100 Mile House), B.C. - This pretty little village is a trading and distribution hub for local ranching and lumbering activities.

0:00 (1:38) Depart Exeter.

0:19 (1:14) Peaceful waters of Lake LaHache stretch along tracks on right at milepost 274.

1:30 (0:00) Arrive Williams Lake at milepost 314.

WILLIAMS LAKE, B.C. - This is the "Cattle Capital of British Columbia," with thousands of critters being shipped, not only to Canada but also to the U.S. Lumber is also important, with large mills in and around this city of 13,000.

0:00 (1:35) Depart Williams Lake.

0:29 (1:12) An airy crossing of Deep Creek takes place at milepost 331 on one of world's highest railway bridges—a 1,200-foot span, 312 feet above water.

0:35 (1:06) Soda Creek, at milepost 541, marks the point from which venerable river steamers plyed Fraser River to Prince George and back—a 260-mile round trip.

0:50 (0:51) At milepost 351, ferry provides autos only way across Fraser River.

1:41 (0:04) On outskirts of Quesnel, Western Plywood plant processes lumber into multi-layered wooden sheets of construction plywood.

1:45 (0:00) Arrive Quesnel.

 QUESNEL, B.C. - This city of 8,000 serves as a regional trade center, and is home for several lumber-oriented industries.

0:00 (1:55) Depart Quesnel.

0:26 (1:28) At milepost 400, cross Cottonwood River Bridge which carries train a lofty 234 feet above that river. In 1921, Pacific Great Eastern Railroad (BCR's predecessor) hoped to cross further downstream and form a link between Quesnel and Prince George. That attempt was thwarted by unstable soil, and it wasn't until 1952 that this spot was crossed at a cost exceeding one million dollars.

0:36 (1:12) At milepost 406, cross Ahbau Creek where silver spike ceremony at north end of bridge celebrated completion of Quesnel-Prince George section.

1:03 (0:52) Canyon Creek Bridge, at milepost 426, was once scene of feverish placer mining activities.

1:36 (0:19) From milepost 451 into Prince George, train is escorted by impressive Fraser River.

1:55 (0:00) Arrive Prince George.

PRINCE GEORGE, B.C. - See page 378.

Vancouver Island Service

The **Malahat Dayliner** runs daily between Victoria and Courtenay. These rail diesel cars make a four-hour morning run to Courtenay and return to Victoria in the afternoon. Sandwiches and beverages can be purchased at Nanaimo and Courtenay during station stops.

Although VIA attempted to terminate this extremely popular service in January 1990, the province of British Columbia went to court to require its continuance. The province won in the lower court, but the case has been appealed.

Mexico

There is probably no uniform description for Mexican train travel. There are some reasonably good trains in Mexico, and there are some unreasonably bad ones—at least by most standards. At times, it may seem as though every positive is offset by at least two negatives. Nothing is predictable except the unpredictable.

There are some developments, however, that offer a glimmer of hope. Mexico has recently embarked upon a program of upgrading many of their main-line trains to Servicio Estrella—or "Star Service." The idea is to make these trains consistently acceptable to U.S. and other foreign tourists. It remains to be seen how effective these efforts will be, but new equipment has been added to many of these trains and early results have been positive. In any event, the Star Service trains are the best Mexico has to offer, and those planning to travel on the Mexican rails would be well-advised to stick to this class of service.

There are reasons for traveling by train in Mexico—and reasons not to. If you are anxious to get to the beaches of Mazatlan, Acapulco or Cancun, and have little interest in seeing the country between here and there, the train is one of the worst choices. On the other hand, if you want to come in contact with the real culture of Mexico, the train offers fine possibilities.

The countryside moves past your window offering scenes ranging from quaint to spectacular, many of which can only be seen from the railroad. Occasional stops of twenty minutes or better allow exploring such out-of-the-way villages as Escobedo or Benjamin Hill.

Economically, the trains south of the border are a real bargain. The price of a first-class coach ticket from Nuevo Laredo on the U.S. border to Mexico City, 781 rail miles to the south, is only about 50,000 pesos. If the dollar is worth 2,700 pesos, that's only $18.50 U.S., or a little more than two cents per mile! A bedroom occupied by two would be approximately twice that amount per person.

The equipment used by the railroads in Mexico is sometimes clean (particularly the sleepers) and sometimes not. On older equipment, it is not unusual for the air conditioning to fail, or for various other mechanical aspects of coaches and sleepers to refuse to function. This should be less of a problem on Star Service trains.

The service on board is not dazzling, but it is provided with a warmth and sincerity that won't always be found on U.S. or Canadian trains. Although porters, waiters and conductors seldom speak more than a few words of English, somehow communication never seems that difficult. Knowing at least some Spanish will come in handy.

The food is acceptable, most meals offered being Continental and not too spicy. Menus on those trains which carry a dining car (coche comedor) are in Spanish and not English. Dining cars serve tasty meals in the old tradition, complete with white tablecloths, but purified water is not always available.

Trains usually leave their origination points quite punctually. Star Service trains seem to have a reasonable on time record, but, as almost anywhere else in North America, don't count on making tight connections. Non-Star Service trains can be particularly tardy, sometimes arriving three or four hours late.

Stations are often situated in the heart of the downtown area, which can be a real help when trying to keep cab fares to a minimum. These buildings are frequently modern, large, busy and rather earthy. The platform areas are often immaculate, but it's best to avoid the station rest rooms. If you enjoy "people watching," stations, such as the one in Guadalajara, offer excellent opportunities.

Making reservations from outside of Mexico is still awkward if made directly with the railroad. That procedure is explained below. Fortunately, however, certain selected travel agents will now make Mexican train reservations; Thomas Cook Travel, with many locations in the U.S. and elsewhere, is one of those agents.

From all of the above, you should be able to know whether Mexican train travel is for you. Although it's not for everyone (what is?), it offers a unique adventure that should be enjoyed by those who are willing to relax and accept what comes with the unpredictable territory.

CLASS OF SERVICE

Mexico's railroads offer reserved first-class and regular first- and second-class coach service on their trains. The difference in cost is not great, but the difference in accommodations is generally significant. On non-Star Service trains, first class coaches ("Primera Clase") are frequently rather attractively refurbished, offering comfortable seats with reclining backs and have air conditioning. (Air can work too well, very well, just barely, not at all, or any combination of these during any given trip.) Second class ("Segunda Clase"), on the other hand, has thinly padded bench seats, no air conditioning, and frequently has a "congested" appearance with various types of baggage ("equipaje") temporarily stored in the aisles. The windows open in lieu of air conditioning, but this feature also permits dust to fog up the cars in more arid climes. For the slight additional cost, first class would normally be the choice. Star Service seating is all reserved first class and newer equipment; these trains are the only ones offering food service. These coaches have airline-style tray tables and reclining seat backs.

Sleeping cars are also available on many trains, and depending on the exact type of accommodation, may cost up to approximately twice that of a first class coach ticket. This is still a bargain, and it is certainly the way to go if the trip is overnight. Crisp, white linens and Pullman virgin wool blankets are the rule. Most sleeping cars are old U.S.-built Pullmans, many similar to Amtrak's Heritage sleepers. It is always advisable to have a flashlight with you, just in case of a lighting circuit failure. Sleeping accommodations include sections (upper and lower berths), roomettes and bedrooms. Roomettes and bedrooms contain their own toilet facilities.

FOOD

Some Star Service trains provide dining-car service, some provide complimentary box lunches, some provide both. The food is quite acceptable. Typical menus are:

	Breakfast
Starters:	Fruit Juices
	Fruit Cup
Entrees:	Huevos Rancheros (or other style eggs)
	Hot Cakes
	Cereal
Beverages:	Coffee, Tea or Milk

	Lunch or Dinner
Wine:	Red or White
Starters:	Consomme
	Fruit
	Soup
Entrees:	Fish
	Chicken
	Filet Mignon
	T-Bone
Dessert:	(Usually peach half or pineapple slice)
Beverages:	Coffee, Tea or Milk

On Star Service trains, meals in the diner are included with sleeping car tickets and box lunches are included with coach tickets. Coach passengers may also go to the diner and purchase meals.

On non-Star Service trains, it is not uncommon for train personnel to go throughout the train selling ham sandwiches or even chicken dinners; however, don't count on it. Also, some stops are long enough to allow passengers to eat outside the train, if they want to be that venturesome. It would be a good idea to take along some sort of survival rations such as hard-shelled fruit, cheese and nuts, or even a box lunch such as those available at some hotels or Mexico City's Buenavista Station.

Purified water is frequently not available, but soft drinks and beer are almost always available on the better trains. It's not a bad idea to take some fresh drinking water along, since you may begin to yearn for something to drink that is bubble free ("sin gas").

CUSTOMS AND CURRENCY

Although crossing the border into Mexico can be done without red tape, to go more than 75 miles beyond the border requires two documents for U.S. and Canadian citizens:

1. Proof of citizenship, such as a passport, voter registration, birth certificate, military identification card or naturalization certificate.

2. An entry permit, commonly called a tourist card, which can be obtained from travel agents, airlines serving Mexico, embassies, Mexican consulates or at entry points. All that is needed to obtain this permit is proof of citizenship.

The Mexican emigration inspector will examine these documents on entry at the border railway station. One copy of the permit will be collected on entry and the remaining copy will be collected upon leaving the country. These permits are free of charge.

Children under 15 may be included on their parents' or guardians' tourist cards.

Many fruits, vegetables and nuts are not allowed into the U.S. from Mexico, and a current listing can be obtained from the U.S. Department of Agriculture.

It is important to accurately declare what you acquired while in Mexico, since failure to do so can subject you to fines and criminal prosecution as well as seizure of the articles involved.

The Mexican peso is a floating currency, which means that the exchange rate can change on a daily basis, and the safest way to get a fair conversion rate is to do so at a bank.

Unlike many Mexican resort areas, the railroads may not accept U.S. currency, so obtaining some pesos before boarding is advisable.

TOURS

Rather than set out on their own, many people prefer to sample Mexican rail travel by way of a tour package. Such tours are offered by various operators, and usually include the spectacular Copper Canyon trip across the Sierra Madre Occidental between Chihauhua and Los Mochis on the Chihuahua Pacific Railroad.

Some examples of available tours that include the popular Copper Canyon are:

-**Tauk Tours** and **Sierra Madre Express of Tucson** (800-666-0346) offer deluxe eight-day tours from Tucson or El Paso. These tours use nicely restored private rail cars which include bedrooms, a dining car, a lounge and specially designed "patio cars" and a dome car that permit excellent viewing and photo taking.

-**Rail Travel Center** (802-527-1788) has a two-week tour in the spring that includes the Canyon and a cruise along the Baja Coast.

-**Let's Travel Tours** (714-787-8350) have offered ten-day tours in March and April using private equipment.

For these and other tours, contact your travel agent, or the tour company directly.

BAGGAGE

Baggage can be checked to be carried in the baggage car, 110 pounds allowed free for each full fare and 55 pounds for each half fare. Stations do not have storage lockers but generally have provisions for holding baggage in a secure area for those who wish this service. Redcaps (their caps are actually tan) are available at the larger stations and will carry baggage to and from the trains for tips.

STATIONS

There are two stations in **Chihuahua.** One is The National Railways of Mexico station serving those trains traveling north and south between Ciudad Juarez and Mexico City. The other is the Chihuahua Pacific Railroad station which is the northeastern terminus for the Copper Canyon trains. Although these stations may someday be consolidated, at this writing both are still in use.

The National Railways of Mexico station, at the northeastern end of Av. Division del Norte, is situated at the north end of the downtown area of Chihuahua. It is a large spacious station with huge murals at each end of the interior of the station. The station has a restaurant, pay phones, cabs and parking.

Ticket windows are sometimes open only a very short period during the day, so it would be best to call the station before attempting to do any business there.

The Chihuahua Pacific (Chihuahua al Pacifico) station, at Mendez and Calle 22A, is situated southeast of the downtown area. Newspapers, postcards and magazines can be purchased just outside the station. There is one pay phone available. Parking is quite limited. Although the closest cab stand is two blocks west of the station, there are normally a few cabs at the station at train times and are taken up rather quickly.

Huehuetoca, Mexico

The **Ciudad Juarez** station, located at Ensuquentes and Francisco Villa, is quite roomy and colorful, with interior walls covered with thousands of small tiles. Non-Spanish-speaking persons can seek assistance at the office labeled "Agente General." There is one pay phone at the entrance to the station. A large parking lot is next to the station. There are also parking lots in both Juarez and El Paso that offer special rates to those wishing to leave their cars for an extended stay in Mexico. There is no official taxi stand, but cabs frequent the station area. The bus station is on 16th Street, about fourteen blocks east of the station.

Guadalajara has a large modernistic station near the downtown area located at the southern end of Calzada Indepencia, with a large attractive fountain in front. It has a newsstand, cab stand, gift shop, limited banking services, baked goods, a deli-type snack bar, restaurant, pay phones, a baggage check area, redcaps and adjacent parking. Local buses stop in front of the station.

In **Monterrey,** the station is not in the best section of town and is about three miles from the downtown area on Av. G ral B. Reyes just north of Av. Colon. This is a very active station with plenty of cabs. There are also pay phones and a baggage check area.

Mexicali's station is about two miles beyond the border in the city, just east of Blvd. Adolfo Lopez Mateos on Calle Ferrocarrileros. It has parking, pay phones, and cabs. Note that this station may be one hour ahead of Pacific Standard Time observed by the rest of Mexicali.

Buenavista Grand Central Station in **Mexico City** is the largest in Mexico. This is a busy station since many trains fan out from the city, so it is always a good idea to arrive early to pick up tickets. Lines can be long at times. Located just a little more than a mile north of the "Pink Zone," it is on Av. Insurgentes Norte at F.C. Mosqueta. This is really a split-level station with a front (or middle) level, a lower level and an upper level.

Entering the front level, one encounters an enormous, marble-floored expanse, broken only by an island of landscaping in the center. There are ticket windows, arrival and departure boards, a snack food store, a very helpful bilingual information clerk, and precious little seating. First class ticket holders proceed through this level to the upper level where there is a waiting area for thru passengers (again with precious little seating), the gates to first class trains, sleeping-car (dormitorio) check-in counters, a newsstand, a restaurant and pay phones. The lower level has second-class ticket windows, waiting area and boarding gates. The baggage counter, a baggage check room and a lunch counter are also in this area.

Outside there are parking, cabs and local buses. Although the station is not in a particularly attractive area of the city, a very nice hotel, the Ponte Vedra, is just across Insurgentes Ave. where rooms are available for about $20 to $30 per day. From the station's west entrance (lower level), just take the yellow catwalk over the street.

Although ticket offices in **Nogales** are located just on the Mexican side at the border-crossing point, the station is about two miles farther south.

The station in **Nuevo Laredo** is about a mile or so from the border. Small and attractive, it has pay phones, cabs and parking.

RESERVATIONS

Reservations are necessary for Star Service trains as well as other first-class coach and sleeper accommodations. Reservations can be made either directly through the railroad or with a few selected travel agents.

When making reservations directly with the railroad, they should be confirmed in writing before you arrive to pick up your tickets. When making reservations, do it well in advance, such as two or three months.

When reservations are confirmed, instructions will be given as to where to send the required fare. The railroad's remittance instructions will state that the funds should be sent by bank cashier's check or money order and in Mexican funds. Tickets will then be

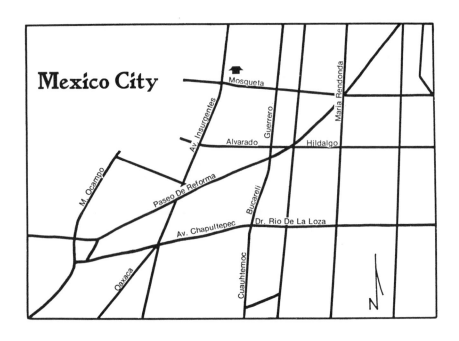

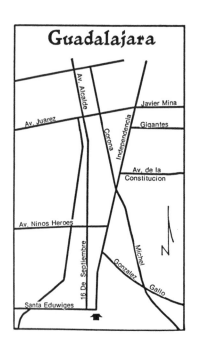

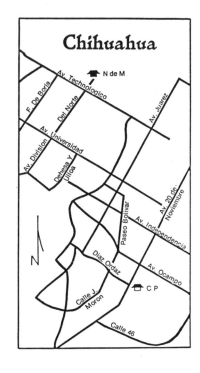

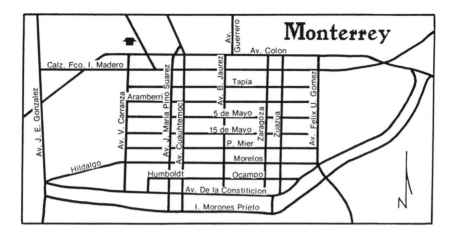

held at the ticket window and can be picked up prior to train departure time. Confirmation notices should be presented at the ticket office window when picking up tickets to help expedite the process. If funds are not received by the time specified, your reservations will be cancelled. At least this is the way it's supposed to work. Service can vary a lot from agent to agent.

When writing the railroad for reservations, include the exact dates of travel, number of passengers, ages of any children and accommodations desired. The National Railways of Mexico requires that such requests should be addressed to the representative at the border gateway where entry is planned, or to the "corresponding officer," depending on the point from where you plan your trip as follows:

-For trips from Mexico City to any point in Mexico, or for trips **from Monterrey, Veracruz, Chihuahua, Urupan and Guadalajara to Mexico City,** send requests to Mr. Javier Sanchez Mendez, Chief Commercial Passenger Department, National Railways of Mexico, Buenavista Grand Central Station, 06358 Mexico, D.F. (Mexico), Tel. 547 86 55.

-From Neuvo Laredo to any point in Mexico, send requests to Mr. Mario Guzman Santana and Mr. Jaime David Chavez Lopez, Commercial Agents, National Railways of Mexico, Passenger Station, Nuevo Laredo, Tamps. (Mexico), Tel. 280 97 or P.O. Box 595, Laredo, Tex. 78042.

-From Ciudad Juarez to any point in Mexico, send requests to Mr. A. Barraza Silva, Commercial Agent, National Railways of Mexico, Ciudad Juarez, Chih. (Mexico), Tel. 225 57 or P.O. Box 2200, El Paso, Tex. 79951.

-From Nogales, Son. to Sufragio, Culiacan, Mazatlan, Tepic, Guadalajara and Mexico City, send requests to Mr. Luis Mejia Wagner, Commercial Agent, Calle Internacional No. 10, Nogales, Son. (Mexico), Tel. 200 24.

-From Guadalajara to Tepic, Mazatlan, Culiacan, Sufragio, Nogales and Mexicali, send requests to Mr. Antonio Velarde Zatarain, Chief Regional Passengers Department, Calle Tolsa No. 336, Guadalajara, Jal. (Mexico), Tel. 12 43 96.

-From Mexicali to Sufragio, Culiacan, Mazatlan, Tepic, Guadalajara and Mexico City, send requests to Mr. Alberto Bazua M., Commercial Agent, P.O. Box 182, Mexicali, B.C. (Mexico), Tel. 57 23 86.

-Between Chihuahua and Los Mochis (Copper Canyon, LaJunta, Creel, Divisadero, Surfragio), send requests to Mr. Oscar Luevano Ceniceros, Chief Regional Passengers Department, P.O. Box 46, Chihuahua, Chih. (Mexico), Tels. 12 22 84 and 15 77 56.

As mentioned earlier, some U.S. travel agents will handle Mexican train tickets for a fee and offer a quicker response and an assurance that the tickets will be at the border when you arrive. In Mexico City, reservations can be made through Wagons-Lits Tourisme Mexicana, 52-5-518-1180 (or, of course, at the station).

Mexico by Rail, P.O. Box 3580, Laredo, Texas 78044 (1-800-228-3225), specializes in obtaining Mexican train tickets and even furnishes border transfers to trains at the Laredo border, issuance of tourist cards, secured parking and general advice on tipping, the water, etc. Many other travel agents such as Thomas Cook, also utilize this company's services in making Mexican rail arrangements. Since the National Railroads of Mexico do not pay commissions, a fee has to be tacked on to the ticket price by the travel agent, making the ticket higher priced than if obtained directly from the railroad. This additional charge, however, is an assurance that you have a ticket when you arrive, as well as confirmation within a matter of days (instead of months, or worse, never).

TIMETABLES
It is possible to obtain condensed timetables of Mexico's major trains by writing the agent in Mexico City listed above. However, for those wanting detailed, complete schedules of Mexican trains, send $10 to Mexico Research, P.O. Box 2858, Riverside, CA 92516, and request their publication *Train Times in Mexico*.

FARES
As noted above, Mexican train fares are a travel bargain. There are no family plans, but children, at least 5 years of age but under 12, are charged half the adult fare (plus a small insurance charge) when traveling with an adult. One child under 5, not occupying a seat or other accommodation, may travel free. There is no savings on round trips, since the fare is two times the one-way fare.

Some sample approximate one-way fares for Star Service coach are:

Nogales-Guadalajara	$12
Chihuahua-Los Mochis	$17
Guadalajara-Mexico City	$11
Mexico City-Oaxaca	$ 6
Mexico City-San Miguel Allende	$ 6
Nuevo Laredo-Mexico City	$18

Sleeping car accommodations, when available, would be about twice these amounts for one person.

STAR SERVICE TRAINS
These are the best trains on the Mexican system. In the late 1980s, Mexico began to upgrade certain trains to help bolster tourism, putting specially built coaches into service, refurbishing sleepers for certain runs and restoring on-board food service.

There is still a shortage of sleeping cars, and at this time only one Star Service train, El Regiomontano between Nuevo Laredo and Mexico City, offers sleeping car service as far north as the border.

Nuevo Laredo to Mexico City
Regiomontano is a daily train, leaving Nuevo Laredo midafternoon and arriving in Mexico City midmorning the following day. Northbound trains are scheduled to leave Mexico City late afternoon and arrive in Nuevo Laredo about noon the following day. The **Regiomontano** carries reserved sleeping cars, a dining car and reserved first-class coaches. Sleeping cars include bedrooms, roomettes and berths.

San Antonio is the closest Amtrak service, and Greyhound has frequent bus service between San Antonio and Laredo. Cabs are available between Laredo and Nuevo Laredo, but allow at least thirty minutes between Nuevo Laredo rail station and the Laredo bus station.

The route covers 780 miles in approximately 18 hours. The roadbed is reasonably good, not unlike much of that found in the U.S. and Canada. The northern portion of this route is typical Mexican desert, with plenty of sand, cactus, mesquite and yucca, and frequently providing spectacular sunsets. After reaching San Luis Potosi, the

Club Car – Regiomontano

scenery gradually becomes greener as the train progresses toward Mexico City.

The terrain remains flat to moderately rolling for the entire trip, and after San Luis Potosi, mountains are always visible in the distance on both sides of the train. Small farms become more numerous as well as cattle and sheep. Crops include corn (it originated in Mexico), milo, pineapple, papaya, coconuts and bananas. Burros are everywhere, and now and then a field is being plowed with oxen. Towns and villages become more numerous and modern as the train nears Mexico City, and finally the last 45 minutes are through the northern suburbs of the city. This last stretch is typically industrial, with some of the most impoverished neighborhoods to be found anywhere.

Mexicali and Nogales to Guadalajara

Del Pacifico is a daily train with southbound sections from both Mexicali and Nogales that join at Benjamin Hill and continue on to Guadalajara. The northbound train from Guadalajara splits at Benjamin Hill with separate sections going to both Mexicali and Nogales. This train is scheduled to allow through-coach connections in Guadalajara with Tapatio, an overnight train between that city and Mexico City, but these connections are less than two hours and should not be relied on.

Del Pacifico carries reserved first-class coaches and a diner (south of Benjamin Hill and between Benjamin Hill and Mexicali) but no sleeping car. Box lunches are complimentary.

Mexicali can be reached by air from the U.S. as well as bus, while Calexico, just on the California side of the border, is also reached by air and bus. Cab service is available between the two towns; the rail station is approximately two miles beyond the border. Nogales, Sonora and Nogales, Arizona can be reached by bus and Nogales, Arizona by air. Cab service is also available between these towns.

The route is 1,336 miles from Mexicali, or 1,094 miles from Nogales, and is covered in a scheduled time of approximately 32 hours from Mexicali, or 26 hours from Nogales. Trains depart Mexicali early morning and Nogales early afternoon arriving in Guadalajara early evening the next day. The northbound train leaves Guadalajara early morning and arrives the next day in Mexicali late afternoon and in Nogales late morning.

The terrain is desert in the northern portion with considerable irrigated farmland near Mexicali. It is the second day southbound that one will find upon awakening that the countryside has become verdant and semi-tropical as the train heads down the coast towards Mazatlan. South of Mazatlan, between Ruiz and Tepic, the route traverses through the prettiest part of the trip as the scenery becomes mountainous and even more tropical. The most spectacular portion of the trip occurs when the train follows the course of the River Grande de Santiago for a short while. After Tepic, the train heads inland and to the higher elevations of Guadalajara.

Scenes of particular interest along the route would include: the numerous cotton fields southeast of Mexicali; a national electric power plant being fueled by natural gas wells which surround the plant, approximately 30 minutes out of Mexicali (right side southbound); the Gulf of California can be seen from time to time, with the best views about four hours out of Mexicali (right side southbound); the town of Benjamin Hill where there is time to get off the train, stretch, and for the more daring, sample some of the Mexican food being cooked at trackside by various vendors; sugarcane, various tropical fruit orchards, and Brahman herds as the train approaches Mazatlan; acres of morning glories and tall orange wildflowers south of Mazatlan; perhaps one of the most beautiful churches in Mexico just to the left of the train (southbound) in the 1584 village of Acaponeta, about two hours south of Mazatlan; the village of Roseta with vendors selling coconuts and fruit juices, four hours south of Mazatlan; approximately four-and-one-half hours south of Mazatlan the River Grande de Santiago set in scenery quite similar to Hawaii including the Indian village of Antonalisco with quaint, thatched roof huts (left side southbound); and in the town of Tepic, which is located at the base of an extinct volcano, the twin-spired Church of Santa Cruz, built in 1750 on a site where it was noticed that grass grew in the form of a cross.

Guadalajara to Mexico City

El Tapatio is one of the best trains in Mexico. It is composed of a large number of sleepers, several reserved first class coaches, and a dining car. Complimentary box lunches are also available. Each way is an overnight run. Train #6 leaves Guadalajara midevening and arrives in Mexico City early the next morning. Train #5 leaves Mexico City midevening and arrives in Guadalajara early the next morning.

Copper Canyon

The **Chihuahua-Pacific** train (Chihuahua to Los Mochis) offers what is often cited as the most scenic train trip in North America (and occasionally called the most scenic in the world). The passage should stir the emotions of even the most galvanized traveler. Numerous waterfalls, multi-colored cliffs and canyons, tropical fruit trees, 36 major bridges and 87 tunnels highlight this journey that follows a tortuous 3,000-mile route from mile-high Chihuahua, crossing the Sierra Madre Occidental Mountains to an altitude of 8,071 feet, and finally descending to Los Mochis at sea level.

The route was originally conceived in the late nineteenth century by private interests in the United States as a rail line linking the Mexican town of Topolobampo on the Pacific Coast of Mexico with Midwestern U.S. markets. However, it was not until November 1961 that the final link was made between Creel and San Pedro in the heart of the remote mountains of northwestern Mexico. This culminated a 50-year effort on this section alone, and was completed only after the Mexican government, with the expenditure of millions of dollars, took over the project. Although it has never become the major freight line envisioned (linking Kansas City with the Pacific), it does provide important access to a canyon that is four times the size of the Grand Canyon where nearly 50,000 Tarahumara Indians live, a people who are recognized for their unusual running abilities.

The Star Service train departs Chihuahua early morning and arrives in Los

Mochis early evening. The return leaves Los Mochis early morning, arriving in Chihuahua early evening. The train carries reserved coaches, and box lunches are served.

For those not wishing to make a round trip through the canyon from Chihuahua, connections can be made with Del Pacifico in Sufragio, about a half hour out of Los Mochis. Ths problem, however—and it would be considered a significant problem by most travelers—is that Del Pacifico arrives in Sufragio (northbound or southbound) about one o'clock in the morning. Neither the town nor the station is a place to sit around and wait several hours in the middle of the night for the next train. A round trip out of Chihuahua seems to work the best, with an overnight in Los Mochis.

The left side of the train, when traveling from Chihuahua to Los Mochis, probably offers more scenery than the right, but if you can't sit on the left, don't worry about it, you can certainly see well enough on the right side. Since the altitude is quite high for long segments of these trips, it is a good idea to take along a warm sweater or jacket just in case.

Tunnel numbers are high on the left side (westbound) as you enter each tunnel, and anyone wishing to keep track could do so easier on that side. Kilometer signs are low on the right side and impossible to see unless you sit against the right hand side and watch very carefully. Also, keep in mind during the winter, if the train should be late, there is more spectacular scenery in daylight hours eastbound than westbound, which may be important to those not wanting to miss a single cliffside or waterfall.

Leaving Chihuahua, the trip starts out on a serene note, passing through farmland, much of which was settled in the early part of this century by Mennonites from Canada. Scenes are quintessential Mexico, with antiquated farm machinery pulled by oxen or burros here and there. But later, the character of the land changes, with lumbering activities in evidence and tropical orchards and wildflowers enhancing the countryside.

Soon the terrain is quite mountainous, and shortly before reaching Divisadero Barrancas, the journey's midpoint, the tracks actually cross over themselves while making a complete loop to gain elevation.

The stop at Divisadero allows passengers to get out to view the Barranca del Cobre—the Copper Canyon. (It obtained its name from the copper mines that operated in the canyon, not from its color.) Forested, sloping sides descend to more tropical areas near the bottom where one can make out the Urique River. If you look carefully, you may be able to see some of the cliff dwellings of the Tarahumara. Baskets, drums, violins and other hand-made objects are sold by the Tarahumara at trackside. Be prompt on reboarding; it's easy to be left behind.

Later in the day, Bahuichivo, the deepest part of the canyon, can be seen from the train, making one's thoughts turn to track maintenance (fortunately, it's well-maintained). Then, a bit later, the train passes next to a spectacular waterfall at Temoris. Although there are many falls along the route, this is clearly the largest. Tunnels and trestles abound along this stretch as the final descent is made to Sufragio, the intersection with the Pacific Railroad and just 40 minutes from the end of the line at Los Mochis.

Ciudad Juarez to Chihuahua

El Rapido de la Fronteraz is a convenient way to reach Chihuahua from the U.S. border (the train's name says it—The Fast One from the Border). This is the only Mexican route that allows a connection (as short as a cab ride) with Amtrak. The Sunset Limited serves the city of El Paso just across the border from Juarez.

The train has reserved first-class seating and box lunches. It leaves Juarez early evening and arrives in Chihuahua four hours later. The return leaves Chihuahua early morning and arrives in Juarez late morning.

Mexico City to San Miguel Allende and Guanajuato

El Constitucionalista is a convenient way to reach the appealing community of

San Miguel Allende from Mexico City. There is reserved first-class seating, and a "box" breakfast or dinner is included in the fare. A dining car is also available for those wishing complete meal service. Northbound trains leave Mexico City early morning and arrive at San Miguel Allende around noon. Southbound trains depart late afternoon and arrive in Mexico City late evening. Recently, the run has been extended northward from San Miguel Allende to San Luis Potosi and Guanajuato.

Piedras Negras to Saltillo and Matamoros to Monterrey

Two Star Service trains are scheduled to meet the Regiomontano south of the border allowing passengers to leave from (or return to) two border towns other than Nuevo Laredo. **El Coahuilense** links the border town of Piedras Negras with Saltillo and **El Tamaulipico** joins the border city of Matamoros with Monterrey. Both trains have reserved first-class coaches and box lunches.

Mexico City to Oaxaca

The **Oaxaqueno** makes an overnight run from Mexico City to the delightful city of Oaxaca, some 300 miles south of Mexico City. Trains make daily departures from each city in the early evening and arrive at the other city early morning the next day. There are sleeping cars, reserved first-class coaches and a diner. Box lunches are also available.

The morning leg into Oaxaca is particularly bucolic. As dawn breaks, the train follows a stream for many miles through a canyon marked with cacti and other more tropical vegetation; an occasional house here and there, a school or a village now and then. Quaint farms begin to appear with a tidiness that is totally lacking in Northern Mexico.

Mexico City to Veracruz

Jarocho makes an overnight run from Mexico City to the historic coastal city of Veracruz. This route has some wonderful scenery, but unfortunately, most of it is passed during the night. Trains depart each city daily in the midevening and arrive at the other city early morning the next day. There are sleeping cars and reserved first-class coaches. Box lunches are served.

Mexico City to Urupan

Purepecha is another overnight train out of Mexico City. It leaves Mexico City late each evening and arrives in Urupan midmorning the next day. One of the stops is the colonial city of Morelia. The train carries sleeping cars and reserved first-class coaches. Box lunches are served.

Mexico City to Zacatecas

San Marqueno Zacatecano is also an overnight train out of Mexico City which travels to Zacatecas. There are daily departures from each city in the early evening with arrivals in the early morning. This train carries sleeping cars, reserved first-class coaches and a diner. Box lunches are also available.

Guadalajara to Manzanillo

The **Colimense** departs Guadalajara early morning each day and is scheduled to arrive at the resort town of Manzanillo late afternoon, seven hours after departure. Trains depart Manzanillo early afternoon and arrive in Mexico City midevening. There are reserved first-class coaches and box lunches.

Zacatecas to Durango

El Centauro del Norte provides service to Durango from Zacatecas where connections are made with the Star Service train between that town and Mexico City. Trains depart Zacatecas for Durango midmorning, two hours after the scheduled arrival of San Marqueno Zacatecano from Mexico City, and arrive in Durango late that afternoon. Returning, trains depart Durango late morning and arrive in Zacatecas late afternoon, about three hours before the San Marqueno departs for Mexico City.

The train carries reserved first-class coaches. Box lunches are served.

Other Trains

Other numerous trains are available in Mexico (see route map) but are generally of poorer quality than those mentioned above.

Equipment

Contrary to the popular notion of many, rail-passenger equipment in the United States is not a patchwork of old and worn-out rail cars being pulled by a hodgepodge of freight engines. Much of it has been freshly designed and built within the last few years, while all of the older equipment still in service has been refurbished and converted from steam to electric heat—vastly increasing reliability and comfort. Long-haul trains west of the Mississippi are now using bilevel Superliner cars giving passengers the ultimate in roominess, comfort and unobstructed high-level viewing of the landscape. It is their height, however, that prevents this equipment from being used in the East where clearances pose a problem. The East is served by both Amfleet rolling stock as well as the older and more traditional cars which Amtrak calls their "Heritage Fleet."

Canada's long-haul equipment, which is the conventional variety similar to Amtrak's Heritage Fleet, has been refurbished but still relies on steam from steam generator cars to supply heat. Many of the shorter runs in Canada have self-propelled rail diesel cars. In the heavily traveled "Corridor" between Quebec City and Windsor, LRC (Light, Rapid, Comfortable) trains are in service to augment other trains that serve there.

Mexico has mostly a mixture of older, conventional equipment on long hauls and makes some use of rail diesel cars on many shorter runs. Maintenance of equipment is also a mixture. Their "Star Service" trains, however, are generally well maintained.

The following is a brief review of the most utilized rolling stock in North America.

Heritage Fleet and Other Traditional Cars - Coaches are equipped with reclining seats which have leg and footrests. Luggage can be stored overhead and often at one end of the car. Rest rooms are also located at one end of the car, generally with ample room for changing clothes. Their heavy construction gives them an extremely smooth ride.

Sleepers in the U.S. offer bedrooms and roomettes. Canada and Mexico not only offer bedrooms and roomettes but also "sections," each with an upper and lower berth. Bedrooms sleep two adults (an upper and lower berth) and can be used as a four-person room by opening a common wall between two bedrooms. Each has a wash basin and an enclosed toilet. Roomettes accommodate one person and have rest room facilities which, unfortunately, cannot be used once the bed is lowered. Sections during the daytime are two facing couches open on the aisle side and make into upper and lower berths at night with heavy curtains between the berths and the aisle. Rest rooms are at the end of the car. Some sleepers have larger bedrooms accommodating three persons called "drawing rooms."

Slumber coaches are offered on a few trains in the East having small compartments providing economic sleeping accommodations for either one or two adults. These compartments include bathroom facilities.

Diners offer complete meal service while lounge cars offer more casual seating for cocktails and snacks.

Dome cars are specially equipped coaches or observation cars with "vista domes" mounted in their roofs, permitting 360-degree viewing. Amtrak operates these cars on The Capitol, Auto Train and The City of New Orleans. The Alaska Railroad and Canada's transcontinental train also have these cars.

Dayniters are on some of VIA's trains. These have reclining seats in coaches that are somewhat more conducive to overnight travel. The fare is slightly higher than VIA's regular coach fare.

Amfleet - This was the first new equipment to go into service in the Amtrak era. Built in the U.S. by Budd, these cars use a strong tubular-shell body and produce a reasonably smooth and quiet ride—with a sleek, almost futuristic appearance. Designed for shorter and medium distance trips, Amtrak has also had to press them into service for longer hauls on some eastern routes. A newer Amfleet II design has been placed into operation with larger windows and more spacious seating for those longer runs. Amfleet includes coaches, diners and cafe cars but no sleepers. Heritage sleepers are used in conjunction with Amfleet cars for overnight runs.

Standard Amfleet coaches have reclining seats but no legrests on the shorter hauls. Overhead luggage storage, reading lights, attractive appointments, and rather small windows create an airliner atmosphere. Longer haul Amfleet cars use reclining seats with legrests and allow more leg room by installing fewer seats per coach.

Amclub seating has only three seats to a row; two on one side of the aisle and one on the other, giving a special luxurious effect. Attendants furnish food and beverage service at your seat with more elaborate menus than those available at the cafe counter. Of course, club fares are higher than coach.

Amdinettes have a cafe counter and tables for light, hot meals and snacks. Trays can be taken to the tables or to coach seats, and some trains offer food service at the tables. Amcafes are coaches with a food and beverage counter in the middle, also offering light meals, sandwiches and other snacks.

Superliners - Coaches are roomy and attractively designed with tasteful appointments. Reclining seats are wide, offer plenty of leg room and have both leg and footrests. Large windows provide excellent viewing and individual overhead reading lights add to the luxury. Folding trays, ala the airlines, are also provided. Luggage can be stored overhead as well as beneath the seats, and extra luggage storage compartments are on the lower level just as you enter. Besides upper-level seating, several seats are on the lower level and available to handicapped travelers who would find the circular climb to the upper level an obstacle. Rest rooms and a ladies' lounge are also on the lower level.

Each sleeping car has five deluxe bedrooms, 14 economy bedrooms, a family bedroom and a special handicapped bedroom. Deluxe bedrooms extend almost the entire width of the car, are on the upper level, have two beds for sleeping two to three people, and include an enclosed bathroom that even has a shower. During the daytime there is a sofa and swivel chair for seating. Economy bedrooms sleep two and are fairly compact, but aisle windows give them a more roomy appearance. These have two berths sleeping a total of two and having facing couches during the day. There is also a very thin closet, a fold-down table and individual comfort controls. Luggage storage is virtually nil. There are no in-room toilet facilities, but there is one bathroom upstairs and several downstairs.

The family bedroom is quite spacious, is on the lower level and has room for up to three adults and two children but no toilet facilities. The handicapped "special" bedroom is on the lower level, can accommodate a wheelchair, will sleep two adults and has a specially equipped rest room. Meals will be delivered to these special rooms to avoid going to the diner which is accessed through the upper levels of the train.

Economy bedrooms one through ten are on the upper level with the lower numbers toward the center of the car while 11 through 14 are downstairs, again with the lower numbers toward the center. You may wish to keep these locations in mind when making reservations since the center of the car gives a smoother ride. Deluxe bedrooms are lettered A through E, with A at the end and E near the middle.

Amtrak is now converting a lower level dressing-bathroom to a public shower on all Superliner sleepers. Also 13 former Superliner coach-baggage cars are being converted to all economy bedroom sleepers.

Lounge/Cafe cars offer splendid viewing from swivel, upper-level chairs through windows that extend from almost floor level upward and wrap into the ceiling overhead. Downstairs there are tables and a snack bar. The viewing from the upper

Superliner Economy Bedroom (daytime)

Superliner Lounge

level of these cars is superb.

Diners have seating for 72 persons at 18 tables, all on the upper level. The kitchen is on the lower level with an elevator arrangement for delivering food to the dining area.

Metroliners - Metroliner Service, Amtrak's high-speed Northeast Corridor service, is provided by specially equipped Amfleet cars pulled by Swedish-designed (but U.S. built) electric locomotives. Older Metroliner trains that were once used for this service are now utilized on short runs in and out of Philadelphia.

Turboliners - Certain service in New York State is supplied by racy Rohr Turboliners. These sleek beauties provide streamlined service between New York City and upper New York State. Designed to run in a five-car consist, power is supplied by diesel-electric "power coaches" at both the front and rear of the train. The center car offers food service and the last car usually has a 2-1 seating configuration, draped windows and Custom Class service. This section is reserved seating and, although more expensive, would be the best choice during the busier holiday seasons. Regular coaches are unreserved and are in standard rows of four.

Rail Diesel Cars - These short-distance standbys are now mostly found in Canada and Mexico. As their name implies, they are self-propelled, diesel-powered coaches, each having the capability of traveling in either direction. Seats are reclining, but no legrests, and there are folding trays similar to the airlines. Food service is generally not available, although snacks or even sandwiches are sometimes offered where these cars make lengthy runs.

Horizon Fleet - These are new coaches and diners, initially being put into service on the busy shorter routes out of Chicago (including to Detroit) and San Joaquin service in California. The windows are small, like Amfleet I, but instead of Amfleet's confining tubular construction, the sides are flat with a brushed aluminum exterior. Bombardier, a Canadian company who now owns the rights to both Budd and Pullman-Standard passenger-car technologies, is constructing these new cars at its Barre, Vermont plant.

Viewliners - A long testing and development phase is ending for Amtrak's newest rail cars, a period which saw prototype sleepers that combined the best of Superliner technology and comfort. These are single-level cars (to allow for Eastern clearances) with two rows of windows that give upper berth occupants their own viewing portals. Prototype sleepers have 14 compartments (double or single), two deluxe bedrooms (with showers) and a handicapped bedroom. Every room has a sink and a toilet as well as luggage storage space under the seats and over the aisles. Aisle-side windows give both the room and aisles a more spacious feeling. This new Viewliner equipment (there will also be coaches and diners) is meant to replace Amtrak's well maintained but aging Heritage Fleet.

LRC Trains - Canada is using these trains in their "Corridor" service. Built by Bombardier, LRC's (Light, Rapid, Comfortable) are designed for high-speed service in heavily populated areas, and have an innovative "power-banking" system that allows a higher speed on curves as the train automatically tilts to the inside. Besides their speed, extreme smoothness of ride is a characteristic.

Superliner Diner

LRC Train

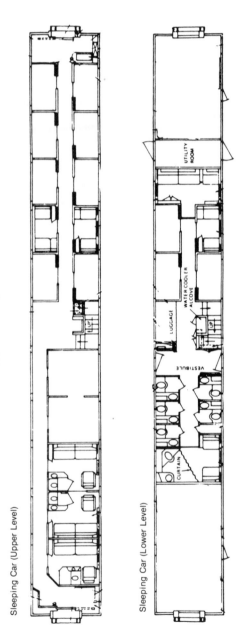

Heritage Sleeper floor plan

Superliner Sleeper

Sleeping Car (Upper Level)

Sleeping Car (Lower Level)

410

Nostalgic Adventures

Recently, North America has experienced a resurgence of railroading from the past. Several private companies have gambled that there is a demand, albeit limited, for luxurious rail travel. They have invested large sums of money in refitting older passenger train cars, and they provide deluxe on-board service to a few pampered travelers.

Besides these five-star adventures, many of which occur at the rear end of regularly scheduled passenger trains, some operators place less emphasis on luxury and more on the destination, such as the Grand Canyon Railway. Still another breed has offered "dinner train" excursions that emphasize service and elegance for a single, gracious dining experience.

A sampling of these offerings is shown below. Contact your travel agent or the tour operators directly.

American-European Express is probably the creme-de-la-creme of the fantasy-on-rails tours. The service and food are strictly gourmet and everything occurs in mahogany-paneled elegance. The trip is offered six times per week between Washington, D.C. and Chicago at the back of the Capitol Limited. The one-way overnight journey is $695 for a single roomette, while bedrooms for two start at $1,080. Meals are included. (There is also a "suggested gratuity.") Call 800-677-4233.

The **California Sun Express** operates "Superdome" cars on the back of the Coast Starlight between San Francisco and Los Angeles. Princess Rail Tours utilizes remade cars that once served on the Olympian Hiawatha (similar to the Princess Alaska tour cars). The decor is swank oak and brass. All passengers are guaranteed a dome seat, and meals are served in an intimate 20-seat dining salon. Each car is entirely non-smoking.

The one-way fare is $179. Stops are permitted at San Luis Obispo and a fare of $99 is charged passengers going only this far. Also available are packages including meals and Hearst Castle tours. Call 800-835-8907.

The **Royal Canadian** will start operation across Canada August 4, 1990 on the CP line. Four trips per month are planned between Vancouver and Toronto. Bedrooms have showers and there is live on-board entertainment. Prices start at $1,885.

The **Sierra Madre Express** runs eight-day trips between Tucson and El Paso through Mexico's famous Copper Canyon. Five cars are utilized, including a dome car and specially designed "patio cars." The fare is $2,400. Call (602) 747-0346.

The **Alaska Railroad** carries tour cars for both Princess and Gray Line of Alaska between Anchorage and Fairbanks. See the Alaska Railroad introduction in this book for more information.

The **Grand Canyon Railway** offers seasonal steam-powered excursions between Williams, AZ and the South Rim of the Grand Canyon. Trains leave Williams early morning and arrive at the Canyon about three hours later. Passengers have about four hours at the Canyon before returning to Williams. The adult round-trip fare is $47. Call 800-843-8724.

The **Napa Valley Wine Train** carries up to 75 passengers on a gourmet dining experience through California's scenic wine country. Trains depart from Napa and make a 38-mile round trip to St. Helena and back in 2½ hours. The food is superb and the basic fare is $25 plus $20 for lunch or $25 for dinner. There is also a "brunch train" on weekends. Call (707) 253-2111. (California only, 800-522-4142.)

The **Texas Limited** offers round-trip excursions to Galveston Thursday through Sunday. Fares are $27.50 Tourist; $37.50 First Class; and $42.50 Dome. Call (713) 522-9090. Trains depart Houston from the Amtrak station and arrive at the rail museum in Galveston.

Appendix

Telephone Numbers for Reservations and Information*

AMTRAK

Boston, MA .... (617) 482-3660
Chicago, IL .... (312) 558-1075
Los Angeles, CA.................... (213) 624-0171
New York City, NY
  (all 5 boroughs) .... (212) 582-6875
Philadelphia, PA .... (215) 824-1600
Washington, DC .... (202) 484-7540
All other U.S. locations 1-800-USA-RAIL
  1-800-872-7245

From Canada 1-800-4AM-TRAK
  1-800-426-8725
For Metroliner Service only 1-800-523-8720

Deaf persons with access to a teletypewriter
can call weekdays, 8:30 am to 8 pm ET:
Nationwide (except Pennsylvania) ...1-800-523-6590
Pennsylvania 1-800-562-6960

VIA RAIL CANADA

Newfoundland:
St. John's, Gander, Grand Falls, Corner Brook,
Stephenville, Bishops Falls. Call your Travel Agent
or nearest TerraTransport Ltd. road cruiser office.
All Other Locations 1-800-561-3926

Prince Edward Island:
All Locations 1-800-561-3952

Nova Scotia:
Halifax 429-8421
All Other Locations 1-800-561-3952

New Brunswick:
Moncton............................. 857-9830
Saint John 642-2916
All Other Locations 1-800-561-3952

Quebec:
Montreal............................. 871-1331
Quebec City 692-3940
James Bay - Call your Travel Agent
or VIA Rail Canada .... (514) 871-1331
All Other Locations 1-800-361-5390

Ontario:
Hamilton 522-7533
Kingston............................. 544-5600
London............................... 672-5722
Ottawa 238-8289
Toronto 366-8411
Windsor 256-5511
Other Area 416, 519 and 613 Calls ...1-800-361-1235
All Area 705 Calls.................1-800-361-1235
All Area 807 Calls.................1-800-561-8630

**Manitoba, Saskatchewan, Alberta,
British Columbia, Yukon and
Northwest Territories:** 1-800-561-8630

People with speech or hearing problems may communicate through telecommunication devices for the deaf (TDD).
The access numbers are: Toronto Area ... 368-6405
All Other Locations 1-800-268-9503

USA: For VIA train information or reservations in the USA, contact your Travel Agent.

*Use the telephone number appearing opposite the city, state or province from which you are calling.

Index